LAW, JUSTICE, AND SOCIETY

LAW, JUSTICE, AND SOCIETY

A SOCIOLEGAL INTRODUCTION

Second Edition

Anthony Walsh
Boise State University

Craig Hemmens
Boise State University

New York Oxford
OXFORD UNIVERSITY PRESS
2011

Oxford University Press, Inc., publishes works that further Oxford University's
objective of excellence in research, scholarship, and education.

Oxford   New York
Auckland   Cape Town   Dar es Salaam   Hong Kong   Karachi
Kuala Lumpur   Madrid   Melbourne   Mexico City   Nairobi
New Delhi   Shanghai   Taipei   Toronto

With offices in
Argentina   Austria   Brazil   Chile   Czech Republic   France   Greece
Guatemala   Hungary   Italy   Japan   Poland   Portugal   Singapore
South Korea   Switzerland   Thailand   Turkey   Ukraine   Vietnam

For titles covered by Section 112 of the US Higher Education
Opportunity Act, please visit www.oup.com/us/he for the latest
information about pricing and alternate formats.

Published by Oxford University Press, Inc.
198 Madison Avenue, New York, New York 10016
http://www.oup.com

Oxford is a registered trademark of Oxford University Press

Library of Congress Cataloging-in-Publication Data

Walsh, Anthony, 1941–
    Law, justice, & society: a sociolegal introduction / by Anthony Walsh,
Craig Hemmens.—2nd ed.
        p. cm.
    Includes index.
    ISBN 978-0-19-975793-0 (alk. paper)
    1. Law—United States. 2. Sociological jurisprudence. 3. Justice, Administration of—
United States.   I. Hemmens, Craig.   II. Title.
KF386.W325 2011
340′.115—dc22   2010037526

Printing number: 9 8 7 6 5 4 3 2 1

Printed in the United States of America
on acid-free paper

*Dedicated to my wife, Grace; my parents, Lawrence and Winifred;
my sons, Robert and Michael; my stepdaughters, Kasey and Heidi;
my grandchildren, Robbie, Ryan, Mikey, Randy, Christopher, Stevie, Ashlyn,
and Morgan and my great grandaughter, Kaelyn—A. W.*

*Dedicated to Mary, Emily, Sera, Amber, and Max, and to all my
students—C. H.*

"What is hateful to you, do not to your fellow man.
This is the law: all the rest is commentary."
Talmud, Shabbat 31a.

BRIEF CONTENTS

PREFACE   xix

ACKNOWLEDGMENTS   xxiii

CHAPTER 1 LAW: Its Function and Purpose   1

CHAPTER 2 JUSTICE AND THE LAW   27

CHAPTER 3 MAKING LAW   57

CHAPTER 4 FEDERAL AND STATE COURTS   87

CHAPTER 5 CRIME AND CRIMINAL LAW   111

CHAPTER 6 CRIMINAL PROCEDURE   135

CHAPTER 7 CIVIL AND ADMINISTRATIVE LAW   163

CHAPTER 8 JUVENILE JUSTICE   197

CHAPTER 9 THE LAW AND SOCIAL CONTROL   223

CHAPTER 10 THE LIMITS OF SOCIAL CONTROL:
            Policing Vice   253

CHAPTER 11 THE LAW AND SOCIAL CHANGE   281

CHAPTER 12 WOMEN AND THE LAW *(by Mary K. Stohr)*   311

CHAPTER 13 RACIAL MINORITIES AND THE LAW   337

CHAPTER 14 COMPARATIVE LAW: Law in Other Cultures   367

APPENDIXES   395

GLOSSARY   415

TABLE OF CASES   437

INDEX   441

DETAILED CONTENTS

PREFACE   xix

ACKNOWLEDGMENTS   xxiii

CHAPTER 1   **LAW: Its Function and Purpose**   1
             Introduction   2
             What Is Law?   2
             The Six Primary Characteristics of Culture and Their
                 Relationship to Law   3
                 1. Beliefs   4
                 2. Values   4
                 3. Norms   5
                 4. Symbols   6
                 5. Technology   7
                 6. Language   8
             The Code of Hammurabi   9
             Early Thinkers about Law   10
                 Plato   11
                 Aristotle   12
                 Thomas Hobbes   12
                 John Locke   14
                 John Rawls   15
             Sociological Perspectives of Law   16
                 Max Weber   17
                 Émile Durkheim   19
             Two Opposing Perspectives: Consensus and Conflict   20
                 The Consensus Perspective   21
                 The Conflict Perspective   22
             Summary   23
             Discussion Questions   25
             References   25

CHAPTER 2   **JUSTICE AND THE LAW**   27
             Introduction   28
             What Is Justice?   28
                 Distributive Justice   28

Retributive Justice   30
Problems with Aristotle's Definition of Justice   33
Legal Realism   34
Where Does Justice Come From?
   Two Perspectives of Law and Justice as Natural   36
      The Transcendental Natural Law Perspective   37
      The Evolutionary Perspective   39
What Is the Relationship of Law to Justice?   41
   Equity   42
Garofalo and Natural Crime   44
The Rule of Law   45
Justice Evolving: Cesare Beccaria and Reform   47
Justice, the Law, and Packer's Models of
  Criminal Justice   48
   The Crime Control Model   49
   The Due Process Model   49
   An Illustration of the Models in Action   50
Summary   51
Discussion Questions   53
References   54
Cases Cited   55

CHAPTER 3   **MAKING LAW**   57
Introduction   57
Common Law   58
Precedent and Stare Decisis   59
Sources of Law   60
Sources of Individual Rights   62
The Constitution   62
The Bill of Rights   63
   First Amendment   64
   Second Amendment   66
   Third Amendment   67
   Fourth Amendment   67
   Fifth Amendment   68
   Sixth Amendment   70
   Seventh Amendment   72
   Eighth Amendment   72
   Ninth Amendment   72
   Tenth Amendment   73
   Other Amendments   73
   Thirteenth Amendment   74
   Fourteenth Amendment   74
   Standard of Review   75
   Incorporation of the Bill of Rights in
     the Fourteenth Amendment   77

Judicial Review   80
    Marbury v. Madison   81
The Process of Amending the Constitution   82
Summary   83
Discussion Questions   84
References   84
Cases Cited   85

CHAPTER 4 **FEDERAL AND STATE COURTS**   87
Introduction   87
Jurisdiction   88
The Federal Courts   90
    District Courts   91
    Courts of Appeals   92
    Supreme Court   94
The State Courts   95
Overview of the Criminal Process   98
    Pretrial Proceedings   98
The Jury and Its Selection   100
    Jury Selection   101
    The Trial   102
    Sentencing   103
    Appeals   103
Court Actors   104
    Judges   104
    Prosecutors   105
    Defense Attorneys   107
Summary   107
Discussion Questions   108
References   109
Cases Cited   109

CHAPTER 5 **CRIME AND CRIMINAL LAW**   111
Introduction   111
What Is Crime?   112
Sources of Criminal Law   114
Limitations on Criminal Law   114
Elements of Criminal Liability   115
    Common Elements of Criminal Offenses   116
Liability Without Fault   119
Inchoate Crimes   119
    Attempt   119
    Solicitation   120
    Conspiracy   120
    Parties to Crime   120
Defenses to Criminal Liability   121

Justification Defenses   121
Excuse Defenses   122
Procedural Defenses: Entrapment   124
Crimes Against the Person   125
Murder   125
Forcible Rape   126
Aggravated Assault   127
Robbery   128
Crimes Against Property   128
Arson   129
Burglary   129
Larceny/Theft   130
Crimes Against Public Order and Morality   131
Summary   132
Discussion Questions   132
References   133
Cases Cited   133

CHAPTER 6   **CRIMINAL PROCEDURE**   135
Introduction   135
Purpose of Criminal Procedure Law   136
Sources of Criminal Procedure Law   137
Search and Seizure Law and the Fourth Amendment   138
The Warrant and Reasonableness Clauses   138
Probable Cause   138
Arrest   139
When an Officer May Arrest   139
Manner of Arrest   139
Types of Seizures   139
Searches   141
Reasonable Expectation of Privacy   142
Exceptions to the Search Warrant Requirement   142
Right to the Assistance of Counsel   146
Right to Counsel During Interrogations and Pretrial
   Identification Procedures   148
Custody   148
Interrogation   149
Circumstances in Which *Miranda* Is Not Required   149
Extension and Application of
   the *Miranda* Warnings   149
Pretrial Identification Procedures   150
The Confrontation of Witnesses Clause   151
The Right to Compulsory Process Clause   152
The Exclusionary Rule   152
Advancing Toward the Exclusionary Rule   153
Curtailing the Exclusionary Rule   155

	Summary	158
	Discussion Questions	159
	References	159
	Cases Cited	160

CHAPTER 7   **CIVIL AND ADMINISTRATIVE LAW**   163

Introduction   164
Differentiating Criminal and Civil Law   164
Tort Law   167
    Tort Categories   169
    Defenses to Liability   170
    Tort Reform   171
Property Law   172
    Interests in Real Property   173
    Interests in Personal Property   174
Contract Law   174
    Elements of a Valid Contract   175
Family Law   177
    Who May Marry Whom?   177
    The Supreme Court and the Right to Marry   178
    Common Law Marriage   179
    Divorce and Annulment   179
    Dividing Property, Child Custody, and
        Spousal Support   180
Administrative and Regulatory Law   181
    Origins and Growth of Administrative Agencies   181
    Legislative Function of Administrative Agencies   185
    Investigatory and Enforcement Function of Administrative
        Agencies   185
    Judicial Function of Administrative Agencies   185
    Environmental Justice   186
    Administrative Law and Corporate Crime   190
    Recent Responses to Corporate Crime   191
Summary   192
Discussion Questions   193
References   194
Cases Cited   195

CHAPTER 8   **JUVENILE JUSTICE**   197

Introduction   197
What Is Juvenile Delinquency?   198
The Extent of Delinquency   198
Developmental Factors and Juvenile Delinquency   200
History and Philosophy of Juvenile Justice   201
    Institutional Control   202
    Childhood in the United States   203

The Child Savers   204
The Beginning of the Juvenile Courts   205
Juvenile Waiver to Criminal Court   207
Extending Due Process to Juveniles   208
   Kent v. United States   208
   In Re Gault   209
   In Re Winship   210
   McKeiver v. Pennsylvania   211
   Breed v. Jones   211
   Schall v. Martin   212
The Juvenile Death Penalty   212
Eroding the Distinction Between Adult and
  Juvenile Court Systems   215
Restorative Justice   215
Summary   218
Discussion Questions   219
References   220
Cases Cited   222

CHAPTER 9   **THE LAW AND SOCIAL CONTROL**   223
Introduction   223
What Is Social Control?   224
A Typology of Social Control   224
The Law as a Social Control Mechanism   226
   Punishment and Deterrence   227
   Other Philosophies of Punishment   229
   Black's Styles of Social Control   231
Social Control and the Criminal Justice System   232
Is the United States Soft on Crime?   233
Plea Bargaining   234
The Death Penalty Debate   235
   Arguments Against the Death Penalty   237
   Arguments Favoring the Death Penalty   238
The Law and Social Control of Political Dissent   240
Therapeutic Social Control: Law and Psychiatry   244
"No Taxation Without Representation!":
  A Case of Judicial Social Control   246
Summary   248
Discussion Questions   250
References   250
Cases Cited   252

CHAPTER 10   **THE LIMITS OF SOCIAL CONTROL:**
                 Policing Vice 253
Introduction   254
What Is a Vice Crime?   254

Homosexuality and Sodomy   256
Prostitution and Commercialized Vice   259
  Should Prostitution Be Decriminalized/Legalized?   261
Pornography/Obscenity   262
Abortion   266
Alcohol and Illicit Drugs   270
  Taming the Beast in the Bottle   271
  Illicit Drugs   273
Conclusion   275
Summary   276
Discussion Questions   277
References   278
Cases Cited   280

CHAPTER 11 **THE LAW AND SOCIAL CHANGE**   281
Introduction   282
What Is Social Change?   282
The Law as a Cause of Social Change   283
Social Movements, the Law, and Social Change   284
British Law and the American Revolution   286
Law and Social Engineering in the Former Soviet Union   288
  Law and the Destruction and
    Reconstruction of the Soviet Family   289
The United States Supreme Court and Social Change   290
  Dynamic and Constrained Views of
    the Supreme Court's Power   291
  The Legitimacy Basis of the Court's Power   292
  Strict Constructionism   294
The Supreme Court's Role in Maintaining the Status Quo   295
  The Fourteenth Amendment and Business Interests   297
The Supreme Court's Role in Inducing Social Change   302
  Bringing the Country Together Through Case Law   302
  The Activism of the Warren and Burger Courts   304
Summary   305
Discussion Questions   307
References   307
Cases Cited   309

CHAPTER 12 **WOMEN AND THE LAW** *(by Mary K. Stohr)*   311
Introduction   312
Feminist Legal Theory   312
Women and Law in History:
  The Birth of Misogyny and Other Triumphs   313
The Relative Value of Citizens:
  The Struggle for Women's Suffrage   316
Woman as Human and Person   320

Rape and Other Misogynous Atrocities   321
Women's Work and Other Legal Matters   322
The UNCEFDW and the Equal Rights Amendment   324
Women's Representation in the Legal Profession   325
The Bias Studies   329
Law, Equality, and Justice   330
Building Understanding   331
Summary   332
Discussion Questions   333
References   334
Cases Cited   336

CHAPTER 13   **RACIAL MINORITIES AND THE LAW**   337
Introduction   337
African Americans   338
   Slavery and the Law   338
   The *Amistad* Case   339
   The *Dred Scott* Case   340
   Emancipation and the Reconstruction Period 341
   The Emergence of Jim Crow Laws   342
   Segregation, Disenfranchisement, and the *Plessy*
     and *Williams* Cases   343
   Lynching and Black Protest   345
   "We Shall Overcome"   346
   Congressional Activity   347
   The Cold War and International Pressure   347
   How Far Have We Come?   348
American Indians   349
   The Early Years   349
   The Marshall Trilogy: Defining Indian Status 350
   The Period of Removal and Physical Genocide 352
   The Assimilation Period and Cultural Genocide 352
   The Beginning of the End of Cultural Genocide
     (With a Few Backward Steps)   354
   How Far Have We Come?   355
Asian Americans   356
   Asian Americans Today   357
Race, Law, and Conflict   357
Is Today's Criminal Justice System Racist?   358
Summary   360
Discussion Questions   362
References   362
Cases Cited   364

CHAPTER 14   **COMPARATIVE LAW: Law in Other Cultures**   367
                  Introduction   368
                  Law in Preliterate Bands and Tribes   368
                  Law in the Modern World: The Four Traditions   370
                       Common Law   371
                       Civil Law   373
                       Socialist Law   379
                       Islamic Law   384
                  The Four Traditions and the Rule of Law   387
                  The Convergence of Systems   389
                  Summary   391
                  Discussion Questions   392
                  References   393

APPENDIX A   Constitution of the United States of America   395

APPENDIX B   Student-Friendly Legal Web Sites   413

GLOSSARY   415

TABLE OF CASES   437

INDEX   441

PREFACE

Law, Justice, and Society: A Sociolegal Introduction (second edition) is a text designed for use in courses such as Law and Social Justice, Introduction to Law, and Sociology of Law. Several aspects of this text are not found in competitive texts. Many texts are written by authors with recognized expertise in only one or two of the areas covered, which results in very good chapters in those areas but which also produces chapters that may contain errors and misunderstandings. This text is a collaborative effort that draws on the expertise of scholars with extensive track records in publishing, teaching, and actual field practice in the topics in this text.

Law per se can be a dry topic when approached from a law school perspective. After all, law schools are in the business of turning out professionals who know how to navigate treacherous legal waters on behalf of their clients. This book is not a law book but rather a book *about* law for students wanting to learn the relationship of law to justice and to society. It is a book about how law as a social institution fits into and shapes other institutions. Most students who take a course such as Law and Justice or Sociology of Law have no intention of going to law school and just want to know the relationship of law to their own disciplines and to themselves as citizens, as well as the functions of law in their society. We are all potential witnesses, jurors, victims, or even offenders.

Chapters 1 and 2 introduce you to the *idea* of law and justice. These chapters discuss the philosophy, history, and sociology of law. We even take a look at how some evolutionary biologists have viewed the law and its origin in nature, as opposed to the view that it is purely a social construction. We ask in these chapters what law and justice is, where it comes from, how it has been conceived in the past, and what its function in society is. You will come away from these chapters realizing that few things in modern life are more important than the law.

Chapter 1 in this second edition includes the addition of perhaps the most important American philosopher of justice in the twentieth century, John Rawls. Chapter 2 includes an extended discussion of legal realism.

Chapters 3 through 8 introduce you to the various aspects of modern American law and justice. Chapter 3 focuses on the process of making law and introduces you to the Bill of Rights. Chapter 4 focuses on the federal and state court systems and the processes that occur within them. Chapter 5 examines criminal law, major crimes, and legal defenses. Chapter 6 looks at criminal procedure, such as the right to an attorney and the exclusionary rule. Chapter 7 covers various aspects of civil and administrative law, such as torts, family law, contract law, and white-collar crime. We have added the important contemporary legal and social issues of gay marriage and environmental justice. Chapter 8 provides insight on the juvenile justice system and the special ways in which it differs from the adult system. This edition adds to chapter 8 an extended discussion of restorative justice.

Chapters 9 through 11 are more sociological and historical in orientation, focusing on how law affects the processes of social change and social control. Chapter 10, new to this edition, fills a gap that a number of reviewers had pointed out. It concerns the limits of law as a social control mechanism and explores some so-called vice crimes and the law's differing approach to them across time and place. Chapter 11 explores how the law has been involved in momentous changes in the United States from before the Revolution to the present day, with special emphasis on the role of the Supreme Court. We also examine the special role of the law in making society possible by its role in social control. A discussion of the role of social movements in the process of social change has been added to this chapter.

Chapter 12 takes on a topic sorely lacking in competitive texts—women and the law. Its author, Dr. Mary K. Stohr, is a major figure in feminist criminal justice circles. She has had criminal justice field experience as a correctional officer and counselor and has served as an expert witness in court cases dealing with women's issues.

Chapter 13 provides an overview of the law as it has been applied to racial minorities in the United States from the earliest days of white settlement to the present. It documents the black fight against slavery and the Indian fight to maintain their cultural independence as well as touching on the Asian experience in the United States. As far as we are aware, this is the only law and society text that devotes a whole chapter to this important topic. This new edition discusses the election of President Barack Obama as it pertains to race relations in contemporary America.

Chapter 14 focuses on comparative law. We learn far more about our own system of law if we know a little about other systems. The chapter looks at law in bands and tribes and in the four major legal traditions in the world today: common, civil, Islamic, and socialist. Students tend to become particularly interested in the practices of non–common law systems.

It is hoped that at the conclusion of a course based on this book students will have achieved the following primary objectives.

1. *An appreciation of the role of law in society.* Law is arguably the most important of all human inventions, based as it is on our innate sense of fairness, decency, and concern for a peaceable and orderly existence. We have striven to provide you with a "feel" for what law means and where it has come from (both in evolutionary and cultural terms). You will come to a deeper understanding of the legal system as a basic social institution and of its relationship to other institutions, such as the family, the economy, and government, and to social control and social change. The limits of the law in trying to prevent change and to police private morality are also discussed.

2. *A basic understanding of the courts, law making, and criminal substantive and procedural law.* This book is an introduction to learning *about* law rather than learning law. Learning law is the process of becoming educated and socialized into the legal profession, whereas learning about law is the process of becoming an informed citizen. The student is given enough detail about the basics of law that every educated adult should know for participation in a democracy. This detail is provided with as little legal jargon as possible.

3. *An appreciation of the concept of the rule of law.* The *rule of law* has been called the most important of all legal concepts. It is imperative that citizens of democracies know what it is, how it has evolved, and the mechanisms in place to ensure its survival. Imbedded in this rule is the relatively modern notion of due process, which involves procedural rules (the legal "dos and don'ts") that must be followed by criminal justice officials to ensure fairness and impartiality in the processing of criminal cases. The evolution of the once-absurd idea of due process is a fascinating story going back as far as the Magna Carta in 1215.

4. *An understanding of comparative law.* Understanding how other cultures view and implement law is one of the most interesting features of the study of law. It has been said that if you only know your own culture, you don't know your own culture. The process of understanding almost anything necessarily involves comparison and contrast. The law in the United States has English common law as its foundation. The most prevalent form of law in the world today is civil, or code, law, which differs in many interesting ways from the common law. However, it differs considerably less from the common law than do Islamic and socialist legal systems.

5. *Knowledge of the law's treatment of minorities and minors.* Racial/ethnic minorities, women, and minors have been excluded from full constitutional protection and historically have been treated in very different ways than have white male adults. This unequal treatment has often been sanctioned and even encouraged by the law. These specialized chapters document how the law has evolved to come to view unequal treatment as morally wrong and how it has gone about rectifying its earlier mistakes.

New to the Second Edition:

-   A chapter on the limits of social control (Chapter 10)
-   Chapter 1, on the function and purpose of the law, has been revised to include a discussion of John Rawls.
-   Throughout the book, new material has been added on the following topics: legal realism, distributive and procedural justice, the politics of law/legislative process, restorative justice, gay marriage, and the Defense of Marriage Act (DOMA).

- Chapter 13, on racial minorities and the law, has been updated to include a discussion of the Obama administration.
- Chapter 7, on civil law, now includes a lengthy discussion of environmental justice.
- The authors have added a detailed table of contents, chapter outlines, and key terms. Additionally, there is now a list of five to seven relevant websites at the end of each chapter.
- Test questions and PowerPoint Presentations have been thoroughly revised.

ACKNOWLEDGMENTS

We would first of all like to thank senior editor Sherith Pankratz, a woman who recognizes excellence when she sees it. That shameless plug aside, Sherith's faith in and commitment to the project is greatly appreciated, as are those of the very able editorial assistant Richard Beck. This tireless duo kept up a most useful three-way dialogue between authors, the publisher, and a parade of excellent reviewers, making this text the best that it could possibly be. Our first and second edition copyeditors, Jeanne Ford and Elliot Simon, spotted every errant comma, dangling participle, and missing reference in the manuscript, for which we are truly thankful, and production editor Marianne Paul made sure everything went quickly and smoothly thereafter. Thank you one and all.

We are also most grateful for the many reviewers who spent considerable time providing us with the benefit of their expertise as the text was revised. Attempting to please so many individuals is a trying task, but one that is ultimately satisfying, and one that undoubtedly made the book better than it would otherwise have been. These expert legal scholars include: Michael Bogner; Cary Federman, Montclair State University; Laura Hatcher, Southern Illinois University; Lenore Molee, Montclair State University; Robert W. Peetz, Midland College; Godpower O. Okereke, Texas A&M University at Texarkana; John Riley, University of Alaska; Nilsa Santiago, John Jay College of Criminal Justice; and several anonymous reviewers.

We also thank graduate students Jonathon Cooper and Hailey Johnson for helping with the test bank and for developing the excellent PowerPoint presentation that accompanies this text. Thanks also to graduate student Marc Ruffinengo for assisting Jonathon with the PowerPoint slides. Thanks especially to Michael Bogner of Chadron State College, who supplied Figures 1.1, 3.1, 3.2, and 6.1.

Finally, Anthony Walsh would like to acknowledge his most wonderful and lovely wife, Grace Jean, for her love and support during this and all the other projects that have taken him away from her. She is a real treasure, the pleasantest of persons, candy for my eye, and the center of his universe.

Craig Hemmens would like to acknowledge the love and support of his wife and colleague, Mary Stohr, and his stepdaughter, Emily Stohr-Gillmore. He would also like to thank his colleague and coauthor, Tony Walsh, for pushing him to get the job done and to avoid the trap of always thinking like a lawyer. Lastly, thanks to all the students who have listened and (hopefully) learned about the role of law in a just society.

LAW, JUSTICE, AND SOCIETY

CHAPTER 1

LAW: ITS FUNCTION AND PURPOSE

The bomb blast sent Jawad Sabah flying from his seat in Ali's tea shop in Baghdad. Jawad went there daily to seek the solace of Sunni Muslim relatives and friends following the brutal gang rape and murder of his wife, Abeer, by a marauding Shiite militia gang six months earlier. He picked himself up dusty but uninjured, saw the flame-engulfed bus, and wailed soulfully at the futility and wickedness of the world around him. The police arrived 15 minutes later and just stood around smoking and waiting for their next call to do nothing.

Jawad wasn't thrilled with life under the brutal dictatorship of Saddam Hussein, but at least Baghdad was relatively safe, and he could drink his tea undisturbed. He remembered the jubilation felt after the Americans over-threw Hussein in 2003, and his brutal police force melted from the scene. He also remembered the foreboding as looting and vengeance killings began to openly occur; three years later, Iraq seems to be plunging ever deeper into chaos. In June 2005, Baghdad had 880 violent deaths *excluding* people killed by car bombs and suicide attacks (McGirk 2005). This translates into a homicide rate 30 times higher than New York City's. What law remains in Baghdad is imposed by the "infidel" Americans or by ineffectual and openly corrupt Iraqi police officers, neither of which can expect to be considered legitimate by those whose behavior they are charged with regulating.

America's attempt to impose democracy on a country whose values, norms, and customs are at odds with it has not worked out well. As of the beginning of 2010, Shiites and Sunnis were still blowing each other up, although things had significantly improved since the troop surge of 2007. If Iraq is to become a viable state, it must afford its people security, stability, and personal safety; these are the things that law is supposed to provide. The Iraqi Constitution (the bedrock of the country's law) is reasonably democratic for that area of the world, but as with all law it is just a set of lifeless state-ments on paper without the will of human actors to give it life. For the law to be more than words on paper it needs the respect and even the awe of all individuals affected by its constraints and obligations. It requires assurances that the police and judicial processes will be open to scrutiny and will pro-vide equal protections for all citizens. Without such things, government loses its credibility, the economy languishes, organized crime flourishes, vigilantism emerges, and innocent people like Jawad are victimized. This chapter explores the cultural underpinnings of law, its functions, and how ancient philosophers and early sociologists have viewed it and introduces the idea of natural law.

INTRODUCTION

When most people think of law, images of the uniformed police officer or of the pomp and circumstance surrounding the criminal courts tend to dominate. If we ponder a little longer, we may conjure up images and smells of large dusty books full of sterile rules and a multitude of archaic Latin terms and phrases and conclude that law is a pretty dull subject. Nothing could be further from the truth! Few topics are broader in scope than the law, and none is more important to social life, as Jawad Sabah would doubtless agree. For better or for worse, law insinuates itself into every aspect of social life, governing the relationship between person and person, institution and institution, and between persons, institutions, and the state; we are all potential victims, witnesses, jurors, and even offenders. The point is that law is a social institution, and to study it is to gain valuable understanding of one's society, its heritage, its values, and its day-to-day functioning.

Law has always been considered of the utmost importance in American life. The excerpt from Abraham Lincoln's Lyceum Address, given in 1838 when he was only 28 years old, makes this abundantly clear:

> Let reverence for the laws, be breathed by every American mother, to the lisping babe, that prattles on her lap—let it be taught in schools, in seminaries, and in colleges; let it be written in Primers, spelling books, and in Almanacs;— let it be preached from the pulpit, proclaimed in legislative halls, and enforced in courts of justice. And, in short, let it become the *political religion* of the nation; and let the old and the young, the rich and the poor, the grave and the gay, of all sexes and tongues, and colors and conditions, sacrifice unceasingly upon its altars. (Basler 2007, 6)

Law justly promulgated and justly applied is the bedrock of individual liberty and social progress. Former legal counsel for the British government, Phillip Allott (2001, 19) augmented Lincoln's awe of the law when he wrote: "In the making of the human world, nothing has been more important than what we call *law*. Law is the intermediary between human power and human ideas. Law transforms our national power into social power, transforms our self-interest into social interest, and transforms social interest into self-interest." Allott is saying that law is a mechanism by which diverse individual and community interests become as close to being the same thing as possible. Law has been a study of endless fascination and the subject of endless debate for generations of philosophers and social scientists—let us join them.

WHAT IS LAW?

What is this thing called law of which Allott is so enamored? The question is a very simple one with a variety of complex answers. The question usually leads to other questions, such as "Where did it come from?" "How did it originate?" "What is it based on?" "Whom does it serve—everyone, or just those with the money and influence to get laws enacted and enforced?" The next two chapters attempt to answer these questions from a number of different perspectives. But before we attempt this, let us first try to define law. The seventeenth-century English philosopher Thomas Hobbes (1952) defined law as "just a statute, commanding those things which are honest, and forbidding the contrary" (chap. 26.1). But law is much more than an aggregate of statutes that multiply promiscuously and then sometimes are sloughed off; "it is crucially the art and technique of applying these heterogeneous [statutes and] norms in the administration of justice" (Murphy 2006, 106). We could go on and on discussing the definitions of law that various thinkers have given us, but we spare you that and offer our own definition: **Law** is *a written body of general rules of conduct applicable to all members of a defined community, society, or culture, which emanate from a governing authority and which are enforced by its agents by the imposition of penalties for their violation*. This definition would not be acceptable to everyone. Nevertheless, it is offered as a working definition so that we may proceed with our endeavor.

Our definition is appropriate for all modern systems of law, but it would not completely fit preliterate societies, since by definition such societies do not possess writing, nor do they typically employ agents to enforce rules of conduct. However, law as a system of proscribed and prescribed behavior is certainly not unique to highly developed societies with written statutes and a formal system of law enforcement. All groups of people living together in organized groups have had at least some type of rudimentary rules for governing conduct. They would not last very long as organized groups if they did not, for law is at the center of all organized social life. Indeed, the word *law* itself has come to us from a variety of Latin and Nordic words meaning "to bind" (people together). People "bound together" share a common culture, and all cultures share certain core elements. Our first task is to see how these common elements are related to law.

THE SIX PRIMARY CHARACTERISTICS OF CULTURE AND THEIR RELATIONSHIP TO LAW

Culture is the totality of learned socially transmitted behaviors, ideas, values, customs, artifacts, and technology of groups of people living in a common society (Schaefer and Lamm 2001). It is the transmission of all sorts of information from generation to generation by nongenetic means. All cultures possess six primary elements: beliefs, values, norms, symbols, technology, and language. These elements represent critical information that maintains and transmits culture across the generations. Without a general consensus about the nature of a shared culture in terms of the six primary elements, the socialization process would be a difficult task indeed. All of these elements are related to one another and, most centrally for our purposes, to the law. Let us take these elements one by one and see how they are related to the law.

1. Beliefs

Beliefs are ideas that we have about how the world operates and what is true and false. Beliefs may be about phenomena that are tangible and observable and things that are not. Information that is observable or verifiable is known as empirical knowledge, which may be derived from scientific experimentation or some other type of experience. For example, although we can scientifically demonstrate that the earth is round and that it rotates around the sun, most people in Christopher Columbus's day were convinced that their "commonsense" information demonstrated that it was flat and that the sun rotated around the earth. However, scientists knew that the world was round long before Columbus's voyage; the Greek mathematician Eratosthenes had calculated its circumference with remarkable accuracy more than one thousand years earlier. In those days, knowledge and news, and hence beliefs, traveled slowly.

Cultures also communicate shared beliefs about intangible, nonobservable phenomenas such as religious and philosophical beliefs relating to "ultimate" questions such as "Who am I?" "What is the purpose of life?" "Where will I go when I die?" and "How can I lead a just and good life?" These questions are not amenable to scientific answers, but they have been answered to the satisfaction of millions by religious, spiritual, and philosophical systems of belief that are even more important to understanding culture and law than are beliefs that are open to verification or falsification. They are more important because they are at the core of human concerns and meaning and because they appease the uncomfortable irritation of doubt.

Laws are often enacted to support our most deeply held beliefs, and as beliefs change over time, so do the laws that support them. When the established doctrine of the Roman Catholic Church was that the earth was the center of the universe and that the sun revolved around it, astronomers who held contrary beliefs were labeled heretics and were in danger of severe punishment or even death if they made their beliefs public (one of the reasons why beliefs traveled slowly back then). Similarly, when the United States Constitution defined a black person, for legal purpose, as three fifths of a person, and slavery was constitutionally permissible, laws were made to protect the "property rights" of slave owners. Now that we have ceased to believe in prescientific astronomical notions or in slavery, laws regarding heresy or property rights over human beings no longer exist in Western societies. Laws against heresy, however, continue to exist in many Islamic societies, and there are remnants of legally sanctioned slavery still existing in some African countries. The point is that if enough people believe something is real, the consequences are often real regardless of the empirical validity of the belief. Witches do not exist (at least not in the stereotypical, broom-flying, spell-casting, potion-making sense), but this empirical truth was of no comfort to the thousands of women legally burned over the centuries because people believed witches did exist.

2. Values

Values refer to normative standards shared by the culture about what is good and bad, correct and incorrect, moral and immoral, normal and deviant. Values are more general and abstract than specific beliefs, although values themselves differ in their generality and specificity. Shared values are an important binding force in culture and an important integrative mechanism that binds the disparate parts of our personalities into a coherent self-concept (Walsh 2006). American values are based on transplanted and modified Western European values. Examples of broad and general "core" values in all Western societies include the Golden Rule, justice, equality, liberty, and the sanctity of life. Even though everyone defines these core values as good, people of different ideological persuasions may have quite different images in their heads when they talk about them. Take the different views of fairness and equality held by conservatives and liberals, for instance. Conservatives view fairness as an equal-opportunity *process*—a nondiscriminatory chance to enter the race—that governments can guarantee via law; liberals tend to see fairness as equality of *outcome*, which implies that all should cross the finishing line at the same time—which no power on earth can guarantee. If everyone is *equally* subjected to the same rules and *equally* judged by the same standards, fairness is achieved, according to conservatives, even if equality of outcome is not. Because they want to achieve greater equality of outcomes, liberals tend to believe in subjecting certain individuals whom they consider disadvantaged to different rules and then judging them by different standards.

3. Norms

There are other rules governing appropriate conduct that are more specific than values known as norms. A **norm** is the action component of a value or a belief patterning social behavior in ways consistent with those values and beliefs. Some norms have serious moral connotations and are known as *mores.* These standards are moral imperatives, and violations of them may be met with chastisement or serious punishment. Less serious norms are called *folkways.* Lacking the moral connotations of mores, folkways are habits that many people conform to automatically, such as the little rules of etiquette when meeting your fiancée's parents.

Laws always reflect the core values and mores of a culture. Western core values are generally those that come from its Jewish/Christian heritage (think of the Ten Commandments and the criminal law: "Thou shalt not kill," "Thou shalt not steal," etc.). Few laws are ever passed that contravene deeply held cultural values without significant opposition from large segments of society. Laws assuring abortion rights, for instance, are so hotly debated because they involve conflicting core values: the sanctity of human life versus a woman's privacy and the liberty to choose what happens to her body. Similarly, the effort to pass a constitutional amendment banning the burning of the American flag (exemplifying the value of patriotism) runs up against the conflicting values of freedom of speech and political protest. Law is thus a social tool in which the norms reflective of a people's deepest values are put down in writing to assure the continuation of patterns of conduct that are deemed socially desirable.

Figure 1.1 illustrates the flow from values and beliefs to law. All societies have behaviors they encourage and discourage through the use of informal rules such as norms. Discouraged behavior may eventually reach a point that society

Figure 1.1 The Progression from Informally Encouraged/Discouraged Behavior to Law

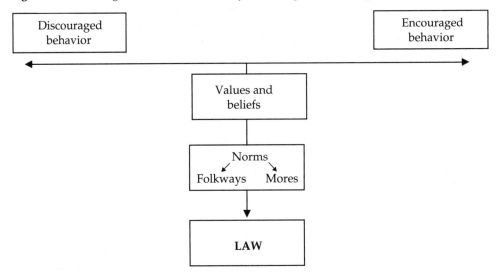

Figure provided by Professor Michael Bogner, Justice Studies Department, Chadron State College (2006).

takes formal action by enacting laws against it and specifying punishments for those who engage in it.

Legal philosophers differentiate between laws that arise from the norms and customs of a given culture, which is known as **positive law**, with a hypothesized universal set of moral standards known as **natural law**. Legal positivism is a theory of law that explains law by examining its cultural context and views law as socially constructed. Legal positivists study the cultural sources of law as it *is* without passing moral judgments; natural law adherents philosophize about the law as it *ought* to be. Believers in natural law view it as standing above and placing limits on what is permissible in positive law, whereas positivists draw a distinction between law and morality. It is not that positivists divorce law from morality. Law and morality are always intertwined to some extent, but positivists aver that it is not necessarily so and that law is law if it has the appropriate authority behind it even if it offends moral sensibilities. Positivists insist that all law is morally relative and must be judged according to the cultural context in which it was made. That is, there are no "good" or "bad" laws judgeable as such outside of their cultural context. The essential feature of law for most positivists is its coerciveness or authoritative power to command compliance with it, not its moral quality (Leiter 2001). Legal positivists may well agree that law should be moral but that we should study law as we find it rather that as we would like it to be.

4. Symbols

Anthropologists and sociologists often refer to nonmaterial culture as symbolic culture. Although the totality of symbolic culture includes nonphysical things such as gestures, language, values, and norms, we concentrate here on physical and tangible **symbols** that are identified with something else less tangible. Symbols are concrete physical signs that "stand for" and signify abstractions that range from the mundane and specific (the little man or woman painted on the restroom door) to those that are suffused with meaning and can evoke the deepest of feelings such as a nation's flag. While the figures on the restroom doors point to something useful, they do not capture our emotion. A flag, while less useful in a day-to-day sense, expresses all that it means to be a part of the nation signified by that piece of cloth. A symbol such as a flag may transcend many cultures so that persons living in different cultures may understand the symbol within their own cultural context. Think of the different emotional responses evoked in Washington, Paris, and Teheran by seeing a mob burning the American flag. The American flag is recognized as a symbol representative of the American nation in each of those cities, although this recognition has vastly different emotional meanings to their citizens.

Symbols are of vast importance to the law, which is, after all, a rather abstract and intangible notion itself. Think of the symbolic meanings involved in being inside an imposing courtroom, viewing robed (and in some countries, bewigged) judges sitting on elevated stages flanked by flags and uniformed law officers. Think of the "sacred" text of the nation's constitution, the pomp, the ritualism, the old-fashioned terminology sometimes used ("Hear ye!"), the formal oaths sworn, all of which symbolically support the notion that the law is of great importance and above any individual. The law must "stand for something" (which is what *symbol* means) that is agreeable to at least the majority of society's members if it is to be considered legitimate. The symbolism surrounding the law helps those who observe it to "feel" its majesty and awesome power, and thus helps to legitimize and sustain it.

5. Technology

Technology is the totality of the knowledge and techniques a people employ to create the material objects of their sustenance and comfort. As Karl Marx was fond of telling us, the different forms of technology employed by a culture (hunting and gathering, agriculture, industrial, postindustrial) create different physical, social, and psychological environments. It should be obvious to all that the way we live and work has profound effects on all aspects of our lives, including our beliefs, values, and symbolic interpretations. The material trappings associated with life in a technologically advanced culture connote a special significance to its members that would not be evident to persons in preliterate societies. The more technologically advanced a society is, the more complex are the relationships among its parts, and the more that society relies on law to monitor those relationships.

Different stages of technology affect the law in at least three ways (Vago 1991). First, it supplies technical inventions and refinements (e.g., fingerprinting, DNA testing, polygraphy, computerized data banks, and closed-circuit TV cameras) that change ways in which criminal investigations are made and the law is applied. Second, technological advances in the media (the ability to televise congressional hearings and courtroom dramas, videotape of police officers beating suspects) may change the intellectual climate in which the legal process is executed. Third, new technology presents the law with new conditions with which it must wrestle. For example, how will the law deal with technology-driven issues such as surrogate motherhood, surgical and chemical "cures" for criminals, pornography and fraud on the Internet, human cloning, and the possible uses and misuses of individual genetic profiles?

The challenges that scientific and technological advances present for the law are different from past challenges because many of these advances (nuclear power, genetic engineering, chemical plants, and so on) have potentially catastrophic risks attached to them. In the past, catastrophes (e.g., disease, natural disasters, and foreign invasion) came overwhelmingly from events external to the affected society and were accepted as normal, inevitable, and beyond the society's control. Modernization and globalization, however, have brought potential catastrophes internally manufactured and with global reach (Giddens, Duneier, and Applebaum 2005). The nuclear accident in Chernobyl, Ukraine, in 1986; the chemical leakage in Bhopal, India, in 1984; and the toxic waste incident in Love Canal, New York, in 1978 are examples of huge manufactured disasters with consequences that extended beyond national boundaries.

Because these and a host of other potential hazards are manufactured and internal rather than natural and external, we have evolved a **risk society**, meaning a society "increasingly preoccupied with the future (and also with safety), which generates the notion of risk" (Giddens 1999, 3). This does not mean that there are more risks today than in the past, although arguably there are, but rather we are more aware that we can do something about them. *Risk* is thus conceptually different from *danger* or *hazard* in the sense that it is bound up with human control and "particularly with the idea of controlling the future" (Giddens 1999, 3). Automobiles are not going to stop pouring excessive carbon dioxide into the air unless the law mandates lower emission levels; the ozone layer will get bigger and global warming will increase unless law mandates control of chlorofluorocarbon and puts a stop to deforestation. But since these things occur cross-nationally, there is little that the legal system of a single country can do except tend to the problems in its own backyard. The point is that whether problems/risks/hazards are addressed by local, national, or international law, law has an increasingly central role in our lives.

6. Language

Language is a vast repository of information about culture; it is in effect the "storehouse of culture." It would be practically impossible to develop any kind of culture as we know it without language. Language is a terribly complex thing, but children learn it almost effortlessly, thanks to Mother Nature's "technology" built in over eons of evolutionary time. Human communication enables us to discuss the simple and the profound, to discuss events and ideas from the past and plan for the future, and it provides a way to convey a wide array of ideas and events to others. Language is part of the great biological leap that separates the human species from other species. Although animals communicate with one another, and some primates can even be taught to communicate in a rudimentary, humanlike way, only humans are able to express and understand abstract ideas through language.

Language is created abstractly and can be added to or modified according to the needs of each culture. Words mean what they mean because culture defines the meanings they denote. In cultures with writing—a symbolic representation of the language—information can be recorded and transmitted to future generations. Language thus becomes the vehicle for cultural evolution. In a very real sense, cultural definitions existing in the language help to create reality for the members of a culture.

Language is related to law in the most obvious way; it provides us with the ability to formulate, articulate, and understand rules of conduct. Without language, none of the other characteristics of culture would be possible; and our behavior would be regulated only by vague visceral feelings of right and wrong impinging on us through anger, fear, anxiety, joy, and empathy. Written language is absolutely necessary to the idea of law because written law warns everyone in advance what is forbidden conduct and what is not. Although preliterate cultures have rules, the simplicity of such cultures necessitates only a few simple rules that everyone understands. The more complex a culture becomes, the more it relies on written codes of conduct. This is a general principle of legal philosophy upheld by all anthropological, historical, and sociopolitical data available to us.

Law, then, is integral to all aspects of culture. Since the dawn of civilization, there has been some form of rules and sanctions designed to ensure socially desirable conduct and thereby bring order to a culture; to define authority and its limits; and to clarify the responsibilities, duties, and obligations members owe to one another. Given the great importance of law, it is not surprising that philosophers, historians, sociologists, and scholars from many other disciplines have debated the nature and function of law for centuries. The ideas of some of these men are discussed in the following sections. We limit ourselves to what these scholars had to say about topics that have the greatest bearing on the content of other chapters in this book and to a brief discussion of one of the earliest and most famous legal codes.

THE CODE OF HAMMURABI

The first legal codes showed that there were well-advanced societies that exhibited signs of mature civilizations many centuries ago. The Code of Hammurabi (Hammurabi was a King of Babylonia who lived from 2123 to 2081 bce) was long acknowledged as the oldest known written code of law. We now know, however, that other documents of this type existed in the area of the Middle East called Mesopotamia, but no other was so broad in its scope. The code was discovered inscribed on a round stele pillar, seven feet four inches high. On the top of the pillar was Shamash, the Sun god, handing the legal code to Hammurabi. On the back and front of the lower portion of the obelisk was the legal code of King Hammurabi. It was not law in the sense that law is understood today, that is, a set of abstract principles applicable to all. Rather, it is a set of judgments originally pronounced to solve particular cases (Bottero 1973). Nor was it an attempt to cover all possible situations as modern codes are; and as far as we know, it was never copied and distributed to those officials charged with the day-to-day administration of Hammurabi's vast kingdom (Sinha 1990). Nevertheless, the system of justice contained in the code showed signs of mature development, although it was obviously quite different from what we would recognize as such today.

The Code of Hammurabi governed relationships in the society related to sexual behavior, property rights, theft, and acts of violence, and its administration was almost exclusively in the hands of the priesthood. The law forbade retaliatory actions and deadly blood feuds among the people, leaving punishments to be dispensed by the King's agents. The "eye for an eye, tooth for a tooth" (*lex talionis*) concept of justice is clearly stated in the code, predating the Old Testament passage familiar to Jews, Christians, and Muslims. The law introduced specified standards of conduct and amelioration by an independent third party to settle disputes. Cruelty and inhuman behavior to those accused of wrongdoing was restricted by the legal code. A written code, theoretically impartial in its application, represented a tremendous advance for society in general and the administration of justice in particular.

Although the laws contained in the code were secular in nature, Hammurabi was wise enough to buttress their (and his) authority with the approval of the gods. The linking of the code to an honored deity was a powerful piece of psychological gilding employed by many others, both before and after Hammurabi. The prologue to the code reads, "Then Anu and Bel delighted the flesh of mankind by calling me, the renowned prince, the god-fearing Hammurabi, to establish justice in the earth, to destroy the base and the wicked, and to hold back the strong from oppressing the feeble: to shine like the Sun-god upon the black-haired men, and to illuminate the land" (Edwards 1971, 23).

EARLY THINKERS ABOUT LAW

The extent to which law has been deemed important in the affairs of humans can be gauged by noting that every social and political philosopher of any stature has felt compelled to comment on it at some length. They have attempted to come to grips with such topics as where law comes from, what its nature is, what it is for, why it is necessary, whom it serves, and what human life would be without it. Philosophical insights have been important in every field of inquiry as a beginning point, as a basis for examining what may or may not be possible, and as a method by which we clarify our terms and organize our thinking. We begin with Plato and his thoughts about natural law and how it is related to positivist law.

Plato

PLATO (427–347 BCE) stands as one of the most influential thinkers in the history of the world. Not only do his writings affect all Western legal systems, his approach to thinking about legal concepts influenced how law is taught and learned in most Western universities. This method of inquiry often used by law professors to teach law became known as the "Socratic method," named after Plato's mentor, Socrates. Rather than define the concepts to be discussed at the outset, Plato's definitions and ideas slowly unfolded in "dialogue" form as he debated them in his imagination with Socrates.

Perhaps Plato's best-known contribution to philosophy is his *theory of forms*. His theory is of interest to us because it helps us to understand the ideas of natural law and of justice developed by later philosophers and legal theorists. For Plato, all philosophy is an attempt to come to grips with **forms,** or *ideas*. Plato's "ideas" are not subjective mental images confined to our minds, but rather they are essences wholly independent of our knowledge about them, which contain the only true and ultimate realities. The objects (including the law) that we perceive through our five senses are only vague, untrustworthy, and transitory copies of these ultimate and eternal realities of the forms. Among the imperfect objects we possess is the law. Only by apprehending the nature and substance of the eternal ideas these copies mimic can humans act with wisdom, and only by conforming to universal principles (forms) can the rules of rightful conduct be determined. The task of lawmakers is thus to gain an understanding of the *form* or *idea* of law so that they can fashion the best possible resemblance of it that humans are capable of making (Lavine 1989).

Although never wavering from his theory of forms, Plato did not neglect to analyze and dissect the palpable world and the "imperfect copies" of reality it contained. Because human beings as they existed in the transitory world were imperfect copies of the idea or the form of humanness, their behavior was less than perfect. To regulate the self-interested, contentious, and sometimes evil behavior of mortals, law was necessary even if it is also less than perfect, as all man-made things are. Plato (1952, 311) offered one of the most comprehensive ideas of law in ancient times in a treatise on government:

> When men have done and suffered injustice and have had experience of both, not being able to avoid the one and obtain the other, they think that they had better agree among themselves to have neither, hence there arise laws and mutual covenants; and that which is ordained by law is termed by them lawful and just. This they affirm to be the origin and nature of justice—it is a mean or compromise, between the best of all, which is to do injustice and not be punished, and the worst of all, which is to suffer injustice without the power of retaliation; and justice being at a middle point between the two, is tolerated not as good but as the lesser evil, and honored by reason of the inability of men to do injustice.

Plato further argued that the state was virtuous, and it was only through the state that the behavior of the citizenry could be regulated. The state was superior to the individual because only it could lay down a set of workable rules to govern the complex behaviors of human beings. Anarchy and chaos would be the inevitable result if law was not present to restrain the insatiable desires of the citizenry. Without the law, human nature would run amok since it always sought to satisfy its appetites without much regard for the concerns of others. Plato felt that humans lacked the power to distinguish good from evil, for if they had the power to comprehend the difference, there would be no need for law. Plato's concept of positivist law and of its necessity due to the insatiable and selfish appetites of human nature would be given its greatest impetus by the British philosopher Thomas Hobbes many centuries later—and later yet by the French sociologist Émile Durkheim.

Aristotle

Aristotle (384–322 BCE) was a pupil of Plato. Aristotle assumed that the state was not only created so individuals could simply live, but so that they could live well. Aristotle agreed with his master that law must be something more than mere convention, a simple codification of custom. As we have seen, this codification of custom—"man-made" law or positive law—is often contrasted with natural law. Aristotle disagreed with Plato on a number of other law-related issues, however. Whereas Plato was an elitist who favored the rule of one man (the "philosopher king") whose great wisdom would guide his understanding and administration of law, Aristotle favored a more egalitarian system in which even the rulers must be subservient to the law. This faith in the common person and in the ultimate authority of the law was a very radical idea, and one that is difficult to find in the writings of any other legal philosopher until it appeared in John Locke's work (see the later section about him) about two thousand years later. He also knew that laws passed by rulers tended to favor the interests of their own class and warned that legislators must guard against these tendencies. Accordingly, the goal of the legislature must be to provide for the greatest happiness of the greatest number (Aristotle 1952). Aristotle's ideas were given impetus by British philosopher and lawyer Jeremy Bentham, who popularized the "greatest happiness for the greatest number" principle in England in the early nineteenth century.

Aristotle equated the concept of law with justice: "Since the lawless man was seen to be unjust and the lawful man just, evidently all lawful acts are in a sense just acts; for the acts laid down by the legislative art are lawful, and each of these we say is just" (Aristotle 1952, 377). Persons acting unlawfully (i.e.,unjustly) receive "too much" from society, and victims (of the unlawful behavior) receive "too little." The goal of law was to balance the proportion so that persons receive what they justly deserve by their actions. These just desserts may be in the form of rewards, if acting justly, or punishments, if acting unjustly. Aristotle's ideas of justice are expanded in the next chapter.

Thomas Hobbes

English philosopher Thomas Hobbes (1588–1679) was perhaps the most important of the seventeenth-century legal philosophers. In his famous book *Leviathan* ("commonwealth" or "state"), we see Hobbes's negative and cynical view of human nature lead him to views of law quite different from those of Plato and Aristotle, although he mirrored Plato in advocating an all-powerful sovereign. In his view, as in Plato's, humans are a selfish and vicious lot concerned only with our own interests. According to Hobbes, in the "state of nature" (i.e., precivilized life), life was a "war of all against all," and was "nasty, brutish, and short." Fear of violence and death under such conditions drove human beings to create a **social contract** with one another to create a state that could protect them from predation and exploitation.

Hobbes had a great concern for order in society (he had witnessed the bloody English civil wars of 1642–1645 and 1648–1649) and argued for a strong sovereign capable of enforcing the social contract and thus providing security from disorder and anarchy. Hobbes disavowed any notion of natural law in the Platonic and Aristotelian senses and was very much a legal positivist. Hobbes argued that natural law, if it exists at all, exists only in the "general conscience" and therefore cannot effect the ultimate end of the law, which is security, until the government is formed: "When a Commonwealth is once settled, then are there actually laws, and not before; as being then the commands of the Commonwealth; and therefore also civil laws: for it is the sovereign power that obliges men to obey" (Hobbes 1952, 131). Justice is thus identified with positive law, the form of which was to be determined by a strong sovereign rather than with some set of universal principles, as in the natural law of Plato and Aristotle. Laws are the commands of the sovereign—nothing more, nothing less. The sovereign's subjects are morally obliged to obey because they are parties to the social contract.

Hobbes's overweening concern for order and security can be gauged by his opinion that *any* government that provided these things for its citizens, by whatever means, was just. According to Deininger (1965, 153):

> The theme in Hobbes's *Leviathan* is that men are normally better off even in a despotic state than they would be in the absence of a political organization. Hobbes believes men are weak and cowardly, even subject to moments of sheer irrationality—thus needing for their protection a political structure which, by its coercive might, can minimize disorder by restraining the rash actions of individuals and groups as well as by laying an obligation to act when security is at stake.

Hobbes was a reactionary whose defense of absolutist monarchy was published in 1661, just twelve years after Charles I was beheaded by the English Parliament for trying to practice what Hobbes preached. In many ways, Hobbes served to galvanize the thoughts of the Parliamentarians of the time about what it was they were fighting for. Hobbes' dislike of individual liberty and freedom of thought and of the press, and his liking for unquestioned obedience to authority and for peace at any costs, provided them with an articulated agenda they could oppose item by item. One person whose work can be construed as a liberal response to Hobbes is fellow English philosopher John Locke.

John Locke

John Locke (1632–1704) held a much more optimistic view of the state of nature and of human nature than Hobbes. Because of his views about the common person and the law, Locke's writings have been interpreted by a number of individuals as providing justification for the Glorious (English) Revolution of 1688, the American Revolution of 1776, and the French Revolution of 1789 (Lavine 1989). In *The Second Treatise on Government* originally published in 1690, Locke described the state of nature as an inferior to the organized political state only because of its lack of law, not because it was "nasty" and "brutish." Nor did he see human nature as inherently violent and selfish. Locke believed that our minds and personalities are like "blank slates" when we arrive in this world; what we become and how we behave is entirely the result of our past experiences interacting with our present circumstances. Locke's conception of the state of nature, human nature, and the necessity of law is captured in the following passage:

> Though man in that state [of nature] has an uncontrollable liberty to dispose of his person or possessions, yet he has not liberty to destroy himself, or so much as any creature in his possession, but where some nobler use than its bare preservation calls for. The state of nature has a law of nature to govern it, which obliges every one; and reason, which is that law, teaches all mankind who will but consult it that, being all equal and independent, no one ought to harm another in his life, health, liberty, or possessions; for men being all the workmanship of one omnipotent and infinitely wise Maker—all the servants of one sovereign master, sent into the world by his order, and about his business. . . . (Locke 1952, 5)

Contrary to Hobbes, Locke postulated that this state of nature had natural laws based on moral obligations which governed conduct and which logically preceded an established political system. This led Locke to one of his most important conclusions regarding the state of nature and the formation of a government. The central question of his *Second Treatise* is "Why would men, living in a state of nature with harmonious relationships form a political system to govern them?"

> Men being, as has been said, by nature all free, equal, and independent, no one can be put out of this estate and subjected to the political power of another without his own consent. The only way whereby any one divests himself of his natural liberty and puts on the bonds of civil society is by agreeing with other men to join and unite into a community for their comfortable, safe, and peaceable living one amongst another, in a secure enjoyment of their properties and a greater security against any that are not of it. This any number of men may do, because it injures not the freedom of the rest; they are left as they were in the liberty of the state of nature (Locke 1952, 54)

For Locke, human beings enjoyed freedom and independence in the prepolitical state of nature, and they do not have to surrender their liberty in order to live in a political community, as Hobbes supposed. Like Hobbes, Locke assumed that individuals enter into a social contract with the government to be governed, but the government must protect individual freedoms, not curtail them in the name of security and order. Furthermore, since the social contract is entered into freely, it can be broken by the governed if the state does not maintain its part of the contract, that is, if it acts despotically and arbitrarily. This principle became extremely important to the American colonists, and later to the framers of the Constitution, who were trying to deal legally with what they considered to be the oppressive laws, policies, and decrees of the British Parliament. The influence of Locke on the writing of such American authors of the Constitution and the Bill of Rights as Thomas Jefferson and James Madison was great (Pojman 1989).

John Rawls

The eminent American legal philosopher John Rawls (1921–2002) theorized broadly about justice from a liberal moral position without being explicit about natural law. However, he did allude to it when he compared law to a scientific theory, stating: "A theory however elegant and economical must be rejected or revised if it is untrue; likewise laws and institutions no matter how efficient and well-arranged must be reformed or abolished if they are unjust" (1999, 3). Laws and institutions must thus be evaluated according to the principles of justice, as scientific theories are judged by truth. Of course, both truth and justice are intangible and open to subjective interpretation.

What is justice for Rawls? Just like the social contract theorists we have discussed, he found it necessary to propose a time in history in which humans did not live in organized political societies. Rawls shapes his theory of justice with the use of a thought experiment conjuring up a hypothetical situation he called the **original position**, which is his version of Hobbes's and Locke's precontractual state of nature. In Rawls's state of nature, however, individuals were neither brutal beasts nor noble savages, but were equal, rational, and self-interested with "a capacity for a sense of justice and for a conception of the good" (Rawls 1996, 19). He wanted to go beyond thinkers like Hobbes and Locke to describe in some detail the nature of the contract in terms of the kind of society the contract would specify. In elucidating the terms of the contract, Rawls appeared strongly to favor equality over meritocracy without belittling the latter. He envisioned a just society as one that arranged social institutions so that even the least advantaged members of society would reap fair benefits (without spelling out exactly what "fair" means in this context) and in which all social positions would be open to all people under conditions of equal opportunity.

However, Rawls seemed uneasy with the idea of equal opportunity as a nondiscriminatory *process* because, as he points out, some individuals have greater natural talents than others, and according to him that is unfair. He asserted that we have done nothing to earn our natural talents, and thus we are not fairly entitled to all the benefits that those talents could bring us. Here he reveals his preference for equality of outcome over equality of opportunity. Rawls was aware that in coming together to write this hypothetical social contract, rational self-interested individuals will try to write it in such a fashion as to privilege themselves and their descendants.

How might it be possible to prevent them from doing this? Rawls asks which principles of justice would rational and self-interested individuals choose to regulate social institutions if they had to choose behind a **veil of ignorance.** By the veil of ignorance, Rawls means that in determining the nature of their society, individuals would not know if they were going to keep any of the ascribed roles (race, class, gender) or achieved roles (student, lawyer, street sweeper) they now have or even their unique talents (intelligence, strength, conscientiousness). In other words, what kind of society would people endeavor to make in complete ignorance of their future place in it? Rawls argues that they would choose exactly the same liberties and opportunities for everyone, because each of them would be that "everyone." They would choose a society in which the most disadvantaged would be afforded help and opportunities because they just might be one of the disadvantaged.

SOCIOLOGICAL PERSPECTIVES OF LAW

For sociologists, the law is one of the six social institutions (the others are the family, education, religion, the economy, and the polity). All institutions make rules regulating conduct, but in modern democratic and secular states, only the rules contained in the law enjoy the enforcement power of the state. In many ways, law serves the purposes of the other institutions, such as regulating what constitutes a legal marriage, defining what is permissible in schools, defining the relationship between church and state, making sure contracts are adhered to, and determining voter eligibility. Because the law serves these purposes, sociologists specializing in the study of these other institutions should have an understanding of the law. Sociologists also recognize that law is written by humans who bring ideological biases and personal baggage with them to the task and thus recognize that laws should be critically analyzed.

Major early sociological luminaries such as Karl Marx, Émile Durkheim, and Max Weber were steeped in law and "regarded the sociology of law as an integral part of social theory" (Schluchter 2002, 257). They were all writing at times when other social institutions appeared to be radically changing, and they sought to understand why. All three saw law as a method of redefining relationships between persons and institutions. But according to their ideological leanings, they viewed law as either greasing the squeaky wheels of change to make the passage quieter for everyone or a weapon to maintain the power and privilege of the few. Marx saw law as an ideological tool justifying the institutionalization of the class system, Weber saw it as the prime mover in society's progress toward rationality and modernity, and Durkheim saw it as the preeminent social fact through which the evolution of all societies can be traced. These early sociologists saw law as both a product and a producer of social change and as a response to, and sometimes a cause of, social unrest. In fact, nineteenth-century sociology was so immersed in the law that Donald Kelly (1990) has characterized modern sociology as "the ghost of jurisprudence past" (275).

Max Weber

Few scholars have had greater influence on contemporary legal thinking than German sociologist and lawyer Max Weber (1864–1920). In his most famous work, *Economy and Society* (1978/1905), Weber argued that the law was different from other kinds of rule-following behavior in three fundamental ways. First, regardless of whether or not persons want to and habitually do or do not obey the law, they face external pressures to do so in the form of actions and threats. Second, these external pressures involve the threat of coercion and force. Third, these threats are carried out by agents of the state charged with that specific duty. Nowhere in Weber's writings do we see allusions to natural law by which unjust laws may be invalidated.

Weber's major interest in both his sociological and legal writings was the increasing rationalization of the world. Weber wanted to explain how the world had changed from a hierarchical world of lords and peasants, overwhelmingly concerned with the afterlife, to a world of technical progress and capitalism firmly planted in this life (Collins and Makowsky 1993). The progress and expansion he saw around him was possible only if the people responsible for it could plan ahead, secure in the knowledge that if all citizens followed certain binding rules, things would happen in a relatively predictable fashion. Without such predictability, economic progress and expansion cannot happen, and the economy is destined to remain at the level of barter. Predictability and progress can only occur under a binding code of conduct rationally derived from the minds of individuals schooled in legal and administrative theory and practice and enforced by a cadre of honest and professional state agents.

Given his interest in rationalization, Weber was very interested in how authorities in various cultures make decisions when confronted with issues of contention and how the decision-making process that was employed accelerated or retarded modernization (rationalization) in those cultures. Weber is perhaps best known in legal circles for his fourfold typology of legal decision making. As you might have guessed, the two fundamentals of Weber's typology are the *rationality* or *irrationality* of legal procedure. Rational procedures rely on logic; nonrational procedures rest on mysticism, faith, or superstitions. Rational or irrational procedures may be either *formal* or *substantive*. *Formality* refers to decision making on the basis of established and inflexible rules and implies the independence of the legal system from other social institutions. *Substantive* decision making takes the substance of individual cases into consideration rather than relying on general legal principles (Turkel 1996). The four methods of legal decision making derived from these elements are next described in more detail:

1. **Substantive irrationality**: This method is the least rational of the four types. It is based on case-by-case political, religious, or emotional reactions on the part of a nonlegally trained person acting without a set of legal principles. The biblical story of King Solomon's decision regarding the custody of a child is an example of this type. Recall that Solomon was asked to solve the dilemma of two women claiming maternity and possession of the same infant. He ordered

the baby to be sliced into two and divided between the women. One woman agreed to this solution, the other begged Solomon to give the infant to her rival. Solomon reasoned that the second woman must be the true mother because of this and that the first woman could not possibly be. He therefore made his decision in favor of the second woman. Because Solomon's decision was shorn of any legal rules, it was irrational; and because it was decided on a case-by-case basis, it was substantive. However, the decision was the essence of justice and wisdom.

2. **Formal irrationality**: This method is based on such things as religious dogma, magic, oath swearing, and trial by combat or ordeal. There are certain formal rules to be followed, but they are not based on reason or logic. The process of oath swearing (discussed in chap. 14) used to settle cases in some Islamic countries is an example of formal irrationality.

3. **Substantive rationality**: This method is guided by a set of internally consistent general principles other than law. Examples of this type would be decision making applied on a case-by-case basis according to the logic of some religious, ideological, or bureaucratic set of rules. The principles that are seen in the Code of Hammurabi indicate that substantive rationality was the method of legal decision making used. Much of American administrative law is of this type when dealing with issues involving complex technological issues (see chap. 7).

4. **Formal rationality**: The most rational and ideal of all four types. This type combines a high degree of independence of legal institutions with a set of general rules and procedures applicable to all. Those who make the decisions on these grounds are monitored by others trained in the law. All Western legal systems fall into this category (Evan 1990). Table 1.1 presents a summary table of Max Weber's decision-making typology.

Although Weber clearly favors Western formal rationality, none of the other three methods are necessarily "wrong" or unjust; all methods must be evaluated in the context of the culture in which they are being used. Weber was primarily concerned with identifying the kind of legal reasoning best suited to modern capitalism and not necessarily passing judgment on these decision-making methods as functional or dysfunctional in the cultural contexts in which they

Table 1.1 *Summary Table of Max Weber's Decision-Making Typology*

	Irrationality	Rationality
Substantive	Decisions made subjectively by nonlegally trained individuals on a case-by-case basis.	Decisions made on a case-by-case basis guided by logically consistent principles (bureaucratic rules, religion, ideology) other than law.
Formal	Decisions based on formal rules that are not based on logic (superstition, magic, ordeals, oath swearing, etc.).	Decisions based on formal logical rules and principles made by legally trained persons bound by those rules but with a high degree of independence.

were employed. As we shall see in the next chapter, cases settled exclusively on the basis of formal rationality may sometimes be at odds with justice.

Émile Durkheim

French sociologist Émile Durkheim (1858–1917), a contemporary of Weber's, was interested in the relationship between types of law and types of society. Durkheim's basic theme is that all societies exist on the basis of a common moral order, not on the basis of rational self-interest as implied in the "social contract" theses of Hobbes or Locke. In his famous book *Division of Labor in Society* (Durkheim, 1960/1893), he set out to examine the effects of the division of labor on social solidarity. By *social solidarity*, Durkheim meant the degree to which people felt an emotional sense of belonging to other individuals and groups. The type and strength of social solidarity depends to a great extent on the kind of economic system a society has and on the stage of its development. Durkheim divided societies into two types: the nonindustrial societies of earlier times, which were characterized by what he called **mechanical solidarity,** and modern or industrial societies, characterized by **organic solidarity**.

In nonindustrial societies, social relations were based mostly on primary group interactions (frequent face-to-face contact with the same people), which tended to result in strong emotional bonds. There was only a simple and limited division of labor in such societies; individual differences were minimized, and all members more or less shared the same worldview. Since people were involved in a limited range of occupations, most people looked at life in the same predictable way. Social relations were personal and uncomplicated for the most part, with strong behavioral norms leaving little leeway for behavior that contravened them. Mechanical solidarity thus grows out of sameness, out of a commonality of experience, and produces a very strong *collective conscience* or *collective consciousness* (in French they mean the same thing; Collins and Makowsky 1993).

With the onset of the industrial revolution and the factory system came a broad division of labor, which resulted in a shift from mechanical to organic solidarity. Durkheim chose the term *organic* to illustrate this type of solidarity because it was consistent with his functionalist view of society as an organism consisting of interdependent parts. Organic solidarity is characterized by *secondary* relationships in which people interact for brief periods to accomplish specific goals such as exchanging services (workers in factories, students in schools, shoppers in stores, repairmen in homes, etc.). The collective consciousness is weakened because of this basically unemotional pattern of temporary and goal-directed interaction. Additionally, because of occupational specialization, people began to conceive of themselves less in terms of the groups to which they belong and more as individuals. Organic solidarity thus grows out of differences and a sense of social interdependence rather than from shared experiences and a common identity.

With changes in patterns of interaction came changes in the form of social solidarity, which in turn generated changes in the law. The greater the complexity of a society and the greater the shift from predominantly primary to secondary interaction, the more laws are required to regulate the different kinds of relationships among citizens. Growth in social and economic complexity almost by definition requires growth in legal complexity. Consider the recent efforts of the Chinese government to modernize and to develop a market economy. From 1979 to 1989, over 3,000 laws were passed or changed in that country in response to these efforts, and the number of lawyers in the country more than doubled (Turkel 1996). In Weber's terms, modern economies demand a formal/rational legal system.

Different types of social solidarity, as well as increasing the reach of civil law, generate changes in the criminal law. In preindustrial societies, the community exercised great power over the life of the individual. The laws of those communities expressed a strong collective conscience, and thus violations generated great moral outrage. Punishment for breaking moral and legal rules demanded extremely harsh penalties, including torture and execution. Durkheim called this pattern of response to violations of the collective conscience *retributive* or *repressive* justice (Durkheim was too Eurocentric here; many preliterate cultures stressed arbitration and reconciliation over harsh punishments). Harsh punishments, according to Durkheim, functioned to reaffirm the righteousness of the moral norms that had been violated. As the collective conscience became weaker under the increased division of labor in industrial societies, so did the strength of collective moral outrage. The lessening of moral outrage led to more tolerant attitudes toward minor rule breakers and to a more humanitarian form of justice that is *restitutive* rather than retributive. We have observed this change from retributive to restitutive justice in Western societies over the past 200 years. The old notions of retributive justice are still in evidence in some Islamic countries that continue to lop off the hands of thieves, stone adulterers to death, and apply the lash to users of alcohol (Fairchild and Dammer 2001).

TWO OPPOSING PERSPECTIVES: CONSENSUS AND CONFLICT

Sociologists who study the law as a social institution and its function as a social control mechanism tend to view it in terms of one of two broad perspectives. Which perspective a scholar favors tends to depend on his or her more fundamental perspective on society. Some scholars view society as basically good, just, and more or less providing equal opportunity for all individuals within it. These people hold what is called the consensus view of society. Others view society as basically unjust, unequal, and discriminatory. These people hold what is called the conflict view. **Consensus** theorists emphasize how society is structured to maintain its stability and view it as an integrated network of institutions (the family, church, school, economy, government) that function to maintain social order and the system as a whole (Schaefer and Lamm 2001). Social stability is also achieved in this view through cooperation, shared values, and the cohesion and solidarity that people feel by being part of a shared culture. Consensus theorists are aware that conflicts often arise in social life, but they stress that such conflicts are temporary and can be and are solved within the framework of shared fundamental values as exemplified by a neutral legal system.

Conflict theorists consider society to be composed of individuals and groups with sharply different interests and to be characterized by conflict and dissention. People and groups everywhere, they maintain, seek to maximize their interests. Since resources are limited, conflict between different individuals and groups is inevitable and continuous. The stability and order that consensus theorists see is only temporary and is maintained by coercion rather than consensus, that is, the ability of more powerful people and groups to impose their will upon the less powerful. The social institutions so lauded by consensus theorists function to maintain the privilege of the few and to keep the many subservient to them (Schaefer and Lamm 2001).

Which view is correct? The simple answer is that it is impossible to say without specifying what society we are talking about. All societies are characterized by both consensus and conflict; it is almost impossible to imagine any society in which they are absent. Max Weber recognized the dual nature of society when he defined law in a manner that encompasses both consensus and coercion: "Laws are 'consensually valid in a group' and are 'guaranteed through a coercive apparatus'" (in Turkel 1996, 8). We have to remember that these two competing models are examples of what sociologists call *ideal types*. Ideal types are abstract conceptual tools that accentuate, purely for analytical purposes, the phenomenon being studied; they lay no claims to mirror the day-to-day reality of any concrete example of that phenomenon. Let us examine law in the context of these two ideal-type models of society.

The Consensus Perspective

All the legal theorists we have encountered thus far have been proponents of the consensus perspective. This perspective views law as basically a neutral framework for patching up conflicts between individuals and groups who primarily share the same set of fundamental values. Law is viewed in a manner analogous to the immune system of the body in that it identifies and neutralizes potential dangers to the social body before they can do too much damage. Thus, law is a just and necessary mechanism for controlling behavior detrimental to peace, order, predictability and stability, and for maintaining social integration. Specific legal codes are assumed to express compromises between various interest groups regarding issues that have been contentious in the past, not to codify the victories of some groups over others. Law is also seen as reflecting the community's deeply held values, and as defining the rights and responsibilities of all those within it, and is a legitimate expression of morality and custom. If coercion is sometimes needed to bolster conscience, it is because the individual, not the law, is flawed. The law is obeyed by the vast majority of people not out of fear, but out of respect, and it is willingly supported by all good people.

Perhaps the main reason why we have not encountered any theorist with a conflict view of the law is that they were all members of privileged classes, which naturally tended to endear them to the status quo. Except for Aristotle's brief note of concern that legislators should guard against laws favoring their own class, any hint in the works of these writers that the law could unfairly serve the needs of the elite comes percolating from below the surface. We see this in Thrasymacus, Plato's antagonist in the dialogue on justice contained in *The Republic and Other Works* (1960, book 1). Thrasymacus argues that the law of any state is merely the legalizing of the interests of the stronger. For the conflict perspective to be given full voice, it had to wait for writers arising from the less privileged classes, which could only come after education became more widespread.

The Conflict Perspective

Underlying the conflict perspective of the law is a view of human nature that sees human beings as basically exploitive and duplicitous creatures (although conflict theorists believe we have become that way because of the greed and egoism instilled in us by living in a capitalist society, not because we are born that way). It also avers that law functions to preserve the power and privilege of the most exploitive and duplicitous among us, not to protect the weak and helpless. The conflict perspective of law rests on the assumptions of conflict sociology, which asserts that social behavior is best understood in terms of struggles and conflicts between groups and individuals over scarce resources. As we have seen, although thinking of social processes in terms of conflict between rival factions (usually between social classes) goes back as far as Plato, the more formal treatment of conflict as a concept traces its origin to the thought of the nineteenth-century German philosopher Karl Marx.

Marxist legal scholars certainly agree with scholars from other perspectives that law exists to settle conflicts and restore social peace but insist that conflicts are always settled in favor of the ruling class in any society, even if it may sometimes look like other segments of society also benefit (e.g., a general tax cut in which the wealthy gain millions while the working person perhaps gains a dollar or two every paycheck). The ruling class always wins out because it is this class that makes the rules governing social interaction. The basic proposition of the conflict perspective was set down by Marx and Engels (1888/1972, 136) in *The German Ideology*: "The ideas of the ruling class are in every epoch the ruling ideas; i.e., the class, which is the ruling material force of society, is at the same time its ruling intellectual force."

For Marx and Engels, society is divided into two classes, the rulers and the ruled. The ruling class—by which Marx and Engels meant the owners of the means of production, that is, factory owners and entrepreneurs—controls the "ruling material force of society." Because these individuals control the means of production, they are able to buy politicians, the media, the church, and all other social institutions that mold social values and attitudes and thus law. The relationship between power and lawmaking as been described (cynically?) as the "Golden Rule," which posits that "Those with the gold make the rules."

Why do the exploited not recognize their exploitation and the ways in which the law supports it? Marx and Engels explained this puzzle with reference to the idea of **false consciousness**. By false consciousness, Marx and Engels meant that the working classes have accepted an ideological worldview that is contrary to their best interests. Workers have been duped into accepting the legitimacy of the law by the ruling classes and are not aware that the law does not serve them. They blindly and docilely obey the law, believing that they are behaving morally by doing so. The ruling class is able to generate the false consciousness of the workers by virtue of its control over key institutions such as education, religion, the media, and of course, the law itself. These institutions define what is right and what is wrong, and they control the flow of information so that it conforms to the worldview of the ruling class.

We do not have to be Marxists, or even liberals, to agree that great wealth confers special privilege on its possessors or that history is replete with class struggles. In Athens in 594 BCE, Plutarch wrote of the great disparity of wealth between classes and the dangerous conflict it generated (Durant and Durant 1968, 55), and President of the United States John Adams wrote that American society was divided into a small group of rich people and a large mass of poor people engaged in a constant class struggle (Adams 1778/1971). Neither do we have to be reactionaries, or even conservatives, to realize that any society without a fairly strong moral consensus will not last very long.

Because both consensus and conflict are ubiquitous and integral facts of social life, we have to address both processes in this book while attempting to remain agnostic with respect to which process "really" characterizes social life in a general sense. It is hoped that it will become plain to the reader that the consensus perspective is most suitable for explaining certain sets of facts and that the conflict perspective is better suited to explaining other sets of facts. We hope that it will also become plain that conflict is as necessary as consensus to maintain the viability of a free society. In fact, conflict may form the very foundation of later consensus in pluralistic societies such as the United States, since justice for all is usually unattainable unless the oppressed agitate strongly for it (Rawls 2003). This principle will be illustrated in subsequent chapters discussing the rights of workers, racial minorities, and women.

SUMMARY

Law is a written body of rules of conduct applicable to all members of a defined community, society, or culture, which emanate from a governing authority and that are enforced by its agents by the imposition of penalties for their violation. We looked at the six primary characteristics of culture and their relationship to law. These characteristics are beliefs, values, norms, symbols, technology, and language. Our discussion of these characteristics showed that law is, and always has been, an integral part of culture. Examining law as a social construct is known as legal positivism.

We have traced thinking across the centuries about various aspects of the law from Hammurabi to the more recent sociological writing of Weber and Durkheim. The law was relatively well developed in Hammurabi's Code, replacing a system of personal vengeance with a system in which a neutral third party was charged with making decisions in both criminal matters and business transactions.

Plato felt that although justice and wisdom were part of the perfect order of the universe, humans could only approach these ideals through reason. Although humans had the capacity to emulate the good and the just, they rarely did. Plato thus reasoned that if law did not exist, society would degenerate into chaos. To some extent, he articulated an idea that was given its greatest impetus about two thousand years later by Thomas Hobbes.

Aristotle equated the concept of law with justice. He assumed a very strong utilitarian interpretation of the law, going much further than Plato in terms of arguing for the rights of ordinary people. For Aristotle, the most important goal of the legislature was to provide for "the greatest happiness of the greatest number" in society. He even offered the "radical" notion that even the rulers of a nation should not be above the law.

Thomas Hobbes disavowed any belief in natural law or justice. He saw the "state of nature" as a warlike state where only the strong survive. Because of this warlike state, people agreed to engage in a social contract in which they surrendered many of their freedoms in exchange for protection. Hobbes argued that the main goal of government under this contract was to provide for the security of the individual and that any state that did so was just by definition. Hobbes believed that the sovereign was an absolute ruler who could employ oppressive tactics in the service of obtaining an orderly society.

The work of John Locke stands in sharp contrast to the work of Thomas Hobbes. Locke both refuted the absolute right of monarchs and reconciled strong government with the liberty of the individual. In contrast with Hobbes's brutish state of nature, Locke's was one in which individuals enjoyed liberty and harmony and was only inferior because it lacked law. States or governments develop and exist by virtue of the social contract, according to the terms of which individuals maintain most of their liberties while voluntarily surrendering to a civil government their power to punish transgressors themselves. He also wrote that when governments overstep their powers, individuals have the right to reconstitute that civil government based on the moral force of natural law. Locke's version of natural law, liberty of individuals, and the proper role of civil society provided the ideas and justifications for the British, American, and French revolutions.

Max Weber asserted that if a society is to advance into a more modern and complex structure, it must be governed by rational law. For the modern capitalistic economy to develop, it needed a predictable and dependable legal system. Natural law may be the philosophical "touchstone" of a society in terms of individual rights and responsibilities, but for any capitalistic complex economy to develop, it must depend on a predictable, rational system of law. Weber's four types of legal decision making, ranked from the least to the most rational, are substantive irrationality, formal irrationality, substantive rationality, and formal rationality.

Émile Durkheim was interested in the relationship between law and social solidarity. He postulated two types of social solidarity, mechanical and organic. Mechanical solidarity is associated with preindustrial societies and grows out of the sameness of everyone's experiences; organic solidarity is associated with industrial societies and grows out of the interdependence of individuals that exists due to an advanced division of labor. The growing complexity of industrialized societies required the increasing reach of the civil law to regulate the great variety of transactions that occur in such societies.

Criminal law also changes with the type of solidarity within a society. Societies characterized by mechanical solidarity have a very strong collective conscience, which leads to great moral outrage when norms are violated and to a retributive or repressive form of justice. A weakening of the collective conscience follows a change to organic solidarity, which leads to the more tolerant and humanitarian restitutive form of justice.

Most sociological students of the law conduct their analyses from one of the two general sociological models of society: the consensus or the conflict models. The consensus model views society as an integrated network of institutions held together by a common set of values. The law is seen as a neutral protector of the continuity and stability of these institutions and values. This perspective also views society as basically good and just. The conflict model holds the opposite view: conflict rather than consensus is the main characteristic of society, and the law serves the purposes of the ruling classes. This view is presented most forcefully in the works of Marx and Engels. We indicated that all societies are characterized by both conflict and consensus, with one process dominating at one time, and the other at another time.

DISCUSSION QUESTIONS

1. What do you think are the main differences between legal rules and other kinds of rules?
2. Give one or two examples of how changing values and/or technology have led to changes in the law.
3. In what ways are (a) Plato and Hobbes and (b) Aristotle and Locke alike in terms of their views of human nature and of the law?
4. Do you believe that the "ruling class" (decide for yourselves who these people may be) unfairly pass laws favorable to themselves and detrimental to the rest of us? If they do, what can we do about it?
5. In what ways can conflict be beneficial to a society? Can conflict actually support consensus?
6. Would you choose to live under a brutal dictator such as Hitler, Stalin, or Saddam Hussein or suffer the chaos of a society without any kind of law?

References

Adams, J. 1778/1971. *In defence of the Constitution of the United States.* Vol. 1. New York: De Capo Press.

Allott, P. 2001. Law and the remaking of humanity. In *Democracy and the rule of law,* edited by N. Dorsen, pp. 19-30. Washington, DC: CQ Press.

Aquinas, T. 1952. *The Summa Theologica.* Chicago: University of Chicago Press.

Aristotle. 1952. *Nicomachean ethics.* Chicago: William Benton.

Basler, R. 2007. Lyceum address. *Abraham Lincoln online.* http://showcase.net/web/creative/lincoln/speeches/lyceum.htm.

Bottero, J. 1973. The first law code. In *Ancient empires,* edited by S. Brandon, pp. 22–28. New York: Newsweek Books.

Collins, R., and M. Makowsky. 1993. *The discovery of society.* 5th ed. New York: McGraw-Hill.

Deininger, W. 1965. *Problems in social and political thought.* New York: Macmillan.

Durant, W., and A. Durant. 1968. *The lessons of history.* New York: Simon and Schuster.

Durkheim, E. 1960 [1893]. *The Division of labor in society.* Translated by George Simpson. New York: Free Press.

Edwards, C. 1971. *Hammurabi, King of Babylonia.* Port Washington, New York: Kennikat Press.

Evan, W. 1990. *Social structure and the law: Theoretical and empirical approaches.* Newbury Park, CA: Sage.

Fairchild, E., and H. Dammer. 2001. *Comparative criminal justice systems.* Belmont, CA: Wadsworth.

Giddens, A. 1999. Risk and responsibility. *Modern Law Review* 62:1-10.

Giddens, A., M. Duneier, and R. Applebaum. 2005. *Introduction to sociology.* New York: Norton.

Hobbes, T. 1952. *Leviathan.* Chicago: William Benton.

Kelly, D. 1990. *The human measure: Social thought in the western legal tradition.* Cambridge, MA: Harvard University Press.

Lavine, T. 1989. *From Socrates to Sartre: The philosophic quest.* New York: Bantam.

Leiter, B. 2001. Legal realism and legal positivism reconsidered. *Ethics* 111:278–301.

Locke, J. 1952. *The second treatise of government.* Indianapolis, Ind.: Liberal Arts.

Marx, K., and F. Engels. 1888/1972. The German ideology. In *The Marx-Engels reader,* edited by R. Tucker. New York: Norton.

McGirk, T. 2005. Killers in the neighborhood. August 21. *Time Magazine Online.* http://www.time.com/time/magazine/article/0,9171,1096488-4,00.html.

Murphy, J. 2006. The lawyer and the layman: Two perspectives on the rule of law. *Review of Politics* 68:101–31.

Plato. 1952. *The dialogues of Plato.* Chicago: William Benton.

———. 1960. *The republic and other works.* Garden City, NY: Doubleday.

Pojman, L. 1989. *Philosophy: The quest for truth.* Belmont, CA: Wadsworth.

Rawls, J. 1996. *Political liberalism.* New York: Columbia University Press.

———. 1999. *A theory of justice.* Oxford: Oxford University Press.

———. 2003. Conflict as a foundation for consensus: Contradictions of industrial capitalism in Book III of Durkheim's *Division of labor. Critical Sociology* 29:295–335.

Schaefer, R., and R. Lamm. 2001. *Sociology.* 7th ed. New York: McGraw-Hill.

Schluchter, W. 2002. The sociology of law as an empirical theory of validity. *Journal of Classical Sociology* 2:257–80.

Sinha, S. 1990. *What is law? The differing theories of jurisprudence.* New York: Paragon House.

Turkel, G. 1996. *Law and society: Critical approaches.* Boston: Allyn and Bacon.

Vago, S. 1991. *Law and society.* 3rd ed. Englewood Cliffs, N.J.: Prentice Hall.

Walsh, A. 2006. Correctional assessment, casework, and counseling. 4th ed. Lanham, Md.: American Correctional Association.

Weber, M. (1978/1905). *Economy and society: An outline of interpretative sociology.* Edited by G. Roth and C. Wittich. Vol. 2. Berkeley: University of California Press.

CHAPTER 2

JUSTICE AND THE LAW

After Adolf Hitler came into power in 1933, he decided that there would be no more flirtation in Germany with such notions as democracy and individual rights. The law would exist only to serve his vision of the state. Nazi Germany would live under the law of power, not the power of law. Just three months later, Jews were dismissed from the civil service, and over the following months and years, they were deprived of everything, even their lives in the death camps scattered across Europe. These acts took place under the cloak of law after 1935 with the implementation of the Nuremberg Laws, which stripped Jews of all legal, civil, social, or political rights and defined them as a separate race under The Law for the Protection of German Blood and Honor.

Do we have a moral right to pass judgment on the customs and laws of another culture that we find repugnant? Because Jewish persecution met every rational criteria for lawmaking by a democratically elected sovereign nation, by what standards would legal relativists condemn such laws? Despite their belief in the relativity of morals, they would have to turn to the ideas of justice embedded in natural law as the basis of their condemnation. This is exactly what the victorious Allies did when they tried Nazi war criminals at Nuremberg. The crimes committed by the Nazis, although legal under positivist Nazi law, violated universal principles of civilized behavior and human dignity.

There were legal theorists at the time who, while not denying that the Nazis deserved punishment, felt that the Nuremberg trials were a travesty, a "victor's justice" conducted in ways that violated many principles of law. For instance, the charge of "crimes against humanity" did not exist prior to the trials; hence, the Allies created an ex post facto (retroactive) crime. The Nazi defendants relied on positivist legal principles to defend themselves by rightfully claiming that they were operating under German law as it existed at the time (because of the Nazi experience, modern German law is very much influenced by natural law).

This illustrates the tensions between the legal positivists and natural law advocates. Positivists claim that the Allies were cloaking their desire for revenge using the language of natural justice and by doing so had violated the rule of law. Believers in natural justice replied that moral standards cried out for retribution and that the Nuremberg trials established a needed international standard of conduct. After reading this chapter, decide if it is wise or not to posit "universal standards" with which all cultures must comply. If so, who gets to define those standards and how might they be enforced?

INTRODUCTION

This chapter discusses questions that philosophers, theologians, and legal scholars have pondered for millennia: "What is justice?" "Where does it come from?" and "What is its relationship to the law?" Justice is one of those great intangibles, like truth, beauty, and love, all recognizable as we experience them in their particular manifestation but awkward to define. Justice, like truth, beauty, and love, is an *ideal*, not an objective "thing" that we can lay our hands on in the sense that the written law is. It is above all a *moral* ideal that persons and social institutions owe one another. By *ideal* we mean to imply that we think of it not as a Platonic "idea" but, rather, as something we must strive to understand and practice as the ultimate goal of the legal endeavor. Let us first try to come to grips with the first question: "What is justice?"

WHAT IS JUSTICE?

The definition of *justice* in Webster's dictionary (like most dictionary definitions) goes around in circles. *Justice* is: "The maintenance or administration of what is just." The dictionary previously defines *just* as "Conforming to a standard of correctness; righteous; merited; deserved" and gives as synonyms the terms *fair* and *upright*. So we are beginning to get an idea of what a general definition might look like, and you are probably all thinking to yourselves that justice is a very desirable thing, which of course it is. Think what life would be like under the maintenance and administration of what is unjust and in conformity with standards opposite of those listed under the definition of *just*.

Although, like *law, justice* is a complex idea with many definitions, we need one in order to proceed. Perhaps the definition that has gained the widest acceptance over the centuries is the one offered by Aristotle 300 years before the birth of Christ: "**Justice** consists of treating equals equally and unequals unequally according to relevant differences" (in Walsh 2006, 125). Similarly, the great Roman Jurist Dometius Ulpanius defined justice as "the constant and perpetual will to allot everyman his due" (in Day 1968, 31). Justice is thus about how we behave toward and treat others and how decisions are made about what type of behavior and treatment is appropriate given our perceptions about what others deserve. With Aristotle's definition in mind, we look at what various legal scholars have considered to be the two components of justice with which Aristotle was most concerned: distributive and retributive justice.

Distributive Justice

Distributive justice is concerned with how a political entity such as a nation-state distributes resources to its members. If there are no good reasons to distribute resources unequally (in the Aristotelian sense, there are no *relevant* differences), then resources should be equally distributed. But of course there are relevant differences with respect to resource distribution, although there may be arguments about just how relevant they are. Distributive justice is about rightful, merited, deserved distribution; it is not about need. A just distribution depends on the individual's contributions and value to the community.

The Marxist principle "From each according to his ability, to each according to his need" does not sit well with Aristotelians. They may agree that it is excellent advice for parents to apply to their children, but it is not a recipe for just government. Two people may have identical needs, but one of them may *deserve* a much greater proportion because of his or her contributions to the community. Dividing the resource pie equally regardless of people's differing contributions to its existence is unjust. Think how students who have done work worthy of an A grade would feel if required to donate their extra points to pull up other students with D's and F's because they "need" the points (an application of the preceding Marxist principle). Is giving each student a C grade regardless of their efforts because they need to pass the class and obtain a respectable grade-point average just? If you think it is, what consequences do you think it will have on the future efforts of students? According to Aristotle's definition, because their differing scores are a relevant difference, grading students unequally is just.

What if rather than talking about test grades we talk about more basic things such as food, clothing, and shelter? For example, is the provision of welfare for the "have-nots" of society just? We are not asking if it is decent or compassionate—we are only asking if it is just. Welfare means that the government has taken money from productive members of society and given it to non-productive members on the basis of the need of the latter. Help for the disabled, the temporarily unemployed, and for the formerly productive who by no fault of their own lack the capacity to function independently is considered just according to Aristotelian criteria because such people have earned it by their past efforts. On the other hand, what about a woman who has three or four children out of wedlock and who has never contributed anything to society? Her need is real, but it is self-induced and thus abusive of the welfare system and exploitive of those whose money is taken from them to support it. Providing such a person with needed resources may be decent and compassionate, but it is not, according to Aristotle's definition, just. Decency and compassion may be strong components of justice, although it is not always necessarily so.

There are times when some persons get less than they deserve because others have acquired more than their share. For instance, it was estimated that in 2001 the average American CEO was paid $13.1 million and that the average pay for the ordinary worker was $24,688 (Peirce 2001). We may agree that the CEO's worth is greater than that of any one line worker, but what relevant difference makes him or her 530 times more valuable? How about athletes and actors, who contribute nothing to the community except entertainment, making more each year than an entire 400-person police force, whose contributions to the community are enormous? While such a situation is reflective of some rather bizarre values, a market economy allows for these kinds of discrepancies in resource distribution. The invisible hand of market capitalism "decides" that a man dunking a ball into a hoop is worth more than 400 individuals putting their lives on the line trying to keep our streets safe, and, like it or not, by the strange logic of a market economy he deserves it. According to Aristotle's concept of justice, it is only when the accumulation of resources is exploitive that it becomes unjust. Athletes and entertainers do not obtain their grossly inflated salaries by exploiting others; fans freely pay to watch them perform. It is the scarcity of something rather than its intrinsic value that determines market price. Water, which is absolutely vital to all life, is far more intrinsically valuable than gold, but it is their respective abundance and rarity that determines their market value. Likewise, line workers and police officers are far more easily replaced than are the rare talents of a corporate CEO or an NBA star.

Exploitation has been a constant feature in the history of humankind, as have attempts to justify it by claiming that its fruits were the due of "naturally superior" people. Anatole France's well-known declaration that "Justice is made to give everyone his due; to the rich his richness, to the poor his poverty," was his caustic reply to Aristotle's "to each his due" concept of justice. However, this is unfair to Aristotle who condemned *undeserved* richness and poverty alike. Democratic governments have long recognized the unjustness of exploitive concentrations of wealth and have taken legislative steps to correct it. As we will see in chapter 11, most democracies have encouraged (or at least allowed) the formation of trade unions to fight workplace exploitation, they have regulated business, and they have sought a more equitable distribution of wealth by implementing a progressive income tax. Because the privileged classes have stoutly resisted such things, none of them occurred without great struggles. However, each of these reforms moved the economic systems of the democracies involved closer to the ideals of distributive justice as most philosophers and social theorists have viewed it.

Retributive Justice

We will be discussing substantive and procedural law at length in a later chapter, but for now it is sufficient to say that substantive law places limits on the actions of individuals (defines acts that are and are not permissible), and procedural law places limits on the agents of the state as they go about the business of enforcing substantive law. **Retributive justice** is concerned with *how* a society's system of law goes about determining guilt or innocence (procedural retributive justice), and then how it goes about determining the proper (just) punishment (substantive retributive justice) for the guilty. We will only concern ourselves for the moment with substantive justice. Like distributive justice, substantive retributive justice is concerned with persons getting what they rightly deserve according to their behavior. To be just, a society must punish with fairness and impartiality, which means that equals must be punished equally, and unequals must be punished unequally according to relevant differences.

The criminal justice system recognizes that one relevant difference that makes people different in terms of deciding punishment is the amount of harm done by a criminal act. Thus, murder, rape, and robbery are punished more severely than petty theft, receiving stolen property, and simple assault. The first three crimes are punished more severely because justice tries to seek a balance between the harm done to the victim and the pain the criminal must suffer.

But is the severity of the crime the only relevant difference that should determine punishment; that is, should all people committing the same crime receive equal punishment? Do you believe that a cardiologist and a laborer are punished equally if they are both fined $100 for speeding? Is there any relevant difference that justifies treating one differently from the other? Although $100 is $100, it is pocket change to the cardiologist, but perhaps one half of the laborer's weekly take-home pay. Just punishment is about equality of pain, not the equality of the instrument (the amount of the fine) used to inflict it because it is the pain that supposedly provides the deterrent effect. Thus, when financially unequal offenders are fined equally, they are not being punished equally and therefore not justly. A just punishment would be one that hurt both parties roughly equally. The day-fine system used in some European countries might accomplish this. Under this system, a convicted person pays a fine equal to a day's pay, which could be $500 per day or $50 per day depending on his or her daily salary. For instance, a Finnish billionaire was fined the equivalent of $216,900 for speeding in 2004, which beat the former Finnish record speeding fine of $148,000 ("Finland millionaire . . ." 2004).

There are many issues related to punishment and justice, the most pressing of which is probably sentencing disparity. If the statutory penalty for a given crime is open ended (say, "up to fifteen years," or from "two to ten years"), the actual punishment an offender receives will depend on the judge's exercise of discretion guided by legal and extralegal factors. The subjective opinions of individual judges as to what constitutes deserved punishment naturally leads to wide sentencing disparities, with "hanging" judges at one extreme and "bleeding heart" judges at the other. Temperamental and ideological differences among judges hardly constitute a relevant difference for determining different penalties for defendants who are roughly similarly situated in terms of the crimes they committed and their criminal records. One of the solutions aimed at minimizing sentencing disparity tried in various jurisdictions is the use of sentencing guidelines.

Sentencing guidelines are a way of operationalizing, or numerically defining, Aristotle's definition of justice by assigning numbers to various aspects of the crime and to characteristics of the offender. Typically, the crime seriousness section assigns points according to (1) the statutory gravity of the crime (first degree, second degree, etc.); (2) whether or not the crime was committed while the defendant was on probation, parole, or bail; (3) the amount of monetary loss; and (4) a series of aggravating (did the crime include "shocking and deliberate cruelty?") or mitigating (did the victim contribute to his or her victimization?) circumstances. The prior record section is typically concerned with (1) number of prior felony and misdemeanor offenses; (2) previous probation, parole, or bail violations; (3) whether the defendant has previously served prison time; and (4) a series of mitigating factors such as voluntary restitution, being a family breadwinner, or being substantially law abiding over a certain period prior to the present offense. Points on both sections are added and applied to a sentencing grid at the point at which the scores intersect. These grids indicate a sentence that may be presumptive or advisory, depending on the jurisdiction.

How did the designers of such guidelines know what the important aspects of the crime and the defendant's character are? In the case of Ohio's felony

Figure 2.1 Felony Sentencing Worksheet

Defendant's Name: _____ Case No. _____

OFFENSE RATING

1. Degree of Offense
Assess points for the one most serious offense or its equivalent for which offender is being sentenced, as follows: 1st degree felony = 4 points; 2nd degree felony = 3 points; 3rd degree felony = 2 points; 4th degree felony = 1 point. __

2. Multiple Offenses
Assess 2 points if one or more of the following applies: (A) offender is being sentenced for two or more offenses committed in different incidents; (B) offender is currently under a misdemeanor or felony sentence imposed by any court; or (C) present offense was committed while offender on probation or parole.

3. Actual or Potential Harm
Assess 2 points if one or more of the following applies: (A) serious physical harm to a person was caused; (B) property damage or loss of $300 or more was caused; (C) there was a high risk of any such harm, damage, or loss, though not caused; (D) the gain or potential gain from theft offense(s) was $300 or more, or (E) dangerous ordinance or a deadly weapon was actually used in the incident, or tis use was attempted or threatened.

4. Culpability
Assess 2 points if one or more of the following applies: (A) offender was engaging in continuing criminal activity as asource of income or livelihood, (B) offense was part of a continuing conspiracy to which offender was party, or (C) offense included shocking and deliberate cruelty in which offender participated or acquiesced.

5. Mitigation
Deduct 1 point for each of the following, as applicable: (A) there was substantial provocation, justification, or excuse for offense; (B) victim induced or facilitated offense; (C) offense was committed in the heat of anger; and (D) the property damaged, lost, or stolen was restored or recovered without significant cost to the victim.

Net Total = Offense Rating

OFFENDER RATING

1. Prior Convictions
Assess 2 points for each verified prior conviction, any jurisdiction. Count adjudications of delinquency for felony as convictions.

Assess 1 point for each verified prior misdemeanor conviction and jurisdiction; count adjudications of delinquency for misdemeanor as convictions. Do not count traffic or intoxication offenses as disorderly conduct, disturbing the peace, or equivalent offenses.

2. Repeat Offenses
Assess 2 points if present offense is offense of violence, sex offense, theft offense, or drug abuse offense, and offender has one or more prior convictions for same type of offense.

3. Prison Commitments
Assess 2 points if offender was committed one or more times to a penitentiary, reformatory, or equivalent institution in any jurisdiction. Count commitments to state youth commission or similar commitments in other jurisdictions.

4. Parole and Similar Violations
Assess 2 points if one or more of the following applies: (A) offender has previously had probation or parole for misdemeanor or felony revoked; (B) present offense committed while offender on probation or parole; (C) present offense committed while offender free on bail; or (D) present offense committed while offender in custody.

5. Credits
Deduct 1 point for each of the following, as applicable: (A) offender has voluntarily made bona fide, realistic arrangements for at least partial restitution; (B) offender was age 25 or older at time of first felony conviction; (C) offender has been substantially law-abiding for at least 3 years; and (D) offender lives with his or her spouse or minor children or both and is either a breadwinner for the family or, if there are minor children, a housewife.

Net Total = Offender Rating

INDICATED SENTENCE
-Circle the box on the chart where the offense and offender ratings determined on the previous page intersect. This indicates a normal sentencing package.

		OFFENDER RATING				
		0-2	3-5	6-8	9-11	12 or more
Offense Rating	6 or More	Impose one of three lowest minimum terms. No probation	Impose one of three highest minimum terms. No probation	Impose one of three highest minimum terms. No probation	Impose one of two highest minimum terms. Make at least part of multiple sentences consecutive. No probation	Impose highest minimum term. Make at least part of multiple sentences consecutive. No probation
	5	Impose one of three lowest minimum terms. Some form of probation indicated only with special mitigation	Impose one of three lowest minimum terms. No probation	Impose one of three highest minimum terms. No probation	Impose one of three highest minimum terms. No probation	Impose one of two highest minimum terms. Make at least part of multiple sentences consecutive. No probation
	4	Impose one of two lowest minimum terms. Some form of probation indicated	Impose one of three lowest terms. Some form of probation indicated only with special mitigation	Impose one of three lowest minimum terms. No probation	Impose one of three highest minimum terms. No probation	Impose one of three highest minimum terms. No probation
	3	Impose one of two lowest minimum terms. Some form of probation indicated	Impose one of two lowest terms. Some form of probation indicated	Impose one of three lowest minimum terms. Some form of probation indicated only with special mitigation	Impose one of three highest minimum terms. No probation	Impose one of three highest minimum terms. No probation
	0-2	Impose lowest minimum term. Some form of probation indicated	Impose one of two lowest minimum terms. Some form of probation indicated	Impose one of two lowest minimum terms. Some form of probation indicated	Impose one of three lowest minimum terms. Some form of probation indicated only with special mitigation	Impose one of three lowest minimum terms. No probation

sentencing worksheet (FSW), a two-year study of the sentencing practices of 60 percent of Ohio's felony judges preceded the design of the FSW (Walsh 2006). The study determined what these judges *as a whole* considered relevant, thus ruling out any idiosyncratic opinions on the matter that individual judges may have. The study also determined what sentences these judges gave *on average* to defendants similarly situated in terms of the FSW's criteria. Averaging sentences pulled the sentences of both the overly lenient and overly severe judges into the middle of the distribution of sentencing possibilities. The averaging of the sentences of more than half of a state's judges combines their wisdom, promotes consistency, and provides other judges with sentencing norms based on the past practices of their peers. Sentencing according to these criteria provides a mean between two equally unjust extremes. Such a practice is probably as close as we can get to the ideal of retributive justice as it is applied to the punishment of wrongdoers. The felony sentencing worksheet is presented in Figure 2.1.

PROBLEMS WITH ARISTOTLE'S DEFINITION OF JUSTICE

Although we have shown a positive attitude about Aristotle's definition of justice as "treating equals equally and unequals unequally according to relevant differences," can you spot a potential problem with it? The big problem rests with defining what *relevant* differences are. Is skin color a relevant difference? If so, we can justify slavery by asserting that we are treating unequals unequally. Early American law considered Africans as being less than human, which, if believed, is a relevant difference and thus a justification for the treatment of Africans as beasts of burden. How about gender, religion, nationality, and sexual orientation? All these statuses have been (and sometimes still are in some countries) considered at one time or another to be relevant differences, thus granting the law permission to treat the disvalued group badly. Perhaps justice will be more fully realized when we view relevant differences exclusively as differences of conduct, not of ascribed statuses such as those mentioned.

Theorists with a conflict perspective on the law would point out a further problem with the Aristotelian view of justice in that even if the *process* of justice is identical for every person brought before the courts, the *result* in terms of equal treatment and equal outcome is impossible under the present socioeconomic and legal systems. Conflict theorists would point out that in a capitalist system and adversarial system of law, "justice" is just another commodity, the quality of which depends on its price. Everyone is entitled to legal counsel in the United States, even paid for by the state if the person is indigent, but only the privileged few can afford the legal superstars of the world. With the aid of great lawyers, the factually guilty may be set free; with poor lawyers, or even good lawyers lacking the incentive of a big fee, the factually innocent may be found guilty. Both outcomes are perversions of justice.

LEGAL REALISM

Unlike natural law and legal positivism, **legal realism** is not a theory or philosophy of law but, rather, the study of legal decision making. Legal realists examine how law is actually applied and the implications of that application. They evaluate law not "as written" but, rather, law "as practiced." After all, law only becomes "real" in the hands of judges and administrators, and it is obviously central to the practice of law for lawyers to understand law as it is understood and applied by its decision makers. For the legal realist, law is indeterminate, by which we mean that law by itself does not fully determine the outcome of a legal action. That is, although legal rules certainly "influence" judicial decisions, they do not determine them in any absolute way, as legal positivists might argue. In other words, positivism is a theory of what is distinctive about a society's legal norms; legal realism is an empirical theory about what judges really do (Leiter 2001). Chief Justice Oliver Wendell Holmes's succinct definition of law sums legal realism up nicely: "The prophecies of what the courts will do in fact, nothing more pretentious, is what I mean by law" (cited in Kidder 1983, 21).

Legal realists maintain that nonlegal reasons such as a subjective judgment of fairness on the part of the judge often explain judicial decisions and by doing so can introduce justice (or injustice) into law. This does not mean that judges can make arbitrary decisions or that legal realism and positivism are incompatible. The former obviously needs the latter if judges are not to stumble into Weber's substantive irrationality. Judges' decisions are guided by positive law even if they are not completely determined by it. Note how the great American eighteenth-century Judge Chancellor Kent cleverly made use of positive law to make decisions he felt were just rather than simply legal:

> My practice was first to make myself . . . master of the facts. . . . [B]y the time I had done this slow and tedious process I was master of the cause [case] & ready to decide it. I saw where justice lay and the moral sense decided the cause half the time, & I then set down to search the authorities until I had exhausted my books, & I might once & a while be embarrassed by a technical rule, but I most always found principles to suit my views of the case. (Kaye 1998, 13–14).

Kent's strategy amounts to judges sending their clerks to the legal parking lot to find a vehicle that will take them from where they are to wherever it is they want to be without breaking down. Miles and Sunstein (2008) provide summaries of many studies showing that judicial decisions are frequently predictable by their political ideology, race, gender, and religion, depending on the nature of the case before them (say, sexual harassment). Judges sitting on appeals courts are also frequently subjected to ideological dampening (a Democrat sitting with two Republicans, or vice versa, will move ideologically toward his or her two colleagues) or amplification (if all judges on a panel are of the same political persuasion, their ideology will be amplified) (Miles and Sunstein 2008).

Of course, if judges go too far in injecting their subjective interpretations into the law as written in order to rationalize their decisions, there are layers of appeals courts to set the matter right, if there can be said to be a "right" ruling. Because of this, only the court of last resort, the United States Supreme Court, has the luxury of deciding cases after the fashion of Chancellor Kent and being assured of not being overturned. For instance, in *Bush v. Gore* (2000), the case that gave the Presidency to George W. Bush, the justices came up with a novel interpretation of the Fourteenth Amendment's equal protection clause (all Florida counties did not count votes in the same way, thus Bush's equal protection rights were violated). Even here a decision is based on a majority vote rather than on the interpretation of a single judge, and they do at least have to have the appearance of following the Constitution (notwithstanding that the Constitution is what the majority of justices say it is). However, the point is that when not adhering strictly to the law as written (or mangling it beyond recognition), most judges are presumably convinced that they are dispensing justice.

We do not wish to be overly cynical in our discussion of legal realism by leaving the impression that it is only characteristics of judges that influence their decisions. Recall that Chancellor Kent considered justice as he saw it to be his guide. It is generally considered that *Muller v. Oregon* (1908) was the first time that the United States Supreme Court openly acknowledged social science data in rendering its decision (Tomkins and Oursland 1991). This case involved a woman who was required to work in excess of 10 hours in one day at Muller's laundry, in violation of an Oregon law forbidding excessive hours for women. Muller was convicted of violating the law and fined. His appeal eventually was heard by the U.S. Supreme Court, which upheld the Oregon statute, in spite of the fact that three years earlier it had upheld the rights of a bakery to work its bakers (all males) 16 hours per day. In Muller, the Court "distinguished" the two cases on the basis of the difference between the sexes. Part of the ruling stated:

> That woman's physical structure and the performance of maternal functions place her at a disadvantage in the struggle for subsistence is obvious. This is especially true when the burdens of motherhood are upon her. Even when they are not, by abundant testimony of the medical fraternity continuance for a long time on her feet at work, repeating this from day to day, tends to injurious effects upon the body, and as healthy mothers are essential to vigorous offspring, the physical well-being of woman becomes an object of public interest and care in order to preserve the strength and vigor of the race.... [H]istory discloses the fact that woman has always been dependent upon man. He established his control at the outset by superior physical strength, and this control in various forms, with diminishing intensity, has continued to the present.

Although this ruling was hailed by women at the time, modern feminists have criticized it for what they consider to be the sexist assumptions that led to the decision as well as on the grounds that it protected only women, not all workers (Tomkins and Oursland 1991).

Legal realism belies the claim that the United States is "a country of law, not men." The hearings on the nomination of Sonia Sotomayor to the United States Supreme Court in 2009 made it plain that decisions of social importance are not made by disembodied, objective judges devoid of passion for one side of an issue or the other. We are not saying that this is right or wrong, only that it is inevitable. Opponents of Sotomayor's nomination made much of her claims of empathy with the less fortunate, thus assuming that she can discard her biases when she dons her judicial robes. The critical issue is not whether judges should rely on their emotions but, rather, whether or not they can empathize with diverse groups of people, not only with groups with whom they identify.

WHERE DOES JUSTICE COME FROM? TWO PERSPECTIVES OF LAW AND JUSTICE AS NATURAL

In this section, we explore two perspectives on why and how law and justice exist in the first place. These two perspectives go beyond the consensus and conflict perspectives, both of which view law as entirely socially constructed and therefore invented rather than discovered. Do we discover law like physicists discover new scientific facts about the physical world, or do we make it up as we go along like novelists making up their plots? Obviously, we make up specific laws relating to given issues as they arise, but what about the more abstract concepts of law and justice, the inner urge that makes people everywhere *want* to apply rules to conduct?

People everywhere not only want to apply rules to conduct, they want to apply rules that are just, if for no other reason that they want to be treated fairly themselves. Is justice inherent in the very nature of humanity in the same sense that physical laws describing the behavior of all inanimate objects are inherent in the universe? Think of the physical laws that are the bases for sciences such as physics and chemistry. These laws create harmony and predictability in the universe; they operated long before humans discovered them; and they continue to operate whether we are aware of them or not. Physical laws are not invented, nor do they evolve from earlier incomplete versions of themselves: they are simply *there*, waiting to be discovered, understood, and applied. The more we understand about the nature of these physical laws, the more we can harness them for human good. Likewise, for those who believe in the existence of moral laws whether or not we have discovered and applied them, the more we search for them and understand them the more just and harmonious our societies will be.

Philosophers have long contemplated the question of whether there are natural laws governing human behavior in the same sense that there are physical laws governing the physical world. The great philosopher Immanuel Kant was one who thought there were when he spoke of the two things he could be absolutely sure of: "The starry heavens above, and the moral law within" (in Thomas 1962, 255). Consider that the first moral statement children make, and often with some force, is "That's not fair!" As Kant may have asked, how do children arrive at that conclusion so readily, and why is it so immediately compelling if the sense of fairness is not somehow within them ready to be activated? Finkel, Harre, and Rodriguez Lopez (2001, 7) call these "not fair" complaints "commonsense justice" because they "are uttered long before children come into contact with any formal introduction to general moral principles."

If there is a natural law, we have to ask ourselves if it is the product of a deity concerned with our well-being or the product of blind evolutionary processes. We are not concerned at present with specific laws but with the concept of law as an overarching regulator of human behavior, an instinct for rule making that is as natural to the human species as language, thought, emotion, and the reproductive urge. Proponents of these two naturalistic perspectives—the *transcendental* and *evolutionary* perspectives—believe that there is a natural basis for law based on an inner voice yearning for justice, although they differ on its source.

The Transcendental Natural Law Perspective

A moral relativist basically believes that whatever is considered right and proper in any given society is morally right even if outsiders might consider some practices of that society (for instance, cannibalism, wife beating, the mutilation of young girls by clitorectomy) to be morally repugnant and thus unjust. Social scientists have long preached against passing moral judgment on cultures other than our own because doing so implies that we are asserting the superiority of our own culture, and to do that supposedly makes us bigots, racists, and ethnocentrics. Since few people like to be called such names, many social scientists are moral relativists (at least publicly). However, there are those who believe that there are absolute moral standards of right and wrong that transcend time and culture and that are universally applicable.

Transcendentalism is a philosophical position that emphasizes the primacy and superiority of the spiritual over the material. It does not deny the reality of the physical world and its human constructs, such as positive law, but asserts that the transcendental (*transcendental* means "above," "beyond," and "exceeding normal human knowledge") realm is more fundamental. Transcendentalists believe that there are timeless and universalistic (natural) laws that transcend the legal interests of one particular society at one particular time in history. In this view, law originates in some transcendental realm and must be followed by all. Because natural law is superior to any human law, it must be followed even if it conflicts with human-made (positivist) law. In other words, the transcendentalist position is that the *ought* of law runs downward from some transcendental realm through jurisprudence (the science and philosophy of law) and education to the individual (Wilson 1998). This perspective agrees with Plato's assertion that as humanity becomes more civilized, learned, and wise, it will discover the nature of this law and apply it for the benefit of all, just as we discover and apply physical laws.

Natural law is a philosophy of law, not a formal set of statutes or procedures. No country has a natural law system in the sense that it has a common law, civil law, or socialist law system, although natural law principles may be woven into the threads of these systems. Many of the precepts contained in the Ten Commandments, considered to be elements of natural law because they are God-given, have been incorporated into most of the world's legal systems, and some scholars consider Islamic law to be a natural law system because it is largely based on the Qur'an (Koran), the Holy Book of Islam, and thus is God-given (Souryal, Potts, and Alobied 1994).

Natural law may be considered "law within the law," a set of moral precepts that tempers the often rigid nature of positivist law with concerns of fairness and justice. Natural law is a set of absolutist principles morally binding on all societies and individuals. The international legal community even has a name for something quite close to this called *jus cogens*, which literally means "compelling" or "higher" law. Although this principle does not explicitly appeal to natural law, it is obviously strongly influenced by it and has been an accepted doctrine in international law since 1986 (Caplan 2003). Advocates of *jus cogens*, like advocates of natural law, insist that any positive law contrary to it is not valid and may even constitute a corruption of law (Danilenko 2003). The ringing passage of the Declaration of Independence that asserts "We hold these truths to be self-evident, that all men are created equal; they are endowed by their Creator with certain inalienable rights," is a well-known example of the use of natural law to invalidate legally constituted English colonial laws of the period. We see more and more nations of the world accepting *jus cogens* standards as our notions of decency and justice evolve.

You might ask yourself who decides when human law is in conflict with natural law. The quick-and-dirty answer is "those with the power to do so." Because natural law is not a set of written statutes and procedures, its advocates must turn to ideas of morality set down in the texts of the various religions in the world or in constitutions modeled on them. As is the case with any idea or principle, transcendental natural law can be used for ends less than fair and noble. Transcendental natural law fits Weber's substantive irrational type of law and has been employed by monarchs and their champions to support the so-called "divine right of kings." According to this philosophy, the king's lawmaking powers issued from God's law, so his decisions could no more be questioned than the will of God himself. Because the issue of whether Parliament's positive formal-rationality lawmaking power or the kings' substantive, irrational, "divine" power should prevail produced much turmoil in England during the seventeenth century, there has always been a certain distrust of the concept of natural law in the English-speaking world (Friedrich 1963).

Natural law has also been used against the idea of the divine right of kings. We may assume that much of the quest for natural law is embedded in the desire to limit the absolute power of the sovereign (or the state). Those seeking limitations of state power have searched beyond positive law (which is, after all, the product of the state) by searching for authoritative principles by which these limitations can be legitimized.

Although many of the early proponents of natural law saw it as God-given, it is not necessary to believe in a deity to believe in the concept. For secular believers in natural law, the "higher" nature of natural law means that its principles are derived from the nature of human beings. In a general sense, natural law means that humans everywhere should be treated with dignity and respect and viewed as intrinsically valuable "ends-in-themselves," not as means to some other end. This is the idea behind the Golden Rule, versions of which exist in all the world's major religions. Humans are assumed to have an innate sense of fairness and justice and to know deep inside when those principles are being violated, even when it is they who are violating them. For proponents of natural law, its universal applicability and unchanging nature rest on this principle.

The Evolutionary Perspective

The **evolutionary perspective** attempts to explain the origins of law and justice with reference to the principles of evolutionary biology. From the point of view of this perspective, law may be considered "natural" because it flows from the evolved nature of *Homo sapiens*. As one evolutionary legal theorist put it, "The ability to formulate, articulate and understand rules, like other regularities that characterize successful species, undoubtedly had a significant impact on subsequent hominid [*hominid* refers to any bipedal primate form from ancestral to modern humans] evolution" (Gruter 1991, 61).

The primary difference between the evolutionary and transcendentalist positions is that evolutionists seek empirical support for their position through the study of the behavior of human and other social species. Instead of viewing natural law as transcendentally imposed from above and molding human choice to its bidding via education and positivist law, the evolutionary position begins with human choice. That is, humans are biologically predisposed to make certain choices because those choices promoted the survival and reproductive success of our distant ancestors. Because of their function, these choices became norms and were eventually codified into positive law. Ancient lawmakers (as we saw with Hammurabi) then attempted to impress on the people that the law originated in some transcendental realm (Wilson 1998).

We do not want to give the impression that this perspective enjoys a privileged position because it is "scientific." Values and laws are statements about what *ought* to be; scientists are also positivists because they are in the business of trying to discover what *is* without investing it with moral overtones. Evolutionary legal theorists do not engage in searches for "law genes," but they do seek to explain law as a by-product of evolved human desires for peace, order, fairness, and predictability. The evolutionary perspective thus attempts to illuminate why law is necessary by illuminating the evolutionary origins of humanity's more offensive traits. (Of course, humans have many nice traits too, but we do not need laws to regulate them.)

When evolutionary theorists refer to something as natural, they do not use the word as a synonym for "good" or "desirable." Philosophers use the term **naturalistic fallacy** to describe the common practice of confusing *is* with *ought* (Jones and Goldsmith 2005). What *is* represents a scientific observation, what *ought to be* is a moral hope. Many disagreeable traits and behaviors were adaptive in the sense that individuals possessing them tended to be more successful in securing mating opportunities and thus passing on those traits to offspring, which is what biologists mean by *reproductive success*. The most successful reproducers contribute disproportionately to any species' gene pool, and over eons of time, their genes (and hence the traits they promote) came to dominate it. These biological truisms point only to what is, not to moral statements about what ought to be.

Evolutionists view any behavior that is found in all cultures at all times, and which is also found in closely related species, to be natural ("arising from nature"). Moral sensibility is a universal trait, although the things that offend it may vary considerably from culture to culture and from time to time. This moral sensibility probably evolved in our species as a counterstrategy to evolved exploitive strategies, and the rules of conduct we have come to call law are manifestations of this moral sensibility. Without a sense of moral outrage we would not react against, and therefore not deter, the murderer, rapist, thief, cheater, and free rider; and any genes inclining individuals to such behavior would have proliferated. Without the evolved sense of moral outrage, we would all be conscienceless psychopaths (Walsh 2006; Weibe 2004).

Moral outrage is probably also the basis for the desire for revenge, which may be considered a necessary evil for humans to make credible threats. If we threaten to break someone's legs if he steals our bananas and do not carry out the threat when he does, the miscreant has no rational reason for not stealing them again in the future. If our distant ancestors made nothing but idle threats, the impulse to take what is not ours would be far stronger than it is today. The more the potential for retaliation is a reality the less likely we are to actually harm one another because the would-be miscreant is likely to take that potential seriously. Moral outrage buttressed by retaliatory action is a plausible candidate as the basis of our sense of justice.

As with any universal desire, the desire to punish has a built-in physiological basis. We recognize justice because we recognize injustice, and we recognize injustice not by reference to positivist standards of law but by *felt* outrage at experiencing injustice. We thus *feel* justice by virtue of our evolved physiology prior to articulating conceptions of it. As Walsh (2000, 853) put it, "The positive feelings accompanying the punishment of those who have wronged us, coupled with the reduction of negative feelings [evoked when we are wronged], provides powerful reinforcement [for punishing], as suggested by the popular saying 'Vengeance is sweet.'"

There is experimental evidence for this from brain imaging studies showing increased blood flow to areas of the brain that respond to reward, suggesting that punishing those who have wronged us provides emotional relief and reward for the punisher (de Quervain et al. 2004). Similar experimental research has provided strong evidence for Durkheim's theoretical insight about the functional role of punishment discussed in chapter 1. This body of research has also concluded that what is called "altruistic punishment" has been crucial for the evolution of cooperation among humans (Fehr and Gachter 2002). For the evolutionary biologist, altruistic punishment is punishment applied by someone who has not been personally wronged for the benefit of those who have. For the rest of us, it is punishment applied by agents of the state on behalf of those who have been wronged.

It is hardly controversial to say that humans have an innate desire for harmony, peace, predictability, fairness, and control in their environments, and to establish ways in which these things can be accomplished. According to the evolutionary perspective, these ways are designed and implemented by human beings, and are thus socially constructed, but the motivations behind them are innate. As

Fikentscher (1991, 317) put it, "If there is a human drive, and instinct for the just, it cannot be separated from the idea of justice and its material contents [the law]."

This *does not* mean that cultural ideas of justice are irrelevant unless they conform to the will of a deity as manifested in holy writings. This is perhaps the major difference between the transcendental and evolutionary perspectives. Think of the former as positing a moral code of immutable *absolutism* and the latter as pointing to moral *universality*, which implies generality but recognizes the possibility of exceptions (Wilson 1998). The evolutionary position asserts that the emotional and intellectual equipment for moral outrage has evolved; it does not specify all the behaviors that will evoke it. If a cultural norm forbids public urination (as in the United States), or the slaughter of cattle (as in India), then people in those cultures will be rightly outraged when these things occur. They will also feel emotionally reassured that justice is done when offending parties are punished. Different cultures shape different expectations and will thus elicit different emotional responses to what seems wrong (Masters 1991; Walsh 2000).

Not all moral outrage is arbitrary and culture bound. Some actions will generate moral outrage at anytime or in any place, which is what we mean by universality. These are the actions that most threatened the survival and reproductive success of our distant ancestors. Public urination and irreverent attitudes toward cattle had absolutely no reproductive consequences in evolutionary environments (nor do they, of course, today), and thus outrage about such things is purely culturally conditioned. Behaviors such as murder, rape, and theft evoke outrage everywhere because these were the most evolutionarily relevant threats our distant ancestors faced.

There are numerous fascinating examples of evolutionary thinking applied to various aspects of law in the literature (e.g., Browne 1997; Cosmides and Tooby 2006), and there is even an organization headquartered at Vanderbilt University called the Society for the Evolutionary Analysis of Law, with an agenda made obvious by its name. However, to appreciate the nuances of such thinking requires a solid background in evolutionary biology, which we cannot provide here. Suffice to say that it is one of the perspectives attempting to account for the "ultimate" origins of law and that its basic ideas are that laws have been devised by all societies as cultural counterstrategies to aspects of human nature conducive to exploitation and that our evolved moral sensibilities provide the basic biological motivation to formulate them.

WHAT IS THE RELATIONSHIP OF LAW TO JUSTICE?

When most people think of justice they probably think of law, but law and justice are not identical. In fact, law professors often get a bit testy if someone mentions justice, and you will find it quite hard to find the term even indexed in most law books. Because it is easier and consistent with their objectives to describe law as it is (legal positivism) rather than evaluate its moral content, most law professors are quite happy to be legal positivists. Law *can* be in accordance with justice, but it can also be the farthest thing from it. Law is in accordance with justice when it respects, cultivates, and protects the dignity of even the lowliest person living under it; it violates justice when it does not. Believers in natural law maintain that it should be the goal of positive law to bring itself into conformity with what is just. We have to be confident that we can find justice and that we can harness it and put it to practical use for the benefit of humankind just as scientists seek to harness the laws of nature and put them to practical use. When all is said and done, it is only through law that justice can be achieved.

Equity

Equity is a term derived from the Latin word for "just" and refers to remedies for wrongs that were not recognized (neither the remedies nor the wrongs) under English common law. In many respects, equity is at the heart of the relationship between justice and law in the English-speaking world and illustrates what we said earlier about law becoming more just as our standards of morality evolve to a higher plane. Equity principles are heavily used in family and contract law since they allow judges to fashion necessary remedies not readily apparent from a reading of legal statutes. The judicial philosophy of Chancellor Kent described earlier is an example of one man's efforts to make law and justice the same thing.

The idea of equity in law in medieval England evolved on parallel tracks with the evolution of the role of the king's chancellor who was essentially the king's most important minister (his "prime minister"). One of the chancellor's responsibilities was to handle petitions from the king's subjects seeking relief from rulings in common law courts. This relief was sorely needed because by the thirteenth century, the common law had become a very inflexible system. Judges frequently applied the same abstract principles and procedural rules rigidly to every case, regardless of the issues involved. They frequently failed to see the *intent* behind precedent as they sought to follow the letter of an ancient ruling rather than its spirit. Judges also failed to realize that ever-changing social circumstances and mores require a dynamic, "living" system of law.

As a result of the rigidity of common law practice, many people felt unjustly treated by the courts and turned to the king (through his chancellor and his staff) to seek justice. This does not mean that the common law of the time was inherently unfair. The law was more incomplete and inflexible than purposely unfair, and equity was conceived of as a corrective for the rigidity and impersonal nature of law. With an increasing number of petitions being filed, an entirely independent court system with its own distinct set of principles and procedures was eventually implemented, known as the **Court of Chancery.** Judges presiding in these courts were directed to view each case as unique, to be flexible and empathetic, and to think in terms of *standards* or *principles* of fairness rather than *rules* of law. Because it was a corrective, many equity decisions were contrary to the principles of the common law as a rational and predictable legal system (Reichel 2005). It is important to note that equity supplemented, not replaced, common law: equity "begins where the law ends; it supplies justice in circumstances not covered by the law" (McDowell 1982, xii). In other words, if justice were to be served in England, the cold formality of common law alone would not suffice. Courts of Chancery were a necessary "add-on" because of the equity defects apparent in the rigid common law at the time.

English monarchs welcomed a court system separate from that of the common law because judges were becoming too independent for their liking, and these separate courts reasserted royal power in legal matters (Fairchild and Dammer 2001). Nevertheless, over the centuries, common law and equity engaged in dynamic cross-pollination to the benefit of both. The common law became fairer and more flexible, and the judges of the chancery courts began relying on rational legal principles and precedent to make equity more predictable. Some of the benefits to each system are given by Reichel (2005, 116): "Common law judges learned that technicalities were not an excuse for reaching obviously wrong decisions, and the chancellors came to understand better the law and its application." They eventually became so alike that formal distinctions between the two courts were removed in 1875, although there are still provisions for separate courts of law and equity in England. Some states in the United States (notably, Delaware) have chancery courts, but most U.S. judges are empowered to hear cases of both law and equity (Abadinsky 2003).

What kinds of legal decisions violate equity, and what exactly is an equity decision? Civil law (i.e., noncriminal law) in the United States throughout most of the nineteenth century was very much oriented toward protecting the legality of contracts between individuals. As long as no specific contract was violated, the defrauding, maiming, and killing of innocent consumers and workers by defective products and dangerous working conditions was not cause for legal action. Victims of defective and/or dangerous products could not sue the manufacturers because the guiding legal principle was *caveat emptor* (let the buyer beware). Companies had no legal duty to be concerned with the welfare of those to whom they sold their products; it was incumbent on buyers to be concerned with their own welfare. Similarly, unhealthy and dangerous working conditions in mines, mills, and factories were excused under the freedom of contract clause of the Constitution. Companies and individuals had entered into a contract to exchange work for wages, with no contractual provisions made for the conditions under which the work was to be done (Abadinsky 2003). American law in this period was as rigid as twelfth-century English law, as judges mechanistically applied legal rules without concern for standards of equity. Equity became more and more a consideration of American courts in the late nineteenth and early twentieth centuries, however, as laws were passed making companies liable for defective products and protecting workers from unsafe working conditions.

The classic American equity case is *Riggs v. Palmer* (1889) because it illustrates the tension between the *rules* of law and the *principles* of equity. Elmer Palmer was to be the major recipient of his grandfather's, Francis Palmer's, large estate upon Francis's death. Fearing that his grandfather was about to disinherit him, Elmer poisoned him. Elmer was investigated, arrested, and convicted for murder and sentenced to ten years imprisonment. Since the will in question had not been changed, Elmer laid claim to the estate, a claim contested by two of Francis's daughters. The law was clear: "No will in writing, not any part thereof, shall be revoked or otherwise altered," and thus the New York Court of Appeals was obliged to uphold the will's validity.

However, the majority of the court reasoned that to allow someone to profit from his crime violated principles of justice and ruled in favor of Mrs. Riggs (daughter of Francis Palmer). Two dissenting judges (clearly legal positivists) argued that judges must look to the law, not moral principles when making decisions. They also argued that the murder was irrelevant to the issue before them because it had already been addressed in other courts, and to deny Elmer the estate that is legally his amounts to additional punishment. Many other legal positivists railed against the decision, declaring it a dangerous precedent because the primary purpose of law is predictability, and predictability is lost if principles trump rules. However, nothing is precedent until it is done for the first time, and now every state has so-called "slayer statutes" that prevent killers from profiting from their crimes. What was once a hotly contested equity *principle* now has evolved into a commonsense *rule* of positivist law.

GAROFALO AND NATURAL CRIME

Perhaps the best example of a specific attempt to "naturalize" elements of the law was Raffaele Garofalo's efforts to formulate a natural definition of crime. Garofalo (1852–1934), an Italian criminologist and legal scholar, was dissatisfied with the positivistic definition of crime ("crime is what the law says it is"). This appeared arbitrary and "unscientific" to Garofalo, who wanted to anchor the definition of crime in something natural and "real," like tying linear measurement to the circumference of the earth, as in the metric system, rather than relying on the arbitrary Anglo-American method of measurement in feet, inches, and miles. Garofalo's definition of crime was to be anchored in human nature, by which he meant that an act should be considered a crime only if it was universally condemned. Such an act, he reasoned, would be universally condemned if it offended the natural sentiments of probity (integrity, honesty) and pity (compassion, sympathy). We see here how Garofalo anticipated many of the points made by evolutionary scientists regarding universal evolved emotional responses to wrongdoing. Natural crimes are evil in themselves (*mala in se*), whereas "man-made" crimes (*mala prohibita*) are wrong only because they have been made wrong by positive law.

Crimes such as prostitution, drug usage, and gambling, while they do cause much social harm, are *mala prohibita* because they are not universally condemned. Not only are they not universally condemned, people actually seek to be "victimized" by prostitutes, drug dealers, and gambling operators. On the other hand, no one ever seeks to be murdered, raped, assaulted, or robbed. These are crimes that are intrinsically evil, and the litmus test for determining *mala in se* status is that no one (except in the most bizarre of circumstances) wants to be a victim of them. These kinds of arguments are often made today by those who would like to see "victimless" (*mala prohibita*) crimes legalized because criminalizing behavior and services that many people want tends to lead to organized crime, police corruption, and a general disrespect for the law. Perhaps the best example from American history we can give for this is Prohibition (otherwise known as the Volstead Act, prohibiting the manufacture and sale of alcohol), which gave the green light to every petty criminal in America to scramble to feed the public's demand for alcohol and to become rich in the process.

THE RULE OF LAW

The only way we can be reasonably assured of integrating important aspects of justice with a legal system is to assure strict adherence to what is called the **rule of law**. The idea of the rule of law appears to have originated with Plato in *Laws* (2000, 89) when he writes, "For that state in which the law is subject and has no authority, I perceive to be on the highway to ruin; but I see that the state in which the law is above the rulers, and the rulers are the inferiors of the law, has salvation, and the very blessings which the Gods can confer." This idea of the rule of law, not of men, evolved in the English-speaking world from the time of the Magna Carta (1215) through the English civil wars (1642–1646 and 1648–1649) and the Glorious Revolution (1688–1689) of the seventeenth century. These struggles of the English people were efforts to gain the freedom from arbitrary government power and from oppressive sovereigns. Struggles for freedom and liberty continued with the American Revolution and Civil War and are still going on today around the world. For this reason, Samuel Donnelly (2006, 42) asserts that "The English-speaking countries of the world are renowned citadels of the rule of law." Donnelly also makes the point that the notion of natural law has been essential for the "advance of the rule of law and the promotion of human rights" (51).

Philip Reichel expresses the idea of the rule of law in the phrase, "laws change but the *Law* must remain" (2005, 175). He illustrates the point by saying that when the English king put people to death (presumably he meant people innocent of any criminal act), he broke the law, but when the Russian tsar did the same thing, he created law. What he meant by this is that the English king was acting within a system that recognized a set of fundamental values and principles that were supposed to be supreme. By violating these principles, the king had set himself above the law and had therefore violated it. The Russian tsar was not operating within such a system of fundamental values and principles, and therefore there were no laws to break. He, rather than the law, was supreme, and thus the law could be bent and twisted to his will. The English king violated both justice and law; the Russian tsar only violated justice.

Although the rule of law can be violated, the fact that it exists serves as a rallying point and source of legitimacy for those who would oppose individuals and governments who violate it. It is primarily for this reason that the rule of law has been called "the most important legal principle in the world" (Chieveley 1997, 760).

According to Reichel (2005), the rule of law contains three irreducible elements:

1. It requires a nation to recognize the supremacy of certain fundamental values and principles.
2. These values and principles must be committed to writing.
3. A system of procedures that hold the government to these principles and values must be in place.

The first element is relatively unproblematic; it is difficult to imagine a modern organized society not recognizing a set of fundamental values that they hold supreme. These ultimate principles may be secular or religious. The second element is also relatively unproblematic. Any culture possessing a written language would be expected to put such important guiding principles into writing so that all may refer to them. Documents containing these principles may be the culture's holy books or a nation's constitution. The third element is much more problematic because it determines if a country honors its fundamental values in practice as well as in theory. At bottom, law is a set of lifeless statements; it has no life apart from human actors. If the law is to be consistent with justice, it can only be so if the procedures followed by the servants of the law are, and are perceived as, fair and equal.

The system of procedures to hold the government to its principles is best articulated by the concept of **due process**. When we speak about something that is due to us, we are usually referring to something that we feel we are rightly entitled to. Due process is procedural justice that is due to all persons whenever they are threatened with the loss of life, liberty, or property at the hands of the state. Due process is essentially a set of instructions informing agents of the state how they must proceed in their investigation, arrest, questioning, prosecution, and punishment of individuals who are suspected of committing crimes. Due process rules attempt to assure that people are treated justly by the state. Unlike distributive justice, due process is not something a person earns by his or her actions; it is something that is due (hence the term) to everyone without exception simply because of their humanity.

To understand what due process means today and how far we have come in implementing it, let us examine what people went through in times when the idea of due process would have been foreign to most people. Imagine you are in France three hundred years ago. Soldiers come to your house in the dead of night, batter down your door, arrest you, and lodge you in a filthy dungeon. Furthermore, imagine that you genuinely do not know why this is happening to you. You try to find out for years while rotting in that dungeon, but no one you ask has the slightest idea. All you and they know is that you are the victim of one of the infamous *lettres de cachet* ("sealed letters"). These letters were issued by the king, his ministers, or some other high-ranking aristocrat, ordering authorities to seize and imprison anyone who had in any way offended them. When (or if) you were finally released, there is nothing you could do about what had happened because it was all perfectly legal under the ***Code Louis*** of 1670, which governed France until the implementation of the *Code Napoléon* in 1804

(Durant and Durant 1963, 16). The *Code Louis* is a perfect example of a system of positivist law being at odds with justice.

JUSTICE EVOLVING: CESARE BECCARIA AND REFORM

These and other injustices found all around Europe did not go unnoticed by many influential thinkers of the period. During the Enlightenment (a historical period typically considered to have begun with the Glorious Revolution in England in 1688 and to have ended with the French Revolution of 1789), a wave of reform sentiment swept Europe. The man generally considered most responsible for this sentiment invading the law and the criminal justice system was an Italian nobleman and professor of law with the impressive name and title of Cesare Bonesana, Marchese di Beccaria. In 1764, Beccaria published what was to become the manifesto for the reform of judicial and penal systems throughout Europe—*Dei Delitti e della Pene* (*On Crimes and Punishment*). The book constituted an impassioned plea to humanize and rationalize the law and to make punishment more reasonable. In other words, it was a plea for both substantive and procedural justice.

Beccaria did not question the need for punishment, but he believed that laws should be designed to preserve public safety and order, not to avenge crime. He also took issue with the practice of secret accusations (*lettres de cachet*) and of keeping the accused ignorant of the charges brought against them, asserting that such practices led to general deceit and alienation in society. He argued that accused persons should be able to confront their accusers, to know the charges brought against them, and to enjoy the benefit of a public trial before an impartial judge as soon as possible after arrest and indictment. If guilty, the criminals' punishment should fit the crime (i.e., be proportionate to the harm done to society), should be identical for identical crimes, and should be applied without reference to the social status of either the offender or the victim.

Beccaria also championed the abolition of the death penalty and the cause of mild and merciful punishment (that is, relative to the barbarous practices of the day, for he did approve of various forms of corporal punishment). Such punishments should only just exceed the level of damage done to society. To ensure a rational and fair penal structure, punishments for specific crimes must be decreed by written criminal codes and the unbounded discretionary powers of judges severely curtailed. The judge's task was to determine guilt or innocence and then to impose the legislatively prescribed punishment if the accused is found guilty. Many of the reforms (especially with respect to the abolition of torture) were implemented in a number of European countries during Beccaria's lifetime (Durant and Durant 1967, 321).

Beccaria's greatest influence was on the European continent. As we have seen, according to Thompson, many of the due process rights we take for granted today had been slowly evolving in England since at least the early thirteenth century. Although we will be discussing due process rights contained in the Fourth, Fifth, Sixth, and Eighth Amendments to the Constitution in their modern American context in much greater detail in chapter 6, it is always interesting to know something about their origins.

The rights we are concerned with involve everything that was denied to the victims of the notorious *lettres de cachet*. These rights are as follows: the right to be secure in your home, to confront your accuser, to know the charges against you, to secure counsel, to be tried by a jury of your peers, and to be free of excessive bail as well as from cruel and unusual punishment. These rights are guaranteed in the United States in the Bill of Rights, which are the first ten amendments to the Constitution. The Bill of Rights did not, of course, arise from nothing; it has a history. As legal historian Bernard Schwartz (1980, 3) put it, "To understand the history of the federal Bill of Rights, one must understand the development of constitutional guarantees of liberty which led up to the 1791 document." The most relevant documents enunciating these guarantees prior to the adoption of the United States Bill of Rights in 1791 are the *Magna Carta* (1215), the *Statute of Winchester* (1275), the *Petition of Right* (1628), and the *Bill of Rights* (1689). The great colonial charters of early America built on the foundation of these documents and contributed considerably to what was eventually to become the United States Bill of Rights as we know it today. The relationship of these documents to the various due process rights will be briefly touched on as we discuss the various rights in a criminal justice context.

As we discuss these various rights, you will find that they have been constantly violated over the centuries by the state and its agents of social control. If they had not been, there would not have been the necessity to continually add to the documents that supposedly guaranteed them for all time. When violations became particularly egregious, however, brave and moral individuals have been able to point to those guarantees to legitimize their complaints and outrage at those violations. **Sir Edmund Coke** (1562–1634), Chief Justice of England during the reign of James II, frequently incurred the king's wrath (he was even imprisoned in the Tower of London for a while) for reminding him that the king was not above the law and that Parliament was not subservient to him. Coke helped to write the 1628 Petition of Right, and he was the first person to suggest a series of written procedures for implementing substantive criminal law; for the latter reason, he is often called the "father of due process" (Boyer 2004). But in the final analysis, these revered documents are only as good as the people entrusted with implementing the principles written therein. A firm commitment to the rule of law on the part of the government, coupled with the people's sense of justice and their political empowerment, makes these precious guarantees more secure than they have ever been before.

JUSTICE, THE LAW, AND PACKER'S MODELS OF CRIMINAL JUSTICE

In 1964, Professor Herbert Packer wrote an article that has influenced just about everyone who has written about the operation of the criminal justice system since then. Packer's two models of the criminal justice system provide a framework for us to explore the relationship between the everyday operation of the criminal justice system and justice itself. We will see that equally moral individuals and societies can hold very different conceptions of justice. The major tension between these two models is a tension between an emphasis on justice for an offended community and on justice for those who offend against it. These alternative conceptions of where the emphasis should properly lie often clash, but out of these clashes sometimes come compromises that elevate standards of justice.

Packer (1964/1997) proposed two "ideal-type" models reflecting different value choices that undergird the operation of the criminal justice system. These two models are the *crime control* and the *due process* models. Ideologically, the crime control model embodies traditional conservative values, and the due process model embodies traditional liberal values.

The Crime Control Model

The crime control model emphasizes community protection from criminals based on the argument that civil liberties can only have real meaning in a safe, well-ordered society. To achieve such a society, it is necessary to suppress criminal activity swiftly, efficiently, and with finality. Swiftness and efficiency demand a well-oiled criminal justice system in which cases are handled informally and uniformly in "assembly-line" fashion. Police officers must arrest suspects, prosecutors must prosecute them, and judges must sentence them "uncluttered with ceremonious rituals that do not advance the progress of the case" (Packer 1996, 4). To achieve finality, the occasions for challenging the process (appeals) must be kept to a minimum. The assumption is that such a process will more efficiently screen out the innocent and that those who are not may be considered "probably guilty." Packer does not want us to think of a presumption of guilt as the conceptual opposite of the presumption of innocence; the crime control model does not advocate a return to the days of *lettres de cachet*. As Packer (1996, 5) put it, "reduced to its barest essentials and when operating at its most successful pitch," the crime control model consists of two elements: "(a) an administrative fact-finding process leading to the exoneration of the suspect, or to (b) the entry of a plea of guilty."

The Due Process Model

If the crime control model can be likened to an assembly line, the due process model can be likened to an obstacle course in which impediments to carrying the accused's case further are encountered at every stage of his or her processing. Police officers must obtain warrants when possible and must not interrogate suspects without the suspect's consent; evidence may be suppressed; and various motions may be filed that may free a factually guilty person. These and other obstacles are placed in the way and prevent the efficient and speedy processing of cases. If the person is convicted, he or she may file numerous appeals, and it may take years to gain closure of the case. The due process model is more concerned with the integrity of the legal process than with its efficiency and with legal rather than factual guilt. Indeed, successful defenses can and have been mounted that have had nothing to do with factual guilt. Factual guilt translates into legal guilt only if the evidence used to determine it was obtained in a procedurally correct fashion. Advocates of the due process model do not place the same degree of trust in agents of the criminal justice system (sometimes with good reason) that crime control advocates do.

Which model do you prefer, and which model do you think best exemplifies the ideals of justice? It is probably correct to say that under a crime control model, more innocent people may be convicted and that under a due process model, more (factually) guilty people will be set free. In the first instance, the individual has been unjustly victimized; and in the second, the community has been unjustly victimized. It is clear that both models have their faults as well as their strengths. The danger of a runaway crime control model is a return to the days when due process was nonexistent. The danger of a runaway due process model is that truth and justice may get lost in a maze of legal ritualism. But as we said earlier, these are ideal-type models that do not exist in their extreme form anywhere in the world in which the rule of law is respected. These models rather lie on a continuum between their extremes. The United States, for instance, has been characterized as operating with a due process model, while Canada has leaned more toward the crime control model (Ellis and Walsh 2000). The underlying values of these two common law countries that help to determine where they sit on the criminal justice continuum are exemplified in the objectives of "life, liberty, and the pursuit of happiness" in America's Declaration of Independence and "peace, order, and good government" in Canada's British North America Act. Both countries have respected civil liberties better than most others throughout their histories, but it is fair to say that Canada has been more conservative in its insistence that civil liberties can have meaning only in an orderly society (Hagan and Leon 1977).

An Illustration of the Models in Action

A famous Supreme Court case that illustrates the "tinkering" that goes on to modify the excesses that might arise with exclusive use of either model is that of *Brewer v. Williams* (1977). This case involved an escaped mental patient named Robert Williams who kidnapped, raped, and murdered a ten-year-old girl named Pamela Powers on Christmas Eve 1968. Two days after the crime, Williams turned himself in to the police in Davenport, Iowa. Because the crime took place in Des Moines, a detective was dispatched to transport Williams from Davenport. At Williams's lawyer's insistence, the detective agreed not to question Williams during the trip. However, the officer was concerned that Pamela's body be found before the snows fell, after which the body may not have been discovered until the following spring. The officer engaged Williams in conversation, during which the officer made statements, but did not ask questions, about how important it was to the family to find Pamela's body so that they could give her a proper Christian burial. This "Christian burial speech" touched whatever spark of decency remained in Williams, who then directed the detective to the girl's frozen body. On the basis of this evidence, Williams was convicted of murder in 1969.

After going through a series of appeals, the case finally reached the United States Supreme Court in 1977. The Court overturned Williams's conviction by a vote of 5-to-4, stating that Williams had not waived his right to counsel during questioning and that the officer's "Christian burial speech" constituted custodial interrogation. It was reasoned that since Williams's confession was obtained in violation of his right to counsel, any evidence obtained on the basis of it (Pamela's body) was inadmissible under the exclusionary rule (there will be much more about this rule in the next chapter). The majority of the Justices were obviously more enamored of legal ritualism than with justice and discounted the mental anguish such a decision would cause Pamela's family. Their blind obedience to legal rules and technicalities remind us of the common law courts in thirteenth-century England. As Chief Justice Burger put it in his strong dissenting opinion, "The result reached by the Court in this case ought to be intolerable in any society which purports to call itself an organized society" (cited in Robin and Anson 1990, 188).

Brewer v. Williams is an example of the excesses of the due process model. However, this case was one of a number of cases involving the boundaries of custodial interrogation from a time when the crime control model ran amok. The most famous of such cases was *Brown v. Mississippi* (1936), which involved the alleged murder of a white man by three black men. All three men were sentenced to death on the basis of confessions obtained under torture (they were whipped and told that the whippings would not stop until they confessed). The injustice to the community inherent in the *Brewer* case can be viewed as one of a number of correctives to the injustices suffered by defendants and typified in the *Brown* case.

The "Golden Mean" between the contending views of justice relative to the issue of confessions was probably reached in *Nix v. Williams* (1984), which enunciated the *inevitable discovery* exception to the exclusionary rule. The Mr. Williams in *Nix v. Williams* is the same Mr. Williams in *Brewer v. Williams*. In affirming Williams's 1969 conviction upon retrial, the Court ruled that search parties looking for Pamela's body would have found it by legal means sooner or later, and thus the fact that it was found because of Williams's confession was irrelevant. Thus, almost sixteen years after the murder, Pamela's family could finally obtain some closure. We might say that the Court had corrected a corrective and that this process of tinkering by successive approximations to broad-reaching justice is the best that mere mortals can hope for.

SUMMARY

We began this chapter by discussing the definition and concept of justice. We chose to concentrate on Aristotle's definition, which states that justice consists of treating equals equally and unequals unequally according to relevant differences. We looked at distributive justice, which is about the fair distribution of resources. A fair distribution of resources is determined not by what persons need but rather by what they deserve by virtue of their efforts and contributions. Retributive justice is concerned with how a society determines guilt or innocence of accused persons (procedural restitutive justice) and the determination of proper punishment for those found guilty (substantive retributive justice). The latter concern involves punishing with fairness and impartiality according to the amount of damage the defendant has done to the community. Sentencing guidelines, which seek to balance the severity of the crime and the defendant's criminal history, can be viewed as instruments designed to decrease sentencing disparity and thereby make punishments more equitable.

We addressed the idea of legal realism, a study of law as practiced rather than as written. We saw how legal decision making is not fully determined by written law but often by judges' subjective interpretations of what is just in a case. Judges may decide the way they are going to rule and then seek justification for their decision in the statutes after the fact.

We then addressed ourselves to the origins of justice, focusing on the transcendental and evolutionary perspectives. Both perspectives assert that there is a "natural law" that may be at odds with positivist law and that can be discovered. The transcendental perspective emphasizes the primacy and superiority of the spiritual over the natural. It posits an absolutist system of natural laws that are binding on all persons at all times. These laws are usually considered "God given," and found in the holy books of the world's religions. The evolutionary perspective views natural law as originating in our evolved human nature. Because humans have evolved a number of deceptive and exploitive traits to achieve goals, we have also evolved a set of counterstrategies for detecting and punishing such behavior. Laws are made to formalize our moral sensibilities. The major difference between the two perspectives (other than the origin of natural law) is that the transcendental perspective views natural law as a set of absolutes, while the evolutionary perspective, although asserting that evolved sensibilities are universal, allows for exceptions regarding what specific behaviors might evoke them.

In discussing the relationship between law and justice, we noted that it is only through law that justice can be achieved. We began by discussing the role of equity in the evolution of the common law. Separate courts of equity evolved in England in the thirteenth century because the common law had become overly rigid and often at odds with justice. These courts of equity, or Courts of Chancery, were directed to be flexible and to decide cases based on standards of fairness rather than on rigid rules of law. It is important to note that equity supplemented rather than replaced common law and that both systems benefited by the cross-pollination of ideas over the centuries.

Raffaele Garofalo's effort to formulate a natural definition of crime was discussed as an example of applying natural law justice to positivist law. A crime is a "natural" crime if it is universally condemned, and it is universally condemned if it offends the natural sentiments of pity and probity. Such natural crimes were termed *mala in se* (evil in themselves) crimes and were contrasted with *mala prohibita* (evil because they are forbidden) crimes.

The rule of law is the only way that we can reasonably assure that we are integrating important aspects of justice into our legal systems. The rule of law contains three irreducible elements: (1) A nation must recognize the supremacy of certain fundamental values and principles, (2) these values must be committed to writing, and (3) a system of procedures holding the government to these principles and values must be in place. The first two principles are relatively unproblematic, but the third, requiring a nation to honor the first two in practice as well as in theory, is much more problematic. The third principle is best articulated by the concept of due process, which is procedural restitutive justice in practice. Due process is not something one earns by exemplary behavior but something that is due to everyone by virtue of their humanity. We contrasted due process with its complete absence under the infamous *Code Louis* that existed in France from 1670 to 1804, when ordinary people had no rights whatsoever. The efforts of Cesare Beccaria to humanize European law by instituting rules of due process were noted, as were the precursors of the due process rights we enjoy in the United States today under the Bill of Rights.

Herbert Packer's two "ideal-type" models of criminal justice are the *crime control* and *due process* models. The former emphasizes the protection of the community from the criminal, and the latter emphasizes the protection of the accused from the state. No modern legal system completely conforms to either of these ideal types. Rather, each system lies on a continuum somewhere between the extremes. Both models can take their positions too far, requiring some legal adjustment. We illustrated this in terms of the crime control model in the torture-confession case of *Brown v. Mississippi* and in terms of the due process model in *Brewer v. Williams*. The excesses of both were eventually righted in subsequent Supreme Court decisions.

DISCUSSION QUESTIONS

1. What do you think Aristotle would have to say regarding the justice/injustice of race- and gender-based quotas in education and employment? Do you agree or disagree with him?
2. Do you find the tremendous inequalities in wealth and in salary structure in our society to be just or unjust? Should salary be based on social usefulness rather than on the market?
3. Do you believe in natural law and natural justice? If so, which of the two positions (transcendental or evolutionary) most convinces you? If you don't believe in either position, where do you think that we got our sense of justice from?
4. Why is law sometimes at odds with justice? Give an example.
5. Relate the rule of law to Packer's models of criminal justice.
6. Go to the *Brewer v. Williams* case at http://www.law.cornell.edu/supct/html/historics/USSC_CR_0430_0387_ZS.html and read Justice Stewart's majority opinion and Justice White's dissent. Choose one position or the other and debate the issue in terms of justice as you understand the concept.

References

Abadinsky, H. 2003. *Law and justice: An introduction to the American legal system.* Upper Saddle River, NJ: Prentice Hall.

Boyer, A. 2004. *Law, liberty, and Parliament: Selected essays on the writings of Sir Edward Coke.* Indianapolis, IN: Liberty Fund.

Browne, K. 1997. An evolutionary perspective on sexual harassment: Seeking roots inbiology rather than ideology. *Journal of Contemporary Legal Issues* 8:5–77.

Caplan, L. 2003. State immunity, human rights, and *jus cogens*: A critique of the normative hierachy theory. *American Journal of International Law* 97:741–781.

Chieveley, Lord Goff of. 1997. The future of the common law. *International and Comparative Law Quarterly* 46:745–760.

Cosmides, L., and J. Tooby. 2006. Evolutionary psychology, moral heuristics, and the law. In *Heuristics and the law*, edited by G. Gigerenzer and C. Engel, pp. 181–212. Cambridge, MA: MIT Press.

Danilenko, G. 2003. International jus cogens: Issues of law-making. *European Journal of International Law.* http://www.ejil.org/journal/Vol2/No1/art3.html.

Day, F. (1968). *Criminal law and society.* Springfield, IL: Charles C Thomas.

de Quervain, D., U. Fischbacher, T. Valerie, M. Schellhammer, U. Schnyder, A. Buch, and E. Fehr. 2004. The neural basis of altruistic punishment. *Science* 305:1254–59.

Donnelly, S. 2006. Reflecting on the rule of law: Its reciprocal relations with rights, legitimacy, and other concepts and institutions. *Annals of the American Academy of Political and Social Sciences*, 603:37–53.

Durant, W., and A. Durant. 1963. *The age of Louis XIV.* New York: Simon and Schuster.
———. 1967. *Rousseau and revolution.* New York: Simon and Schuster.

Ellis, L., and A. Walsh. 2000. *Criminology: A global perspective.* Boston: Allyn & Bacon.

Fairchild, E., and H. Dammer. 2001. *Comparative criminal justice systems.* Belmont, CA: Wadsworth.

Fehr, E., and S. Gachter. 2002. Altruistic punishment in humans. *Nature* 415:137–40.

Fikentscher, W. 1991. The sense of justice and the concept of cultural justice. *American Behavioral Scientist* 34:314–334.

Finkel, N., Harre, R., and J. Rodriguez Lopez. 2001. Commonsense morality across cultures: Notions of fairness, justice, honor and equity. *Discourse Studies* 3:5–27.

Finland millionaire gets $216,900 speeding fine. 2004. *Idaho Statesman*, February 11, p. 2.

Friedrich, C. 1963. *The philosophy of law in historical perspective.* Chicago: University of Chicago Press.

Gruter, M. 1991. *Law and the mind: Biological origins of human behavior.* Newbury Park, CA: Sage.

Hagan, J., and J. Leon. 1977. Philosophy and sociology of crime control: Canadian-American comparisons. *Sociological Inquiry* 47:181–208.

Jones, O., and T. Goldsmith. 2005. Law and behavioral biology. *Columbia Law Review* 105:405–498.

Kaye, J. 1998. Commentaries on Chancellor Kent. *Chicago-Kent Law Review.* http://www.courts.state.ny.us/history/elecbook/kent/pg1.htm.

Kidder, R. 1983. *Connecting law to society.* Englewood Cliffs, NJ: Prentice Hall.

Leiter, B. 2001. Legal realism and legal positivism reconsidered. *Ethics* 111:278–301.

Masters, R. 1991. Naturalistic approaches to the concept of justice. *American Behavioral Scientist* 34:289–313.

McDowell, G. 1982. *Equity and the Constitution: The Supreme Court, equitable relief, and public policy.* Chicago: University of Chicago Press.

Miles, T., and C. Sunstein. 2008. The new legal realism. *University of Chicago Law Review* 75:831–51.

Packer, H. 1964/1997. Two models of the criminal process. In *A criminal procedure anthology*, edited by S. Wasserman and C. Snyder, pp. 3–9. Cincinnatti, OH: Anderson.

Pierce, N. 2001. Urban polarization as unfair as executive compensation. *Idaho Statesman*, September 8, p. 9.

Plato 2000. *Laws*. Edited and translated by B. Jowett. Amherst, NY: Prometheus.

Reichel, P. 2005. *Comparative criminal justice systems: A topical approach*. 4th ed. Upper Saddle River, NJ: Prentice Hall.

Robin, G., and R. Anson. 1990. *Introduction to the criminal justice system*. 4th ed. New York: Harper & Row.

Schwartz, B. 1980. *The roots of the Bill of Rights*. Vol. 1. New York: Chelsea House.

Souryal, S., D. Potts, and A. Alobied. 1994. The penalty of hand amputation for theft in Islamic justice. *Journal of Criminal Justice* 22:249–65.

Thomas, H. 1962. *Understanding the great philosophers*. New York: Doubleday.

Tomkins, A., and K. Oursland. 1991. Social and scientific perspectives in judicial interpretations of the Constitution. *Law and Human Behavior* 15:101–20.

Walsh, A. 2000. Evolutionary psychology and the origins of justice. *Justice Quarterly* 17:841–64.

———. 2006. Evolutionary psychology and criminal behavior. In *Missing the revolution: Darwinism for social scientists*, edited by J. Barkow, pp. 225–68. Oxford: Oxford University Press.

Weibe, R. 2004. Expanding the model of human nature underlying self-control theory: Implications of the constructs of self-control and opportunity. *Australian and New Zealand Journal of Criminology* 37:64–84.

Wilson, E. 1998. The biological basis of morality. *Atlantic Monthly* 281 (April):53–70.

Cases Cited

Brewer v. Williams, 430 U.S. 387 (1977).

Brown v. Mississippi, 297 U.S. 278 (1936).

Bush v. Gore 531, U.S. 98 (2000).

Muller v. Oregon, 208 U.S. 214 (1908).

Nix v. Williams, 467 U.S. 431 (1984).

Riggs v. Palmer, 115 NY 506 (1889).

CHAPTER 3

MAKING LAW

Dollree Mapp was at home early one spring morning in 1957 when Cleveland, Ohio police officers stormed into her office without a search warrant. They were looking for a suspect in a recent bombing, but all they found were some pornographic books and pictures. She was charged with possession of obscene materials and convicted over her protest that the search of her home violated her Fourth Amendment right to be free from "unreasonable" searches and seizures and that the evidence seized during the search should be excluded from trial. The trial and appeals courts denied her claim, noting that the U.S. Supreme Court had previously held, in *Wolf v. Colorado* (1949), that while the Fourth Amendment applied to the states through the due process clause of the Fourteenth Amendment, the remedy for violations of the Fourth Amendment, exclusion of the unlawfully seized evidence, did not apply to the states.

In *Mapp v. Ohio* (1961), the U.S. Supreme Court overruled *Wolf v. Colorado* and held that the remedy of the exclusionary rule should in fact be applied to the states, along with the right to be free from unreasonable searches and seizures. The Court admitted this decision meant it was ignoring the principle of *stare decisis*, which says that prior decisions should govern future decisions, and that courts should be consistent in their interpretation of the law. The Court felt it had to do this, however, because in the decade after *Wolf v. Colorado* was decided, the states had refused to apply other remedies for violations of the Fourth Amendment, thus rendering, for all practical purposes, the protections of that provision of the Bill of Rights meaningless.

INTRODUCTION

We have previously explored why law exists and explained its existence by noting that people need a mechanism for enforcing order and resolving disputes peacefully. Laws are created by a legislature, provide rules to guide conduct, and are a means of resolving disputes and maintaining order through the medium of the courts. In this chapter, we discuss the historical development of the law, focusing on the Anglo-American concepts of the **common law**, much of which had been developed in England by the thirteenth century, and the related concepts of precedent, *stare decisis*, and the role of the judge in creating, interpreting, and applying the law.

The Western legal tradition may be traced to the Code of Hammurabi. This is the first known written legal code, and it expressed a retributivist "eye for an eye" philosophy. Roman law, the next major codified set of legal principles, was influenced heavily by Babylonian legal principles. *The Twelve Tables* (450 BCE) was the first entirely secular written legal code (the Code of Hammurabi was very much a religious as well as secular code). During this time, law began to change its focus from being a mechanism for resolving private disputes to viewing crimes as offenses against society as well as against the victim.

COMMON LAW

The spread of the Roman Empire brought Roman law to Western Europe, but it had minimal impact on English common law. The Norman Conquest of England in 1066 brought feudal law, which provided the basis for common law, to England. During the following several hundred years, England slowly developed what came to be known as the common law system. After the Norman Conquest, the new rulers established new forms of government, including courts of law. By the reign of **Henry II** (1154–1189), who is often referred to as the "father of the common law," a body of law had been developed and applied nationally. Decisions were written down, circulated, and summarized. The first systematic attempt to collect and explain these decisions was compiled under the supervision of Henry's Chief Justice **Ranulf de Glanvill** in a book titled *Treatise on the Laws and Customs of the Realm of England,* around 1188. This book details the transition from what was essentially the substantive irrationality decision making of pre–Norman England to adherence to formal legal rules (Turner 1990). The result was a more unified body of law, which came to be known as common law because it was in force throughout the country.

The next important document in the evolution of common law was the **Magna Carta** ("Great Charter") of 1215. The Magna Carta was a document drawn up by English barons to limit the power of the sovereign (specifically, the notorious King John of Robin Hood fame) and to assert certain rights. Contained in the document are the first dim glimpses of many of the rights we take for granted today, such as the right to trial by jury, proportionality of punishment, and the privilege against self-incrimination. Although King John's acquiescence to the provisions of the charter was a victory for the barons, it meant little at the time for the common person.

Henry de Bracton's *On the Laws and Customs of England,* written between 1250 and 1260, built on Glanvill's work and furthered the "commonality" of common law. Bracton was a high-ranking judge in England who was enamored of the idea that common law was based on case law decided on ancient custom rather than on authoritative codes imposed on people from above. The common law is thus judge-made law. That is, it was law created by judges as they heard cases and settled disputes. Judges wrote down their decisions and in doing so, attempted to justify them by reference to custom, tradition, history, and prior judicial decisions. *On the Laws* was essentially a compilation of these judicial rulings made over the previous decades, arranged to show how precedent may guide future rulings. For this reason, Bracton is often referred to as the father of case law (Stramignoni 2002).

As judges began to rely on previous judgments, they developed the concepts of "stare decisis" and precedent. Of course, for there to be precedent, there must be prior decisions. At first, judges made decisions without referring to other cases or courts. They simply heard the case and decided the appropriate outcome based on their understanding of the law as they had learned it through the reading of legal treatises. But as time went by, judges came to rely on prior decisions as a means of justifying their decision in a particular case.

PRECEDENT AND STARE DECISIS

Under the common law system, every final decision by a court creates a precedent. This precedent governs the court issuing the decision as well as any lower, or inferior, courts. The common law system, developed in England, was brought to America by the early colonists. Many of the principles of common law, including precedent and a belief in stare decisis, remain in force today in American courts. Thus, all courts in a state are bound to follow the decisions of the highest court in the state, usually known as the state supreme court. All courts in the federal court system are bound to follow the decisions of the U.S. Supreme Court. This is the notion of precedent.

Precedent is binding only on those courts within the jurisdiction of the court issuing the opinion. Thus, a decision of the Idaho Supreme Court is not binding on any court in Wyoming. Wyoming courts are not subject to the jurisdiction or control of Idaho courts and thus are free to interpret the law differently from Idaho courts, if they see fit to do so. Decisions from courts in other jurisdictions, while not binding, may be persuasive, however. This simply means that another court may give consideration and weight to the opinion of other courts. Thus, a Wyoming court may consider, if it chooses, the judgment of an Idaho court, or an American court can consider the judgment of a British, Australian, New Zealand, or any other common law court. Courts may do this when faced with an issue that they have not dealt with before but that other courts have examined.

Stare decisis means "let the decision stand" (Black 2001). Under the principle of stare decisis, if there is a prior decision on a legal issue that applies to a current case, the court will be guided by that prior decision and apply the same legal principles in the current case. Stare decisis, then, is the principle behind establishing the value of prior decisions, or precedent. It is a principle that assures us that if an issue has been decided one way, it will continue to be decided that way in future cases. Through a reliance on precedent and the principle of stare decisis, common law courts were able to provide litigants with some degree of predictability regarding the courts' decisions.

Precedent establishes a legal principle, but not every pronouncement that a court makes in a ruling establishes precedent. Pronouncements that do are known as *ratio decidendi* ("the reason for the decision"). Ratio decidendi is the legal principle, or rationale, used by the courts to arrive at their decisions. Additional supporting statements are called **obiter dicta** ("things said by the way") or simply dicta. These statements are other legal or nonlegal arguments used to support the ratio decidendi and do not constitute precedent.

Precedent is not necessarily unchangeable. Judge-made law may be set aside, or overruled, by an act of the legislature if the constitution permits the legislature to do so. Additionally, the court that issued the precedent may overrule it, or a higher court may reverse the decision of a lower court. If an intermediate-level appeals court decides an issue one way and the losing party appeals to a higher appeals court (such as a state supreme court), that higher court may reverse the decision of the lower court. Higher-level courts are not bound by the judgments of lower courts. They are bound only by the decisions of courts above them in the court structure. Chapter 4 contains a discussion of federal and state court systems.

Stare decisis, then, involves a respect for and belief in the validity of precedent. Precedent is simply the influence of prior cases on current cases. Understandably, courts are reluctant to reverse decisions they made previously, as this is a tacit admission of error. Courts do so, however, when presented with a compelling justification. Thus, stare decisis is not an inflexible doctrine but merely the general rule. There are always exceptions as with most areas of the law.

Alternatively, rather than expressly overrule a prior decision, a court may instead seek to *distinguish* the prior case from the present case on grounds that the facts are slightly different. By doing so, the court can avoid overruling a prior decision while coming to what it considers the proper result in the present case. Until a decision is expressly overruled, it stands as an accurate statement of legal principles or "good law."

No discussion of the evolution of common law is complete without a discussion of English judge and philosopher **William Blackstone**. For Blackstone, laws were creations of God waiting to be discovered via the use of reason. Blackstone's four-volume work, *Commentaries on the Laws of England* (1765–1769), was the definitive work on common law for at least the next century. In these volumes, Blackstone organized common law into four parts: (1) the rights of individuals (procedural law), (2) public wrongs (substantive criminal law), (3) private wrongs (torts), and (4) property rights (law of contracts).

Blackstone had a tremendous influence on the Founding Fathers and on the philosophy behind the Declaration of Independence. This included the rights of Englishmen, indictment of the Crown, the prohibition of taxation without representation, and the ringing natural law phases such as "self-evident" and "unalienable rights"—all were from Blackstone (Bailey 2006). Blackstone's works were so influential in the shaping of America that the great American historian Daniel Bernstein commented, "[N]o other book except the Bible played a greater role in the history of American institutions (Bailey 2006, 5).

SOURCES OF LAW

There are several primary sources of law. These include judge-made law (common law) and legislative law (this includes the Constitution, statutes, ordinances, and administrative regulations). There are other sources for what constitutes appropriate conduct, such as religion and ethics, which were discussed in chapter 1. The focus here, however, is on the forms of the law. Note from Figure 3.1 that the United States Constitution sits above and governs all lawmaking beneath it. There is order and precedent among the sources of law such that the Constitution overrides a statute, and a statute, if consistent with the Constitution, overrides judge-made law.

Legislation is enacted by the legislature under the authority granted to it by the Constitution. A **constitution** creates a government—it literally *constitutes* the government. Legislatures are given authority to act in certain areas, and within these areas, they may pass legislative enactments or bills, often referred to as statutes, which are collected into codes, such as the penal code of **criminal law.**

Legislators, sometimes referred to as lawmakers, quite literally make law. Acts of the legislature are not, however, lawful per se. In other words, just because a legislature passes a bill does not mean the bill is a lawful exercise of the legislature's authority. Acts of the legislature may not limit the constitution under which the legislation was created. For instance, the U.S. Congress may not lawfully pass legislation that abridges the Fourth Amendment.

Who decides when the legislature has acted beyond the scope of its authority? In the United States, it is the Supreme Court that has the final say as to the constitutionality of statutes passed by either state or federal legislatures. This is known as the power of judicial review and is discussed in greater detail later in this chapter.

Administrative regulations are another form of legislation, which, under certain circumstances, may have the force of law. This means that they will be enforced by the courts just like a statute. Administrative regulations are issued either by agencies of the executive branch, which derive their authority from a delegation of power by the executive branch, or by independent agencies, created through a delegation of power from the legislature. Examples include regulations affecting food and drugs and occupational safety requirements. Both the federal government and state governments issue administrative regulations. Administrative law is discussed in more detail in chapter 7.

Figure 3.1 The Sources and Types of Law

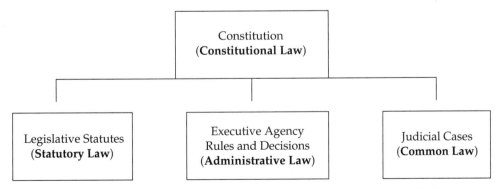

Figure provided by Professor Michael Bogner, Justice Studies Department, Chadron State College (2006).

Statutes are frequently written broadly, leaving administrative agencies with the task of filling in the blanks. Agencies are empowered to do this through the delegation of authority to them by the executive or legislative branch. Common examples include the Department of Health and Human Services and the Department of Veterans' Affairs. Violation of an administrative regulation generally is not treated as a crime but rather as a civil violation (see chapter 7). Like broadly written statutes, the U.S. Constitution leaves much room for interpretation. For example, the Fourth Amendment prohibits "unreasonable searches and seizures." But what is unreasonable? What constitutes a search or a seizure? There are no easy answers to these questions, and the U.S. Supreme Court has struggled to define the terms, as we will see in chapter 6.

Why are statutes ambiguous? Why does the legislature not write more clearly and explain exactly what it means? There are several reasons. First, it is difficult to define, in a few sentences, something involving human conduct—there is an almost infinite range of possible actions by individuals.

Second, legislators are politicians, and politics involves compromise. Thus, a statute may be written so that it appeals to the greatest possible number of legislators, but in doing this, the language of the statute may be watered down and made less precise rather than more so. This is particularly likely to happen when dealing with controversial issues. Politicians may decide to leave it to the courts to define more clearly the terms of a statute. While judges in some jurisdictions hold office for life and cannot be removed simply for declaring legislation void, in many states, judges are elected and thus are subject to removal if the electorate does not approve of their interpretation of legislation.

SOURCES OF INDIVIDUAL RIGHTS

There are several sources of individual rights in the United States. These include federal and state constitutions, case law, court rules, and legislation. Individual rights are those possessed by the individual, which protect him or her from others as well as the government. Examples include freedom of speech, freedom of religion, and the right to counsel. The Constitution, particularly the Bill of Rights, is the primary source of individual rights. While states are free to provide more individual rights than the United States Constitution does, neither Congress nor a state may enact a law that abridges a federal constitutional right. This is because the Constitution is paramount; it is the supreme law of the United States.

THE CONSTITUTION

The Continental Congress (the colonists' first attempt to form a unified national government) was formed through the adoption of a document called the **Articles of Confederation** in 1781. This was the first attempt at creating a unified United States, but it was a failure, in large part because the national government created by the Articles of Confederation was virtually without power relative to the power held by the individual states. It lacked the authority to tax, to raise an army, or to force the states to comply with any mandates. The first president of the Continental Congress was John Hanson, who held the title of "President of the United States." Despite his grand title, Hanson was little more than a chairperson, and he is now little more than a footnote to history despite being the first "first" President of the United States.

In 1787, the Continental Congress invited delegates from the thirteen original states (Rhode Island declined to attend) to meet in Philadelphia to write a new Constitution to replace its Articles of Confederation. If the national governing body's lack of power was to be rectified and a truly *United* States realized, the delegates knew that the new nation would need a strong central government. Supporters of a strong centralized government were called Federalists, and supporters of a weak central government were called "states rightists."

The result of the convention in Philadelphia was the creation of the U.S. Constitution. The Constitution is different from ordinary legislation in that it is primarily concerned with establishing the powers and limits of the government, both between the branches of government and between the government and the individual citizen (Amar 1998). The Constitution itself contains few protections of individual rights. The only individual rights mentioned in the Constitution are the right to seek a writ of **habeas corpus** (a document challenging the legality of a person's detention), the prohibition on **bills of attainder** (legislation imposing punishment without trial), and the prohibition on **ex post facto** laws (legislation making prior conduct criminal). These are discussed more fully in chapter 5.

When the Constitution was submitted to the states for ratification, several states were reluctant to ratify it without more clear-cut protections of individual rights. In response to these concerns, the Bill of Rights was added. These provisions were initially drawn up by James Madison. His proposals were condensed into ten amendments, commonly referred to as the Bill of Rights. With the addition of these ten amendments, the Constitution was ratified by the original thirteen states in 1791. The complete texts of the Constitution and the Bill of Rights are provided in Appendix A.

THE BILL OF RIGHTS

The first eight amendments set out twenty-three individual rights. These rights include protections against government action of all kinds. These rights originally were intended to apply only to actions by the federal government. The Bill of Rights was added to reduce the apprehension of states' rights supporters who feared a strong central government would infringe on the rights of citizens of the states (Anastaplo 1995). Not until the twentieth century were the provisions of the Bill of Rights applied to actions of state governments through a process referred to as incorporation. This is discussed later in the chapter after an examination of the most significant provisions of the Bill of Rights, beginning with the first amendment. (See Table 3.1.)

Table 3.1 *Constitutional Rights of Americans*

Constitutional Article or Amendment	Rights
Article 1, Section 9	Habeas corpus, no bills of attainder, no ex post facto laws
First Amendment	Freedom of speech, press, and assembly, freedom of and from religion
Second Amendment	Bear arms
Third Amendment	Freedom from quartering soldiers
Fourth Amendment	Freedom from unreasonable searches and seizures, warrants based on probable cause and stated with specificity
Fifth Amendment	Grand jury indictment, freedom from double jeopardy and self-incrimination, rights to face accusers, to due process, and to just compensation for takings
Sixth Amendment	Rights to speedy trial, to impartial jury, to be informed of charges, to face accusers, to obtain witnesses on your behalf, and to an attorney
Eighth Amendment	Freedom from excessive bail or fines and from cruel and unusual punishment
Ninth Amendment	Listing of right does not imply absence of other rights, e.g., right to privacy
Thirteenth Amendment	Freedom from slavery
Fourteenth Amendment	Right to citizenship of native-born people, right to equal protection of the law, right to be free of laws that abridge the privileges and immunities of citizens, right to due process
Fifteenth Amendment	Right to vote regardless of race
Seventeenth Amendment	Right to vote for senators
Nineteenth Amendment	Right to vote regardless of sex
Twenty-Sixth Amendment	Right to vote for persons eighteen years old or older

First Amendment

Congress shall make no law respecting an establishment of religion, or prohibiting the free exercise thereof; or abridging the freedom of speech, or of the press; or the right of the people peaceably to assemble, and to petition the Government for a redress of grievances.

The First Amendment covers the freedoms of religion, speech, press, and assembly. It is not surprising that the first provision of the Bill of Rights deals with these topics, as religion was a primary force in the settling of America. Religion held a central position in people's lives in England in the 1500s and 1600s. Religion was also very important to the colonists, so much so that several colonies had their own established or quasi-established religion (Feldman 2005). Many bloody conflicts were waged over which religion should be the official religion of England. The colonists sought to avoid such conflicts and to avoid persecution for their religious beliefs. If their particular colony's religion could not be established as the official religion of the whole nation, then it was best not to have any religion established as the nation's official religion. Freedom of speech and the press as well as the freedom to assemble peacefully were all issues of great concern for the colonists prior to the American Revolution.

With respect to religion, there are two guarantees in the First Amendment: the government shall neither establish an official, state-supported religion, nor shall the government interfere with individuals' religious practices. The essence of these two clauses is that the government is not to be in the business of either promoting or destroying religion. Whereas the state was heavily involved in religion in England, the founding fathers wanted the U.S. government to stay out of the business of religion entirely (Anastaplo 1995).

The first guarantee is often referred to as the Establishment Clause. This creates what the Supreme Court has referred to as a "wall of separation between church and state" (*Everson v. Board of Education* 1947). This does not mean the government cannot be involved in religion to some degree, but the Supreme Court has stated that any statute affecting religion is valid only if three conditions are met: (1) The statute must have a secular (nonreligious) purpose, (2) the primary purpose of the statute must be neither pro- nor antireligion, and (3) the statute must not foster "excessive" government entanglement with religion (*Lemon v. Kurtzman* 1971).

This does not mean the freedom to worship is absolute. Otherwise valid government regulations, which incidentally restrict religious practices, are permitted. For example, a state may ban polygamy under its authority to enact health and safety regulations, even though this at one time imposed a restriction on the religious practices of some Mormon sects; or it can forbid the use of mind-altering substances in prisons, notwithstanding that by doing so, it may infringe on religious practices of some Native American inmates.

The freedom of speech is one of the most treasured rights possessed by Americans. This right has been accorded great, but not total, weight by the Supreme Court. Thus, the Supreme Court has held that the freedom of speech includes the right to say things that may anger others, including so-called hate speech, or speech directed at minority groups. The Court also has held that the freedom of speech includes not just verbal statements but written statements and some physical acts. These physical acts, when intended to make a point, are referred to as "symbolic speech" or "expressive conduct." Examples include signs, picketing, and the burning of the American flag (*Texas v. Johnson* 1989).

Freedom of speech is not absolute, however. The Supreme Court has held that the government can regulate obscenity (*Miller v. California* 1973) and speech that is likely to provoke a violent response is referred to as "fighting words" (*Chaplinsky v. New Hampshire* 1942). Commercial speech (speech contained in advertising, song lyrics, books and magazines, and so forth) may be regulated to a greater degree than so-called "political" speech (*Virginia State Board of Pharmacy v. Virginia Citizens Consumers Council, Inc.* 1976). In general, however, the Supreme Court looks with disfavor on attempts to curb any kind of speech. Instead, the Court repeatedly has endorsed the view of Justice Oliver Wendell Holmes that society is improved by permitting a "free marketplace of ideas."

In a very real sense, the First Amendment forms the nucleus of the other rights found in the Bill of Rights. The Framers went beyond their English ancestors in drafting the American Bill of Rights in the areas of freedom of religion, speech, and the press. Although virtually everything in the Bill of Rights having to do with criminal justice was taken from the various English documents discussed in chapter 2, there was nothing analogous to these three freedoms contained in them.

Second Amendment

> *A well regulated Militia, being necessary to the security of a free State, the right of the people to keep and bear Arms, shall not be infringed.*

The Second Amendment provides citizens with the right to "keep and bear arms," and states that this right shall not be "infringed." The right to bear arms was one of only two "individual" rights (the other being the right to petition) contained in the English Bill of Rights that the Framers took as their guideline for crafting the American Bill of Rights. Opponents of gun control legislation seize on this Amendment as support for their claim that the state may not limit the use and possession of firearms (Kates 1983; Williams 1991). The history of the Amendment suggests this may not be completely accurate; the Supreme Court repeatedly has held that states may regulate firearms, upholding legislation that prohibits the possession of certain weapons and that requires firearm registration.

The history behind this Amendment suggests it was intended, at least in part, not to allow individuals to possess any weapons they wanted as protection against other individuals but to allow the states and groups of citizens (a militia) to have weapons to protect themselves against oppression by the federal government (Levinson 1989). There was a great concern at the time of the passage of the Bill of Rights that the federal government might become oppressive, and allowing states to form militias would not be of much use if the federal government previously had outlawed weapons. At this time, there were no public stores of weapons, so if the federal government were to prohibit private ownership, states would be unable to fight back, as their citizens all would be unarmed to some degree.

In 2008, in *District of Columbia v. Heller*, the Supreme Court held that the Second Amendment protected the rights of *individual* gun owners, and is not just a right of states or the people to create and arm militias. The case arose after the District of Columbia, in response to a tremendous amount of gun violence, enacted what its supporters acknowledge was the strictest gun control law in the country. It placed stringent restrictions on the ownership of firearms, including requiring person who lawfully owned guns to keep those guns unloaded and disassembled or locked in their homes. Heller and several others brought suit, claiming the law violated their Second Amendment right to bear arms.

Justice Scalia, writing for a narrow 5-4 majority, asserted that the opening clause of the Second Amendment referring to the need of militias to be armed was merely one of the reasons for an individual right to bear arms. Justice Scalia focused a portion of his opinion on the role of handguns in self-defense, suggesting that self-defense was a fundamental right as well. Justice Scalia's opinion emphasized, as is his wont, historical analysis, in a lengthy 64 page opinion. The decision raised more questions than it answered, however. It will take further litigation to determine just what the decision will mean to state efforts to regulate the purchase of firearms and handguns, and firearm registration policies. The decision appears to allow for regulation, but sets no standard for evaluating that regulation. Justice Scalia said the decision is not meant to cast doubt on the constitutionality of laws prohibiting gun ownership by felons or the possession of firearms in sensitive areas such as schools. Writing for the four dissenters, Justice Stevens charged the majority with misreading the historical record, ignoring Supreme Court precedent, and judicial activism.

Third Amendment

No Soldier shall, in time of peace be quartered in any house, without the consent of the Owner, nor in time of war, but in a manner to be prescribed by law.

The Third Amendment is another amendment that was a product of its times. Prior to the Revolution, English troops sometimes were housed in the homes of private citizens against the wishes of the homes' owners. The Third Amendment makes such a practice unconstitutional by expressly forbidding the quartering of soldiers in private homes against the wishes of the owner at any time. A similar clause prohibiting the billeting of soldiers and sailors is contained in the English Petition of Right of 1628.

Fourth Amendment

The right of the people to be secure in their persons, houses, papers, and effects, against unreasonable searches and seizures, shall not be violated, and no Warrants shall issue, but upon probable cause, supported by Oath or affirmation, and particularly describing the place to be searched, and the persons or things to be seized.

The Fourth Amendment is the provision of the Constitution that stands most directly between the individual citizen and the police. This amendment forbids "unreasonable" searches and seizures and requires the existence of "probable cause" before warrants may be issued or a search or seizure may take place. Warrants are required to describe the subject of their search with "particularity." The particularity requirement is a response to the British practice in colonial times of issuing general warrants. General warrants allowed British customs inspectors to search for virtually anything, anywhere, at any time (Cuddihy 1990). The colonists, especially those engaged in smuggling, found this practice most distressing, and it was one of the prime precipitating factors in the American Revolution.

Requiring probable cause to search or seize was the Founding Fathers' attempt to limit the ability of the police to interfere at will in the lives of individual citizens. Instead, they must have some reasonable amount of evidence that the person has engaged in criminal activity. We refer to this degree of proof as *probable cause*. Probable cause is a fair probability that a crime has occurred. It is less than proof beyond a reasonable doubt but more than a simple hunch.

The Fourth Amendment does not forbid all searches and seizures but rather requires that they be reasonable. The obvious question then is what is reasonable? Courts have struggled mightily to define this phrase, and much of the law of criminal procedure is devoted to its explication. Criminal procedure is discussed in detail in chapter 6.

Fifth Amendment

No person shall be held to answer for a capital, or otherwise infamous crime, unless on a presentment or indictment of a Grand Jury, except in cases arising in the land or naval forces, or in the Militia, when in actual service in time of War or public danger; nor shall any person be subject for the same offence to be twice put in jeopardy of life or limb; nor shall be compelled in any criminal case to be a witness against himself, nor be deprived of life, liberty, or property, without due process of law; nor shall private property be taken for public use, without just compensation.

The Fifth Amendment provides a number of protections for individual citizens. These include the right to an indictment by a grand jury, freedom from double jeopardy (defined later), the right to due process and just compensation, and the privilege against self-incrimination. These rights are all associated with the criminal trial. Many of the provisions of the Fifth Amendment were born out of reaction to practices in Europe during the Middle Ages. The Star Chamber (a notorious and oppressive court in England characterized by secrecy and torture devoted to obtaining self-incrimination by confession was abolished by Parliament in 1641) and the Spanish Inquisition are examples of intrusive activities by governments during this time, when arrested individuals had few rights, and torture and forced confessions were common. Such practices made their way to American shores as evidenced by the Salem witch trials.

The Fifth Amendment requires that a person be indicted by a grand jury before he or she may be tried on a criminal charge. A **grand jury** is a group of citizens, selected in a fashion similar to a petit (trial) jury, who listen to the case presented by a prosecutor and determine whether there is sufficient evidence to bind the defendant over for trial. The purpose of the grand jury is to ensure the government does not prosecute individuals without some proof of guilt. Thus, the grand jury is meant to serve as a check on the power of the government, serving as a barrier standing between the individual citizen and the government.

An **indictment** is a document formally charging the defendant with a crime handed down by a grand jury after hearing the evidence presented by the prosecutor. The requirement of an indictment before criminal prosecution is one of a handful of provisions in the Bill of Rights that has not been incorporated into the Fourteenth Amendment and applied to the states. In *Hurtado v. California* (1884), the Supreme Court expressly held that the right does not apply to state criminal trials, and this decision never has been overruled. Nonetheless, a number of states either require indictment by statute or state constitutional provision or provide prosecutors with the choice of seeking an indictment or proceeding through an information. An **information** is a substitute for an indictment, and it is filed directly with the court by the prosecutor, thus bypassing the grand jury.

The Fifth Amendment also prohibits placing someone in **double jeopardy**. This means a jurisdiction may not (1) prosecute someone again for the same crime after the person has been acquitted, (2) prosecute someone again for the same crime after the person has been convicted, and (3) punish someone twice for the same offense. This does not mean a state may not try someone again if the first trial ends in a mistrial or a hung jury. A **mistrial** may be declared if a legal error occurs during a trial that unfairly prejudices the defendant. The trial is then thrown out and a new one held at a later date. A **hung jury** occurs when the trial jury is unable to reach a unanimous verdict in a case that requires unanimity. Not all jurisdictions require a unanimous verdict in civil or criminal cases. In those states where the verdict must be unanimous, if the jury is deadlocked and the judge believes that further deliberations would be pointless, he or she may excuse the jury and order a new trial. This is similar to a declaration of mistrial. In these situations, there has been neither an acquittal nor a conviction. An **acquittal** occurs when a jury votes unanimously that the defendant has not been proven guilty "beyond a reasonable doubt," which is the burden of proof in a criminal case. An acquittal, or "not guilty" verdict, does not necessarily mean that the defendant did not commit the crime for which he or she was charged; it simply means that the state was unable to meet the high burden of proof necessary for conviction. Additionally, if a conviction is overturned on appeal, the state may retry the person, as the reversal on appeal is not an acquittal.

While the double jeopardy clause bars multiple punishments for the same offense, there are exceptions. Under the **dual sovereignty doctrine**, a person can be prosecuted in both federal and state court for same offense or in the courts of different states for the same offense if certain circumstances surrounding the offense occurred in more than one state. An example of this might be a person who is kidnapped and beaten in Ohio who is then taken to Michigan and shot. Double jeopardy does not apply in these situations because a different sovereign, or jurisdiction, is prosecuting the person. However, a person may not be tried for the same crime in both a municipal court and a state court, as these two courts derive their authority from the same source—the same state constitution.

The Fifth Amendment also protects individuals from being forced to incriminate themselves. The privilege against self-incrimination, so familiar to those who have watched television shows and seen police officers read **Miranda warnings** to suspects, is a right we often take for granted today but that did not exist in early common law. The privilege allows a defendant to refuse to speak to police about the crime charged, the right to counsel, and to refuse to testify at trial. Furthermore, the prosecution is barred from commenting on a defendant's refusal to testify, as the Supreme Court has determined that doing so would limit the privilege against self-incrimination by suggesting that asserting a constitutional right was somehow evidence of something to hide (*Griffin v. California* 1965).

The privilege against self-incrimination is not total, however. The Supreme Court has held that the privilege protects a person from compelled testimonial communications, which is a fancy legal phrase meaning "spoken admissions" (*Malloy v. Hogan* 1964). The privilege does not apply to the obtaining of evidence from a suspect by other means, such as taking blood samples, fingerprints, or requiring his or her presence in a lineup.

The Fifth Amendment also provides for due process of law. Exactly what constitutes due process of law is much debated. Essentially, due process means the state must follow certain procedures, designed to protect individual rights, before they deprive an individual of his or her liberty or property. Due process is discussed in greater detail in chapters 2 and 6.

The "taking clause" of the Fifth Amendment involves the circumstances in which the state or federal governments can seize private property for public use under the principle of **eminent domain**. "Public use" is usually thought of in terms of building needed roads, bridges, and parks, which are literally for the use of the public. In a classic conservative-liberal issue, state and local governments across the country have been seizing private property (with just compensation) and selling it to private developers for nominal sums. Conservatives see this as violation of sacred property rights, and liberals see it as a justifiable use of government power to fit a broader definition of "public use." Private development of seized land increases property values and provides work, both of which increases a government's tax revenues and is therefore considered a public benefit. The most famous of such cases decided by the Supreme Court is *Kelo v. City of New London* (2005) in which the Court, split strictly along ideological lines, ruled in favor of New London's right to condemn homes in a ninety-acre blue-collar neighborhood and sell the land to a private developer. (The Kelo decision held that the Fifth Amendment's "public use" is equivalent to "public purpose," which is equal to "economic purpose.")

Sixth Amendment

> *In all criminal prosecutions, the accused shall enjoy the right to a speedy and public trial, by an impartial jury of the State and district wherein the crime shall have been committed, which district shall have been previously ascertained by law, and to be informed of the nature and cause of the accusation; to be confronted with the witnesses against him; to have compulsory process for obtaining witnesses in his favor, and to have the Assistance of Counsel for his defence.*

The Sixth Amendment, like the Fifth, contains a laundry list of rights. These rights are associated with the criminal trial and include the right to a speedy trial, the right to a public trial, the right to a trial by an impartial jury, the right to notice of the charges against oneself, the right to representation by counsel, and the right to confront the witnesses against oneself.

The right to a speedy trial means that the defendant must be brought to trial without "unnecessary delay" (*Barker v. Wingo* 1972). In the Barker case, there was a five-year delay between Barker's indictment and trial. A five-year delay is hardly "speedy," but in upholding his conviction, the Supreme Court ruled that "speedy" is determined on "an ad hoc balancing basis, in which the conduct of the prosecution and that of the defendant are weighed." In other words, there is no inflexible rule defining "unnecessary delay." A whole host of factors such as the reason for the delay and its length must be considered on a case-by-case basis. In Barker's case, the Court essentially said that five years was not excessive because Barker had not actually asked for a speedy trial!

In response to the concerns of civil libertarians following the Barker decision, the U.S. Congress passed the Speedy Trial Act of 1974 which set a specific time limit of one hundred days from arrest to trial. This act only applies to federal cases, but most states have enacted similar legislation. However, considerable "wriggle room" still exists, and if push comes to shove, states can always fall back on less stringent constitutional law provided by *Barker* that trumps statutory law (Schmalleger 2006).

The right to a public trial means defendants have a right to have the public attend the trial if they so wish. The right to notice of the charges against the defendant simply means the prosecution must inform the defendant prior to trial what it is he or she is accused of so a defense may be prepared. This can occur through the filing of an information or the handing down of an indictment by the grand jury. Both these rights emanate from the traditional Anglo-Saxon distrust of secrecy in government as a menace to liberty (again, think of the *Code Louis*, *lettres de cachet*, the Star Chamber, and the Spanish Inquisition).

The right to a trial by an impartial jury means the right to a jury, selected from the community where the crime occurred, which is not predisposed to believe the defendant is guilty. In other words, the members of the jury need not be unaware of the events which led to the trial, but they must not have formed an opinion as to the guilt (or innocence) of the accused: this is the presumption of innocence so valued by common law legal tradition. Trial by jury is an ancient right, mentioned in the Assize of Clarendon (1166) and affirmed in the Magna Carta (1215; Anastaplo 1995).

The Sixth Amendment also provides for the assistance of counsel. The Supreme Court has interpreted this right to include the right to assistance of counsel at any proceeding deemed to be a "critical stage" in the fact-finding process, not only at trial (*Kirby v. Illinois* 1972). Precisely what constitutes a critical stage is subject to some dispute, but it includes the preliminary hearing, the arraignment, the trial itself, and the right of appeal.

The Supreme Court also has determined that the right to counsel means indigent persons who cannot afford to hire a lawyer must be provided one at the state's expense, so long as the defendant faces the possibility of incarceration for six months or more. Additionally, the Supreme Court has held that the right to counsel includes the right to the *effective* assistance of counsel (*Strickland v. Washington* 1984).

The right to counsel was first recognized in the Statute of Merton in 1236. Of course, this right was not nearly as useful to the accused as it is today. Accused persons were permitted to have relatives or friends counsel them. Free men had the right to an attorney (such as there were in those days) unless charged with a felony or with treason.

Seventh Amendment

In Suits at common law, where the value in controversy shall exceed twenty dollars, the right of trial by jury shall be preserved, and no fact tried by a jury, shall be otherwise re-examined in any Court of the United States, than according to the rules of the common law.

The Seventh Amendment provides for the right to a trial by jury in federal civil trials. This Amendment applies only to federal trials; it has not been incorporated into the Fourteenth Amendment by the Supreme Court.

Eighth Amendment

Excessive bail shall not be required, nor excessive fines imposed, nor cruel and unusual punishments inflicted.

The Eighth Amendment prohibits several things, including excessive bail and cruel and unusual punishment. Both of these prohibitions are written broadly, and the courts have struggled with interpreting them.

As for the prohibition on excessive bail, this provision does not expressly state that bail must be set in all cases—it just says bail cannot be excessive. What constitutes excessive bail varies widely, but according to the Supreme Court, it is bail set at a figure higher than necessary to ensure the presence of the defendant at trial (*Stack v. Boyle* 1951). While the Eighth Amendment does not clearly provide for a right to bail, such a right existed in common law (a clause in the Statute of Westminster of 1275) and has been codified in state statutes. Bail does not have to be granted, and the Supreme Court has ruled that a person considered to be a threat to public safety may be denied bail (*United States v. Salerno* 1987).

The prohibition on cruel and unusual punishment limits the type and form of punishment imposed by a state after conviction of a crime. It prohibits torture as well as punishment that is disproportionate to the offense. The cruel and unusual punishment clause does not prohibit the death penalty, as it is deemed to be in accord with contemporary standards of decency, and as the death penalty existed at the time of the passage of the Eighth Amendment

Ninth Amendment

The enumeration in the Constitution, of certain rights, shall not be construed to deny or disparage others retained by the people.

The Ninth Amendment simply states that the listing of some rights in the Constitution should not be construed as a listing of all the rights retained by individual citizens. In other words, the rights provided in the Bill of Rights should not be taken as the *only* rights that citizens have—they are merely *some* of the rights retained by the people (Massey 1995). This is similar to the natural law or natural rights approach discussed in chapter 2.

The obvious question is, if the Bill of Rights is not all inclusive, what exactly are the other rights retained by the people? The Supreme Court has struggled to provide a framework for delineating these rights, as the discussion on incorporation that follows indicates.

In at least one case, the Supreme Court expressly mentioned the Ninth Amendment as providing a basis for giving individual citizens other, unenumerated rights, such as a right to privacy (*Griswold v. Connecticut* 1965). Griswold was the director of the Planned Parenthood League of Connecticut, and he and the league's medical director had been found guilty of dispensing birth control advice and devices (both then illegal in Connecticut), for which they were fined $100 each.

In overturning their conviction, the Supreme Court affirmed that the right to privacy is a very important right while acknowledging that it is not specifically mentioned anywhere in the Constitution. In their ruling, they appealed to an old English case (*Entick v. Carrington* 1765) in which the British High Court's opinion rested heavily on a "natural" right to privacy. Justice Douglas, who delivered the Court's majority opinion in *Griswold*, stated that the specific constitutional guarantees of the Bill of Rights "have penumbras [incompletely lighted areas] formed by emanations from these guarantees that help give them life and substance." In other words, although the right to privacy is not specifically mentioned in the Constitution, such a right can be logically deduced from the rights that are. *Griswold* was a very important step to *Roe v. Wade* (1973), granting abortion rights to women under the principle of privacy, and to *Lawrence v. Texas* (2003), outlawing sodomy statutes under the same principle. Thus, the Ninth Amendment has more social importance than it is often given credit for.

Tenth Amendment

The powers not delegated to the United States by the Constitution, nor prohibited by it to the States, are reserved to the States respectively, or to the people.

The Tenth Amendment has been largely ignored by the Supreme Court. It simply states that the rights not delegated to the federal government by the Constitution are reserved for the states or individual citizens. This is simply the principle of federalism and constitutionalism; the federal government is a government of enumerated powers. This means it has no authority unless so granted by the Constitution, and where the federal government has no authority, the states and individual citizens retain the authority.

Other Amendments

In addition to the individual rights enumerated in the Bill of Rights, several other later-enacted constitutional amendments directly implicate individual rights. These included the Reconstruction Amendments, passed shortly after the Civil War and intended to protect the recently freed slaves from abuse at the hands of state governments. The Reconstruction Amendments include the Thirteenth, Fourteenth, and Fifteenth Amendments. While initially intended to prevent the Southern states from limiting the rights of the recently freed slaves, today these

Amendments, particularly the Fourteenth, are used to protect all citizens from state actions that impinge on constitutional rights.

Thirteenth Amendment

Neither slavery nor involuntary servitude, except as a punishment for crime whereof the party shall have been duly convicted, shall exist within the United States, or any place subject to their jurisdiction. Congress shall have power to enforce this article by appropriate legislation.

The Thirteenth Amendment prohibits slavery in the United States. It has been used since then to uphold civil rights legislation passed by Congress to prevent racial discrimination by private citizens. Where other amendments prohibit discrimination by state governments, there is no such limiting language in the Thirteenth Amendment. Courts have interpreted it as not merely outlawing slavery but forbidding so-called "badges of slavery," or practices intended to keep blacks at lower social and economic levels than whites (Tribe 1988).

Fourteenth Amendment

All persons born or naturalized in the United States, and subject to the jurisdiction thereof, are citizens of the United States and of the State wherein they reside. No State shall make or enforce any law which shall abridge the privileges or immunities of citizens of the United States; nor shall any State deprive any person of life, liberty, or property, without due process of law; nor deny to any person within its jurisdiction the equal protection of the laws.

The Fourteenth Amendment is a very long amendment having five sections. We include only the first section here, which has to do with individual rights. It is an important amendment because it is the first that specifically forbids states from mistreating their citizens. Although the Bill of Rights was intended to apply only to actions of the federal government, after the Civil War, congressional leaders realized that individual states were just as capable of oppressing individual citizens as was the federal government (Klarman 2004). They responded by enacting the Fourteenth Amendment, which forbids states from denying citizens due process of law or equal protection of the laws. These two clauses have dramatically altered the way that states deal with citizens.

The due process clause is identical to the clause in the Fifth Amendment. It has been interpreted to incorporate the various provisions of the Bill of Rights, making them applicable to the states. The equal protection clause has been interpreted to preclude states from making unequal, arbitrary distinctions between people. It does not ban reasonable classifications, but it does prohibit classifications that are either without reason or based on race, gender, national origin, or religion. These are sometimes referred to as **suspect classifications** (Tribe 1988). To put it another way, where the law limits the liberty of *all* persons, it is a due process question; where the law treats *certain classes of people* differently, it is an equal protection question.

Not all classifications are a violation of equal protection. States may treat people differently if they have a legitimate reason to do so. Thus, states may refuse to issue a driver's license to a minor or limit the age at which a person may lawfully consume alcoholic beverages. Classifications based on age are not suspect (meaning likely illegal), if (1) the state can demonstrate an interest in the health and safety of minors who are a peculiarly vulnerable segment of society, and (2) there is no history of "invidious" discrimination against minors as there is for minorities and women. Furthermore, juveniles are seen as possessing fewer rights, or lesser rights, than adults. Thus, a juvenile curfew might be upheld, whereas a general curfew including adults would be struck down.

Standard of Review

In constitutional law, the outcome of a case is often determined as much by the standard of review the court employs as by the facts of the case. Not all of the individual protections set forth in the Bill of Rights are accorded the same respect. Rather, there is a hierarchy of rights. The court employs either a strict scrutiny or rational basis review, depending on whether a fundamental right is implicated or a suspect classification is impacted (Tribe 1988).

Fundamental rights are those freedoms the Supreme Court has determined are "essential to the concept of ordered liberty," rights without which neither liberty nor justice would exist (*Palko v. Connecticut* 1937). Examples include virtually all of the various provisions of the Bill of Rights as well as the Fourteenth Amendment guarantees of due process and equal protection. To date, the Supreme Court has held that only race and religion are suspect classifications in all circumstances, although gender, illegitimacy, and poverty occasionally have been treated as suspect classifications (Tribe 1988).

Under **strict scrutiny** review, the state may not enact legislation that abridges a fundamental right unless (1) it has a compelling interest that justifies restricting a fundamental right, and (2) the legislation is "narrowly tailored" so that the fundamental right is not abridged any more than absolutely necessary to effectuate the state's compelling interest. An example of a compelling interest is the state's interest in the health and safety of its citizens. Additionally, the Supreme Court requires that for legislation to be narrowly tailored, there must exist a sufficient nexus between the legislative body's stated interest and either the classification drawn or the means chosen to advance the state's compelling interest.

This standard of review is referred to as the strict scrutiny test because the Court looks closely at the purpose and effect of the legislation rather than merely accepting the claims of the legislature that the legislation is needed or accepting the legislation as presumptively valid (Tribe 1988). The reason for employing a higher standard of review when legislation impacts on a fundamental right or suspect classification is that closer analysis is required when individual liberties are threatened. The burden of proof is on the government to prove the constitutionality and necessity of legislation exposed to a strict scrutiny test.

Laws involving quasi-suspect classifications such as gender and legitimacy are reviewed under the **intermediate scrutiny** standard. A law is upheld (passes

Figure 3.2 Standards of Judicial Review

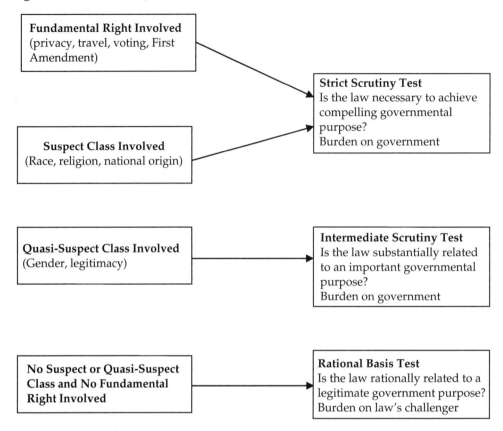

Figure provided by Professor Michael Bogner, Justice Studies Department, Chadron State College (2006).

constitutional muster) if the Court finds that it is *substantially related* to an *important* government purpose. The burden of proof lies primarily with the state under this standard of review.

    If neither a fundamental right nor a suspect classification is implicated, a state may enact legislation abridging that right or impacting that class so long as there is a rational basis for the legislation. This standard of review generally is referred to as the **rational basis test** since under it, the Court will not strike down legislation that appears to have some rational basis. The Court does not look closely at the effects of the legislation, unlike the strict scrutiny test. Under this standard of review, state actions are presumptively valid (Tribe 1988). This standard of review is obviously a much easier one to pass. The legislature need not choose the best possible means; it merely must appear that it has chosen means that are not wholly unrelated to the achievement of the legislative purpose. Figure 3.2 differentiates between the standards of review.

Incorporation of the Bill of Rights in the Fourteenth Amendment

As previously stated, originally the Bill of Rights applied only to the federal government, and state and local governments were not bound by its various provisions. This was because at the time of the adoption of the Constitution, there was a fear of a strong centralized government. State governments were viewed much more favorably, and many state constitutions contained protections of individual rights similar to those in the Bill of Rights. In 1833, the Supreme Court, in *Barron v. Baltimore* (1833)—the first Bill of Rights case coming a surprising forty-two years after its ratification—expressly held that the Bill of Rights applied only to the federal government.

The *Barron* case involved the clause of the Fifth Amendment that forbids governmental taking of private property without just compensation. Barron wanted this clause applied to the states since the city of Baltimore had essentially taken his property without compensation. The Supreme Court dismissed his claim, stating that the amendment did not apply to the states and therefore that the Court lacked jurisdiction in the matter. This cased showed that without the application of the Bill of Rights to the states, individuals would have no recourse to higher authority if the states violated their rights.

After the Civil War and the failed attempt by the Southern states to secede from the Union, federal legislators felt it was necessary to amend the Constitution to provide greater protections for individuals from the actions of state governments. There was in particular a fear that the Southern states would attempt to limit the ability of the recently freed slaves to become equal citizens. The result was the passage in 1868 of the Fourteenth Amendment.

The Fourteenth Amendment, as discussed earlier, contains three clauses: the privileges and immunities clause, the due process clause, and the equal protection clause. The essence of each of these clauses is that they bar states, not the federal government, from infringing on individual rights. The Amendment was expressly intended to control state action, but it was unclear exactly how far it went. The original spur for it was a desire to protect the rights of the freed slaves, but the language of the Amendment was broad and not specifically limited to state actions infringing on the rights of blacks.

An early attempt to apply the language of the privileges and immunities clause to persons other than the recently frees slaves failed in the *Slaughterhouse cases* (1873). At issue was a Louisiana state statute passed by a highly corrupt state legislature, granting one corporation a monopoly on slaughterhouse business (Ross 2003). The petitioners (the person or persons bringing the suit) argued that the privileges and immunities clause should be interpreted as prohibiting unreasonable restrictions on business because the restriction in question deprived them of their right to pursue their lawful trades. The Supreme Court sided with the monopoly, emphasizing that the due process clause should not be a source enabling judges to nullify laws they considered unreasonable (despite the financial gain some legislators realized from the monopoly, there were genuine public health concerns involved). It has been argued that the Court's decision was intended to protect blacks by emphasizing that the Fourteenth Amendment was meant specifically for them (Ross 2003), but the Court's "hands off" stance regarding state legislation actually left them at its mercy (see chapter 12).

During the later part of the nineteenth century, however, the Supreme Court began to use the due process clause of the Fourteenth Amendment to strike down state action involving economic regulation. Due process rights are said to extend beyond procedural rights (discussed fully in chapter 5) to encompass **substantive due process** as well. Under the principle of substantive due process, legislatures cannot pass laws that infringe on substantive rights such as free speech and privacy (this is the legal theory under which the privacy rights applied in *Griswold, Roe, and Johnson* were based). This sounds all very liberal until we realize that the Supreme Court has used the principle repeatedly to hold that states could not impose regulations such as minimum wage laws and child labor laws on private businesses because doing so violated due process. The violation of due process consisted of the regulation or taking of a right such as the right to work or to enter into a contract.

During the 1930s, the use of the due process clause to protect economic interests fell into disfavor, in part because the Supreme Court used it to strike down much of President Roosevelt's New Deal legislation, which was intended to ease the burden of the Great Depression. At the same time, however, the Supreme Court began to use the due process clause of the Fourteenth Amendment to protect individual rights from state action. Beginning in the late 1930s, the Supreme Court incorporated most of the provisions of the Bill of Rights into the Fourteenth Amendment's due process clause and applied them to the states. Many of the criminal law provisions were applied to the states during the 1960s by the Supreme Court under the leadership of Chief Justice Earl Warren (Domino 1994).

By **incorporation** we mean that the justices interpreted the due process clause of the Fourteenth Amendment, which says no state shall deprive a person of life, liberty, or property without "due process of law," as prohibiting states from abridging certain individual rights. Many of these rights are included in the Bill of Rights, hence these rights were included (or incorporated) in the definition of due process. Various Supreme Court justices have advocated different approaches to incorporation during the twentieth century. These are discussed next.

Total Incorporation

Under the total incorporation approach, the due process clause of the Fourteenth Amendment made the entire Bill of Rights applicable to the states. In essence, the phrase "due process of law" was interpreted to mean "all of the provisions of the Bill of Rights." This approach has never commanded a majority of justices on the Court. However, a prominent supporter of this approach was Justice Hugo Black.

Total Incorporation Plus

As the name implies, the total incorporation plus approach goes a step further than the total incorporation approach. Under total incorporation plus, the due process clause of the Fourteenth Amendment includes all of the Bill of Rights and, in addition, includes other, unspecified rights. A principal advocate of this approach was Justice William Douglas who argued that the various provisions of the Bill of Rights created a "penumbra" (*Griswold v. Connecticut* 1965) in which the whole was greater than the sum of the parts. That is, the individual rights contained in the Bill of Rights, when examined together, create other rights. Thus, he argued the various provisions limiting the ability of the government to intrude into a person's private life (such as the Fourth Amendment prohibition on unreasonable searches and the Third Amendment prohibition on quartering troops in private residences) created a general right to privacy.

Fundamental Rights

In *Twining v. New Jersey* (1908), the Supreme Court suggested that some of the individual rights in the Bill of Rights might be protected from state action, not because the Bill of Rights applied to the States but because these rights "are of such a nature that they are included in the conception of due process of law." This became known as the fundamental rights or ordered liberty approach. Under this approach, there is no necessary relationship between the due process clause of the Fourteenth Amendment and the Bill of Rights. The due process clause has an independent meaning that prohibits state action that violates rights "implicit in the concept of ordered liberty" or those rights that are "fundamental" (*Palko v. Connecticut* 1937). Exactly what constitutes a fundamental right is left to the justices considering the history and tradition of the law. Additionally, justices considered the "totality of the circumstances" of each case in determining whether a right is fundamental. This approach provides justices with greater discretion, and they may interpret it either narrowly or broadly. This approach enjoyed strong support on the Court until the late 1960s. A principal advocate of this approach was Justice Felix Frankfurter.

Selective Incorporation

The selective incorporation approach combines elements of the fundamental rights and total incorporation approaches in modified form and is the approach that seems to predominate in most Supreme Court cases. This approach favors a piecemeal, gradual, and selective method of incorporation. Selective incorporation rejects the notion that all of the rights in the Bill of Rights are automatically incorporated in the due process clause of the Fourteenth Amendment but does look to the Bill of Rights as a guide to the meaning of due process. Selective incorporation rejects the "totality of the circumstances" component of the fundamental rights approach and instead incorporates rights deemed fundamental to the same extent and in the same manner as applied to the federal government.

As an example, the Supreme Court in *Wolf v. Colorado* (1949) held that the Fourth Amendment was fundamental and applied it to the states but decided that the exclusionary rule was not fundamental and therefore does not apply to the states. Thus, state law enforcement officials were told by the Court that they must

Table 3.2 *Summary of Incorporation Theories*

Total Incorporation	Total Incorporation Plus	Selective Incorporation
Intent: To make all provisions of the Bill of Rights applicable to the states.	**Intent:** To protect rights enumerated in the Bill of Rights plus certain unenumerated rights.	**Intent:** To incorporate provisions of the Bill of Rights in a careful and discriminative way.
Justification: Due process clause of the Fourteenth Amendment	**Justification:** The totality of the rights in the Bill of Rights created a penumbra over the law.	**Justification:** Only fundamental rights should be incorporated; nonfundamental rights should be left as state concerns.

obey the Fourth Amendment, but a failure to do so would not result in the exclusion of evidence obtained through a violation of the Fourth Amendment. In *Mapp v. Ohio* (1961), under selective incorporation, the Court held both the right (freedom from unreasonable searches) and the means of enforcing the right (the exclusionary rule) were part of the due process clause of the Fourteenth Amendment.

Selective incorporation became popular in the 1960s with the Warren Court. A principal advocate was Justice William Brennan. While selective incorporation accepted the idea that the due process clause protects only "fundamental rights" and that not every right in the Bill of Rights is necessarily fundamental, over time it has led to the incorporation of virtually everything in the Bill of Rights. The criminal protections not yet included are the right to an indictment by a grand jury and the prohibition on excessive bail. The Second and Seventh Amendments have not been incorporated.

It should be noted that because the Supreme Court has deemed incorporation necessary, it does not mean that most of these rights did not already exist in the states. Many states had rights in their state constitutions that were even more protective of individual rights than those in the Bill of Rights in some instances. For instance, a number of states had privacy rights in such matters as abortion and the bearing of arms long before the Court's "discovery" of "penumbras."

Table 3.2 presents a summary of incorporation theories.

JUDICIAL REVIEW

Given the varied sources of law, and the ambiguous language of many statutes and constitutional provisions, it is inevitable that laws will come into conflict or interpretations of statutes will differ. When this happens, who decides which law is paramount? In the United States, the answer to that question is the courts through the power of judicial review.

Judicial review simply means the court has the power to examine a law and determine whether it is constitutional. To make this determination, judges must examine the law and compare it with the Constitution. This requires them to interpret the language of both the statute and the Constitution. If the judge determines the law is constitutional, he or she upholds the law; if not, he or she declares it unconstitutional and therefore void.

For example, the Fourth Amendment prohibits "unreasonable" searches. Suppose a state legislature passes a law allowing police officers to search anyone they encounter on a public street. Is this law constitutional? Or does it violate the prohibition on unreasonable searches? To answer this question, judges must examine the history and meaning of "unreasonable" as contained in the Fourth Amendment. They do this by examining precedent.

Judicial review is not specifically provided for in the Constitution. Rather, judicial review is judge-made law. *Marbury v. Madison* (1803) established the authority of the U.S. Supreme Court to engage in judicial review of the acts of the other branches of government. The Supreme Court stated in *Marbury* that it was the duty of the judiciary to interpret the Constitution and to apply it to particular fact situations. The Court also said that it was the job of the courts to decide when other laws (acts of Congress or state laws) were in violation of the Constitution and to declare these laws null and void if they were. This is the doctrine of judicial review.

One fact of which we must be aware is that the law is not like mathematics in which all students who apply the correct algorithm with care will inevitably arrive at the correct solution to the problem. Law is preeminently a human endeavor, and the "correct" solution to a legal problem depends on all kinds of human foibles, eccentricities, and interests. It is for this reason that the existence and extent of judicial review has been hotly debated from the very beginning of the United States, as we shall see in future chapters.

Marbury v. Madison

Marbury v. Madison is perhaps the most important case ever decided by the Supreme Court because it established the authority of the high court. Article III of the Constitution created the Supreme Court, but it did not discuss whether the Supreme Court could review legislation or interpret the Constitution.

At the time of the adoption of the Constitution, there was heated debate concerning which branch of government had the authority to declare an act void. There were three suggestions on how to handle such a situation: (1) each branch within its sphere of authorized power has the final say; (2) the Supreme Court has the final say, but only as to the parties in cases before the court; and (3) the Supreme Court has the final say. This controversy was finally resolved by the opinion in *Marbury*. An examination of the case provides insight into this controversy and how the Supreme Court handled the situation.

The facts of *Marbury v. Madison*:

1. President Adams, a Federalist, appointed forty-two of his fellow Federalists as justices of the peace for the District of Columbia just days before turning over the office to incoming President Thomas Jefferson, a Democrat. Adams's secretary of State, John Marshall, delivered most of the commissions to the newly appointed justices of the peace, but failed to deliver Marbury's.

2. The newly elected president's secretary of state, James Madison, refused to deliver Marbury's commission, so Marbury applied directly to the Supreme

Court for a writ of mandamus (a writ compelling public officials to perform their duty). The Supreme Court was granted original jurisdiction in such matters by the Judiciary Act of 1789. The Supreme Court agreed to hear the case but was unable to hear it for fourteen months because Congress passed a law that stopped the Supreme Court from meeting.

3. In 1803, the Supreme Court reconvened, heard the case, and decided Marbury was entitled to his commission but that the Supreme Court could not issue a writ of mandamus. Chief Justice John Marshall (formerly Adams's secretary of state!) wrote the opinion of the court.

Marshall said, (1) Marbury was entitled to his commission, as he had a legal right that was not extinguished by the change in office of president; (2) a writ of mandamus was a proper legal remedy for enforcing Marbury's right; (3) however, the Supreme Court lacked the constitutional authority to issue such a writ. The Judiciary Act of 1789 gave the Supreme Court original jurisdiction in such cases, but this grant of authority to the Supreme Court was unconstitutional because Article III of the Constitution defined Supreme Court jurisdiction.

The Judiciary Act of 1789 had the effect of changing (by enlarging) the jurisdiction of the Supreme Court, but Congress cannot pass a statute that changes the Constitution. The only way to change the Constitution is through a constitutional amendment (see next section). As stated by Chief Justice Marshall, "an act of the legislature, repugnant to the Constitution, is void." In other words, the Constitution is superior to congressional legislation.

Prior to the decision in *Marbury*, Democrats argued that the Supreme Court lacked the authority to declare acts of other branches of the federal government unconstitutional, while Federalists supported judicial review. If the Supreme Court had issued a writ of mandamus, it could not have forced Madison to honor it. The Supreme Court thus was faced with a serious challenge to its authority. Marshall's opinion saved the court's prestige while allowing the Democrats to claim a political victory (not having to appoint any more Federalists as justices of the peace). What is more important, the decision established as law the idea that the Supreme Court has the authority to review the constitutionality of congressional activity (and presidential acts)—this is judicial review.

This was obviously a major victory for the Supreme Court, and although opposed at the time, it was accepted at least in part because the result in the case was satisfactory to opponents of a strong Supreme Court. The Supreme Court did not use the power of judicial review to invalidate congressional legislation again until 1857, when it ruled the Missouri Compromise unconstitutional (discussed in chapter 13), so Congress had little reason to complain.

THE PROCESS OF AMENDING THE CONSTITUTION

We have discussed at some length the most important amendments that impact individual liberty in this chapter without touching on the process by which these amendments come into being. The Constitution may be changed—or a Supreme Court ruling overturned if the Court does not itself overturn it—only by a constitutional amendment. A constitutional amendment may be passed only by following one of two procedures set forth in Article V of the Constitution. The first process involves two-thirds of both houses of Congress passing a resolution calling for an amendment. If the resolution passes both houses, the proposed amendment must be ratified (approved) within seven years by three-fourths of the states. The second method involves two-thirds of the states voting to call for a convention at which a constitutional amendment can be proposed. All twenty-seven amendments (out of thousands that have been proposed) have been added to the constitution using the first process.

The Eleventh Amendment, passed in 1795, is particularly interesting for a number of reasons, not the least of which is that it was passed in response to the Supreme Court's very first constitutional decision (*Chisholm v. Georgia* 1793). The issue before the Court was whether the State of Georgia is subject to the jurisdiction of the United States Supreme Court and the federal government. The case involved a citizen of South Carolina suing Georgia for payment of goods supplied to the state during the Revolutionary War. Georgia refused to appear before the court, claiming sovereign immunity (a doctrine precluding a suit against a sovereign government without its consent), which meant that it thus was not liable to be sued. Article III of the Constitution plainly states that federal courts have jurisdiction to decide cases "between a State and citizens of another State," and therefore, the Court ruled against Georgia's sovereign immunity claim and for Chisholm's claim for compensation.

Many states objected to this ruling, claiming that were they liable for debts incurred during the Revolutionary War, they would face financial ruin. The Eleventh Amendment was therefore passed both to prevent further such suits and, perhaps more importantly, to assert the sovereignty of the states. This amendment reads:

> The Judicial power of the United States shall not be construed to extend to any suit in law or equity, commenced or prosecuted against one of the United States by Citizens of another State, or by Citizens or Subjects of any Foreign State.

Nevertheless, both the federal government and the states may, and often do, waive their right not to be sued. Whenever the issue has arisen in Supreme Court cases, the ruling has always favored the sovereign immunity of the states, although dissenting opinions have consistently asserted that the states surrendered their sovereign immunity when they ratified the U.S. Constitution.

SUMMARY

In this chapter, we have discussed the historical development of the law with a particular focus on the concepts of common law, precedent, stare decisis, and judicial review. We also have examined the sources of law, focusing primarily on the U.S. Constitution and the Bill of Rights. The Bill of Rights provides many of the individual rights that American citizens have. We also have discussed the means by which the Bill of Rights, originally applicable only to the federal government, has been applied to the states through the due process clause of the Fourteenth Amendment.

Associated with incorporation is the concept of judicial review. This is a tremendously important concept in the law, for it is judicial review that gives to the courts the power to declare acts of other branches of government void as unconstitutional. Without this power, the courts would be unable to provide an important check on the action of the executive and legislative branches of government.

The American system of government was designed expressly by the Founding Fathers with checks and balances among the branches of government. Nonetheless, judicial review is a controversial subject, as many feel it gives the courts too much power vis-à-vis the other branches of government, and it allows democratically elected leaders to be obstructed. The question students should ask in deciding whether they support the concept of judicial review is who else can provide a check on the other branches of government?

The law, in the end, is what we in society make it. Whether it is written by judges or legislators, it can be changed in one way or another. It is the responsibility of individual citizens to be aware of their rights and the law and to ensure no branch of government is too powerful at the expense of the others.

DISCUSSION QUESTIONS

1. What is common law, and what role does precedent and stare decisis play in the development of the law?
2. How did the Bill of Rights come to be applied to the individual states?
3. What is the power of judicial review, and how was it developed?
4. Why was the Bill of Rights adopted, and what rights are contained in it?
5. What are the different standards of review in constitutional law, and when are they used?
6. Given the Supreme Court's "discovery" of penumbras in the Bill of Rights, such as the right to privacy, should this right be extended to assisted suicide for terminally ill patients and/or access to marijuana for medical purposes? Why or why not?
7. Go to http://www.earlyamerica.com/review/spring97/blackstone.html about Sir William Blackstone and discuss his impact on American institutions.

References

Amar, A. 1998. *The Bill of Rights*. New Haven, CT: Yale University Press.

Anastaplo, G. 1995. *The amendments to the Constitution: A commentary*. Baltimore: Johns Hopkins University Press.

Bailey, G. 2006. Blackstone in America: Lectures by an English lawyer become the blueprint for a new nation's laws and leaders. *Early American Review*. http://www.earlyamerica.com/review/spring97/blackstone.html.

Black, H. 2001. *Black's law dictionary.* 5th ed. Minneapolis, MN: West.

Blackstone, W. 1765–1769. *Commentaries on the law of England.* 4 vols. London: Routledge.

Cuddihy, W. 1990. *The Fourth Amendment: Origin and original meaning.* Unpublished doctoral dissertation, Claremont, CA: Claremont College.

Domino, J. 1994. *Civil rights and liberties.* New York: HarperCollins.

Feldman, N. 2005. *Divided by God: America's church-state problem—and what she should do about it.* New York: Farrar, Straus and Giroux.

Kates, D. 1983. Handgun prohibition and the original meaning of the Second Amendment. *Michigan Law Review* 82:204–279.

Klarman, M. 2004. *From Jim Crow to civil rights: The Supreme Court and the struggle for racial equality.* New York: Oxford University Press.

Levinson, S. 1989. The embarrassing Second Amendment. *Yale Law Journal* 99:637–709.

Massey, C. 1995. *Silent rights: The Ninth Amendment and the Constitution's unenumerated rights.* Philadelphia: Temple University Press.

Ross, M. 2003. *Justice of shattered dreams: Samuel Freeman Miller and the Supreme Court during the Civil War era.* Baton Rouge: University of Louisiana Press.

Schmalleger, F. 2006. *Criminal justice today.* 9th ed. New York: Prentice Hall.

Stramignoni, I. 2002. At the margins of the history of English law: The institutional, the socio-political and the "blotted out." *Legal Studies* 22:420–47.

Tribe, L. 1988. *American constitutional law.* Mineola, NY: Foundation Press.

Turner, R. 1990. Who was the author of Glanvill? Reflections of the education of Henry II's common layers. *Law and History Review* 8:97–130.

Williams, D. 1991. Civic Republicanism and the citizen militia: The terrifying Second Amendment. *Yale Law Journal* 101:550–623.

Cases Cited

Barker v. Wingo, 407 U.S. 514 (1972).
Barron v. Baltimore, 32 U.S. 243 (1833).
Chaplinsky v. New Hampshire, 315, U.S. 568 (1942).
Chisholm v. Georgia, 2 U.S. 419 (1793).
District of Columbia v. Heller, 554 U.S.—(2008).
Entick v. Carrington, 19 Howell's State Trials 1029 (1765).
Everson v. Board of Education, 330 U.S. 1 (1947).
Griffin v. California, 380 U.S. 609 (1965).
Griswold v. Connecticut, 381 U.S. 479 (1965).
Hurtado v. California, 110 U.S. 516 (1884).
Kelo v. City of New London, 545 U.S. 108 (2005).
Kirby v. Illinois, 406 U.S. 682 (1972).
Lawrence v. Texas, 539 U.S. 558 (2003).
Lemon v. Kurtzman, 403 U.S. 602 (1971).
Malloy v. Hogan, 378 U.S. 1 (1964).
Mapp v. Ohio, 367 U.S. 643 (1961).
Marbury v. Madison, 1 Cranch 137 (1803).
Miller v. California, 413 U.S. 15 (1973).
Palko v. Connecticut, 302 U.S. 319 (1937).
Roe v. Wade, 410 U.S. 113 (1973).
Slaughterhouse cases, 83 U.S. 36 (1873).
Stack v. Boyle, 342 U.S. 1 (1951).
Strickland v. Washington, 466 U.S. 668 (1984).

Texas v. Johnson, 491 U.S. 397 (1989).
Twining v. New Jersey, 211 U.S. 78 (1908).
United States v. Salerno, 481 U.S. 739 (1987).
Virginia State Board of Pharmacy v. Virginia Citizens Consumers Council, 425 U.S. 748 (1976).
Wolf v. Colorado, 338 U.S. 25 (1949).

CHAPTER 4

FEDERAL AND STATE COURTS

The Supreme Court comprises eight associate justices and the chief justice. The justices are nominated by the president, confirmed by the Senate, and serve for life, or until they choose to retire from the bench. There is no standard career path that one can follow to become a justice. Many Supreme Court justices served as judges in the United States Courts of Appeal, while others served as judges on state supreme courts. Others come to the high court without any prior judicial experience. Some were law professors, others senators with a great deal of political experience.

One of the most unique justices, in terms of background and life experiences, was William O. Douglas. He served on the Court longer than any other justice, from 1939 to 1975. Prior to joining the Supreme Court, he was a distinguished law professor at Columbia and Yale, and he served as chairman of the Securities and Exchange Commission under President Franklin Roosevelt. His experience in academe and in politics provided him with fairly typical credentials for a Supreme Court justice. What made him stand out from other justices was his approach to life. He grew up poor in Yakima, Washington, and was one of the first Supreme Court appointees to come from the West. Throughout his life, he maintained a love for the West and the outdoors, leaving Washington immediately after the close of the Supreme Court's term in June to spend the summer months in the mountains of Washington. Because Supreme Court justices have duties that require them to review documents throughout the summer months, this meant the Supreme Court clerk's office had to find a way to deliver documents to Justice Douglas, often very quickly. Today, with ATVs, the Internet and cell phones, getting in touch with someone, even someone living in a cabin in a remote area of Washington state, is not that difficult. But in the 1940s and 1950s, this sometimes meant sending Supreme Court clerks on horseback into the wilds of Washington state to find Justice Douglas. Justice Douglas on more than one occasion reviewed important court documents in front of a campfire while clerks waited to obtain his decision and signature on the paperwork.

INTRODUCTION

Justice is something we all seek for ourselves and for others, and while we may have different ideas about what constitutes justice, in America, the place where people go to obtain justice is the court system. The many different types of courts all share the feature of doing justice. Courts provide several functions while dispensing justice, depending on the case. The overarching purpose of the courts is to "do justice" by providing all parties with due process of law. Courts settle disputes by providing a forum for obtaining justice and resolving disputes through the application of law (Meador 1991). In the courts, injured parties may be heard, and the state may seek to punish wrongdoers; private parties may seek redress in civil court, and the state may seek to punish violators of the criminal law in criminal court. While the courtroom is obviously not the only place that people may go to settle disputes, Americans traditionally have not been reluctant to turn to the courts for redress. The courts are used much less frequently in other cultures, such as in China, where social control is exercised less formally (we explore this in chapter 13).

Second, courts make public policy decisions. Policy making involves the allocation of limited resources (such as money, property, or rights) to competing interests. The United States has a long tradition of settling difficult policy questions in the courtroom rather than in the legislature (Perry 1994). This is because politicians, fearful of harming their reelection prospects, often avoid settling complex and/or difficult problems. Additionally, the rights of minorities often are unprotected by the legislature, so courts are forced to step into the breach. Finally, there is an acceptance of litigation as a tool for social change.

Examples of how the U.S. Supreme Court has shaped social policy include striking down economic reforms during the Great Depression, the extension of criminal procedural rights to defendants, race relations and school desegregation, reapportionment, and abortion (Wasby 1993). Law and social change itself is the subject of chapter 10.

Third, courts serve to clarify the law through interpretation of statutes and the application of general principles to specific fact patterns (Abraham 1987). Courts are different from the other branches of government in many ways, but perhaps the most significant difference is that courts are reactive: courts do not initiate cases but rather serve to settle controversies brought to them by others— plaintiffs and defendants, in legal parlance.

In this chapter, we discuss the role and structure of the federal and state courts with emphasis on the role of the U.S. Supreme Court, the court of last resort. The court systems of the various states and the federal system share a number of characteristics but also can be quite different. Some examples of different court systems are provided to illustrate these similarities and differences. We include in the discussion trial and appeals courts as well as courts of limited jurisdiction. Frequently, issues arise concerning the interplay of federal and state courts. After our discussion of court structure, we include a discussion of the trial process, focusing on the criminal trial.

JURISDICTION

To appreciate how and why court systems are set up the way they are, it is important to understand the concept of jurisdiction. The term *jurisdiction* comes from the Latin *juris* ("law") and *dicere* ("to speak") and denotes the legal authority or power of a court to hear, pronounce on, and decide a case. A court's juris-diction is conferred by statute or constitution. There are four primary types of jurisdiction: personal, subject matter, geographical, and hierarchical (Shreve and Raven-Hansen 1994).

Personal jurisdiction involves the authority of the court over the person. A court may acquire personal jurisdiction over a person if that person comes in contact with the court, either by being a citizen of the state or by committing an act or acts that contravene the laws of that state.

Subject matter jurisdiction involves the authority conferred on a court to hear a particular type of case. Some courts may hear only a specified type of case. Examples include traffic court, juvenile court, and probate court. Thus, a juvenile court would hear only matters involving juveniles. Smaller jurisdictions often do not have such courts, instead combining all the specialized courts into one court because of limited resources.

Geographical jurisdiction refers to the authority of courts to hear cases that arise within specified boundaries, such as a city, county, state, or country. Sometimes this is referred to as *venue*. For a court to have jurisdiction over an event, that event must have taken place in whole or part within the geographical jurisdic-tion of the court. Thus, a person who kills someone in New York could not be prosecuted in North Carolina for that killing. The proper forum would be in New York. Furthermore, the proper court within New York would be the county in which the killing occurred.

Precisely where a crime occurs is not always clear-cut. For instance, a person may be kidnapped in Mississippi and taken to Texas. In this case, the kidnap-ping is a continuing offense—that is, each state into which the victim is taken could charge the kidnapper with a crime. Furthermore, both states may pros-ecute without violating the prohibition on double jeopardy, as they are each sep-arate sovereign governments. This means each state derives its authority from a different source—its own state constitution. While two states can prosecute a person for the same offense, a state and a county in that state cannot do so, as the county derives its jurisdiction from the same source as the state (that state's constitution).

Within each state there are jurisdictions, usually defined by county bound-aries. A state crime must be tried both within the proper state and the proper district within the state. Occasionally, a defendant in a criminal case may request a change of venue. Such a request must be based on evidence that it is impos-sible for the defendant to get a fair trial in the original court, perhaps because of substantial adverse publicity.

Hierarchical jurisdiction involves the division of responsibilities and functions among the various courts. There is original and appellate jurisdiction, as well as limited and general jurisdiction, as follows.

General jurisdiction means a court has the authority to hear a variety of cases, that it is not limited to hearing only a particular type of case. An example is the state trial court, which often has the authority to hear all manner of civil and criminal cases. *Civil cases* involve a dispute between two private parties, such as over contract or property law. *Criminal cases* involve prosecution of an individual by the state for violating state criminal law.

Original jurisdiction means the power of the court to hear the case initially. For example, in federal court, all felony-level cases begin in the district court, while a suit between two states would start at the Supreme Court level. The court of original jurisdiction is where trials take place.

Appellate jurisdiction means the power of the court to review a decision of a lower court. Appeals courts may affirm or reverse lower court judgments and either enter a new judgment or send the case back down to the lower court for reconsideration in light of its decision. Appellate courts do not conduct a retrial; rather, they generally are limited to a review of the trial record to determine if there were any major legal errors. The court hears oral argument by the attorneys for each side and reads legal briefs filed with the court and bases its decision on these materials rather than on new evidence.

THE FEDERAL COURTS

Essentially, there are two court systems in the United States: the court systems of the fifty states and the federal court system. Federal courts are sometimes referred to as *Article III Courts* because they are established by Congress pursuant to its authority to create "inferior" or lower courts under Article III of the U.S. Constitution. The jurisdictions of the federal and state courts frequently overlap, as what may be a crime in a state is also punishable under federal law (such as bank robbery). The principles drawn up by the Constitutional Convention in 1787 created a government with three branches—the legislature, the executive, and the judicial. The duties of each branch were set forth in a separate article of the Constitution. The duties of the judicial branch were listed in Article III. This article established the Supreme Court and authorized "such inferior courts as Congress" chose to create. Neither the number of members of the Supreme Court nor the form of any potential "inferior" courts was described.

At first the idea of creating inferior federal courts met with much resistance from supporters of states' rights who were afraid that federal courts would infringe on the jurisdiction and authority of state courts. Anti-federalists sought limitations on Article III for the same reason they sought a bill of rights: they feared a strong central government. On the other hand, several contributors to the *Federalist Papers* (a series of articles written by James Madison, Alexander Hamilton, and John Jay arguing for ratification of the Constitution) argued for a strong federal court system as a bulwark against the actions of a democratically elected legislature. These writers saw the Constitution as the paramount law of the land and believed it the job of the courts to interpret it and prevent the legislature from passing laws that may infringe on constitutional rights, which they saw primarily as property rights (Kelly, Harbison, and Belz 1983).

With the independence of the United States, one of the first acts of the newly elected Congress was to pass the Judiciary Act of 1789. This act established Supreme Court membership at six justices. The act also created three federal circuit courts and thirteen district courts, one in each of the original states. From this, an entire federal system has grown and today encompasses some thirteen federal circuit courts and several hundred district courts. The first set of inter-mediate-level appellate courts with purely appellate jurisdiction was established more than one hundred years later, in 1891.

The federal court system today consists of three primary tiers: district courts, courts of appeal, and the Supreme Court. Each of these courts has different functions. These are discussed in the following sections.

District Courts

The district court is the trial court, the court of original jurisdiction, for the federal court system. There are currently ninety-four federal judicial districts. Each state has at least one district court. Some, such as California and Texas, have as many as four (see Figure 4.1). With minor exceptions, no judicial district crosses state lines (Meador 1991).

In each district, there is a U.S. District Court. The number of judges in each court ranges from two to twenty-eight, depending on the population of the individual district. There are approximately 650 federal district judges, all of whom are appointed for life. Within each district court, there are subordinate judicial officers referred to as federal magistrates. These officers conduct preliminary proceedings in cases before the district court and issue warrants. Judgments entered by magistrates are considered judgments of the district court. Federal magistrate courts are similar to courts of limited jurisdiction in state courts (Smith 1992).

Figure 4.1 The Federal Judicial Circuits.

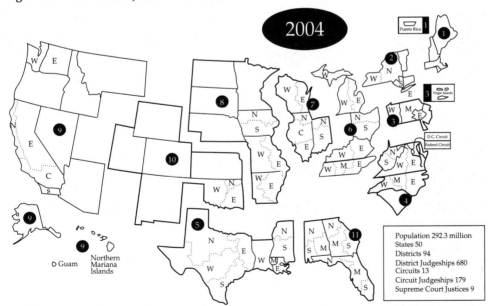

Source: Wheeler R. & C. Harrison: *Creating the Federal Judicial Systems* (3rd Edition). Washington, D.C. Federal Judicial Center, 2005.

Federal district courts have original jurisdiction over both civil and criminal cases involving federal statutes. Their jurisdiction is defined by both the Constitution and federal statute. District courts conduct trials for all federal criminal offenses and have jurisdiction to hear civil cases where there is diversity of citizenship between the parties. *Diversity of citizenship* refers to the situation where the opposing parties are from different states.

Until recently, much of the federal court docket was comprised of civil cases, but in recent years, this balance has begun to shift. Congress in recent years has greatly increased the number of federal crimes. Consequently, while the number of civil cases filed in federal district court still far outnumbers criminal cases, criminal trials take up a significant portion of the district court's time. In 2003, there were 259,962 cases filed with the federal district courts. Crimes tried in federal courts include many types of white-collar crimes, kidnapping, bank robbery, mail fraud, and civil rights abuses. The current "war on drugs" and the illegal immigration crisis have added greatly to the federal courts' burdens, together comprising about 60 percent of criminal cases heard by them (Bohm and Haley 2007). Mainly because of these two issues, some jurisdictions have been forced to postpone all civil proceedings to deal with the backlog of criminal cases. The Constitution requires a "speedy trial" in criminal cases, and consequently, criminal cases take precedence, often delaying civil cases for significant periods of time.

Federal district courts are not courts of general jurisdiction. Rather, they have jurisdiction to hear only those types of cases specified by acts of Congress, and Congress may authorize the district court to hear only those cases and controversies specified in Article III of the Constitution. The majority of cases in federal court deal with claims arising out of federal law, either civil or criminal. These may be based on federal statutes or the Constitution.

The other major category of cases in federal courts are civil cases arising out of the court's diversity jurisdiction. District courts are authorized to hear any civil matter, even if it involves state law, if the amount in question exceeds $75,000 and the parties are diverse: that is, if they are citizens of different states. Federal courts were given diversity jurisdiction originally because the Founding Fathers feared state courts would be biased in favor of their residents when presented with a suit between a resident and a nonresident. Allowing the nonresident to shift the case to federal court was seen as a means of ensuring a fair trial (Kelly et al. 1983).

Federal judges are appointed for life; they hold office "during good behavior." Furthermore, their salary cannot be reduced during their term of office. This protects the independence of the federal judiciary and sets it apart from state court judges, most of whom are appointed or elected to a defined term of years.

Courts of Appeals

The next level in the federal system comprises the courts of appeals. These courts also are referred to as circuit courts. There are thirteen courts of appeals: eleven for the fifty states, one for the District of Columbia, and one for the federal circuit.

The jurisdiction of the Court of Appeals for the Federal Circuit is defined by statute to include appeals from several federal administrative agencies, patent claims, and decisions of the Claims Court and the Court of International Trade, two specialized federal trial courts. The District of Columbia has its own appeals court in part because of the large volume of cases filed in the District of Columbia.

The eleven remaining courts of appeals are organized on a territorial basis, with each covering several states. For instance, the Eleventh Circuit encompasses the states of Florida, Georgia, and Alabama, while the Ninth Circuit, the largest of the courts of appeals, includes the states of Alaska, Hawaii, California, Nevada, Arizona, Idaho, Oregon, Washington, and Montana, as well as Guam and the Northern Marianas Islands.

The number of judges on each of the courts of appeals varies from six in the First Circuit to twenty-eight in the Ninth Circuit. Appeals are heard by three-judge panels. The makeup of these panels is constantly changing so that Judge A does not repeatedly sit with Judge B. If there are conflicting decisions involving the same legal issue between two panels, the entire circuit may sit *en banc* (meaning "as a group") and rehear the case. This obviously can be a bit unwieldy in those circuits that have a large number of judges; consequently, federal law permits courts of appeals with more than fifteen active judges to sit en banc with less than all of their members (Meador 1991). The Ninth Circuit may hold en banc hearings with as few as eleven of its twenty-eight judges. As with district court judges, Courts of Appeals' judges are appointed for life.

Figure 4.2 displays the federal court system.

Figure 4.2 The Federal Court System

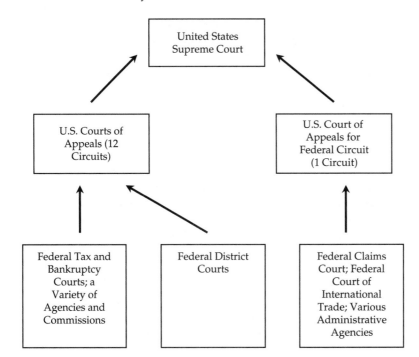

Supreme Court

The third and final tier in the federal court system is the Supreme Court. This is the court of last resort for all cases arising in the federal system as well as all cases in state courts that involve a federal constitutional issue. All Supreme Court decisions regarding constitutional law are precedents that bind all lower federal and state courts. Only future Supreme Court decisions or a constitutional amendment can overturn a Supreme Court decision, although the Court usually respects its own precedents. The Supreme Court has original jurisdiction over a very small number of situations, including suits between states, suits between the United States and a state, and suits between a state and a foreign citizen. These rarely occur, and if they do, they are typically disputes between states. The bulk of the Court's docket is comprised of cases taken on appeal from either the federal court of appeals or the state supreme courts (Wasby 1993).

The Court's appellate docket is almost entirely discretionary—that is, the Court may choose which cases it takes and which it refuses to hear. This is very different from trial courts and lower appeals courts, which must hear cases brought before them. Parties seeking to appeal to the Supreme Court petition for a writ of certiorari. A **writ of certiorari** is an order to the lower court to send the record of the case up to the Supreme Court. The justices vote whether to accept a case. If four or more justices vote to accept a case, it is placed on the Court's docket. This is known as the **rule of four** (Wasby 1993). If the Court elects to hear an appeal, it issues the writ to the lower court, requesting the case be sent up to it. If four votes to accept are not obtained, the petition for a writ of certiorari is denied, and the decision of the lower court is left undisturbed, meaning it is left as is. Typically, when the Court refuses to grant certiorari, it does so because there is no difference of opinion on the issue that is the subject of the case among the circuit courts or because no federal constitutional issue is raised. Refusal to accept an appeal is not considered a decision on the merits of the case and has no binding precedential value. It simply means that the Court has chosen not to hear the case, for whatever reason (Brigham 1987). Only about 2 percent of petitions to the Court are granted certiorari.

The Supreme Court Justices

The law is inherently conservative, and so are most of its servants. The conservatism of the law is plain in its respect for precedent and predictability (and hence the status quo). The conservatism of the Court is apparent in the composition of its members since the Court's beginning. As of 2009, there have been 112 justices, of whom 92 have been white, Protestant, and male. Forty-six years after its inception, the Court had its first Catholic, Roger Taney, appointed in 1835. Only ten other Catholics have served on the Supreme Court, five of whom—Anthony Kennedy, Antonin Scalia, John Roberts, Samuel Alito and Sonia Sotomajor—are serving presently. It was not until 1916 that the first Jew, Louis Brandeis, was appointed. There have been four other Jewish justices, including a current member, Ruth Bader Ginsburg. It was not until 1965 that the first black man, Thurgood Marshall, was appointed. Upon Marshall's retirement, the second black justice, Clarence Thomas, was appointed. The first female, Sandra Day O 'Connor, was appointed to the Court in 1981, just eight years shy of the two-hundredth anniversary of the Judiciary Act of 1789. She was joined in 1993 by the Court's second female member (and fourth Jewish member), Ruth Ginsburg. Justice O'Connor retired in 2006 and was replaced by Samuel Alito. Sonia Sotomajor become the third female to serve on the Supreme Court when she was appointed in 2009.

Currently, the Court is composed of nine justices, one of whom is designated the Chief Justice. John Roberts became Chief Justice in 2005 following the death of former Chief Justice William H. Rehnquist. Congress has the authority either to enlarge or reduce the number of justices on the Supreme Court, and has done so at times in the past. Congress has not changed the number of justices in more than one hundred years; however, it seems unlikely Congress would try to do so now in the face of a long-standing tradition of having nine justices on the Court.

While created as a third branch of the federal government, the Supreme Court did not immediately establish a significant presence in the affairs of the country. In fact, there was so little for the Court to do that the first chief justice, John Jay, resigned to take a position as an ambassador. It was not until the term of John Marshall that the Supreme Court was able to establish its role in the government. Today, the Supreme Court plays a significant role in public affairs (Cooper 1988).

THE STATE COURTS

While it is the federal courts (particularly the Supreme Court) that capture much of the attention of the media and the general public, the reality is that state courts are the workhorses of the American judicial system. State courts currently process in excess of one hundred million cases a year. These range from the most serious of criminal cases to complex civil litigation and to the run-of-the-mill divorce case or traffic ticket.

The structure of state courts is much more varied than the structure of the federal court system. The fifty states have created a multiplicity of court structures. Some court systems are unified and clearly organized; others are a jumble of overlapping jurisdiction and confusion. In this section, we present a "typical" state court system.

The most common state court system is comprised of four levels, or tiers, of courts. There are courts of limited jurisdiction, courts of general jurisdiction, intermediate appellate courts, and a final appellate court or court of last resort. Although most states only have one court of last resort, Texas has two—one for civil appeals (Texas Supreme Court) and one for criminal appeals (Court of Criminal Appeals). The Texas court hierarchy is presented in Figure 4.3.

Courts of limited jurisdiction are those courts that deal with the less serious offenses and civil cases. These courts are referred to by a variety of names, including justice of the peace court, magistrate's court, municipal court, and county court. These lower courts handle a wide variety of matters, including minor criminal cases, traffic offenses, violations of municipal ordinances, and civil disputes under a certain amount, usually $1,000.

Figure 4.3 The Texas State Court System

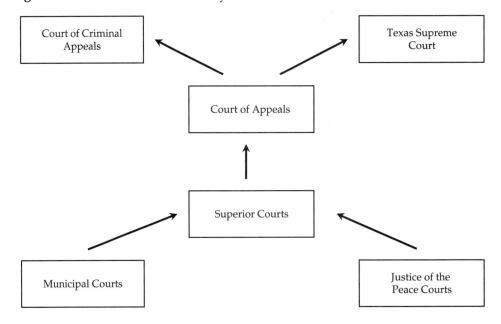

On the criminal side, these courts also may be responsible for issuing search and arrest warrants and conducting the preliminary stages of felony cases, such as the preliminary hearing and arraignment. On the civil side, these courts may handle a variety of matters, including juvenile delinquency, family law, and probate.

Proceedings in lower courts are often more informal in nature than they are in appellate courts or trial courts. Generally, there is no right to trial provided in these courts. If losing parties wish to appeal adverse decisions, they must do so through a **trial de novo** in the court of original jurisdiction. A trial de novo is not like a standard appeal where the higher court concerns itself only with a review of the trial record and consideration of any possible legal errors. Instead, a trial de novo is an entirely new trial. Lower courts are not courts of record—that is, there is no constitutional requirement to provide an official, verbatim recording or transcript of the proceedings. The only official document is the judgment of the court.

While courts of limited jurisdiction receive very little attention, they are important for several reasons. First, for many citizens, they are the only experience that person will have with the court system. Second, these courts process a tremendous number of cases, and there are many of these courts. The National Center for State Courts reports that there are almost fourteen thousand lower courts, and these courts process more than seventy-five million cases each year. Third, these courts often are involved in the crucial early stages of criminal cases, in the issuance of warrants, and the determination whether to set bail and to hold the suspect over for trial. A warrant may be for a search or an arrest. A search warrant authorizes police to search a particular place for certain items named in the warrant. An arrest warrant commands the police to take into custody the person named in the warrant. Bail is the amount of money the defendant in a criminal case turns over to the court or its agents as assurance that he or she will return for trial. If the defendant fails to voluntarily return for trial, the bail may be forfeited.

All of this is complicated by the fact that many judges in lower courts are not lawyers. While legal training may not be necessary to determine whether someone is guilty of speeding, it is hard to see how someone without legal training can be expected to know what constitutes probable cause in issuing a search or arrest warrant.

The next level in a typical state court system includes the courts of general jurisdiction. These are the trial courts for civil and criminal matters. They are also courts of original jurisdiction in that it is here that trials for felonies are held. *Felonies* are defined in most jurisdictions as crimes for which the possible punishment includes a sentence of imprisonment for at least one year. Generally, they are authorized to hear any matters not exclusively designated for courts of limited jurisdiction. In some states, they even may have concurrent jurisdiction with lower courts on some matters such as misdemeanors. They also may hear appeals, in the form of a trial de novo, from lower courts.

Trial courts usually are referred to as district court, circuit court, or superior court, although at least one state, New York, refers to its trial court as the Supreme Court and its court of last resort as the Court of Appeals. The precise workload of the trial courts varies by jurisdiction. In less populous areas, the trial court may hear all manner of cases, including civil and criminal. In other more populated areas, there may be a greater specialization, with one court handling only felony trials and another handling only civil matters.

To date, at least thirty-eight states have two levels of appellate courts, consisting of an intermediate appellate court and a court of last resort (Meador 1991). Intermediate appellate courts are largely a creation of the twentieth century. As jurisdictions became more crowded and court dockets increased, officials saw a need to relieve the state supreme court of the burden of hearing all appeals of right. The states that have not created an intermediate court tend to be either very small or not very densely populated.

The intermediate appellate courts are referred to by a variety of names, but by far the most common is the court of appeals. The primary purpose of the intermediate court of appeals is to hear felony appeals of right. An appeal of right is an appeal that state legislatures permit all criminal defendants as a matter of law and occurs after a final order has been entered by the trial court. There is no constitutional right to appeal a guilty verdict, but all fifty states and the federal government provide for an appeal of right either by statute or state constitutional provision. The number of judges on the intermediate appellate court varies, and many states have more than one intermediate appellate court.

The court of last resort is in most states called the state supreme court. Forty-eight states have one court of last resort; two states (Oklahoma and Texas) have two. These states have a court of last resort for all civil cases and a court of last resort for all criminal cases. The number of judges on the court of last resort varies by state from three to nine.

The court of last resort usually hears the majority of appeals on a discretionary basis, similar to the U.S. Supreme Court. This allows them to control their docket and focus on cases involving significant legal issues. The exception is those states that do not have an intermediate appellate court and, in other states, death penalty cases. In states without an intermediate appellate court (usually the smaller, less populous states), the state supreme court is the only appellate court and thus is mandated by law to hear all appeals. Most states also require their supreme court to hear all appeals in cases involving the death penalty. This is provided as an extra safeguard, as the punishment in these cases is obviously the most severe punishment, and the states wish to be absolutely sure the defendant has received a fair trial.

For most cases, the state supreme court is the end of the line, the final arbiter of the dispute. The only option for a losing party in the state supreme court is to appeal directly to the U.S. Supreme Court, and to do so, the party must be able to identify a legal issue that involves the U.S. Constitution or a federal law.

OVERVIEW OF THE CRIMINAL PROCESS

Pretrial Proceedings

The criminal process begins either with the filing of a complaint or arrest. A **complaint** is simply an accusation on a formal document that may be filled out by an officer or a private citizen accusing a specified person or persons of committing a specified act or acts. If an arrest is made first, a complaint will be sworn out afterwards usually by the arresting officer. The complaint serves as the charging document for the preliminary hearing.

Search and arrest warrants are obtained by police officers who first must fill out an affidavit stating the facts relied on to create what is called probable cause. There must be probable cause to arrest or search. **Probable cause** is a legal concept referring to the amount of proof a police officer must have to search or arrest someone. This is discussed further in chapter 6. After individuals are arrested, they are booked. **Booking** is an administrative procedure, and it involves making an entry in the police blotter at the station indicating the suspect's name, arrest time, offense, and the taking of fingerprints and photographs.

The first court appearance is referred to as the **initial appearance** and takes place in a municipal or justice of the peace court. Once a person is arrested, the individual must be brought before a magistrate "without unnecessary delay." It is here that suspects are informed of their constitutional rights as well as the nature of the charges against them, and a bail decision is made as to whether it will be granted and, if so, how much to set it at.

The next stage in the proceedings is the preliminary examination or **preliminary hearing**. Here the magistrate determines if there is probable cause to believe that an offense was committed and that it was the defendant who committed it. If probable cause is established, the defendant is "bound over" for trial. When a defendant is bound over, it means that a trial date is set and the defendant is notified of the pending charges. The preliminary examination is a formal adversarial proceeding, conducted in open court. The Supreme Court has defined it as a "critical stage" of the prosecution, which means the defendant has a right to have his or her lawyer present.

Charges may be filed against a defendant either by an information filed by the prosecutor or by an indictment issued by a grand jury. An information is prepared and signed for by the prosecutor. It is adequate if it informs the defendant of the facts and the elements of the offense for which the individual is charged. It is a substitute for a grand jury indictment and is a more efficient way to proceed, as it eliminates the need to organize a grand jury and present evidence. The Fifth Amendment requires the federal government to proceed through an indictment, handed down by a grand jury. This clause of the Fifth Amendment is one of the few that has not been applied to the states so states may use an information instead (*Hurtado v. California*, 1884). A little less than half of the states require an indictment. Twelve states require indictment by a grand jury only for felonies, while three states require indictment by a grand jury only for capital offenses. Four states require indictment by a grand jury for all felonies and misdemeanors (del Carmen 2007).

The typical grand jury has twenty-three people, and proceedings are not open to the public. The only persons present aside from the members of the grand jury are the district attorney and any witnesses whom the attorney calls. Some states follow the federal model and seat grand juries of twenty-three members; other states seat anywhere from six to twenty-three members. Few states require grand juries in all felony cases, and in some states, a grand jury is formed at the discretion of the prosecutor. Since the grand jury hears only evidence presented by the state, and the defense does not have the opportunity to challenge the information, it is a relatively rare occurrence when a grand jury does not return an indictment. The rationale behind requiring an indictment by a grand jury is that this body can act as a check on an overzealous prosecutor, preventing him or her from prosecuting cases for which there is not sufficient evidence.

In reality, the grand jury today is a "rubber stamp" unlikely to refuse to indict anyone. This does not necessarily mean it is not achieving its purpose of preventing improper prosecutions, however, as its very existence may prevent prosecutors from taking shaky cases to the grand jury. In this way, the grand jury does check the prosecutor's power.

The next step in the process is the arraignment, a formal hearing before a felony court where defendants are again informed of the charges against them and advised of their rights. At this time, the defendant enters a *plea*, which is the defendant's response to the charge against him or her. Possible pleas include guilty (by far the most common plea), not guilty, standing mute, and no contest. **Standing mute** means that the defendant is refusing to plead. In these instances, the court enters a not guilty plea on behalf of defendant, thus preserving the constitutional right to trial. A no contest plea, also referred to as **nolo contendere**, means the defendant accepts whatever punishment the court would impose on a guilty defendant but refuses to admit liability. A no contest plea is frequently used by defendants who fear being exposed to civil liability for their criminal misdeeds, and a guilty plea would so expose them.

A fourth possible plea, not accepted as a valid option in all states and only conservatively allowed in the federal system, is the **Alford plea**. An Alford plea is one in which the defendant enters a guilty plea but denies having committed the crime to which he or she is pleading. The reason that the Alford plea is not recognized in some states and only reluctantly accepted in special circumstances in others is that when a defendant enters a plea of guilty, he or she is expected to so state on the record. Judges do not take it lightly when defendants say they are guilty on the one hand and then assert their innocence on the other. As famous British jurist Lord Birkett responded to a defendant who said, "As God is my judge, I'm innocent": "He isn't. I am; you're not."

THE JURY AND ITS SELECTION

Juries have played a crucial role in the common law almost from its beginnings. Its modern form started to take shape during the reign of Henry II when the ecclesiastical (church) courts banned trial by combat and by ordeal in their courts (Macnair 2006). Trial by combat meant that parties literally fought each other, and trial by ordeal meant ordeals such as carrying hot coals for a certain distance. Victorious combatants and ordeal sufferers whose wounds did not fester within three days were said to have been favored by God, the ultimate judge, and thus innocent (Shapiro 2002).

Early jurors were composed of what were known as "knowledgeable witnesses." These were "good and lawful" men who could provide testimony relating to what they knew about the events and persons involved in the case. They also sat in judgment as well, so the outcome of a case was the result of collective "witness/judgment" wisdom (Macnair 2006). The number of jurors necessary for a case to be heard was settled in favor of the old Anglo-Saxon custom of twelve men. Why the number twelve was chosen has been the topic of much speculation, and Horowitz and Willging (1984, 165) supply a rationale we find satisfying: "Twelve apostles, twelve tribes of Israel, twelve patriarchs, twelve officers in Solomon's court, twelve months in a year, are among the credentials it has as a number of unusual potency."

Gradually juries began to be composed of disinterested parties rather than individuals with special knowledge of the case or of the parties involved. Unlike the continental systems of law, in which professional judges were finders of both law and fact, since the time of Edward I (1239–1307) the common law system has been one in which matters of law were the domain of the judge, while matters of fact were the domain of juries, although there are exceptions. That is, judges made sure that the trial process followed legal rules and procedures and instructed jurors on the law, but only jurors could be finders of fact, meaning only they were to determine the meaning of the evidence provided by both sides of a dispute

(Shapiro 2002). This is the concept of the jury that was imported into the United States by the early colonies, and we continue to view it this way today.

Jury Selection

When defendants (suspects become defendants once officially indicted) plead not guilty, the next step in the process is the trial itself. Once a trial date is set, jury selection begins. The jury is selected from the eligible members of the community, who are selected at random, usually from voting records or automobile registration records. These records are used to obtain as complete a list as possible of all the residents of a community. The legal term for summoning jurors is the **venire**, which is Latin for "to cause" or to "make come" (to the courthouse). Prospective jurors are examined by the judge and/or the attorneys for the prosecution and defense to determine whether they have any bias, prejudice, or interest that would prevent the potential juror from being impartial. This process of questioning the jurors is referred to as the **voir dire**, which literally means "to speak the truth."

While the stated purpose of the voir dire is to obtain an unbiased jury, in reality, each side seeks not only to excuse potential jurors who are biased against their side but to keep on the jury those individuals who are biased toward their side. Many attorneys are so averse to impartial juries that they may employ the services of professional **jury consultants** to make sure they do not get one. These consultants employ the theories and methods of social science to help them determine what type of person is more likely to favor their side.

Jury consultants are expensive and are mainly used in civil cases involving millions of dollars. In criminal cases, their use is confined to the very rich and/ or celebrity defendants such as Robert Blake and O. J. Simpson (both of whom beat strong cases against them). They may also be used by defendants who exemplify a particular social or political cause and are able to garner monetary support from supporters of those causes. Examples include the trial of Philip Berrigan and six other anti–Vietnam war activists (the Harrisburg Seven, accused of conspiring to kidnap then secretary of state Henry Kissinger and to destroy selective service records) and of Joan Little, a black female charged with killing a white jailer she claimed tried to rape her. The Harrisburg Seven jury was loaded with individuals with antiestablishment and antiwar attitudes, and the Joan Little jury was stacked with supporters of the feminist and black civil rights movements. The defense prevailed in both cases, apparently far more on the basis of the jurors' ideology than on the facts of the evidence presented to them (Kressel and Kressel 2002).

Both the prosecution and the defense may seek to remove by challenge potential jurors they feel may be biased against them. Jurors may be **challenged for cause** in which a valid reason for wanting to dismiss an individual is shown to the court's satisfaction, or they may be removed through the use of a peremptory challenge. A **peremptory challenge** is one for which no reason need be given. While challenges for cause are unlimited, peremptory challenges are usually limited to a certain number. The Supreme Court has held that peremptory challenges may not be used to exclude potential jurors on the basis of race (*Batson v. Kentucky* 1986) or gender (*J. E. B. v. Alabama* 1994).

The Supreme Court also has held that the jury need not be composed of the traditional twelve members since there is no constitutional requirement for such a number. Juries with as few as six members have been approved for both civil and criminal trials (*Williams v. Florida* 1970). Furthermore, there is no constitutional requirement that the jury verdict be unanimous, even in criminal cases. The Supreme Court has approved both 9–3 and 10–2 verdicts (*Johnson v. Louisiana* 1972; *Apodaca v. Oregon* 1972); however, juries consisting of fewer than twelve members must render unanimous verdicts (*Burch v. Louisiana* 1979). Finally, the requirement of a "jury of one's peers" has been interpreted simply as requiring the jury be selected from the community where the crime takes place. It does not mean the jury must share any other similarities with the defendant. Initially, the principle of a trial by one's peers proclaimed in the Magna Carta meant that nobles should be tried by nobles and commoners by commoners.

The Trial

Once the jury is selected and sworn in, the trial can begin. Before the trial begins, various motions may be filed by attorneys for each side. A motion is simply a request made to the court asking it for something, such as a granting a continuance, the suppression of evidence, or dismissal of the case. After any motions have been granted or denied, the first step in a jury trial is the making of opening statements—first by the prosecution, because it has the burden of proof, and then by the defense. The defense may choose to reserve its opening statement until after the prosecution has presented its evidence. This is referred to as the prosecution's case-in-chief. During this phase, the prosecution must establish each element of the crime charged beyond a reasonable doubt.

Once the prosecution has presented its evidence and called its witnesses, the defense has an opportunity to present its case-in-chief. The defense is not required to put on any case, but if the defense chooses to, it may raise several types of defenses. These include an alibi or an affirmative defense such as insanity or self-defense. These defenses are addressed in chapter 5. The prosecution may then choose to rebut the defense's case.

Next are closing arguments in which each side has the opportunity to sum up its case. Here, the prosecution gets to go last since it has the burden of proof. After closing arguments or, in some jurisdictions, before them, the judge will give the jury instructions on the applicable law. These include instructions on the elements of the crime charged, the presumption of innocence, and the burden of proof—which in criminal trials is proof beyond a reasonable doubt.

Once the jury has received its instructions, it retires to the jury room to deliberate. It remains there until a verdict is reached. In most jurisdictions, criminal verdicts must be unanimous despite the Supreme Court's ruling that unanimity is not constitutionally required. In these jurisdictions, failure to achieve a unanimous verdict (a "hung jury") means the case is declared a mistrial. If this occurs, the defendant may be retried without violating the prohibition against double jeopardy because the case never reached a conclusion. Alternatively, the prosecutor may decide that the state cannot win its case and dismiss the charges.

Sentencing

If a jury returns a verdict of not guilty, the defendant is set free. The constitutional prohibition on double jeopardy prevents the state from prosecuting the defendant again for the same act. If the verdict is guilty, then sentence must be imposed. In most instances, the judge imposes sentence, the exception being death penalty cases in which the jury in most states traditionally imposes the sentence. An interesting case strictly affirming the separation of roles between judges and jurors was handed down by the Supreme Court in 2002 (*Ring v. Arizona* 2002). Ring was convicted by the jury of killing an armored car driver in a robbery. A separate hearing called the penalty phase (which is constitutionally required in a death penalty case) was then held before the judge alone to determine sentencing. After hearing testimony, the judge found that the aggravated circumstances of the murder warranted the death penalty. The problem the Supreme Court found with this is that the aggravated circumstances heard by the judge constituted facts, and the truth and importance of matters of fact is the domain of juries. The Court thus vacated Ring's death sentence. This ruling affected only the eight states in which judges alone imposed the death penalty.

In other kinds of cases, the sentence is usually not handed down immediately after the verdict. Instead, the judge orders a presentence investigation report (PSI) written by officers in a probation department. This report contains information about the offense, the offender's personal and criminal history, medical and psychological information, and any other pertinent information used to guide the officer in making his or her sentencing recommendation and to guide the judge in actually imposing the sentence. The PSI thus contains facts discovered by the PSI investigator that are then conveyed to the sentencing judge, along with a sentencing recommendation based on them. Since these facts are not available to a jury, unless the PSI is written on a case that was plea bargained, and thus no jury is involved, this opens the door for another *Ring*-type ruling by the Supreme Court in the future.

A number of different sentences are possible. These include probation, a suspended sentence, or a fine. Factors influencing the sentence include the information contained in the PSI, the attitude of the defendant, and the defendant's prior criminal and personal history. In recent years, there has been a move to increase sentence length and require incarceration, with the result being a tremendous increase in the number of persons incarcerated. However, probation (which may be paired with fines and some jail time) is still the most common sentence in the United States (Bohm and Haley 2007).

Appeals

Once a person has been convicted and sentenced, there are two ways to challenge the trial outcome. A defendant may file either a direct appeal or an indirect appeal, also known as a writ of habeas corpus. Habeas corpus translates as "you have the body," and the writ requires the person to whom it is directed to either produce the person named in the writ or release that person from custody. There is no federal constitutional right to an appeal, but every state allows a direct appeal, either by statute or state constitutional provision.

The writ of habeas corpus is considered an indirect appeal because it does not directly challenge the defendant's conviction but instead challenges the authority of the state to incarcerate the defendant. The state defense to a habeas writ is based on the conviction, however—that is why the defendant has been incarcerated. Habeas corpus is an ancient legal remedy, dating back at least to the Magna Carta. It often is referred to as the "Great Writ."

There is no time limit for filing a habeas petition, unlike direct appeals, which in most jurisdictions must be filed within a set period, usually several months. However, Congress recently has restricted the use of habeas corpus by imposing time limits on federal habeas petitions if there is evidence of intentional delay by the defendant that injures the prosecution's case. Additionally, Congress and the Supreme Court have restricted habeas corpus by imposing limits on how such appeals are filed and pursued, such as requiring that inmates include all their appealable issues in one writ rather than doing separate, consecutive writs for each issue (Maahs and Hemmens 1998).

COURT ACTORS

There are three key actors in court: judges, prosecutors, and defense attorneys. It is important to understand what they do and how they do it so we can better understand why courts function the way they do and how courts can be improved.

Judges

The judge serves as a referee, responsible for enforcing court rules, instructing the jury on the law, and determining the law. Judges are expected to be completely impartial. Trial judges have tremendous power to control a case, although they do not actively participate in the trial by questioning witnesses or the defendant, as do judges in many non–common law legal systems.

As a whole, judges are not representative of American society. Just like their counterparts on the U.S. Supreme Court, they are mostly white, male, and upper middle class. Women and minorities are underrepresented, not only with respect to their numbers in American society but with respect to their proportion in the legal community. A number of commentators have argued that this results in bias, either intentional or unintentional. Others have suggested that even if bias does not exist, there is a perception among many segments of the population that justice is not obtainable because minorities and women are underrepresented on the bench (Graham 1990; Slotnick 1988).

There are three common methods of selecting judges. These include appointment, election, and the merit system. Different jurisdictions use different methods of selecting judges. Some jurisdictions use more than one method, while others, such as the federal system, use only one method. Appointment by the chief executive of the jurisdiction (the President of the United States or the governor of an individual state) is the oldest method of selecting judges. All thirteen of the original colonies used it, and it is used today in the federal system and about twenty states. Table 4.1 presents methods of selecting judges for courts of general jurisdiction in all fifty states and the name each state employs for their courts of general jurisdiction.

Election of judges became popular during the 1830s when Democrats under the leadership of Andrew Jackson gained control of Congress from the Federalists. Jackson and his supporters believed wholeheartedly in popular democracy and thought appointment of judges to be undemocratic (Slotnick 1988). Georgia (1824) was the first state to implement judicial elections. As seen in Table 4.1, currently twenty-nine states use popular elections to select judges.

These elections take one of two forms. Some states have *partisan* (meaning aligned with a particular party) elections in which candidates for judicial office run in the party primary and their political affiliation is listed on the ballot. Thirteen states use this method. In sixteen other states, judges are selected in nonpartisan elections in which no political affiliation is listed. In two states, South Carolina and Georgia, judges are elected by the legislature.

A third method of selecting judges is the merit system. This system is based on a system originally developed by the American Judicature Society in 1909 and endorsed by the American Bar Association in 1937. It was first adopted by Missouri in 1940; consequently, it sometimes is referred to as the Missouri plan (Slotnick 1988).

The merit system has become popular only recently. In 1960, only four states used the system, but by 1998, about half the states used it. The merit system has three parts. First, a nonpartisan nominating commission selects a list of potential candidates based on the candidates' legal qualifications. Second, the governor makes a selection from this list. Finally, the person selected as a judge stands for election (this is referred to as *retention*) within a short time after they are selected, usually within one year.

Prosecutors

Under the early common law, there were no public prosecutors. Instead, private citizens were responsible for litigating their criminal cases. Private prosecution gave way to public prosecution as society came to view crime as an offense not just against the person but against society as well. Today, private prosecution is no longer permitted in any state. In its place are prosecutor's offices. There are more than 25,000 prosecutors today, although about half of them are part-time (primarily in small jurisdictions).

The Judiciary Act of 1789 provided for a U.S. attorney for each court district who was appointed by the president. In 1870, Congress authorized the creation of the Department of Justice, with an attorney general and assistants. The attorney general, a political appointee, is an administrator who sets prosecution priorities for deputy attorney generals. Deputy attorney generals are appointed by the president and confirmed by the Senate and serve at the pleasure of the president. Assistant U.S. attorneys are not political appointments.

State prosecutors are called by various names, such as district attorney, solicitor, county attorney, state's attorney, and commonwealth attorney. State

Table 4.1 *Methods of Selecting Judges for Courts of General Jurisdiction and Names Given to Courts of General Jurisdiction by State*

Election	Name	Nominating commission	Name	Appointed by governor	Name
Alabama (P)	Circuit	Alaska	Superior	Maine	Superior
Arkansas (P)	Circuit	Arizona	Superior	New Hampshire	Superior
California (N)	Superior	Colorado	District	New Jersey	Superior
Florida (N)	Circuit	Connecticut	Superior	Rhode Island	Superior
Georgia (N)	Superior	Delaware	Superior		
Idaho (N)	District	Hawaii	Circuit		
Illinois (P)	Circuit	Iowa	District		
Indiana (P)	Circuit	Kansas	District		
Kentucky (N)	Circuit	Maryland	Circuit		
Louisiana (P)	District	Massachusetts	Superior		
Michigan (N)	Circuit	Nebraska	District		
Minnesota (N)	District	New Mexico	District		
Mississippi (P)	Circuit	Utah	District		
Missouri (P)	Circuit	Vermont	Superior		
Montana (N)	District	Wyoming	District		
Nevada (N)	District				
New York (P)	Supreme				
North Carolina (P)	Superior				
North Dakota (N)	District				
Ohio (N)	Common Pleas				
Oklahoma (N)	District				
Oregon (N)	Circuit				
Pennsylvania (P)	Common Pleas				
South Carolina (L)	Circuit				
South Dakota (N)	Circuit				
Tennessee (P)	Circuit				
Texas (P)	District				
Virginia (L)	Circuit				
Washington (N)	Superior				
West Virginia (P)	Circuit				
Wisconsin (N)	Circuit				

Note: P = Partisan election; N = Nonpartisan election; L = Election by legislature. Election, *N* = 31 (13 partisan, 16 nonpartisan, 2 legislature); nominating commission, *N* = 15; appointment by governor, *N* = 4.

prosecutors are usually elected officials with appointed assistants who do most of the trial work. Only four states (Alaska, Connecticut, Delaware, and New Jersey) do not have an elected district attorney. The district attorney's duty is to prosecute cases in the name of the people but also to do justice by pursuing only those who have committed crimes. District attorneys have tremendous power to decide whether or not to prosecute, and this power is largely unreviewable, meaning that there are few real or meaningful restrictions on prosecutorial discretion.

Defense Attorneys

Defense attorneys are expected to represent their client as effectively as possible, while acting within the rules of court. The right to counsel existed in common law and in state constitutions. The Sixth Amendment codified this right. The Supreme Court has interpreted the Sixth Amendment requiring the right to counsel as applying at any "critical stage" of the prosecution, not just at trial. Thus, a defendant has been held to have the right to counsel at a lineup, which takes place after indictment; at the preliminary hearing; and during pretrial discovery.

The role of defense counsel is primarily (1) to ensure that the defendants' rights are not violated (intentionally or in error); (2) to make sure the defendants know all their options before they make a decision; (3) to provide the defendants with the best possible defense, without violating ethical and legal obligations; (4) to investigate and prepare the defense; and (5) to argue for lowest possible sentence or best possible plea bargain (Uphoff 1992).

There are several types of defense counsel. These include privately retained counsel, public defenders, and court-appointed counsel. Private attorneys are attorneys selected and paid for by the defendant. Public defenders are hired by the state but work for defendants who cannot afford to hire their own lawyer. An appointed attorney is a private attorney who is paid by the state on a case-by-case basis to represent indigent defendants.

A fourth method of providing indigent offenders with counsel is the contract system. Under this system, a number of private law firms may enter bids to serve as a sort of subcontractor to the courts in the area covered by the court's jurisdiction. This system is usually utilized in lightly populated counties, and the contract typically goes to the lowest bidder.

While the Supreme Court has held that there is a right to counsel, the Court has not held that this means a right to the counsel of your choice in all cases. A person who can afford to hire a lawyer may do so; those who cannot afford a lawyer will be provided one, but there are limits on when the appointment will occur, and the defendants have little or no say in who is selected to represent them.

SUMMARY

In this chapter, we have provided an overview of both the federal and state court systems, and we have examined the key actors in the court system (judges, prosecutors, and defense attorneys). We also have provided an overview of the trial process from arrest to sentencing. While these may seem like "basic" materials to some, they are crucial components of the legal system. One cannot understand how justice is done if one does not understand how cases are dealt with and who is involved in the justice process. It is crucial that students under-stand not only the stages in the process, but the roles played by those involved at each stage.

The United States has essentially fifty-one court systems—one federal system and fifty state systems. While there are many similarities between these systems, there are also differences—in both how the process works and how the partici-pants in the process are selected. Different states have different court arrange-ments. Some states have elected judges, while others (and the federal system) rely on appointed judges. These differences are important factors in how justice is distributed in the courts.

The criminal trial process has many stages, and each stage is important. At each stage, the prosecution is called upon to demonstrate to the court that there exists sufficient evidence to hold the defendant over for further proceedings; this burden increases from "probable cause" to, eventually, "proof beyond a reasonable doubt." At each stage, the prosecution and defense reveal some of the information they have; by the time the trial is through, both sides have had the opportunity to present to the fact finder (usually a jury) all the evidence in their possession. The jury is then called upon to render a verdict. The appeals process provides a degree of protection for defendants who have been convicted—this close scrutiny of the trial process is unparalleled in the world. The appeals process is set up to determine whether there were mistakes made at trial that caused a miscarriage of justice.

While justice may be an elusive concept, one with different meanings for dif-ferent people in the United States, it is clear that the court system is intended to provide a forum for doing justice. There are many different types of courts, but all share this common feature. Courts serve as a forum for settling disputes between private parties, as a means of prosecuting individuals who break the law, and as a place where public policy sometimes is made. The common refrains "I'll sue you" and "I'll take it all the way to the Supreme Court" are evidence that courts are a popular forum.

DISCUSSION QUESTIONS

1. What are the different types of jurisdiction?
2. What are the different stages in the criminal trial process, and why is each important?
3. What are the different methods for selecting judges, and what are the advantages and disadvantages of each?
4. What are the ethical problems involved in the use of jury consultants? Does it result in one system of justice for the rich and another for the poor?
5. If a jury verdict of guilty is not unanimous, does that mean that there was reasonable doubt? If so, do you think nonunanimous verdicts violate the Sixth Amendment?
6. Should Supreme Court Justices be elected and therefore responsible to the people for their rulings? Why or why not?

References

Abraham, H. 1987. *The judiciary: The Supreme Court in the governmental process.* 7th ed. Boston: Allyn & Bacon.

Bohm, R., and K. Haley. 2007. *Introduction to criminal justice.* 4th ed. Boston: McGraw-Hill.

Brigham, J. 1987. *The cult of the court.* Philadelphia: Temple University Press.

Cooper, P. 1988. *Hard judicial choices.* New York: Oxford University Press.

del Carmen, R. 2007. *Criminal procedure: Law and practice.* Belmont, CA: Wadsworth.

Graham, B. 1990. Judicial recruitment and racial diversity on state courts. *Judicature* 74: 28–34.

Horowitz, I., and T. Willging. 1984. *The psychology of law: Integrations and applications.* Boston: Little, Brown.

Kelly, A., W. Harbison, and H. Belz. 1983. *The American Constitution: Its origins and development.* 6th ed. New York: Norton.

Kressel, N., and D. Kressel. 2002. *Stack and sway: The new science of jury consulting.* Boulder, CO: Westview Press.

Maahs, J., and C. Hemmens. 1998. The Prison Litigation Reform Act and frivolous section 1983 suits. *Corrections Management Quarterly* 2:90–94.

Macnair, M. 2006. Vicinage and the antecedents of the jury. *Law and History Review* 17:1, 24–41. Online: http://www.historycooperative.org.

Meador, D. 1991. *American courts.* St. Paul, MN: West.

Perry, M. 1994. *The Constitution in the courts.* New York: Oxford University Press.

Shapiro, B. 2002. Testimony in seventeenth-century English natural philosophy: Legal origins and early development. *Studies in History and Philosophy of Science* 33:243–63.

Shreve, G., and P. Raven-Hansen. 1994. *Understanding civil procedure.* 2nd ed. New York: Matthew Bender.

Slotnick, E. 1988. Review essay on judicial recruitment and selection. *Justice System Journal* 13:109–24.

Smith, C. 1992. From U.S. magistrates to U.S. magistrate judges: Developments affecting the federal district courts' lower tier of judicial officers. *Judicature* 75:210–15.

Uphoff, R. 1992. The criminal defense lawyer: Zealous advocate, double agent, or beleaguered dealer? *Criminal Law Bulletin* 28:419–56.

Wasby, S. 1993. *The Supreme Court in the federal judicial system.* Chicago: Nelson-Hall.

Cases Cited

Apodaca v. Oregon, 406 U.S. 404 (1972).

Batson v. Kentucky, 476 U.S. 79 (1986).

Burch v. Louisiana, 441 U.S. 130 (1979).

Hurtado v. California, 110 U.S. 516 (1884).

J. E. B. v. Alabama ex rel T.B., 511 U.S. 127 (1994).

Johnson v. Louisiana, 406 U.S. 356 (1972).

Ring v. Arizona, 536 U.S. 584 (2002).

Williams v. Florida, 399 U.S. 78 (1970).

CHAPTER 5

CRIME AND CRIMINAL LAW

Ms. Cogdon suffered from occasional bouts of sleepwalking and night-mares. She had spoken to her doctor about these events, and he had pre-scribed her a sedative and suggested she consider psychiatric counseling. One night, Ms. Cogdon spoke with her daughter, Pat, about the possibility that the country would get involved in the war in Korea. She then went to bed. That night, Ms. Cogdon dreamed that there was a war going on around her house and that soldiers had entered the house and were attacking her daughter Pat. When she awoke, she was in her neighbor's house. When she returned home, she discovered her daughter Pat was dead. It turned out Ms. Cogdon had been sleepwalking and had gone outside to the woodpile, picked up an axe, come back into the house, gone into Pat's room, and struck her twice in the head with the axe, killing her.

Ms. Cogdon was arrested and tried for the murder of her daughter. She admitted administering the blows that killed her daughter and did not claim that she suffered from a mental disease or insanity. Instead, her defense to the charge was that she did not "act" in killing her daughter because she was asleep. The criminal law generally requires that for a person to be held liable for committing a crime, there must be evidence that that person committed a voluntary act. Ms. Cogdon argued that because she was asleep, her obtain-ing the axe and striking her daughter with it were not voluntary acts. Rather, they were involuntary, products of her dream and her sleepwalking.

The jury accepted Ms. Cogdon's account, and voted to acquit her, on the grounds that her actions were not truly voluntary.

INTRODUCTION

In this chapter, we discuss the basic elements of criminal law, sometimes referred to as substantive law. *Substantive law* is the law of crimes as compared to *procedural law* (discussed in chapter 6), which are the rules the state must fol-low when investigating suspects or prosecuting someone who has committed a crime. **Substantive law** is defined by statute, and it prescribes (what we should do) and proscribes (what we should not do) various types of conduct. It is that code of conduct that all in a society are expected to follow, such as prohibitions on murder, assault, or burglary. Criminal laws are enforced by the state, and violation of the criminal law is treated as an act against the state and the individual victim. The primary purpose of criminal law is thus to protect the public from harm by punishing harmful acts that have occurred and seeking to forestall harm by forbidding conduct that may lead to it.

WHAT IS CRIME?

A frequently quoted definition of crime is that of Paul Tappan (cited in Walsh and Ellis 2007, 3), who defined it as "an intentional act in violation of the criminal law committed without defense or excuse, and penalized by the state." This is a legal definition with five components: **crime** is an (1) *act* in violation of (2) a *criminal law* for which (3) a *punishment* is prescribed; the person committing it must have (4) *intended* to do so and to have done so without legally acceptable (5) *defense* or *justification*. Defining crime is not the same as defining gravity or photosynthesis because unlike these natural phenomena, crime is defined into existence rather than discovered. By this we mean that crimes can be defined into and pass out of existence by human beings. This does not mean that there is no harmful substance to them independent of human definitions of them as such, but we do have to be aware that what are crimes at one time or in other cultures may be considered virtues at other times or in other cultures.

For instance, the Harrison Narcotics Act of 1914 created a large class of criminals overnight by, in effect, criminalizing the sale, possession, or use of "narcotics." Although the wording of this act, clearly states that it was intended to ensure the orderly marketing of narcotics, it was soon interpreted and acted upon as prohibiting them (Goode 2005). Prior to the act, there were few restrictions on these substances, many of which were sold in pharmacies and elsewhere as cures for all kinds of ailments. Crimes also pass out of existence. Committing sodomy or burning the American flag could get a person imprisoned in many states until fairly recently. Statutes criminalizing sodomy were ruled unconstitutional by the Supreme Court in *Lawrence v. Texas* (2003), as were anti-flag-burning statutes in *Texas v. Johnson* (1989).

Despite the arbitrariness of many criminal statues, there is a core of acts that are universally condemned and criminalized. According to the International Criminal Police Organization (Interpol), acts such as murder, rape, assault, and theft are criminalized in every one of its 125 member nations (Ellis and Walsh 2000). These are crimes we previously defined as mala in se crimes, or crimes that are inherently harmful because they generate strong emotional responses in all victims of them. Acts not considered mala in se may or may not be criminalized in a particular place at a particular time according to the social attitudes surrounding those acts at the time. All socially harmful acts run the risk of criminalization, but only some make the cut.

A crime is a subcategory of all harmful acts. Figure 5.1 helps to distinguish between the various subcategories. First we have the largest circle, containing all harms, personal and social, criminal and noncriminal. Some harmful acts such as

Figure 5.1 *Mala in Se* and *Mala Prohibita* Crimes as Subsets of all Harms.

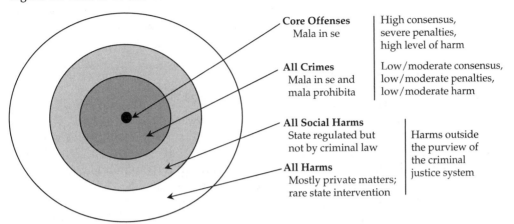

Core Offenses
Mala in se

High consensus,
severe penalties,
high level of harm

All Crimes
Mala in se and
mala prohibita

Low/moderate consensus,
low/moderate penalties,
low/moderate harm

All Social Harms
State regulated but
not by criminal law

Harms outside
the purview of
the criminal
justice system

All Harms
Mostly private matters;
rare state intervention

Source: A. Walsh and L. Ellis (2007). *Criminology: An Interdisciplinary Approach*. Thousand Oaks, California: Sage/Pine Forge Press. Reprinted with permission.

drinking to excess are considered nobody's business except the person engaging in them unless he or she creates a public annoyance by doing so. The next largest circle contains all social harms that are regulated by the state but not by the criminal justice system. These acts are typically regulated by civil law or administrative bodies (see chapter 7). The next circle contains all crimes, both *mala prohibita* and *mala in se*, and the final circle contains the "core" mala in se crimes.

Walsh and Ellis (2007) differentiate mala in se from mala prohibita in terms of three concepts that are arrayed on continua from low to high: consensus, seriousness (corresponding to severity of penalty), and harm. There is little consensus among people on the seriousness of crimes such as prostitution and smoking marijuana, social harm is minor, and penalties are relatively light. There is universal consensus, however, that mala in se crimes such as murder and rape are wrong; it is also obvious that such crimes cause high levels of social harm, that they are extremely serious offenses, and that as such they carry severe penalties.

Part I offenses in the Federal Bureau of Investigation's annual report known as the **Uniform Crime Reports** (UCR) are major mala in se crimes. The UCR defines these eight crimes (murder, rape, robbery, aggravated assault, burglary, larceny/theft, motor vehicle theft, and arson) and reports their annual incidence. There are also a large number of other offenses reported in the UCR known as Part II offenses. These are a mixture of mala prohibita offenses, such as gambling and prostitution, and a number of other offenses that are less serious mala in se offenses, such as simple assault. The incidence of Part I offenses are those offenses known to the police whether or not an arrest was made for them; the much more numerous Part II offenses are only reported if an arrest was made.

While different jurisdictions define criminal acts, defenses, and penalties differently, there are similarities that traverse jurisdictional boundaries. Common characteristics of criminal law include a description of prohibited conduct, a list of the penalties prescribed for those who violate the law, and the provision of certain defenses to criminal liability. Conviction carries with it the community's formal condemnation. It is this final element that sets criminal law apart from civil law, which involves disputes between private parties.

SOURCES OF CRIMINAL LAW

Criminal law is derived from a variety of sources, including state and federal constitutions, state and federal statutes, and common law. Treason is the only crime specifically mentioned in the U.S. Constitution. The bulk of criminal law is located in state statutes, variously referred to as penal or criminal codes. Much of the states' criminal codes are derived originally from common law crimes.

Around the middle of the nineteenth century, states began to codify common law, enacting criminal codes that set forth in one location the law of crimes. Some states still recognize as crimes those acts defined as such by common law even though they have not seen fit to codify them. A growing source of criminal law is federal criminal law. Traditionally, law enforcement has been left largely to the states, but as criminals become more sophisticated, and their actions have an impact outside of their local community, Congress has acted to criminalize additional activities, including selling drugs and kidnapping. Needless to say, these acts are crimes under state law as well. Statutes define the elements (the various parts) of a crime more specifically than was the case under common law.

LIMITATIONS ON CRIMINAL LAW

A state cannot criminalize any conduct it chooses. The due process clause of the Fourteenth Amendment has been interpreted by the Supreme Court to mean both procedural and substantive due process. **Substantive due process** essentially means that there are limits to what conduct the law may seek to prohibit. Specifically, the due process clause forbids the passage of laws that infringe on the substantive rights of individuals, such as the rights to free speech and assembly, because such rights are fundamental and necessary for ordered liberty.

The legal theory of substantive due process is the underlying theory for the privacy rights extended in *Griswold v. Connecticut* (1965; access to birth control information and devices), *Roe v. Wade* (1973; abortion), and *Lawrence v. Texas* (2003; sexual practices). As with the concept of crime, however, what does and does not come under the umbrella of substantive due process shifts around uneasily. For instance, early in 2006, South Dakota lawmakers approved a ban on abortion except to save the life of a pregnant woman (Nieves 2006). This would have been a direct challenge to *Roe v. Wade*, but South Dakotans rejected it in the November 2006 elections.

There are a number of other legal limitations on criminal law. Criminal laws that are either overly broad or vague (such as a law that prohibits anyone from "being about in public without a clear purpose") may be declared unconstitutional. A criminal law violates the **overbreadth doctrine** when it fails to narrowly define the specific behavior to be restricted. For instance, banning the sale of obscene materials is permitted, but a statute banning the sale of any and all material related to sexual activity would be overbroad.

A statute is **void for vagueness** if it fails to clearly define both the act prohibited and the appropriate punishment in advance. A statute must give fair notice to both law enforcement and citizens on exactly what conduct is forbidden by it so as to limit arbitrary enforcement and provide individuals with fair warning of what they lawfully may do (*Papachristou et al. v. City of Jacksonville* 1972). *Fair notice* simply means letting people know what is (and is not) permitted.

Criminal statutes also must not restrict due process or equal protection. Due process refers to the idea that laws must be enforced in a fair and nonarbitrary manner. Equal protection means that the state cannot enact or enforce laws aimed at restricting the rights of individuals who are members of suspect classifications, which are groups that have historically been ill-treated. According to the Supreme Court, these groups include racial minorities and, in some circumstances, women (*J.E.B. v. Alabama* 1994).

The Eighth Amendment bars "cruel and unusual punishment." This has been read by the Supreme Court to require that punishments be proportionate to the crime committed. Hence, the death penalty is appropriate only in cases where a murder has been committed (*Gregg v. Georgia* 1976). The Eighth Amendment does not require that each jurisdiction punish an offense in precisely the same manner. Nor does the concept of proportionality mean what it seems. The Court has allowed states to impose sentences of life in prison for habitual felons, even when the underlying felonies involve nothing more serious than obtaining a total of less than $230 over a fifteen-year period by false pretenses (fraudulent use of a credit card and writing bad checks) in three separate incidents (*Rummel v. Estelle* 1980). Needless to say, there are many who would define such a draconian sentence for such a trivial set of offenses as cruel and unusual.

Other constitutional limitations on criminal law, which are raised less frequently, include a prohibition on *ex post facto* laws and *bills of attainder*. **Ex post facto** laws are those passed "after the fact," meaning that the event occurs first and then it is criminalized. For example, if abortion becomes illegal in a state after July 25, 2007, an abortion provider could not be prosecuted for performing one on July 24 but could if he or she performed one on July 26. The ex post facto provision also forbids increasing the penalties for a crime after it has already been committed. Ex post facto laws that benefit the defendant are applied retroactively, however. Hence a person sentenced to death in a state that subsequently abolishes the death penalty will benefit from having the sentence commuted to life imprisonment. **Bills of attainder** are laws that impose punishment without a trial. Such bills were issued under old English common law for crimes against the state such as treason and marked the accused as "attainted" (morally contaminated).

ELEMENTS OF CRIMINAL LIABILITY

Criminal law does not punish individuals for all harms done, nor does it prohibit certain acts and thoughts that many may consider reprehensible, such as refusing to aid a drowning person or hating someone for the color of his or her skin. Criminal liability attaches, in most instances, only when there exists both a criminal act and the intent to commit it, which together are the cause of harm to another. There are five elements of criminal liability, each of which must be established beyond a reasonable doubt. Taken together, these comprise the body of the crime, or **corpus delicti**.

Common Elements of Criminal Offenses

1. Actus Reus (Criminal Act)

There must be an act for criminal liability to attach. The law does not punish evil thoughts alone—it is only when these thoughts are acted on that they may be punished. There are three forms of the criminal act, or **actus reus,** meaning a guilty act: (1) voluntary bodily movements, (2) an omission in the face of a duty to act, and (3) possession.

Voluntary movements occur by virtue of the actor's free will, without coercion and with awareness of the actor's conduct. This excludes involuntary bodily movements such as reflexive actions or unconscious activity (such as sleepwalking). Words may constitute acts in some cases, such as solicitation to commit a crime or threatening someone. The state may not punish someone on the basis of his or her status alone. For example, the Supreme Court has said that it is unconstitutional to punish someone for being a drug addict, a status (*Robinson v. California* 1962), but lawful to punish someone for being drunk in public, an act, even if the person suffers from chronic alcoholism (*Powell v. Texas* 1968).

A failure to act, or omission, is generally not subject to sanction, even if morally reprehensible. However, there are two narrow circumstances where failing to act may result in criminal liability. These include a failure to perform a legal duty (such as failing to register a handgun when the law requires it or failure to pay income taxes) and failure to intervene to prevent serious harm when there exists a special relationship between the parties (as in the case of parents and children).

Possession itself may constitute a criminal act if the person has some knowledge that what he or she possesses, such as an illegal weapon or child pornography, is illegal. While possession is passive, the act of acquiring possession requires action, and retaining possession in the face of awareness that it is unlawful to possess the item is similar to an omission.

2. Mens Rea (Criminal Intent)

Criminal liability generally does not attach based on actions alone. There also must exist some sort of guilty mind or **mens rea.** The rationale for this requirement is that society does not wish to punish unavoidable accidents. Modern criminal law recognizes several levels of intent, with varying levels of punishment associated with them. While the language varies by jurisdiction, many states track the language of the *Model Penal Code*, promulgated by the American Law Institute (1962). *Mens rea* is a sticky concept, for how can one person know what is in the mind of another? Nevertheless, *mens rea* must be proven, so the guilty mind is inferred from the circumstances surrounding the criminal act.

Criminal motive and criminal intent are different things. *Intent* refers to the mental purpose or desire to commit a certain act; *motive* refers to the cause, or reason why the act was committed. While some degree of intent is required for criminal liability to attach, there is no requirement that the prosecution prove motive, although it is commonly done as a means of explaining the act to the jury because it helps to clarify intent. Thus, prosecutors will frequently prove not only all the elements of an offense (such as murder) but provide a reason or motive why the defendant would want to kill the victim, such as anger or greed.

The **Model Penal Code** sets forth four levels of intent: purposeful, knowing, reckless, and negligent. A person who acts *purposefully* does so consciously, with the intent to commit a certain act or produce a certain result. The person is virtually certain of the results of his or her conduct. A person acts *knowingly* when he or she is practically certain of the result to follow from this conduct. The person possesses knowledge of what he or she is doing but lacks the premeditation and determination of one who acts purposefully. One acts *recklessly* when the individual acts with awareness of the risk involved but without the certainty of knowledge that harm will follow.

Criminal culpability is based on the conscious creation of risk of harm rather than the intent to harm. **Negligence** is the unconscious creation of a risk of harm. Negligent actors are those who should have been aware that they were creating a substantial and unjustifiable risk of harm. This standard is an objective one— if the "reasonable" person would have been aware of the risk of harm, then the negligent person is responsible for being aware of his or her conduct.

There is one other form of intent developed at common law, known as the doctrine of transferred intent. This *doctrine of transferred intent* applies to situations where a person intended to harm A but in error harmed B. To prevent the defendant from escaping liability by claiming that he or she did not intend to hurt B and that therefore the element of intent is missing, courts developed the concept of transferred intent. The concept means that the intent to harm a person who is not actually harmed is transferred to the person who is. Thus if Jeremy shoots at Dave with the intention of harming him but misses and kills Andy instead, under the doctrine of transferred intent Jeremy's intent (to kill Dave) is transferred to Andy, so that he cannot claim he is not guilty of a crime because he did not intend to kill Andy.

3. Concurrence

Concurrence is simply the union of the criminal act (*actus reus*) and criminal intent (*mens rea*). The criminal intent must set the criminal act in motion. Acts not generated by criminal intent do not constitute criminal conduct. For instance, Dick and Jane live in the same apartment complex and are in the habit of walking into each other's apartment unannounced to visit. One day Dick walks into Jane's apartment to ask her if she has any spare marijuana since he is all out. He finds that Jane is not home, so he rummages around looking for her stash of pot.

Finding none, he decides to take her new stereo and pawn it for drug money. In this case, Dick could not be charged with burglary because burglary requires that a person enter a structure by "force or fraud." Since he had consent to enter Jane's home at any time, he did not enter by force or fraud. The criminal intent to steal Jane's stereo occurred only after he had entered and found her not at home, not before, as required to prove the crime of burglary. Dick could only be prosecuted for larceny/theft, which carries a less severe penalty than burglary, because *mens rea* was formed only after entry into Jane's apartment.

4. Causation

Causation is the legal principle that the criminal act is the act that is the cause of the harm. There are two types of causation: factual and legal. **Factual cause** refers to the idea that "but for" the actor's conduct, the harm would not have occurred. It is an initial act that sets a series of other acts in motion that leads to some harm. Factual causation is a necessary but not sufficient element for the imposition of criminal liability. A legal cause also must exist.

Legal cause, also referred to as **proximate cause,** is not as straightforward as is factual cause. For all practical purposes, in the vast majority of criminal cases, they are the same thing. The issue of proximate causation only becomes relevant when some additional acts not under the accused person's control or which he or she could not reasonably foresee intervene between the factual cause and the harm ultimately caused. Another way to view proximate causation is the proximity ("nearness") in time between the accused's actions and the ultimate degree of harm caused to the victim. The question often asked in such cases is "For which act does it seem fair and just to hold the actor accountable?" Consequences of an act that are not reasonably foreseeable to the actor are "intervening causes" and serve to relieve the actor of some degree of criminal liability.

An example might be if Mr. Smith struck Mrs. Smith with his fist and broke her tooth. When Mrs. Smith went in to have her tooth replaced, the dentist, drunk from having too many margaritas at lunch, accidentally gave her too many drugs and she died as a result. While it is true that Mr. Smith is in some ways the "cause" of his wife's untimely demise, since if he had not punched her she would not have gone to the dentist, most would agree that the dentist's behavior was not reasonably foreseeable to Mr. Smith. Therefore, Mr. Smith would not be liable for his wife's death simply for setting in motion an unlikely chain of events. He could, of course, be held liable for assault.

5. Harm

Harm is simply the result of the act, the injury to another. Harm occurs in all crimes, even in so-called "victimless" crimes. Harm may be physical, as in murder, or mental, as in threatening someone with some form of harm. There can be no liability without harm, although this harm may be to society in general rather than to a specific individual. The state even may criminalize acts that ostensibly harm only the actor, such as suicide, prostitution, or drug abuse. Such acts, of course, can harm others involved with the actor (spouses, parents, children) far more seriously than many other criminal acts, such as robbery or assault.

LIABILITY WITHOUT FAULT

There are a few instances where criminal liability may attach without proof of criminal intent. These include strict liability and vicarious liability. Strict liability is an important tort law (discussed in chapter 7) concept but also is used in the criminal arena when there is a strong public interest involved to justify eliminating the *mens rea* requirement. **Strict liability** imposes accountability without proof of criminal intent in situations where society deems it fair to do so. Statutory rape (consensual sexual intercourse between an adult and a minor) provides an example. It does not matter whether the adult knew the correct age of the minor, or even if the minor told the adult that he or she was of consenting age—criminal liability still attaches to the adult. Minors are considered not legally capable of giving sexual consent, and society has deemed it important to protect minors from exploitation, even at the expense of eliminating the *mens rea* requirement for the commission of a crime. The age of consent varies across nations and across states, with some as high as eighteen, but the most typical age of consent is sixteen.

Vicarious liability refers to the imputation of accountability from one person to another, usually the individual's superior. Here, liability is based not on a person's act but on the individual's relationship to the person who committed an illegal act. It eliminates the criminal act requirement for the second actor by imputing the first actor's intent to this individual. It is different from strict liability, which eliminates the necessity of proving mens rea. An example would be the liability of correctional administrators for the actions of the officers they are supervising. In some instances, a supervisor may be held accountable for the actions of his or her subordinates. This form of liability attaches only in civil cases, never in criminal cases.

INCHOATE CRIMES

Crimes that occur in preparation for an offense are called **inchoate crimes**. The adjective *inchoate* means "to begin" or "to partially put into operation." Although in reality inchoate crimes are anticipatory and incomplete crimes, legally they are completed crimes in which criminal liability exists even though the contemplated act or actions never take place. There are three types of inchoate crimes: Attempt, solicitation, and conspiracy.

Attempt

In early common law, it was not a crime to attempt but fail to complete a criminal act. As the law developed, however, the doctrine of attempt developed as a means of controlling both potentially dangerous persons and activities. For one to be liable for attempting to commit a crime, there must be proof of the specific intent to carry out an act that constitutes a crime. General intent, meaning the person's general disposition to commit criminal acts at any time or against any person when the opportunity arises, is not sufficient. As criminal law does not punish evil thoughts alone, there must be some evidence of a specific intention to commit an overt act in the pursuance of the intended crime. Courts generally require evidence of "some step" or "substantial steps" (see *Model Penal Code*; American Law Institute 1962) that constitute perpetration of the criminal act.

Solicitation

Solicitation involves the intent to induce another to commit a crime. There must be words or some action of inducing, accompanied by the intention to induce—joking about a crime is not enough. The solicited crime need not actually be committed for there to be solicitation. Thus, a crime has occurred as soon as Lilly asks Billy the biker to kill her husband. Billy need not actually kill Lilly's husband, or need not take any steps at all to do so for Lilly to have committed a crime. The crime is in Lilly's asking of Billy to commit a crime. Billy has not committed any crime if he refuses the solicitation.

Conspiracy

A **conspiracy** is an agreement between two or more people for the purpose of committing a crime. If Lilly and Billy seriously make plans to kill Lilly's husband, then both are guilty of conspiracy to commit murder. As with solicitation, the intended crime need not occur for the conspiracy to be committed—in most jurisdictions, it is enough if there is an agreement for an unlawful purpose. Some jurisdictions require in addition some act in furtherance of the conspiracy. A coconspirator may be held liable for the actions of others in the conspiracy, even if he or she is unaware of their offenses.

Parties to Crime

The doctrine of **complicity** sets forth the situations where more than one person may be held liable for criminal activity. Complicity still requires all the elements of criminal liability but allows liability to attach for someone else's conduct. Common law recognized four parties to a crime: (1) principles in the first degree (those who commit the act), (2) principles in the second degree (present when the crime occurred, acting as lookouts, getaway drivers, etc.), (3) accessories before the fact, and (4) accessories after the fact. Complicity includes accessories both before and after the fact, so long as they are aware that a crime will occur or has occurred.

Accessories before the fact are individuals not present at the crime but who facilitated it in some way such as providing plans, information, or weapons. Accessories after the fact are individuals who aid the principles in some way after the crime has been committed by hiding them or their criminal gains, or providing them with information useful in avoiding capture. Modern statutes have eliminated the distinction between principles and now make them, as well as accessories before the fact, equally culpable accomplices. The statutes do retain the distinction between principles and accessories after the fact, however.

DEFENSES TO CRIMINAL LIABILITY

There are several defenses to criminal liability. A **defense** is a response made by a defendant to the complaint, which, if successful, allows the defendant to avoid criminal liability. A defense may take the form of an *alibi* where the defendant asserts he or she is not the person who committed the act charged. An alibi is different from the other defenses because the defendant is claiming innocence, whereas the other defenses admit committing the act, but the defendant is raising one of two affirmative defenses—justification or excuse.

Affirmative defenses are those in which the defendant has the burden of production and the burden of persuasion. The **burden of production** refers to the duty to produce evidence. In every criminal case, the prosecution must introduce evidence showing the defendant, in all likelihood, committed the crime with which he or she has been charged. Failure to produce such evidence will result in a dismissal of the case. The burden of persuasion refers to which side has to "prove" its case. Again, in criminal cases, the prosecution has the burden of persuasion and must prove its case to the jury beyond a reasonable doubt. When the defense is asserting an affirmative defense, however, both burdens shift from the prosecution to the defense. Generally, the burden of persuasion for affirmative defenses is by a preponderance of the evidence, although in some states, a higher burden is imposed for certain defenses, such as the insanity defense. Affirmative defenses may result in acquittal, a reduction of the charge, or serve to mitigate the punishment.

Justification Defenses

A **justification defense** is one in which the defendant admits he or she is responsible for the act which occurred but claims that under the circumstances, the act was not criminal. Examples of common justification defenses include self-defense, consent, and execution of public duties.

Self-defense

Self-defense may be successfully claimed if the defendant can demonstrate that he or she used force to repel an imminent, unprovoked attack, in the reasonable belief that he or she was about to be seriously injured. The defendant may only use as much force as is necessary to repel the attack. There are a number of limitations and exceptions to the general rules of self-defense. These include the *retreat doctrine*, which states that a person must retreat rather than use deadly force if doing so is possible without endangering the person's life. The *castle doctrine*, on the other hand, states that persons attacked in their home need not retreat from a potentially deadly invasion and/or attack. States differ as to which doctrine defines their stance vis-à-vis self-defense claims. Self-defense also may apply to the defense of others, and in some circumstances to the defense of property.

Consent

Consent is a defense to some crimes, albeit a controversial one. Most jurisdictions provide that persons may consent to suffer what otherwise would be an actionable injury. What acts a person can consent to suffer are quite limited, however, and it must be demonstrated that the consent was voluntary, knowing, and intelligent. As we have seen, the consent of a minor to have sex with an adult is not considered voluntary, knowing, and intelligent and would therefore not be a legally permissible consent offense. An example of voluntary, knowing, and intelligent consent is that of the professional athlete who chooses to engage in activity where injury similar to an assault may occur.

Execution of Public Duties

Agents of the state, such as police officers or soldiers, are permitted to use reasonable force in the lawful execution of their duties. This defense allows the use of deadly force under the proper circumstances and allows police to engage in activities that are otherwise criminal if they are doing so as part of their law enforcement efforts, such as posing as a drug dealer. The most controversial element of this defense is police killings, since officers are limited to the circumstances under which deadly force can be used (*Tennessee v. Garner* 1984).

Excuse Defenses

An **excuse defense** is one in which a defendant admits that what he or she did was wrong but argues that under the circumstances, he or she is not responsible for the improper conduct. Examples include duress, intoxication, age, and insanity.

Duress

Duress may be raised at a defense in a limited number of situations. These vary by jurisdiction but generally include situations involving the threat of serious, imminent harm to oneself, where the act is less serious than the threatened harm. Thus, a person is acting under duress when he commits a robbery to avoid being killed by the person holding him hostage. Duress is allowed as a defense under the rationale that those forced to commit a crime in such circumstances do not act voluntarily, so there is no actus reus component. Another explanation is that subjugation to the will of another removes the mens rea component (Dressler 1995). The duress defense excuses only minor crimes in some states, whereas in others, it excuses all crimes except murder.

Intoxication

There are two forms of intoxication, voluntary and involuntary. Voluntary intoxication never provides a complete defense but may negate the mens rea component for an offense requiring the specific intent by reducing the degree of the crime charged in some states. In other states, the rule is that the voluntary act of drinking establishes voluntariness and thus cannot be used as any kind of mitigation. It also may be used in mitigation of the penalty. Involuntary intoxication may provide a defense if it can be shown that the actor was unaware that he or she was being drugged. In such cases, the actor is excused because he or she is not responsible for becoming intoxicated; consequently, it would be unfair to hold him or her liable for the resulting uncontrollable action. The Supreme Court has held that due process does not require that states allow the defense of intoxication (*Montana v. Egelhoff* 1996).

Age

Historically, youth has been treated as a defense to criminal liability on the ground that persons below a certain age lack the requisite mental capability to form mens rea. Under the common law, there was a presumption that children under the age of seven years were incompetent. Today, the various jurisdictions define the age of majority (when one becomes an adult) at varying ages. Those classified as juveniles are dealt with not in the criminal justice system but rather in the juvenile justice system. The *parens patriae* doctrine of the juvenile court, which essentially means that the state acts as a parent to the child (discussed further in chapter 8), is slowly giving way to an increased desire to treat juveniles similarly to adult offenders.

Insanity

Insanity is a legal term to describe mental illness, which excuses criminal liability by impairing mens rea. Mental illness and legal insanity are not the same things. A person can be judged mentally ill by medical standards and sane by legal standards, and vice versa. The insanity claim is probably the most controversial of all defense strategies, although it is rarely used except in cases of capital murder because few defendants believe that being locked up in a mental institution for an indefinite period is preferable to being locked in prison for a definite period. There are several different legal tests for insanity; all of these have been criticized as either too difficult or too easy to establish (Dressler 1995).

The first renowned case in which the modern insanity defense was successfully mounted was in *Rex v. Hadfield* in 1800 in England. John Hadfield was an ex-British soldier who had received a head wound and had a great dislike of his monarch, George III. Convinced that George was preventing the second coming of Jesus, Hadfield took a shot at George, missed him, and was tried for high treason. Upon hearing testimony of expert witness, the judge halted the trial and ordered Hadfield sent to a mental institution (Hawthorn 2000).

Another British case, *Rex v. M'Naghten* (1843) cemented the modern insanity defense. This time, the intended target of an assassination attempt was Prime Minister Robert Peel. M'Naghten missed Peel and hit Peel's secretary, Edward Drummond, who subsequently died. M'Naghten was found not guilty by reason of insanity and sent to a mental institution. This case became the foundation for insanity defenses around the world. The **M'Naghten rule** is also known as the right–wrong test, meaning that the M'Naghten standard for insanity is realized if a defendant did not know either what he or she was doing or that it was wrong. Other tests are briefly mentioned in the following list:

- **Durham rule**: This test is also known as the *products test*. The Durham standard is met when the act was the product of the defendant's mental illness. Note that it goes beyond the right–wrong test to include mental disease or defects. Almost all states have abandoned the Durham test as too broad.

- **Irresistible impulse**: Many states have appended this test to the right–wrong test, thus adding a behavioral to a cognitive component. The irresistible impulse is defined as the inability to control one's conduct. This defense was successfully employed in 1994 by Lorena Bobbitt, who was on trial for cutting off her husband's penis while he slept. The defense claimed that Lorena's irresistible impulse to sever her husband's penis arose because she saw the penis as the symbol of the fear and humiliation she suffered at the hands of her husband (Schmalleger 2006).
- **Substantial capacity test**: The substantial capacity standard is defined as when the defendant lacks substantial capacity to appreciate the wrongfulness of his or her conduct or to know how to control it.

Following the uproar over the 1982 acquittal by reason of insanity of John Hinckley, who had wounded President Ronald Reagan in an assassination attempt, Congress passed the Insanity Defense Reform Act of 1984, and the states made a variety of changes to their insanity laws. These included dropping the defense altogether, shifting the burden of proof, changing their commitment and release rules, and, more generally, by adopting a "guilty but mentally ill" (GBMI) defense. A GBMI verdict maintains defendants' criminal liability, and hence criminal sentence, but mandates psychiatric treatment for them. Several states and the federal courts have limited the use of the insanity defense or altered the burden of proof in establishing the defense. Federal courts, for instance, require that the defense establish insanity by clear and convincing evidence rather than the standard usually applied to affirmative defense, a preponderance of the evidence.

PROCEDURAL DEFENSES: ENTRAPMENT

There are a number of other defenses against liability called procedural defenses. These are defenses in which it is claimed that somewhere along the line in processing the case, the criminal justice system violated the defendant's due process rights. These defenses include double jeopardy, denial of speedy trial, and use of illegally seized evidence. These issues are discussed elsewhere in the text, so we will not go into them here. We will, however, discuss entrapment, a defense that is increasingly being raised by defendants caught in drug stings and Internet sexual enticement stings (Johnson 2006).

The Supreme Court laid out two rules of entrapment in *Sherman v. U.S.* (1958), stating that **entrapment** occurs when (1) the crime is the result of "the creative activity" of law enforcement, and (2) the prosecutor cannot prove beyond a reasonable doubt that the defendant was "independently predisposed" to commit the crime. Creative activity, such as stings and decoy operations, is therefore permissible if used to trap individuals who were predisposed (i.e., had a preexisting inclination) to commit the crime for which they were arrested. If a person steals money from the pocket of a police officer acting as a drunk lying in the gutter, or if he or she consistently sells stolen property at a pawnshop operated by the police, that person has demonstrated predisposition. As one judge was famously heard to remark, "Traps must distinguish between the unwary innocent and the unwary guilty."

CRIMES AGAINST THE PERSON

Crimes are frequently categorized on the basis of the type of act. Under this approach, there are crimes against the person, crimes against property, crimes against society, and crimes against morality. Each of these categories encompasses a wide range of conduct. Crimes against the person often are ranked among the most serious offenses.

Murder

The FBI (2005, 15) defines **murder** as "the willful (non-negligent) killing of one human being by another." There were 16,137 murders in the United States in 2004, a rate of 5.5 per 100,000 people. Murder is a subcategory of homicide, a broad, all-inclusive term for any killing of another human being. Definitional issues include what is a human being, when is someone alive (or dead), and what types of homicide are deserving of punishment. The issues of when life begins and ends are difficult moral and ethical questions, and they pose legal problems as well. Some states criminalize the killing of an unborn fetus, while others require the baby be born alive and then die before a killing is considered to have occurred. Determining when life ends is made more difficult as medical science has made it possible for severely injured persons to live indefinitely, hooked up to life support devices. Under common law, death was defined as when the heartbeat stopped, but many states now define death as occurring when there is an irreversible cessation of brain function.

The *Model Penal Code* distinguishes between lawful killings (such as those committed in self-defense or public duty) and unlawful killings, or criminal homicides. There are three forms of criminal homicide—murder, manslaughter, and negligent homicide. Under common law, murder generally was defined as the killing of another person, with malice aforethought. Malice aforethought means an intentional, premeditated (planned) killing. Murder is today defined by the *Model Penal Code* as a killing that occurs (1) purposefully, or (2) knowingly, or (3) recklessly under circumstances exhibiting extreme indifference to human life. As these comprise three distinct levels of intent, murder is graded into first degree and second degree. First-degree murder encompasses those killings that are deliberate and premeditated. Second-degree murder includes any killings that are intentional but not premeditated or planned.

States and courts differ on how planned and how premeditated a crime must be to be considered first-degree murders. Some consider it a period of careful and thoughtful consideration and the formulation of some preconceived design for carrying out the crime, while others hold that premeditation is formed the minute the intention to kill is formed. Many such "instantly premeditated" murders can actually be worse than a murder that takes place after months of planning.

For instance, someone who forms an instant urge to rape and kill a child for no other reason than sheer wanton bloodlust and does so has surely committed a more atrocious act than an abused wife who carefully plans how to do away with her husband and does so.

Manslaughter is a second category of criminal homicides and includes both voluntary and involuntary manslaughter. **Voluntary manslaughter** is an intentional killing that occurs either (1) under a mistaken belief that self-defense required the use of deadly force or (2) in response to adequate provocation, while in the sudden heat of passion (Dressler 1982). Adequate provocation under common law included instances such as where a husband caught his wife in the act of committing adultery. Today, *adequate provocation* is defined as a killing that occurs after such provocation as the law deems sufficient—that which could cause a reasonable person to react violently. Examples include catching a spouse in adultery, being assaulted, and someone trespassing in one's home. Words alone are not considered sufficient to create adequate provocation. **Involuntary manslaughter** is a criminal homicide where an unintentional killing results from a reckless act.

Negligent homicide, the third category of criminal homicide, is an unintentional killing in which the defendant should have known that he or she was creating a substantial risk of death by his or her conduct, which itself deviated from the ordinary level of care owed to others (American Law Institute 1962). The most common example is negligent driving, and in some jurisdictions, there is a separate offense such as vehicular homicide.

Another type of murder is felony murder, a category ranked as first-degree murder in some states and second-degree in others. Under the **felony murder** *rule*, an individual may be held liable for an unintended killing that occurs during the commission of a dangerous felony, such as robbery or rape. In most states, felony murder is treated as second-degree murder. There is no requirement of intent to either kill or inflict serious injury. It is enough if the person was engaged in what is considered a dangerous felony or a felony in which serious injury is a reasonably foreseeable outcome.

There are a number of offenses against the person aside from murder and manslaughter. These offenses, while less serious than killing, nonetheless are treated seriously in criminal law, as they involve harm of one form or another to a person. Among these are assault and battery, robbery, and a myriad of sexual offenses including rape, sexual assault, and child sexual abuse. These offenses, while different in form, all share the common denominator of direct harm to a person inflicted by the actor.

Forcible Rape

The FBI (2005, 27) defines forcible rape as "the carnal knowledge of a female forcibly and against her will." This definition includes attempts to commit rape but excludes statutory rape (consensual sex with an underage female) and the rape of males. Rapes of males are classified as either assaults or other sex offenses depending on the circumstances of the crime and the extent of physical injury.

Under common law, rape was defined as "carnal knowledge by a man of a woman who is not his wife, forcibly and without her consent." This definition created several interesting holes in the law: only men were capable of rape, only women could be raped, men could not rape their wives, the only act that constituted rape was vaginal intercourse, and there must be evidence of both force and resistance to force. All fifty states have formally abolished the so-called marital rape exception, although if a rape takes place within the context of marriage in some states, it is considered a factor mitigating the seriousness of the charge and severity of the punishment (Belknap 2001).

Many states have rewritten their statutes using gender-neutral language so that the crime applies to acts committed by men and women and to acts committed against men and children and have relaxed the common law requirement that a woman physically resist her attacker on the ground that requiring her to do so simply put her at risk of additional harm. There also has been an attempt to limit the sort of evidence that can be introduced at trial. Rape shield statutes restrict the introduction into evidence of a victim's sexual history. The *Model Penal Code* follows this approach, focusing instead on the conduct of the defendant. This aligns the elements of rape law more closely with the elements of modern assault law, which do not focus on the conduct of the victim. Some states no longer classify the crime as rape but instead use the phrase "sexual assault" (*Texas Penal Code*, 2005).

Other sexual offenses, which are currently the subject of much public debate, include child sexual assault. Recent highly publicized cases involving allegations of child sexual abuse and the increase in the number of reports of sexual assaults on children by both family and strangers have heightened public awareness and led to a toughening of child sexual abuse laws. While the elements of these laws track closely the elements of rape law, the punishment accorded these is often even more severe. While the Supreme Court in *Coker v. Georgia* (1976) declared that the death penalty was a punishment disproportionate to the offense of rape of an adult woman, several states (for example, Louisiana) have recently enacted statutes providing for the death penalty in cases involving the rape of a young child. Whether these laws will withstand constitutional scrutiny remains to be seen.

Aggravated Assault

The FBI (2005, 37) defines aggravated assault as "an unlawful attack by one person upon another for the purpose of inflicting severe or aggravated bodily injury." As opposed to simple assault, aggravated assault is an assault in which a weapon such as a knife or gun is used, although the use of personal weapons such as hands and feet can result in a charge of aggravated assault if they cause great bodily harm. Aggravated assault is the most common felony violent crime, accounting for 62.5 percent of all Part I violent crimes in 2004. Each incident of aggravated assault carries the potential threat of becoming a murder. It has been claimed that without the speedy access to modern medicine we enjoy today, many aggravated assault victims would have ended up as murder victims (Harris et al. 2002).

Under common law, there was a clear distinction between the offense of assault and the offense of battery. Assault was either (1) an attempt or (2) a threat to inflict immediate harm by a person with the present means of carrying out the attempt or threat. No physical contact was necessary for an assault to take place—it was enough if the victim reasonably feared for his or her safety, or if the assailant attempted to complete the assault. A completed assault in which there was actual bodily contact was considered a *battery*. A battery under common law was defined as unjustified, offensive physical contact of some sort. It could be a blow from a fist, being spit upon, or being shot. There must have been an intention to make contact. Today, many jurisdictions have merged the offenses of assault and battery, referring to both as assault, and grading what was assault under common law as a less serious form of the offense.

Robbery

The FBI (2005, 31) defines robbery as "the taking or attempted taking of anything of value from the care, custody, or control of a person or persons by force or threat of force or violence and/or putting the victim in fear." Robbery is thus larceny by force and is thus classified as a violent rather than property offense. It is the most serious form of larceny, as it involves an offense against both property and person. Any force or threat of force constitutes "force" for purposes of imposing criminal liability for robbery. A taking of property accomplished by the threat of future harm to person, property, or reputation is *extortion*.

Robbery carries a more serious penalty than any other crimes except murder and rape in every state in the union because the act of taking property from someone who has it in his or her custody entails a strong risk of violence. We might mention that while a pickpocket takes personal assets from another's care, custody, or control, there is no force or threat of force because the person is not usually aware of the theft until later. The offense of pocket picking is classified as a larceny/theft, a crime against property.

CRIMES AGAINST PROPERTY

Crimes against property encompass a broad spectrum of activities. The most common include burglary, trespass, arson, theft in its myriad forms, forgery and uttering, and receiving stolen property. While crimes against the person receive the bulk of media and public attention, the reality is that crimes against property are far more common. The 2005 UCR reports that fully 88.3 percent of crimes reported to the police were property crimes. At early common law, there was only the crime of larceny, but as society developed and criminals devised new ways to deprive people of their possessions, the law responded by creating new offenses. Because the law of theft developed so haphazardly, these theft offenses were confusing and hard to distinguish from one another. Today, many states have done away with the variety of theft offenses and lump together all crimes involving the unlawful obtaining of property as larceny.

Arson

Arson is defined by the FBI (2005, 61) as "any willful or malicious burning or attempting to burn, with or without intent to defraud, a dwelling house, public building, motor vehicle or aircraft, personal property of another, etc." Arson is setting fire to a structure with the intent to burn the structure, in whole or in part. Under early common law, arson applied only to the burning of the dwelling of another. The definition of the crime was soon expanded to cover any structure, including one's own home and nonresidential buildings. Most jurisdictions grade arson so that the burning of an occupied structure is first-degree arson, and the burning of an unoccupied structure is second-degree arson. Some jurisdictions have expanded arson to cover the burning of personal property (such as vehicles) as well as structures, and this is generally treated as third-degree arson. There must exist intent to burn, which excludes negligent acts but includes reckless conduct.

Burglary

The FBI (2005, 45) defines burglary as "the unlawful entry of a structure to commit a felony or theft." Burglary is a crime committed against the home. Since the earliest common law, the dwelling has been afforded special protection from entry by both agents of the state and uninvited guests. The definition of burglary has changed over time, as society has developed and conditions have changed. In early common law, burglary could take place anywhere that was likely to attract people, including public places. Gradually, burglary was limited to home invasions, and by the seventeenth century, burglary was defined as the breaking and entering of the dwelling of another at night with the intention of committing a felony inside the dwelling. Each of these six elements had its own unique meaning. Burglary was restricted to nocturnal home invasions on the theory that invasions at such times were more likely to result in greater harm to the occupants, who were more likely to be home at the time. Nighttime entry is no longer a necessary element, although almost all states differentiate between burglaries of a home taking place at night (aggravated, or first-degree, burglary) and those that take place during the day or of a structure other than the home.

It is important to note that burglary is not entry alone—there must be an *unlawful* entry accompanied by the present intent to commit another crime once inside. Thus, stealing a television from your neighbor's house is not necessarily burglary unless you had the intent to remove the television *before* entering the house (the concurrence of *actus reus* and *mens rea*). Going into someone's house or simply onto their property unlawfully without the intention to commit any additional acts is trespass.

Today, burglary is much more broadly defined in most jurisdictions. It may occur at all hours of the day, and is not limited to dwellings, but also may occur in virtually any structure. In fact, burglary statutes across the country are such a confusing mixture of laws covering such a wide variety of conduct that many acts are considered burglary. The element of "unlawful entry" enables shoplifting to be classified as burglary if the suspect is unwise enough to admit that he or she entered the store for the specific purpose of stealing. A variety of incidents that have actually resulted in burglary charges and convictions include pumping gas and leaving without paying, stealing popcorn from a sidewalk stand, stealing from a locked glove compartment, and taking a few coins from a pay phone. Regardless of state statutes, "burglaries" (such as shoplifting) that do not fit the FBI definition must be reported to the FBI as larcenies.

Larceny/Theft

The FBI (2005, 49) defines larceny/theft as "the unlawful taking, leading, or riding away from the possession or constructive possession of another." The unwieldy phrase and concept of "constructive possession" refers to circumstances in which the victim may still have possession of the item in question (e.g., a credit card), but someone else has stolen the number and can thus use it without the victim's consent.

Under common law, larceny was the unlawful taking and carrying away of another's personal property, with the intent to permanently deprive the rightful owner of its possession. This definition encompassed takings that occurred by force and takings that occurred without the knowledge of the owner. It was not larceny if someone deprived some other person of property under any other circumstance. As society evolved and people began to rely on others to do business, personal property was placed in the custody of another for a limited purpose. Thus, person X might give a bank clerk $100 to deposit in person X's bank account. If the clerk kept the money for himself or herself instead, it was not larceny, as there was no wrongful taking—person X willingly handed over the money to the clerk. Courts soon responded to this strange situation by enlarging the definition of larceny. Larceny is defined broadly today and includes taking by stealth, by fraud, and by false pretenses. Under common law, each of these was a separate offense, but today, in many jurisdictions, they all are classified as larceny. This trend follows the *Model Penal Code* approach of consolidating common law theft offenses.

All the elements of larceny have been significantly broadened over the years. The "taking" element is satisfied when an actor gains brief control over an item, either directly or indirectly. The "carrying away" element is satisfied if the item is moved even a slight distance from its original location. The "personal property" element has been expanded to cover both personal and real property (note: *personal* property is anything that is movable; *real* property is land and anything growing out of or affixed to it). There still must be intent to deprive a person permanently of his or her property. A temporary misappropriation of the property of another is not larceny but is punishable as a lesser offense. Teenagers who steal a car and then abandon it (thus showing no intent to gain permanent possession of it) will probably be charged with joyriding. Motor vehicle theft is a larceny, but it is considered different enough from other larceny/thefts to warrant a separate classification in the UCR. Most jurisdictions now grade larceny based either on the method of taking or the value of the property taken.

According to the value of the item(s) stolen, larceny/theft is classified either as grand theft or petty theft, the former being a felony and the latter a misdemeanor. The distinction varies from state to state, but it is under $1,000 in every state. The value of the property is considered to be its value at the time it was stolen, not its replacement value. Because of the wide variation among the states regarding the grand/petty cutoff point, the FBI does not make that distinction in its annual report of the number of larceny/thefts.

CRIMES AGAINST PUBLIC ORDER AND MORALITY

Crimes against persons and property have readily identifiable victims. There are other acts that are classified as crimes but for which the victim is less readily identifiable. These acts fall into one of two categories: crimes against public order and crimes against public morality. Crimes against public order are those in which the injury is to the peace and order of society. These include disorderly conduct, unlawful assembly, and vagrancy. Crimes against morality, or public morals crimes, are those in which the moral health of society is injured. These include consensual sexual acts such as fornication, adultery, prostitution, and obscenity.

People who commit public order offenses generally do not direct their conduct at specific individuals. Public order offenses are frequently challenged as constitutionally invalid because they place limits on cherished individual rights such as freedom of assembly and privacy. States must take care to craft public order legislation carefully so that it does not impermissibly limit constitutionally protected conduct. Statutes that do so often are struck down by courts on the grounds of vagueness or overbreadth.

According to early common law decisions, it was a crime to disturb the public tranquility. This was referred to as breach of the peace. Today many states have codified it as disorderly conduct. This is a catchall phrase and has been held to include acts as diverse as public drunkenness, vagrancy, playing loud music, and fighting. Disorderly conduct in a group setting generally is referred to as *unlawful assembly*. This includes groups assembled in public without the necessary permits as well as riots. Vagrancy is a crime developed in feudal England after the Black Death to control the peasants and tie them to their lords. Vagrancy laws made it a crime to move about the country without proof of employment. Today, courts often determine vagrancy statutes to be unconstitutionally overbroad (*Papachristou et al. v. City of Jacksonville* 1972).

Public morals offenses involve acts committed by consenting adults but which society has chosen to prohibit as immoral even if freely engaged in. Examples include fornication, adultery, bigamy, and prostitution. Most public morals offenses involve the regulation of sexual activity in some form. While these acts all involve consenting adults, some argue that, in fact, consent is not freely given by some (as in the case of prostitution) or that such conduct diminishes the moral capacity of society and hence is deserving of criminalization as a means of eliminating or at least reducing such activity.

SUMMARY

In this chapter, we have discussed the basic elements of criminal law as well as the purposes of criminal law and sources and limitations on it. Criminal law governs much of human activity today. According to social contract theory, when human beings abandoned their solitary existence for the benefits of living among others, they gave up some of their individual rights to the state in return for the benefits they gained from living in society. Criminal law is the formal means by which society attempts to control the conduct of individuals. Informal means of social control still exist and are often effective, but when informal means fail, criminal law exists to deal with society's transgressors.

Criminal law has developed as society has developed. Definitions of crimes have changed and new offenses have been created in an attempt to maintain a rational set of rules by which society can function and individuals within society are protected from others. What is legal may vary across the years and by culture, but all societies with a written criminal law share many similarities.

The issues with which scholars, judges, and juries continue to struggle involve the limits of the criminal sanction. How much can society expect the criminal to accomplish? When is it fair and just to hold individuals accountable for their conduct and to subject them to criminal sanctions? Determining not only when liability should attach, but also the appropriate level of punishment, are difficult choices, involving policy considerations, legal doctrine, and morality.

In this chapter, we have attempted to explain not only what constitutes a particular crime, such as murder or arson, but also to explain why certain acts are crimes and others are not and why we assess blame differently depending on the circumstances of each event and the mental state of the defendant. There are no easy answers in this area.

DISCUSSION QUESTIONS

1. What are some of the prominent limitations on criminal law?
2. What are the five elements of the corpus delicti, and why must each be proven?
3. What is the difference between an excuse defense and a justification defense?
4. What are the major categories of crimes, and how are crimes classified?
5. What are the four levels of intent in the *Model Penal Code*, and how do they differ from one another?
6. One day Mr. Smith receives an e-mail from an unknown person named "Julie" who informs Smith that she has viewed his Web site and found him to be most attractive. After several e-mail exchanges, Smith asks "Julie" to meet him and have sex. She agrees to do so but then informs him that she is only fifteen years old. Upon hearing this, Smith then calls the meeting off. "Julie" sends several more e-mails imploring Smith to meet her and have sex. He finally agrees, but when he arrives at the meeting place and identifies himself, he finds that "Julie" is a police officer, who then arrests him for

soliciting sex from an underage minor. Does Smith have a good entrapment defense? Was he predisposed to engage in sex with a minor?

References

American Law Institute. 1962. *Model penal code*. Philadelphia: The Institute.

Belknap, J. 2001. *The invisible woman: Gender, crime, and justice*. Belmont, CA: Wadsworth.

Dressler, J. 1982. Rethinking heat of passion: A defense in search of a rationale. *Journal of Criminal Law and Criminology* 73:421–79.

———. 1995. *Understanding criminal law*. 2nd ed. New York: Matthew Bender.

Ellis, L., and A. Walsh. 2000. *Criminology: A global perspective*. Boston: Allyn & Bacon.

Estrich, S. 1986. Rape. *Yale Law Journal* 95:1087.

Federal Bureau of Investigation. 2005. *Crime in the United States, 2004: Uniform crime reports*. Washington, DC: U.S. Government Printing Office.

Goode, E. 2005. *Drugs in American society*. 6th ed. Boston: McGraw-Hill.

Hart, H. 1958. The aims of the criminal Law. *Law and Contemporary Problems* 23:401–44.

Harris, A., S. Thomas, G. Fisher, and D. Hirsch. 2002. Murder and medicine: The lethality of criminal assault 1960–1999. *Homicide Studies* 6:128–66.

Hawthorn, C. 2000. "Deific decree": The short, happy life of a pseudo-doctrine. *Loyola of Los Angeles Law Review* 33:1755–1810.

Johnson, J. 2006. *The entrapment debate: Are undercover investigations egregious conduct of law enforcement*. http://www.grayarea.com/entrap.htm.

Nieves, E. 2006. *S.D. abortion bill takes aim at Roe*. http://www.washingtonpost.com.

Schmalleger, F. 2006. *Criminal justice today*. 9th ed. New York: Prentice Hall.

Texas Penal Code, Chapter 22 (assaultive offenses). 2005. Longwood, FL: Gould.

Walsh, A., and L. Ellis. 2007. *Criminology: An interdisciplinary approach*. Thousand Oaks, CA: Sage/Pine Forge Press.

Cases Cited

Bowers v. Hardwick, 478 U.S. 186 (1986).
Coker v. Georgia, 433 U.S. 584 (1977).
Gregg v. Georgia, 428 U.S. 153 (1976).
Griswold v. Connecticut, 381 U.S. 479 (1965).
J.E.B. v. Alabama, 511 U.S. 127 1419 (1994).
Lawrence v. Texas, 539 U.S. 558 (2003).
Montana v. Egelhoff, 518 U.S. 37 (1996).
Papachristou et al. v. City of Jacksonville, 410 U.S. 156 (1972).
Powell v. Texas, 392 U.S. 514 (1968).
Rex v. Hadfield, 27 Howell's State Trials 1281 (1800).
Rex v. M'Naghten, 8 Eng. Rep. 718 (1843).
Robinson v. California, 370 U.S. 660 (1962).
Roe v. Wade, 410 U.S. 113 (1973).
Rummel v. Estelle, 445 U.S. 263 (1980).
Sherman v. U.S., 356 U.S. 369 (1958).
Tennessee v. Garner, 471 U.S. 1 (1984).
Texas v. Johnson, 491 U.S. 397 (1989).

CHAPTER 6

CRIMINAL PROCEDURE

Police officers in Wisconsin obtained information that Steiney Richards was selling large quantities of cocaine out of a hotel room. They obtained a search warrant for Richards's hotel room and went to execute it in the middle of the night. A police officer, dressed as a maintenance worker, knocked on Richards's door and asked to come in. Richards refused to admit the officer, and shut the door. The police then broke down the door and entered the room. They apprehended Richards and discovered a large amount of cocaine hidden in the ceiling of the bathroom. Richards was charged with drug possession.

At trial, Richards claimed the police entry of his hotel room without any notice of who they were or why there were there violated the Fourth Amendment, which prohibits "unreasonable" searches and seizures. He argued that the common law "knock and announce" rule requires police to give notice of their presence and purpose before entering a dwelling to conduct a search. The police in this case admitted they did not knock and announce, but argued the search was nonetheless reasonable because Richards was suspected of selling drugs and that experience indicated drug dealers were dangerous, so telling Richards they were police officers might cause him to try to harm them to prevent their entry into his hotel room. The Supreme Court has held that when police obtain evidence in violation of the Fourth Amendment, that evidence is inadmissible at trial. The trial court held that the police entry without notice was reasonable.

Richards appealed all the way to the United States Supreme Court. The Supreme Court noted that the common law knock and announce rule was part of the "reasonableness" requirement of the Fourth Amendment and that police must generally knock and announce before entering a dwelling to execute a search warrant. They refused to create a blanket exception to the knock and announce rule for drug search warrants for fear that doing so would essentially eliminate the knock and announce requirement in all drug cases, without proof that all drug dealers were inherently dangerous. In this case, they balanced the competing interests of law enforcement and civil liberties of citizens.

INTRODUCTION

Whereas the substantive criminal law we discussed in the previous chapter sets forth the appropriate behavior for all citizens, criminal procedure law discussed

135

in this chapter sets forth the appropriate behavior for agents of the state as they go about their business responding to criminal activity. Procedural rights are derived from the due process clause in the Fifth and Fourteenth Amendments. Due process is a tremendously important concept in American law. It is perhaps the single most powerful phrase in the law used to prevent governments from unjustly depriving individuals of liberty (remember the infamous *Code Louis*?). The primary purpose of procedural law is to implement this very important concept. Whereas criminal law sets forth the appropriate code of conduct for all citizens, criminal procedure comprises the rules that govern the manner in which the state may go about depriving an individual of his or her liberty. Balancing the rights of the individual and the authority of the state and its agents is a difficult but crucial process.

A question that concerns all democratic societies is how much authority to grant to the state vis-à-vis the individual citizen. Both the state and the individual, being imperfect entities, need controlling. Human nature being what it is, people will offend against one another to the overall detriment of the state, and power being what it is, the state will abuse it to the detriment of all within it. Social contract theory as enunciated by Thomas Hobbes and John Locke posits that by choosing to live among others, individuals give up some of their liberties and permit the state to intervene in their lives. But how much intervention and in what manner the state may do so are vital questions with which the courts have struggled over the centuries.

PURPOSE OF CRIMINAL PROCEDURE LAW

As we saw in chapter 2, there are two competing models of the criminal justice system—the due process and crime control models—and that the history of criminal procedural law has been a constant pendulum swing between these two models. Recall that the due process model is concerned primarily with the protection of individual privacy even at the expense of factually guilty parties occasionally evading justice. The due process model emphasizes the importance of the formal legal process as a means of ensuring mistakes are kept to a minimum, and it operates on the presumption of innocence. The underlying premise of this model is that truth at any price is too costly for liberty to endure. The crime control model primarily is concerned with the reduction of crime and the protection of public order. It emphasizes the use of discretion and police power as a means of quickly and efficiently investigating and screening cases, and it operates on the presumption that most likely a defendant is guilty.

Criminal procedure law attempts to balance the differing goals of these two models, but it is a zero-sum game: Granting the police greater power to investigate crime means reducing individual liberty and privacy, while increasing individual rights may result in suspects who are factually guilty going free because the state is unable to prove legal guilt beyond a reasonable doubt, the burden of proof in criminal cases. The words of the famed English legal scholar, Sir William Blackstone, sum up the primary sentiment shared by advocates of the due process model: "It is better that ten guilty persons escape, than that one innocent suffer."

SOURCES OF CRIMINAL PROCEDURE LAW

The legal foundation for most criminal procedural decisions is the U.S. Constitution, including the Bill of Rights and the Fourteenth Amendment. The Bill of Rights sets forth twenty-three individual rights, and the Fourteenth Amendment guarantee of "due process" has been interpreted by the U.S. Supreme Court to incorporate much of the Bill of Rights. As we pointed out in chapter 3, the Bill of Rights originally was conceived as applying only to the federal government; but during the twentieth century, the Supreme Court interpreted the due process clause of the Fourteenth Amendment as including, or incorporating, many of the individual rights contained in the Bill of Rights, thus making these rights applicable to the states. These include most of the procedural criminal provisions of the Fourth, Fifth, Sixth, and Eighth Amendments.

Other sources for criminal procedure law are state constitutions and federal and state statutes. States are free to provide more individual rights than the federal constitution, but states cannot deny or diminish any federal constitutional rights. In the past, states were seen as perhaps less protective of the rights of criminal suspects than the federal government, yet in the last two decades, a number of state courts have interpreted their state constitutions as providing greater protections of individual liberties than the federal government. To say that a piece of legislation passes constitutional muster is to say only that it passes minimal standards of fairness.

Other sources of criminal procedural law come from the provisions of the Bill of Rights, in particular the Fourth, Fifth, and Sixth Amendments. Courts frequently are asked to interpret the meaning of these amendments and to apply them to current fact situations. The Fifth Amendment prohibits compelling people to testify against themselves. But does requiring someone to take a Breathalyzer test or give a blood sample constitute testimony when the results may be used against him or her at trial? The Fourth Amendment prohibits the unreasonable seizure and search of persons, places, and effects, but what is an "effect"? And what is "unreasonable"? Courts must answer these questions to determine when the police have exceeded the scope of their authority, either intentionally or unintentionally.

The U.S. Supreme Court has the final word on the constitutionality of any state action that is challenged as violating a constitutional right. Consequently, much of criminal procedure law comes from Supreme Court decisions. As courts decide only the case before them, and do not issue policy directives, criminal procedure law has developed fitfully, on a case-by-case basis. Much of criminal procedural law has been written in the past fifty years since the Supreme Court began to apply the provisions of the Bill of Rights to the states, which conduct the bulk of criminal investigation and prosecution.

SEARCH AND SEIZURE LAW AND THE FOURTH AMENDMENT

Search and seizure law is governed in large part by the Fourth Amendment, which states that citizens have a right to be free from "unreasonable" searches and seizure and that warrants shall be issued only upon a showing of "probable cause." These two portions of the amendment sometimes are referred to as the reasonableness clause and the warrant clause (LaFave 1996).

The Warrant and Reasonableness Clauses

The warrant clause states that all warrants must be based on probable cause and must describe the place to be searched or the person to be seized with "particularity." *Particularity* means that the warrant must make clear on its face who or what is to be searched or seized, so as to limit the discretion of the police officer.

The Supreme Court has interpreted the reasonableness clause to allow searches without warrants, provided there exists both probable cause and an "exigent circumstance" (meaning a critical or urgent situation) that justifies the failure to obtain a warrant. These exigent circumstances, or exceptions to the warrant requirement, have been spelled out by the Court on a case-by-case basis and apply to a variety of situations (Amar 1994). Examples of such situations might be officers chasing a suspect into the suspect's home to apprehend him before he or she can initiate actions that might make an arrest more problematic, such as obtaining a weapon, building barricades, or destroying evidence.

Probable Cause

Probable cause exists when "the facts and circumstances within the officers' knowledge and of which they had reasonably trustworthy information are sufficient in themselves to warrant a man of reasonable caution in the belief that an offense has been committed" *(Brinegar v. United States* 1949). The Supreme Court has acknowledged that probable cause is a "fluid concept," meaning that it can ebb and flow to meet a variety of specific circumstances *(Illinois v. Gates* 1983). Probable cause does not require absolute certainty, or even a great likelihood—it is enough if there is a "fair probability" of criminal activity.

To compare, the burden of proof in a criminal trial is "beyond a reasonable doubt," which often is equated with near certainty, while the burden of proof in a civil trial is a preponderance of the evidence, which is simply more likely than not. While it is difficult to accurately quantify or precisely define the levels of proof (Hemmens, del Carmen, and Scarborough 1997), probable cause is similar to the "preponderance of the evidence" standard in civil trials and significantly less than what is necessary to obtain a criminal conviction.

ARREST

The Fourth Amendment prohibits unreasonable seizures. Seizure is a broader term than arrest, which does not encompass all detentions. *Seizure* involves the exercise of dominion or control by the police over a person or item. What standards determine when a detention has occurred? According to the Supreme Court, a *detention* occurs when a reasonable person, viewing the particular police conduct as a whole and within the setting of all the surrounding circumstances, would have concluded that the police in some way had restrained his or her liberty so that the person was not free to leave (*Michigan v. Chesternutt* 1988). Thus, in strictly legal terms, it is the perception of the detained individual, not the police officer that determines if a detention has occurred.

When an Officer May Arrest

Individuals may be arrested pursuant to an arrest warrant, or a police officer may arrest an individual without a warrant if the officer has probable cause to believe a criminal act has occurred. Warrantless arrests generally are allowed only for misdemeanors committed in the presence of the officer and for felonies either when the crime is committed in the presence of the officer or the arrest occurs outside a private dwelling. Police may not make a warrantless arrest in a private dwelling unless there are exigent circumstances or they have consent to enter (*Payton v. New York* 1980). This consent must be given by a person who has the legal authority to do so, such as a legal adult resident of the dwelling.

Manner of Arrest

Police officers may use whatever force is reasonable under the circumstances to make an arrest. Deadly force is permitted only when it is necessary to protect life. Deadly force may be used to prevent escape only if the officer has probable cause to believe the suspect poses an immediate threat of serious harm to the officer or others (*Tennessee v. Garner* 1985).

Police officers executing an arrest (or search) warrant at a private dwelling are required to "knock and announce" their presence and purpose and provide occupants of a dwelling a reasonable amount of time to answer the door. This common law principle has been endorsed by the U.S. Supreme Court, which also has indicated that the common law exceptions to the knock and announce rule apply (*Wilson v. Arkansas* 1995). These exceptions, or instances when the police may ignore the rule of announcement, are when there is reason to believe escape is likely, evidence will be destroyed, or officers may be injured if notice is given (Hemmens 1997).

Types of Seizures

Police may ask questions of anyone in public, and doing so does not constitute an arrest or even a seizure. In such "on-the-street encounters," citizens remain free to leave and even ignore the police officer's question. While doing so may arouse suspicion and/or resentment, it does not create probable cause for an arrest.

Some encounters with the police do not rise to the level of an arrest but are more intrusive than mere on-the-street encounters. These types of detentions, sometime characterized as "seizure tantamount to arrest," do not require probable cause but do require more than mere suspicion. These encounters are classified as seizures but not full arrests. Examples include traffic stops, border searches for drug couriers, and stop and frisks on the street (LaFave 1996).

Stop and Frisk

A "stop and frisk" involves a police officer stopping people in public and questioning them as to their identity and activity, followed in some circumstances by a limited "pat-down" search of their outer clothing. Stop and frisk procedures were endorsed by the U. S. Supreme Court in *Terry v. Ohio* (1968) and sometimes are referred to as "Terry stops" or "investigative detentions." In *Terry*, the Court attempted to balance the interests of law enforcement with individual rights in situations where police do not have probable cause to arrest but do possess some inkling of criminal activity based on the intuition they develop from years of experiences. This level of proof has been referred to by the Court as "reasonable suspicion." This level of proof has been defined by the Supreme Court as "a less demanding standard than probable cause . . . that can be established with information that is different in quantity or content . . . [and it] can arise from information that is less reliable" (*Alabama v. White* 1990).

While a stop and frisk is not an arrest, it is a form of search and seizure. Consequently, the Fourth Amendment does apply. As the stop is not an arrest, and the frisk is not a full search, the Court has determined that probable cause is not necessary. Rather, all that is needed is "reasonable suspicion." There are two distinct parts of the encounter—the stop and the frisk.

To stop an individual, a police officer must have reasonable suspicion, in light of his or her experience, that a crime has occurred or is about to occur. Such an "investigatory stop" must be temporary and no longer than necessary under the circumstances to achieve its purpose. Police officers may ask questions intended to dispel any suspicions and alleviate any fears they may have during these investigatory stops.

A frisk does not automatically follow from a stop. If, and only if, the investigatory stop does not allay an officer's reasonable fear about his or her safety or the safety of others, then the officer may conduct a frisk of the detained individual. The Supreme Court has made clear that the sole purpose of a frisk is for the protection of the officer. It is not meant to be a fishing expedition to ferret out evidence of criminal activity. The frisk itself is defined as a pat-down of the suspect's outer clothing. Any object that the officer reasonably believes may be a weapon may be properly seized and may provide probable cause for arrest on the charge of carrying a concealed weapon. The Supreme Court has referred to this as the plain feel doctrine (*Minnesota v. Dickerson* 1993). If the object is not a weapon but rather something that is typically used in the commission of some crime (e.g., burglary tools), the item would be admissible evidence of attempted burglary. Officers may not, however, manipulate items they feel in or under the outer clothing in an attempt to discern what those items are when they are plainly not weapons. If an officer seizes contraband without following these guidelines, the contraband cannot be used as evidence at trial. The officer does not have to return the contraband to the suspect, however, but instead may keep it and turn it over to his or her superior officer.

Vehicle Stops

Vehicles, by virtue of their mobility, present a particularly difficult situation for both law enforcement and the courts. A seizure occurs every time a vehicle is stopped, even if the purpose of the stop is limited (*Delaware v. Prouse* 1979). While every vehicle stop is a seizure, not every seizure of a vehicle necessitates either probable cause or a warrant because the nature of most routine traffic stops is not very intrusive. Generally, police must have at least reasonable suspicion of criminal activity to stop a vehicle. Exceptions are roadblocks to check for drunk driving or illegal aliens and to check licenses and registration papers. In these instances, the Supreme Court has allowed police to stop cars absent any individualized suspicion of wrongdoing and justified this determination by balancing the "slight" intrusion of the stop against the public interest served by the seizure (*Michigan Department of State Police v. Sitz* 1990).

Once an officer has stopped a vehicle, he or she is authorized to ask the driver to exit the vehicle. This is true even if the stop is for a minor traffic violation. Additionally, if the officer reasonably fears for his or her safety after the driver has exited the vehicle, the officer may conduct a frisk for weapons (*Pennsylvania v. Mimms* 1977). Additionally, officers may order passengers out of the vehicle as well, even when there is absolutely no indication of wrongdoing on the part of the passenger (*Maryland v. Wilson* 1997). The officer also may request vehicle registration and other licensing documents, examine the vehicle identification number, and ask questions of both the driver and occupants. If a person legally stopped by a police officer refuses to identify himself or herself, that person may be arrested. The officer also may seek consent to search the vehicle without informing the driver that the initial stop is over and the driver is free to leave (*Ohio v. Robinette* 1997).

SEARCHES

A search is the examination of an individual's house, person, or effects to discover items related to criminal activity. *Effects* include papers, cars, and other like items. Items sought may include contraband, fruits of the crime, instrumentalities of the crime such as weapons, burglar's tools, or the getaway car, or evidence of the crime. The Fourth Amendment only applies to areas where persons have a reasonable expectation of privacy such as in a person's home; Fourth Amendment rights do not generally apply with the same force in public locations because people have a lesser expectation of privacy in public (*Katz v. United States* 1967).

Reasonable Expectation of Privacy

The concept of "reasonable expectation of privacy" is a relatively recent addition to criminal procedural law. Until the *Katz* decision in 1967, courts seeking to determine when a "search" had occurred focused on whether police conduct infringed on a property interest (meaning an area afforded constitutional protection). If so, then the police conduct constituted a search and the protections of the Fourth Amendment applied. The decision in *Katz* abandoned the focus on property interests in favor of a consideration of the expectation of privacy the individual and society had in a given situation.

A "reasonable expectation of privacy" has subjective and objective components: (1) the subject of the search must have a subjective expectation of privacy, and (2) society must view that expectation as reasonable.

Exceptions to the Search Warrant Requirement

Search Incident to Arrest

While police are generally required to obtain a search warrant, the Supreme Court has held that a variety of exigent circumstances justify a warrantless search. There are also several actions that are not considered searches so that the Fourth Amendment does not apply. These exceptions have been developed by the Supreme Court on a case-by-case basis. Each is discussed in turn.

Police officers executing a valid arrest of a suspect may conduct a full search both of the suspect and of the area within the suspect's immediate control (*Chimel v. California* 1969). This search must occur at the same time as the arrest. The scope of the search includes anywhere on the person and the "lunge area," or immediate vicinity of the suspect. For instance, police arresting someone in a house may search the room in which the arrest occurs, but cannot, under the search incident to arrest exception, search other rooms in the house.

The justifications for this exception include officer safety, prevention of evidence destruction, and prevention of escape. The search incident exception applies to all custodial arrests regardless of the severity of the offense for which the person is being arrested. So long as the person is being taken into custody, a search incident may be performed. The exception does not apply to situations such as traffic stops, which are detentions but in which no arrest occurs.

Consent

If police obtain an individual's consent to search, there is no need for probable cause or a search warrant. A search conducted pursuant to consent is not a search for Fourth Amendment purposes—that is, the Fourth Amendment simply does not apply. Police may ask anyone for consent to search without any basis for doing so. However, there are some limitations on consent searches. First, consent must be both voluntary and intelligent. That is, the police must demonstrate that a suspect's consent was not obtained as the result of coercion or force and that the suspect knew what he or she was doing. Police are not required to inform suspects of their right to refuse consent, however. Second, consent may be limited to a particular area or time and may be withdrawn at any time. Third, valid consent to search may be obtained only from a person with the apparent authority to consent, such as the owner and resident (not absent landlord) of a home or driver of a car (Hemmens and Maahs 1996).

For a long time, the courts had applied the so-called co-occupant consent rule. This rule meant that warrantless searches could be conducted and contraband seized belonging to a resident of a home who was someone other than the person granting consent if the person granting consent was an adult validly residing in the home. This rule was overturned by the Supreme Court in *Georgia v. Randolph* (2006) in which it ruled that a co-occupant could not give consent to search over the objections of another co-occupant who is present. The *Randolph* decision was narrowly scripted on the physical presence of a co-occupant who is objecting to the search. It does not necessarily apply to a co-occupant who is absent from the premises at the time his or her co-resident grants consent.

Vehicles

The Supreme Court has ruled that the inherent mobility of vehicles eliminates the necessity of obtaining a search warrant in many instances (*Carroll v. United States* 1925). The Court also has noted that there is a lessened expectation of privacy in a vehicle that is in public. While the warrant requirement is relaxed, the probable cause requirement is not. To search a vehicle without a warrant, the police must be able to (1) demonstrate that there exists probable cause to search and (2) establish that the vehicle is mobile. This mobility creates the exigency justifying relaxation of the warrant requirement.

When a police officer arrests the driver of a car, he or she may conduct a warrantless search of the passenger compartment of the car, including any containers, which reasonably may hold a weapon or evidence of the crime for which the driver has been arrested. "Container" means any item capable of holding something, including luggage, boxes, bags, and the glove compartment or other like receptacles (*New York v. Belton* 1981). However, officers cannot search any person in the passenger compartment other than the person or persons being arrested. The passenger compartment includes the entire interior of the car, but excludes the trunk and engine compartment (if these are not readily accessible from the passenger compartment).

This search may be conducted after the officer has placed the driver in the police cruiser for transport to the police station (*Chimel v. California* 1969). This rule applies to all custodial arrests, regardless of the nature of the offense. It does not apply to traffic stops or other detentions in which the driver is not being taken into custody. If, however, the police observe contraband or other evidence in the passenger compartment during a lawful traffic stop, the item may be seized under the plain view doctrine (see next section).

Many police departments as a matter of policy impound and/or inventory vehicles after the driver is arrested. This procedure is intended to protect the property of the arrestee as well as the department from lawsuits alleging theft of personal property within the vehicle. The Supreme Court has upheld warrantless inventory searches so long as they are routinely conducted by the department and not done as a pretext to search for evidence or contraband (*Florida v. Wells* 1990). The Court also has upheld warrantless searches conducted of impounded vehicles, even when the driver has not been arrested (*South Dakota v. Opperman* 1976).

Because a person traveling on a public roadway does not have a reasonable expectation of privacy, surveillance, including the installation of electronic tracking devices, is permissible. Monitoring of these devices is not permissible when the vehicle is in a private dwelling, however, as there is a heightened expectation of privacy in a dwelling or on private property (*United States v. Karo* 1984).

Plain View

According to the plain view doctrine, objects are subject to seizure if they are in the plain view of an officer who has a legal right to be in a position to see them (*Harris v. United States* 1968). The plain view doctrine is not actually an exception to the Fourth Amendment but rather another instance in which the protections of that amendment simply do not apply—when officers lawfully observe something, they are not conducting a "search" for Fourth Amendment purposes. Hence, no warrant or probable cause is required. The Supreme Court at one time suggested such observations must be "inadvertent" (accidental rather than purposeful) but has retreated from that requirement (*Horton v. California* 1990).

The plain view doctrine is just that—it is limited to seizure of items an officer sees. It does not apply to items discovered by touch, smell, or any other of the senses. Evidence discovered by the other senses may be admitted under one of the other exceptions to the warrant requirement. For instance, if an officer smells evidence of a methamphetamine being cooked in someone's house, he or she must obtain a warrant to search for the methamphetamine the officer knows to be there on the basis of olfactory evidence. The meth lab was not in plain view and therefore, could not be seized in the absence of a warrant. In addition, police may use tools that aid them in their observation, such as a flashlight (*Texas v. Brown* 1983). Furthermore, the officer must be lawfully present at the spot where he or she observes the item. If an officer enters a dwelling illegally, the officer may not take advantage of the plain view doctrine. Finally, it must be "immediately apparent" that the item observed is seizable, either as contraband, evidence of a crime, or as the fruits of a crime (*Arizona v. Hicks* 1987).

Open Fields

Certain areas outside the home are classified as "open fields." Items in "open fields" do not fall under the protection of the Fourth Amendment, as they are not "house, papers and effects" (*Hester v. United States* 1924). As with items in plain view, items in open fields may be seized without a warrant or probable cause. Unlike the plain view doctrine, police need not be lawfully in an area considered open fields to seize an item observed there—under this doctrine, officers may seize and use in court evidence they obtain while trespassing.

"Open fields" is a misleading term, as these areas literally need not be either open or a field. Rather, *open fields* simply refers to everything that is *not* defined as being within the curtilage. *Curtilage* is the land and buildings immediately surrounding and intimately associated with a dwelling. These include fenced areas incorporating the house, garages, and other buildings used primarily for domestic purposes, such as a shop or washroom. Curtilage is, essentially, an extension of the home. Any land that is deemed outside of the curtilage is "open fields." This doctrine applies to fields, forests, and other land formations equally (LaFave 1996). While the curtilage is considered protected by the Fourth Amendment, it does not receive the level of protection afforded the interior of the home. The Supreme Court has permitted aerial surveillance of the curtilage on the theory that there is not the same expectation of privacy in the curtilage as inside the home (*California v. Ciraolo* 1986).

Abandoned Property

Abandoned property is not protected by the Fourth Amendment, as the person abandoning it has evinced a willingness to give up control and dominion of the item. It belongs to no one. Consequently, abandoned property may be seized without a warrant or probable cause. The key is determining when abandonment has occurred. This depends on where the item is discarded and the intent of the person discarding the item.

Intent to abandon may be inferred from the manner in which the item is discarded. Items tossed to the ground accompanied by a statement such as "I don't want this" clearly have been abandoned, as have items left behind and not retrieved for a substantial period of time. Intent to abandon also may be inferred from the location of the abandonment. A textbook left behind in a classroom may have been abandoned, but it is unclear without further information. Items thrown in the trash in public are considered abandoned, but items thrown in the trash on private property are not considered abandoned until the trash is placed outside the curtilage of the home for regular collection (*California v. Greenwood* 1988).

Special Needs of Law Enforcement

This exception is actually a series of exceptions to the search warrant requirement. It is applied in cases that are a mixture of criminal investigation and conduct by other public agencies not related to the police. Examples include searches of students by school authorities, searches of closely regulated businesses, and searches of probationers and parolees. In these instances, the Court has held that searches may be conducted both without a warrant and on less than probable cause and without individualized suspicion (such as having focused suspicion on a particular individual).

Because individuals on probation or parole waive their Fourth Amendment search or seizure rights, probation and parole officers may conduct searches at any time without a warrant and without the probable cause needed by police officers. However, the Supreme Court has stated that if a probation order is written in such a way that provides for submission to a search "by a probation officer or any other law enforcement officer," then the police gain the same rights to conduct warrantless searches and searches based on less than probable cause as probation and parole officers (*United States v. Knights* 2001).

Figure 6.1 Flow of Procedural Reasoning in Search and Seizure

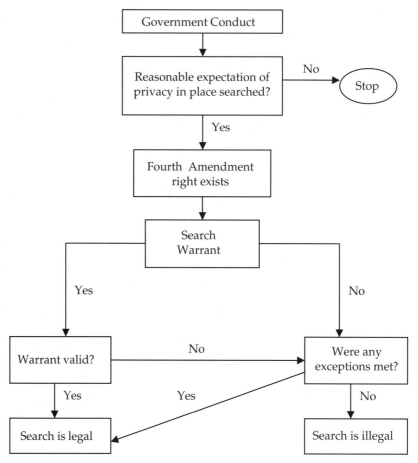

Figure provided by Professor Michael Bogner, Justice Studies Department, Chadron State College (2006).

The justification for such searches varies according to the subject of the search, but they have in common the Court's willingness to balance the limited intrusion on individual rights against the heightened public interest in the subject (such as school security and product safety), with the governmental interest outweighing the principle of *de minimis* (literally, *the least*), or negligible, intrusion on individual liberty (Stuntz 1992).

Figure 6.1 shows the flow of procedural reasoning expected in search and seizure cases. Stage 1 consists of asking if a reasonable expectation of privacy exists, and Stage 2 asks if warrant requirements were met.

RIGHT TO THE ASSISTANCE OF COUNSEL

Procedural law would be a pretty empty exercise in rhetoric if there was no mechanism in place for assuring that it is followed. Accused individuals who are knowledgeable about the nature and extent of their rights and who are competent enough to assert and protect them are few and far between. This is why the right to the assistance of legal counsel is specifically enumerated in the Sixth Amendment. This right was long interpreted as a prohibition against the government denying defendants who wanted and could afford the services of a lawyer to assist them in their defense rather than as an affirmative right.

Starting in the 1930s, the Court started to expand the meaning of the assistance clause to its present form in *Powell v. Alabama* (1932). Powell and eight other black youths were charged with raping two white girls. No defense attorney was assigned to the case until the day of the trial, which took place only twelve days after the boys' arrest. The so-called Scottsboro boys were represented by Stephen Roddy and Milo Moody. According to Linder (2006, 1), "Roddy was an unpaid and unprepared Chattanooga real estate attorney who, on the first day of trial, was so stewed he could hardly walk straight. Moody was a forgetful seventy-year-old local attorney who hadn't tried a case in decades." Eight of the nine youths were convicted and sentenced to death; the ninth, a twelve-year-old boy, was sentenced to life imprisonment.

The case eventually reached the Supreme Court on the basis that the youths were effectively denied their liberty interests by virtue of receiving essentially no legal assistance at trial. The Supreme Court reversed their convictions on Fourteenth Amendment due process grounds because at the time, the Sixth Amendment and its attending rights did not apply to state proceedings since the Sixth Amendment had not been incorporated (Hemmens, Worrall, and Thompson 2004). *Powell* held that due process requires the appointment at government expense of defense attorneys for indigent defendants facing capital charges. Although *Powell* was limited to death penalty cases, it provided the groundwork for extending the right to counsel for all indigent defendants facing serious felony charges in federal courts (*Johnson v. Zerbst* 1938).

The *Johnson* ruling was not made applicable to the states, although by this time many states did provide the right to legal counsel for indigent defendants. In *Gideon v. Wainwright* (1963), the Supreme Court ruled that the right to counsel was so fundamental to the American system of justice that it should be applied to the states based squarely on the Sixth Amendment.

Gideon was charged with burglary, and he requested that an attorney be appointed to assist him in his defense because he was indigent. The trial court refused his request, stating that Florida law only required the appointment of government-funded lawyers to indigent defendants potentially facing the death penalty. The Supreme Court remanded the case stating that "any person haled [sic] into court, who is too poor to hire a lawyer, cannot be assured of a fair trial unless counsel is provided for him." Gideon was acquitted at retrial, where he was represented by a competent lawyer.

To further clarify the circumstances under which an accused indigent defendant has the right to government-provided counsel, the Supreme Court seized on *Argersinger v. Hamlin* (1972). Indigent defendant Argersinger was convicted in Florida of carrying a concealed weapon (a misdemeanor), without the assistance of counsel, and sentenced to ninety days in jail. On vacating Argersinger's conviction, the Court established that any indigent defendant facing incarceration for a felony or a misdemeanor must be represented by counsel.

RIGHT TO COUNSEL DURING INTERROGATIONS AND PRETRIAL IDENTIFICATION PROCEDURES

One of the most important sources of evidence in a criminal investigation is the suspect. A significant number of cases are solved through obtaining a confession from the suspect; many others are solved in large part through the use of eye-witness identifications of the perpetrator. While the Fourth Amendment governs most search and seizure situations, it is the Fifth and Sixth Amendments that regulate situations involving interrogation of criminal suspects and identification procedures.

The Fifth Amendment provides that persons shall not be compelled to incriminate themselves. While self-incrimination cannot be compelled, it is permitted. The standard for admissibility of a confession has historically been voluntariness. Precisely what constituted a voluntary statement has developed over the years. The Supreme Court has determined that police use of physical force to obtain a confession rendered it involuntary. Later, the Court declared involuntary those confessions obtained after extended interrogation in isolation and those obtained through the use of mental coercion. In 1964, the Court held that a criminal defendant had a right to counsel once the police investigation "is no longer a general inquiry, but has begun to focus on the defendant" (*Escobedo v. Illinois* 1964).

Two years later, in *Miranda v. Arizona* (1966), the Supreme Court held that evidence obtained by the police during a custodial interrogation of a suspect could not be used at trial unless the suspect first was informed of both his privilege against self-incrimination and his right to counsel. *Miranda* is probably the most controversial criminal procedure decision ever handed down by the Supreme Court, in part because police feared it would lead to a dramatic reduction in confessions and because the decision went beyond just declaring one particular police practice unconstitutional.

The Court did not merely hold that police must inform suspects of their rights, the Court set forth exactly what the police should say: suspects must be told (1) that they have a right to remain silent, (2) that anything they say can be used against them in court, (3) that they have a right to have an attorney present during questioning, and (4) that if they cannot afford an attorney, one will be appointed for them prior to any questioning. Any person subject to custodial interrogation is entitled to the so-called *Miranda* warning.

Custody

Miranda warnings are required when there is a custodial interrogation. Custody has been defined as when the suspect "has been subjected to a formal arrest or equivalent restraints on his freedom of movement" (*California v. Beheler* 1983). It is fairly obvious when a full arrest has occurred. The more difficult situation is determining when a person has been deprived of his or her freedom in a significant way. The test is whether a reasonable person in the suspect's position would conclude that he or she is not free to leave. Factors considered by the courts in this determination include the actions of the police, the location of the encounter, and the time of the encounter.

Interrogation

Miranda warnings are not triggered by custody alone, however. The warnings are required only when there is both custody and interrogation. What then, is interrogation? Interrogation occurs (1) when police are asking questions the answers to which may incriminate and (2) in circumstances in which the police, through their actions, create the "functional equivalent" of an interrogation. The police create the functional equivalent of an interrogation when they engage in activity they "should know is reasonably likely to evoke an incriminating response from a suspect" (*Rhode Island v. Innis*, 1980).

Figure 6.2 summarizes the major cases in the evolution of the right to the assistance of counsel.

Circumstances in Which *Miranda* Is Not Required

There are a number of situations in which *Miranda* warnings need not be given. If there is not both custody and interrogation, *Miranda* warnings are not required. Examples of situations the Court has held do not constitute custody include routine traffic stops (*Berkemer v. McCarty* 1984), and sobriety checkpoints (*Michigan State Police v. Sitz* 1990). Examples of situations the Court has held do not constitute interrogation include conversations between two officers in the vicinity of the suspect, situations where someone volunteers a statement without prompting, routine questioning of persons at the scene of a crime, questions intended to clarify an ambiguous response, questions that are part of a stop and frisk, and when there is a threat to public safety (*New York v. Quarles* 1984).

Extension and Application of the *Miranda* Warnings

The Supreme Court has decided a number of cases involving the *Miranda* warnings. The Court has held that once suspects have invoked their right to remain

Figure 6.2 Summary of Steps in the Evolution of the Right to the Assistance of Counsel

Powell v. Alabama (1932) Indigent defendants have right to free counsel in capital cases.	Johnson v. Zerbst (1938) Indigent defendants charged with serious felonies in federal courts have right to free counsel.	Gideon v. Wainwright (1963) Sixth Amendment applied to the states. Indigent defendants have right to free counsel in all felony cases.
Argersinger v. Hamlin (1972) Indigent defendants have right to free counsel in misdemeanor cases as well as felony cases if facing incarceration.	Escobedo v. Illinois (1964) Suspects have right to counsel when the police cease making general inquiries and focus on a particular individual.	Miranda v. Arizona (1966) Suspects must be informed of right to counsel, as well as other rights, before custodial interrogation.

silent, until they meet with a lawyer, police may not question them further unless the suspects initiate further communication (*Edwards v. Arizona* 1981). The Court also has held that once suspects invoke their right to counsel, they may not be questioned about any other offense unrelated to the offense for which they were arrested and about which they have asserted their right to remain silent (*Arizona v. Roberson* 1988). While these decisions clarify and extend *Miranda*, most of the decisions have restricted the reach of *Miranda* as originally interpreted.

The failure of the police to inform a suspect that an attorney, retained for him or her without his or her knowledge by a family member, was attempting to reach him or her does not invalidate a confession obtained by the police because the suspect did not know he or she had a lawyer (*Moran v. Burbine* 1986). Police posing as an inmate need not provide *Miranda* warnings to a suspect in jail before asking him or her incriminating questions because the location where the questioning is taking place is assumed to have no coercive atmosphere (*Illinois v. Perkins* 1990).

Requesting a lawyer at a bail hearing is not considered an invocation of the right to counsel for crimes with which the suspect had not yet been charged because the request is construed as limited to the Sixth Amendment right to counsel at trial, not as an invocation of the Fifth Amendment right to counsel prior to questioning (*McNeil v. Wisconsin* 1991). If police obtain a voluntary, but unwarned, confession, they may remedy any possible problems with the confession by giving proper *Miranda* warnings and obtaining a waiver of rights signed by the suspect and then obtain the confession again, even though the suspect may not realize the initial confession was inadmissible (*Oregon v. Elstad* 1985).

An illegally obtained confession also may be admitted at trial if it is used solely to impeach the testimony of the defendant (*Harris v. New York* 1971). In other words, if during a trial, a defendant asserts his or her innocence, an illegally obtained confession in which the defendant admitted guilt may be used as evidence that the defendant's trial testimony is not to be trusted. However, it may not be used as evidence of the defendant's guilt.

Finally, the rights mentioned in the *Miranda* warnings may be waived by the suspect so long as the written waiver is "knowing, intelligent, and voluntary," meaning that the suspect is fully informed and understands the possible consequences of waiving his or her rights and does so free of any form of coercion in the form of threats or promises.

Pretrial Identification Procedures

Police long have acknowledged that a pretrial confrontation of a criminal suspect and the witness is both a common and effective investigatory tool. Eyewitness identifications are notoriously unreliable, however, and the Supreme Court has held that a criminal defendant has a right to counsel not only at trial but at any "critical stage" in the criminal proceedings. Reconciling the competing interests of individual liberty and crime investigation has led to some unusual results in this area. According to two decisions, decided five years apart, the Supreme Court held that a suspect has a right to counsel at a lineup if it occurs after criminal charges have been filed (*United States v. Wade* 1967) but that no right to counsel exists if the lineup takes place prior to charges being filed (*Kirby v. Illinois* 1972). The rationale for providing the right to counsel at a postindictment lineup is that such an event now constitutes a "critical stage" in the prosecution. Because there is the potential for prejudicial error at such events, a lawyer can help to make sure the procedure is conducted properly and, if it is not, the defendant has a record by which to challenge the identification procedure at trial (Grano 1974).

THE CONFRONTATION OF WITNESSES CLAUSE

The confrontation clause in the Sixth Amendment states that the accused has the right "to be confronted with the witnesses against him," that is, to challenge via cross-examination any witnesses hostile to him or her. This affords the defense the opportunity to test the credibility of hostile witnesses and prevents the use of hearsay statements made outside of the courtroom (*ex parte* evidence). Ex parte absent witness statements are common in civil law but prohibited in criminal trials.

The right to confrontation was the issue in *Pointer v. Texas* (1965). Pointer and a codefendant were arrested and charged with the robbery with violence of one Kenneth Phillips. During the course of the proceedings, Phillips left Texas and indicated that he would not return. During the trial, the state offered Phillips's written testimony into evidence, to which the defense objected on the grounds that it was being denied the opportunity to confront Phillips. The judge overruled, stating that the defense had the opportunity to confront at the preliminary hearing. Pointer was convicted and the Texas Court of Appeals affirmed. The U.S. Supreme Court disagreed, however, when it remanded the case and made the confrontation clause obligatory on the states.

The Court further clarified (some would say "further muddied") the interpretation of the clause in *Crawford v. Washington* (2004). Crawford had stabbed one Kenneth Lee during an argument. Both Crawford and his wife, Sylvia, corroborated each other's story initially, but in a second interview, Sylvia's statement differed as to her husband's self-defense claim. During the trial, Crawford invoked his marital exception privilege, which prevented Sylvia from testifying at the trial, but the state was allowed to introduce her *ex parte* statements into evidence because of the "unavailability" of the witness. Crawford was convicted of assault with a deadly weapon and the Washington Supreme Court affirmed.

The U.S. Supreme Court reversed his conviction, declaring that statements of absent witnesses may be admitted only when the witness is unavailable (which Sylvia was if the marital exception rule is to be honored) or if the defense had prior opportunity to cross-examine (recall that in *Pointer*, the Court brushed aside the fact that the defense had had such an opportunity). The Court ruled that "unavailable" should be read to mean that the witness is "demonstrably unable to testify in person."

The confrontation clause does not absolutely guarantee the right to face-to-face confrontation at trial even if the hostile witness is fully capable of being there.

The right can be denied when denial serves an important policy and where reliability is otherwise assured. An example of this would be in cases involving the sexual molestation of very young children where the children's testimony is corroborated by an examining physician or social worker following strict procedural guidelines.

THE RIGHT TO COMPULSORY PROCESS CLAUSE

This clause of the Sixth Amendment indicated that accused persons have the right "to have compulsory process for obtaining witnesses in his favor." This right essentially means that defendants have the right to compel favorable witnesses to appear in court to testify on their behalf. One of the purposes of the discovery process (the procedure in which there is the reciprocal obligation of the prosecution and the defense to allow the other side to "discover" the strength of each other's cases and to inspect and copy items relevant to the case) is to uncover potentially favorable witnesses. These witnesses are then summoned to court via a subpoena, which is a written order issued by a judicial officer to appear in court at a designated time and to bring any relevant documentation or other evidence as may be required.

To obtain compulsory process, the defendant must show the relevance of the proposed witness's testimony and/or evidence and that such testimony would not be cumulative, that is, prove the same point already in evidence over and over again. An example of this would be to call multiple witnesses to testify that the defendant was at a party when the crime occurred. Note that cumulative evidence is not the same as corroborating evidence. Corroborating evidence is evidence used to prove the same general point but which comes from a separate source that strengthens, adds to, or confirms evidence already existing.

The compulsory process clause was made applicable to the states in *Washington v. Texas* (1967). In this case, Jackie Washington and Charles Fuller were convicted of murder. Fuller was tried first, and Washington sought to secure Fuller's testimony, which he claimed was vital for his defense. Texas statutes prevented a coparticipant in a crime from testifying for the defense (but not for the prosecution). Washington's conviction ensued and was upheld on appeal.

In reversing and remanding, the Court stated that the state had arbitrarily denied Washington "the right to put on the stand a witness who was physically and mentally capable of testifying to events that he had personally observed, and whose testimony would have been relative and material to the defense."

THE EXCLUSIONARY RULE

The exclusionary rule provides that any evidence obtained by the government in violation of the Fourth Amendment guarantee against unreasonable searches and seizures is not admissible in a criminal trial for the purpose of proving guilt. It is a judicially created remedy for violations of the Fourth Amendment, not a rule logically derived from the Fourth Amendment. The rule, the reason for its existence, the method and scope of its implementation, its social consequences, and the exceptions to it have all been the subjects of fiery legal debate from its beginnings. Opponents of the rule feel it absurd to throw out valid evidence because of the way it was obtained. For instance, two vocal opponents of the rule estimate that 150,000 criminal cases, including 30,000 violent cases, are dismissed or dropped annually in the United States due to the inadmissibility of clearly probative evidence in accordance with the demands of the rule (Meese and DeHart 1997). On the other hand, proponents feel that without a means of enforcing the Fourth Amendment guarantee, the amendment is reduced to a "form of words," as Justice Clark said in *Mapp v. Ohio* (1961).

ADVANCING TOWARD THE EXCLUSIONARY RULE

The first hint of something like an exclusionary rule from the Supreme Court came in *Boyd v. United States* (1886). This case involved the compulsory production of some business papers that revealed a conspiracy to defraud the customs revenue service, rather than a search and seizure, although the Court likened it to one. Boyd's conviction was overturned and the case remanded to the lower courts where the evidence provided by Boyd's papers was to be excluded. The Court reasoned that Boyd had been compelled to be a witness against himself (by being forced to produce the papers in question) based on the prohibition of such in the Fifth Amendment.

In *Adams v. New York* (1904) the plaintiff was arrested for possessing illegal lottery tickets and relied on *Boyd* to have his conviction overturned. The Supreme Court held that the circumstances of *Boyd* did not apply and stated that the fact that the materials were seized illegally "is no legal objection to the admission of the evidence." The Court further stated that how the evidence was obtained was a collateral matter for which the trespasser (the arresting officer) "may be held responsible civilly, and perhaps criminally, but his testimony is not thereby rendered incompetent." In their decision, the Court upheld the guiding principle of the common law that "evidence is evidence, is evidence." This is still the guiding principle in most other common law systems in which the judiciary is reluctant to police the police, considering such action to be an unwarranted intrusion into the business of a separate branch of government. Unlike American judges who today *must* exclude illegally obtained evidence (with the exceptions noted later), judges in these countries have discretionary power to exclude evidence obtained under questionable circumstances. However, it is not usual for them to do so since they apparently feel, in common with the Justices in *Adams*, that other remedies would best serve the interests of justice (Reichel 2005).

Boyd came up again in *Weeks v. United States* (1914). Fremont Weeks had been convicted on the basis of evidence (like *Adams*, the evidence related to illegal lotteries as well as seizing a number of private items) seized in two warrantless searches of his home and sought to have his conviction overturned. On this occasion, the unanimous decision of the Court held that the evidence seized in an illegal manner should have been excluded by the trial court and remanded the case back. Thus, the contentious exclusionary rule was born.

However, the exclusionary rule only applied to evidence illegally obtained by federal law enforcement officers for use in federal criminal prosecutions. Because of this limitation, state law enforcement officers were still free to seize evidence illegally without fear of its exclusion in state criminal proceedings. Additionally, evidence seized illegally by state police could be turned over to federal law enforcement officers for use in federal prosecutions, as the federal law enforcement officers were not directly involved in the illegal seizure. The fruits of illegal activities of federal officers could likewise be turned over to state law enforcement for prosecution. This was known as the "silver platter" doctrine, meaning that evidence was simply being given to law enforcement agencies unencumbered by the rule (LaFave 1996).

An offspring doctrine of the exclusionary rule that further aggravated its critics is known as the *fruit of the poisonous tree*. This metaphorical phrase denotes that as probative evidence discovered by way of an illegal search, arrest, or interrogation is inadmissible because of the exclusionary rule, any later evidence derived from any of these illegal procedures must also be excluded. For instance, if Jack is interrogated illegally and on the basis of that illegal interrogation officers obtain a warrant to search his home and there find incriminating evidence, that evidence is inadmissible even though the search was conducted with a valid warrant. The idea behind the concept is that if the tree (the original illegality) is "poisoned," then the fruit (subsequent evidence derived from it) is "tainted" (*Nardone v. United States* 1939). As with the exclusionary rule itself, this rule only applied at the time to the federal courts.

The next important case in the evolution of the exclusionary rule was *Wolf v. Colorado* (1949). Julius Wolf, a practicing physician, was convicted of performing illegal abortions on the basis of evidence taken from his office in a warrantless search. In *Wolf*, the Supreme Court applied the Fourth Amendment against the states, incorporating it into the Fourteenth Amendment. However, the Court refused to apply the remedy of the exclusionary rule, leaving the enforcement of the Fourth Amendment up to the individual states. Thus Wolf's conviction was affirmed.

Twelve years later, in *Mapp v. Ohio* (1961), the Court took the step it failed to take in *Wolf* and applied the exclusionary rule to the states. The home of Dollree Mapp had been searched without a search warrant because she was suspected of harboring a bombing suspect. The police did not find the suspect, but they did find a number of pornographic materials in a trunk, and she was arrested, convicted, and imprisoned. Curiously, she appealed her conviction primarily on her First Amendment rights to free expression, but the Court brushed this issue aside in favor of her Fourth Amendment rights. The Court reversed her conviction and applied the exclusionary rule to the states because it acknowledged the states had failed to provide adequate remedies for Fourth Amendment violations committed by state police officers.

The Court also stated that the exclusionary rule is designed to serve at least two purposes: the deterrence of police misconduct and the protection of judicial integrity. In recent years, however, the Court has emphasized almost exclusively the deterrence of police misconduct, leading to the creation of several exceptions to the rule. While courts and commentators have suggested there are alternate means of enforcing the Fourth Amendment, such as civil suits for damages, criminal prosecutions of police engaged in illegal activity, and administrative sanctions, the Supreme Court concluded in *Mapp* that these means of enforcing the Fourth Amendment were ineffectual. Note that the term "illegal" in this context does not necessarily mean a criminal act; rather, it usually means a violation (knowingly or unknowingly) of some constitutional procedural rule.

Curtailing the Exclusionary Rule

As previously noted, the exclusionary rule has been severely criticized by a number of courts and commentators. Prior to its application to the states in *Mapp*, Justice Cardozo voiced the most quoted critical opinion of it in *People v. Defoe* (1926): "There has been no blinking at the consequences [of applying the exclusionary rule]. The criminal is to go free because the constable blundered." Despite its many critics over the years, the exclusionary rule has not been overruled. However, the Supreme Court has carved out several exceptions to the rule over the years and has held that there are a number of proceedings in which the exclusionary rule does not apply.

Proceedings in Which the Exclusionary Rule Is Not Used

Both the *Weeks* and *Mapp* decisions involved criminal trials. The Supreme Court has been reluctant to extend the exclusionary rule to other proceedings, even if there is a potential for loss of liberty. The Court has held that the exclusionary rule does not apply in civil cases and grand jury investigations, and a number of lower courts have concluded that the rule does not apply to probation and parole revocation hearings. Illegally seized evidence may be admitted in a criminal trial if the purpose for admitting the evidence is not to prove guilt but rather to impeach a defendant's testimony (Hemmens and del Carmen 1997).

The Standing Exception

In *Rakas v. Illiniois* (1978), the Supreme Court held that to claim Fourth Amendment protection, a defendant must have standing. To have *standing* means that a person has the right to bring legal action by virtue of being personally harmed. For instance, a person who is legally present in someone else's home (but not a resident) when the police conduct an illegal search and discover incriminating evidence belonging to that person, he or she does not have standing to seek redress in the courts because he or she cannot claim a legitimate expectation of privacy in someone else's home (he or she has not been harmed by an invasion of privacy). That person does, of course, have an expectation of privacy with regard to searches of his or her person in that home.

In *Rakas*, the petitioner appealed his conviction on armed robbery charges on the basis that police had illegally searched a car in which he was the passenger and found shells in the glove compartment and a sawed-off rifle under the front passenger seat and therefore not in plain view. Rakas had moved to suppress the rifle and shells on Fourth Amendment grounds, but the trial court denied the motion because Rakas lacked standing to object to the lawfulness of the search of the car because he did not own either the car or the rifle and shells. The Supreme Court upheld the finding of the Illinois court.

Independent Source Exception

Under the *independent source exception*, evidence may be admitted if knowledge of that evidence is gained from a source that is entirely independent from a source tainted by illegality (*Segura v. United States* 1984). In *Segura*, police illegally entered the petitioner's apartment and remained there for nineteen hours awaiting a search warrant. When the warrant arrived, the police conducted a search and found cocaine and evidence of trafficking. The state court disallowed evidence derived from the initial illegal search but allowed evidence found during the execution of the warrant. The Supreme Court ruled that the information on which the warrant was secured came from sources independent of what the officers had seen upon illegal entry and it was known to them well before their entry (it had come from an informant previously arrested who told police that he bought drugs from Segura). The Court affirmed Segura's conviction.

Attenuation Exception

Under the attenuation exception, illegally obtained evidence is admissible if there is less than a clear causal connection between the illegal police action and the evidence, that is, if the means of obtaining the evidence is sufficiently remote from the illegality. In *Wong Sun v. United States* (1963), there was a convoluted chain of events starting with illegal police entry into a laundry. The proprietor of the establishment told the police that another party had been selling drugs, who in turn implicated the proprietor and Wong Sun. Wong Sun was illegally arrested (his arrest was a fruit of the poisonous tree since the laundry had been illegally entered), arraigned, and released on his own recognizance. Some time later, Wong Sun voluntarily returned and confessed and was subsequently convicted.

Wong Sun claimed that because the entry into the laundry had been ruled illegal and evidence seized there inadmissible as poisoned fruit and since his own arrest was therefore illegal and had he not been arrested, he would never have returned and made a confession, his conviction should be overturned. The Supreme Court disagreed, saying that the connection between the arrest and Wong Sun's confession had "become so attenuated as to dissipate the taint." In other words, the impact of the initial illegality on Wong Sun's confession had been weakened (attenuated) by time and subsequent events and was therefore allowable. The Court did, however, remand the case back to the district court for a new trial based on the fact that his conviction was primarily the result of his confession.

Good Faith Exception

The exceptions we have looked at so far have been essentially about the admissibility of evidence obtained indirectly from police misconduct and may be considered exceptions to the fruit of the poisonous tree doctrine rather than of the exclusionary rule per se, which deals with evidence directly obtained by such conduct. The good faith and inevitable discovery exceptions to be discussed next, on the other hand, are exceptions to the exclusionary rule proper.

In *United States v. Leon* (1984), the Supreme Court held that evidence obtained by the police acting in *good faith* is admissible. Based on an anonymous informant's tip, police officers applied for and received a search warrant to search Leon's home, where they found large quantities of illegal drugs. Leon was indicted, but a judge concluded that the affidavit for the search warrant did not establish the probable cause necessary to issue the warrant and that the evidence obtained could not be used at Leon's trial (it was the "fruit of the poisonous tree"). The government appealed to the Court, claiming that the police had acted in good faith. The Court agreed, stating that the exclusionary rule is not a right but a remedy applied to deter illegal police conduct. In cases such as *Leon*, the majority argued, the rule cannot deter where the police act in good faith based on a warrant issued by a judge since an officer cannot reasonably be expected to question the judge's probable cause determination. Some of the Justices' dicta in *Leon* made it evident that they were not overly keen on the exclusionary rule: that is, it is "costly to society"; "Guilty defendants go unpunished and people lose respect for the law"; and "The benefits of the exclusionary rule are uncertain."

The Court has extended this rationale to allow the introduction of evidence obtained by the police acting in good faith reliance on an arrest warrant issued that is later discovered to be void. For instance, in *Arizona v. Evans* (1994), Evans was pulled over for a traffic offense and found to have an outstanding arrest warrant. Based on this, the officer arrested Evans, performed a search incident to arrest, and found drugs on him. Unbeknownst to the officer, the arrest warrant had been voided, but the clerk failed to remove it from the computer. Thus, the arrest was invalid, and also the subsequent search arising from that arrest was invalid also. The court admitted the evidence despite the fact that it was obtained by an unlawful search because the officer did not know that the warrant was invalid and relied in "good faith" on the records.

The rationale for the good faith exception is that excluding evidence obtained by police who have not knowingly violated the Fourth Amendment and who relied in "good faith" on other actors in the criminal justice system does not serve the purpose of deterring police misconduct, the primary goal of the exclusionary rule. The good faith exception does not apply to errors made by the police themselves, even if the errors were entirely inadvertent—it applies only to situations where the police relied on others such as magistrates and clerks who, it later turns out, made a mistake.

Inevitable Discovery Exception

The *inevitable discovery* exception permits the introduction at trial of evidence that was illegally obtained by police officers if the police can demonstrate that they would have eventually discovered the evidence by legal means. This ruling was based on the murder/rape case discussed in chapter 2 to illustrate the interplay between the due process and crime control models of criminal justice (*Nix v.*

Figure 6.3 Summary of the Evolution of the Exclusionary Rule

Advance of the Exclusionary Rule

Boyd v. U.S. (1886)	Adams v. N.Y. (1904)	Weeks v. U.S. (1914)	Nardone v. U.S. (1939)	Wolf v. Colorado (1949)	Mapp v. Ohio (1961)
Hint of an exclusionary rule based on the Fifth Amendment.	Affirmed common law principle that evidence is evidence.	Formulated the exclusionary rule for federal cases.	Fruit of the poisonous tree first announced.	Applied the Fourth Amendment to states but not the exclusionary rule.	Applied the exclusionary rule to states.

Retreat from the Exclusionary rule

Wong Sun v. U.S. (1963)	Rakas v. Illinois (1978)	Segura v. U.S. (1984)	U.S. v. Leon (1984)	Nix v. Williams (1984)
Evidence is admissible if it is attenuated by it being sufficiently remote from the initial illegality.	Defendant must have standing to claim Fourth Amendment protection.	Evidence is admissible if obtained from a source independent of any initial police illegality.	Evidence is admissible if officers acted in good faith based on the actions of others (i.e., judges, legislators, etc.)	Evidence is admissible if it would have inevitably been discovered by legal means.

Williams 1984). The burden is on the police to prove they, in fact, would have discovered the evidence lawfully even if they had not acted illegally.

Figure 6.3 traces the evolution of the exclusionary rule from significant cases that advanced it to significant cases that have curtailed it.

SUMMARY

In this chapter, we have discussed the sources of criminal procedure and the various protections afforded criminal defendants by the Constitution and the Bill of Rights. In particular, we have focused on the Fourth, Fifth, and Sixth Amendments. We have discussed the meaning of "unreasonable" in the Fourth Amendment as well as "search" and "seizure." These terms sometimes mean something different legally than they do in general usage. The Supreme Court has carved out a vast body of law dealing with the meaning of the Fourth, Fifth, and Sixth Amendments. There are exceptions to virtually everything, and law enforcement officers are expected to be familiar with the nuances of the law. Individual citizens also would do well to know their rights!

Due process of law is a very important legal concept. It is one of the strongest defenses that individual citizens have against their government. Criminal procedure, the rules the government must obey when it seeks to deprive a person of his or her liberty, is a direct outgrowth of the concept of due process.

Criminal procedure law is constantly evolving, as police resort to new tactics and technologies in their war on crime. The courts, as interpreters of the Constitution, continually are struggling to maintain the proper balance between the competing interests of law enforcement and individual privacy. The Bill of Rights provides a number of broad individual protections, and the Supreme Court has endeavored to develop more precise, understandable parameters of these protections.

The Fourth Amendment prohibits unreasonable searches and seizures, but the Court has not applied this standard blindly, developing the concepts of "reasonable suspicion" and permitting techniques such as stop and frisks. In some instances, the Court has created clear specific rules for police conduct, such as the exclusionary rule and the *Miranda* warnings. In other instances, the Court has resorted to a case-by-case mode of analysis, sometimes leaving law enforcement unsure of what is permitted in a particular case. This confusion to some degree is unavoidable, as the abstract legal doctrines that comprise criminal procedure law constantly are challenged by new technologies, new fact patterns, and a changing political climate. The Supreme Court is both a legal and political institution, and its decisions invariably are affected to some degree by public opinion about crime—what is "unreasonable" today may not have been unreasonable fifty years ago.

DISCUSSION QUESTIONS

1. What is the meaning of due process of law?
2. What is the difference between the crime control model and the due process model of criminal justice?
3. What is the meaning of probable cause?
4. What are the major exceptions to the search warrant requirement, and what do they allow a police officer to do?
5. What is the exclusionary rule, and why does it exist?

References

Amar, A. 1994. Fourth Amendment first principles. *Harvard Law Review* 107:757–809.

Blackstone, W. 1769. *Commentaries on the laws of England.* 4 Vols. Chicago: University of Chicago Press.

Grano, J. 1974. *Kirby, Biggers* and *Ash*: Do any constitutional safeguards remain against the danger of convicting the innocent? *Michigan Law Review* 72:717–55.

Hemmens, C. 1997. The police, the Fourth Amendment, and unannounced entry: *Wilson v. Arkansas. Criminal Law Bulletin* 33(1):29–53.

Hemmens, C., and R. del Carmen. 1997. The exclusionary rule in probation and parole revocation proceedings: Does it apply? *Federal Probation* 61(3):32–46.

Hemmens, C., R. V. del Carmen, and K. E. Scarborough. 1997. Grave doubts about "reasonable doubt": Confusion in state and federal courts. *Journal of Criminal Justice* 25(3):231–51.

Hemmens, C., and J. Maahs. 1996. Reason to believe: When does detention end and a consensual encounter begin? An analysis of *Ohio v. Robinette. Ohio Northern Law Review* 23(2):309.

Hemmens, C., J. Worrall, and A. Thompson. 2004. *Significant cases in criminal procedure.* New York: Oxford University Press.

LaFave, W. R. 1996. *Search and seizure: A treatise on the Fourth Amendment.* 3rd ed. Minneapolis, MN: West.

Linder, D. 2006. *The trials of the "Scottsboro Boys."* http://www.law.umkc.edu/faculty/projects/FTrials/scottsboro/SB_acct.html.

Meese, E., and R. DeHart. 1997. The imperial judiciary… and what Congress can do about it. *Policy Review.* http://www.policyreview.org/jan97/meese.html.

Reichel, P. 2005. *Comparative criminal justice systems: A topical approach.* 4th ed. Upper Saddle River, NJ: Prentice Hall.

Stuntz, W. J. 1992. Implicit bargains, government power, and the Fourth Amendment. *Stanford Law Review* 44:553–617.

Cases Cited

Adams v. New York, 192 U.S. (1904).

Alabama v. White, 496 U.S. 325 (1990).

Argersinger v. Hamlin, 407 U.S. 25 (1972).

Arizona v. Evans, 514 U.S. 1 (1994).

Arizona v. Hicks, 480 U.S. 321 (1987).

Arizona v. Roberson, 480 U.S. 675 (1988).

Berkemer v. McCarty, 468 U.S. 420 (1984).

Boyd v. United States, 116 U.S. 616 (1886).

Brinegar v. United States, 338 U.S. 160 (1949).

California v. Beheler, 463 U.S. 1121 (1983).

California v. Ciraolo, 476 U.S. 207 (1986).

California v. Greenwood, 486 U.S. 35 (1988).

Carroll v. United States, 267 U.S. 132 (1925).

Chimel v. California, 395 U.S. 752 (1969).

Crawford v. Washington 541 U.S. 36 (2004).

Delaware v. Prouse, 440 U.S. 648 (1979).

Edwards v. Arizona, 451 U.S. 477 (1981).

Escobedo v. Illinois, 378 U.S. 748 (1964).

Florida v. Wells, 495 U.S. 1 (1990).

Georgia v. Randolph 547 U.S. 103 (2006).

Gideon v. Wainwright, 372 U.S. 335 (1963).

Harris v. New York, 401 U.S. 222 (1971).

Harris v. United States, 390 U.S. 234 (1968).

Hester v. United States, 265 U.S. 57 (1924).

Horton v. California, 496 U.S. 128 (1990).

Illinois v. Gates, 462 U.S. 213 (1983).

Illinois v. Perkins, 495 U.S. 292 (1990).

Johnson v. Zerbst, 304 U.S. 458 (1938).

Katz v. United States, 389 U.S. 347 (1967).

Kirby v. Illinois, 406 U.S. 682 (1972).

Mapp v. Ohio, 467 U.S. 643 (1961).

Maryland v. Wilson, 519 U.S. 408 (1997).

McNeil v. Wisconsin, 501 U.S. 173 (1991).

Michigan v. Chesternutt, 486 U.S. 567 (1988).

Michigan Department of State Police v. Sitz, 496 U.S. 444 (1990).

Minnesota v. Dickerson, 508 U.S. 366 (1993).

Miranda v. Arizona, 384 U.S. 436 (1966).

Moran v. Burbine, 475 U.S. 412 (1986).

Nardone v. United States 308 U.S. 338 (1939).
New York v. Belton, 453 U.S. 454 (1981).
New York v. Quarles, 467 U.S. 649 (1984).
Nix v. Williams, 467 U.S. 431 (1984).
Ohio v. Robinette, 117 519 U.S. 33 (1997).
Oregon v. Elstad, 470 U.S. 298 (1985).
Payton v. New York, 445 U.S. 573 (1980).
Pennsylvania v. Mimms, 434 U.S. 106 (1977).
People v. Defoe, 150 N.E. 585 (1926).
Pointer v. Texas, 380 U.S. 400 (1965).
Powell v. Alabama, 287 U.S. 45 (1932).
Rakas v. Illinois, 439 U.S. 128 (1978).
Rhode Island v. Innis, 446 U.S. 291 (1980).
Segura v. United States, 468 U.S. 796 (1984).
South Dakota v. Opperman, 428 U.S. 364 (1976).
Tennessee v. Garner, 471 U.S. 1 (1985).
Terry v. Ohio 392 U.S. 1 (1968).
Texas v. Brown, 460 U.S. 730 (1983).
United States v. Karo, 468 U.S. 705 (1984).
United States v. Knights, 534 U.S. 112 (2001).
United States v. Leon, 468 U.S. 897 (1984).
United States v. Wade, 388 U.S. 218 (1967).
Washington v. Texas, 388 U.S. 14 (1967).
Weeks v. United States, 232 U.S. 383 (1914).
Wilson v. Arkansas, 514 U.S. 927 (1995).
Wolf v. Colorado, 338 U.S. 25 (1949).
Wong Sun v. United States, 371 U.S. 471 (1963).

CHAPTER 7

CIVIL AND ADMINISTRATIVE LAW

In 1978, three teenage girls, Judy and Lyn Ulrich and their cousin Donna, were driving to church in Indiana when their Ford Pinto was rear-ended. Gas spilled out and caught fire, condemning the trapped girls to horrible fiery deaths. Ford knew that Pintos had gas tanks that easily ruptured in rear-end collisions of over twenty-five miles per hour. The company also knew that the problem could have been fixed for $11 per vehicle but decided against doing so because accountants estimated that not fixing it would result in about 180 burn deaths and 1,200 serious burn injuries, which would cost Ford $49.5 million dollars in lawsuits and other claims. In comparison, fixing the problem would cost $137 million, so Ford reasoned that to do so would be fiscally unsound and bad business.

A former Ford engineer claimed that 95 percent of the 700 to 2,500 people who died in Pinto crashes would have survived had the problem been fixed. If even the lower figure is true, the Ford executives who made the decision to ignore the problem may be the worst serial murderers in history (remember, by their own calculations, they knew a certain number would die because of their decision). Yet no Ford executive was ever imprisoned for this reckless disregard for human life; their cost-benefit analysis was even used to lobby against federal fuel leakage standards to show how unprofitable they would be!

Ford Motor Company was criminally charged with the deaths of the Ulrich girls, but Ford won their case on a technicality (Ford subsequently paid the Ulrich family $22,500 in a civil suit); this was the one and only time the criminal courts were involved.

The reason is that corporate wrongdoing falls under the rubric of administrative law, and complaints about corporations by individuals are decided in civil courts. In this chapter, you will read how civil and administrative law complements criminal law. The assumption of civil law is that acts that are not criminal can also be harmful and need a venue to be adjudicated. The changing legal climate of today would probably see Ford being charged criminally, civilly, and administratively.

INTRODUCTION

So far we have concentrated on law and justice as it pertains to criminal matters, but social order, social control, and social justice require that the law also concern itself with other harmful or potentially harmful acts that society has seen fit to regulate but that are outside the purview of the criminal justice system. Law is not only about redressing harms already done; it is also about trying to prevent them and trying to ensure fairness and predictability in everyday life. Law provides rules about how individuals, agencies, and corporations should conduct themselves, aimed at protecting individuals and society at large from anything that may harm them, such as defective products and polluted air and water. Law tells us how to conduct business, it monitors the contractual promises we make, it regulates business practices, it tells us who we may or may not marry, who gets what if a marriage breaks up, and myriad things, all of which fall under the broad umbrella of civil law. **Civil law** is private law, in that it governs transactions between nongovernmental entities, such as corporations and private individuals. Public law involves the regulation of the various relationships between and among the government and private parties, such as corporations and private individuals. Although criminal law is part of public law, we address only noncriminal administrative law in this chapter.

DIFFERENTIATING CRIMINAL AND CIVIL LAW

Many disagreements arise between and among citizens and institutions concerning matters such as property, contracts, and personal injuries. These disputes are resolved through civil law, although certain harms may fall into both criminal and civil categories. As the social contract theorists we met in chapter 1 argued, participants in the social contract must be willing to sacrifice some potential for personal gain to provide an environment conducive to the protection of important liberties for all. Civil law serves this important end, designed as it is to provide remedies for individuals harmed by others, to manage social conflict, and to restore social harmony. Reduced to its bare bones, civil law defines the rights and duties that all individuals owe to all other individuals.

Civil law is divided into five major categories: torts, property, contracts, family, and juvenile law. While there is a great deal of overlap among these categories, the categories each contain their own substantive law and procedures. Cases involving personal injury to person or property are called *torts. Property law* focuses on the ownership and acquisition of property through conveyances and inheritances. *Contract law* deals with the enforceability of private agreements between individuals and between organizations. *Family law* is the set of laws involving marriage, child custody, and other issues arising in personal relationships, and *juvenile law* applies to laws regulating the behavior of minors. The following pages focus on four of the five major fields of civil law (juvenile law is covered separately in the next chapter). These subjects, along with criminal law and criminal procedure, are typically covered during the first year of law school, as they are the foundation of civil law in this country.

Like the criminal justice system, the civil justice system relies on substantive law, procedural law, and precedent. That is, civil law is set by both legislative action and judicial decisions. However, there are a variety of important distinctions that make civil law different from criminal law. In a civil case, a complaint is filed by a private party, known as the **plaintiff,** rather than by a prosecutor, because the injured party is a private citizen, not the state. Occasionally, however, the government may be involved in a civil suit, either as a plaintiff or defendant. At the termination of a civil trial decided in favor of the plaintiff, redress may be in the form of monetary damages, injunctions, or **specific performance** (particular actions the defendant must perform). There can be no penalty inflicted by the state such as imprisonment or probation in a civil action. However, the court may order the sheriff to execute the judgment order by seizing and selling a losing defendant's property to satisfy the judgment. The defendant, of course, may appeal the verdict or the judgment to a higher court.

The cases against football and movie star O. J. Simpson provide us with examples of the differences between the criminal and civil law. In 1994, O. J. Simpson was arrested and criminally charged with the murders of his former wife, Nicole Brown-Simpson, and Ronald Goldman. Simpson was acquitted after a lengthy and highly publicized criminal trial. However, the victims' families (the plaintiffs) filed a wrongful death suit against Simpson in civil court. Simpson was found by the jury in the civil trial to be "responsible" for the deaths of Brown and Goldman.

Why was Mr. Simpson found culpable in the civil case when he was acquitted in the criminal case? Much of the reason has to do with the different standard of proof requirements in criminal and civil law. As you know by now, a conviction in a criminal trial requires proof beyond a reasonable doubt, while civil courts require proof by a preponderance of the evidence. **Preponderance of the evidence** simply means that the evidence indicates that it is more likely than not that the defendant committed the wrongful act. If we were to quantify this concept, preponderance would mean a 51 percent or greater probability that the defendant was responsible for the alleged harm. This is a much lower standard of proof than what is required in a criminal trial. This lower standard of proof is justified on the grounds that the defendant does not stand to lose a fundamental right (life or liberty) in the event of an adverse decision.

The standard of proof is ratcheted up a few notches in some states under certain circumstances to a standard known as **clear and convincing evidence**. This standard establishes proof falling somewhere between the traditional standards of "preponderance of the evidence" and "beyond a reasonable doubt." The cases in which this standard is applied are typically those in which punitive as well as compensatory damages are being sought or in cases of involuntary civil commitment.

Punitive damages, also known as exemplary damages, are damages awarded in excess of compensatory damages and are intended to serve as a punishment and to discourage the conduct of the type the defendant displayed. For instance, the jury in the Simpson civil case awarded the Brown and Goldman families millions of dollars in punitive damages because the jury found Simpson to be responsible for the deaths of Brown and Goldman.

Involuntary commitment is the use of legal means to commit someone to a mental institution against his or her will. Both punitive damages and involuntary commitment decisions against a civil defendant can be seen as quasi-criminal penalties in that persons are being deprived of liberty or property, and thus some states reason that a standard of proof closer to the criminal law standard is warranted.

Another difference is that in criminal cases, the burden of proof is always on the state, whereas in a civil case, it is initially on the plaintiff to prove the allegation. After the plaintiff's evidence has been heard, the burden then shifts to the defense to offer evidence to refute the plaintiff's case. There are fewer hung juries in civil cases than in criminal cases, both because of the lower standard of evidence and because more states allow nonunanimous jury verdicts in civil cases (Melone and Karnes 2003).

Additionally, the rights afforded criminal defendants under the Fourth, Fifth, and Sixth Amendments do not apply to civil defendants. Evidence excluded in a criminal trial can usually be introduced in civil cases, such as the DNA and other physical evidence excluded in Simpson's criminal trial but included in his civil trial. Defendants have no right to remain silent (doing so is tantamount to forfeiting the case), and the right to cross-examine witnesses hostile to the defendant's case is diminished in that a witness's

Table 7.1 *Summary of Major Distinctions Between Criminal and Civil Law*

Distinction	Criminal Law	Civil Law
Who is the legal victim?	The state	The individual
Who initiates Action?	State or federal prosecutor	Private party or parties known as plaintiffs
Issue before the courts	Did the defendant violate a criminal code?	Did the defendant cause harm to the plaintiff(s)?
Standard of proof	Beyond a reasonable doubt	Generally, *preponderance of evidence,* sometimes extended to *clear and convincing evidence*
Who has the burden of proof?	The prosecution	Initially the plaintiff, but both parties must "prove" their cases.
What is the remedy sought?	Punishment—probation, jail, prison, death.	Money or other compensation, punitive damages, resolution of conflict
Rights of the defendant	All rights enumerated under the Fourth, Fifth, Sixth, Eighth, and Fourteenth Amendments	Amendments do not apply to private matters; they are rights owed only by the state to individuals.
Who has the right to appeal an adverse decision?	The defendant	Both the plaintiff and the defendant

deposition (recorded verbal evidence sworn under oath for later use in court) may be read into evidence in his or her absence. There is no legal obligation for the state to provide an attorney for indigent defendants in civil cases since it is not the state that is bringing the case to court. A final important difference is that whereas only the defendant can appeal an adverse decision in a criminal case, in civil law, either party can appeal given the presence of adequate legal grounds to do so.

Table 7.1 summarizes the major distinctions between criminal and civil law.

TORT LAW

The term tort comes from the Latin *tortus*, meaning "a wrong." **Tort law** is the body of law associated with harm caused to plaintiffs by the action or inaction of defendants other than breaches of contract, which are dealt with in contract law. A wide range of harms is covered under the tort rubric such as invasion of privacy, personal injury, medical or legal malpractice, product liability, or simple trespassing. Many torts had their origins in criminal law and may still overlap with it in that a wrong may be remedied in both criminal and civil courts. Tort law is thus similar to criminal law in that it deals with persons who have been harmed by other persons. Unlike criminal law, however, tort law does not seek to punish the wrongdoer but to help the injured party gain financial recompense, even if the wrongdoer has already been punished for the same wrong in criminal court. The purpose of tort law is to determine what harm has been done to someone, and how best to remedy that harm, to put the person harmed back as close as possible to the position he or she was in before the harm occurred. Damages are awarded to those harmed by wrongdoers. These damages are typically monetary, but may in some situations include a court order to perform certain acts or to cease performing certain acts.

Tort law provides the bread and butter of most lawyers because torts constitute by far the majority of cases brought before American courts. Tort cases are even more likely than criminal cases to be settled prior to trial. One study of almost 397,000 civil cases (about 67 percent of them being tort cases) in state courts located in seventy-five of the nation's most populous counties found that a mere 3 percent of them went to trial (Cohen and Smith 2004; see Figure 7.1). Another study found that only 2 percent of the 98,786 tort cases in federal courts in fiscal year 2002–2003 went to trial (Cohen 2005).

Tort cases are not as "sexy" as criminal cases, and we only hear about them when we find huge amounts being awarded to plaintiffs on the basis of what are ostensibly dubious claims. Such claims included the woman who sued McDonalds for millions of dollars because she spilled a cup of their hot coffee on herself, the woman who sued the estate of her psychotherapist because he did not refer her to an alternate therapist before he committed suicide, or the overly sensitive bank robber who sued police for humiliating him by laughing at his purple penis, made that way when the booby-trapped bag carrying his swag exploded and deposited purpled dye thereon.

Figure 7.1 Highlights of Jury Trial Outcomes of Tort, Contract, and Real Property Cases in 2001.

• During 2001, a jury decided almost 75% of the 12,000 tort, contract, and real property trials in the nation's 75 largest counties. Judges adjudicated the remaining 24%. Tort cases (93%) were more likely than contract cases (43%) to be disposed of by jury trial.

• The 11,908 civil trials disposed of in 2001 represents a 47% decline from the 22,451 civil trials in these counties in 1992.

• In jury trials, the median award decreased from $65,000 in 1992 to $37,000 in 2001 in these counties.

• Two-thirds of disposed trials in 2001 involved tort claims, and about a third involved contractual issues.

• Overall, plaintiffs won in 55% of trials. Plaintiffs won more often in bench trials (65%) than in jury trials

(53%) and in contract trials (65%) more than in tort (52%) or real property trials (38%).

• An estimated $4 billion in compensatory and punitive damages were awarded to plaintiff winners in civil trails. Juries awarded $3.9 billion to plaintiff winners, while judges awarded $368 million. The median total award for plaintiff winners in tort trials was $27,000 and in contract trials $45,000.

• Punitive damages, estimated at $1.2 billion, were awarded to 6% of plaintiff winners in trials. The median punitive damage award was $50,000.

• Plaintiffs prevailed in about a fourth (27%) of medical malpractice trials. Half of the 311 plaintiffs who successfully litigated a medical malpractice claim won at least $422,000, and in nearly a third of these cases, the award was $1 million or more.

Source: T. Cohen and S. Smith 2004. *Civil trial cases and verdicts in large counties, 2001 (April)*. Bureau of Justice Statistics.

A person can be held liable for a harm done both in civil and criminal courts regardless of the outcome of the criminal case. This does not constitute double jeopardy because double jeopardy applies to the prospect of additional criminal trials leading to additional punishments (loss of life or liberty). Because only the state can legitimately punish by depriving a person of life or liberty and because the state was not a party in the O. J. Simpson civil case, there is no danger of punishment (defendants may face punishment, including imprisonment, however, if they ignore the judgment of the court). Certainly the award of several million dollars to the plaintiffs was painful to Simpson, and certainly the plaintiff relied on the power of the state to enforce the verdict, but there is never a question of double jeopardy in civil cases following an acquittal because civil cases concern private matters.

This does not mean that a plaintiff can again bring suit against the same person for the same tort in the event that he or she did not prevail in the case. The civil law protection corresponding to the double jeopardy protection in criminal law is known as ***res judicata*** ("thing decided"). This principle means that once the case has been through all possible appeals, it is decided forever. Circumstances in which *res judicata* do not apply include those in which perjury or witness tampering affected the verdict or in cases where it can be shown that all legal issues involved were not fully litigated. Since no such exceptions apply to double jeopardy, *res judicata* is not fully equivalent.

Tort Categories

There are three primary categories of torts: *intentional* acts, *negligent* acts, and acts for which there is *strict liability*. These categories are defined based on the intent of the defendant. The O. J. Simpson civil suit tort case was based on the claim of "wrongful death" caused by Mr. Simpson. In tort cases, *intent* is presumed when an action takes place and is differentiated from *motive* (the term used in criminal cases) because *civil intent* is simply the desire to cause the consequences, not the reason for having that desire. However, many of the defenses to criminal intent also serve as defenses to civil intent (such as self-defense).

Intentional torts include acts in which the defendant (referred to as the *tortfeasor*) deliberately causes harm to another person or their property. An example of an intentional tort is assault and battery (again, a criminal matter that may also be pursued in civil court by victims seeking monetary compensation).

Negligence is "conduct which falls below the standard established by law for the protection of others against unreasonable risks of harm" (Kionka 1988). For negligence to exist, the plaintiff must prove that (1) the defendant had a duty to act in a certain way, (2) the defendant breached that duty, and (3) this breach of duty was the cause of the plaintiff's injury.

The typical standard of care is referred to as **ordinary care**. This is the degree of care expected from the "reasonable person." Often, negligence cases hinge on the "reasonable person" standard. That is, did the defendant act the way a reasonable person should have acted to prevent the harm from occurring?

Another important element in tort cases is *causation*. In addition to the requirement that the tortfeasor owe a duty to the victim is the requirement that the victim be able to show that the tortfeasor's actions were the cause of the victim's injuries. As in criminal law, there are two types of causation—*actual cause* and *proximate cause*. Actual cause is also called *"but for" cause*. If the injury would not have occurred but for the defendant's action, then there exists actual cause. Proximate cause is also called legal cause. This is the requirement that the defendant's action be not only the actual cause but that society is willing to hold the defendant responsible. There can usually be no intervening causes; that is, the acts of a third person that come between the original negligent act and the harm do not excuse the original act.

The 1955 Connecticut case of *Lubitz v. Wells* is a good example of a failed negligence claim. In this case, James Wells left one of his golf clubs in his back yard. His son, while playing with his neighbor, Judith Lubitz, picked up the golf club and swung the club, attempting to hit a rock. In doing so, he accidentally struck Judith's chin with the club. Suit was brought against Mr. Wells for negligently leaving a dangerous instrument in a place where children might find and play with it. The court held that a golf club did not constitute an "intrinsically dangerous" item such that a reasonable person should not leave one lying in his or her own backyard and found for the defendant.

Strict liability torts are cases in which the plaintiff need not prove that the defendant acted intentionally or negligently. Liability is established if it can be shown that the plaintiff was injured and the defendant was the cause of the injury. Strict liability is typically applied to situations where a person chooses an activity that creates a risk of harm to others. For instance, torts concerning injuries sustained due to drunk drivers are included in this category. The courts have ruled in a number of cases that drunk drivers are strictly liable for the harm caused by their actions while driving drunk. In these cases, there is no need to prove intent or negligence. Another example of an area in which strict liability has been applied is in the ownership of animals. Generally, the owners of domestic animals are strictly liable for any injuries that their animals may cause even if they took all precautions against an animal (say, a pit bull) getting loose.

Defenses to Liability

In addition to challenging issues such as causation and duty of care, tort defendants may raise other, affirmative defenses. These include contributory negligence, comparative negligence, and several other defenses. **Contributory negligence** is a doctrine, once preeminent but now falling into disfavor, that holds that if an injured party was in any way partially responsible for his or her injuries, then he or she is barred from recovering from a tortfeasor. So, if two parties are both negligent, neither may sue the other. This doctrine has fallen out of favor, as society has come to recognize that a tortfeasor should not get a "free pass" simply because the injured person was partially to blame.

Comparative negligence is a doctrine that attempts to apportion the responsibility among each party. For instance, if Frank is injured by Bill's negligent conduct, but the court determines Frank was also negligent (say 25 percent responsible), then he may only recover for the percentage of his injuries caused by Bill—in this case, 75 percent.

Defenses to torts include **consent** and **immunity**. A person may consent to being harmed by another person, although the law typically does not allow a person to give valid consent to serious harm. Some parties may be immune from suit. As we discussed in chapter 3, historically, under the doctrine of sovereign immunity, governments could not be sued by their citizens. Most governments have relaxed this defense and now allow citizens to sue the government in many (but not all) circumstances. Judges are also immune from civil suits for judicial actions such as placing a dangerous man, who subsequently kills someone, on probation. They can, of course, be sued for actions that fall outside of their judicial duties. Some other court officials also enjoy limited immunity when performing quasi-judicial duties, such as a probation officer performing a presentence investigation inadvertently omitting information that would have precluded the judge from placing the dangerous man on probation.

Tort Reform

Tort reform is essentially about efforts of insurance companies and their clients to get Congress to pass laws severely limiting what they see as frivolous lawsuits and exorbitant punitive damages awarded by jurors who see civil trials as "poor David" v. "deep-pocket Goliath" battles. Tort reform has been a hot-button social issue for the past two decades that has pitted lawyers against insurance companies, Republicans against Democrats, and pundits of all persuasions against one another. Each side plants its flag on the moral high ground by claiming that their position on the issue is in accordance with a more just civil law system.

One of the first things we should note is that the tort reform issue is driven by "headline" cases, such as the McDonald's coffee spill case mentioned earlier. In this case, the woman in question was burned so badly as to require skin grafts, the coffee was being served forty to fifty degrees hotter than in most other establishments, and McDonald's knew this because they had received numerous previous complaints (Melone and Karnes 2003). The case of the woman wanting to sue her therapist was thrown out, and the "purple-penis" case is apparently an urban legend dreamt up (like many others) in e-mail land (Mencimer 2004). Judges have always had discretion to throw out cases without merit, and huge awards are extremely rare. Figure 7.1 provides highlights from a nationwide study of jury trial outcomes of tort, contracts, and real property cases over a twelve-month period. As seen in Figure 7.1, in 2001, if a plaintiff won (the outcome 55 percent of the time), the median compensatory award was $27,000, and punitive damages were awarded to a mere 6 percent of the winning plaintiffs who received a median award of $50,000.

Further, the golden age of the American "sue the bastards" tradition appears to have passed. The 2001 data presented in Figure 7.1 represent a 48 percent decrease from data from the same seventy-five counties obtained in 1992 (Cohen and Smith 2004), and tort trials declined 79 percent in federal courts from 1983 to 2003 (Cohen 2005). This can be attributed to a number of factors. The "golden age" included the asbestos cases in the 1980s, the Dalkon Shield (an intrauterine birth control device), silicon breast implants, and tobacco cases in the 1990s. Antitort reformers argue that the declining number of tort cases shows that civil litigation is effective in forcing business to take greater care about the products it puts on the market.

Proponents of tort reform insist that all they want is to place caps on excessive punitive damages, claiming that they drive businesses and medical professionals out of business, force insurance premiums up, and generally increase prices for everyone. For instance, physicians in high-risk specialties such as obstetrics and neurosurgery may pay as much as $133,000 per year for malpractice insurance, which has led to a number of them leaving the profession or moving to states or countries with punitive damage caps, and hence lower insurance premiums (*Lancet* Report 2003). This leaves patients without physicians and/or drives the prices charged (and hence medical insurance) by these physicians sky high. A number of studies have shown that states that cap malpractice awards have lower health care expenditures for patients with no corresponding loss of medical efficiency (reviewed in Hellinger and Encinosa 2006).

PROPERTY LAW

Property law in the United States is largely a product of the English common law. Many of the legal doctrines used to decide property cases were first developed by the English courts in the seventeenth and eighteenth centuries, although many changes have since been made. Justice, in the case of property law, most often is defined as the protection of ownership rights. The law has been written and used to protect the owners and possessors of property.

The legal term *property* varies somewhat from the common usage. In a legal sense, **property** means the right of possession or ownership. Property includes personal property, such as an automobile or a television; real property, defined as land or permanent attachments to land; and intellectual property, defined as ideas or concepts developed by an individual or group. In each case, legal property means the right of ownership or control over the item, land, or idea in question (Dukeminier and Krier 1988). The following two cases are examples of property law in action.

The case of *Pierson v. Post* (1805) shows that even 200 years ago Americans were willing to litigate almost anything. In 1804, Lodewick Post took his hounds hunting in New York. After a short time, his dogs found and gave chase to a fox. As Post was approaching the fox in the final stages of the chase, a man named Pierson shot the animal and carried it away in full sight of Post. The question that came before the Supreme Court of New York in 1805 concerned the point at which a hunter of wild animals gains property rights over the hunted animal. This question turned on the legal issue of control. Did Post have control over the fox, or was it still "fair game"? According to the court, property rights over wild animals begin only at the time of absolute control. In this case, Post did not have absolute control over the fox, and therefore, Pierson's act, however discourteous, did not violate any property rights that Post could claim.

The issue in *City of Oakland v. The Oakland Raiders* (1982) revolved around the 1980 decision of the owner of the Oakland Raiders football team to move the team to Los Angeles. The city of Oakland fought the move by arguing the city had a property right in the team. A California statute authorized cities to acquire, through the power of eminent domain, any property necessary to carry out any of its powers or functions. This primarily includes items that have a valid public use, such as land for building roads and highways. The city of Oakland argued that the Raiders football franchise served the valid public purposes of recreation and commerce, and on this basis claimed that it could seize the team through the power of eminent domain. The California Supreme Court determined that allowing the city to the take ownership of the football team would unnecessarily restrict business owners in the enjoyment of their property. The court determined that it would be unjust to constrict business in such a fashion regardless of the claims of the city, and the Raiders moved to Los Angeles (they have since moved back to Oakland).

Interests in Real Property

In common law, a number of different types of interests (or rights) in real property were developed by the courts, largely in response to changes in how people used the land. These interests include freehold estates. A **freehold estate** is one wherein a person owns a piece of property. They are distinguished from nonfreehold estates, which typically involved only a right to use property (as in a rental agreement). Types of freehold estates include a fee simple estate and a life estate.

A **fee simple estate** is an interest in real property that ends when the person dies—at which time the interest reverts to the original owner of the property. A **fee simple absolute estate** is one in which the property interest does not revert to the original owner. This is the type of property interest that is most commonly used in the United States.

It is of course possible for more than one person to own an interest in real property, as when a husband and wife both own their home. When multiple parties each own an equal share of a piece of real property, they have a **tenancy in common**. If one of the parties dies, under the right of survivorship, that person's interest in the property may be transferred to the surviving party.

There are a number of other issues involving real property, such as air and subsurface rights. It is possible for a landowner to sell the rights to the air above his or her land or the right to use or extract materials from below the land (such as minerals or water). A landowner may also grant an easement to someone. An **easement** is a limited right to use the property of another for a particular purpose, without adversely affecting the ownership rights of the land owner. For example, if Williams owned some land that surrounded land owned by Dawson, Dawson could not legally cross Williams's land to get to his property. Williams could grant Dawson an easement to cross his land, however. This easement could prescribe where Dawson could cross William's land and for how long such a right would continue.

While real property is typically transferred either by gift or sale, it is possible for a person to acquire an interest in another's property simply by using it. Under the doctrine of **adverse possession**, if Smith openly and exclusively uses all or a portion of land owned by Jones for a specific period of time (traditionally for at least seven years), then at the end of that time period, he may file suit to obtain the land. The purpose of adverse possession is to encourage people to use their property and to take steps to protect it from encroachment.

Property owners are generally well protected by the law, however. While the doctrine of adverse possession exists, it is very easy to prevent a claim of adverse possession, and it only affects property that has been abandoned by the original owner. While the rights of property owners are protected, the law does impose some duties on owners of real property.

Under the nuisance doctrine, a property owner may not use his or her property in such a way that it has an unreasonable, adverse affect on other property owners. Thus, a homeowner may be prevented from operating a slaughterhouse in a residential area, as such a use of the property does not comport with surrounding uses.

Property owners have a duty to keep their property in reasonably safe condition and to take reasonable steps to protect those who come onto the property, including trespassers, from harm. Until the twentieth century, a trespasser had no rights, and if they were injured while trespassing on another's property, they could not sue for damages. This is no longer the case, as courts have recognized that landowners have a duty to keep their property free of dangers that a trespasser could not be expected to discover.

Interests in Personal Property

Personal property includes any tangible item not connected to the land. This includes automobiles, books, televisions, money, and the like. These are sometimes referred to as *movables*. It does not include land or items permanently attached to the land (such as trees or buildings) or intangible items, such as patents or copyrights. A person may of course own personal property and transfer that personal property permanently to another, either by sale or gift.

Personal property may also be the subject of a temporary transfer of possession. When a person transfers possession of an item to another for a particular purpose, with the understanding that the property will be returned at a later time, a **bailment** is created. A bailment involves the transfer of possession but not ownership. When Marlene takes her skirts to the cleaners, for example, she gives the skirts to the counterperson, who gives Marlene a receipt. When Marlene returns, she presents the receipt, pays the bill, and is given her skirts. Marlene did not transfer ownership of her shirts to the cleaners, nor did she give the skirts to the cleaners to use as they see fit; she merely transferred possession to the cleaners for the limited purpose of having them cleaned.

CONTRACT LAW

Contract law is the law governing the conduct of business. **Contracts** are defined as legally enforceable promises. They are formal agreements between two or more parties voluntarily undertaken that make certain promises in exchange for other specified promises. Thus, contract law is concerned with determining the legality of written and spoken agreements between citizens, groups, agencies, and corporations. Many thousands of contracts are arranged and agreed to in both public and private enterprises each day. Fundamental to the operation of any business is the ability to conduct business transactions. Imagine the chaos of a world in which there were no expectations about business agreements and what constitutes a legally binding contract. It would be very difficult to conduct any type of arranged deal without some common understanding of contracts. Contract law provides this common understanding.

Much of the law concerning contracts is now guided by the **Uniform Commercial Code**. The Uniform Commercial Code is designed to standardize trade and contract practices among merchants and businesses. In the English-speaking world, law concerning the trade and sales of goods and property had historically fallen under the governance of common law. Until the nineteenth century, merchant law was the standard for legal practice. This law was the result of merchant dealings and common law precedent concerning fairness. In 1893, the British Law of Sales was introduced as statute. In the United States, work began on a code of commerce separate from the British law of sales in the 1940s, which resulted in the first version of the Uniform Commercial Code in 1952. Since this time, the code has been adopted in all states except Louisiana, which has a civil (or code) law system similar to France. The Uniform Commercial Code codifies a variety of principles already established by common law.

Elements of a Valid Contract

Every contract has similar elements. These include at least two parties to the contract, both of whom are capable of signing a contract (meaning they have legal capacity). In addition, both parties must agree to the terms of the contract, and there must be a promise supported by consideration. Promises are the backbones of contracts and become legally binding when supported by legal considerations. Consideration is essentially the *reliance* by a party to the agreement. Put simply, a contract generally consists of two or more parties making promises to one another. It becomes legally binding when one or more of the parties relies on the promise of the other. Contracts can be either written or verbal and meet the following requirements:

- *Two-party requirement:* There must be two parties to a contract. A person cannot make a contract with himself or herself. While this may seem obvious, it is nonetheless a requirement of contract law.

- *Legal capacity requirement:* Only the person whom the law recognizes as capable of being a party to a contract may sign a valid contract. This means a person must be mentally competent and be an adult. A person who is "underage" cannot sign a binding contract. The same is true for persons who suffer from a mental problem that limits their ability to understand what they are doing, regardless of age.

- *Assent requirement:* Both parties to a contract must agree to the terms of the contract and must indicate this assent. This requirement is intended to ensure that both parties to a contract understand its terms and are aware that a contract is being created. Assent may be given verbally or in writing and must be objectively reasonable. This means that an agreement made in jest is not a valid contract; likewise, negotiations do not, in and of themselves, constitute a contract.

  Assent is often described as involving an *offer* and an *acceptance*. One party makes an offer to be bound by a contract; if the other party agrees, then a valid contract may be created. If a promise is made in exchange for performance, a unilateral *contract* is created. If a promise is made by both parties, then a *bilateral contract* is created.

- *Legality requirement*: Fraudulent contracts in which one party clearly intends to defraud the other, or illegal contracts, such as the promise to pay a certain amount of money for the delivery of contraband goods, are not legally enforceable.

Another concept crucial to the study of contract law is the notion of *good faith*. In most contract negotiations, there is an assumption that all of the parties are making promises that they mean to keep and that these promises are made based on a common understanding of what will be required to meet the obligations incurred according to standards of fair dealing in trade. Finally, it is considered a *breach of contract* when the terms of a contract are not met.

The 1973 Massachusetts case of *Sullivan v. O'Connor* is an example of contract law in action. Sullivan was an entertainer who relied on her appearance for her living. She entered into a contract with O'Connor, a plastic surgeon, to have reconstructive surgery performed on her nose to enhance her beauty and improve her public appeal. Originally, the contract called for Sullivan to have two surgeries performed by O'Connor to have her rather prominent nose shortened. Sullivan actually had to go through three surgeries, and the end result was a nose that was not satisfactory to her. It was determined that further surgery could not repair the nose. Sullivan sued O'Connor for breach of contract. O'Connor made a "good faith" argument, asserting that he had done the best he could with the "resources" (Sullivan's nose) provided and thus fulfilled his part of the bargain. Nevertheless, the Massachusetts Supreme Court held that the promise made by the surgeon to make Sullivan's nose appealing was enforceable, and that Sullivan could recover not only the costs of the failed surgeries but also damages based on the worsening of the condition after the contractual breach.

However, legal contracts can be voided without penalty under certain circumstances. In a classic "rich man/poor man" Supreme Court case (*National Labor Relations Board v. Bildisco & Bildisco* 1984), the Court ruled that a business could relieve itself of a labor contract (i.e., breach the contract) if a Chapter 11 bankruptcy petition had been filed, even before a bankruptcy court had approved or rejected the petition. Chapter 11 bankruptcy laws are designed to limit business failures by allowing the reorganization of business debts toward this end. In itself this is a positive thing, but the additional uses it was put to after *Bildisco* had had tremendous social impact. Numerous other companies found the Court's permitting of employers to unilaterally breach a collective bargaining contract to be extremely attractive. The threat of such contract breaches left union employees with few protections against loss of their collectively bargained contract rights, and companies all over the United States engaged in an orgy of union busting armed with the Court's *Bildisco* ruling (Walsh 1988).

FAMILY LAW

The family is the basic institution of any society, and therefore the state is a third party in every marriage. Because of this, we should expect all societies to have laws designed to protect the integrity of marriage. **Family law** today is conciliatory rather than accusatory in that there is no necessary judgment of right or wrong but rather an effort to arrange an outcome that comes as close as possible to pleasing everyone involved. Family law is focused largely on the entering into and dissolution of marriages and other interpersonal relationships and the resultant changes in fiscal and personal responsibilities between the parties. There are no national family laws but rather a number of different state laws that have different implications for married couples. Nevertheless, there are several requirements for a valid marriage, such as the obtaining of a marriage license from the state. Included with the license may be a blood test and a waiting period. Additionally, marriage vows must be exchanged in the presence of someone who is legally permitted to acknowledge the marriage, such as a minister or judge, and the marriage vows must be witnessed. Primary issues in family law are briefly addressed in the following sections.

Who May Marry Whom?

Marriage is a legal contract that carries with it rights and responsibilities for both parties; as a contract it must meet certain requirements to be considered legally valid, just as with any other contract. A person must be eighteen years of age or older to get married without parental permission in almost all states. Certain exceptions may apply, such as pregnancy, but this is the general rule. A person under legal age is considered incompetent to enter into a marriage contract. Other incompetencies precluding the issuance of a marriage license include mental deficiencies, such as insanity, and being under the influence of intoxicating substances at the time of application.

Closely related persons, such as brothers and sisters, parents and children, or cousins, may not enter into a marital contract. Any such marriages fraudulently entered into would make the parties eligible for the criminal charge of incest. The final requirement is that neither party be currently married to someone else. If a person already married marries someone else, he or she is guilty of bigamy, which carries a penalty of up to five years' imprisonment in most states (Shakespeare said that the *real* penalty for bigamy is two wives, but in today's climate of political correctness he would be taken to task for saying that).

The Supreme Court and the Right to Marry

The first of the few cases involving the scope of the right to marry came before the Supreme Court in *Reynolds v. United States* (1878). George Reynolds, a Mormon, had been convicted of bigamy in Utah. He claimed the right to multiple marriages as his religious duty, but the Court ruled that religious duty was not a valid defense against a criminal indictment. In *Skinner v. State of Oklahoma* (1942) the Supreme Court stated that the right to marry was a "basic civil right." But in adding that "Marriage and procreation are fundamental to the very existence and survival of the race," it was implicitly defining marriage as something that only opposite-sex partners can enter into. (*Skinner* was actually a case about castration for an inveterate criminal offender; marriage came into it only because castration would prevent procreation).

Loving v. Virginia (1967) is particularly interesting in that it overturned a number of state statutes denying the right to marry on racial grounds. Richard Loving, a white man, and Mildred Jeter, a black woman, were residents of Virginia but had to leave the state to get married. On their return to Virginia, they were arrested for violating Virginia's antimiscegenation law (law against interbreeding involving persons of different races) and sentenced to one year of imprisonment, which was suspended on condition that the Lovings leave Virginia. The Supreme Court eventually heard the case and ruled that distinctions based on race were "odious" and must be subject to "the most rigid scrutiny" under the equal protection clause of the Fourteenth Amendment. In *Zablocki v. Redhail* (1978), the Court ruled that "deadbeat dads" had a right to marry (Redhail was denied a marriage license based on the fact that he was seriously in arrears with his child support payments from a previous marriage), and in *Turner v. Safley* (1987) the Court ruled that even prison inmates have a fundamental right to marry.

If, as the Court has declared in the preceding cases, the right to marry is part of the fundamental "right of privacy" implicit in the Fourteenth Amendment, why has this right not been extended to same-sex couples who wish to marry? According to the federal **Defense of Marriage Act** (DOMA) passed by Congress in 1996, only opposite-sex couples can legally be married. After Vermont passed laws allowing same-sex couples civil unions (not the same as marriage but valid for the purpose of state benefits for partners and inheritance rights), almost all states that did not already have laws prohibiting same-sex marriage initiated such laws modeled on DOMA. As of the writing of this edition, the only states that allowed gay marriage were Connecticut, Iowa, Massachusetts, New Hampshire, and Vermont. Other states are not required to recognize these marriages.

In 2008, the California Supreme Court ruled that same-sex marriage was permissible under the California constitution, and among those who did marry were Arthur Smelt and Christopher Hammer. In the same year the voters in California passed Proposition 8, which amended the California Constitution to end the right of same-sex couples to marry there. In 2009, Smelt and Hammer filed a lawsuit against California and the United States of America, arguing that both DOMA and Proposition 8 are unconstitutional. The suit alleges that DOMA violates a laundry list of rights, such as due process and equal protection, free speech, privacy, and one we have not addressed so far in this book, called the

Full Faith and Credit Clause of Article IV of the Constitution, which states: "Full Faith and Credit shall be given in each State to the public Acts, Records, and judicial Proceedings of every other State." In other words, Smelt and Hammer are alleging here that because other states are not required to recognize another state's same-sex marriage, this clause is violated, as is their right to travel as a married couple.

Despite President Obama's personal support for gay marriage rights, the Department of Justice (DOJ) filed briefs in support of DOMA (the DOJ is obliged to defend suits against federal acts). In August of 2009, Federal District Judge David O. Carter dismissed the case on jurisdictional grounds without ruling on the constitutional merits of DOMA. The case is to be refiled, however, and currently a number of other suits regarding gay marriage in the United States are pending.

The United States Supreme Court has not yet had the opportunity to rule on a same-sex marriage case, and it is anyone's guess what such a ruling might be. If precedent is anything to go by, and barring a constitutional amendment banning gay and lesbian marriage, it seems likely that the Court will rule such marriages constitutional. It may split hairs, however, and note that, unlike race, sexual orientation is not a protected category (but neither are prison inmates or dead-beat dads) and therefore cases involving homosexuals are not subject to the strict scrutiny standard as in *Loving*. The Court may also appeal to the *Skinner* ruling, defining marriage in terms of its relationship to the requirements of procreation, to avoid granting gay marriage constitutional status. We will further discuss the law's attitude toward homosexuality in chapter 10.

Common Law Marriage

Common law marriage may be established by couples cohabiting and acting in every way as though married (owning property in common, filing joint income taxes, etc.) even though they have not been through a formal wedding ceremony and have no license. Such marriages are recognized as valid if established in states allowing them, but thirty-nine states have abolished such marriages. The primary reason that most states have abolished common law marriage is that they recognize marriage to be a legal contract that carries with it rights and responsibilities for both parties and that too many opportunities exist for evading responsibilities, fraud, and all manner of legal complications if one of the couple dies, deserts, or defaults on the implied contract. For instance, common law spouses may have to go to court to establish that all the elements of a common law marriage existed in their relationship before he or she may gain access to a spousal right, such as access to the other spouse's pension or the inheritance of his or her property.

Divorce and Annulment

Just as there are licensing requirements for marriage, the dissolution of the marital contract by divorce or annulment requires legal grounds. Grounds (legally acceptable reasons) for divorce are divided into *no-fault* (such as irreconcilable differences) and *fault* categories. All states now have **no-fault divorce**, meaning that there is no assumption of fault by either marriage partner for the marital breakup. Some states retain fault-based divorce in addition to their no-fault grounds. Fault grounds, which were traditionally such things as adultery, cruelty, desertion, insanity, and alcoholism, are used in states retaining fault for issues such as child custody and financial settlements, even if a no-fault divorce has already been granted.

Marriages may also be annulled. An **annulment** is a legal declaration that a marriage never existed because the legal requirements for a valid marriage were not met. An annulment can be obtained if someone lacked the legal ability to consent to marriage (underage, mentally incompetent, drugged, already married, etc.). Other grounds include impotence and concealing a sexually transmitted disease or pregnancy from a union with some other person.

Dividing Property, Child Custody, and Spousal Support

Marriage is a partnership in the same sense that Smith and Jones's landscaping business is, and the dissolution of the partnership requires a determination of who gets what out of the partnership when it dissolves. Statutes governing property division vary by state, but they can generally be grouped into two types: *dual property* and *all property* models, with most following the dual-property model. In the **dual-property** model, the courts consider assets held jointly (acquired during the marriage) by the spouses, and separate assets each brought with them to the marriage, inherited, or received as gifts during the marriage. If separate property is not commingled with joint assets, courts will typically recognize the separate ownership of the individual spouse and it will not be divided along with joint marital assets. In **all-property** states, the courts typically divide all property owned by either spouse at the time of the divorce equally.

In marriages with children that end in divorce, the courts also have to decide the emotional and often acrimonious issue of child custody. In some cases, one spouse (usually the husband) voluntarily gives up custody to his former wife, but when a battle ensues, the courts in all fifty states are charged with making their decisions with the preeminent concern being the best interests of the child.

Child support is an area of family law that has grown in scope and consequence. Child support is based on the custodial status of the parents. That is, after the legal breakup of a family with children, the courts often are asked to require that the parent without primary physical custody assist with the financial burden placed on the parent with primary physical custody. Most often, the amount of support is based on a calculation of income and the costs associated with child rearing. Many states have complex formulas established to determine an equitable settlement that includes aggregate family income and time spent with each parent.

The twentieth century was a time of growth and change in the realm of family law. The traditional patriarchal family was challenged by a variety of social changes. The role of women changed in our society, as well as throughout the Western world, and this change has had an impact on expectations about the nature of family structures and responsibilities.

Additionally, technological changes in the areas of childbirth and pregnancy have contributed to the demand for legal changes. For instance, modern practices such as artificial insemination and surrogate motherhood bring up issues never dreamt about fifty years ago. If a man donates his sperm, or if a woman carries the fertilized egg of another woman, what are their legal claims to the child? These issue have been accompanied by an increased need to identify and define family law. Divorce is more common in the United States than ever before, and this has resulted in child custody and support issues that have been, until recently, largely left untouched by legal code or statute.

ADMINISTRATIVE AND REGULATORY LAW

Administrative law (or regulatory law) is a branch of public law involving governmental administrative agencies whose activities include the making, enforcement, and adjudication of specific regulatory agendas such as clean air, health standards, and occupational safety. Note that administrative agencies *make* administrative law, *enforce* it, and *adjudicate* it. In essence, this means that administrative agencies combine the governmental roles of the legislative, executive, and judicial branches of government in one agency. These agencies have a huge impact on everyone's life because they regulate just about everything we see, hear, taste, touch, smell, or breathe. It is for this reason that administrative agenices have been termed "the fourth branch of government" (Vago 1991, 84) and the "shadow government" (Samuels 2006, 232).

Article 1, section 8, of the United States Constitution grants Congress the plenary (complete) power to regulate commerce, although care is taken not to trespass on the reserved powers of the states granted by the Tenth Amendment. Prior to the twentieth century, the operating principles of the United States government vis-à-vis business were *laissez-faire* (literally, "leave do"; i.e., leave business alone to do what it will) and *caveat emptor* ("let the buyer beware"). Both of these principles essentially amounted to injunctions against governmental interference with business on behalf of public interests. During the twentieth century, things turned around dramatically to the point that, for better or for worse, the government's unofficial operating principles may be defined as *interférez tout* ("interfere with everything") and *caveat venditor* ("let the seller beware").

Origins and Growth of Administrative Agencies

The United States has seen explosive growth in administrative/regulatory agencies since 1789. The first such agencies were more like executive branch bureaucracies such as the Bureau of Customs or the Bureau of Indian Affairs. According to the U.S. Attorney General's Committee *Final Report* (1941, 8) on administrative agencies, there were just eleven in existence prior to the close of the Civil War. The first regulatory agency in the modern sense of an agency making, enforcing, and adjudicating its own rules independent of the executive branch of government was the Interstate Commerce Commission, created in 1887 in response to unfair railroad tariffs. However, this agency protected businesses against other businesses (as did the Sherman Anti-Trust Act of 1890), and the interests of the general public tended to be ignored.

Administrative agencies grew rapidly in number under President F. D. Roosevelt's New Deal legislative programs in the 1930s "to address the vast economic and social crises wrought by the Depression" (Fenster 2005, 70). The *Final Report* listed fifty-one such agencies in 1941. New Deal legislation, and the agencies created to oversee it, came up against fiece opposition from Republicans and business interests. George Shepard (1996, 1562) called this fight "a pitched political battle for the life of the New Deal." The issue fought over was the expansiveness of the federal government: Should the government intervene on behalf of its people, or would such an extension of its already considerable power eventually lead to a centrally planned economy and the dictatorship that implies (Shepard 1996)?

New Deal opponents saw regulatory agencies as rapacious bureaucrats who made decisions on a case-by-case (substantive rationality) basis rather than on the foundation of precedent and formal/rational rules (Schiller 2005). In response to this criticism, Congress passed the **Administrative Procedure Act** (APA) of 1946, which established the basic procedural standards for federal agencies, letting them know how they may propose and establish their regulations and how they may go about adjudicating violations of them. The APA also outlined the process for the federal courts to review agency decisions should the occasion arise. These procedures formalized what was previously rather arbitrary and "placed many courtlike procedural requirements (cross-examination, rules of evidence, formal records) on agency adjudication" (Schiller 2005, 112). In essence, the APA represented a compromise allowing for the expansion of governmental power while somewhat quieting conservative concerns about federal dictatorship.

Most people today would probably agree that government regulation is a very good thing in terms of protecting their health, safety, civil rights, and wealth, even though the Office of Management and Budget (OMB; 2003) estimates that the cost associated with federal protections costs the taxpayer between $38 billion and $44 billion per year. However, as all good cynics would expect, all agencies self-reported greater benefits (from $135 to $218 billion) to the public than costs in this report.

Table 7.2 presents a single page from the OMB report that lists the agency, benefits, costs, and brief "other information." The agencies represented there are only a small part of the 170 federal agencies (a 233 percent increase from the 1941 total) and commissions listed on the White House (2006) Web site. Many of these agencies are duplicated at the state level, and altogether, these state and federal agencies employ almost twenty million people (Samuels 2006). It is no wonder, then, that administrative law touches most of us more intimately than criminal or civil law, through an alphabet soup of agencies. The gas or electricity we perk our coffee with in the morning are regulated by various state public utilities commissions overseen by the FERC (Federal Energy Regulatory Commission); the food you have for breakfast and the pills you take afterwards were grown, raised, manufactured, and packaged under the regulations of the

Table 7.2 *Estimates of Benefits and Costs (in 2001 dollars) for Selected Federal Administrative Agencies.*

Rule	Agency	Benefits	Costs	Other information
Manufactured Home Construction and Safety Standards on Wind Standards.	HUD	$63,726,314 annually	$412,106,180 annually	The cost estimates do not include costs associated with "out of pocket expenses related to deductibles or non-covered losses" (RIA, pp. 1–2). Non-quantified benefits include: "purcased by damage to or destruction of their manufactured homes. Fourth, residents who choose to remain in their units during storms will suffer fewer injuries and deaths" (RIA, p. 1) Discount rate used = 6.64 percent (RIA, p. 8) Basis for public benefit assessment: Hurricane Andrew (RIA, p. 9).
Designate Critical Habitat for Four Endangered Colorado River Fishes.	DOI	Net benefit: $7.92 million.		Increase employment by 710 jobs, increase earnings by $6.62 million, increase government revenue by $3.20 million from 1995–2020 (59 FR 13374–).
Occupational Exposure to Asbestos.	DOL–OSHA	Reduction in annual cancer risk: 2.12 cancer deaths in general industry, 40.48 cancer deaths in construction industry. 14.2 cancers among building occupants. Reduction in asbestosis: 14 cases annually.	$361.4 million annually	Non-quantified benefits include: avoided cases of asbestosis for building occupants and others secondarily exposed, reduced risks of cancer and fires (from rags contaminated with solvent), more rapid building reoccupation, reduced probability of asbestos-related lawsuits (RIA, pp. 52–57).
Financial Responsibility for Water Pollution (Vessels).	DOT–USCG	525.316 barrels of oil not spilled (NPV).	$451,440,918 (NPV)	Timeline of the analysis: 1996–2025; Discount Rate: 7%; $1996.

(Continued)

Table 7.2 *Continued*

Rule	Agency	Benefits	Costs	Other information
Antidrug Program for Personnel Engaged in Specified Aviation Activities.	DOT–FAA	$206.64 million (NPV)	$138.13 million (NPV)	Timeline of the analysis: 1994–2003 (RIA, p. 12); $1992 (RIA, p. 12); Discount rate = 7% (RIA, p. 20).
Controlled Substances and Alcohol Use and Testing.	DOT–FHWA	Reduced fatal accidents: $680 million in 1st year, $952 million per year in 2nd and subsequent years. Reduced injury cost: $152.4 million in 1st year, $213.4 million per year in 2nd and subsequent years assuming the highest deterrence scenario. Reduced property damage: $47.5 millioin in 1993, $65.5 million per year from 1994–2002. Reduced traffic delays: $3.5 million in 1993, in $4.9 million per year thereafter asssuming highest deterrence rate. Reduce other costs of free-way accidents; $1.9 million in 1995 and $2.7 million thereafter.	$93,947,750 in 1995, and $92,453,950 per year in 1996 and thereafter.	

Note: DOI = Department of the Interior. DOL = Department of Labor. DOT = Department of Transportation. FAA = Federal Aviation Administration. FHWA = Federal Highway Administration. HUD = Housing and Urban Development. USCG = United States Coast Guard.

Source: *Office of Management and Budget (2003).* Report to Congress on the costs and benefits of federal regulations. *Washington, D.C.: U.S. Government Printing Office.*

FDA (Food and Drug Administration); the car you drive to work must conform to EPA (Environmental Protection Agency) standards; and the highway you drive on is overseen in general terms by the NHTSA (National Highway Traffic Safety Administration). We could go on for pages, but the picture is clear—administrative law is everywhere.

Legislative Function of Administrative Agencies

Administrative law is the body of law created by the administrative agencies themselves based on authority granted them by laws enacted by Congress. These laws are the rules, regulations, procedures, orders, and previous decisions of agency courts. These laws apply only to the businesses and activities that fall under the specific areas of responsibility and expertise of the agency. For instance, the Securities and Exchange Commission (SEC) only has power to regulate activities related to the stock exchange and securities markets. Congress has authorized regulatory agencies to create their own rules because it has realized that it lacks the knowledge to create specific rules pertaining to highly technical subject matter with which many agencies deal. Congress makes broad laws (e.g., employers must not discriminate on the basis of race or gender; companies may not pollute the air beyond a certain level; automobiles must be safer) and delegates the specific details to agencies with personnel who have a professional knowledge of their agency's area of responsibility. However, as the Supreme Court has held, filling in the details of law is not lawmaking per se, and thus Congress and state legislatures have oversight powers over the decisions of the agencies operating under their mandates (Friedrichs 2001).

Investigatory and Enforcement Function of Administrative Agencies

Congress has also empowered regulatory agencies to investigate violations of agency rules and to devise ways of enforcing them. Agencies may go about these functions by requiring annual reports from the businesses they regulate, conducting on-site inspections, or investigating complaints from workers or competing businesses. For examples, the SEC requires companies to report profits and losses that may lead to the uncovering of fraud, the Occupational Safety and Health Administration (OSHA) may visit dangerous work sites for signs of unsafe working conditions, and the Office of Equal Opportunity (OEE) will investigate charges of workplace discrimination when members of protected categories (racial minorities and women) complain that they are victims of it. OSHA, for instance, with a 2004 budget of $468 million, has 1,100 inspectors and claims to have cut workplace fatalities by 60 percent and occupational injuries/illness rates by 40 percent since its inception in 1971. In 2004, OSHA reported that its inspectors identified 86,708 violations, for which violators were fined a total of $85,192,940 (Occupational Safety and Health Administration 2005).

Judicial Function of Administrative Agencies

Most disputes and regulatory infractions are settled informally by voluntary settlements. Agencies prefer such settlements because they relieve the agency of expensive investigations and court hearings. If matters cannot be settled informally, the regulatory agency holds a hearing presided over by an administrative judge, who is an expert on, or at least substantially knowledgeable about, the substantive matter at hand. Although more informal that a criminal or civil trial, the proceedings of an administrative hearing are governed by the APA's procedural rules. Both parties to a dispute are entitled to be represented by attorneys, but hearings take place without juries. The administrative judge (or examiner) is thus both the finder of fact and of the administrative law to be applied.

If losing parties in such a hearing so chose, they can appeal their case to the more formal civil law system. However, because they lack the often complex and technical substantive knowledge of an administrative examiner, judges are reluctant to preside over such cases. If an administrative ruling is overturned by the courts, it is based on points of law (the administrative law was not correctly interpreted; the examiner exceeded his or her authority or was obviously biased) rather than on fact. Courts are extremely reluctant to overrule administrative judges, however, and almost always defer to their special expertise. In *National Cable & Telecommunications v. Brand X Internet Services* (2005), the Supreme Court even went as far as to hold that federal agencies are free to "overturn" federal court rulings bearing on interpretations of regulatory statutes unless the court's interpretation is the only one possible (presumably to be determined eventually by the Supreme Court itself).

Since 1984, courts have applied what has come to be known as **Chevron deference** to appeals from administrative court hearings. Chevron deference is a phrase coming from a Supreme Court case (*Chevron U.S.A., Inc. v. Natural Resources Defense Council, Inc.* 1984) in which the Court was asked to clear up an ambiguity in some provisions of the federal Clean Air Act. The Natural Resources Defense Council (NRDC), a private evironmental protection group, challenged the EPA's interpretation of the Clean Air Act when it allowed Chevron Oil to use equipment not meeting the NRDC's interpretation of the act. The Court held in this case that courts must defer to an administrative agency's interpretation of its own rules because Congress has granted them such authority. If there is ambiguity or gaps in the statutes, however, the federal courts may then decide if an agency's interpretation was "reasonable."

Environmental Justice

Accompanying the increasing concern for justice in many areas of American life since the 1960s is a concern for environmental justice, one that is overseen by the Environmental Protection Agency (EPA), the largest of the regulatory agencies just discussed. The EPA defines **environmental justice** as follows:

> Environmental Justice is the fair treatment and meaningful involvement of all people regardless of race, color, national origin, or income with respect to the development, implementation, and enforcement of environmental laws, regulations, and policies. EPA has this goal for all communities and persons across this Nation. It will be achieved when everyone enjoys the same degree of protection from environmental and health hazards and equal access to the decision-making process to have a healthy environment in which to live, learn, and work.

This definition is couched in due process rather than in distributive justice terms, in that a clean and healthy environment is viewed as something due to everyone simply by virtue of sharing a common planet. Environmental justice is an ideal that is difficult to attain because everyone does not enjoy "the same degree of protection" from unhealthy environments, although the effort is being made through environmental laws and regulations.

The Development of Environmental Laws and Regulations

In the 1960s, polluted Lake Erie was considered "dead," the Cuyahoga River in Cleveland "spontaneously burst into flame," and a number of other, similar events gave birth to the modern environmental movement. When the first Earth Day was held in 1970, it was clear that Americans had had enough of environmental degradation. Environmental laws existed before the 1960s, but the most effective protections were passed after the late 1960s. Beginning in 1969 with the signing into law of the National Environmental Policy Act (NEPA) and continuing through the 1970s with the Clean Air Act (1970) and the Clean Water Act (1972), the government began to put teeth into the public desire for a clean and healthy environment (Simonsen 2007).

NEPA's main requirement was that agencies in charge of new government projects must submit environmental impact statements detailing their effects on the environment. Additional relevant acts passed around this time included provisions regulating the handling and disposal of hazardous waste (Resource Conservation and Recovery Act), the control of toxic chemicals (Toxic Substances Control Act), and the identification and cleanup of hazardous waste sites (Comprehensive Environmental Response, Compensation and Liability Act). These acts all provided for criminal prosecution and/or civil penalties for violations.

States and localities have also passed laws to protect the environment, modeled after federal laws, though the laws and their enforcement vary widely because local governments shape their laws around the types of businesses and industries within their borders (Epstein 1998). For instance, if oil production is a major industry in a county, then the state and/or county environmental laws, and hopefully their enforcement, will be focused on concerns over oil's use and the likelihood of leaks and of waste oil's being dumped in waterways or into the soil.

Enforcement of Environmental Laws

Local police and prosecutors are not trained to enforce environmental laws and do not view such enforcement as a priority. Thus the involvement of citizens, advocacy groups, and the media in reporting environmental abuses and pushing for prosecutions and cleanup has been vital. The EPA, the largest regulatory agency in the federal government, is charged with many duties, though it has tended to center its regulatory focus on the areas of air and water pollution and hazardous waste and chemicals (Burns and Lynch 2004). The EPA divides its enforcemental tasks into the three areas: civil, cleanup, and criminal.

- *Civil enforcement*: Serves a number of important goals, including returning violators to compliance and deterring misconduct in others, eliminating or preventing environmental harm, and preserving a level playing field for responsible companies that abide by the laws.

- *Cleanup enforcement:* Deals with sites where there's been a release or a threat of release of hazardous substances into the environment.

- *Criminal enforcement*: Used against the most serious environmental violations as well as those that include egregious negligence or conduct involving intentional, willful, or knowing disregard of the law.

Whether enforcement involves federal, state, or local laws and regulations, certain common problems confront enforcers. It is not always clear whether a violation is criminal or civil; and because the alleged violators/criminals may be powerful and provide jobs and taxes for the local community, regulatory agencies are often reluctant to enforce the laws fully. Corporate entities are often rich and powerful, and politicians are frequently elected with campaign funds largely donated by corporations.

Most federal and state regulations allow for both civil and criminal enforcement, but with few exceptions regulatory agencies tend to pursue civil rather than criminal penalties. The choice is related to the difficulty prosecuting environmental crimes, due to the frequent lack of evidence tying a corporate actor to the decision to commit the offending act. This, plus the frequent lack of the political will to enforce regulations, often results in offenses' being punished with fines rather than with criminal sanctions (Burns, Lynch, and Stretesky 2008). When the violator is a governmental entity, the reluctance to enforce regulations is likely tied to the fact that local governments cannot do anything to remedy the situation without resorting to unpopular tax increases.

Burns and Lynch (2004) note that support for environmental protection has waxed and waned across presidential administrations since 1970, when the EPA was created through executive order by President Nixon. The Nixon administration had a largely positive influence on environmental regulation; the Ford administration was too short-lived to have much influence; the Carter administration, though sympathetic to environmental regulation, provided mixed messages by weighing the benefits of pro-business versus a pro-environment stance. Burns and Lynch (2004) argue that the pro-business/antiregulatory stance of the Reagan administration damaged the EPA immensely, although under the aegis of Reagan appointee William Ruckelshaus, lead was removed from gasoline and the dangerous pesticide ethylene dibromide was removed from the market. President George H. Bush also had a mixed record on the environment, at one point pushing to strengthen the Clean Air Act, but at another opening up wetlands to development. President Clinton, though bringing much hope of environmental reform into office, was a disappointment, in that the EPA's research staff was reduced during his tenure. In the latter part of his second administration, the EPA was engaged in the greater protection of endangered species and the protection of public lands.

President George W. Bush has been deemed the worst president on environmental issues, taking a hard-line stance from the beginning (Burns, Lynch, and Stretesky 2008). Bush "reversed a campaign pledge to control carbon

dioxide emissions from power plants; ...announced that the U.S. would withdraw from the Kyoto Protocol on climate change; sought to open the Arctic
National Wildlife Refuge to oil exploration; withdrew the EPA's new arsenic-
in-drinking-water standards; and had the boundaries of 19 National Parks
redrawn to encourage oil exploration" (Burns and Lynch. 2004, 95). At the time
of this writing it is difficult to characterize how the Obama administration will
influence the functioning of the EPA, although he did make promises during
his campaign to strengthen environmental protections and regulation. Part of
Obama's stimulus bill included $6 billion for upgrades in sewer systems around
the country.

Environmental Crime

Environmental crimes are primarily offenses committed by business interests,
such as the dumping of tons of toxic waste in rivers, lakes, and ocean, failing to
repair or prevent toxic mercury emissions from smokestacks, and the inclusion of
harmful chemicals such as lead in products such as lipstick and children's toys.
Many of these corporate crimes have far-reaching health and safety effects that
harm millions of people and other living creatures. Regardless of whether they
are criminally or civilly prosecuted, defendants are typically tried under principles of strict liability (recall that strict liability is a legal doctrine relaxing the
mens rea requirement and makes persons responsible for damages their actions
or products cause, regardless of any malignant intent). In fact, the classic strict
liability case involved an environmental wrong when water from a man's textile
mill reservoir overflowed and flooded the mine shafts of another in nineteenth-
century England (*Rylands v. Fletcher*, 1868).

The classic American case cementing the use of the strict liability criteria for polluters is *United States v. Weitzenhoff* (1994). This case involved two
managers of a Honolulu sewage treatment plant (Michael Weitzenhoff and
Thomas Mariani) who were convicted of dumping nonbiodegradable waste
into the ocean on forty different occasions, in violation of the Clean Water
Act. Each of the defendants was sentenced to prison; thus subsequently
appealed their convictions on the basis of statutory vagueness. The Ninth
District Circuit Court denied their appeal, basically stating that regardless of
the alleged vagueness of the statute, the defendants should have known what
they were doing was wrong. The defendants then appealed their case to the
United States Supreme Court, but the Court denied certiorari, thus allowing
the convictions to stand.

Despite the lesson of *Weitzenhoff*, according to a recent study using EPA data
(Duhigg 2009), the single biggest violators of the Clean Water Act are local governments with inadequate sewer systems. As populations have exploded in cities
and suburbs, their infrastructure, like sewer systems, have not always expanded
to accommodate this growth. Unlike corporations, these governmental entities are
not making a profit off polluting, but they are polluting enough that hundreds
of their citizens are sickened by waterborne illnesses. "More than a third of all
sewer systems...have violated environmental laws since 2006....Thousands of
other sewage systems operated by smaller cities, colleges, mobile home parks and

companies have also broken the law. But few of the violators are ever punished" (Duhigg 2009, A18).

As was noted in chapter 1, we have evolved a "risk society" that is preoccupied with safety and the future and with the sense that we can control the future by attending to the dangers and hazards engendered by scientific and technological advances. We can only do this with law and regulation, but history has shown us that the law is a sluggish creature often requiring a kick to stir it. Social movements have arisen in response to the many environmental disasters of the twentieth century to provide that kick. Many other potential environmental disasters loom for the twenty-first century, so vigilance must be maintained. As always, the law is required to mediate the often-competing claims of businesses and environmentalists as tensions between economic and environmental concerns wax and wane. When the economy is buoyant, unemployment is low, and energy prices are low, everyone sympathizes with the greens, but when the opposite situations obtain, environmental concerns tend to be sacrificed to the needs of the economy.

Administrative Law and Corporate Crime

In its annual Uniform Crime Reports (UCR), the FBI provides the nation with a count of the mayhem that occurred on the streets of America the previous year. Except for forgery/counterfeiting, fraud, and embezzlement (usually relatively minor crimes committed by individuals or small groups), however, white-collar crimes are conspicuously absent from the annual crime tally. The FBI has a Congressional mandate to collect and report the "in your face" crimes committed on America's streets, but there is no mandate to collect and report crimes that occur in America's suites.

Conflict theorists would explain this by pointing out that the people who define the seriousness of criminal acts are the same people who have large vested interests in many of the businesses that commit the acts we call corporate crime. Corporate entrepreneurs and "their representatives play an active part in crafting the laws and regulatory standards that circumscribe their conduct. Through monetary contributions and social contacts, they gain access to legislators to ensure their views are made known and taken seriously" (Shover and Hochstetler 2000, 294). It is also true that some administrative agencies are dominated by the businesses they supposedly regulate because many regulators come from, and eventually expect to go back to, those very businesses.

But let us not be too cynical; tallies of occupational and corporate wrongdoings *are* collected and distributed each year by state and federal regulatory agencies (we briefly mentioned OSHA's annual report earlier). Because agencies do not come under the jurisdiction of the United States Justice Department, however, they lack criminal enforcement powers beyond assessing fines. If an agency's investigation uncovers criminal violations as opposed to merely regulatory violations, it can refer cases for criminal prosecution.

There are many complications and practical difficulties in recognizing and reporting corporate crime. As Walsh and Ellis (2007, 398) point out:

> With common street crime we have a body lying in the street, a house burgled, a dazed mugging victim, or a car stolen. These easily understood and defined discrete events quickly come to the attention of the police, who then record them and set out to find the perpetrators.... many victims [of white-collar crimes] do not even know they have been victimized, and the sequence of events is often quite the opposite.

In other words, with white-collar crime, investigators may start with a suspicion that something has happened, then try to find out what, and then try to find out who is responsible. Serious corporate crimes such as the Enron, WorldCom, and Adelphi Communication frauds prosecuted in the early 2000s, are incredibly complex and require thousands of hours and millions of dollars to unravel.

Recent Responses to Corporate Crime

In the past, very few corporate crooks were the recipients of truly meaningful sanctions. Take the Savings and Loan (S & L) scandal that occurred in the 1980s following the deregulation of the S & Ls. Multiple bank executives looted their own banks of up to $473 billion, a sum many times greater than losses from all the "regular" bank robberies in American history put together (Calavita and Pontell 1994). Two of the biggest players in this scandal were sentenced to less than two years imprisonment for stealing $20 million in one case and $30 million in another (Reiman 1998).

But things are beginning to change. As a result of Congressional hearings and public outcries following the scandals of the early 2000s, Congress passed and President George W. Bush signed into law the **Sarbanes-Oxley Act** (SOA) of 2002. This act authorized a huge increase in the Security Exchange Commission's (SEC) budget to $776 million, and an additional two hundred employees were hired to carry out the SOA mandates (American Institute of Certified Public Accountants, 2004, 6). The act and its provisions have enhanced the morale of the previously underfunded SEC, which now sees its role as more proactive rather than simply reactive (Burr 2004). The SOA requires company chiefs to personally vouch for their company's financial disclosures, ensuring that they can no longer hide behind a "plausible deniability" ("I didn't know what was happening") defense.

A separate act titled **White-Collar Crimes Penalty Enhancement Act** creates new securities offenses with significantly enhanced penalties. It also relaxes some procedural evidentiary requirements for prosecutors who formerly had to prove "willfulness" in white-collar cases (i.e., prove beyond a reasonable doubt that the defendant took some action knowing that it violated a specific law). Prosecutors now have only to show that defendants did what they did, period, which has always been the standard in other criminal cases ("Ignorance of the law is no excuse"). Relaxed standards for proving obstruction of justice (and penalties of up to twenty years for conviction) are also included. This should make it easier for loyal and otherwise guiltless employees attempting to shield their employers to reveal what they know to investigators.

According to Lowell and Arnold (2003, 228), "Congress clearly intended to send a message to the law enforcement community to be tougher on violators of business law and regulations. Further, Congress's message will echo to prosecutors and sentencing judges who will avail themselves of the new SOA maximums or use previously available means to enhance maximum penalties." SEC investigators and prosecutors are clearly taking advantage of the tools provided them by SOA. One commentator remarked, "Today, prosecutors are driven to go after corporate fraud with an almost evangelical zeal" (Burr 2004, 10). Sentencing judges also appear to be matching that zeal, perhaps indicating that the days of leniency for white-collar criminals are over. In July 2005, Bernard Ebbers, ex–WorldCom CEO, was sentenced to twenty-five years in prison for his role in the $11 billion fraud; in June 2005, John Rigas, founder of Adelphia Communications Corporation, was sentenced to fifteen years and his son Timothy to twenty years for their roles in yet another massive fraud; in September 2005, Tyco executives Dennis Koslowski and Dennis Swartz were sentenced to eight and twenty-five years, respectively; and in October 2006, Enron CEO Jeffrey Skilling was sentenced to twenty-four years and four months for his part in the massive Enron fraud. Finally, in June 2009, Bernard Madoff was sentenced to 150 years' imprisonment for his massive $13 billion-plus Ponzi scheme.

SUMMARY

Civil law is law designed to address private wrongs and is composed of tort, contract, property, family, and juvenile categories. There are many differences between civil and criminal law, the most important being the lower "preponderance of evidence" standard of proof. Tort law is law regarding wrongs committed against private citizens, which may also be crimes that have already been prosecuted in criminal courts. There are a variety of tort categories that mirror criminal categories (e.g., intentional versus negligent wrongs) as well as a similar variety of defenses to liability.

Tort reform is about the efforts of certain business interests to limit what they consider frivolous lawsuits and to place caps on punitive damages. Tort reform should lead to cheaper insurance premiums and cheaper services for consumers from those who pay huge premiums to cover lawsuits. On the other hand, punitive damages have a way of forcing businesses to be more careful about what they place on the market and forcing service providers to more closely monitor their work.

Property law is law about the rights of ownership or possession of personal (movables, such as furniture and automobiles), real (buildings, houses), and intellectual (ideas, songs, abstract creations) property. It also has to do with the responsible use of property and how it can be used, disposed of, given away, or inherited.

Contract law is the law covering the conduct of business. A contract is a legally binding promise of one party to do or provide something to one party in exchange for a similar promise from the other party. There are a number of requirements that must be met for a contract to be legal: two parties, capacity, assent, and legality. If the terms of a contract are not met, it is considered a breach of contract, for which the injured party can seek legal redress.

Family law has to do with such issues as the legal requirements for a valid marriage, the duties and responsibilities of the parties in the marriage, the dissolution of the marriage, and issues of alimony and child support. A contentious issue at present is gay marriage. The Defense of Marriage Act defines marriage as something that can only occur between opposite-sex partners. However, the Supreme Court has ruled a number of times that marriage is a fundamental right, although it has never yet ruled on gay marriage.

Administrative or regulatory law is public law dealing with the relationship of governmental administrative agencies' oversight of business. There has been a huge growth of administrative agencies since the birth of the country, with a particularly large increase taking place in the 1930s. This growth took place against the sharp opposition of Republicans and businesses who saw agency regulation as the first step toward a communist-like planned economy and as unwarranted intrusion. Democrats saw agency oversight as simply protecting public interests. A compromise was reached with the passage of the Administrative Procedure Act, which placed procedural constraints on agency oversight activities.

Administrative agencies have been empowered by Congress to create law, enforce it, and adjudicate it within their special area of expertise. If an agency uncovers violations within its oversight purview, it may require offending parties to cease and desist and may assess fines against them. Most such violations are settled informally, but quasi-judicial hearings may be held if they are not settled informally. If accused parties do not like the agency's ruling, they may take the case to civil court. However, these courts typically defer to agency rulings under the so-called Chevron deference rule.

Administrative investigation and adjudication is often the first step in uncovering corporate (white-collar) crime. If a corporation is found to be engaging in criminal activities (as opposed to regulatory violations), the administrative agency refers the case to the appropriate criminal justice agency for prosecution. White-collar criminals have traditionally been treated leniently compared with the treatment of ordinary street criminals, but with the economic scandals of the early 2000s, this began to change. In 2002, Congress passed the Sarbanes-Oxley Act, and the White Collar Crimes Penalty Enhancement Acts, designed to provide the SEC and the criminal justice system with greater ability to investigate, prosecute, and punish white-collar crooks.

DISCUSSION QUESTIONS

1. How does civil law differ procedurally from criminal law?
2. In light of the different standards of proof in civil versus criminal law, would you favor a "preponderance of evidence" standard of proof in

criminal trials over the "beyond a reasonable doubt" standard? Defend your position.
3. Discuss your opinion about tort reform; that is, should there be strict caps on punitive damages?
4. In light of previous Supreme Court cases on the right to marry, does the government's anti–gay marriage stance make legal sense?
5. The tension between Democrat and Republican and between liberal and conservative are in evidence in their respective opinions about the expansiveness of administrative law. In your opinion, where does public protection stop and unwarranted government intrusion begin?
6. Should corporate criminals be punished as severely as street criminals? How about massive fines for companies committing illegal acts? What if those fines bankrupt the company, resulting in the loss of hundreds of jobs?

References

AICPA. 2004. American Institute of Certified Public Accountants *Summary of the Sarbanes-Oxley Act of 2002.* http//www.aicpa.org/info/sarbanes_oxley_summary.htm.

Burns, R., and M. Lynch. 2004. *Environmental crime: A sourcebook.* New York: LFB Scholarly Publishing.

Burns, R., M. Lynch, and P. Stretesky. 2008. *Environmental law, crime and justice.* El Paso, TX: LFB Scholarly Publishing.

Burr, M. 2004. SEC gains power, prestige in post Enron era. *Corporate Legal Times,* December, pp. 10–13.

Calavita, K., and H. Pontell. 1994. Savings and loan fraud as organized crime: Toward a conceptual typology of corporate illegality. *Criminology* 31:519–48.

Cohen, T. 2005. *Federal tort trials and verdicts, 2002–2003.* Washington, DC: Bureau of Justice Statistics.

Cohen, T., and S. Smith. 2004. *Civil trial cases and verdicts in large counties, 2001.* Washington, DC: Bureau of Justice Statistics.

Duhigg, C. 2009. Sewers at capacity, waste poisons waterways. *New York Times,* Monday, November 23, pp. A1, A18.

Dukeminier, J., and J. E. Krier. 1988. *Property.* 2nd ed. Boston: Little, Brown.

Epstein, J. 1998. Despite the lesson of *Weitzenhoff* state and local environmental enforcement. In *Environmental crime: Enforcement, policy, and social responsibility,* (edited by M. Clifford, pp. 145–68). Gaithersburg, MD: Aspen.

Fenster, M. 2005. The birth of a "logical system": Thurman Arnold and the making of modern administrative law. *Oregon Law Review* 84:69–146.

Friedrichs, D. 2001. *Law in our lives.* New York: Oxford University Press.

Hellinger, F., and W. Encinosa. 2006. The impact of state laws limiting malpractice damage awards on health care expenditures. *American Journal of Public Health* 96:1375–81.

Kionka, E. 1988. *Torts.* St. Paul, MN: West Publishing.

Lancet Report. 2003. Insurance loss leaves doctors scrambling for coverage. *Lancet* 362:376.

Lowell, A., and K. Arnold. 2003. Corporate crime after 2000: A new law enforcement challenge or déjà vu? *American Criminal Law Review* 40:219–40.

Melone, A., and A. Karnes. 2003. *The American legal system: Foundations, processes, and norms.* New York: Oxford University Press.

Mencimer, S. 2004. False alarm. *Washington Monthly,* October. http://www.washingtonmonthly.com/features/2004/0410.memcimer.html.

Occupational Safety and Health Administration. 2005. *OSHA facts—December 2004.* http://www.osha.gov/as/opa/oshafacts.html.

Office of Management and Budget. 2003. *Report to Congress on the costs and benefits of federal regulations.* Washington, DC: U.S. Government Printing Office.

Reiman, J. 1998. *The rich get richer and the poor get prison.* 5th ed. Boston: Allyn & Bacon.

Samuels, S. 2006. *Law, politics, and society.* Boston: Houghton Mifflin.

Schiller, R. 2005. "Saint George and the dragon": Courts and the development of the administrative state in twentieth-century America. *Journal of Policy History,* 17:110–24.

Shepard, G. 1996. Fierce compromise: The Administrative Procedure Act emerges from New Deal politics. *Northwestern Law Review* 90:1557–1683.

Shover, N., and A. Hochstetler. 2000. Crimes of privilege. In *Criminology: A contemporary handbook,* edited by J. Shelly, pp. 287–319. Belmont, CA: Wadsworth.

Simonsen, C., ed. 2007. *The essentials of environmental law.* 3rd ed. Upper Saddle River, NJ: Pearson/Prentice Hall.

United States Attorney General's Committee. 1941. *Final report of the Attorney General's Committee on Administrative Procedure.* Washington, DC: U.S. Government Printing Office.

Vago, S. 1991. *Law and society.* 3rd ed. Englewood Cliffs, NJ: Prentice Hall.

Walsh, A. 1988. "The people who own the country ought to govern it": The Supreme Court, hegemony, and its consequences. *Law and Inequality* 5:431–51.

Walsh, A., and L. Ellis. 2007. *Criminology: An interdisciplinary approach.* Thousand Oaks, CA: Sage.

White House, the. 2006. *Federal agencies and commissions.* http://www.whitehouse.gov/independent-agencies.html.

Cases Cited

Chevron U.S.A., Inc. v. Natural Resources Defense Council, Inc., 467 U.S. 837 (1984).

City of Oakland v. The Oakland Raiders, 646 P.2d. 835 (1982).

Loving v. Virginia, 388 U.S. 1 (1967).

Lubitz v. Wells, 113 A.2d. 147 (1955).

National Cable & Telecommunications v. Brand X Internet Services, 545 U.S. 967 (2005).

National Labor Relations Board v. Bildisco & Bildisco, 465 U.S. 513 (1984).

Pierson v. Post, 3 Cal. R. 175, 2 Am. Dec. 264 (1805).

Reynolds v. United States 98 U.S. 897 (1878).

Rylands v. Fletcher, L.R. 3 H.L. 330 (1868).

Sullivan v. O'Connor, 296 N.E.2d. 183 (1973).

Skinner v. State of Oklahoma, Ex. Rel. Williamson, 316 U.S. 535 (1942).

Turner v. Safley, 482 U.S. 78 (1987).

United States v. Weitzenhoff, 35 F.3d 1275 (9th Cir. 1994).

Zablocki v. Redhail, 434 U.S. 374 (1978).

CHAPTER 8

JUVENILE JUSTICE

Both Jon Venables and Robert Thomson came from severely deprived and abusive single-parent homes in Liverpool, England. On February 12, 1993, Jon and Robert, both then ten and one-half years old, abducted two-year-old Jamie Bulger from a Liverpool shopping mall, beat him, sexually molested him, and killed him, leaving his body on train tracks to be mutilated. The abduction was caught on closed-circuit TV, and both boys were arrested and charged as adults with murder. The trial took place in an atmosphere of intense national rage and grief. Both boys were convicted and ordered to serve a minimum of 10 years, the first 8 in a juvenile facility.

In 1999, the boys' lawyers appealed their case to the European Court of Human Rights (a supranational court with jurisdiction among all European Union countries), claiming that they had not received a fair trial. The Court agreed, stating that the trial took place in a charged atmosphere and that the boys should not have been tried as adults. The boys were released in 2001 without serving one day in an adult prison. The British government paid an estimated $8 million to furnish them with new homes and identities (they had received numerous death threats). By way of contrast, the Bulgers were given only $15,000 in victim compensation.

Keep this case in mind as you read about juvenile behavior and early efforts to deal with it humanely. When you read about juveniles being transferred to adult court in the United States for far less heinous crimes, think about the contrast between American and European attitudes toward juvenile crime and punishment. How much more protection are juveniles entitled to? How far should the government go to protect them after release, if at all?

INTRODUCTION

This chapter addresses the history and current practices of juvenile justice in the United States. We will see that society has come a long way in its understanding and treatment of its children and youths (collectively known as juveniles) since ancient times. Our evolving understanding of childhood and the sometimes-emotional turmoil of adolescence has led to a system of justice for juveniles that is different from the adult system. Juvenile justice today falls under the umbrella of the civil law rather than of the criminal law, and as such there are a number of differences in the way juvenile offenders are processed through the courts as compared with adult offenders. Juveniles who commit acts that are criminal when committed by adults are considered a separate class of offenders called **delinquents.** The term *delinquent* comes from the Latin for "to leave undone" and conveys the notion that the juvenile has *not done* something he or she *was supposed to do* (behave lawfully) rather than *done* something he or she *was not supposed to do* (behave unlawfully). This subtle difference reflects the presumably rehabilitative rather than punitive thrust of American juvenile justice.

WHAT IS JUVENILE DELINQUENCY?

Juveniles have historically been subject to laws that make some actions illegal for them that are legal for adults, such as smoking, not obeying parents, and not attending school. Such acts are called **status offenses** because they apply only to individuals of a particular status—that of a juvenile—and to distinguish them from offenses that are violations of the criminal law. Status offenses are proscribed because juveniles are assumed to lack the requisite ability to appreciate the long-term consequences of their behavior and are therefore in need of protection from themselves. Acts such as smoking, drinking alcohol, and having sex can have negative effects that juveniles often fail to recognize. Acts such as disobeying parents and school truancy can seriously jeopardize juveniles' future acquisition of suitable social roles (Binder, Geis, and Bruce 2001). If parents cannot or will not shield their children from harm, then operating under the ostensibly benign philosophy of juvenile justice, the juvenile system takes it as its duty to become a substitute source of discipline and training for responsible adulthood.

Status offenses constitute the largest proportion of juvenile offenses and thus consume an inordinate amount of juvenile courts' time and resources (Bynum and Thompson 1999). For this and other reasons, some states have relinquished juvenile court jurisdiction over such acts to other social service agencies. In states that have not relinquished jurisdiction over status offenders, terms such as "child in need of supervision" (**CHINS**) or "person in need of supervision" (PINS) tend to be used to distinguish status offenders from juveniles (delinquents) who have committed acts that are crimes when committed by adults.

THE EXTENT OF DELINQUENCY

The public image of juvenile offenders tends to be fueled by sensationalized media accounts of atypical cases such as the outburst of school shootings in Arkansas, Kentucky, and Oregon that occurred in the late 1990s (Lawrence and Mueller 2003). However, juveniles do commit a disproportionate percentage of the FBI's Uniform Crime Report (UCR) Part I index crimes. Krisberg (2005, 2) indicates that we have actually witnessed a steady decline in juvenile offending since 1994, and that youth under eighteen account for "only" 13 percent of arrests for violent crime. This is true, but "youths under eighteen" are only about 6 percent of the American population (United States Census Bureau 2004) and thus are overrepresented among those arrested for violent crimes. In 2005, youths under eighteen years of age accounted for 15.5 percent of Part I index violent crimes, and 28.9 percent of Part I index property crimes and are thus overrepresented by about 2.5 times among violent offenders and about 4.5 times among property offenders.

Figure 8.1 presents a graph showing arrest rates by age in the United States in 1999. Although the height of the peak differs somewhat from year to year, the same pattern—that is, a sharp rise beginning around puberty that rises steadily until the mid-teens and then falls off— is present each year and in every country arrest statistics are kept (Walsh and Ellis 2007).

No discussion of juvenile delinquency can proceed without noting that some degree of antisocial behavior is normative for juveniles. It is a time when youths are "feeling their oats" and seeking to cast off parental apron strings to become their own persons. During this period, the young are seeking their identities in an increasingly complex and confusing world and are asking themselves who they are, what their place in society is, and where they are going. The juvenile courts are thus dealing with individuals at a time in their lives when they are most susceptible to antisocial behavior. Individuals (especially males) who *do not* engage in some form of antisocial behavior are statistically in the minority (Moffitt and Walsh 2003). Looking at data from twelve different countries, Junger-Tas (1996) concluded that delinquent behavior is a part of growing up and that the peak ages for different types of crimes were similar across all countries (fourteen to fifteen for vandalism, sixteen to seventeen for property crimes, and eighteen to twenty for violent crimes).

Figure 8.1 Arrest rates per 100,000 in the United States by Age in 1999.

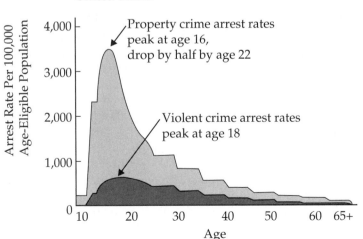

Source: L. Ellis and A. Walsh, *Criminology: A global perspective* (2000), p. 109. Reprinted with permission.

This has always been so. Shakespeare had a shepherd in *The Winter's Tale* express the wish that youth could be put to sleep between the ages of ten and twenty-three: "for there is nothing in between but getting wenches with child, wronging the ancientry, stealing, fighting" (Walsh 2006, 399). Why this sharp rise in antisocial behavior has been a constant across time and cultures has been something of a mystery to criminologists who have long admitted that they cannot explain it by any known set of sociological or psychological variables (Gottfredson and Hirschi 1990; Walsh and Beaver 2008). However, work in the neurosciences over the past fifteen to twenty years has thrown much light on the topic. We briefly discuss some of this evidence because, as we shall see, the courts are making some important decisions in juvenile justice influenced by neuroscience data on the juvenile brain (Garland and Frankel 2006).

DEVELOPMENTAL FACTORS AND JUVENILE DELINQUENCY

The New York Academy of Sciences' 2003 conference on adolescent brain development provided some key messages that help us to understand adolescent behavior (White 2004, 4):

1. Much of the behavior characterizing adolescence is rooted in biology intermingling with environmental influences to cause teens to conflict with their parents, take more risks, and experience wide swings in emotion.

2. The lack of synchrony between a physically mature body and a still maturing nervous system may explain these behaviors.

3. Adolescents' sensitivities to rewards appear to be different than in adults, prompting them to seek higher levels of novelty and stimulation to achieve the same feeling of pleasure.

Puberty marks the onset of the transition from childhood to adulthood and is accompanied by a tenfold to twentyfold increase in testosterone in males, a hormone linked to aggression and dominance seeking (Ellis 2003). Neurotransmitters such as dopamine that excite behavior increase during this period, while inhibitory transmitters such as serotonin decrease (Collins 2004; Walker 2002). The brain is also undergoing a period of physical reorganization that slowly refines the neural circuitry to its adult form during this period (Walker 2002). For instance, the prefrontal cortex (PFC) is getting its final coat of a fatty substance called myelin to insulate various brain structures that are important for the speedy transmission of information. The PFC is the brain's "CEO," serving functions such as modulating emotions from the brain's emotional centers and making reasoned judgments and plans. In a nutshell, the adolescent brain is immature, and as neuroscientist Richard Restak (2001, 76) put it, "The immaturity of the adolescent's behavior is perfectly mirrored by the immaturity of the adolescent's brain."

The point is that there are *physical* reasons why adolescents do not evidence the same level of judgment that adults do and why they tend to assign faulty attributions to situations and to the intentions of others. A brain on "go slow" superimposed on a hormone-driven physiology on "fast forward" may explain why "teenagers often find it difficult to gauge the meanings and intentions of others and to experience more events as aversive during adolescence than they did as prepubescent children and will do so again as adults" (Walsh 2002, 143). Around about the age of twenty-two, when the brain reaches its adult state in most people, more adultlike personality traits emerge (McCrae et al. 2000, 183). To put this in the context of justice policy, by far the most successful "treatment" for delinquency is simply growing older. It is against this backdrop that we discuss the history and philosophy behind juvenile justice.

HISTORY AND PHILOSOPHY OF JUVENILE JUSTICE

While it may seem odd that the juvenile justice system is considered a branch of civil law, the reason that it is will become clear as we discuss its historical development. Throughout much of history, young children have been considered not much different from property, and as such, civil law has been critical to the development of juvenile justice. Also important to our discussion is the concept of *culpability,* which describes the level to which persons are held legally responsible for their actions. The minimum legally defined age of criminal responsibility was defined at common law as seven (it is now ten in British common law) and is the age of responsibility in most states, but it ranges from six in North Carolina to ten in Arkansas, Colorado, Kansas, Pennsylvania, and Wisconsin (Snyder et al. 2003, 2). The idea of reduced culpability for children is a relatively new one. Throughout much of history, there were no special allowances for children when it came to determining culpability and punishment, and there are records of children as young as six being housed in jails and prisons with adults and even being executed for relatively minor offenses (Schmalleger 2003).

The social conception of children is a fundamental consideration in the study of juvenile justice. The control of children's behavior has historically been the responsibility of the family, particularly of fathers. Children were considered the property of their fathers, who were invested with the authority to maintain discipline within the family as they saw fit. The ancient Romans used the term *patria potestas* (literally, *fatherly power*) to describe the power of the father over his family. He had power of life or death over his children and as such, could sell them into slavery, abandon, or even kill them, although punishments were sometimes prescribed for fathers who exercised their power arbitrarily (Binder et al. 2001). Because children held no special status in society, there was no special status given to youthful offenders. Fathers were accountable for the actions of children under their control and were responsible for their punishment when they misbehaved.

Toward the end of the fourth century, there developed a trend toward limiting the power fathers had over their children in Roman society, as the cultural ideal of *paterna pietas* ("fatherly love") became prominent. While this ideal did not dramatically change the nature of juvenile treatment, it indicated a gradual shift toward a more benign method of attempting to control the behavior of the young. However, there were still no separate rules or regulations for children, no separate system to deal with youthful offenders, and few laws as to how much or what types of punishment a father could inflict upon his children.

Under the increasing influence of the Christian church during the Middle Ages, there was a gradual lessening of the brutal nature of the treatment of children. Church doctrine held that children under the age of seven could not be held responsible for spiritual transgressions because they had not yet reached the age of reason. The English courts of the period came to accept this doctrine and exempted children below this age from criminal responsibility as well. Additionally, they afforded special status to children between the ages of seven and fourteen, during which period children could only be held criminally responsible and treated as adults if it could be shown that they were fully aware of the consequences of their actions. Fourteen was the cutoff age between childhood and adulthood for the purpose of assigning criminal responsibility because individuals were considered rational and responsible enough at this age to marry (Springer 1987).

Institutional Control

Although parents retained the primary responsibility for the behavior of their children, the impetus toward greater state involvement had been in evidence since the formation of the English chancery courts (or courts of equity) in the thirteenth century. These courts adopted the doctrine of *parens patriae*, which literally means *father of his country* or, more loosely but more correctly in a practical sense, "state as parent." *Parens patriae* gave the King, by virtue of his role as symbolic father of all his subjects, the right to intercede and act in the best interest of the child or any other legally incapacitated persons such as the mentally ill. This philosophical shift in the treatment of juveniles meant that the state and not the parents had the ultimate authority over children. It also meant that children who fell under the jurisdiction of the courts could be removed from their families if judged to be delinquent, abandoned, or in need of the care and protection that their parents were unwilling or unable to provide and placed in the custody of the state (Schmalleger 2003).

The parental control model was not completely lost in the transition. In keeping with this model, children without parents or with inadequate ones were assigned to foster families through a system known as **binding out**. While the idea of binding out is the precursor of modern adoption, the practice was more akin to indentured servitude because children were generally only accepted by families who could profit from their labor. Children whose parents could not control them or who were simply too poor to provide for them were apprenticed to richer families, generally land-owning farmers, who used them for domestic or farm labor. It was during this time that the first laws directed specifically at children were established, including laws that condemned begging and vagrancy (Sharp and Hancock 1995).

The concern over vagrancy and laziness moved the English authorities to create workhouses in which "habits of industry" were to be instilled in their youthful residents, who were typically vagrants and beggars. The first one, opened in 1555, was a converted palace called Saint Bridget's Well, which was subsequently shortened to *Bridewell*. Despite its regal origins, Bridewell soon became a prison-like institution. Nevertheless, it was considered so successful that in 1576, the English Parliament passed a law establishing **Bridewells**, or workhouses, in every English county (Whitehead and Lab 1996). The idea behind the Bridewells was that youth were trainable and malleable, and if vagrant youths were removed from the negative influences of street life, they could be taught proper work habits and become contributors to society.

While originally established as training schools, Bridewells were soon filled with all types of problem children. It was not uncommon for parents to place their own children in these institutions in the hope that their experiences there would reform them and help them to develop a work ethic. The directors of these institutions often used the children as a cheap source of labor for their own economic gain and were often cruel and harsh in their treatment of them (Krisberg and Austin 1993).

Childhood in the United States

The British colonization of the United States provided an additional way to deal with delinquent British youths, many of whom were sent from the Bridewells to the colonies as indentured servants, sometimes without parental notification or support. Due to labor shortages in the colonies, many destitute and rebellious youth were promised wealth and happiness in the New World. They earned their passage to the colonies by agreeing to work for their employers for a specific term, usually four years, and were considered the legal property of their "owners" (Krisberg and Austin 1993).

The economy in the United States took a downturn in the early 1800s, limiting opportunities available in the infant factory system of the Northeastern United States for the increasing number of poor immigrants arriving in the country. Unemployment was rife during this period, and the streets of many big cities were cluttered with destitute and unwanted children who engaged in illegal activities to survive. The problem was particularly bad in large urban areas such as New York and Boston, which did not have the resources to deal with the rising number of juveniles requiring state supervision. At that time, children who were arrested for any antisocial act, including vagrancy and begging, were placed in the same jails as adult offenders.

In response to this situation, a number of concerned New York citizens formed a group known as the *Society for the Prevention of Pauperism*. The idea motivating the actions of this group was the belief that the primary causes of criminal behavior were economic, and therefore, if children were provided with food, shelter, and vocational training, they would choose to become productive citizens rather than thieves and beggars. Based on this assumption, and following the Bridewell model, the New York House of Refuge was established in 1825 to house orphans, beggars, vagrants, and juvenile offenders. Not long after, several other cities, counties, and states established their own homes for "the perishing and dangerous classes" as they were thought of (Binder et al. 2001, 202).

Children assigned to these houses were to remain there until those in charge determined that they were reformed, and criteria for admission were often arbitrary. For instance, parents could place their children in residence for such offenses as idle and disorderly behavior. Given this situation, it soon became clear that the courts would have to create standards for admission and control, which they did in *Ex Parte Crouse* (1838). (The term *ex parte* designates a hearing in the presence of only one of the parties to a case.) This case challenged the power of magistrates to remove children from their parents and send them to these institutions. The subject of the case, a child named Mary Ann Crouse, was placed in the Pennsylvania House of Refuge by her mother against the wishes of her father (Whitehead and Lab 1996). Her father argued that it was unconstitutional to incarcerate a child without a jury trial. Citing the *parens patriae* doctrine, the Pennsylvania supreme court ruled that parental rights are superseded by the "best interest of the child" doctrine, as those interests were viewed by the courts. This landmark decision brought the ideals of the English chancery courts as they pertained to juveniles to America, thus establishing *parens patriae* as settled law in American juvenile jurisprudence (del Carmen, Parker, and Reddington 1998).

While the purpose of the Houses of Refuge was to train and care for children, in practice they looked very similar to the Bridewells. Children lived highly disciplined lives and were required to work at jobs that brought income to the institution. The indeterminate nature of children's residence allowed the institutions a great deal of latitude in their treatment of them. Throughout the nineteenth century, children placed in these institutions were exploited, worked long hours, often received little or no training, and were frequently mistreated (Whitehead and Lab 1996).

The Child Savers

As the nineteenth century drew to a close, there emerged a growing discontent with government corruption and inefficiency among the rising and increasingly influential middle classes. This dissatisfaction generated a group of concerned individuals collectively referred to as **Progressives** who called for the professionalization of public service. In the later part of the nineteenth century, a group of well-funded and highly educated liberal reformers (mostly females) known as the **Child Savers** began an ideological attack on the Houses of Refuge, which they saw as punishment-oriented rather than rehabilitation-oriented. Central to their attack was the belief that juveniles could be molded into better citizens through religious instruction and training them to satisfy their basic needs through honest labor and thrift. Reformers argued that children should be deinstitutionalized and placed in settings that provided a more family-like atmosphere where they could be taught the value of hard work and social conformity. Most often the type of intervention suggested for wayward children was their placement with farm families in the Western United States.

It was thought that since criminal environments breed criminals, a dramatic change to more wholesome surroundings was the best solution to the problem of juvenile delinquency. These farm families were often idealized as "God's reformatories" (Mennel 1973).

The motives of many reformers may have been less altruistic than they might initially appear, for many of them held beliefs similar to those held by the people who created the Bridewells in sixteenth-century England. Many of them believed the poor to be innately criminal and that poverty was a sign of personal defects such as laziness and feeblemindedness. It was also believed that the presence of destitute and vagrant children in neighborhoods contributed to their decline, and for this reason, it served the public interest to rid the city of them.

The Beginning of the Juvenile Courts

Regardless of their motives, the Child Savers created an impetus for change in the way juvenile offenders were handled. It became increasingly obvious that the solutions applied by the criminal courts were not working with children. Adult criminal courts were not equipped to apply the doctrine of *parens patriae* in a fashion consistent with the spirit of its philosophy. In 1899, Cook County, Illinois, enacted the first Juvenile Court Law providing for a separate court system for juveniles, and by 1945, every state in the union had established juvenile court systems (Hemmens, Steiner, and Mueller 2003). In establishing these courts, the legislation both created a class of offenders separated by their age status and a nonadversarial courtroom process using civil law standards of proof, that is, "preponderance of evidence" rather than the more restrictive "beyond a reasonable doubt." Juvenile judges were afforded a great deal of latitude in determining how "the best interests of the child" were to be achieved. In principle, the juvenile court was supposed to emphasize an individualized approach to youthful offending, tailoring each case to the unique characteristics and needs of the child rather than simply matching sentences to offenses. In practice, however, it gave judges wide latitude to impose their own private views of morality on children.

The ideal (not necessarily the day-to-day practice) of the juvenile courts in the early twentieth century was best described in 1909 by Judge Julian Mack as cited by Mark Small (1997, 120):

> The child who must be brought into court, of course, should be made to know that he is face to face with the power of the state, but he should at the same time, and more emphatically, be made to feel that he is the object of its care and solicitude. The ordinary trappings of the courtroom are out of place in such a hearing. The judge on the bench, looking down upon the boy standing at the bar, can never evoke a proper sympathetic spirit. Seated at desks, with the child at his side, where he can on occasion put his arm around his shoulder and draw the lad to him, the judge, while losing none of his judicial dignity, will gain immensely in the effectiveness of his work.

This kind of judicial solicitude is probably no longer in evidence in any juvenile court in the land, where the judge, surrounded by all the trappings Judge Mack called "out of place," does indeed "look down upon the boy."

The creation of a separate system of justice for juveniles brought with it a set of terms (euphemisms, if you like) describing the processing of children accused of committing delinquent acts that differentiated it from the adult system. These terms reflect the protective and rehabilitative nature of the juvenile system in contrast with the punitive nature of the adult system. To illustrate these differences, in Table 8.1, we follow Tony, age nineteen, and his younger brother, Craig, age fifteen, as they are processed through the adult and juvenile court systems after being apprehended for robbery in 1960. The italicized terms are the parallel terms used in their respective courts; for example, in Item 1, Tony is *arrested* and Craig is *taken into custody*. Tony receives all due process rights guaranteed to him by the Bill of Rights; Craig receives none of these since he is processed in accordance with civil law procedure (as we shall see, however, juveniles are now entitled to most due process rights). What Craig does receive is the "solicitous protection" of the court under the *parens patriae* philosophy, which is cold comfort when he was similarly incarcerated against his will for longer than his brother, notwithstanding that it was in a "training school" rather than in a prison. Note that the age of majority (when one becomes an adult) was twenty-one in the 1960s.

Table 8.1 *Major Distinctions Between the Juvenile and Adult Systems in the United States*

Tony's Trip Through the Adult System	Craig's Trip Through the Juvenile System
1. Tony is *arrested* and taken to jail.	1. Craig is *taken into custody* and taken to the juvenile detention center.
2. The prosecutor seeks an *indictment* or *information* charging Tony with robbery.	2. The prosecutor *petitions the court* for an adjudication of delinquency.
3. The *defendant* (Tony) is *arraigned* and *pleads* guilty, not guilty, or no contest to the charge.	3. The *respondent* (Craig) receives a *hearing* and *admits or denies* the charge in the petition.
4. Tony pleads not guilty and receives a *jury trial*, which is an adversarial process open to the public.	4. Craig denies and receives an *adjudicatory hearing*, which is a nonadversarial process generally not open to the public.
5. The jury returns a verdict of *guilty* using the "beyond a reasonable doubt" standard.	5. The judge *adjudicates* Craig *delinquent*, generally using the "preponderance of evidence" standard of proof.
6. A *presentence investigation report* is written.	6. A *predispositional* or *social inquiry report* is written.
7. Tony is *incarcerated* in *prison* for five years.	7. Craig is *detained* in a *training school* for "the remainder of his minority" (age twenty-one).
8. Tony is *paroled* after serving four years and is supervised by an adult probation/ parole officer.	8. Craig is released at age twenty and receives *aftercare* under the tutelage of a juvenile probation officer.

JUVENILE WAIVER TO CRIMINAL COURT

Under certain circumstances, juveniles can be **waived** (transferred, or bound over) to adult criminal court where they are subject to criminal prosecution and punishments. When juveniles are waived to criminal court, they lose their status as minors and become legally culpable for their alleged crime. The simple philosophy underlying juvenile waivers seems to be "Do adult crime, do adult time." A transfer to adult court is called a waiver because the juvenile court waives (relinquishes) its jurisdiction over the child in question to the adult system. Waivers are designed to allow the juvenile courts to transfer to a more punitive system those juveniles over a certain age who have committed particularly serious crimes or who have exhausted the juvenile system's resources in trying to rehabilitate chronic offenders.

Alarm and disenchantment crystallized into a "get tough" philosophy in which every state allowed some form of waiver, and the practice increased by 400 percent in the 1980s over what it was in the 1970s (Steiner and Hemmens 2003). Juveniles become increasingly more likely to be waived if they are chronic offenders approaching the upper age limit of their state's juvenile court's jurisdiction. It should be noted that only about 1.5 percent of juvenile cases nationwide are waived to the criminal courts (Schmalleger 2003, 352).

There are three primary ways in which juveniles can be waived to criminal court.

1. **Judicial waiver** occurs when a juvenile court judge decides according to his or her own discretion after a "full inquiry" that the juvenile should be transferred. At present, forty-eight states allow for judicial discretionary waivers. In some states, there are mandatory waivers for some offenses, but the juvenile system is involved in that juvenile judges must determine if the criteria for a mandatory waiver are met. A third form of waiver under this heading is the presumptive waiver. In this type, the burden of proof is on the juvenile to prove that he or she is amenable to treatment and therefore should not be waived, not on the prosecutor to prove that he or she should be waived. This is similar to the burden of proof shift in criminal courts when the defendant claims insanity.

2. **Prosecutorial discretion** or *direct file* allows prosecutors to file some cases in either juvenile or adult court. In such cases (usually limited by age and seriousness of the offense), the prosecutor can file the case directly with the adult court and bypass the juvenile court altogether. Fourteen states and the District of Columbia allow prosecutorial discretion waivers.

3. **Statutory exclusion** or *legislative waiver* indicates instances in which state legislatures have statutorily excluded certain offenses (the most serious ones) from the juvenile courts for juveniles over a certain age, which varies from state to state. These automatic waivers exist in thirty-one states.

The presumed social benefits of waivers (deterrence and reduction of crime) have not materialized. Studies have shown that juveniles waived to adult courts are more likely to recidivate than youths adjudicated for similar crimes in juvenile court, although we suspect that this is because the most delinquent-prone youths are waived (Butts and Mitchell 2000). Neither does a waiver necessarily guarantee a more punitive disposition. Waived juveniles who commit violent crimes are likely to be incarcerated, but juveniles waived for property and drug offenses often receive more lenient sentences than they would have received in juvenile courts (Butts and Mitchell 2000). It is easy to see how juries and adult court judges would be more reluctant to convict and/or send nonviolent minors to adult institutions than a juvenile judge would be to adjudicate them delinquent and send them to a juvenile institution.

EXTENDING DUE PROCESS TO JUVENILES

Under the philosophy of *parens patriae*, juvenile courts viewed their mission as one of helping troublesome, neglected, or abandoned children to overcome their difficulties, not to punish them. Yet children were being punished and often in arbitrary ways that would not be tolerated in the adult system. Critics argued that the *parens patriae* doctrine allowed too much latitude for courts to restrict the rights of juveniles. It was also argued that because the actual practice of juvenile corrections was still very similar to adult correctional practices at the time in that it was punitive and that since the courts could remove juvenile rights to liberty, juveniles should be afforded the same due process protections as adults. Nevertheless, in a number of early cases, state courts generally held that the doctrine of *parens patriae* was suitable and proper for the treatment of children and that any problems concerning juvenile court operation were considered problems of implementation rather than of philosophy (Whitehead and Lab 1996).

The United States Supreme Court maintained a hands-off policy with regard to juvenile issues until 1948 in *Haley v. Ohio*. On October 14, 1945, a storekeeper in Canton, Ohio, was shot to death in his store by one of two boys. The petitioner, fifteen-year-old John Harvey Haley, served as a lookout for the other two older boys. Haley was not allowed to see his mother for five days after his arrest, and there was evidence that he was beaten by the police in long interrogation sessions during the course of which he confessed. He was subsequently sentenced to life imprisonment, partly on the basis of that confession. The issue before the Court was whether the due process clause of the Fourteenth Amendment prohibits the use of coerced confessions against juveniles. The Court ruled that the Fourteenth Amendment does prohibit the police from violating the due process clause in obtaining confessions from juveniles and that confessions obtained in this fashion are inadmissible in court.

Kent v. United States

The *Haley* case dealt with the actions of the police, not with the operation of the juvenile courts. In *Kent v. United States* (1966), we have the first instance in which the Supreme Court provided oversight to juvenile court proceedings, marking a steady shift away from the juvenile courts' traditional operating principle of *parens patriae*. Morris Kent first came to the attention of the juvenile court of the District of Columbia when he was fourteen years old, charged with several burglaries and a purse snatching. In 1961, when he was sixteen years old, he broke into a woman's apartment, raped her, and stole her wallet. Fingerprints left at the scene identified him as the culprit, and during interrogation, he admitted several other similar offenses. Because of the seriousness of the offense and Kent's chronic delinquency, the juvenile judge decided that the case warranted waiver to adult court for prosecution. The code of the District of Columbia allowed juvenile court judges to waive jurisdiction and transfer to adult criminal court children over the age of sixteen charged with a serious crime after a "full investigation." The judge in the Kent case read "full investigation" to mean private consultation and reflection on police reports and the predisposition report. He held no hearing and denied Kent's counsel access to Kent's social service file.

The adult court found Kent not guilty of two counts of rape "by reason of insanity," and he was consigned to a psychiatric hospital (he was still there at the time of the Supreme Court hearing in 1966). However, he was found guilty of six counts of housebreaking and robbery, for which the judge sentenced him to thirty to ninety years in prison. Had Kent remained in juvenile court, he could have been sentenced to a maximum of five years (the remainder of his minority). Kent appealed, arguing that the waiver process had not included a "full investigation," no findings were made, no reasons were stated for the waiver, and counsel was denied access to the files upon which the juvenile judge presumably relied to make the waiver determination. Kent's appeal to the Unites States Court of Appeals was denied, and the case came before the United States Supreme Court.

In the majority opinion remanding Kent's case to district court, Justice Abe Fortas called the waiver decision a "critically important stage" in the juvenile process and added that "there is no place in our system of law for reaching a result of such tremendous consequences without ceremony—without hearing, without effective assistance of counsel, without a statement of reasons. ... the admonition to function in a 'parental' relationship is not an invitation to procedural arbitrariness." Justice Fortas also noted that under the philosophy of *parens patriae*," there may be grounds for concern that the child receives the worst of both worlds: that he gets neither the protections accorded to adults nor the solicitous care and regenerative treatment postulated for children." The Court thus determined that juveniles must be afforded certain constitutional rights, and in doing so, it began formalizing the juvenile system into something akin to the adult criminal courts (Hemmens et al. 2003).

In Re Gault

The *Kent* decision opened the door for a close inspection of juvenile courts by the Supreme Court, which heard a second case concerning the civil rights of juveniles one year later in *In Re Gault* (1967). (The Latin phrase *In re* literally means "in the matter of," and is used in nonadversarial proceedings.) In 1964, fifteen-year-old Gerald Gault was taken into custody following a complaint by a neighbor that he had made lewd and indecent remarks during a phone call. The worst of these remarks were "Are your cherries ripe today?" and "Do you have big bombers?" (Butts and Mitchell 2000 176). For these obviously adolescent and relatively innocuous remarks, Gault was adjudicated delinquent and sentenced to a total of six years in the State Industrial School. An adult convicted of the same offense would have faced a $5 to $50 fine and a maximum of sixty days in jail. The court never resolved the issue of whether Gault actually made the call because the alleged victim did not appear at the adjudicatory hearing.

The United States Supreme Court used this case to establish five basic constitutional due process rights for juveniles: (1) the right to proper notification of charges, (2) the right to legal counsel, (3) the right to confront witnesses, (4) the right to privilege against self-incrimination, and (5) the right to appellate review, all of which had been denied to Gault. The Court determined that "[f]ailure to observe the fundamental requirements of due process has resulted in instances, which might have been avoided, of unfairness to individuals and inadequate or inaccurate findings of fact and unfortunate prescriptions of remedy." Justice Fortas took some robust stabs at the doctrine of *parens patriae* in this case, calling it a phrase that has "proved to be a great help to those who sought to rationalize the exclusion of juveniles from the constitutional scheme; but its meaning is murky and its historic credentials are of dubious relevance." He also likened the juvenile court's proceedings against Gault to a "kangaroo court."

It is important to note that in extending due process rights to juveniles and introducing more formalized procedures into juvenile courts, the major tenets of *parens patriae* have not been voided. What has changed is the previously almost unbridled discretion of juvenile authorities. It is also important to note that the due process protections extended under Gault do not automatically apply in all cases; rather, they only apply in an adjudication hearing that is likely to result in a juvenile's deprivation of liberty (Hemmens et al. 2003).

In Re Winship

A third significant Supreme Court case involving the juvenile court is *In Re Winship* (1970). In 1967, twelve-year-old Samuel Winship was accused of stealing $112 from a woman's purse taken from a locker. Since the juvenile court system was developed from civil law, the standard of proof required for conviction was the civil system's "preponderance of the evidence." Winship was adjudicated delinquent in a New York court based on this standard and was ordered to spend eighteen months in a state training school. Winship appealed his case to the New York Supreme Court, which denied it on the grounds that a delinquent adjudication is not a conviction, that it affects no rights or privileges such as the right to vote or hold office, and that because juvenile proceedings are not criminal proceedings, there can be no deprivation of due process. (Perhaps in this decision we can appreciate Justice Abe Fortas's point about the murkiness of *parens patriae* and how its collection of euphemisms can be used in ways far from being "in the best interests of the child.")

In Justice Brennan's majority opinion reversing Winship's conviction, he noted that despite the euphemisms employed by the juvenile courts, a conviction is a conviction and that deprivation of liberty is deprivation of liberty no matter what name the places of confinement go by. The Court ruled that when the possibility of commitment to a secure facility is a possibility, the "beyond a reasonable doubt" standard of proof must extend to juvenile adjudication hearings. The Court ruled that although juvenile proceedings are civil in nature, the "preponderance of evidence" standard must be upgraded when the possibility of deprivation of liberty exists.

McKeiver v. Pennsylvania

In 1968, sixteen-year-old Joseph McKeiver was charged with robbery, larceny, and receiving stolen goods. McKeiver was represented at the adjudication hearing by counsel and he requested a jury trial, which was denied. He was adjudicated delinquent and was placed on probation. He lost all appeals in lower courts and eventually appealed to the Supreme Court. The sole issue before the Court in *McKeiver v. Pennsylvania* (1971) was "Do juveniles have the right to a jury trial during adjudication hearings?" The Supreme Court ruled that they are not, thus backing away somewhat from their due process momentum and reaffirming *parens patriae* to some extent. In delivering the Court's majority opinion, Justice Blackmun wrote, "The imposition of the jury trial on the juvenile court system would not strengthen greatly, if at all, the factfinding function, and would contrarily, provide an attrition of the juvenile court's assumed ability to function in a unique manner. It would not remedy the defects of the system … and would once again tend to place the juvenile squarely in the routine of the criminal process." Justice Blackmun added that "If in its wisdom, any State feels the jury trial is desirable in all cases or in certain kinds, there appears to be no impediment to installing a system embracing that feature." The Court did not rule that the states cannot provide juveniles with this due process right, only that they are not constitutionally required to do so.

Breed v. Jones

Breed v. Jones (1975) recommenced the Supreme Court's program of applying due process rights to juveniles. Gary Jones was a chronic delinquent who was charged with armed robbery in 1970 when he was seventeen years old. A petition was granted alleging Jones had committed the acts outlined in the petition, and subsequently an adjudicatory hearing was held on this matter. At the hearing, the judge found that the allegations in the petition were true (in effect, meaning that Jones was guilty), and continued the proceedings for a dispositional hearing upon completion of the predisposition report. At the disposition hearing, the judge ruled that Jones was not amenable to treatment available to the juvenile court and ordered him transferred (waived) to adult court.

Jones's counsel petitioned for a writ of habeas corpus before the juvenile court and then the California Court of Appeal, alleging a claim of double jeopardy in violation of the Fifth and Fourteenth Amendments. Both courts denied the petition, stating that jeopardy did not attach to his adjudicatory hearing. The case finally arrived at the Supreme Court, which in a unanimous decision declared that double jeopardy did indeed attach to Jones's adjudicatory hearing. Remember, although the adjudicatory hearing is nominally a civil process and not technically a trial, it is the functional equivalent of a trial in that a "finding of fact" against the respondent can result in a substantial loss of liberty. The Court essentially ruled that Jones was subjected to the burden of two trials for the same offense and therefore the double jeopardy clause of the Fifth Amendment had been violated. Practically, the ruling meant that a waiver to adult court cannot occur after jeopardy attaches, and jeopardy attaches at the adjudicatory hearing when evidence is first presented.

Schall v. Martin

Gregory Martin, age fourteen, was arrested in 1977 and charged with armed robbery, assault, and possession of a weapon. Martin was held in detention pending adjudication because the court determined that he was at "serious risk" of further criminal activity if released. He was adjudicated delinquent after spending fifteen days in detention. His attorney filed a writ of habeas corpus challenging the constitutionality of preventative detention while awaiting a fact-finding hearing. The issue before the Supreme Court in *Schall v. Martin* (1984) was whether the preventative detention of a juvenile charged with a delinquent act is constitutional. The Court ruled that preventative detention of juveniles was constitutionally permissible because it serves a legitimate state interest in protecting both society and the juvenile from the risk of further crimes committed by detainees while awaiting their hearing. In effect, this ruling established that juveniles do not enjoy the right to bail consideration and reasserted the *parens patriae* interests of the state in promoting the best interests of the child.

THE JUVENILE DEATH PENALTY

The greatest moral issue associated with juvenile justice is the application of the death penalty to individuals who committed their crimes when they were juveniles. From 1973 to 2003, twenty-two juvenile offenders were executed in the United States; thirteen (59 percent) of them in Texas (Streib 2003). It should be noted that the ultimate penalty has only been applied to persons who committed their murders when they were juveniles in particularly heinous and depraved ways. The issue has gone before the Supreme Court on four occasions.

The first occasion was *Eddings v. Oklahoma* (1982). In 1977, Monty Lee Eddings, age sixteen, and several companions stole an automobile to run away from their homes. Sometime during the trip Eddings was pulled over by an Oklahoma Highway Patrol Officer. When the officer approached Eddings's car, Eddings shot and killed the officer with a shotgun. After Eddings was arrested and found guilty, the state presented three aggravating circumstances that it maintained warranted the death penalty. The judge allowed only Eddings's youthful age to be entered as a mitigating factor and not other factors, such as the abusive treatment he received at home. In vacating Eddings's death sentence, the Supreme Court ruled that in death penalty cases, the courts must consider any and all mitigating factors in deciding whether to impose the death sentence, although the Court did not rule on how judges should weigh the relevance of those factors.

The next such case was *Thompson v. Oklahoma* (1988). William Thompson, age fifteen, was one of four persons charged with the brutal murder of his former brother-in-law. All four persons were found guilty and sentenced to death. The Supreme Court granted certiorari to consider whether a sentence of death for a crime committed by a fifteen-year-old is cruel and unusual punishment. In effect, Thompson's attorney was asking the Court to draw the line at an age below which it was constitutionally impermissible to execute juveniles. Using the "evolving standards of decency that marks the progress of a maturing society," the Court drew the line at sixteen, hence sparing Thompson's life.

The case before the Court in *Stanford v. Kentucky* (1989) involved even more heinous murder circumstances. Kevin Stanford, age seventeen, and his accomplice repeatedly raped and sodomized a female during and after their commission of a robbery at a gas station, after which they drove her to a secluded area where Stanford shot her in the face and in the back of her head. In a 5–4 decision, the Supreme Court ruled that if states choose to execute juveniles who were sixteen or seventeen at the time of the commission of their crimes, it was constitutionally permissible. The *Thompson* and *Stanford* cases taken together thus set the minimum age for the execution of juveniles at age sixteen.

There were certain indications in Stanford that some of the justices were anxious to revisit the juvenile death penalty issue again as soon as possible and that their intention was to eventually rule it unconstitutional. Their opportunity came sixteen years later, when they heard *Roper v. Simmons* (2005). Seventeen-year-old Christopher Simmons and two younger accomplices burglarized a home, kidnapped the owner of the home, tied her up, beat her, and threw her alive off a high bridge into the river below to drown. Simmons had been saying to friends before the crime that he wanted to commit a murder and bragged about having done so afterwards.

Simmons was sentenced to death for this heinous crime, but had his sentence overturned by the Missouri Supreme Court. The state of Missouri then petitioned the United States Supreme Court to reverse this decision. In a 5–4 decision, the Court decided to redraw the age line at eighteen, under which it was constitutionally impermissible under the Eighth Amendment prohibition against cruel and unusual punishment to execute anyone. This case brought a blizzard of *amicus curiae* ("friend of the court") briefs, which are briefs presented to the Court arguing in support of one side or the other by interested parties not directly involved with the case. Parties filing amicus briefs in favor of Simmons included the European Union, the American and British Bar Associations, the American Medical and Psychological Associations, and fifteen Nobel Prize winners. Six states filed amicus briefs in favor of Roper (superintendent of the prison in which Simmons was incarcerated), arguing in support of capital punishment for juveniles.

In writing the majority opinion, Justice Kennedy noted that the United States was the only country in the world that gives official sanction to the juvenile death penalty and that such a penalty contravenes the United Nations Convention on the Rights of the Child, which every country in the world has ratified save Somalia and the United States. (As Justice Scalia noted in his dissent, however, whether all these countries honor the Convention in practice as well as on paper is open to question). Kennedy also noted the neurological evidence of the immaturity of the adolescent brain but went to some length to announce that neither this information nor the opinion of the world community was controlling on the Court's decision.

Supreme Court decisions have to have at least the appearance of being based on constitutional grounds. Statements devoid of strictly legal reasoning are relegated to dicta (which you recall are nonbinding explanatory statements). The Court cannot justify decisions with statements such as "the scientific evidence compels us," or "world opinion demands." This would be politics, not law. Thus, the majority opinion cited *Atkins v. Georgia* (2002) in which the Court ruled that the execution of the mentally retarded constituted cruel and unusual punishment under the Eighth Amendment because of the lesser degree of culpability attached to the mentally challenged and noted that such reasoning should have even greater power applied to juveniles. The court also cited state legislation by noting that a national consensus against executing juveniles existed, as evidenced by the fact that the plurality of states (thirty) either bar execution for juveniles or have banned the death penalty altogether. Finally, Kennedy noted that United Kingdom laws were particularly relevant to the case given the English origins of the Eighth Amendment. He noted that United Kingdom law banned the juvenile death penalty as cruel and unusual in 1930 and subsequently banned the death penalty in its entirety.

Figure 8.2 presents a summary of Supreme Court cases altering the nature of juvenile court proceedings from *Kent* (1966) to *Simmons* (2005).

Figure 8.2 Supreme Court Cases Altering the Nature of Juvenile Court Proceedings, 1966–2005

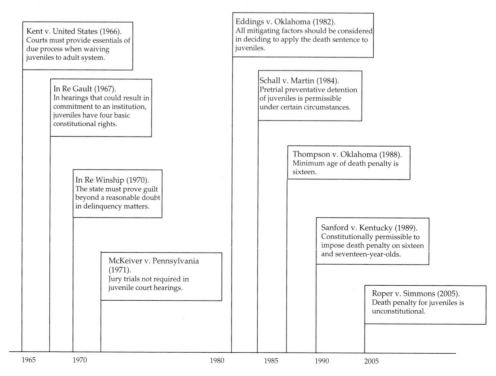

ERODING THE DISTINCTION BETWEEN ADULT AND JUVENILE COURT SYSTEMS

In their dissenting opinions in *Winship*, Justices Burger and Stewart complained that this decision, along with the *Kent* and *Gault* decisions, were eroding the differences between juvenile and criminal courts; in effect, they were criminalizing juvenile courts. These rulings have clearly helped to create a juvenile court system that more closely reflects the procedural guidelines established in adult criminal courts. Juveniles have given up some benefits, such as the informality of solicitous treatment, a high level of confidentiality, and the sealing of their juvenile records, to gain others (formal due process rights). Only time will tell if this convergence of systems results in more just outcomes for juveniles than they received under unmodified *parens patriae*.

One interesting example of extending adult criminal standards to juveniles is the application of the provisions of the 1996 Megan's Law to them. **Megan's Law** (named for Megan Kanka, age seven, who was kidnapped, raped, and murdered by a twice-convicted sex offender), requires law enforcement agencies in all fifty states to register sex offenders in their area. The law requires adjudicated delinquent sex offenders as well as convicted adult sex offenders to register with law enforcement agencies as sex offenders for the rest of their lives. You may agree that such a consequence is appropriate for a seventeen-year-old boy convicted of raping a toddler, but should it apply to a twelve-year-old boy who mooned a group of younger children or to a juvenile who grabs the breasts of a female classmate in the lunchroom? Megan's Law has been applied to cases such as these, thus making no distinctions between predatory sex offenders and incidents that we used to pass off as adolescent playfulness (Trivits and Repucci 2002). Surely not all sex offenses are created equal, and to treat them as if they were trivializes the experiences of the truly brutalized while at the same time elevating the youthful peccadilloes to the point where any of our sons and brothers could be stigmatized for life. This is not meant to excuse the behaviors just described or to belittle how the targets of those behaviors may have felt about their experiences; it is just a reminder of the principle of proportionality.

RESTORATIVE JUSTICE

Because of high levels of recidivism among juvenile and adult offenders as well as the skyrocketing costs of incarceration, alternative forms of dealing with them have emerged. One of the major innovations emerged from an Office of Juvenile Justice and Delinquency Prevention (OJJDP) grant that called for strategic development of juvenile justice policies and models based on the philosophy that juvenile crime is a social problem best handled using a variety of social resources. One of the major consequences that emerged from this grant has been the application of a concept called *restorative justice* in juvenile corrections (and often in adult corrections as well) over the past quarter century (Bazemore and Umbreit 1994).

Restorative justice may be defined as "every action that is primarily oriented toward justice by repairing the harm that has been caused by the act" and "usually means face-to-face confrontation between victim and perpetrator, where a mutually agreeable restorative solution is proposed and agreed upon" (Champion 2005, 154). Even though relatively new in Western correctional systems, it has been claimed that the concept is an ancient one, although there are a multitude of competing histories and claims as to where it originated, what it was to accomplish, and how it was to do it (Sherman and Strang 2002).

Much of the appeal of restorative justice, according to Kelly Richards (2005, 384), is not so much attributable to the failure of other correctional philosophies, as others have claimed but, rather, to the widespread acceptance of other concepts of contemporary culture, such as "self-help, New Age, therapy, and recovery." In other words, the general cultural acceptance of the therapeutic "And how did that make you feel?" sentiment set the stage for the academic and correctional acceptance of restorative justice. The "healing" approach also gained impetus when various victim's rights movements emerged in the 1970s (Bazemore and Umbreit 1994). Richards (2005) also follows many others in asserting that the origins of restorative justice have been mythologized and romanticized by accounts that tend to resurrect images of the "noble savage" behaving in far more "civilized" (nonpunitive) ways than peoples in contemporary societies and that advocates of restorative justice sometimes slip into viewing the offender as a victim.

All previous models, whether retributive or rehabilitative in orientation, were "offender driven" (what do we respond to the offender?) and ignored the needs of victims and of the community. These older models held the legal position that the victim of a crime was the state and that the debt incurred by the offender was owed to society. Restorative justice defines crime and delinquency as offenses committed by one person against another, not against a bloodless state, and by doing so personalizes justice by engaging the victim, the offender, and the community in a process of *restoring* the situation to its preoffense status as far as possile. Thus, restorative justice gives equal weight to the needs of offenders, victims, and the community (Bazemore and Umbreit, 1994). The philosophy of restorative justice was formally endorsed by the American Correctional Association in 1994 and again in 2004 (Walsh 2006).

Under the general philosophical rubric of restorative justice emerged a model for juvenile probation known as the *balanced approach*. The balanced approach focuses on three equally important components for the sanctioning of juvenile offenders. First, juveniles are to be held accountable for their actions. Central to this notion is creating awareness among offenders of how their actions impact their victims and the community. In addition to the usual dispositional treatments, there is a greater focus on restitution and community service. The second component under the balanced approach is community protection. This element addresses directly the growing public fear of crime by focusing on community-based programming and surveillance designed to limit nonproductive time for juveniles while maintaining supervision levels. Examples of this ideal include midnight basketball programs and after-school programs. Both have shown success in providing "voluntary incapacitation" for participants (Mueller and Heck

1997). The balanced approach also provides for the development of employment and educational skills for juvenile offenders through competency development programs.

An integral part of the restorative justice balanced approach is victim–offender reconciliation programs (VORPS). These programs bring offenders and victims together (voluntarily) in face-to-face meetings that are mediated by a trained mediation counselor to iron out ways in which the offender can right the harm done to the victim. Victims are afforded the opportunity to let offenders know how their victimization has hurt them and affected their lives, and offenders are able to put a face to what was otherwise an abstract victim. These meetings may spark rehabilitative feelings of guilt and empathy in offenders who may have never previously experienced such feelings following their delinquent or criminal behavior. As part of the process, a contract is worked out between victim, offender, and mediator laying out what the offender has to do in order to repair the damage he or she has caused. This contract (usually involving monetary restitution and verbal and written apologies) is monitored for compliance by the mediator, who will make a report to the court if necessary. It is assumed that VORPS may assuage some of the rage and helplessness often felt by crime victims and thus lead to psychological closure for them. VORPS have been extremely successful, with one study reporting that 97 percent of victims involved in them express satisfaction (Coates 1990). Similar positive results have been found in Britain, Canada, and Germany, with a few negative results muddying the water a bit (reviewed in Walsh 2006).

As part of their overall mission, the OJJDP has embraced the balanced approach to restorative justice for juvenile offenders, and many states have followed suit (Lauen 1997; Carter 2006). Current juvenile justice policy ranges broadly from state to state. Several authors have suggested that the lack of continuity in juvenile treatment has led to a system with no common understanding of the developmental stages associated with children (Krisberg and Austin 1993). Further, it is clear that there is no commonly accepted theory or philosophy about what causes juvenile delinquency, and therefore policy seems to be a hodgepodge of stopgap interventions sprinkled with crime control ideals (see S. Walker 1998). Criminologists have constructed a variety of theories concerning human behavior and the causes of crime, but these causes are rarely addressed in modern juvenile justice policy, and perhaps they should not be, since these theories are often poles apart in their assumptions about human nature. However, if these theories can integrate the harder and more sophisticated data coming from the neurosciences (for instance, those mentioned at the beginning of this chapter) and the biosocial sciences in general, we will have more cause for optimism.

Restorative justice is not meant to replace traditional methods of dealing with delinquents and criminals but, rather, to complement them. The method can be slotted into a graduated system of sanctioning that begins with restorative solutions and escalating into more coercive methods for offenders who persist in victimizing others (Braithwaite 2006). For instance, for a first offender who has committed a minor crime, the strategy might be to treat the matter outside of the traditional justice system and entirely in restorative terms (mediated by a court official, such as a probation officer, of course). This could be escalated to formal probation for a subsequent offense, then to electronic monitoring, and finally to incarceration if the offender persists. However, because restorative justice is about victims as well as offenders, there may still be restorative aspects attached to specific cases even if the offender is incarcerated. As Sherman and Strang (2002, 88) put it: "Offenders would be subjected to increasing constraints on their freedom if they persisted in crime, but they would always be encouraged to meet with their victims [if victims so desire] to explain their crime and offer to make amends."

How well does restorative justice work? The answer depends on what we wish to accomplish and for whom. First and foremost we wish to reduce recidivism. The general consensus is that restorative justice works best for low-risk offenders with a capacity for empathy and remorse but also that it can work well as a valuable entrée into other rehabilitative programs for higher-risk offenders who focus on criminogenic risk factors (Lilly, Cullen, and Ball 2007). A study assessing the overall effects on recidivism from thirty-two different studies found that 72 percent of those studies reported that restorative justice participants were less likely to recidivate than nonparticipants, although the effect was weak (Latimer, Dowden, and Muise 2001). The same researchers found that, among thirteen studies testing victim satisfaction with the process, only one study reported victim dissatisfaction and overall that participating victims reported greater satisfaction with their case outcomes than nonparticipating victims. Of course, these findings have to be viewed in terms of self-selection bias. That is, both victims and offenders take part in restorative processes on a voluntary basis, and they are therefore at least partially open to the goals of the process. Nevertheless, restorative justice is another weapon in the correctional armamentarium that, although having only minor effects on most offenders, at least gives the previously neglected victims a voice in the justice process that they appear to appreciate.

SUMMARY

Juvenile justice stems from civil law and as such the commonalities between the two are readily visible. The juvenile system deals with both status offenses and delinquency; the former is only applicable to juveniles, and the latter are crimes if they were committed by an adult. Until recently, proof standards and courtroom procedures were much the same for both categories. However, recent Supreme Court decisions have created a juvenile justice system that more closely reflects the adult criminal justice system, especially in cases involving serious delinquent behavior.

It was noted that juveniles commit a disproportionate number of both property and violent crimes, and this has always been true across time and cultures. Recent scientific evidence relates this situation to the hormonal surges of puberty juxtaposed with an adolescent brain undergoing numerous changes. Although most adolescents commit antisocial acts, only a small proportion continue to commit antisocial acts after brain maturation is completed. This evidence was presented to the Supreme Court in a 2005 juvenile death penalty case.

The history of juvenile justice has three distinct periods. Originally, Western culture relied heavily on parents to control children. As society has changed, so have the expectations regarding juvenile delinquency. Institutional control of wayward youth was the model from the mid-1500s until the inception of the juvenile courts. In the United States, this occurred in the late 1800s and early 1900s. The juvenile court model, following the doctrine of *parens patriae*, continues today. However, recently there has been a movement away from the broad discretion formerly accorded to juvenile courts to a model that more closely reflects the constitutionally granted protections afforded to adult offenders. Much of this change has issued from the increased waivers of juveniles to adult courts and from the often-arbitrary control juvenile justice authorities have exercised over juveniles.

The due process "revolution" in juvenile courts beginning with *Kent v. United States* (1966) is summarized in Figure 8.1. Some commentators deplore this trend as having criminalized the juvenile courts; others applaud it as assuring that juveniles are afforded due process rights and that they are not treated arbitrarily. *Parens patriae*, under which the "best interests of the child" are to be protected, has not disappeared altogether, however. Restorative justice is a promising compromise between the punitive approach of the adult courts and the sometimes overly protective nature of some juvenile courts in the past.

DISCUSSION QUESTIONS

1. How does the civil law differ procedurally from the criminal law in juvenile courts?
2. Discuss the development of childhood as a separate class of citizen in Western culture.
3. Discuss the doctrine of *parens patriae* in relation to the development of the juvenile court system in the United States.
4. Should the courts seriously consider the hormonal and neurological evidence as valid legal defenses reducing (not eliminating) culpability for juveniles?
5. Do you agree with the majority opinion in *Roper v. Simmons*? Support your arguments with reference to Justice Kennedy's affirming opinion or Justice Scalia's dissenting opinion. Both opinions are available by typing in the case name in any Web search engine.
6. Do you think that restorative justice is workable? In what circumstances would and would it not be?

References

Bazemore, G., and M. Umbreit. 1994. *Balanced and restorative justice.* Washington, D.C.: Office of Juvenile Justice and Delinquency Prevention, U.S. Department of Justice.

Binder, A., G. Geis, and D. Bruce. 2001. *Juvenile delinquency: Historical, cultural, and legal perspectives.* Cincinnati, OH: Anderson.

Braithwaite, J. 2006. Narrative and "compulsory compassion." *Law and Social Inquiry* 31:425–46.

Butts, J., and O. Mitchell 2000. Brick by brick: Dismantling the border between juvenile and adult justice. *National Institute of Justice 2000: Vol. 2. The nature of crime: Continuity and change.* Washington, D.C.: National Institute of Justice.

Bynum, J., and W. Thompson. 1999. *Juvenile delinquency: A sociological approach.* Boston: Allyn & Bacon.

Carter, K. 2006. Restorative justice and the balanced approach. In *Correctional assessment, casework, and counseling,* 4th ed., edited by A. Walsh. pp. 8–11. Lanham, MD: American Correctional Association.

Champion, D. 2005. Probation, parole, and community corrections. 5th ed. Upper Saddle River, NJ: Prentice Hall.

Coates, R. 1990. Victim-offender reconciliation programs in North America: An assessment. In *Criminal justice, restitution, and reconciliation,* edited by B. Galaway and J. Hudson. Monsey, NY: Criminal Justice Press.

Collins, R. 2004. Onset and desistence in criminal careers: Neurobiology and the age-crime relationship. *Journal of Offender Rehabilitation* 39:1–19.

del Carmen, R., V. Parker, and F. Reddington. 1998. *Briefs of leading cases in juvenile justice.* Cincinnati, OH: Anderson.

Ellis, L. 2003. Genes, criminality, and the evolutionary neuroandrogenic theory. In *Biosocial criminology: Challenging environmentalism's supremacy,* edited by A. Walsh and L. Ellis, pp. 13–34. Hauppauge, NY: Nova Science.

Ellis, L., and A. Walsh. 2000. *Criminology: A global perspective.* Boston: Allyn & Bacon.

Garland, B., and M. Frankel. 2006. Considering convergence: A policy dialogue about behavioral genetics, neuroscience, and law. *Law and Contemporary Problems* 69:101–13.

Gottfredson, M., and T. Hirschi. 1990. *A general theory of crime.* Stanford, CA: Stanford University Press.

Hemmens, C., B. Steiner, and D. Mueller. 2003. *Significant cases in juvenile justice.* New York: Oxford University Press.

Junger-Tas, J. 1996. Delinquency similar in Western countries. *Overcrowded Times* 7:10–13.

Krisberg, B. 2005. *Juvenile justice: Redeeming our children.* Thousand Oaks, CA: Sage.

Krisberg, B., and J. Austin 1993. *Reinventing juvenile justice.* Newbury Park, CA: Sage.

Latimer, J., C. Dowden, and D. Muise. 2001. *The effectiveness of restorative justice practices: A meta-analysis.* Ottawa, Canada: Department of Justice Canada.

Lauen, R. 1997. *Positive approaches to corrections: Research, policy, and practice.* Lanham, MD: American Correctional Association.

Lawrence, R., and D. Mueller. 2003. School shooting and the man-bites-dog criterion of newsworthiness. *Youth Violence and Juvenile Justice* 1:330–45.

Lilly, J., F. Cullen, and R. Ball. 2007. *Criminological theory: Context and consequences.* Thousand Oaks, CA: Sage.

McCrae, R., P. Costa, F. Ostendorf, A. Angleitner, M. Hrebickova, M. Avia, J. Sanz, M. Sanchez-Bernardos, M. Kusdil., R. Woodfield, P. Saunders, and P. Smith. 2000.

Nature over nurture: Temperament, personality, and life span development. *Journal of Personality and Social Psychology* 78:173–86.

Mennel, R. 1973. *Thorns and thistles.* Hanover, NH: University of Hanover Press.

Moffitt, T., and A. Walsh. 2003. The adolescence-limited/life-course persistent theory of antisocial behavior: What have we learned? In *Biosocial criminology: Challenging environmentalism's supremacy,* edited by A. Walsh and L. Ellis, pp. 125–144. Hauppauge, NY: Nova Science.

Mueller, D., and C. Heck. 1997. The neutral-zone as one example of community wide problem solving. In *Community policing in a rural setting,* edited by Q. Thurman and E. McGarrell. Cincinnati, OH: Anderson.

Restak, R. 2001. *The secret life of the brain.* New York: Dana Press and Joseph Henry Press.

Richards, K. 2005. Unlikely friends? Oprah Winfrey and restorative justice. *Australian and New Zealand Journal of Criminology* 38:381–99.

Schmalleger, F. 2003. *Criminal justice today.* 5th ed. Englewood Clifffs, NJ: Prentice Hall.

Sharp, P., and B. Hancock. 1995. *Juvenile delinquency: Historical, theoretical, and societal reactions to youth.* Englewood Cliffs, NJ: Prentice Hall.

Sherman, L., and H. Strang. 2007. *Restorative justice: The evidence.* London: Smith Institute.

Small, M. 1997. Juvenile justice: Comments and trends. *Behavioral Sciences and the Law* 15:119–24.

Snyder, H., R. Espiritu, D. Huizinga, R. Loeber, and D. Petechuck. 2003. *Prevalence and development of child delinquency.* Child Delinquency Bulletin Series. Washington, DC: U.S. Department of Justice, Office of Juvenile Justice and Delinquency Prevention.

Springer, C. 1987. *Justice for juveniles.* Washington, DC: U.S. Department of Justice, Office of Juvenile Justice and Delinquency Prevention.

Steiner, B., and C. Hemmens. 2003. Juvenile waiver 2003: Where are we now? *Juvenile and Family Court Journal* 54:1–24.

Streib, V. 2003. *The juvenile death penalty today: Death sentences and executions for juvenile crimes, January 1, 1973–June 30, 2003.* http://www.law.onu.edu/faculty/streib.

Trivits, L., and N. Repucci. 2002. Application of Megan's Law to juveniles. *American Psychologist* 57:690–704.

United States Census Bureau. 2004. *Statistical abstracts of the United States.* http//:www.census.gov/prod/2004pubs/03statab/vitstat.pdf.

Walker, E. 2002. Adolescent neurodevelopment and psychopathology. *Current Directions in Psychological Science* 11:24–28.

Walker, S. 1998. *Sense and nonsense about crime and drugs: A policy guide.* 4th ed. Belmont, CA: Wadsworth.

Walsh, A. 2002. *Biosocial criminology: Introduction and integration.* Cincinnati, OH: Anderson.

———. 2006. *Correctional assessment, casework, and counseling.* 4th ed. Lanham, MD: American Correctional Association.

Walsh, A., and K. Beaver. 2008. The promise of evolutionary psychology for criminology: The examples of gender and age. In *Evolutionary forensic psychology,* edited by J. Dunteley and T. Shackleford. Oxford: Oxford University Press.

Walsh, A. and L. Ellis. 2007. *Criminology: An interdisciplinary approach.* Thousand Oaks, CA: Sage/Pine Forge Press.

White, A. 2004. *Substance use and the adolescent brain: An overview with the focus on alcohol.* Durham, NC: Duke University Medical Center.

Whitehead, J., and S. Lab. 1996. *Juvenile justice: An introduction.* Cincinnati, OH: Anderson.

Cases Cited

Atkins v. Georgia, 536 U.S. 304 (2002).
Breed v. Jones, 421 U.S. 517 (1975).
Eddings v. Oklahoma, 445 U.S. 104 (1982).
Ex Parte Crouse 4 Whart. 9 (Pa. 1838).
Haley v. Ohio, 332 U.S. 596 (1948).
In Re Gault, 387 U.S. 1 (1967).
In Re Winship, 397 U.S. 358 (1970).
Kent v. United States, 383 U.S. 541 (1966).
McKeiver v. Pennsylvania, 402 U.S. 528 (1971).
Roper v. Simmons, 112 S.W. 3rd 397 (2005).
Schall v. Martin, 104 U.S. 2403 (1984).
Stanford v. Kentucky, 492 U.S. 361 (1989).
Thompson v. Oklahoma, 487 U.S. (1988).

CHAPTER 9

THE LAW AND SOCIAL CONTROL

Frank Walters was knifed to death outside a London nightclub on October, 12, 2002; John Creeger was taken into custody for his murder three days later. Police were able to make the arrest (and subsequent conviction) of Creeger because the murder and Creeger's flight from the scene in a taxicab were caught on three of the thousands of CCTV (closed-circuit TV) cameras situated in London. Creeger's image was checked against thousands of faces in a database and quickly identified.

In 1890, a Harvard Law Review article expressed concerns about privacy issues emanating from the invention of photography. One wonders how the authors would react if resurrected into our post-9/11 world of wall-to-wall surveillance. It is estimated that an urban citizen in the United Kingdom. is caught on camera an average of 300 times per day, and big cities in the United States are catching up. The rationale for this hi-tech surveillance is the prevention and detection of crime, particularly terrorism. As the Creeger case testifies, CCTV cameras can be very useful in detecting crime, but to civil libertarians it all smacks of Big Brother.

Then there is the USA Patriot Act, which has greatly enhanced the government's power to spy on its citizens in the name of deterring and detecting terrorists. All of this surveillance increases the sense of security for those who trust the government but decreases it for those who do not. Do we really care how many times a day we are caught on camera if the bad guys are caught on them too and brought to justice? What about our right to privacy? How much of it are we willing to give up in the name of safety? Benjamin Franklin once wrote, "Those who would give up an essential liberty for temporary security deserve neither." But then Franklin did not live in an age of weapons of mass destruction. When reading this chapter, we ask you to consider the delicate balance between government's power and responsibility to exercise social control and our constitutionally guaranteed rights to privacy.

INTRODUCTION

If law has one overriding function, it is social control. This is evident in the central philosophical question in sociology: "How is society possible?" *Society* is a name we give to the product of countless interactions carried on by people living within some geographical and political boundary. These interactions involve the energy of diverse individuals pursuing their personal interests in interaction with others pursuing their personal interests. This being so, it is not surprising that social life is rife with potential antagonism, conflict, and competition: rich against poor, environmentalist against developer, minority against majority, conservative against liberal, me against my neighbor, ad infinitum. If people are to live together peacefully, there must be some method for containing, organizing, or channeling human energy to produce cooperation and integration rather than conflict and disintegration. In other words, societies need the formal mechanism of social control that we call law.

WHAT IS SOCIAL CONTROL?

We define **social control** *as any action, either deliberate or unconscious, that influences conduct toward conformity, whether or not the persons being influenced are aware of the process.* The term *control* can be used as a noun to denote restriction and supervision and as a verb to denote regulation and restraint. The primary function of the law is to establish and maintain social control through a system of codified rules and regulations. But social control is a much broader concept than the law because there are other informal mechanisms of social control that are more effective, such as the informal socialization process that helps to develop our consciences.

It is not only peaceful coexistence that makes society possible, it is peaceful and *predictable* coexistence that makes it possible. To the degree that members of a society abide by group rules and expectations, they will be able to know with some degree of certainty what others will do in a variety of situations. Social life would be impossible without at least a modicum of predictability. To increase peace, predictability, and social unity, societies need mechanisms for minimizing nonconformity and deviance and for maintaining social order. Tolerance of nonconformity is a mark of a democratic society, but if such nonconforming behavior hammers too hard at the heart of deeply held standards of right and proper behavior, if it jeopardizes our feelings of safety, security, propriety, and freedom, those who conform to society's mores have a right to defend themselves against it.

A TYPOLOGY OF SOCIAL CONTROL

We may classify social control along two dimensions: direct versus indirect and formal versus informal. Direct control is coercive, and indirect control is persuasive and voluntary. Direct control is exemplified by the effect of the presence of the police officer—the uniformed symbol of law and control—on the behavior of those aware of the officer's presence. Those who might want to steal that video or run that red light will not do so if they perceive the presence of the officer.

People prevented from illegal behavior only by the threat of the officer are externally (directly) controlled. People who behave well regardless of the presence of an officer are controlled indirectly because they have internalized a belief in the rightness or wrongness of various acts. Indirect control is better than direct control because those who are directly controlled only can be trusted to behave well when they are being watched, but indirectly controlled individuals watch themselves. Of course, these two forms of control are not mutually exclusive; each supports and reinforces the other.

Informal control begins with the socialization process in which we internalize rules of proper conduct. Internalized rules provide us with an internal self-regulating thermostat we call a conscience, which makes us feel guilty, anxious, and uncomfortable when we misbehave and happy and self-righteous when we behave well. Few of us are so self-controlled that we do not deviate from the norms of expected behavior at some time or another. Controls set us at odds with our hedonistic human nature; there is more truth than we are willing to acknowledge in the old saying that "Everything I like is either illegal, immoral, or fattening." Plato (1960, 47) made the same point more eloquently some twenty-five hundred years ago: "The universal voice of mankind is always declaring that justice and virtue are honorable, but grievous and toilsome; and that the pleasures of vice and injustice are easy of attainment, and are only censored by law and opinion."

Being "censored by opinion" is informal censure—the merest raising of the eyebrows, the snub, the frown, the cold shoulder, the dismissal, the dressing down. This kind of control depends on whether we value the opinions and affections of others and on our range of significant others. Sometimes the power of significant others to control our behavior may play second fiddle to people and ideas we may never meet. The "stars" we see in movies and on the athletic fields are much admired by the young, and many young people strive to emulate these heroes with whom they will never have direct contact.

Many different kinds of socially harmful behaviors such as drug use and sexually promiscuous behavior are tired conventions among the Hollywood set, and through the influence of the media, they have done much to destigmatize, and perhaps even glamorize, these behaviors. Stigmatization is still a powerful social control (try lighting a cigarette in a nonsmoking area if you doubt this). Stigmatizing formerly acceptable behavior (for example, smoking in public places) and destigmatizing the formerly unacceptable (for example, unwed motherhood), certainly has contributed powerfully to dramatic changes in the prevalence of these behaviors over the last two or three decades.

Stigma and other informal means of social control usually suffice in societies that are homogeneous with respect to important social parameters such as race, language, and religion, but they become less so in direct proportion to the growth of diversity along these dimensions, a fact that we have seen emphasized over and again by the great social and legal thinkers. Complex and heterogeneous societies also need social peace and predictability to function properly and may have to turn to alternative methods to get it. As informal controls prove inadequate, our vices are more likely to be censored by more formal means. Formal control is the kind of structured impersonal control exercised by the state via the law.

THE LAW AS A SOCIAL CONTROL MECHANISM

Legal sociologist Donald Black (1976, 107) put the relationship between formal and informal controls well when he stated that "law varies inversely with other forms of social control." In other words, as informal controls exercised by the family, church, school, and neighborhood weaken, increasing reliance is placed on formal legal controls.

Black gives the examples of juvenile law, which is less punitive than adult law in part because juveniles are subject to more informal controls by parents and teachers than are adults. Black's proposition explains the greater legal intervention in families of juveniles where parental authority is weak or in families where fathers are absent. The tendency of juvenile authorities to more often retain juveniles from broken homes in custody and to release children from intact homes to the care of their parents is often interpreted as unfairly discriminating against poor children while favoring children from intact homes. But in terms of Black's proposition about the inverse relationship between formal and informal controls, this practice makes sense. Juvenile authorities make calculations about the amount of control exercised over the child by informal means. If this amount is deemed inadequate, then legal controls are substituted for those lacking from other sources. In a very real sense, frequent and widespread use of the law to contain deviant behavior is a measure of the extent of the weakening of the more fundamental social institutions: the family, church, and school.

The fundamental distinctions between direct versus indirect and formal versus informal control allows us to bring the concept of social control more sharply into focus. These two dichotomies create four separate social control mechanisms: **direct/formal**, **direct/informal**, **indirect/formal**, and **indirect/informal**. To illustrate these separate (but often significantly overlapping) mechanisms, we use an incident in Nathaniel Hawthorne's novel, *The Scarlet Letter*, a book familiar to most students.

In this novel, Hester Prynne had been found guilty of adultery and bearing a child out of wedlock by the authorities of the seventeenth-century Massachusetts Bay Colony. The Colony was a very close-knit and homogeneous community, which means that there was strong and widespread agreement about the norms of acceptable behavior. Indicative of the seriousness with which Hester's behavior was viewed, among the various penalties discussed by women viewing her trial were branding with hot irons and death, "for the shame she has brought on us all." As far as they were concerned, Hester had violated the values that underlie the family, the very basis of society, and must be punished so that others may not be tempted to do as she did. Her judges sentenced her to forever endure the scorn of her community and to forever wear the badge of shame on her dress—an elaborately embroidered letter *A*, branding her as an adulteress. Her transgression was so great as to warrant the direct intervention of formal law, but her actual punishment was to be direct but informal "social" punishment—the reproach and ostracism of all who knew of her shame. Figure 9.1 illustrates the social control typology.

Figure 9.1 Social Control Typology Applied to Hester Prynne's Punishment

	Formal	**Informal**
Direct	Hester's arrest, trial and sentencing by agents of the state	Social shame and ridicule suffered by Hester
Indirect	The threat of legal sanctions perceived by onlookers ("it could happen to me")	Norms reinforced by viewing and participating in Hester's punishment

Punishment and Deterrence

Citizens of the Massachusetts Bay Colony believed that sexual activity outside of marriage was such a serious offense that the norms forbidding it had been codified into law, and the law provided penalties for violations. The people viewed the exercise of legal power against Hester as legitimate, that is, right and just *as defined by those affected by that power*. Thus, the legitimacy of any law (and by extension, the power to enforce it) rests at bottom with those affected by the power, not those who exercise it.

Adultery, while still a crime carrying the possibility of imprisonment in some states and in the armed forces, no longer—rightly or wrongly—is considered any business of the state by the majority of Americans. Most American citizens would probably consider any enforcement of adultery statutes resulting in imprisonment of the participants to be an illegitimate use of state power today.

When people violate the rules of acceptable behavior, they usually feel guilty in proportion to the level of disapproval attached to the violation. But the internal restraints of guilt and anxiety are not always strong enough to allay deviant temptations, and there are those who lack effective internal restraints altogether. It always has been considered wise to augment internalized rules with the tangible experience of punishment. Just as praise and rewards express social approval and value, punishment expresses social condemnation. As Brubaker (1993, 81) put it, "Punishment, like praise, publicly expresses our determinations of what people deserve." Hester's punishment functioned in her community to reaffirm and define the boundaries of acceptable behavior, and thus was directed just as much at onlookers as at Hester herself. Those who witnessed her shame were reinforced in their belief in the correctness of the social norms, more so because they themselves participated in the various actions and gestures of ostracism and contempt that constituted Hester's punishment. Thus, the *direct and formal* control over Hester functioned simultaneously as a powerful *indirect and informal* control for others.

Deterrence has long been considered the primary function of punishment and is defined as the prevention of deviant and criminal acts by the use or threat of punishment. Deterrence may be either *specific* or *general*. **Specific deterrence** refers to the effect of the imposed punishment on the future behavior of the person punished. If the offender desists from future criminal activity, we say the punishment worked; if he or she continues to engage in crime, we say that it did not. There is evidence that punishment in the form of imprisonment is not a significant deterrent for the majority of offenders, although it does appear to have an impact on white-collar criminals and minor blue-collar offenders for whom there exist informal social controls (Seigel 2006).

The influence of punishment on specific individuals being punished has a lot to do with the **contrast effect**. The contrast effect is the contrast between the circumstances of punishment and the offender's usual life. Incarceration is a nightmarish contrast for those who previously enjoyed the company of a loving family and the security of a valued career. Such people are aware of this, and thus the mere prospect of experiencing the embarrassment of public disgrace that threatens the families and careers of those who have invested time, effort, and emotional energy in acquiring and nurturing them is a strong deterrent. This is why having a strong stake in conformity is such a powerful mechanism of informal social control. On the other hand, for those lacking strong family ties and a commitment to a legitimate career, punishment has little effect because the disparity between the punishment and their normal lives is minimal. As Bob Dylan sang, "When you ain't got nothin', you got nothin' to lose."

General deterrence refers to the preventive effect of punishment on those who have witnessed it but not personally experienced it (e.g., Hester Prynne's witnesses). Convicted and punished offenders serve as examples to the rest of us of what may happen if we violate the law. Radzinowicz and King (1979, 296) asserted that "People are not sent to prison primarily for their own good, or even in the hope that they will be cured of crime. Confinement is used as a measure of retribution, a symbol of condemnation, a vindication of the law. It is used as a warning and deterrent to others. It is used, above all, to protect other people ... from the offender's depredations."

Some people may insist that our moral conscience and not the threat of punishment keeps us from committing criminal acts. Such a view invests the human conscience with an essence independent of its origins and maintenance. Conscience is the name we give to the internalized moral content of our social groups. It admonishes us to conform to the obligations implied by its contents and makes us feel anxious, guilty, and ashamed when we act contrary to it. But how long would we feel these pangs of conscience and trust them to keep us in check were it not for Plato's censorship by "law or opinion"? Plato argued that it is only the real threat of punishment—physical, psychological, or both—that keeps any of us honest. As one wag has suggested, "Locks exist to keep honest folks honest; they present no problem for the dishonest." We may all have different thresholds for crossing the line from honesty to dishonesty, but few of us are immune from doing so altogether.

To illustrate his point, Plato (1960, 43–44) recounts the allegory of a good and honest shepherd named Gyges, employed by the king of Lydia. One day, Gyges descended into an opening in the earth made by an earthquake and found a gold ring there. While sitting around the campfire that night with other shepherds, he chanced to turn the ring and became invisible. Upon turning it again, he reappeared and noted with pleasure that he could disappear and reappear at will. Thus armed, Gyges went to the royal palace, seduced the queen, and conspired with her to murder the king and usurp the throne. Plato asserted that given such an opportunity to be free of the prying and censorious eyes of others, to be free of both formal and informal social controls, "no man can be imagined to be of such an iron nature that he would stand fast in justice" (44).

The anonymity of the modern city functions as a kind of ring of Gyges, rendering us "invisible" to the censorious judgments of others. As so many social theorists have pointed out, the city frees us from the social controls exercised by the close-knit communities of yesteryear. We have seen that the use of law as a social control mechanism varies inversely with the loss of more informal and effective methods of social control. To the extent that this is true, the use of law to control behavior becomes a measurable marker of the failure of other forms of control.

The failure of informal controls can be roughly gauged by comparing the size of the legal profession in the United States with those of other countries. Abadinsky (2003) tells us that more than fifty thousand lawyers are admitted to the bar in the United States each year and that the United States has one lawyer for every 345 people compared to one for every 1,220 in the United Kingdom and one for every 9,000 in Japan. Americans have been encouraged to rely on law as an acceptable form of dispute resolution, and perhaps the number of lawyers in the United States is as much a sign of cultural evolution as it is of the lack of informal mechanisms of control. Americans continue to file millions of legal actions each year to keep each new batch of lawyers occupied. These legal actions involve everything from the Supreme Court hearing death penalty appeals to debtors and creditors fighting over a few dollars in small claims court.

Other Philosophies of Punishment

There are other theories or philosophies of punishment besides deterrence that we should discuss briefly. A philosophy of punishment involves justifying the imposition of a painful burden on unwilling subjects. When we justify something, we are providing reasons for doing it in terms of morality ("It's the right thing to do") and in terms of the goals we wish to achieve ("Do this and we'll get that"). Legal scholars have traditionally identified three other major objectives or justifications for punishing criminals besides deterrence: retribution, incapacitation, and rehabilitation/reintegration.

Retribution

Retribution is the justification for punishment exemplified by the "eye for an eye" concept. It is a "just desserts" model that demands that punishment match the degree of harm inflicted on victims; minor crimes deserve minor punishments, and more serious crimes deserve more serious punishment. This is the most honestly stated justification for punishment because it posits no secondary purpose for it, such as the reform of criminals or deterring them from further criminal behavior. California is among the states that have explicitly embraced this justification in their criminal codes (California Penal Code Sec. 1170a): "The Legislature finds and declares that the purpose of imprisonment for a crime is punishment" (cited in Barker 2006, 12).

Retribution as presently conceived is not Durkheimian revenge "that ceases only when exhausted." Rather, it is constrained revenge curbed by proportionality and imposed by neutral parties bound by laws mandating respect for the rights of individuals against whom it is imposed. Logan and Gaes (1993, 252) go so far as to claim that only retributive punishment "is an affirmation of the autonomy, responsibility, and dignity of the individual." By holding offenders responsible and blameworthy for their actions, we are treating them as free moral agents, not as mindless victims of fate.

Incapacitation

Incapacitation refers to the inability of incarcerated criminals to victimize people outside the prison walls. Its rationale is aptly summarized in James Q. Wilson's (1975, 391) trenchant remark: "Wicked people exist. Nothing avails except to set them apart from innocent people." It goes without saying that incapacitation "works" while criminals are incarcerated. Elliot Currie (1999) uses robbery rates to illustrate, stating that in 1995 there were 135,000 inmates in state and federal institutions whose most serious crime was robbery and that each robber on average commits five robberies per year. Had these robbers been left on the streets, they would have been responsible for an additional 135,000 × 5, or 675,000, robberies on top of the 580,000 actual robberies reported to the police in 1995. The morality and goals justification in this philosophy of punishment is simple social defense.

Rehabilitation

The term *rehabilitation* means to restore or return to constructive or healthy activity. The rehabilitative goal is based on a medical model that used to view criminal behavior as a moral sickness requiring treatment. Now this model views criminality in terms of "faulty thinking" and criminals in need of "programming" rather than "treatment." Although the goal is the same as that of deterrence, it is different from it in that the goal is to change offenders' attitudes so that they come to accept that their behavior was wrong, not to deter them by the threat of further punishment.

Reintegration

The goal of reintegration is to use the time criminals are under correctional supervision to prepare them to reenter the free community as well-equipped to do so as possible. In effect, reintegration is not much different from rehabilitation, but it is more concrete and pragmatic, focusing on concrete programs, such as job training, rather than psychological attitude change.

Table 9.1 presents a summary of the key elements of the punishment philosophies discussed in terms of justifications, strategies, focus, and their images of offenders. The commonality they all share is the prevention of crime.

Table 9.1 *Summary of Key Elements of Different Punishment Philosophies*

	Retribution	Deterrence	Incapacitation	Rehabilitation	Reintegration
Justification	Moral: Just desserts	Prevention of further crime	Risk control Community protection	Offenders have correctable deficiencies	Offenders have correctable deficienciesr
Strategy	None: Offenders simply deserve to be punished	Make punishment more certain, swift, and severe	Offenders cannot offend while in prison	Treatment to reduce offenders' inclination to reoffend	Concrete programming to make for successful reentry into society
Focus of Perspective	The offense and just desserts	Actual and potential offenders	Actual offenders	Offenders' faulty thinking patterns	Offenders' concrete needs to reintegrate into society
Image of offenders	Free agents whose humanity we affirm by holding them accountable	Rational beings who engage in cost/benefit calculations	Not to be trusted but to be constrained	Good people who have gone astray Will respond to treatment	Ordinary folk who require and will respond to concrete help

Adapted with permission from M. Stohr, A. Walsh, and C. Hemmens, 2009. *Corrections: A text reader.* Thousand Oaks, CA: Sage.

Black's Styles of Social Control

Donald Black (1976, 5) identified four legal "styles" of social control: *penal, therapeutic, compensatory,* and *conciliatory.* The latter two styles are dealt with elsewhere in this book in the context of civil law. Briefly, the **compensatory style** involves some breach of obligation resulting in an accused debtor and an alleged victim. The solution necessary to restore social harmony is payment of the debt. The **conciliatory style** usually involves a breach in a harmonious relationship between two people who are now disputants (for example, husband and wife in a divorce suit). There is no necessary consideration of who is right or wrong, only a concern for a fair and reasonable resolution of the problem.

Our concern in this chapter is with the penal and therapeutic styles. The **penal style** is one in which a person has violated some aspect of the penal code (has committed a crime) and is thus subject to punishment. The **therapeutic style** is one in which a person's unacceptable conduct is considered "sick" and in need of treatment rather than the result of willful misbehavior deserving of punishment. These styles often overlap, such as when a convicted offender is deemed in need of psychiatric or substance abuse treatment. The penal style shares with the compensatory style the characteristic of being *accusatory* in that there is a victim and a wrongdoer. The therapeutic style shares with the conciliatory style the characteristic of being *remedial* (legal means are used to remedy a situation for which blame is not usually legally assigned).

The penal style of social control assigns blame to individuals for their actions and punishes them accordingly. The law assumes rational individuals engage in cost-benefit analysis ("How will I benefit from this behavior, and what might it cost me?") before they act. It follows from this rational view of human nature that the law must do what it can to tip the scale against criminal behavior by attempting to make the costs of crime outweigh its benefits by punishing those convicted of criminal acts to a degree commensurate with the damage caused. This view invests criminals with a capacity for calculation exceeding that of most individuals but pays tribute to their capacity for moral responsibility.

Opposing this view are those who want to blame everyone and everything for crime—except the criminal. Such people question the efficacy, or even the morality, of punishment because for them, crime is "caused" by some factor in the environment (capitalism, racism, poverty, and so forth) that oppresses, degrades, and humiliates the underclass while ignoring the crimes of the rich and powerful. From this viewpoint, forces external to them determine the behavior of criminals; therefore, to punish them is to divert attention from the "true" causes of crime. Less radical advocates of this position stress personal characteristics of the typical criminal rather than some aspect of the social environment. They stress that individuals with such characteristics as low IQ and impulsiveness are not likely to engage in rational cost-benefit analyses.

The personal and environmental factors just mentioned influence the probability of criminal behavior, but, rightly or wrongly, the law acts *as if* criminal activity is the product of free choice. This is the only possible stance the law can take; it cannot wait for "root causes" of crime to be identified and eradicated before it responds to it. To the extent that our behavior is determined, punishment or the threat of punishment becomes part of the bundle of determinants, and as we have already said, the social control function of punishment is not confined to the person being punished.

SOCIAL CONTROL AND THE CRIMINAL JUSTICE SYSTEM

The criminal justice system—the machinery set up by the state to manage the criminal courts, law enforcement, and corrections—is the quintessential example of direct-formal social control, having been designed specifically for that purpose. The criminal justice system is the mechanism that enforces the laws deemed necessary for the safety and protection of society. The American criminal justice system is designed primarily to prevent injustice rather than to promote justice. In enforcing rules to prevent injustice, however, it simultaneously promotes justice. Yet the criminal justice system has come in for much criticism both from conservatives (it "coddles criminals") and liberals (it is "racist and discriminatory"). In general, conservatives would like to change the system by cracking down on criminals, increasing the severity of punishment, and eliminating so-called "legal technicalities" that sometimes allow factually guilty criminals to go free. The liberals' more optimistic view of human nature leads them to want to change the system in the direction of more reliance on rehabilitation, treatment programs, and greater use of community-based alternatives to prison (Walsh and Ellis 2004).

IS THE UNITED STATES SOFT ON CRIME?

The belief that the United States is soft on crime is pervasive; but is it accurate? It is not if our incarceration rate means anything. Figure 9.2 shows the incarceration rates per 100,000 population for selected countries in 2004 (Mauer 2005). Only Russia comes close to touching the U.S. rate, and the closest any modern Western nation comes to the U.S. rate is England and Wales, with a rate five times lower. American sentences also tend to be longer than those of other democracies (Siegel 2006).

In fairness to the "soft on crime" view, the rate per 100,000 *citizens* incarcerated is not the same as the rate per 100,000 *criminals* incarcerated. Incarceration rates are determined by dividing the number of people incarcerated per 100,000 people (criminals and noncriminals alike) in the population. These calculations are

Figure 9.2 Comparing International Incarceration Rates Mid-Year 2004.

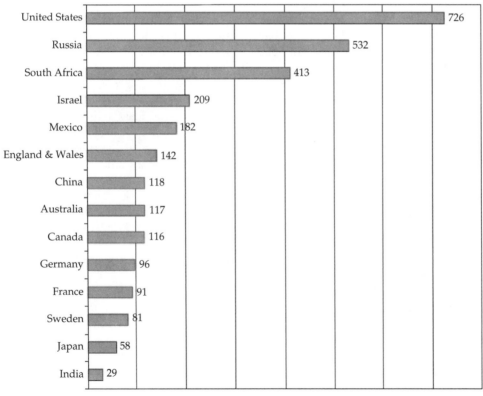

Incarceration Rate (number of people in prison per 100,000 population)

Source: The Sentencing Project (Mauer 2005). Reproduced with permission.

useless for assessing the question at hand. We need to know the rate per 100,000 *criminals*, but we have no idea how many criminals there are in the United States, let alone in other countries. We can look at crime rates as a rough approximation, however. Mauer (2003) points out that our homicide rate is about five times that of England and Wales, which matches our five times greater incarceration rate. When it comes to property crimes, however, the U.S. rate is about in the middle of the pack of nations (less than in Britain, for instance), yet burglars serve an average of 16.2 months in prison in the United States compared with 6.8 months in Britain and 5.3 months in Canada (Mauer 2003). Compared to other democracies, then, we are probably hard on crime, but we are softer than authoritarian countries such as China or Saudi Arabia, countries we will be discussing in chapter 13.

PLEA BARGAINING

The accused can mitigate the severity of punishment by cooperating with the prosecutor and engaging in **plea bargaining** (pleading guilty in exchange for a lighter sentence). About 90 percent of all felony suspects plead guilty rather than have their day in court (Siegel 2006), which raises some legal and moral issues. Conservatives condemn plea bargaining as unwarranted leniency because criminals are punished for crimes that bear little resemblance to the ones actually committed. Liberals criticize plea bargaining as a practice that coerces suspects to surrender their Sixth Amendment right to a trial, their Fifth Amendment privilege against self-incrimination, and their right to any subsequent appeal of their conviction (because they have admitted their guilt).

It would seem that plea bargaining offers something for everyone while leaving no one completely satisfied. The victim may be the least satisfied, but he or she has the satisfaction of certain conviction and at least a modicum of punishment for the victimizer. The police enjoy a benefit from a plea bargain in that they are saved from numerous appearances in court. Judges and prosecutors benefit by the speedy and efficient clearing of cases, and the community as a whole saves the cost of a trial. Even criminals gain when their plea bargains result in more lenient treatment than they otherwise may have received. Thus, while the plea bargaining process draws a lot of criticism, the principal parties in the legal drama appear quite comfortable with it.

The parties most immediately involved—the prosecutor and the defendant—have the greatest incentive to use the plea bargain. The pressure on prosecutors with huge caseloads is great, and this may sometimes lead them to threaten defendants with dire consequences if they refuse to bargain. The Supreme Court upheld the constitutionality of such threats in *Bordenkircher v. Hayes* (1978). Hayes had been indicted for forgery, a crime for which the maximum penalty in Kentucky was ten years. The prosecutor offered to recommend five years if Hayes pled guilty, which he refused to do. The prosecutor then informed Hayes that he would seek a second indictment of him as a habitual offender if he insisted on a trial. Hayes still refused, was indicted as a habitual offender, and sentenced to life imprisonment. An appeals court overturned

Hayes's conviction as a habitual offender, but the U.S. Supreme Court reaffirmed his conviction and declared that in the tit-for-tat world of plea bargaining, there was no element of punishment or injustice in what the prosecutor did since Hayes was free to accept or reject his offer.

It is not only prosecutors who may become vindictive about a defendant's refusal to accept a plea agreement. Judges have been accused of operating according to the "You take some of my time, I'll take some of yours" rule (Uhlman and Walker 1980). No wonder that "experienced" defendants are anxious to bargain, but what about those who insist on their due process rights? "Such defendants may be viewed as disruptive, as lacking in any show of contrition and, therefore, deserving of more severe treatment. If convicted, they will receive sentences in excess of the norm" (Abadinsky 2003, 229).

Although it is true that defendants who go to trial receive more severe sentences if convicted, this is to be expected because these defendants are being sentenced for a more serious crime than are those who pled guilty in exchange for a charge reduction or for a specific sentence. But there still appears to be an element of punishment attached to noncooperation. Adjusting for the effects of prior record, crime seriousness, and charge reduction, one study found that defendants found guilty at trial were 4.76 times more likely to be imprisoned than those who pled guilty, and among those who went to prison, trial defendants received an average of 13.5 more months than plea defendants (Walsh 1990a). We cannot say with certainty if these differences represent a penalty tacked on to the sentences of those defendants audacious enough to demand their constitutional rights or whether it represents a reward in the form of leniency for those kind enough not to "waste" the court's time. However, the pressures to plea bargain show those additional social control mechanisms exist even in contexts where one would think control is already maximized.

THE DEATH PENALTY DEBATE

The death penalty has been subjected to intense scrutiny over the past three decades. Given the social, political, and philosophical issues surrounding it, and particularly the finality of the sentence, it is reasonable that this ultimate form of social control should be hotly debated, although throughout much of our history, the death penalty has been considered a normal and legitimate form of punishment. It remains highly popular with the American public today, with the federal government and thirty-seven of the fifty states retaining it. Polls consistently show that between 65 percent and 75 percent of the American public favors its retention (Radelet and Borg 2000).

Legal opposition to the death penalty has revolved around the Eighth Amendment's prohibition of cruel and unusual punishment. Very few challenges to the penalty arose until the NAACP (National Association for the Advancement of Colored People) and the ACLU (American Civil Liberties Union) waged a joint attack on it beginning in the early 1960s. As a consequence of their efforts, pending executions throughout the country were suspended awaiting the Supreme

Court's word on the matter. The word came down in *Furman v. Georgia* (1972) in which the Court decided that the death penalty per se was not unconstitutional but rather that the arbitrary and discriminatory way in which it was imposed did violate the Eighth Amendment.

Because the criteria for imposing the penalty rather than the penalty itself were found to be unconstitutional, death penalty states began the process of changing their sentencing procedures. Some states introduced the bifurcated (two-step) hearing process, the first to determine guilt (the trial) and the second to impose the sentence with a full hearing of aggravating and mitigating circumstances, which argue for or against the imposition of the death penalty. Other states removed sentencing discretion and made the death penalty mandatory for certain types of homicide.

In *Gregg v. Georgia* (1976), the Supreme Court upheld the constitutionality of the bifurcated hearing, but on the same day, the Court also decided against mandatory death sentences in *Woodson v. North Carolina* (1976). Other noteworthy death penalty cases include *Coker v. Georgia* (1977) in which the Court struck down the death penalty for rape as "grossly disproportionate" and *Penry v. Lynaugh* (1989) and *Stanford v. Kentucky* (1989) in which the Court allowed the imposition of the death penalty on the mentally retarded and on juveniles, respectively. However, the Court reversed itself on Eighth Amendment grounds in the matter of the execution of the mentally retarded in *Atkins, v. Virginia* (2002) and in the matter of executing juveniles in *Roper v. Simmons* (2005). In *Atkins,* six justices concluded that the overwhelming disapproval of the world community must be considered a relevant factor (although not a controlling factor) in determining the imposition of capital punishment on mentally retarded individuals, and as we have seen, similar reasoning was apparent in *Simmons.* Much to the chagrin of constitutional conservatives such as Justice Scalia, the

Figure 9.3 Executions in the United States 1976–2006.

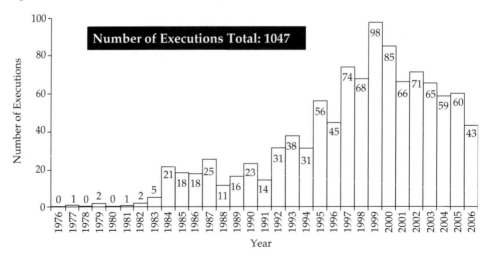

Source: Death Penalty Information Center, *Facts about the death penalty* (2007).

plurality of the Supreme Court seems to be increasingly respecting international *jus cogens* norms.

The death penalty is relatively rarely carried out in the United States today. As illustrated in Figure 9.3, there were 3,366 prisoners under a sentence of death in 2006, and 43 were executed (Death Penalty Information Center 2007). Of those under sentence of death in 2006, 45 percent were white; 42 percent black, 11 percent Hispanic, and 2 percent other races. Only 1.6 percent of death row inmates were women. Among people sentenced to death from 1977 to 2005, 16 percent of whites sentenced to death have been executed compared to 11 percent of Hispanics and blacks (Snell 2006).

Arguments Against the Death Penalty

Opponents of capital punishment view it as a barbaric anachronism that the United States shares with such countries as China and Iran. All other democracies except Japan have abolished it. On this issue, we have distanced ourselves from countries most like ourselves in other respects and associated ourselves with countries holding values usually considered antithetical to ours. According to Amnesty International (2006), in 2005, four countries (China, Iran, Saudi Arabia, and the United States) accounted for 94 percent of the world's *known* executions. China, Iran, and Saudi Arabia have repeatedly demonstrated lack of respect for the dignity of human life, and opponents of capital punishment argue that our "evolving standards of decency" should preclude the United States from being associated with them in any way.

Proponents of capital punishment often cite its supposed deterrent effect, but opponents say that there is no sound evidence that it is a deterrent. Friedman (1984, 214) points out that while capital punishment may function as a deterrent in societies that use it frequently, mercilessly, and without much legal ado, "It cannot work well in the United States, where it is bound to be rare, slow, and controversial." Studies conducted to assess the issue "have failed to support the hypothesis that the death penalty is a more effective deterrent to criminal homicide than long term imprisonment" (Radelet and Borg 2000, 45). Given this reality, and if deterrence is the only rationale for capital punishment, then it is argued that we should join the other democracies and leave governmental killing of citizens to nondemocratic regimes. Even Russia and South Africa, our two closest incarceration rate competitors, have abandoned the practice (Radelet and Borg 2000).

Not only does capital punishment not serve as a deterent, say death penalty abolitionists, executions actually may "cause" a slight rise in the homicide rate due to the "brutalization effect" (Siegel 2006). Advocates of the brutalization argument like to point to what they see as the contradictory message that is sent by the state killing people to teach other people that killing is wrong. The brutalization effect is said to have its influence on "fringe" killers through this message, which abolitionists interpret as saying that it is proper to kill someone who has wronged you. According to abolitionists, killing criminals puts a society sanctioning such treatment on the same moral level as the murderer.

Death penalty advocates often cite their belief that execution is cheaper than holding people in prison for life. Opponents point out that a sentence of death is actually financially more costly to the taxpayer than a sentence of life imprisonment without the possibility of parole. It has been estimated that the total cost of trials and appeals prior to the day of execution (which may be as long as ten to twenty years after the sentence is passed) is between $3 million and $5 million, which is about five times the cost of lifetime imprisonment (Albanese 2005). Thus, capital punishment is not only morally reprehensible, it is fiscally unsound.

The most telling argument against capital punishment, one that must give pause to even its most ardent advocates, is the possibility of executing the innocent. The mere possibility of such an occurrence is abhorrent to abolitionists. Erroneous convictions in capital cases, while rare, occur more often than we would like to think. Careful research has turned up 350 convictions in capital cases in this century that later were determined to have been erroneous, including cases in which "victims" later turned up alive and well (Radelet and Bedau 1988). Later data (Dieter 2004) reveal that 116 convicted people have been exonerated and freed from death rows across the country since 1976. There are many instances of incompetent defense attorneys who miss potentially important evidence and even vindictive prosecutors who purposely hide exculpatory evidence from the defense (Albanese 2005). Because such mistakes and illegalities occur, and since death is irreversible, the death penalty must be abolished, opponents maintain.

Yet another argument is that human life is sacred, and thus no person has the right to take any other person's life. To do so is to play God who, according to this argument, has the sole right to decide when a person's life is to be ended. When the state steps in to kill convicted criminals, it is both denying the sanctity of life and playing God. This is why "leaders of Catholic, most Protestant and Jewish denominations are strongly opposed to the death penalty, and most formal religious organizations in the United States have endorsed statements in favor of abolition" (Radelet and Borg 2000, 54).

Arguments Favoring the Death Penalty

Supporters of capital punishment agree that there have been few convincing studies demonstrating a deterrent effect of capital punishment in the United States, but they argue that if the death penalty were imposed with greater certainty and frequency, we may be able to demonstrate such an effect. The deterrence studies that have been conducted examine all homicides, but the majority of homicides are crimes of passion for which the death penalty is not an option. Studies should be conducted only on the effect of capital punishment on homicides committed with deliberation and premeditation. These death penalty-eligible homicides are by definition crimes that the perpetrators have thought about (premeditated) and thus presumably have thought about the penalty also.

Under conditions of uncertainty regarding either/or questions (God either exists or he does not; the death penalty either deters or it does not), we can only place our bets on the option that promises the most advantageous outcomes. *If*

the death penalty deters, and we choose to use it, we prevent the death of innocent victims. If we do not choose to use it, we will be party to the murders
of those victims. If the death penalty *does not* deter, and we choose to execute
murderers, we have gained nothing, and the only cost we have sustained are
the lives of those who deserved to die anyway. This cost-benefit assessment
(what society stands to lose versus what it stands to gain under these conditions)
places the burden of proof squarely on the shoulders of those who wish to abolish the death penalty, not on its proponents. In other words, society stands to
gain more by retaining the death penalty *if* it deters than it stands to gain if the
death penalty does not deter and we abolish it; thus, the onus must be on those
who wish to deprive society of this alleged protection to prove their case more
convincingly.

One study of the criminal activity of thirty-nine convicted murderers *after*
they had served their time for their murders found that between them, they had
122 arrests for serious violent crimes (including 7 additional murders), 218 arrests
for serious property crimes, and 863 "other" arrests (DeLisi 2005, 165). Had these
thirty-nine murderers been executed, much social harm in the form of pain, suffering, and economic loss would have been averted. Death penalty advocates may
agree with abolitionists, however, that the same harms would have been averted
had they been sentenced to life without parole.

Death penalty advocates may agree that it is more costly to impose a sentence of death than one of life imprisonment but claim that this is only because
of the seemingly interminable appeal process. Limiting appeals and bringing the
case quickly to closure would save taxpayers' money and perhaps also enhance
the deterrent effect of the death penalty. The Supreme Court has moved in the
direction of placing limits on death penalty appeals in *Coleman v. Thompson*
(1991), but we have seen little evidence that limitations have actually occurred.
Inmates executed in 2005 were on death row an average of twelve years and
three months, fifteen months longer than in 2004 (Snell 2006).

Death penalty advocates reject the argument that the use of capital punishment in the United States places this country on the same moral plane as authoritarian countries using it. Both the Nazis and the allies invaded France but for
two very different reasons. The moral equivalency of physically equivalent acts
is not automatically valid. If someone restricts your freedom, binds you, and
forcibly transports you to a place of captivity, it is called "kidnapping," and it is
a crime. If a police officer does the same thing to you, it is called "arrest." The
officer, as a legitimate holder of legal authority, is representing the moral order of
society and is acting in its name as is the state executioner. Arrest is a moral and
legitimate social reaction to some immoral harm done to society. The death penalty is also a moral and legitimate social reaction to an immoral act. Thus, death
penalty advocates argue that the moral difference between *arrest* and *kidnapping*
is the same as the moral difference between *execution* and *murder*.

Those who argue that the imposition of the death penalty is racially biased
and therefore should be abolished erroneously conflate the justice, usefulness,
and morality inherent in the death penalty with its maldistribution among
those eligible to receive it (van den Haag 1993). If the death penalty appears

discriminatory, in *McClesky v. Kemp* (1987), the Supreme Court ruled that statistical aggregates indicative of it do not per se establish a violation of the Eighth or Fourteenth Amendments in individual cases. Maldistribution is certainly unjust, but it does not make those who received the death penalty any less deserving of it. The solution to biased sentencing is equity in sentencing, which implies neither the abolition nor the retention of capital punishment. Proponents of capital punishment argue that equity in sentencing (given similarly situated defendants, of course) should be achieved by imposing more death sentences, not by imposing the death penalty on no one (van den Haag 1993).

The prospect of an innocent person being executed is troubling to proponents of capital punishment. However, the figure cited most often by abolitionists of 350 innocent convictions is misleading. Radelet and Bedau (1988) did indeed list 350 erroneous *convictions*, but only 25 of them actually were executed, and the 116 exonerated individuals reported by the Death Penalty Information Center were, after all, exonerated. Mistakes are made in all human activities, but before we give up any of these activities, we generally weigh the cost and benefits of doing so. Death penalty advocates believe the benefits of retaining this ultimate form of social control outweigh the benefits of abolishing it. Given more accurate greater evidence gathering and evaluating techniques (such as DNA testing) and greater scrutiny of the criminal justice system by the public, the media, and watchdog groups such as the Innocence Project (a nonprofit legal clinic that takes on postconviction cases dealing with DNA evidence), the likelihood of innocent defendants being executed today is much less than it has been in the past.

THE LAW AND SOCIAL CONTROL OF POLITICAL DISSENT

A government's need to control extremes of political dissent is even more important than its need to control crime. The rights to free speech and assembly enshrined in the Bill of Rights imply the right to dissent, but there are limits to what even democracies will tolerate in the form of dissent. All governments, regardless of political persuasion, wish to hold on to the reigns of power and attempt to do so through various mechanisms of social control. There are important differences in these mechanisms among authoritarian, totalitarian, and democratic regimes, however. Authoritarian governments demand conformity to a single party line but not political participation, thus maintaining a distinction between public and private life. Penalties are extracted from citizens only for opposition, not for failing to contribute. Totalitarian regimes do not permit political neutrality, thus blurring the public/private life distinction. All must participate in the political process, no matter how banal it is—such as the ritual of voting for unopposed candidates. Democracies maintain the distinction between public and private lives by encouraging but not requiring political participation and by allowing for political plurality. Democratic governments thus exercise less control over political dissent than other forms of government.

This does not mean that democratic governments will allow all forms of political nonconformity, or that they do not attempt to maintain themselves in power. Although the law is a tool used by legitimate holders of political power to hold on to that power, if the reigns of power are to be turned over to others, there are also rules to accomplish this in an orderly and peaceful manner. In democratic nations, power is transferred periodically between political parties whose legitimate claim to power is not challenged.

However, if political entities outside of the mainstream, such as the American Communist Party, claim legitimacy and a place in the political power race, parties of established legitimacy generally view it as a threat to the social and political order. Both the Republican and the Democratic parties are in effect committed to the preservation of each other. When such threats are perceived, many different methods may be used to combat them, such as the force of arms, physical harassment, public opinion, and election laws that limit participation. One or all forms may be, and have been, used to counter threats to the political status quo in the United States.

It has been claimed that relative to other democracies, the United States does not have a very good reputation for tolerating political dissent. As Jethro Lieberman (1972, 74) put it, "The United States has a long history of welcoming dissent in the abstract and punishing it in the concrete." And Seymour Lipset (1964, 321) has written that "more than any other democratic country, the United States makes ideological conformity one of the conditions for good citizenship." Whether or why the United States is less politically tolerant than other democracies is not a question we explore here. Perhaps it is necessary for new nations lacking a long cultural heritage (and thus lacking a natural conformity born of tradition) to go to greater lengths to ensure political conformity through more formal controls in the same way that it uses law to ensure social conformity in the absence of strong informal controls. Any new political force that may be perceived as a threat to a growing feeling of national unity runs the risk of suppression. The ink was barely dry on the Constitution when the first new political force in the United States felt the sting of political suppression. This new political entity was the Democratic-Republican Party, or simply the Republican Party, as members preferred to call it. The Republican party had a number of its members and supporters prosecuted under the 1798 Sedition Act for criticizing the Federalist government. The act, however, had the effect of uniting the Republican party and did much to gain Republican Thomas Jefferson the presidency in the 1800 election (Brinkley et al. 1991, 186). Note that this party was not the forerunner of the modern Republican Party, which was founded in 1854 as an antislavery party.

Populist or "fringe group" third parties in the United States can be tolerated because they generally are wrapped around a single central issue (the gold standard, the federal deficit, and so forth), none of which seriously threaten the political, social, and economic status quo. However, parties such as the socialist and communist parties, which do threaten the status quo, especially when they achieve a significant following as they did in the early 1900s, are a different proposition.

By 1919, the American Socialist Party had become a serious threat to established political power and as such became the target of extraordinary efforts to crush it. As Charles Dunn (1982, 234) explains: "After the Socialists won control of some thirty-two municipal governments, their headquarters in several cites were ransacked, their funds confiscated, their leaders jailed, and their newspapers denied mailing privileges. Winning candidates were even denied seats in state legislatures and Congress." The combined effect of these tactics was to destroy socialism as a viable political alternative in the United States. Yet, according to Dunn (1982, 235), the FBI burglarized the offices of the Socialist Workers Party no less than ninety-two times from 1960 to 1966. What happened here to the rule of law, to free speech, and to other constitutional protections? Political scientist Michael Parenti (1977, 203) answers: "When change threatens the rule, the rules are changed."

A more welcome method of destroying the appeal of threatening third parties is to co-opt what is most appealing to the public about their political platforms. Milton and Rose Friedman (1980) noted long ago that almost every item on of the economic platform of the American Socialist Party platform of 1928 has been adopted in the United States. Among the reforms and benefits the platform called for was a forty-hour work week, unemployment benefits, Social Security pensions, public works, legalization of trade unions, child labor laws, and the establishment of government unemployment offices. These and many other items in the platform have been so integrated into American life that few today would call them "socialist" or "un-American."

Wartime constitutes another period in which governments tend to forget such niceties as civil liberties, although they usually are careful to use the law to suppress them. President Wilson's administration made far-reaching use of the law to assure political conformity after the United States entered World War I. The Espionage Act of 1917, which very broadly defined the term "espionage," allowed the post office to confiscate any "seditious material." The Sabotage and Sedition Acts of 1918 made it illegal for anyone to publicly express opposition to the war or to criticize the president or Congress. The great majority of the American people apparently supported these acts as legitimate exercises of state power since many citizens joined groups to root out those who criticized the war or high government officials. The main targets of these groups were the socialists and communists, who opposed the war on principle. The activities of these groups are summarized by Brinkley and Colleagues (1991, 678):

> [The American Protective League] . . . enlisted the services of 250,000 people, who served as "agents"—prying into the activities and thoughts of their neighbors, stopping men on the street and demanding to see their draft cards, opening mail, tapping telephones, and in general attempting to impose unity of opinion on their communities. Attorney General Thomas W. Gregory described them approvingly as a "patriotic organization." Other vigilante organizations—the National Security League, the Boy Spies of America, the American Defense Society—performed much the same function.

These patriotic snoops functioned as a form of grassroots social control. Any person, or any groups of persons, whose philosophy ran counter to the official line had to be extremely careful, for the eyes and ears of orthodoxy were everywhere. The situation described in the preceding quotation reminds us of the Hitler Youth, Germany's system of "block wardens" during the Nazi period, and of Chinese "neighborhood committees" (see chapter 13). The big difference in America is that these conditions were temporary aberrations that had sprung up in response to unusual circumstances. When the war was over, things more or less reverted to normal.

This return to normalcy did not apply to the continued threats to the American political order perceived as coming from communists and socialists. When the constitutionality of wartime legislation was challenged, the Supreme Court proved once again that the judiciary is situated firmly in the camp of the political status quo. In *Schenck v. United States* (1919), the Court upheld the constitutionality of the Espionage Act and set forth the famous "clear and present danger" test for determining when it is permissible to curtail First Amendment rights. In *Gitlow v. New York* (1925), even while asserting the First Amendment right to freedom of speech and binding the states to it, the Supreme Court upheld the conviction of Benjamin Gitlow, a socialist convicted of passing out seditious (antiwar) pamphlets in New York.

Cold wars as well as hot ones can move the government to feel that it is in "clear and present danger" and thus needs to defend itself by limiting freedom of speech. The Smith Act of 1940, the Internal Security Act of 1950, and the Communist Control Act of 1954 were attempts to control and destroy the American Communist Party. The Communist Control Act has never been tested before the Supreme Court, but the Smith Act was declared constitutional in *Dennis v. United States* (1951), and a provision of the act making it a crime to belong to the Communist Party was upheld in *Scales v. United States* (1961). The Internal Security Act, which required the Communist Party to register with the attorney general as an agent of a foreign state, was upheld in *Communist Party v. Subversive Activities Control Board* (1961). Although a number of these rulings later were qualified, these decisions point to the political nature of the Supreme Court.

Threats to the nation tend to lead to greater state power, which it rarely relinquishes after the threat is passed. Some individuals have expressed the fear that the passage of the **USA Patriot Act** on October 11, 2001, in response to the horrendous terrorist attacks of September 11, 2001, is the beginning of the end of American civil liberties. The act grants federal agencies greater authority to track and intercept private communications as well as greater powers to the Treasury Department to combat corruption and prevent money laundering and creates new crimes, penalties, and procedures for use against domestic and foreign terrorists (Doyle 2002). Other people feel that if the Patriot Act prevents another September 11, it is all right with them. After all, if you are not engaged in any of the preceding activities, what have you to fear?

While no one suggests that law enforcement is interested in intercepting e-mail exchanges of chili recipes or listening to your call home asking for money, the ACLU fears that the inclusion of domestic terrorism in the Patriot Act's

244 *Law, Justice, and Society: A Sociolegal Introduction*

definition of terrorism has great potential for abuse. The ACLU claims that the definition is broad enough to encompass the activities of several legitimate activist groups such as Greenpeace, Operation Rescue, and Environmental Liberation that are often thorns in the side of the "establishment" and that it could put participants at risk for the same enhanced criminal penalties and asset forfeitures applied to genuine terrorists (American Civil Liberties Union 2002). Furthermore, the ACLU does not believe that innocents caught up in a net could seek relief from the courts because as Greenberg (1980, 357; emphasis in original) points out, "From the Alien and Sedition Acts during the administration of John Adams, up to the present, *the Supreme Court has never declared unconstitutional any act of Congress designed to limit the speech of dissidents.*"

Let us not be overly critical. Every nation has the right, indeed, the obligation, to protect and preserve those things it values from perceived threats. Certainly, many communists and socialists were imprisoned for their beliefs, and that is unconscionable in a democracy, but challenges to the status quo in many other countries have been treated much more severely. The Soviet Union executed more than six million of its citizens holding favorable attitudes toward capitalism (Hosking 1985). The current threat from Islamic terrorism may be just as dangerous, but the law has evolved a more tolerant attitude since the days of the communist threat, and most certainly since the time of World War I. No one is being prosecuted or persecuted for his or her written or spoken opposition to the Patriot Act, and no one is likely to.

THERAPEUTIC SOCIAL CONTROL: LAW AND PSYCHIATRY

Among the institutions devoted to social control is the psychiatric hospital. Psychiatry and its concepts of mental health and mental illness are potentially means of achieving social control in conjunction with the legal system. By definition, a mentally ill person does not conform to the behavioral expectations of society and may be referred for treatment. This "medicalization of deviance" has many critics who stress the negative side, but we should not lose sight of its positive side. If nonconformity is causing serious disruptions of individuals' lives, or if the mentally ill are a danger to themselves or to others, then the state has a duty under the doctrine of *parens patriae* to intervene. Since the goal of psychiatry is to cure and control, not punish, it is the quintessential example of Black's therapeutic social control.

On the other hand, there is real danger in saying that "by definition, a person who does not conform to the behavioral expectations of the group is mentally ill." Psychiatric disorders have a definite organic basis, and no one would dispute that these people are in need of treatment. There are those, however, who consider the whole concept of *mental* illness to be bogus, a myth used to label socially disvalued behaviors (drunkenness, drug abuse, homosexuality, and belonging to organizations such as communist or socialist parties). Placing psychiatric labels on such behavior legitimizes the use of a form of social control called psychiatry (Jones 2004). Vago (1991, 148) illustrates the social control function of psychiatric hospitals:

> It is not surprising to find that many state mental hospitals include people who have committed trivial misdemeanors or who have not been convicted of any crime at all, but have been sent there for "observation." The police and courts may refer individuals whose behavior appears odd for psychiatric examination, and if they are found to be "insane," they can be confined in a mental hospital against their will for long periods, in some cases, for life.

The former Soviet Union made widespread use of psychiatric labeling to justify locking up dissidents in mental hospitals. The ideology of Soviet psychiatry has been stated as follows: "Personal mental adjustment is to be found in the submerging of one's wishes and desires to the needs of the group or society, in the assumption that society has rights against the individual and not vice-versa" (Horowitz 1984, 230). The task of Soviet psychiatrists "was to identify and *treat* political dissent" (Grimm 1977, 136). "Treatment" often consisted of the involuntary administration of drugs, and one could not be considered "cured" until deemed to be in conformity with political orthodoxy, deviation from which served as the sole definition of the "illness" in the first place. We are not talking about persons with a genuine inability to cope with the realities of everyday life but rather about persons who voiced their opposition to the regime one time too many.

Responding to criticisms made by the American Psychiatric Association (APA), Soviet psychiatrists defended themselves by suggesting that the Americans look to their own misuses of the art. Among the cases they cited were those of Ezra Pound, the poet, who criticized American involvement in World War II, and General Edwin Walker, an outspoken critic of American intervention in Central America, both of whom ended up in an insane asylum (Grimm 1977). They also defended themselves on the grounds that their involvement saved "patients" from a worse fate in a prison camp. The ethical dilemma of where to place their loyalty (to the patient or the state) may apply to psychiatrists and psychologists everywhere when they are employed by the state. As is the case with their Russian counterparts, American mental health professionals see their role in the criminal justice system as humanitarian, standing as scientific, morally neutral buffers between a possibly mentally ill defendant and a nonscientific judiciary bent on punishing the sick and the well alike.

Others with less charitable views see American psychiatrists and psychologists as tools of the state providing scientific authority to legitimize the state's decisions (Jones 2004). Researchers find it strange that almost all criminal defendants referred to mental health professionals by the courts end up with some sort of psychiatric label attached to them. Scheff (1964) and Walsh (1990b) found that all referrals in their respective samples received a label indicative of some form of mental illness. Either referring judges are remarkably adept at spotting psychiatric problems or psychiatrists are remarkably adept at spotting what judges want and supplying the appropriate label. Holman and Gaston (1987) found that clients referred by organizations that favored more severe labels (for example, the courts) were more likely to get more severe psychiatric labels than those referred by other organizations. This offers support for those who believe that mental health professionals paid by the state may unwittingly serve as agents of social control (Jones 2004).

The idea that people who engage in deviant behavior are sick and require treatment is illuminated in the case of sex offenders. In 1997, the U.S. Supreme Court upheld a Kansas statute (*Kansas v. Hendricks* 1997) aimed at keeping certain sex offenders behind bars under civil commitment laws *after they have served their prison terms* if they demonstrate "mental abnormality" or "personality disorder." The decision paved the way for other states and for the federal government to pass similar involuntary confinement laws. Prior to 1990, civil commitments were limited to those said to suffer from mental illness, but to cover sex offenders, several states have loosened their criterion for commitment to "mental abnormality" as opposed to "mental illness." The phrase "mental abnormality" can be used to cover any kind of behavior or thinking that we disapprove of, and its use is "reminiscent of Soviet policies that institutionalized dissidents" (Grinfeld 2005, 2). Whatever your thoughts about sex offenders are, the *Hendricks* decision created a special category of individuals defined as "abnormal" who may be punished indefinitely for what they *might do* if released.

"NO TAXATION WITHOUT REPRESENTATION!": A CASE OF JUDICIAL SOCIAL CONTROL

Most people in the United States feel that the use of power to enforce rules is legitimate because the law itself is seen as legitimate. Even when obeying the law hurts, as in compliance with income tax laws, few people, even as they curse and complain about their unfairness, deny that income tax laws are legitimate. Tax laws are legitimate because we know that taxes are necessary if the government is to function and provide the many services that private citizens cannot supply for themselves. Legislative bodies constitutionally levy taxes, supposedly with the consent of the people. If the majority of the people do not consider those taxes legitimate, then mechanisms exist to replace legislators most responsible for levying them. Thus, vesting the ability to tax in elected bodies is a precept vital for the democratic control of public institutions.

A violation of this precept occurred in Kansas City, Missouri, in 1983. Federal district court judge Russell Clarke had ruled that the Kansas City, Missouri, School District had been operating a de facto segregated school system (mainly as a result of "white flight" to the suburbs) and ordered it to remedy the situation as required by federal law. The remedy involved the building of so-called "magnet schools" that would attract white suburban students back to the inner city. The facilities in these magnet schools were described by Justice Kennedy in his dissent in the case (*Missouri v. Jenkins* 1990):

> Every school would have a 2,000 square-foot planetarium; greenhouses and vivariums; a 25-acre farm with an air-conditioned meeting room for

104 people; a model United Nations wired for language translation; broadcast capable radio and television studios with an editing and animation lab; a temperature controlled art gallery; movie editing and screening rooms; a 3,500 square-foot dust-free diesel mechanics room; 1,875-square foot elementary school animal rooms for use in a zoo project; swimming pools; and numerous other facilities.

The Kansas City Municipal School District responded to Clarke's ruling by saying that it did not have the funds (an initial total exceeding $200 million) to implement the scheme. After certain considerations were made, Clarke ruled that it must find the money and ordered the school district's property tax levy raised from $2.05 to $4.00 per $100 of assessed property value and later to $4.96 (Gewertz 2000). Thus homeowners in the school district had their property taxes doubled, and then a further 24 percent added later, all by judicial fiat—not even George III was that bold! Among the "injuries and usurpations" listed against King George in the Declaration of Independence was that he imposed "taxes on us without our consent"; "No taxation without representation!" was the rallying cry of the Revolution.

Taking their case to the United States Supreme Court, attorneys for the state of Missouri argued that surely the doubling of taxes by order of an unelected, life-tenured federal judge (or more correctly, Clarke had ordered county commissioners to do so under pain of contempt of court) violates all fundamental precepts of democratic control; surely the ruling violated Article III of the Constitution laying out the boundaries of judicial power, and surely the due process clauses of the Fifth and Fourteenth Amendments were violated by depriving citizens within the Kansas City Municipal School District of property "without due process of law."

The Supreme Court, in a 6–3 decision, was not impressed by these arguments. In authoring the Court's opinion, Justice White reiterated that the Kansas City Municipal School District was segregated, that *Brown v. Board of Education* (1954, discussed in the next chapter) required desegregation, and that the *Brown* decision placed the onus on local authorities for solving the problems of segregation. Since they had not done so, it was then incumbent on the judiciary to implement the constitutional requirement of *Brown* via a **writ of mandamus** (a court order compelling a public official to do his or her duty) compelling the school district to levy taxes adequate for compliance. That the taxation remedy impacted on homeowners within the district presented no problem of conscience to the Court because the ruling "places the responsibility for solutions to the problems of segregation upon those who have themselves created the problems," wrote Justice White. By fleeing to the suburbs, white homeowners were deemed to be responsible for segregation and thus should be financially responsible for the solution.

Justice Kennedy's scathing dissent considered the ruling an insult to all Americans who wish the best for their children and who strive to obtain it by their own efforts. He also considered it to be the federal bullying of a local government and its people, a usurpation of the power of one branch of government (the judiciary) of the powers constitutionally vested in the legislature, and a clear violation of due process:

> Perhaps the KCMSD's Classical Greek theme schools emphasizing foren-sics [the art or study of argumentative discourse] and self-government will provide exemplary training in participatory democracy. But if today's dicta become law, such lessons will be of little use to students who grow up to become taxpayers in the KCMSD.

As of mid-1993, the price tag for these schools had exceeded the normal school budget by $1.3 *billion*, and at one point 44 percent of the K–12 education budget was being spent on the 9 percent of students enrolled in the Kansas City and St. Louis magnet schools (Ciotti 1998). Despite such funding, magnet school students were consistently outscored on all indices of academic achievement by pupils in Missouri's underfunded nonmagnet schools, and many magnet schools even lost state accreditation (Gewertz 2000).

A second trip to the Supreme Court (*Missouri v. Jenkins II* 1995)—based on Missouri's reluctance to provide large across-the-board salary increases to mag-net school teachers given the continued failures of their students and again argu-ing that underachievement was not attributable to de facto segregation—found a sympathetic ear in the Court. The Court reasoned that school segregation was no longer *de jure*, as it had been at the time of *Brown*, but was now the result of other social forces. The Court also reasoned that the state had done everything practicable to remedy the segregation problem and expressed its wish to see con-trol of the schools back in the hands of local authorities. This case did not neces-sarily invalidate the 1990 ruling. Courts are reluctant to give the impression they are ignoring precedent and so narrowly tailor their opinions to the specific issue at hand while at the same time endeavoring in their dicta to make other inten-tions known. However, it was the beginning of the end of the seventeen-year magnet school experiment, which finally ended in 1999.

This case provides an example of the awesome power of the law to exert social control despite the opposition of the overwhelming majority of citizens. Social control by any number of means is a necessity in all societies, but the agents of control from time to time may overstep the boundaries of legitimate power, and even legitimate power sometimes may be excessively and inappropri-ately applied. There are those who abhor and resist social control of any kind on ideological and/or temperamental grounds, but when social controls are consis-tent with norms of fairness and with human dignity, they exist for the benefit of us all. A society that does not hold its citizens to standards of decent behavior is a society in trouble.

SUMMARY

Social control is a necessary process that makes human existence relatively peace-ful and predictable. Social control involves all those mechanisms that influence people to conform to the behavioral expectations of the social group through direct (coercive) or indirect (voluntary) means as well as by formal or informal means. Informal means include any means that make clear that those observing our conduct disapprove of it, for example, the social snub, ostracism, direct confrontation, and so forth. Formal means are those means exercised by duly authorized agents of social control whose specific mandate is to control behavior (for example, agents of the criminal justice system).

Most of us are controlled indirectly and informally, meaning that we rely on internalized norms of conduct (conscience) to regulate our behavior. As society becomes more complex and diverse, our conscience (our informal social control) is weakened. The more we are freed of voluntary and informal restraints on our behavior, the more our behavior is likely to be controlled by direct and formal means. The use of law to control citizen behavior is a measure of the moral strength or weakness of a society.

Violations of the law often result in punishment, which is supposed to have a deterrent effect (both on those experiencing the punishment and on those witnessing it), thus preventing future violations. Whether deterrence "works" depends on a host of factors such as the strength of our conscience, how personally rewarding our transgressions are, what we have to lose if our transgressions are discovered, and our ability to recognize and weigh the costs and benefits of transgressions.

Among Black's four styles of social control are the penal and therapeutic styles. Although these styles often overlap, the former style denotes the control exercised over those who have violated the criminal codes; the latter style denotes controls exercised over those who also have violated behavioral expectations but against whom blame has not been placed. Blame is assigned and punishment applied in the first instance because the offender is held responsible for his or her actions, but blame is withheld in the second instance because the controlee is considered mentally ill and in need of treatment rather than punishment.

The criminal justice system's reason for being is to exert social control. There are many issues within this system that are highly controversial, such as plea bargaining, the death penalty, and differential sentencing. The race issue looms large in the latter two issues, with some scholars supposing that the criminal justice system is racist and therefore that minority defendants are treated more harshly than white defendants. There is evidence both for and against the proposition that the criminal justice system is racist.

Suppressing political dissent is even more important to defenders of the status quo than suppressing crime. Even democracies have their ways to limit the political competition among parties, which are not too ideologically separate. The United States generally is considered less tolerant of political dissent than are most other democracies. This intolerance is particularly in evidence during times of war or other threats from abroad, such as the communist threat. During such times, Congress often has passed legislation limiting the free speech and activities of political nonconformists. The Supreme Court never has declared any of this legislation unconstitutional.

Psychiatry is an effective form of "scientific" social control—what better way to control dissidents than to label them mad? This form of social control was practiced extensively in the former Soviet Union. Soviet psychiatrists often defended their conduct from criticism by foreign psychiatrists by asserting that their "treatment" was a humanitarian alternative to the prison camp. Western psychiatrists defend themselves from accusations that they are the servants of the agents of social control by also citing humanitarian concerns. Certainly, psychiatry can be used for good purposes, but by its very nature, it is highly susceptible to misuse.

A particularly egregious example of social control by the judiciary was exercised by a federal judge in Kansas City, Missouri, in 1983. He ordered the doubling of property taxes in the Kansas City school district to fund so-called "magnet schools." These schools were viewed as a method of desegregating Kansas City schools by attracting white students from the suburbs to the many benefits that would be available at the schools. Issues of legality, fairness, and justice were brushed aside by the Court in favor of the one overriding concern—the implementation of *Brown v. Board of Education*. These issues were discussed from the perspective of Justice Kennedy, who wrote the dissenting opinion.

DISCUSSION QUESTIONS

1. Name two or three factors that may contribute to decreased social cohesiveness. What, if anything, can we do to minimize their impact?
2. Was Hester Prynne's punishment justified for the sake of maintaining family values as the Puritans viewed them?
3. Do you think that most people (including yourself) would act as Gyges did if they had found such a ring?
4. What are your thoughts on the greater use of law in the United States to stifle political opposition than in other democratic countries? Do you think this is true today?
5. After you have thought through all the arguments presented, both pro and con, on the death penalty, what is your position on it? Give your reasons.
6. What are your thoughts about *Missouri v. Jenkins*? Should a judge have that much power? What might have been an alternative solution to implementing *Brown v. Board of Education*?

References

Abadinsky, H. 2003. *Law and justice: An introduction to the American legal system.* 5th ed. Upper Saddle River, NJ: Prentice Hall.

Albanese, J. 2005. *Criminal justice.* 3rd ed. Boston: Pearson.

American Civil Liberties Union. 2002. *How the USA Patriot Act redefines "domestic terrorism."* Retrieved from http://www.aclu.org/national.

Amnesty International. 2006. *Death sentences and executions in 2005.* http://web.amnesty .org/web/web/nsf/print/.

Barker, V. 2006. The politics of punishing: Building a state governance theory of American imprisonment variation. *Punishment and Society* 8:5–32.

Black, D. 1976. *The behavior of law.* New York: Academic Press.

Brinkley, A., R. Current, F. Freidel, and T. Williams. 1991. *American history: A survey.* New York: McGraw-Hill.

Brubaker, S. 1993. In praise of punishment. In *Taking sides: Clashing views on controversial issues in crime and criminology,* edited by R. Monk. Guilford, CT: Dushkin.

Ciotti, P. 1998. Money and school performance: Lessons from the Kansas City desegregation experiment. *Policy Analysis* 298:1–25.

Currie, E. 1999. Reflections on crime and criminology at the millennium. *Western Criminology Review* 2. Retrieved from http://wcr.somoma.edu/v2nl/currie.html.

Death Penalty Information Center. 2007. *Facts about the death penalty.* www.deathpenaltyinfo. org.

DeLisi, M. 2005. *Career criminals in society.* Thousand Oaks, CA: Sage.

Dieter, R. 2004. *Innocence and the crisis in the American death penalty.* www.deathpenaltyinfo. org.

Doyle, C. 2002. The USA Patriot Act: A sketch. Washington, DC: Congressional Research Service, Library of Congress.

Dunn, C. 1982. *American democracy debated.* Morristown, NJ: Scott, Foresman.

Durkheim, E. 1951. *The division of labor in society.* Glencoe, IL: Free Press.

Friedman, L. 1984. *American law: An introduction.* New York: Norton.

Friedman, M., and R. Freidman. 1980. *Free to choose: A personal statement.* New York: Harcourt Brace Jovanovich.

Gewertz, C. 2000. A hard lesson for Kansas City's troubled schools. *Education Week,* April 22, 1–5.

Greenberg, E. 1980. *The American political system: A radical approach.* Cambridge, MA: Winthrop.

Grimm, R. 1977. Brain control in a democratic society. In *Issues in Brain/Behavior Control,* edited by W. Smith and A. Kling. New York: Spectrum Books.

Grinfeld, M. 2005. Sexual predator ruling raises ethical, moral dilemmas. *Psychiatric Times* 16:1–4.

Hawthorne, N. *The Scarlet Letter.* Boston: Hayes Barton Press.

Holman, J. and R. Gaston. 1987. Interorganizational influences on mental health diagnoses: A macro-level study of the labeling process. *Sociological Perspectives* 30:180–200.

Horowitz, A. 1984. Therapy and social solidarity. In *Toward a general theory of social control,* edited by D. Black. Vol. 1. New York: Academic Press.

Hosking, G. 1985. *The first socialist society: A history of the Soviet Union from within.* Cambridge, MA: Harvard University Press.

Jones, E. 2004. Sexually violent predator laws: Psychiatry in service to a morally dubious enterprise. *Lancet* 364:50–51.

Lieberman, J. 1972. *How the government breaks the laws.* Baltimore: Penguin.

Lipset, S. 1964. The sources of the "radical right." In *The radical right,* edited by D. Bell. Garden City, NY: Anchor.

Logan, C. and G. Gaes. 1993. Meta-analysis and the rehabilitation of punishment. *Justice Quarterly* 10:245–63.

Mauer, M. 2003. *Comparative international rates of incarceration: An examination of causes and trends.* Washington, DC: The Sentencing Project.

———. 2005. *New incarceration figures: Growth in population continues.* Washington, DC: The Sentencing Project.

Parenti, M. 1977. *Democracy for the few.* New York: St. Martin's Press.

Plato. 1960. *The republic and other works,* translated by B. Jowett. Garden City, NY: Dolphin.

Radelet, M., and H. Bedau. 1988. Fallibility and finality: Type II errors and capital punishment. In *Challenging capital punishment: Legal and social science approaches*, edited by K. Haas and J. Inciardi. Newbury Park, CA: Sage.

Radelet, M., and M. Borg. 2000. The changing nature of death penalty debates. *Annual Review of Sociology* 26:43–61.

Radzinowicz, L., and J. King. 1979. *The growth of crime: The international experience.* Middlesex, England: Penguin Books.

Scheff, T. 1964. The societal reaction to deviance: Ascriptive elements in the psychiatric screening of mental patients in a Midwestern state. *Social Problems* 11:401–13.

Siegel, L. 2006. *Criminology.* 9th ed. Belmont, CA: Wadsworth Publishing Company.

Snell, T. 2006, December. Capital punishment, 2005. *Bureau of Justice Statistics Bulletin.* Washington, DC: National Institute of Justice.

Uhlman, T., and N. Walker. 1980. He takes some of my time; I take some of his: An analysis of judicial sentencing patterns in jury cases. *Law and Society Review* 14:323–39.

Vago, S. 1991. *Law and society.* Englewood Cliffs, NJ: Prentice Hall.

van den Haag, E. 1993. The ultimate punishment: A defense. In *Taking sides: Clashing views on controversial legal issues*, edited by M. Katsh. Guilford, CT: Dushkin.

Walsh, A. 1990a. Standing trial versus copping a plea: Is there a penalty? *Journal of Contemporary Criminal Justice* 6:226–36.

———. 1990b. Twice labeled: The effects of psychiatric labeling on the sentencing of sex offenders. *Social Problems* 37:375–89.

Walsh, A., and L. Ellis. 2004. Ideology: Criminology's "Achilles' heel?" *Quarterly Journal of Ideology* 27:1–25.

Wilson, J. 1975. *Thinking about crime.* New York: Vintage.

Cases Cited

Atkins v. Virginia, 536 U.S. 304 (2002).

Bordenkircher v. Hayes, 434 U.S. 357 (1978).

Bowers v. Hardwick, 478 U.S. 110 (1986).

Brown v. Board of Education, 347 U.S. 483 (1954).

Coker v. Georgia, 433 U.S. 584 (1977).

Coleman v. Thompson, 501 U.S. 722 (1991).

Communist Party v. Subversive Activities Control Board, 367 U.S. 1 (1961).

Dennis v. United States, 341, U.S. 494 (1951).

Furman v. Georgia, 408 U.S. 238 (1972).

Gitlow v. New York, 266 U.S. 652 (1925).

Gregg v. Georgia, 428 U.S. 153 (1976).

Kansas v. Hendricks, 138 U.S. 521 (1997).

McClesky v. Kemp, 481 U.S. 279 (1987).

Missouri v. Jenkins, 495 U.S. 33 (1990).

Missouri v. Jenkins II, 515 U.S. 70 (1995).

Penry v. Lynaugh, 492 U.S. 302 (1989).

Roper v. Simmons, 112 S.W. 3rd 397 (2005).

Scales v. United States, 367 U.S. 203 (1961).

Schenck v. United States, 249 U.S. (1919).

Stanford v. Kentucky, 492 U.S. 361 (1989).

Woodson v. North Carolina, 428 U.S. 280 (1976).

CHAPTER 10

THE LIMITS OF SOCIAL CONTROL: POLICING VICE

In 1996, Majed Al-Timimy, twenty-eight, and Latif Al-Husani, thirty-four, Iraqi refugees living in Lincoln, Nebraska, decided that it was about time that they were married. A fellow Iraqi refugee told Majed and Latif that he had two daughters who would make good wives that he wanted to marry off. His offer was gratefully accepted, and a Muslim cleric was flown in from Ohio to perform the joint ceremony. Everyone concerned was happy that the proceedings were done right, according to Iraqi Islamic custom. Some months after the wedding, one of the brides ran away; her concerned husband dutifully reported it to the police. It was at this point that American and Iraqi norms of morality clashed head on, because the two brides Majed and Latif had married were 13 and 14 at the time of their marriages. Individuals less than seventeen years old cannot marry under Nebraska law, so the runaway report became a criminal confession. The girls' parents were arrested and charged with child endangerment, and Majed and Latif were arrested and charged with multiple counts of statutory rape.

The Iraqi community was shocked and outraged that these men were arrested and could face up to fifty years in prison simply for engaging in a marriage on which all parties had agreed. An Iraqi woman (who was herself married at twelve in Iraq) interviewed by the police swore that both girls were excited and happy about the wedding. As we have seen, however, minors below the age of consent cannot by definition give consent. Because of the doctrine of strict liability, Majed and Latif's ignorance of Nebraska law meant nothing to the prosecutor, so they were charged, found guilty, and sentenced to four to six years in prison. They were paroled in 2000, with one of the conditions of their parole being that they have no contact with their "wives."

Were the actions of these men despicable and immoral child sex abuse or simply normal, unremarkable, marital sex with females who happened to be a little too young for contemporary American moral tastes? Why can something that is legally and morally permissible in one culture be severely punished in another? We discussed this question briefly in Chapter 5, but we greatly extend it in this chapter in the context of so-called vice crimes. Most such crimes (or at least acts that are and/or have been defined as crimes) are sexual in nature, such as homosexuality, sodomy, pornography, and of course underage sex. The questions asked in this chapter include whether these actions are really harmful, to whom, and to what extent. We will see that the law has vacillated wildly on these things and learn how the law's reach has lengthened and shortened at various times in our history.

INTRODUCTION

A few years ago in Idaho, one of America's most libertarian ("Get the government off my back") states, there was a popular bumper sticker that said: "Do it now before they make it illegal." This sticker nicely illustrates humanity's split personality with respect to things that may both attract and repel us. Being hedonistic we seek a wide variety of sensual pleasures, but also being censorious with moral pretentions, we may want to deny certain pleasures to others. If we are attracted to the forbidden, we keep it secret while openly condemning others similarly attracted; virtue is practiced in public, vice behind closed doors. This chapter focuses on the role of law in regulating vice crimes and asks what the limits of societal control over the individual should be.

WHAT IS A VICE CRIME?

What constitutes vice varies significantly across time and culture, as our opening vignette demonstrates. Those who are morally outraged by cultures that allow girls as young as twelve to marry and become sexually active may feel smug about the moral "superiority" of the United States, where presently no state has an age of consent of less than sixteen. Such has not always been the case, however. As Lawrence Friedman (2005, 446) reminds us: "In 1885, no state had an age of consent above twelve—in the vast majority, the age was still ten (seven in Delaware!)." If that seems too distant, take the case of rock singer Jerry Lee Lewis, who in 1957 married his thirteen-year-old cousin, which was not too far out of the ordinary in the American South at the time (Baltakis 2002). Jerry Lee, who was twenty-two years old when he married, would find himself in prison today, but in 1957 his marriage was perfectly legal. This illustrates how the fickle sands of the law constantly blow this way and that over the moral terrain.

A **vice crime** is any consensual act that offends the moral standards of the community that has defined the act as worthy of condemnation and legal control. Vice crimes cover a smorgasbord of offenses, some of which have been variously called *public-order offenses, consensual offenses, victimless crimes,* or even *nuisance offenses.* Vice being the opposite of virtue, in earlier times proponents of criminalization asserted that such acts must be punished and suppressed simply because they are immoral; opponents of criminalization countered on grounds of moral relativism. In modern times the whole concept of morality is losing its cachet, so proponents of criminalization have turned to arguments based on harm; that is, vice should not necessarily be regulated because it is immoral but because it causes harm (Harcourt 1999). People calling themselves progressives or liberals have also turned to harm arguments to support decriminalization, but they focus on harms *caused* by enforcing vice laws rather than on the harms caused by the prohibited acts.

Because of the shift of emphasis from morality to harm, a key term in our definition of a vice crime is *consensual*, meaning that parties in the activity have freely agreed to take part in it because they find it pleasurable or rewarding in one way or another. Such acts include prostitution, gambling, illicit drug use, and adultery. Because these acts are consensual, some prefer to refer to them as *victimless,* since any harm that may arise from such activities accrues only to those who freely choose to engage in them. If the law interferes with those engaging in such activities, it is, according to some, an unwarranted and patronizing infringement on their liberty.

This argument rests on something called the *harm principle*. This principle was addressed in Chapter 5 when we examined the elements of a crime that the prosecutor has to prove to obtain a guilty verdict. In that chapter we said that there could be no legal liability without harm, but in this chapter we extend the discussion of harm to encompass social and philosophical issues. The issue of harm is central to a discussion of vice crimes in which questions are asked such as "Who is harmed?" "What is the nature of the harm?" and, most importantly, "Is the harm caused by criminalizing the act worse than the harm caused by the act itself?"

The harm principle was best enunciated by the British philosopher John Stuart Mill in his famous essay *On Liberty*, first published in 1859. It is Mill's conception of harm that has been the basis for debating the limits of societal tolerance in academia and in the courts ever since its publication. According to Mill, the **harm principle** is as follows:

> The sole end for which mankind are warranted, individually or collectively, in interfering with the liberty of action of any of their number, is self-protection. That the only purpose for which power can be rightfully exercised over any member of a civilised community, against his will, is to prevent harm to others. His own good, either physical or moral, is not sufficient warrant. He cannot rightfully be compelled to do or forbear because it will be better for him to do so, because it will make him happier, because, in the opinion of others, to do so would be wise, or even right....The only part of the conduct of anyone, for which he is amenable to society, is that which concerns others. In the part which merely concerns himself, his independence is, of right, absolute. Over himself, over his own body and mind, the individual is sovereign (1913, 6).

For Mill, then, you should enjoy the liberty to swing your arms in any and all directions, and the liberty to do so should only be constrained by force of law when your arms come too close to someone else's nose. This is one of the core principles of both libertarianism and liberalism. If you pull your arm out of joint swinging it, you have only harmed yourself, and that should be no one's business but yourself, because you did not victimize anyone—your actions were victimless.

The term *victimless* is popular among advocates of vice decriminalization or legalization, but the term invites rancorous debate because vice crimes are far from victimless (Mill recognized this and was by no means a radical libertarian). Leaving aside the fact that vice participants are harming themselves, the real victims are often third-party innocents. The man who brings a sexually transmitted disease back to his wife after visiting a prostitute, the man who gambles away the family's money, and the woman who takes illicit drugs during her pregnancy are all causing great harm to many other people. Rather than victimless, vice crimes are better conceived of as consensual mala prohibita acts that always have the potential for causing harm to others besides to the person engaging in them.

All vice offenses cause some harm, but the debate today revolves around the question of whether or not the harm caused is great enough to warrant siphoning off criminal justice resources that could be applied to more serious crimes and/or whether the harm is great enough to justify the state's interfering with the privacy rights of citizens. For instance, adultery (sexual intercourse of a married person with someone other than his or her spouse) is an act of betrayal, which may cause untold hurt, pain, and anger in the spouse betrayed as well as damage to children in the marriage. Adultery is so seriously disruptive to society (because the family is the basic institution of any society) that it has been considered a serious offense worthy of the death penalty by many cultures around the world in conformity with the Old Testament's *Leviticus* 20:10, which proclaims: "And the man that committeth adultery with another man's wife, even he that committeth adultery with his neighbour's wife, the adulterer and the adulteress shall surely be put to death." Adultery is still a capital crime in certain Islamic countries, and it once was in England and the American colonies for a brief period in the seventeenth and eighteenth centuries, although the death penalty was rarely carried out (Greenstein 2004).

In the early part of the twentieth century, however, several cities instituted special "morals courts" to deal with adultery and fornication (sex between unmarried adults). No less than 500 such cases were prosecuted in Chicago's Morals Court in 1914 (Friedman 2005, 569), but such courts disappeared after too many prominent citizens became candidates for prosecution. Adultery is still technically a crime in the United States, with some states mandating that only the married party be prosecuted and others mandating prosecution for both parties. Although rarely enforced, penalties range from as low as a $250 fine (a misdemeanor) in many states to five years' imprisonment (a felony) in Illinois (State Adultery Laws 2009). With 21 percent of married men and 12.5 percent of married women admitting they had committed adultery at least once (Greenstein 2004) (and these are just the honest ones), imagine the impact on the criminal justice system and on society as a whole if these laws were enforced with any semblance of vigor.

HOMOSEXUALITY AND SODOMY

In modern legal usage, **sodomy** is anal sex between two men *or* a man and a woman, although a number of antisodomy statutes in the United States and elsewhere have considered sodomy synonymous with homosexual conduct. In the 1920s, most states expanded the definition of sodomy to include fellatio (mouth–penis contact), and a few states also included cunnilingus (mouth–vagina contact) in their definition (Canaday 2008). Interestingly, cunnilingus between two women has never been considered a crime in English common law because lawmakers could not envision women doing such a thing. In an 1811 case from Scotland the very thought was considered an "oxymoron" by the House of Lords (the upper house of the British Parliament) since "the crime here alleged has no existence" (Painter 2005, 6).

As with adultery, the image of homosexuality and sodomy in Christianity, Judaism, and Islam arose from *Leviticus* 20:13, which says, "If a man also lie with mankind, as he lieth with a woman, both of them have committed an abomination: they shall surely be put to death; their blood shall be upon them." Sodomy is not mentioned in the passage, but it has been taken for granted that when two men "lieth" together that is what they are doing. However, according to ten history professors who submitted an *amicus curiae* brief in a sodomy case (recall that these "friends of the court" briefs are submitted by individuals or groups who are not a party to the case offering relevant information about the matter before the court), sodomy has *not* been considered historically to be synonymous with homosexuality (Chauncey et al. 2003). They gain support from early Christian writers such as Thomas Aquinas, who considered sodomy to "cover any genital contact intended to produce orgasm except penile–vaginal intercourse in an approved position" and/or sexual activity that "could not result in procreation regardless of the gender involved" (Chauncey et al. 2003, 5).

Throughout most of European history same-sex sexual behavior was considered a sin to be dealt with by the ecclesiastical courts rather than a crime, although from time to time this was punctuated with secular interference and criminalized. In general, however, people who engaged in homoerotic behavior were seen not as a special class of people but, rather, as ordinary folks who engaged in "unnatural acts" (Canaday 2008). It was not until 1869 that the term *homosexual* was coined and when homosexuals began to be seen as a distinct category of persons (Burr 1993), thus marking the beginning of the focus on the actors (homosexuals) rather than the act (sodomy). With the coining of the term and with the classification of people into it, legal statutes began to equate sodomitic sex with homosexuality. As Chauncey and his colleagues (2003, 10) assert: "Only in the late nineteenth century did the idea of the homosexual as a distinct category of person emerge, and only in the twentieth century did the state begin to classify and penalize citizens on the basis of their status as homosexuals."

The law's stance toward homosexuality and homosexuals was also influenced by the rise of psychiatry in the mid- to late nineteenth century. For many years homosexuality was considered by the American Psychiatric Association (APA) to be a disease. Burr (1993, 2) tells us that "[b]y the 1940s homosexuality was discussed as an aspect of psychopathic, paranoid, and schizoid disorders." Up to and including the 1940s, many states had draconian "treatment" strategies for homosexuals, with some gay males being subjected to such things as electric shock treatment, aversion therapy, castration, and in rare instances lobotomies (an incision in the frontal lobe of the brain to sever certain nerve tracts) and hysterectomies for lesbians (Burr 1993; Painter 2005).

The APA removed homosexuality from its list of mental diseases in 1973 and now considers it to be a normal variant of human sexuality and has characterized it as a "sexual preference," which implies choice. Bringing choice into the debate suggests that things could be otherwise, enabling moralists to bombard homosexuals with religious exhortations and offers of counseling that would help them to see that their "choice" was the wrong one. The term most often used today, however, is *sexual orientation*, in recognition of the growing scientific consensus that the roots of homosexuality are biological (Savolainen and Lehmann 2007). Homosexuals no more choose their sexual orientation than do heterosexuals; i.e., attraction to their own sex is part of their biological constitution and can no more be changed by religious exhortations or counseling than a heterosexual can be browbeaten into becoming homosexual.

Despite the evolving tolerance for homosexuals in society and the evolving respect for privacy rights, the majority of states still had antisodomy laws on their books through the 1990s, some exclusively targeting homosexual sodomy. With the onset of the AIDS epidemic in the 1980s, laws against homosexual conduct were enforced, in the name of reducing harm, not moral repugnance. For instance, many cities closed gay bathhouses (where indiscriminate sexual activity took place with multiple partners) because of the potential harm associated with exchanging bodily fluids containing HIV, the virus that causes AIDS (Harcourt 1999).

In 1986 the Supreme Court upheld the Georgia antisodomy law in *Bowers v. Hardwick* (1986). Hardwick and another male were arrested after they were found engaging in mutual oral sex by a police officer who had entered Hardwick's apartment to serve a misdemeanor arrest warrant for an unrelated offense. The local prosecutor declined to press charges, but Hardwick sued the Georgia attorney general (Bowers), hoping to have the sodomy law declared unconstitutional. The case eventually wound up in the Supreme Court, with Hardwick claiming that his privacy rights had been violated (Carpenter 2004). Using the rational-basis standard of review ("Is there a bona fide state interest served by the statute?") the Court sided with Georgia, although the written opinions made it quite clear that the Justices' moral inclinations had trumped evolving constitutional law. However, the decision could be considered more kindly in the context of the AIDS epidemic, which was creating a moral and medical panic in the 1980s and was then considered exclusively a gay disease; it was even called "gay-related immune deficiency syndrome" (GRIDS) at the time.

In 2003, eighteen states still had laws on the books forbidding consensual sodomy regardless of the sex of the partners or even marital status, and four other states had antisodomy laws aimed at homosexuals only. The Supreme Court overruled its *Bowers* decision in *Lawrence v. Texas* (2003) and invalidated all remaining sodomy statutes throughout the United States. In this case, John Lawrence and Tyron Garner were caught engaging in anal sex in Lawrence's apartment by a deputy sheriff responding to a false report of a "weapons disturbance" in the apartment. They were arrested, convicted, and fined $200 each.

The men appealed their conviction on privacy grounds and on Fourteenth Amendment equal protection grounds because the Texas law prohibited sodomy between same-sex partners but not between opposite-sex partners and was thus unconstitutional (Carpenter 2004).

Justice Anthony Kennedy wrote the majority (6–3) opinion in *Lawrence*, and he turned again to international precedent, as he did in writing the *Roper* opinion outlawing the death penalty for juveniles. He wrote that the Court's reasoning in *Bowers* had "been rejected by the European Court of Human Rights [ECHR]," and that other nations have taken action consistent with an affirmation of the protected right of homosexual adults to engage in intimate, consensual conduct." In referring to the ECHR, Kennedy reminded us that England and Wales had legalized consensual homosexual activity in 1967 and Scotland in 1980. In a case cited by Kennedy—*Dungeon v. The United Kingdom* (1980)—the ECHR invalidated Northern Ireland's sodomy laws on privacy and human rights grounds. Thus, for better or for worse, *Lawrence* finally brought United States law into conformity with laws governing privacy rights in other Western Democracies.

PROSTITUTION AND COMMERCIALIZED VICE

Prostitution and commercialized vice is defined by the FBI's *UCR Handbook* as: "The unlawful promotion of or participation in sexual activities for profit. To solicit customers or transport persons for prostitution purposes; to own, manage, or operate a dwelling or other establishment for the purpose of providing a place where prostitution is performed; or to otherwise assist or promote prostitution" (FBI 2004, 142). This offense thus covers people who sell their sexual services, those who recruit them, those who solicit clients for them, and those who house them. The common term for a procurer and panderer is *pimp* and for the keeper of a brothel is *madam*. There were 38,812 arrests nationwide for prostitution and commercialized vice in 2007 (FBI 2008), which doubtless constitutes only the tiniest fraction of all such offenses.

Prostitution may be succinctly defined as the provision of sexual services in exchange for money or other tangible reward, and a *prostitute* as a person who engages in prostitution as a source of income. Exchanging sexual favors for some other valued resource is as old as the species, and prostitution has long been referred to as the world's oldest profession. Attitudes about the "profession" throughout history have ranged from one extreme to the other. Many ancient societies employed prostitutes in temples of worship with whom worshipers "communed" and then deposited an offering into the temple coffers, just like Christians take bread and wine and contribute to the collection basket. The earliest-known writings on prostitution are contained in Hammurabi's Code, in which prostitutes seemed to have enjoyed something of a privileged status, because 6 of its 282 codes specifically mention the rights of prostitutes (King 2009).

It was not unusual for many high-born women in ancient Greece who had fallen on hard times to become high-class courtesans called *hetaerae* who supplied their wealthy clients with stimulating conversation as well as sexual services. The lower classes had to content themselves with the brothel-based *por-nae* or the prettier and more entertaining *auletrides*, who would make house calls (Bullough 1976). This ancient Greek hierarchy of sex workers is mirrored in modern America, with the *hetaerae* working for elite escort services, *auletrides* working for less selective services, and the brothel prostitutes being our *pornae*. The only legal brothels in the United States are in certain counties of Nevada, where prostitution cohabits comfortably with other cherished vices. Rhode Island has legalized prostitution but not brothels, but de facto brothels probably exist in every city in the United States, masquerading as massage parlors.

Prostitution has been regarded throughout much of American history as a "necessary evil." During the American Revolution camp-followers who serviced the sexual needs of the troops were tolerated, and the term *hooker* is apparently derived from the women who serviced the Union troops commanded by General Joseph Hooker during the Civil War (Hagan, 2008). Prostitutes were particularly active in the old west, where women were a rare commodity. However, the scourge of venereal disease and the grip of Victorian morality marked a change in American attitudes in the latter part of the nineteenth century, at which time many jurisdictions criminalized prostitution. In 1910 the federal government got into the act when Congress passed the White-Slave Traffic Act (the Mann Act), prohibiting "white slavery" (prostitution) and making it a felony to transport females across state lines for immoral purposes.

The period between 1920 and 1940 was a period of "judicial enforcement of Victorian sexual norms," in which "most judges...adopted a tough stance toward prostitution and justified their actions based on their concern to preserve 'high moral standards'" (Harcourt 1999, 151–52). This stance is exemplified by the circumstances of the only prostitution case to come before the U.S. Supreme Court (*Mortensen* v. *United States*, 1944). In 1940, the petitioners, Mr. and Mrs. Mortensen, were convicted of transporting women across state lines for immoral purposes under the Mann Act. The Mortensens, who ran a brothel in Grand Island, Nebraska, had traveled to Salt Lake City, Utah, accompanied by two of their prostitute employees. Although there was no evidence that the trip was anything other than a vacation to visit Mr. Mortensen's parents, all parties were convicted in District Court. In 1944, the United States Supreme Court overruled the convictions, stating that they were improperly charged under the Mann Act because all evidence showed that the journey in question was an innocent vacation.

In 1998 the U.S. Supreme Court avoided ruling on the legal status of prostitution by denying certiorari to an appeal made by a prostitute calling herself Jane Roe II alleging that Florida's prostitution laws violated her "fundamental right to privacy" pursuant to the Supreme Court's "discovery" of privacy rights in *Griswold* and *Roe*. Roe II's certiorari application was based on an Eleventh Federal District Court's affirmation of the Florida Supreme Court's decision that prostitution did not fall under the umbrella of privacy as currently understood (*Roe v. Butterworth*, 1997). The district court asserted that the state's rational interest in criminalizing prostitution was to protect the sanctity of marriage and that privacy is a concept that can only apply to fundamental rights implicit in the concept of ordered liberty.

What are the harms of prostitution, and are they sufficient to warrant state intervention? Most of the harms are obvious, ranging from the Continental Army's concern about the spread of venereal disease to the modern feminists' concern about the exploitation of women. Prostitutes help spread deadly diseases, and they are certainly open to exploitation and violence perpetrated by their customers and their pimps. The seamy world of prostitution is also closely related to the drug market, to other forms of serious criminality, and to neighborhood blight and with the exploitation of children.

Perhaps the worst exploitation is that of trafficking women (and even children) from poor countries to work in the brothels of rich countries. Some of these women come with their eyes wide open, but most others are duped, coerced, or forced. Even so-called voluntary migrants are forced to sell themselves into the quasi-slavery of prostitution due to the poverty and lack of opportunities in their countries of origin (Raymond 2003). Some make the argument that legalizing or decriminalizing prostitution would eliminate many of these problems, and others that doing so would make them worse.

Should Prostitution Be Decriminalized/Legalized?

As sordid as we may feel that prostitution is, it has always been with us and presumably always will be. If we can't stop it, perhaps we should legalize it or decriminalize it. When the Greek lawmaker Solon (638–559 BC) legalized and taxed it, he was widely praised by the citizenry: "Hail to you Solon! You bought public women [prostitutes] for the benefit of the city, for the benefit of the morality of a city that is full of vigorous young men who, in the absence of your wise institution, would give themselves over to the disturbing annoyance of better women" (Durant 1939, 116). The taxes on prostitution enabled Athens to build the temple to Aphrodite, the Goddess of love, and the open availability of prostitutes provided its "vigorous young men" safe outlets for their urges. Legalizing prostitution thus means that it becomes a legitimate occupation and that the state can regulate (licensing brothels and prostitutes, determining where they can be located, requiring regular health checkups, etc.) and tax them, as it does in Nevada. In other words, legalization refers to the use of law to control prostitution by determining the legal conditions under which it can operate.

The Netherlands provides an example of a country that has legalized prostitution. All parties—the prostitutes, pimps, procurers, and customers—are legally sanctioned as long as they remain in prescribed areas. The downside, and it is a truly obnoxious downside, is that various studies have found that about 70 percent of Dutch prostitutes are trafficked in from poorer countries, because legalization has greatly expanded the demand for a variety of "exotic" females (Raymond 2003). There is no evidence that legalization has stemmed trafficking in the Netherlands; rather, it has tended to increase it.

Decriminalization, on the other hand, simply means the removal of laws against prostitution without imposing regulatory controls on it. This is a kind of "blind eye" stance toward prostitution. Decriminalization is the stance favored by the ACLU and prostitution rights groups such as COYOTE (Call Off Your Old

Tired Ethics) who oppose legalization since it requires regulation and further stigmatizes the "profession" (Weitzer 1999). The police tolerance (and evidently the public's) of massage parlors in our cities constitutes de facto decriminalization in the United States. Decriminalization basically means business as usual for prostitutes, and it saves many millions of taxpayers' dollars not expended arresting, prosecuting, and punishing women, most of whom are in the "business" because they perceive few alternatives or who may have been forced into it by pimps on whom they rely for love, protection, and drugs (Tutty and Nixon 2003).

The United Kingdom is an example of a country that has decriminalized prostitution. In the U.K., women are not penalized for selling sexual favors, but all third-party activities, such as pimping, procuring, and in any way living off "immoral earnings," are criminalized. A prostitute may not solicit in the street (if she or he does, then she or he is liable for prosecution for public disorder, not prostitution); thus the police target their resources exclusively on controlling street prostitution. For a prostitute to be strictly legal, that individual must work independently, and for the place of business not to be considered a brothel, the prostitute must employ no more than a maid and/or receptionist (West 2000). Whether prostitution is legalized or decriminalized, however, one inevitable upshot has always been an increase in demand as more men come to see it as no big deal ("It's legal, so it must be OK") or to engage in it because there is no longer risk of arrest.

A third option is practiced by Sweden. The Swedes have decriminalized prostitution but have maintained laws criminalizing the purchasing of prostitutes' services. If a prostitute and the john (customer) are caught engaging in sex, the john is arrested and the prostitute sent on her or his way. Since many customers are married or otherwise respectable members of society, an arrest experience has a very large deterrent effect. An American study of arrested johns found that only 18 out of 2,200 (0.8 percent) men arrested for soliciting were arrested again for soliciting over a four-year period, a truly remarkably low recidivism rate (Weitzer 1999).

PORNOGRAPHY/OBSCENITY

Although the terms *pornography* and *obscenity* are used interchangeably in everyday speech, they are somewhat different concepts in law. In concurring with the majority of the United States Supreme Court in overturning the conviction of a theater manager for showing a movie the courts of Ohio deemed obscene, Justice Potter Stewart famously declared that he could not define obscenity, "But I know it when I see it" (*Jacobellis v. Ohio*, 1964). The courts certainly have had difficulty wrestling with what constitutes pornography/obscenity, and although we all "know it when we see it," we still need reasonable definitions in order to proceed. We define **pornography** as the depiction of sexual behavior in pictures, writing, film, or other material intended to cause sexual arousal. **Obscenity** is a legal term for any subcategory of pornography that is not constitutionally protected, such as child pornography. Pornography is related to prostitution, and literally means "the writings of whores." We can think of consumers of pornography as vicariously engaged in prostitution, since they are using the material to assist their sexual arousal, and the actors depicted in the pornography have been paid to facilitate that arousal.

We have certainly traversed far on the moral seas since 1960, when the book *Lady Chatterley's Lover* was banned in Britain and the United States because of its sexually explicit language. The courts agreed that the book was obscene, but the bans were lifted in both countries because it was also considered to have redeeming literary qualities. Because of the publicity surrounding the case, the book became an instant bestseller, but certainly not for its "redeeming literary qualities." The objectionable language in the book is now heard dozens of times in movies and in many rap songs, which are arguably musical pornography (think of Lil' Wayne grabbing his crotch as he sings the chorus of his hit record "I Wish I Could Fuck Every Girl in the World"). Photographer Robert Mapplethorpe even had a museum exhibition funded by National Endowment for the Arts that featured homoerotic pictures that included one man urinating into the mouth of another. The exhibit was widely defended by cultural mandarins as art, prompting some to quip that the difference between art and pornography is a government grant.

The guiding common law principle has historically been the so-called *Hicklin test*, derived from the English case *Regina v. Hicklin* (1868). In this case the court ruled that the law can ban anything that "depraves and corrupts those whose minds are open to such immoral influences and into whose hands a publication of this sort might fall." This rule held even if a book had literary merit if any part of it fit the ruling. The Hicklin test prevailed until obscenity was more strictly defined as material whose dominant theme appeals to the prurient interest of the average person according to contemporary community standards (*Roth v. United States*, 1957).

In *Miller v. California* (1973) the Court reaffirmed that obscenity is not protected speech and offered a way to define it. It established the so-called **Miller Test,** which specifies that to be considered obscene (1) the material must appeal to prurient interests as determined by the "average person" applying "contemporary community standards." (2) It must describe-illustrate sexual activity in a "patently offensive" way. And (3) it has to lack any serious literary, artistic, scientific, or political value. This is a truly fuzzy definition that permits everything and nothing, depending on what a local jury or court considers prurient, patently offensive, and lacking in serious value. The material sold in "adult" stores everywhere surely fails the Miller Test, making the distinction between obscenity and pornography meaningless.

Pornography in all its forms has been strongly criticized by religious leaders and conservatives as eroding moral standards by representing deviant sexuality as normal and separating sex from love and marriage. It is also criticized by feminists as an evil that is insulting and demeaning to women, a mechanism by which cultural meanings of sexuality and women are distorted, a cause of rape and child molestation, and exploiting the lowest moral depths of those who make it and those who consume it. At the same time, however, feminists tend to oppose most forms of censorship, and most feminists, according to Beverly Brown (2007, 78), oppose sexual morality as "the other of liberalism [i.e., sexual morality is a conservative value]."

Defenders of pornography claim that it does not cause *direct* harm and that only direct harm should be prohibited, according to the harm principle (this argument is analogous to the *causation* principle, i.e., the legal or proximate cause as opposed to the factual or "but for" ultimate cause discussed in Chapter 5). This argument notwithstanding, we punish imprudent acts all the time according to their potential for harm. People driving drunk or recklessly do not cause any direct harm most times they drive drunk or recklessly, but they are punished if caught by the traffic cop because the *potential* for harm is ever present, and it is that potential that justifies state intervention.

Both conservatives and liberal feminists have thus criticized pornography on the basis of the actual and potential harm that it does. Rather than contending with harm claims, defenders of pornography have shifted their emphasis to the freedom of speech clause of the First Amendment. Thanks to the existing national appetite for pornography, pornographers have deep pockets with which to fight any acts, laws, or ordinances designed to curb their trade (according to a CNBC program *Porn: Business of Pleasure*, which aired on September 5, 2009, porn profits are at least $13 billion a year in the United States). The pornographers have won practically all their battles, other than those involving child pornography, based on free speech arguments. In a famous pornography case heard by the United States Seventh Circuit Court of Appeals (*American Booksellers v. Hudnut*, 1984) that invalidated an Indianapolis, Indiana, antipornography ordinance passed explicitly on the basis of the harm it does, Judge Easterbrook wrote:

> [We] accept the premises of this legislation [that pornography causes harm]. Pornography is a systematic practice of exploitation and subordination based on sex which differentially harms women. The bigotry and contempt it produces, with the acts of aggression it fosters, harm women's opportunities for equality and rights. Yet this simply demonstrates the power of pornography as speech. All of these unhappy effects depend on mental intermediation. Pornography affects how people see the world, their fellows, and social relations.

In other words, while the Court agreed that pornography is harmful, it is harm that clearly "demonstrates the power of pornography as speech" to the Court. The First Amendment thus becomes a sort of verbal jujitsu by which the strength of the harm argument is turned against itself. Easterbrook's statement that the "unhappy effects" of pornography depend on "mental mediation" reflects the legal/factual distinction in the causation principle and essentially means that those effects must first clear the sieve of individual interpretation, and it is this thought process that constitutes speech. Even child pornography is not outside the protection of the First Amendment as long as the images of children presented are "virtual" children (computer generated) rather than real (*Ashcroft v. Free Speech Coalition*, 2002). Thus freedom of speech trumps harm.

There is one harm claim, however, that is difficult to reconcile with the actual data: that pornography causes rape. This is the most serious of the harm claims, and it is epitomized by the feminist slogan "Pornography is the theory, rape the practice." However, according to longitudinal data from the various National Crime Victimization Surveys (NCVS) conducted by the Bureau of Justice Statistics, there has been a steady and significant drop in self-reported rape victimization that roughly coincides with the emergence of explicit pornography in the late 1960s and early '70s, as Figure 10.1 clearly demonstrates. No one claims that the easy availability of pornography has *caused* a substantial drop in rape in the United States, but those who claim a causal relationship between rape and pornography will not welcome these data. However, these are nationally aggregated data, and by no means do they disprove the claim that some individuals have been motivated to rape women or molest children by pornography; it all depends on Judge Easterbrook's "mental mediations."

Free speech is our most valuable freedom and must be protected by any means. The free speech clause of the First Amendment is both the foundation and the crown jewel of the Bill of Rights, without which all the other rights contained therein would be impotent. The question is how far should the free exercise of this right be allowed to go? There is abundant evidence that the Founding Fathers meant the clause to cover political and religious speech and that they were very much opposed to obscenity (Stone et al. 1999, 189). As we are frequently reminded, however, the Constitution is a living document that evolves with the times. Opponents of the death penalty are ever willing to remind us that "evolving standards of decency" should no longer permit us to execute murderers. By the same token, those who are convinced that morality is important social cement might consider the law's current stance on pornography as indicative of society's "evolving standards of *in*decency." Many who oppose pornography aver that too much emphasis has been placed on the protection of individual rights and not enough on the rights of that collection of individuals we call

Figure 10.1 U.S. National Rape Rates Per 1,000 Persons Aged 12 and Above Over a Thirty-Year Period

Source: Bureau of Justice Statistics (2009). Rape rates have been stable in recent years.

"society." British lawmaker Patrick Devlin's (1965, 22) position expressed next is reminiscent of sociologist Emile Durkheim's concern about the role shared morality plays in social solidarity:

> [T]he law exists for the protection of society. It does not discharge its function by protecting the individual from injury, annoyance, corruption, and exploitation; the law must protect also the institutions and the community of ideas, political and moral, without which people cannot live together. Society cannot ignore the morality of the individual any more than it can his loyalty; it [society] flourishes on both and without either it dies.

We should note that we cannot from this position use the argument that if someone takes offense at pornography, then he or she should close the book, turn off the television, avoid the movie, or avert the eyes, because the harm claim is a general one about the society as a whole, not about any one individual. We should also note that in no country is free speech an absolute. In the United States we limit many kinds of speech and expression, including libel, false advertising, advertising content, speech intended to incite panic or riot, blackmail/extortion notes, threatening letters, as well as a few other things, and do so on the basis of the harm principle. Indeed, the courts have upheld ordinances against billboards and the like containing explicit advertising for pornography, leading to the curious situation that the law allows more regulation of the advertising of the product than of the product itself.

ABORTION

Few issues more strongly divide modern America and raise more hackles than the abortion issue. Analogies such as comparing abortion to the Holocaust on one side and characterizing its prohibition as slavery on the other abound at the zealous extremes of the debate. Such hyperbole makes it difficult to offer a definition without causing offense to one side of the issue or the other. We offer a definition of abortion here that is as value neutral as we can make it: **Abortion** is the intentional termination of a pregnancy by the removal or expulsion of an embryo/fetus from the uterus resulting in its death. Some individuals view this "termination" as simply a medical procedure analogous to removing a tumor, while others see it as the murder of an unborn child.

When abortion was prohibited throughout the United States and elsewhere it was considered a vice crime, although it hardly fits those parts of the standard definition of vice that describes it as a pleasurable experience that people habitually seek to repeat. There is nothing pleasurable about the abortion experience, and surely no one wants to repeat it. The terms *victimless* and *consensual* for describing the act are also problematic and bring angry outcries from abortion opponents. Pro-life advocates maintain that the embryo/fetus/potential human being/human being (one can take one's pick of the descriptors) is very much a victim, although it cannot complain to the law about it. Kaplan (1988, 153) asserts that the term *consensual* is no better than *victimless* since "[i]t merely underscores that the fetus, which the foes of abortion regard as a human being, has not consented to anything." This leaves us with having to assume that abortion has been characterized as a vice crime because of its link with illicit sex or perhaps to prevent it from falling into a more serious category, such as murder or manslaughter, during the years in which it was legally prohibited (Stuntz 2000).

As long as women have become pregnant without having the support of a committed mate (and sometimes even when they do), they have sought abortion. In the ancient world abortion was induced by a variety of herbal potions or by such physical means as pressure applied to the abdomen by binding or hitting, jumping from considerable heights, or lifting heavy weights. As with sodomy and prostitution, attitudes regarding abortion have fluctuated across the centuries. The first laws regulating abortion are found in the Code of Hammurabi, which stipulated fines for causing "miscarriage" (King 2009). In the Middle Ages and into the last third of the nineteenth century, abortion during the early stages of pregnancy was generally accepted in western Europe, with exceptions from time to time and place to place. The point at which it became prohibited was at the *quickening*, the first discernible movement of the fetus, which usually occurs around the fourth month of pregnancy. However, in the late nineteenth century, public opinion about abortion changed. In 1869 the Roman Catholic Church prohibited abortion under any circumstances for its members.

The attitude toward those who performed abortions was generally more severe than toward those seeking them, as is illustrated by the case of Eleanor Beare in England, who was indicted in 1732 for "destroying the Foetus in the Womb of Grace Belfort, by putting an iron instrument up into her body, and thereby causing her to miscarry" (*Rex v. Beare*, 1732). Counsel for the Crown opened his case with the following statement:

> Gentlemen…the Misdemeanor for which the Prisoner stands indicted, is of a most shocking Nature; to destroy the Fruit in the Womb carries something in it so contrary to the natural Tenderness of the Female Sex, that I am amazed how ever any Woman should arrive at such a degree of Impiety and Cruelty, as to attempt it in such a manner as the Prisoner has done, it has really something so shocking in it, that I cannot well display the Nature of the Crime to you: It is cruel and barbarous to the last degree.

At the instigation of religious leaders and the American Medical Association, by the turn of the twentieth century every state prohibited abortion at any stage of pregnancy except where a woman's life was at risk (Garrow 1998). Enforcement was slack, however, and various estimates put the number of illegal abortions performed at around 1 million per year in the 1960s (Rosenberg 1991). Many of these abortions were performed by either shady or reformist physicians, but many were also performed in dangerous and unsanitary conditions by any individual claiming expertise in such matters. Because of the conditions under which they were performed, it was estimated that 5,000 women died each year from illegal abortions (Stuntz 2000), although the true number may have been many more. Publicity surrounding the plight of these women created a growing opposition to abortion laws, and after *Griswold* the stage was set to challenge abortion laws in the Supreme Court on privacy grounds.

By 1973 seventeen states had amended their abortion laws to allow abortion under certain conditions (rape, incest, health risks, and so on), but most still had restrictive laws. In *Roe v. Wade* (1973) the U.S. Supreme Court gave women the right to unlimited access to abortion in the first trimester (thus back to the old common law rule about the "quickening"), allowed the states to regulate abortion in the second trimester, and permitted states to prohibit it in the third trimester unless the life or health of the mother was at risk. In the case of *Doe v. Bolton* (1973), argued on the same day as *Roe*, in invalidating Georgia's abortion laws the Supreme Court ruled that a woman may obtain an abortion after *viability* (the point at which the fetus is able to survive outside the womb) only if it was necessary to protect her health.

Ever since the *Roe* and *Doe* (both pseudonyms) decisions, the Court has been fine-tuning abortion law. In 1980 it upheld the Hyde Amendment, which restricted Medicaid funding for abortions to cases of rape or incest (*Harris v. McRae*, 1980); in 1989 it upheld a Missouri statute banning the use of public facilities and employees to perform abortions, as well as the requirement that physicians test for fetal viability beginning at twenty-four weeks of pregnancy (*Webster v. Reproductive Health Services*, 1989). These decisions were seen by pro-choice advocates as retreats from the promise of *Roe*. On the other hand, in *Planned Parenthood v. Danforth* (1976) the Court overturned a Missouri law that required married women to get their husband's consent before they could obtain an abortion, and in *Hodgson v. Minnesota* (1990) it invalidated a law requiring that both parents be informed before a minor could obtain an abortion. These rulings were viewed by pro-lifers as violating paternal and parental rights, respectively.

In *Planned Parenthood of Southeastern Pennsylvania v. Casey* (1992) the Court overturned the trimester scheme it introduced in *Roe* in upholding a Pennsylvania act requiring (1) a woman seeking an abortion to give "informed consent" to it after being provided with information about the possible risks and complications involved and to notify her spouse of her intentions; (2) minors to have parental consent, and (3) a 24-hour waiting period before obtaining an abortion. There was also a provision imposing reporting requirements on abortion facilities. In other words, it was now permissible for states to regulate abortion before as well as after fetal viability.

Nothing splits the two opposing camps more bitterly than the issue of partial-birth abortion. Partial-birth abortion is done by partially extracting the fetus from the vagina, collapsing the skull, and extracting the brain. A Nebraska law defined this as "killing the child" and made it a felony. A Nebraska abortion physician named Leroy Carhart challenged the law as unconstitutional in *Stenberg v. Carhart* (2000). The Court agreed with Carhart and struck down the Nebraska law. According to Justice Stephen Breyer: "All those who perform abortion procedures using that method must fear prosecution, conviction, and imprisonment [which places] an undue burden upon a woman's right to make an abortion decision." The depth of feeling that this form of abortion brings out can be gauged by Justice Antonin Scalia's scathing dissent: "[T]he notion that the Constitution of the United States...prohibits the States from simply banning this visibly brutal means of eliminating our half-born posterity is quite simply absurd."

As a result of the *Stenberg* decision, The United States Congress entered the fray by passing the *Partial-Birth Abortion Ban Act* of 2003. This act contained the following two research findings that were crucial to the promulgation of the act.

(1) A moral, medical, and ethical consensus exists that the practice of performing a partial-birth abortion—an abortion in which a physician delivers an unborn child's body until only the head remains inside the womb, punctures the back of the child's skull with a sharp instrument, and sucks the child's brains out before completing delivery of the dead infant—is a gruesome and inhumane procedure that is never medically necessary and should be prohibited.

(2) Rather than being an abortion procedure that is embraced by the medical community, particularly among physicians who routinely perform other abortion procedures, partial-birth abortion remains a disfavored procedure that is not only unnecessary to preserve the health of the mother, but in fact poses serious risks to the long-term health of women and, in some circumstances, their lives. As a result, at least 27 States banned the procedure as did the United States Congress which voted to ban the procedure during the 104th, 105th, and 106th Congresses.

As a result of this act, a number of states, including Nebraska, reinstituted partial-birth abortion bans. The same Dr. Leroy Carhart who was the petitioner in *Stenberg v. Carhart* was then joined by other abortion providers in challenging the constitutionality of the act. After a round of appeals in lower courts, the case eventually found its way to the U.S. Supreme Court as *Gonzales v. Carhart* (2007). The Court found that the Partial-Birth Abortion Ban Act passed constitutional muster. The Court did not overturn *Stenberg* but, rather, distinguished it from *Gonzales* (recall that when a court "distinguishes," it is saying that although the present case is similar to a prior case, the prior case is not overruled because of significant differences between the prior and present cases). The Court held that the Nebraska statute at issue in *Stenberg* was more ambiguous than the later federal statute at issue in *Gonzales*. Legal cynics among us might say that the real difference that "distinguished" *Stenberg* from *Gonzales* was the replacement of moderate Justice Sandra Day O'Connor with conservative justice Samuel Alito, since both cases were 5–4 decisions. This once again illustrates how the theoretically neutral law serves practical ideological positions.

It is perhaps the partial-birth issue that has significantly changed the attitudes of Americans about abortion over the last fifteen years. In 1995, 56 percent of Americans considered themselves pro-choice and 33 percent considered themselves pro-life. By 2009, more Americans considered themselves pro-life (47 percent) than pro-choice (46 percent). There are relatively few people at the moral extremes, however. Only 21 percent thought that abortion should be legal under any circumstances, and only 18 percent thought that it should be illegal in all circumstances (Saad 2009). Given these figures and recent court decisions, we may well see a return to pre–*Roe v. Wade* abortion laws if the Supreme Court decides that abortion is entirely a matter for the individual states to legislate on.

If we leave out the issue of the status of the fetus/child and thus the bitter issue of "termination" versus "killing" (which is impermissible for the pro-life side, since the status of the fetus/child is precisely, and possibly the only, issue at hand), we may ask what the other harms involved are. A number of studies have shown that women who undergo abortion are significantly more likely to be diagnosed with a range of mental disorders, such as clinical depression, substance abuse, bipolar disorder, and suicidal ideation (Cougle, Reardon, and Coleman 2003; Fergusson, Horwood, and Ridder 2006), although other sources claim that the risk of these things is low (American Psychological Association 2005).

One particularly contentious "benefit" of legalized abortion, according to a study conducted by Donohue and Levitt (2001) that managed to upset liberal pro-choice advocates ("It smacks of eugenics and racism") as well as conservative pro-lifers ("The idea that something positive can come from abortion is bizarre"), is that it contributed significantly to the large reduction in crime in the United States in the mid-1990s/early 2000s. Donohue and Levitt (2001, 379) summarize their study as follows:

> Crime began to fall roughly 18 years after abortion legalization. The 5 states that allowed abortion in 1970 experienced declines earlier than the rest of the nation, which legalized in 1973 with *Roe v. Wade*. States with high abortion rates in the 1970s and 1980s experienced greater crime reductions in the 1990s. In high-abortion states, only arrests of those born after abortion legalization fell relative to low-abortion states. Legalized abortion appears to account for as much as 50 percent of the recent drop in crime.

The essence of the argument is that were it not for legalized abortion many thousands of unwanted children would have been born and that this unwantedness is a major predictor of criminality. Unwanted children are likely to grow up in poor single-parent homes and to be at significant risk for abuse and neglect. Additionally, legal abortion reduced the size of the birth cohort, so there will be fewer young males in the high-crime ages to victimize others when they grow up. Although this argument has intuitive appeal (fewer children born into criminogenic environments obviously means less crime down the road), it is also possible that legalized abortion may have actually increased the number of unwanted children because as abortion rates were going up, so was the rate of births to unmarried mothers (Lykken 1995). In other words, the legal availability of abortion granted females license to engage more freely in unprotected sex.

ALCOHOL AND ILLICIT DRUGS

Ben Franklin, arguably the wisest of our Founding Fathers, once wrote: "Beer is proof positive that God loves us and wants us to be happy." Franklin was not alone in praising the Almighty for the gift of alcohol. The ancient Egyptians credited the god Osiris with inventing beer, the ancient Chinese considered it a gift from Heaven, and the Babylonians and Indians are among the ancients who worshiped wine goddesses (McGovern 2003). Humans certainly have a fondness for ingesting substances that alter our moods; we swallow, gulp, sniff, inhale, and inject with such relish that it suggests sobriety is a difficult state for us to tolerate. Among all the diverse substances used to change our moods, alcohol is definitely the favorite route to Franklin's happy state. We drink to loosen our tongues, to be sociable, to liven up our parties, to feel good, to sedate ourselves, and to anesthetize the pains of life. With the help of alcohol we can reinvent ourselves as superior beings; the timid become bold, the tongue-tied loquacious, and the diffident confident.

If alcohol is God's gift to humanity, its abuse is humanity's gift to Satan. Of all mood-altering substances, alcohol is the one most directly linked to crime, especially violent crime (Martin 2001). At least 70 percent of American prison inmates (Wanberg and Milkman 1998) and 60 percent of British inmates (McMurren 2003) are alcohol and/or drug addicted. Police officers spend more than half of their active time on alcohol-related offenses, and about one-third of all arrests in the United States are for alcohol-related offenses (Mustaine and Tewkesbury 2004). About 75 percent of robberies and 80 percent of homicides involve a drunken offender and/or victim, and about 40 percent of other violent offenders in the United States had been drinking at the time of their offense (Martin 2001). The U.S. Department of Health and Human Services (2009) estimates the annual cost of alcohol abuse to society to be a staggering $185 billion ($244 billion in 2009 updated for inflation). According to Alcohol Alert (2009), an organization dedicated to reducing drunk driving, there were 15,387 alcohol-related traffic fatalities on U.S. highways in 2007, or 37 percent of all fatal traffic accidents.

Another major problem is the number of neurological disorders that result from mothers drinking while pregnant, known as *fetal alcohol spectrum disorders* (FASD), the most serious of which is *fetal alcohol syndrome* (FAS). The prevalence of FASD in the United States is around 1 percent of live births (Manning and Hoyme 2007). Fetal alcohol syndrome has a number of readily identifiable physical abnormalities associated with it, because prenatal alcohol exposure adversely effects the migration and hookup of neurons in vital brain areas in the developing fetus (Goodlett, Horn, and Zhou 2005). The behavioral symptoms of FAS include low IQ, hyperactivity, impulsiveness, poor social, emotional, and moral development, and a highly elevated probability of alcoholism (Jacobson and Jacobson 2002). Each of these deficits is linked to high levels of antisocial behavior and criminal offending independent of FAS, but FAS individuals are almost always saddled with them all. There are many other problems associated with alcohol, but the problems addressed here are evidence enough that alcohol is the cause of more obvious harm than all of the other vice crimes combined.

Taming the Beast in the Bottle

More beer was drunk in Europe by children and adults of both sexes in premodern times, simply because it was safer to drink than water, which in those unsanitary days had to be boiled before it could be consumed (McGovern 2003). Beer was also less potent (about 1 percent alcohol, compared to most of today's beers, which average around 3.5 percent), so most of the problems associated with alcohol abuse arose from strong liquor such as gin and rum. The first recorded attempt at the prohibition of alcohol in North America was made by the Massachusetts Colony in 1657; it was aimed only at those products, not at beer (Blue 2004). However, and Ben Franklin notwithstanding, throughout the history of colonial and postcolonial America there have been efforts to prohibit all kinds of alcohol use both for health and moral reasons because it was associated with saloons in which gambling, prostitution, and violence were ever present.

Although the stirrings of temperance movements had existed since the Revolution, the first to have any real impact was the Massachusetts Society for the Suppression of Intemperance, formed in 1828. By the time of the Civil War, thirteen states had passed laws prohibiting the sale of alcohol, with several other states considering it (Augst 2007). After the Civil War the United States saw a rapid increase in prohibitionist sentiment. The Prohibition Party was founded in 1869, the Women's Temperance Union in 1874, and in 1881 Kansas became the first state to outlaw the sale of alcohol. Enforcement of prohibitionist laws was left primarily to the informal but effective methods of religious individuals, such as Carrie Nation, a bulldog of a women who led others of her ilk into saloons with a Bible in one hand and a battle-axe in the other to do "God's work" by laying waste to "murder mills, hell holes, and the donkey bedmates of Satan" (Carver 1999, 31).

The sentiment for prohibition grew to a crescendo with the entry of the United States into World War 1 in 1917, because many of the most prominent breweries had German names, such as Schlitz and Pabst. It was in 1917 that Congress approved a resolution for a constitutional amendment prohibiting the production, sale, transportation, or importation of alcoholic beverages in the United States and sent it to the states for ratification. Ratification was completed in 1919, and in January 1920 the Eighteenth Amendment became effective. The Amendment was supplemented by the Volstead Act of 1919, and together they constituted what became known as **Prohibition**—the "noble experiment." The Volstead Act defined intoxicating liquor as anything containing more than 0.5 percent alcohol and allowed a certain amount of wine and/or cider of that potency to be made at home. Despite Prohibition's rapid passage, greased by anti-German sentiment, it was nevertheless "the fruit of a century-long series of temperance movements springing from deep roots in the American reform tradition" and a culture that "was deeply hostile to alcohol" (Blocker 2006, 233).

That "deep hostility to alcohol" might be better characterized as a deep hostility to other people's use. The public's thirst for alcohol, no longer served by legitimate breweries and the neighborhood bar, was now quenched at a higher price by organized crime and the neighborhood speakeasy. Even President Warren Harding, who was publically a "dry" (pro-Prohibition), served liquor at White House social functions and was thus, like thousands of other Americans, privately a "wet" (Stuntz 2000). Yet in 1928 Americans elected staunch Prohibitionist Herbert Hoover over A1 Smith, who was just as staunchly its opponent. Support for Prohibition waned after the 1929 stock market crash, which produced the Great Depression. Its opponents claimed that Prohibition was costing the government millions of dollars in its enforcement efforts and at the same time causing it to lose millions in revenue.

The economic argument won the day, and in December 1933 the Twenty-First Amendment repealed the Eighteenth Amendment, making it the only amendment to be repealed by the ratification of another. Thus ended the noble experiment aimed at stopping the evils of drink, reducing crime, emptying the prisons, reducing the tax burden, and improving health. It ended up doing quite the opposite: It allowed organized crime to flourish and to corrupt countless government officials, produced more dangerous and potent homemade brews, filled the prisons, and gnawed at government revenue.

Illicit Drugs

The manufacture, sale, and abuse of nonprescription drugs such as cocaine and heroin remains the only vice addressed in this chapter that is not currently legal, quasi-legal, or so tolerated that it is de facto legal. Alcohol is a legal and socially acceptable way of drugging ourselves today, but the use of what once fell under the umbrella term of *narcotics* is not. This was not always the case, for many of the drugs now banned have been legitimately used in religious rituals, for medical treatment, and for recreation around the world and across the ages. There is a reference to the opium poppy as "the plant of joy" in Mesopotamia from around 3000 BC, and the early Egyptians used opium in their religious ceremonies (Davenport-Hines 2002).

At the turn of the twentieth century, most drugs now considered illicit were widely used in the United States and around the world with minimal or nonexistent regulation (Wodak 2007). Sigmund Freud was an avid consumer of cocaine and ecstatic about its medicinal properties. With the public not fully aware of the dangers of addiction, many substances were openly advertised and sold as cures for all sorts of aliments and for refreshing "pick-me-ups." The most famous of these refreshments was Coca-Cola, which until 1903 was made with the coca leaf (used to process cocaine) and kola nuts (hence the name). There were many medicines on the market containing cocaine (e.g., Cocaine Toothache Drops), and others, such as Mother Barley's Quieting Syrup, used to soothe infants and children, contained laudanum, which was essentially opium.

Attitudes toward drug use in America gradually began to change as physicians and lawmakers came to understand more fully the addictive powers of many of these substances. Although earlier federal and state acts had aimed at specific practices and substances (such as opium smoking in opium dens), the **Harrison Narcotics Act** of 1914 was the benchmark act for changing America's attitudes toward drugs. According to Richard Davenport-Hines, "By the early 1920s, the conception of the addict changed from that of a middle-class victim accidentally addicted through medicinal use, to that of a criminal deviant using narcotics (or stimulants) for pleasure" (2002, 14). Although the Harrison Act did initially reduce the number of addicts (estimated at around 200,000 in the early

1900s), it also spawned criminal black market operations and ultimately many more addicts. Three years after the ~~passing of the act, a Cong~~ressional report found: "The 'dope peddlers' appeared to have established a national organization, smuggling the drugs in through seaports or across the Canadian or Mexican borders....The wrongful use of narcotic drugs has increased since the passage of the Harrison Act" (in Casey 1978, 11).

Drugs hijack the brain and produce more powerful, rapid, and predictable effects on its pleasure centers than alcohol. The Drug Enforcement Administration (DEA) estimates that 5 million Americans suffer from drug addiction and that about 55 percent of today's youth have used some form of illegal substance (2003, 13). Addiction is not an invariable outcome of drug use any more than alcoholism is an invariable outcome of drinking. Among those who experiment with drugs are some who are genetically predisposed to develop addiction, just as others are "sitting ducks" for alcoholism (Robinson and Berridge 2003).

Illicit drugs are intimately related to criminal activity. According to the Arrestee Drug Abuse Monitoring Program (Zhang 2004), 75 percent of all male and female arrestees test positive for at least one drug. However, drug abuse does not appear to *initiate* a criminal career, although it does increase the extent and seriousness of one. As Menard, Mihalic, and Huizinga (2001, 295) explain: "Initiation of substance abuse is preceded by initiation of crime for most individuals (and therefore cannot be a cause of crime). At a later stage of involvement, however, serious illicit drug use appears to contribute to continuity in serious crime, and serious crime contributes to continuity in serious illicit drug use."

The link between drugs and crime is largely driven by their illegality, not by their pharmacological effects. Violence induced by illicit drug use is rare compared with violence induced by alcohol, and is most likely to occur *after* the effects of the drugs have worn off, leaving the users stressed, irritable, and paranoid. Just as the underworld stepped in to supply the demand for alcohol during Prohibition, it steps in today to supply drugs. The real link between drugs and violence is associated with "traditionally aggressive patterns of interaction within the system of drug distribution and use" (Goldstein 1985, 497). In other words, violence is an integral part of "doing business"—the growing, processing, transporting, and selling of drugs and the bribery and corruption of law enforcement officials and politicians. A number of terrorist groups are financing their operations through lucrative drug trafficking.

On the streets of the United States, drug violence is most closely linked with gang battles over control of territory (control of drug markets). The National Institute of Justice (1991) estimated that in 1988 about 80 percent of the homicides in the District of Columbia were drug-related, and the dramatic increase in homicides beginning in the mid-1980s has been attributed to the emergence of crack cocaine and the subsequent recruitment of armed and dangerous young males to sell it (Blumstein 1995). Crimes such as shoplifting, burglary, robbery, and prostitution are often committed by addicts to finance the high cost of their drugs.

The criminalization of acts such as sodomy and abortion generated many court cases challenging the legality of the statutes forbidding them, indicating that a significant portion of the population believe that such statutes overstep the bounds of government control of private behavior. There have been no Supreme Court cases challenging the states' right to criminalize illicit drugs, which probably indicates that there is widespread agreement that the manufacture and sale of such substances is morally wrong and is the cause of much harm. It is clear that the use of illicit drugs is very harmful to individuals, their families, and society (Nutt et al. 2007). What is even clearer, however, is that the "war on drugs," just like Prohibition, is the cause of more harm than it prevents. Most countries have abandoned their own wars on drugs today and reverted to harm-reduction policies (i.e., policies aimed solely at minimizing harm). The United States is among only a handful of countries that reject harm-reduction programs favored by agencies such as the World Health Organization (WHO) and the United Nations Children's Fund (UNICEF) (Wodak 2007). Such programs involve syringe-exchange programs, drug-substitution programs (such as methadone for heroin), and, most importantly, decriminalizing drug use. According to Alex Wodak (2007, 61): "No country which has started harm reduction programs has ever regretted that decision and then reversed their commitment."

CONCLUSION

The behaviors addressed in this chapter illustrate the limits of social control by the use of law. As any economist will attest, efforts to prohibit exchanges that are mutually consensual and rewarding are doomed to failure. Criminalizing such acts is really an exercise in morality politics, in which legislative bodies have responded to the publically held values of segments of the population who consider the acts to be perverse. As we pointed out at the beginning of this chapter, however, private behavior often diverges dramatically from public statement about that behavior. History is replete with examples of evangelical ministers caught in adultery or cavorting with prostitutes, with macho opponents of gay rights cruising gay bars and even presidents or future presidents of the United States drinking or sampling illicit drugs when those substances were illegal. Legislative bodies and courts are thus responding to a level of opposition to a variety of vices that simply is not there.

This is not to deny the harms inherent in the various vice crimes, but we have to realize that for many social problems there are no solutions, only trade-offs. Advocates of either legalizing or decriminalizing a particular vice are not promoting it; they are simply recognizing the trade-off nature of trying to deal with it so that it causes the least amount of harm. Presumably, not even the most addicted person would recommend drug use as a good and desirable thing; but given the fact that drugs are here to stay and that there are always people who will abuse them, the question is really one of a cost/benefit analysis of continuing the war versus seeking peace and compromise.

We are repeating many of the mistakes of Prohibition with the war on drugs, such as providing organized crime with a lucrative market, the corruption of officials, huge increases in imprisonment rates, many deaths from adulterated products, and recruitment of our children by addicts who sell to them to finance their own addiction. It may be that economic arguments will win the day, as they did with Prohibition, and lead us along the path many other modern nations have trod to combat the scourge of drugs. Redefining alcohol prohibition as an issue of economics and corruption helped to repeal this well-meaning moral experiment. The moral argument vis-à-vis drugs cuts both ways. Is it more moral to punish the use of admittedly bad substances or to minimize their harmful effects by dealing with them so that they do the least amount of harm?

SUMMARY

Although the law is designed to control deviance, it may occasionally bite off more than it can chew. This chapter has addressed some of those behaviors that seem impervious to any legal threats that a democratic government can make. Acts that have been defined as vice crimes are rewarding to those that engage in them, just as ordinary crimes such as robbery are. The major difference is that vice crimes are mala prohibita, in that both parties have freely consented to engage in them because it is mutually rewarding, whereas robbery is malum in se.

Based on John Stuart Mill's harm principle, vice crimes are defended as acts that should be beyond the reach of the law, since they are said to be consensual or "victimless." However, we have seen that many vice crimes can be extremely harmful, and thus the debate is not about harm/no harm but, rather, about the ratio of harms caused by vice to the amount caused by trying to enforce bans on it. Some vice crimes, such as fornication and adultery, are so widespread that any serious attempt to enforce prohibitions against them is just not possible. In fact, trying to regulate vice is so difficult, expensive, and opposed that the manufacture and sale of addictive drugs is the only vice discussed in this chapter that remains meaningfully criminalized.

Sodomy was historically considered any sex act meant to result in orgasm other than sex for reproductive purposes, but in the late nineteenth century it came to mean primarily homosexual sexual activity. With the American Psychiatric Association's changing attitudes about homosexuality (evolving from a disease, to a choice, and to a biological given), the remaining antisodomy statutes of all states were ruled unconstitutional in *Lawrence v. Texas* in 2003.

Prostitution has had a checkered existence in the United States. It has been alternatively viewed as a necessary evil (in towns with few women) to being damned as a destroyer of marriages and a carrier of disease and death. The arguments about prostitution have revolved around legalization or decriminalizing. Legalizing it means that the state can regulate and tax it; decriminalization simply means that it is just another activity of no interest to the state. Although prostitution is technically illegal everywhere in the United States except Rhode Island and parts of Nevada, it is tolerated in almost every community as long as prostitutes stay off the street.

Pornography is legal in the United States, protected by the First Amendment; obscenity is not. However, where the line between them, or even whether there is such a line, is debatable. The test for obscenity outlined in *Miller* clearly fits almost all products and activities readily available by mail, DVD, cable TV, the Internet, and even live sex shows. The courts have agreed that pornography is harmful but also that it is this very harm that qualifies it as speech, and it is therefore protected. The immense amount of money spent on pornography/obscenity testifies to its popularity, which leads those of a more communitarian bent to decry the moral decline of the United States.

Abortion is the former vice crime that incites the most heated debate. It seems that as of 2009 the pro-life and pro-choice factions are about evenly divided in the United States. Abortion was allowed by common law up until the time of the detection of the first fetal movement (the quickening), but by the turn of the twentieth century every state prohibited it except when the woman's life was at risk. Because of the alarming rate of illegal abortions that led to death, public opinion about abortion began to change in the 1960s. In 1973, the Supreme Court gave women the right to abortion in the first trimester and allowed the states to regulate it in the second trimester and to prohibit it during the third unless the life or health of the mother was at risk. The biggest issue today is that of partial-birth abortion, a brutal method of abortion that the U.S. Congress has forbidden by an act the Supreme Court has upheld.

Alcohol is so popular and ubiquitous today that it is difficult to realize that it was once considered as evil as narcotics in the United States and prohibited. Few people would dispute that alcohol abuse causes more harm than perhaps all the other vices combined, but this fact, plus the fact that it is perfectly legal today, points dramatically to the difficulties in trying to control vice legally. The prohibition of the manufacture, sale, and consumption of alcohol in 1920 ushered in a wild decade of criminal activity in which gangs battled for the control of the illicit alcohol market. In fact, prohibition actually made worse practically all the problems it was supposed to solve. We are arguably repeating the mistakes of Prohibition with today's "war on drugs." Many other democracies are dealing with their drug problem by treating it as a medical rather than a criminal problem, and they aim at minimizing the undoubted harm of drugs.

DISCUSSION QUESTIONS

1. Why are many people hypocritical about vice (publically condemning but privately practicing)?
2. Is the harm principle alone sufficient to determine the illegality of an act?
3. Give reasons why prostitution should or should not be legalized or decriminalized.
4. In what sense can pornography be considered speech protected by the First Amendment?
5. Give the reasons why you are pro-choice or pro-life.
6. Should the United States decriminalize/legalize drugs? What do you think would be the consequences of doing so?

References

Alcohol Alert. 2009. *2007 drunk driving statistics.* http://www.alcoholalert.com/drunk-driving-statistics .html.

American Psychological Association. 2005. *APA Briefing Paper on the Impact of Abortion on Women.* Available at http://www.rcrc.org/pdf/APA%20document.pdf.

Augst, T. 2007. Temperance, mass culture, and the romance of experience. *American Literary History.* 19:297–323.

Baltakis, A. 2002. Jerry Lee Lewis and his marriages: An excuse to attack rock and roll. *Journal of American Culture* 25:51–56.

Blocker, J. 2006. Did prohibition really work? Alcohol prohibition as a public health innovation. *American Journal of Public Health* 96:233–43.

Blue, A. 2004. *The complete book of spirits: A guide to their history, production and enjoyment.* New York: HarperCollins.

Blumstein, A. 1995. Youth violence, guns, and the illicit-drug industry. *Journal of Criminal Law and Criminology* 86:10–36.

Brown, B. 2007. Pornography and feminism: Is law the answer? *Critical Quarterly* 34:72–82.

Bullough, V. 1976. *Sexual variance in society and history.* Chicago: University of Chicago Press.

Bureau of Justice Statistics. 2009. Rape rates have been stable in recent years. http://www.ojp.gov/bjs/glance/rape.htm.

Burr, C. 1993. Homosexuality and biology. *The Atlantic Monthly,* March: 47–65.

Canaday, M. 2008. The strange history of sodomy laws. *The Nation.* Posted on AlterNet at: http://www.alternet.org/module/printversion/99092.

Carpenter, D. 2004. The unknown past of *Lawrence v. Texas. Michigan Law Review* 102:1464–1527.

Carver, F. 1999. With Bible in one hand and battle-axe in the other: Carrie A. Nation as religious reformer and self-promoter. *Religion and American Culture* 9:31–65.

Casey, E. 1978. *History of drug use and drug users in the United States.* Schaffer Library of Drug Policy. http://www.druglibrary.org/schaffer/History/CASEY1.htm.

Chauncey, G., N. Cott, J. D'Emilio, E. Freedman, T. Holt, J. Howard, L. Hunt, M. Jordan, E. Kennedy, and L. Kerber. 2003. *Amicus brief of history professors in the matter of* John Geddes Lawrence and Tyron Garner v. State of Texas. Online at www.findlaw.com.

Cougle, J., D. Reardon, and P. Coleman. 2003. Depression associated with abortion and childbirth: A long-term analysis of the NLSY cohort. *Medical Science Monitor* 9:105–12.

Davenport-Hines, R. 2002. *The pursuit of oblivion: A global history of narcotics.* New York: W.W. Norton.

Devlin, P. 1965. *The Enforcement of Morals.* Oxford: Oxford University Press.

Donohue, J., and S. Levitt. 2001. The impact of legalized abortion on crime. *Quarterly Journal of Economics* 116:379–420.

Drug Enforcement Administration. 2003. *Drugs of Abuse.* Arlington, VA: U.S. Department of Justice.

Durant, W. 1939. *The life of Greece.* New York: Simon & Schuster.

Federal Bureau of Investigation. 2004. *Uniform Crime Reports handbook.* Washington, DC: U.S. Government Printing Office.

———. 2008. *Crime in the United States: 2007.* Washington, DC: U.S. Government Printing Office.

Fergusson, D., L. Horwood, and E. Ridder. 2006. Abortion in young women and subsequent mental health. *Journal of Child Psychology and Psychiatry* 47:16–24.

Friedman, L. 2005. *A history of American law.* New York: Simon & Schuster.

Garrow, D. 1998. *Liberty and Sexuality: The Right to Privacy and the Making of* Roe v. Wade Berkeley: University Of California Press.

Goldstein, P. 1985. The drugs/violence nexus: A tripartite conceptual framework. *Journal of Drug Issues* 15:493–506.

Goodlett, C., K. Horn, and F. Zhou. 2005. Alcohol teratogenesis: Mechanisms of damage and strategies for intervention. *Developmental Biology and Medicine* 230:394–406.

Greenstein, J. 2004. Sex, lies and American tort law: The love triangle in context. *Georgetown Journal of Gender and the Law* 1: 723–62.

Hagan, F. 2008. *Introduction to Criminology.* 6th ed. Thousand Oaks, CA: Sage.

Harcourt, B. 1999. The collapse of the harm principle. *Journal of Criminal Law and Criminology* 90:104–109.

Jacobson, J., and S. Jacobson. 2002. Effects of prenatal alcohol exposure on child development. *Alcohol Research and Health* 26:282–86.

Kaplan, J. 1988. Abortion as a vice crime: A "what if" story. *Law and Contemporary Problems* 51:151–79.

King, L. 2009. Hammurabi's code of laws. http://prostitution.procon.org/sourcefiles/Hammurabi.pdf.

Lykken, D. 1995. *The antisocial personalities.* Hillsdale, NJ: Lawrence Erlbaum.

Manning, M., and H. Hoyme. 2007. Fetal alcohol syndrome disorders: A practical clinical approach to diagnosis. *Neuroscience and Biobehavioral Review* 31:230–38.

Martin, S. 2001. The links between alcohol, crime and the criminal justice system: Explanations, evidence and interventions. *American Journal on Addictions* 10:136–58.

McGovern, P. 2003. *Ancient wine: The search for the origins of viniculture.* Princeton, NJ: Princeton University Press.

McMurren, M. 2003. Alcohol and crime. *Criminal Behavior and Mental Health* 13:1–4.

Menard, S., S. Mihalic, and D. Huizinga. 2001. Drugs and crime revisited. *Justice Quarterly* 18:269–99.

Mill, J. 1913. *On Liberty.* London: Longmans, Green.

Mustaine, E., and R. Tewksbury. 2004. Alcohol and violence. In *Violence: A contemporary reader,* edited by S. Holmes and R. Holmes pp. 9–25. Upper Saddle River, NJ: Prentice Hall.

National Institute of Justice. 1991. *Annual report on adult arrestees: Drugs and crime in America's cities.* Washington, DC: U.S. Department of Justice.

Nutt, D., L. King, W. Saulsbury, and C. Blakemore. 2007. Development of a rational scale to assess the harm of drugs of potential misuse. *The Lancet* 396:1047–53.

Painter, G. 2005. The sensibilities of our forefathers: The history of sodomy laws in the United States. http://www.glapn.org/sodomylaws/sensibilities/introduction.htm.

Raymond, J. 2003. Ten reasons for not legalizing prostitution and a legal response to the demand for prostitution. *Journal of Trauma Practice* 2:315–32. Available online at: http://www.prostitutionresearch.com/laws/000022.html.

Robinson, T., and K. Berridge. 2003. Addiction. *Annual Review of Psychology* 54:25–53.

Rosenberg, G. 1991. *The hollow hope: Can courts bring about social change?* Chicago: University of Chicago Press.

Saad, L. 2009. U.S. abortion attitudes closely divided. Gallop Poll results available at http://www.gallup.com/poll/122033/U.S.-Abortion-Attitudes-Closely-Divided.aspx.

Savolainen, V., and L. Lehmann. 2007. Genetics and bisexuality. *Nature* 445:158–59.

State Adultery Laws. 2009. http://christianparty.net/adulterylaws.htm.

Stone, G., L. Seidman, C. Sunstein, and M. Tushnet. 1999. *The First Amendment.* New York: Aspen Law and Business.

Stuntz, W. 2000. Self-defeating crimes. *Virginia Law Review* 86:1871–99.

Tutty, L., and K. Nixon. 2003. Selling sex? It's really like selling your soul. Vulnerability to and the experience of exploitation through child prostitution. In *Being heard: The experience of young women in prostitution,* edited by K. Gorkoff and J. Runner, pp. 29–45. Black Point, Nova Scotia: Fernwood.

U.S. Department of Health and Human Services. 2009. *Updating estimates of the economic costs of alcohol abuse in the United States.* Center for Substance Abuse Treatment. http://www.maine.gov/dhhs/osa/pubs/us/2009/costoffset.pdf.

Wanberg, K., and H. Milkman. 1998. *Criminal conduct and substance abuse treatment: Strategies for self-improvement.* Thousand Oaks, CA: Sage.

Weitzer, R. 1999. Prostitution control in America. *Crime, Law, and Social Change* 32:83–102.

West, J. 2000. Prostitution: Collectives and the politics of regulation. *Gender, Work, and Organization* 7:106–18.

Wodak, A. 2007. Ethics and drug policy. *Psychiatry* 6:59–62.

Zhang, Z. 2004. *Drug and alcohol use and related matters among arrestees, 2003.* Washington, DC: National Institute of Justice.

Cases Cited

American Booksellers Assn., Inc. v. Hudnut, 475 U.S. 1001 (1986) and 98 F. Supp. 1316 (S.D. Ind. 1984).

Ashcroft v. Free Speech Coalition, 535 U.S. 234 (2002).

Bowers, v. Hardwick, 478 U.S. 110 (1986).

Doe v. Bolton 410 U.S. 179 (1973).

Dudgeon v. The United Kingdom. App. n. 7525/76. ECHR Strasbourg (1980).

Gonzales v. Carhart, 550 U.S. 124 (2007).

Harris v. McRae, 448 U.S. 297 (1980).

Hodgson v. Minnesota, 497 U.S. 417 (1990).

Jacobellis v. Ohio, 378 U.S. 184 (1964).

Lawrence v. Texas, 41 S.W. 348 (2003).

Miller v. California, 413 U.S. 15 (1973).

Mortensen v. United States, 322 U.S. 369 (1944).

Planned Parenthood v. Danforth, 428 U.S. 52 (1976).

Planned Parenthood of Southeastern Pennsylvania v. Casey, 505 U.S. 833 (1992).

Regina v. Hicklin, L.R. 3 Q.B. 360 (1868).

Rex v. Beare, 1 Ld. Raym. 414 (1732).

Roe v Butterworth. 958 F. Supp. 1569 (S.D. Fla.) (1997).

Roe v. Wade, 410 U.S. 113 (1973).

Roth v. United States, 354 U.S. 476 (1957).

Stenberg v. Carhart, 530 U.S. 914 (2000).

Webster v. Reproductive Health Services, 492 U.S. 490 (1989).

CHAPTER 11

THE LAW AND SOCIAL CHANGE

In February 1932, future British Prime Minister Winston Churchill was knocked down by a cab as he crossed Fifth Avenue in New York. Churchill had a flask of whiskey on his person, which made this great man a criminal in the United States. This strange state of affairs existed because of the National Prohibition Act, passed in 1919 to enforce the Eighteenth Amendment's prohibition of the manufacture, sale, or importation of alcoholic beverages. Temperance and abstinence movements had existed for decades before this based on the fact that unbridled drinking was the cause of many of society's problems, particularly crime. In passing the act, the law was responding to demands for change in an important area of social life. Activists of all persuasions agitate for change, and sometimes the law puts its stamp of approval on their goals by passing acts and making favorable judicial decisions.

The intention, of course, was to severely limit drinking and thus to limit the evils associated with it. Unfortunately, good intentions often have unintended consequences that few people see beforehand. What the U.S. Congress did in 1919 was to give every petty criminal gang in the country the green light to unlimited expansion and riches. In many ways, it literally kick-started organized crime in the United States and ushered in a decade of gang wars and widespread corruption. Prohibiting alcohol made it more exciting to imbibe it in the speakeasies that sprang up everywhere; there were a number of cases in which people were poisoned by bad liquor, and there was apparently no letup in incidents of spousal or child abuse.

Given that what lawmakers do may "misfire" in many ways, is there a danger in using law to regulate morality? The danger was clear during Prohibition; are we doing the same thing today by criminalizing drugs such as marijauna and cocaine? What are the limits of law in producing social change; does law lead or follow? More importantly, what are the *principled* limits of law in social change? These are some of the questions to keep in mind as we examine the role of law in social change.

INTRODUCTION

In the last chapter we discussed so-called vice crimes and society's efforts to control them. When a society experiences frequent violations of its normative standards and its capacity or willingness to control this deviance is limited, social change may occur and the boundaries of acceptable behavior may be redefined and redrawn. In the last chapter we saw that changes of this nature occur frequently as American Society defines and redefines what is considered acceptable behavior. Every time society decides that the formerly unacceptable is acceptable or the formerly acceptable is now unacceptable it is engaging in social change. The changes discussed in that chapter revolved around personal and moral issues, such as pornography and abortion; this chapter deals with broader issues of a social, political, and economic nature, although these issues also have large moral elements attached to them.

WHAT IS SOCIAL CHANGE?

Social change may be defined as any relatively enduring alteration in social relationships, behavior patterns, values, norms, and attitudes occurring over time. Some changes may seem trivial, but they may aggregate and interact with other trivial and nontrivial changes to produce patterns of behavior and values that may appear grotesquely alien to individuals born in an earlier period. Because of the sheer complexity of modern societies and the intricate interaction of their component parts, each small change generates its own momentum, gathering speed in a chain reaction as each change generates more change. The sheer pace of modern social change can leave some of us giddy and confused, alienated and afraid.

There was a time in history when people lived out their lives with nary a hint of social change. Norms, customs, values, and practices endured essentially intact through each individual's short journey from cradle to grave. Small and isolated cultures are like small and isolated gene pools—they tend toward equilibrium. Ideas are "inbred" and produce only small "mutations" from the standard ideas available; there are just so many permutations possible from a limited pool of either genes or ideas. As we saw in chapter 1 when discussing the concept of a risk society, for much of human history, large-scale social changes usually originated outside the culture and came in the form of wars, invasions, famines, pestilence, and climate changes but rarely from within the culture itself. Such cultural continuity is psychologically comforting, conferring as it does a sense of meaning and continuity on the lives of people experiencing it. The comfort of habit is one of the reasons that many people resist change, even if change may be desirable on moral grounds, and they occasionally enlist the law in their endeavors to do so.

Those who most stoutly resist social change are usually those who profit most from society as it exists (e.g., business owners resisting organized labor) or who feel most psychologically threatened (e.g., racists resisting integration). Alternatively, changes such as the emergence of legalized pornography and abortion in the late 1960s to early 1970s may be resisted because "it's just not right," meaning that the change is perceived as being at odds with traditional values. Tensions occur when the pressures of change collide with established norms, and these tensions occasionally lead to the emergence of xenophobia, racism, and religious intolerance. Most social changes, however, tend to work themselves out without conflict of any kind, and most changes that do generate conflict are usually resolved in courts of law in modern societies.

THE LAW AS A CAUSE OF SOCIAL CHANGE

Historically, the law has played only a minor role in social change compared with other causes, but its role has hugely increased over the past two centuries. The law is mostly reactive rather than proactive in social change; that is, it reacts to social forces rather than sets such forces in motion. At other times, the law, as an independent source of power, functions as the instrument of social change. There is a tendency to view law as functioning as a barrier to change because it consists for the most part of norms and customs that have been codified, and norms and customs, almost by definition, are resistant to change. Indeed, the very slowness of social change in preindustrial society is what made custom a sufficient basis for formal systems of law. But is custom a sufficient basis in a modern society, and if not, what will replace it, and what does it mean for social change? The tension inherent in these questions was well put over a century ago by the Conservative British Prime Minister Benjamin Disraeli: "The great question is, not whether you should resist change which is inevitable, but whether that change should be carried out in deference to the manners, the customs, the laws, and the traditions of the people, or in deference to abstract principles and arbitrary and general doctrines" (cited in Ashford 1990, 46).

When the law no longer enjoys an organic relationship with custom, according to some theorists, society is in the process of cultural fracture (Bonsignore et al. 1989). Thinkers of this persuasion believe that the active use of law to generate social change is wrong and self-defeating unless that law is a natural extension of social custom. The law is supposed to be close to the heartbeat of the people, a palpable manifestation of their moral sentiments. If law is to be an instrument of change, it should be limited to the removal of some specific defect, not to chase utopian dreams of social perfection. This is an inherently conservative view of the law and one that tends to be held by those who call for a return to "traditional values" and for laws supporting and enforcing them. Such a call may be laudable in a less diverse society than the United States, but many feel that returning to "traditional values" in this country means returning to the customs of white Anglo-Saxon America—which may be fine if you are white, Christian, and male.

This should not be construed as a condemnation of the mainstream cultural traditions of the United States; they are still meaningful, and they have produced a wealthy, decent, and honorable society. But many Americans were never part of this cultural tradition to begin with, so they can hardly be expected to support a "return" to it. The United States is a heterogeneous stew of many different cultural traditions and customs today, which means that American law, if it is to be perceived as fair, cannot be based on the customs and morality of just one group. Non–European American groups tend to look at the role of law quite differently, hoping that it can be used as a valid tool to change custom, not defend it. For them, law should be responsive to injustices suffered by them and it should legislate and enforce social reforms. In other words, law based on universalistic principles of justice should regulate social behavior, not the customs of one particular subset of society that are defended by positivist law. As the law becomes more involved in social life, it faces major challenges, chief among which is how to preserve law without offending cultural pluralism. That is, the law built on Anglo-American moral traditions must validate itself by effecting principles of justice in ways understood and appreciated by all minority groups as well as the mainstream.

There is a reciprocal relationship between law and social change. Sometimes social conditions give rise to changes in the law, and sometimes changes in the law give rise to changes in social conditions. We must remember that law is not an isolated phenomenon; it is an integral and inextricable part of culture and society. This is perhaps more true of the United States than any other country. As long ago as 1835, the French philosopher and political commentator Alexis de Tocqueville (1945, 330–31) noted that nearly all American politicians are trained in the law, that legal language and attitudes saturated American culture, and that almost any issue of any importance sooner or later becomes a "subject for judicial debate."

SOCIAL MOVEMENTS, THE LAW, AND SOCIAL CHANGE

We may consider the role of law in social change to be most often facilitative rather than causative; that is, it serves as a conduit guiding the progress of some reform that is already in the works for other reasons. Those "other reasons" almost invariably involve organized groups of ordinary people making realistic claims on their government to advance their collective interests. When enough people are involved in this process we call it a social movement. A classic definition of a **social movement** is that of Charles Tilly (1984, 306), who defined it as "a sustained series of interactions between powerholders and persons successfully claiming to speak on behalf of a constituency lacking formal representation, in the course of which those persons make publicly visible demands for changes in the distribution or exercise of power, and back those demands with public demonstrations of support."

Law provides a very important part of the terrain for social movements to exploit when pursuing their goals because most social movements rely on claims of rights denial to frame their grievances. Few things are more powerful in recruiting and mobilizing individuals and in creating a common identity than to sharpen their sense of rights deprivation. As Frances Zemans (1983, 694) asserts: "What the populace actually receives from government is to a large extent dependent upon their willingness and ability to assert and use the law on their own behalf." In other words, only when the wheel squeaks will it get some oil. But the law can turn a deaf ear to the squeak, so it is up to individuals in the move-ment to crank up the volume by extralegal means. As Wilson and Cordero (2006, 327) put it: "Combining rights consciousness with a bill of rights and a will-ing and able judiciary improves the outlook for a rights revolution, but material support for sustained pursuit of rights is still crucial." This extralegal "material support" refers to tactics employed by various social movements, which include media campaigns, strikes, protest marches, and other forms of disruptive tactics that reach the ears of politicians and judges and may persuade them to apply the legal oil can.

The contentious politics of social movements pursuing rights and other interests depend to a large extent on democracy, since dissent in nondemocratic societies is rarely tolerated. As we have previously noted, conflict is actually functional in a democratic society because it is a way in which rightful claims of justice are brought to the fore and recognized. Charles Tilly (2004, 36), perhaps the foremost modern theorist of social movements, claims: "Democratization promotes the formation of social movements"; i.e., democracy not only tolerates dissent in the form of social movement, it promotes it. He goes on to say that social movements as we know them had their origins in early eighteenth-century Britain and the United States and that the British slavery abolition movement has "some claim" to be the first social movement. Before there was a free press and other methods by which information could be shared quickly with many others, and before there was an independent judiciary interpreting a Constitution, social movements intended to address grievances were unlikely to go anywhere, even if initiated, without resorting to widespread violence. Tilly (2004) makes a case for the American Revolution as a series of small social movements for limited reforms being largely ignored until they coalesced into violent revolution.

Once a social movement is observed successfully making its rights claim, other, previously silent groups are aroused in what has been called a "contagion effect" (McCann 2006, 26). Of course, there is an ebb and flow of contagion effects, depending on the historical period, with some periods being much more "contagious" than others. As we shall see in the last part of the chapter, the period between 1953 and 1986 was particularly active when the United States Supreme Court under Justice Earl Warren and Justice Warren Burger was respon-sive to justice claims. Think of the cascade of legislation and court cases that rode in on the coattails of the demands of minorities, women, and gays over the past fifty or sixty years. Law legitimized their demands (at least, many of them) in specific and rational ways and provided sanctioning provisions for those who would deny them. Law functions to legitimize change, to smooth the way, and to grease squeaky wheels of opposition to change. Examples of the role of law (both as a block and a facilitator) in the success or failure of social movements are dispersed throughout this book. The century-long fight for worker's rights is featured strongly in this chapter. The rights of gays and lesbians were addressed in chapters 7 and 10, abortion rights were addressed in chapter 10 (a successful movement that has generated a counter right-to-life social movement), women's rights are treated in chapter 12, and minority racial/ethnic rights are addressed in chapter 13.

Figure 11.1 Flowchart Illustrating Typical Role of Law in Social Change

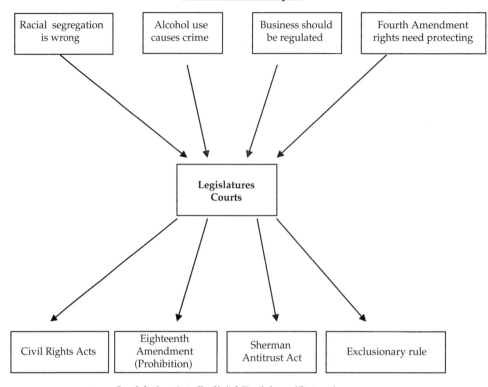

Figure 11.1 illustrates the typical relationship between law and social change with some important examples. The relationship can be viewed as a series of social demands (inputs) flowing into legislatures and courts to be digested and coming out the other end as law (outputs). It will become clear that law, through legislative policy and judicial fiat, may have become a major player in the social change game within the industrialized democracies of the world as they attempt social engineering; "attempted social change, through law, is a basic trait of the modern world," writes Friedman (1975, 277). This function of law is the focus of the present chapter, beginning with the role of law in helping to create the United States.

BRITISH LAW AND THE AMERICAN REVOLUTION

Anyone who is reluctant to credit the law with much of a role in social change might ponder the possibility that were it not for a number of British legal decisions in the eighteenth century, the American colonies may have remained loyal to the mother country. Most of us are aware of the many pieces of British legislation following the French and Indian Wars. Many of those laws were designed to make the American colonists pay their share of the expense of that war, which was, after all, fought to defend them. These included the Mutiny Act of 1765 (requiring colonists to provision and maintain the army), the Sugar Act of 1774 (designed to eliminate illegal sugar trade between the colonies and the French and Spanish West Indies), and the Stamp Act of 1765, imposing a tax on every printed document in the colonies. Colonists used British law to oppose these acts; serving on grand juries, they refused to return indictments against violators.

The **Proclamation Act** of 1763 was particularly galling to many prominent colonists. This act forbade white settlement west of the Appalachians in conformity with a peace treaty with the Ottawa Indians. Powerful land speculators such as George Washington, William Crawford, and Benjamin Franklin had invested heavily in the Ohio valley, which the Proclamation ceded to the Indians. This did much to cause many of these speculators "to favor an independent American government, which might look more kindly on their real estate plans" (Woodin, 1974, 43).

In addition to these legislative acts, there were also judicial rulings that may have contributed to the fracture between Britain and the American colonies. Two famous slavery cases—*Somerset v. Stewart* (1772) and *Joseph Knight v. Wedderburn* (1778)—heard in England and Scotland, respectively—may have been instrumental in propelling the more reluctant southern states into the revolution (Parrillo 2003). The *Somerset* case involved a slave named James Somerset who was taken to England by his Virginian master, Charles Stewart. Somerset escaped, was captured again, and held aboard ship for transportation to Jamaica. Lord Chief Justice Mansfield issued a writ of habeas corpus preventing Somerset's departure from England and requiring Stewart to present him to the court. The legal issue involved was whether or not a slave can be considered free because of his sojourn on free soil. Justice Mansfield declared that he could, and in doing so, he berated slavery as so odious that "[w]hatever inconveniences, therefore, may follow from the decision, I cannot say this case is allowed or approved by the law of England; and therefore the black must be discharged" (cited in Klingberg 1968, 39).

Mansfield's decision applied only to England, Wales, and Ireland, but it set the precedent for *Knight*, decided in 1778. *Knight* had the effect of outlawing slavery from every part of the British Isles and by extension, many jurists of the time believed, throughout the British Empire (this did not actually occur until 1833). Such a possibility, if enforceable, would have been entirely unacceptable to the Southern American colonies whose way of life rested heavily on slavery. According to Donnelly (2006, 40) these cases were "the starting point for the falling dominos that led to the abolishment of slavery, and [to] affirmative action in the United States." We cannot know for sure the part these two decisions actually played in these subsequent events, but they do point to the "ripple" effect of law on so many aspects of human life.

Unlike the other great revolutions in France and Russia, the American Revolution was quite a legal affair: "[T]he American Revolution was a reluctant uprising staged by men who were exceptionally dedicated to the English constitution" (Johnson 2006, 3). Many revolutionaries took the position that the separation from Britain was a legal separation and that the Declaration of Independence was a political bill of divorce based on legal grounds found in the English constitution (Johnson 2006). The principle that the constitution is sovereign, not the reigning monarch, was settled in the Glorious Revolution of 1688, which cost James II his crown. The offenses charged against George III in the Declaration of Independence were all offenses against British law. The rebellious colonists reasoned that since the sovereignty of the law over the monarch had been established, and since George III was now placing himself above the law, the colonists had a legal right to revolt. In the minds of many of the leading figures of the American Revolution, they were loyal to the precedent established by the Glorious Revolution of their forefathers in England (Johnson 2006).

LAW AND SOCIAL ENGINEERING IN THE FORMER SOVIET UNION

The history of the Soviet Union provides an excellent case example to contrast with the discussion of the role of law in bringing about social change in the United States. Before the 1917 revolution, Russia had a system of law codes analogous to those of France and Germany (Reichel 2005). The history of prerevolutionary Russia shows that the law can delay, if not altogether stifle, the "natural" tides of social change. That Czarist Russia failed to survive is a vindication of conservative philosopher Edmund Burke's dictum that "[a] state without the means of some change is without means of its conservation" (in Ashford 1990, 46). After the fall of the czar and the formation of the Soviet Union in 1922, the situation was reversed. Rather than using law to stifle social change, the Soviets used it to force social change. These changes and attempted changes provide the best case example available for examining the strengths and weaknesses of law as a vehicle of social change.

A student of the history and political development of the United States is well advised to study the United States Constitution because it has served as a set of guiding principles for the role of law in social change throughout American history. A study of Soviet constitutions (there have been five of them since 1918) would not yield similar benefits, for it would be difficult to discover general legal principles that would help us to understand the profound changes that occurred there in the twentieth century. The various Soviet constitutions have been longer and more detailed (the 1977 version had 173 articles) than the U.S. Constitution (seven original articles and twenty-seven amendments). The twenty-seven amendments to the U.S. Constitution have occurred over little more than two hundred years; the Russian constitution (the one that existed prior to Boris Yeltsin's new democratic constitution) had been amended, on average, once a day from 1990 to the enactment of the new Constitution of the Russian Federation in December 1993 ("Stalin or Yeltsin?" 1993).

Although quite unlike anything made in Philadelphia, all Soviet constitutions guaranteed certain rights; but unlike their American counterpart, they also set forth certain obligations. We may consider these Soviet constitutions to be preeminently political weapons changed on whim rather than documents enunciating a society's organizing principles. Nevertheless, although the Soviet state subordinated the rule of law to politics, the four Soviet constitutions served the purposes of all **constitutions,** which accomplish the following:

1. Legalize the existing political order and legitimize its ideology.
2. Provide a framework for the administration of government.
3. Regulate social and institutional behavior.
4. Enumerate national goals and aspirations.

The Russian experience shows that written constitutions are not a guarantee of political freedom. Nevertheless, Soviet leaders went to great lengths to make Soviet policy making conform to formal rationality processes so that their social experiments would be perceived in the West as legitimate (Hosking 1985). Officially, the legal process in the Soviet Union was an example of formal rationality; but in actuality, it was administered in concert with substantive irrationality, with the substance provided by Marxist ideology. "Legal" decisions were often made by revolutionary tribunals on an ad hoc basis to conform to the will of the Communist party (Reichel 2005). The use of vague concepts like "counter revolutionary" and "enemy of the people" allowed for the creation of "instant" offenses not designated as crimes in any penal code (*ex post facto* laws). Such practices are expressly forbidden in common law but justified by the Soviets as necessary to preserve the revolution.

Law and the Destruction and Reconstruction of the Soviet Family

A cliché we often hear is that "you can't legislate morality." Although legislators around the country continue to try to do just that, the American experience with prohibition, the drug wars, changing sexual mores, and so on, which we discussed in chapter 10, tends to support the cliché. However, you would not find much support for such a position in the former Soviet Union. The Soviet government viewed law as a force for social change that could and would mold the attitudes and behaviors of the people in any way the government deemed appropriate. The Soviet idea of the role of law in social change places the "emphasis not on whether the job can be done, but rather on how to go about doing the job" (Barry and Barner-Barry 1978, 136). The ultimate goal was the "dictatorship of the proletariat," in which such bourgeois vestiges as law would not be needed. Recall that Marx considered law to be nothing more than the codified ideology of the ruling class; in the Soviet utopia there would be no ruling class and therefore no need for law.

During the early days of the new Soviet state, Western concepts of law were thrown out in favor of **Soviet legalism**, a principle defined as "strict and unflinching observance and fulfillment of Soviet laws by all organs of the socialist state and public organizations institutions and all citizens, in all circumstances, and at all times" (Barry and Barner-Barry 1978, 135). One of the biggest attempted changes involved the family, the basic institution of any society. Because the family is the transmitter, defender, and modeler of the old order, destroy the family and you destroy society as it is presently constituted. The Soviet regime was committed to destroying the "bourgeois family," declaring it to be based on the "paternalistic" notion of property-based bourgeois marriage that exploited women. To destroy the family, the party passed legislation making abortion available on demand, legitimized unmarried cohabitation, made divorce available on demand, and encouraged "free love" as the "essence of communist living" (Hazard, Butler, and Maggs 1977, 470).

These laws had devastating consequences. "Free love" combined with quick and easy divorce resulted in hundreds of thousands of fatherless children roaming the streets who "formed into gangs, attack[ing] and rob[bing] people in the street, or even invad[ing] and ransack[ing] apartment blocks" (Hosking 1985, 213). When the Soviets assessed the damage, they quickly reversed themselves and wrote profamily laws extolling the family and the sanctity of marriage, denouncing divorce, and praising the joys of parenthood. Thus the formerly reviled became praised, and the formerly praised (e.g., "free love") redefined and reviled as "bourgeois."

Overall, the Soviet experience points to both the power of law to induce social change and to its limits. Large-scale and wholesale changes can be written into law, but lacking the legitimacy of custom, they may have to be enforced by strong police tactics. Law is a much more efficient instrument of social control and social change if it relies on legitimacy rather than brute coercion. The fact that the authorities did a 180-degree turn on family law points out that law follows as well as leads social change, even in totalitarian systems.

THE UNITED STATES SUPREME COURT AND SOCIAL CHANGE

Law has been characterized by Talcott Parsons (1977, 11) as an "intellectual stepchild" of sociologists engaged in studying social change. Parsons was puzzled by this neglect because he saw law as the "single most important key to understanding problems of social integration" and by extension, social change (52). As previously indicated, law is an increasingly more important source of social change in the modern world, especially in the United States where the law has its hands in every process.

The ultimate source of law in the United States is the Constitution, but as Chief Justice Charles Evans Hughes's famous dictum makes clear, "The Constitution is what the Supreme Court says it is." Thus the Supreme Court is the ultimate legal authority in the United States, and to the extent that constitutional law is the source of social change, the Court is the source of that change. As phrased by Weinberg and Weinberg (1980, 261): "the Supreme Court's role has been central to the relationship between law and social change." In examining the record of the Supreme Court, we will find much that supports both the conflict and the consensus theories of law, for the Court has issued a number of rulings that both prevented and generated important social change. We will first examine how the Court has used its power to prevent the working classes from achieving social and economic justice and then how it has used the same power to generate social justice in many noneconomic spheres of American life.

Dynamic and Constrained Views of the Supreme Court's Power

In a very influential book, Gerald Rosenberg (1991) presented two views on the extent of the Supreme Court's ability to induce social change: the dynamic and the constrained. The **dynamic view** maintains that the Court can be more effective than other government institutions in bringing about social change because it is free of election concerns and can thus act in the face of public opposition. Supreme Court justices are unelected and life-tenured, so they cannot be removed from office by public disapproval of their actions as politicians can. Likewise, individuals and groups who may be disadvantaged in the legislative process coming before the Court in pursuit of just social change do so on the basis of constitutional issues regardless of their "connections or position" (Rosenberg 1991, 23). Nevertheless, Rosenberg favors the constrained view.

The **constrained view** avers that the Court can rarely produce significant social change because of three important constraints. The first constraint is the bounded nature of constitutional rights. There are therefore only a limited number of issues that can come before the Court, but this constraint can be overcome if there is ample case precedent in the general direction of the proposed change. For instance, the right to privacy "discovered" by Justice Douglas under the "penumbra" of the Bill of Rights in *Griswold v. Connecticut* (1965) granting access to birth control devices was used to grant abortion rights in *Roe v. Wade* (1973). The second constraint is that the Court lacks the necessary independence from the other branches of government. This essentially means that the Court must rely on the cooperation of those branches to enforce its rulings. Overcoming this constraint necessitates the support of a large segment of the Congress and the executive branch. The third constraint is that it lacks the tools to develop policies and implement decisions for significant change. This constraint may be overcome with public support, or at least low levels of public opposition.

Rosenberg reminds us that the judicial process operates at the intersection of law and politics and thus is not the all-powerful institution some think it to be. It is indeed difficult to find a case in which the Court has ruled in favor of major social change in which the three constraints had not been overcome in the ways Rosenberg suggests. The Court does lack the tools to implement its rulings and relies on the other branches to provide those things for it. Like most dichotomies, however, this one may be drawn too rigidly. Sometimes the Court's rulings can reflect the dynamic view and sometimes the constrained view. To the extent that the Court reflects dynamism, it relies on one very important resource: legitimacy.

The Legitimacy Basis of the Court's Power

Constrained by its lack of the power of the purse (legislative branch) and the sword (executive branch), the Supreme Court must rely more on the power of legitimacy to gain compliance than either of the other two branches. **Legitimacy** is the ability to command compliance with rules despite the lack of objective means to compel it. Weber (1968) used the term "authority" to refer to this kind of legitimate power, and he proposed three ideal-types: *traditional, charismatic, and rational-legal*. Any of these three types is considered sufficient in itself to confer legitimacy, but the Supreme Court enjoys them all. Given that Supreme Court justices are neither elected by nor accountable to the people, it is important that we examine this idea of legitimacy upon which the power of the Court ultimately rests. Whether we think of the Court as an almost divinely inspired creator and guardian of American rights (Taylor 1990) or as "at once the most powerful, and the most irresponsible of all the men in the world who govern other men" (Rodell 1955, 4), the concept of legitimacy is central to our understanding of it.

Woven as it is into the fabric of American history, the Court is legitimized by **traditional authority.** Established by Article III of the Constitution, it is almost as old as the Republic itself, and it is as difficult to imagine the United States without the Supreme Court as it is to imagine Great Britain without the monarchy. Tradition has a powerful hold on the psychology of any people, and they obey traditional authority because it is often invested with a kind of quasi-divine inspiration and perhaps because "it has always been there." Unless something very seriously wrong with the institution is brought to public attention, there is rarely any questioning of traditional authority.

Traditional authority may be maintained even in the face of criticism if it is buttressed by **charismatic authority**, a form of authority "generated by exceptional, unusual, and even quasi-supernatural qualities attributed to individuals or institutions" (Corbin and Walsh 1988, 76). Robert Taylor (1990, 42), who describes the Supreme Court as "a priesthood that governs," paints a rather dramatic picture of the process of the justices' decision making and of the awesome consequences of those decisions. Note that all this occurs after the Court has decided for itself, in true autocratic manner, which of the numerous petitions brought before it that it wants to hear (less than 1 percent annually).

> No public hearings are then held, only arguments for the various sides, and these are strictly timed and can, at the Court's pleasure, be dispensed with altogether. Then follows secret deliberations . . . and finally, the promulgation of an entirely new law, valid across the nation and virtually immune to repeal. A law may upset the established customs and practices of an entire culture; it may abruptly make criminal conduct legal . . . or render criminal what has previously been permitted; or it may force upon lower jurisdictions policies radically at odds with those that

have the support of the people and with what had been long established there—and all this without warning . . . as in the most rigid despotism.

Taylor (1990, 41) is not criticizing the Court for its alleged despotism; on the contrary, he feels that the Court provides us with opportunities to exercise our "needs" for deference and servility, "to bow down to persons and things." Such a statement may offend, but the Court's legitimacy does rest to some extent on the quasi-religious myths and symbols associated with it and with the Constitution. Myths and symbols are designed to arouse such feelings of worshipful reverence in the beholder. The legitimizing effect is more in evidence when these aloof justices in their marble palace interpret the Constitution than when they are dealing with issues of statutory construction: "Just as the magisterial statements of the Papacy are more compelling for Roman Catholics when they come *ex cathedra*, the Supreme Court's rulings may have more legitimacy when symbolically connected to the U.S. Constitution" (Corbin and Walsh 1988, 77).

The refusal of the Court to allow television cameras behind the "purple curtain," their refusal to grant interviews, and their affected haughty, grave, and imperious demeanor (compare their demeanor with that of members of Congress during the next State of the Union address) all contribute to that special impression of priestly "otherworldliness." There are those who feel that the Court should divest itself of its aura of myth, mystery, and arrogance: "Since the isolation treasured by most of the justices mutes the Court's voice in national politics," write Levine and Becker (1980, 273), "we urge, as a start, that the Court give up its haughty posture and begin making serious attempts to relate to the American public." Notwithstanding the fact that the last thing in the world the Court is designed to do is "relate to the American public," if the fiction of the Court were to be exposed, "it would soon raise questions of legitimacy, and thus undermine both the Court and the impact of its decisions" (Cox 1981, 206).

The final form of legitimizing authority is **rational-legal**. Beneath all the priestly garb and symbolism, the Court's authority is preeminently rational-legal, which is authority derived from rules rationally and legally enacted. The Supreme Court is provided for in Article III of the Constitution, but just how far its power was intended to stretch is a matter of contention. Some legal scholars assert that the Framers of the Constitution intended some form of judicial review of the constitutionality of federal and state legislation, while others assert that it is clear that they never meant the Court to have the power to void acts of Congress. As we have seen, the Court itself did not assert the power of judicial review until Chief Justice John Marshall explored the Court's power in this regard in *Marbury v. Madison* in 1803.

Legal scholars may argue all they want about the constitutionality of judicial review, but as Rosenberg (1991) reminded us, realistically, the Court could not void anything without the cooperation of the other two branches of government. This cooperation is forthcoming because the other branches find the Court to be more useful than a nuisance. As we saw earlier, legislative bodies are often confronted with "touchy" subjects that they would rather not deal with in a decisive manner. They often deal with such issues by legislation so vague and ambiguous that no clear use can be made of it. They are only too pleased to allow judges, who do not need to worry about reelection, to "interpret" legislation and thus to engage in judicial lawmaking (Abadinsky 2003). This de facto abdication of leg-islative bodies from their proper role as lawmakers, and the concomitant usurpation of that role by the judiciary, is seen by many as a major threat to the validity of the American political system, which is supposed to be one in which those who govern are accountable to the governed (Lewis 1999).

Strict Constructionism

The heated and sometimes hostile Senate interrogations of Supreme Court nominees we witness on television bring to the fore the question of the scope and limitations of judicial power. Conservative presidents tend to nominate justices who believe that the Court's task is to take the Constitution as it finds it. **Strict constructionism** asserts that judges must not place their own interpretations on the Constitution, even if by adhering to this philosophy the consequences would be personally abhorrent to them. A strict constructionist is a constitutional fundamentalist in the same sense as those who believe in the literal and unerring truth of the Bible are religious fundamentalists. In deciding a case, the constructionist looks for "original intent," meaning that he or she will peruse relevant material in an effort "to discover what the collective intention of the Framers was on disputed matters of interpretation" (Dworkin 1985, 38). With sufficient historical data and insight, it is presumed that he or she will discover the "true" intent of the Framers. Strict constructionism is in a sense legal positivism applied to the Constitution.

A Supreme Court dominated by strict constructionists would have very little role in social change because by adhering to original intent, they would be captives of eighteenth-century thinking. This leads to an interesting hypothetical question: Since slavery, at least the principle of people as property, was recognized as legitimate under the Constitution (Article 1, Section 2), would slavery still be a fact of American life if its legality had been ruled on by successive strict constructionist Courts throughout American history? The Court put its stamp of approval on slavery in *Scott v. Sandford* in 1857, and because strict constructionists supposedly take the Constitution as they find it no matter how personally repugnant they may find slavery to be, slavery would still be with us if the rulings of the Supreme Court were all that mattered.

Strict constructionists would not be disturbed by the specter we have raised and would find it absurd. Slavery would no more be present in the United States than it would in any other Western society, regardless of any strict constructionist Supreme Court rulings. Constructionists would point out that important equity (justice) issues are the proper domains of Congress, not the Court. Congress can amend the Constitution in ways that accord with contemporary views of decency and morality, but until it does so, constructionists argue, the justices are bound to find in the Constitution only that which is there. Chief Justice Taney put it this way in *Scott*: "If any of its [the Constitution's] provisions are deemed unjust, there is a mode described in the instrument itself by which it may be amended; but while it remains unaltered, it must be construed now as it was understood at the time of its adoption."

It was the executive branch's Emancipation Proclamation of 1863, legally cemented by the legislative branch's passage of the Thirteenth Amendment in 1865, that made slavery illegal, not a judicial ruling of unconstitutionality. When the demands of justice rise above the demands of law, it is the legislature that should break the chains of law, not the judiciary. Constructionists understand how difficult it is to discover any kind of original intent or to be a servant to literal interpretations of the Constitution as though it were somehow of divine origin, but they believe that any stance other than strict constructionism leads to judicial activism. **Judicial activism** is a term used pejoratively when judges make rulings that critics perceive as based on a particular ideological agenda rather than the law. Critics of judicial activism say that it means judicial governance, which is a clear violation of the Constitutional separation of powers.

Whether we view a Court ruling as conforming to the original intent of the Framers or as an example of judicial activism depends, if we are honest about it, on how it accords with our views on the matter before the Court. If the Court's ruling agrees with our opinions, then we believe the justices correctly interpreted the Constitution; but if it does not, we may angrily dismiss it as judicial activism. Depending on the issue and the ruling (whose ox is being gored), either liberals or conservatives may accuse the justices of voting their ideological biases (being judicial activists), and of course, both sides would be correct. Few legal scholars are naïve enough to believe that personal ideology does not strongly and sometimes decisively affect a justice's ruling. Should anyone doubt it, consider the 5–4 ruling strictly along ideological lines that effectively gave the disputed presidential election of 2000 to George W. Bush (see chapter 2 discussion of legal realism) in *Bush v. Gore* (2000).

THE SUPREME COURT'S ROLE IN MAINTAINING THE STATUS QUO

An extreme concentration of wealth leads inevitably to de facto plutocracy (the rule of the wealthy) functioning beneath the surface of the official government regardless of its political philosophy. Concentrated wealth defiles the very ideas of justice and democracy, for it gives the wealthy far more influence on the political process than their numbers warrant. This fact has been recognized by all democratic governments (at least by governments rising from the working classes), and they have responded to demands for democratic social change in three important ways: (1) they have encouraged working class efforts to form unions so that business interests can be confronted on a more equal footing, (2) they have ameliorated harsh exploitation by regulating the activities of the business class, and (3) they have sought to redistribute wealth by the implementation of a system of progressive income tax (Galloway 1982). These equity mechanisms have been resisted everywhere by the wealthy classes and their political parties but nowhere else in the democratic world more successfully than in the United States where the Supreme Court has assiduously guarded their interests.

We discussed the inherent conservatism of the Court in chapter 4; what about the nature of the document they are charged with preserving and interpreting? We might say that Supreme Court justices are servants to the Constitution in the same way that priests are the servants of the gospels. If this is indeed the case, then the ideological composition of the Court should not matter. But of course it does; presidents are not known for appointing justices who are hostile to presidential ideology. Presidents are aware there is nothing they may do short of asking Congress to declare war that has such far-reaching effects on the nation than the appointment of a Supreme Court justice. The ideological composition of the Court is in many ways more important than the content of the "gospel" because they interpret what is written there and often do so in ways diametrically opposed to the interpretations offered by previous Courts. As Michael Parenti (1977, 251) put it:

> There is an old saying that the devil himself can quote the Bible for his own purposes. The Constitution is not unlike the Bible in this respect, and over the generations Supreme Court Justices have shown an infernal agility in finding constitutional justification for the continuation of almost every inequity and iniquity, be it slavery or segregation, child labor or the sixteen-hour day, state sedition laws or federal assaults on the First Amendment.

It is unnecessary to be more critical of the Founding Fathers than to say that they showed no pronounced enthusiasm for democracy. John Jay's (the first Chief Justice of the Supreme Court) prophetic statement, "The people who own the country ought to govern it," was for many historians and political scientists a statement that exemplified the predominant sentiment of those at the Continental Convention where the main issue appeared to be whether people or property should rule (Galloway 1982). According to Richard Hofstadter (1948, 3), "The men who drew up the Constitution in Philadelphia in 1787 had a vivid Calvinistic sense of human evil and damnation and believed with Hobbes that men are selfish and contentious." A corollary of this is that human nature is not to be trusted, and thus democracy is not to be trusted unless limited by boundaries advantageous to men of position and property. Analyses of the characters and philosophies of the Founding Fathers, as well as of the Constitution itself, lead many authorities of all political persuasions to view the Constitution as first and foremost an economic document strongly favoring the moneyed classes. Galloway (1982) and Parenti (1980) cite many statements by Framers such as James Madison, John Adams, and Alexander Hamilton regarding their image of the "class struggle," a struggle that was very real to them.

"Scratch a fervent believer in judicial supremacy" wrote Max Lerner (1939, 474), "and like as not you will find someone with a bitterness about democracy. The two are as close as skin and skeleton." Between twenty-five and thirty-two of the forty delegates at the Constitutional Convention favored judicial review in one form or another (Dunn 1978). Students should ask themselves why so many delegates favored such an antidemocratic method of settling disputed matters. Those with a conflict view of social relations might cite the Golden Rule ("Those with the gold make the rules"). Having important decisions made by unelected officials based on an inherently economically conservative document safeguards privileges. If elected officials made the ultimate decisions, they might be swayed by public opinion, which may not necessarily be the opinions of the moneyed classes. Perhaps the untimely occurrence of the populist Shays' Rebellion (a six-month-long armed insurrection among Massachusetts farmers led by Revolutionary War veteran Captain Daniel Shays) that occurred just prior to the signing of the Constitution in 1787 crystallized the antidemocratic sentiments of the Framers. This occurrence probably goaded them into taking preemptive action against any future populist movements (Richards 2003).

A less cynical interpretation is that the Declaration of Independence and the Constitution were radically democratic documents by the standards of the time and reveal that the Founding Fathers were at least procedural and principle democrats. The Founding Fathers also foresaw the problems of unfettered democracy ("the tyranny of the majority") and applied some restraints to it; these restraints protect the rights of minorities of all kinds, not just the rights of the economically privileged. After all, the United States is a republic—a representative or indirect form of democracy—and not a democracy in the purest sense of the word. The informed conservative view may be summarized as acknowledging that the moneyed classes have benefited most from Constitutional protection but deemphasizing this in favor of pointing out how racial and ethnic minorities have benefited from its protection also (although as we see in chapter 13, the Court's protection of minorities is a relatively modern thing).

The Fourteenth Amendment and Business Interests

Thus the Constitution may not be a tool of the "ruling class," but it has always been a bastion for the upper classes of society. In its battle to protect the economic elite from the demands of workers, the Court has relied heavily on Article I, Section X of the Constitution, which forbids states to pass any laws "impairing the obligation of contracts." The first use of this clause was in 1810 in *Fletcher v. Peck*, which involved wealthy New England speculators who bribed members of the Georgia legislature in 1795 to make land grants to them. When the conspiracy was uncovered, a later Georgia legislature rescinded the earlier legislation.

John Peck had sold some of the land in question to Robert Fletcher. The issue before the Court was whether the contract between Fletcher and Peck could be invalidated by Georgia. The Supreme Court ruled that the Georgia legislature could not annul contracts or grants made by previous legislative acts. Thus, rich speculators were able to keep the land in what Galloway (1982, 40) called a "classic rich-poor issue." The members of the Court who set the obligation of contract precedent are described by Leo Pfeffer (1965, 41): "All were members or representatives of the propertied, creditor classes, and all believed that the purpose of government was to protect the rights of property against the covetous depredations of the lower classes."

Although there were a number of other such "contract" cases, we will move forward to a further milestone in the history the Court's defense of the status quo: the passage of the Fourteenth Amendment in 1868. This amendment was passed by a Republican-controlled Congress in response to discriminatory Black Codes passed by Southern states during Reconstruction (see chapter 13). The Fourteenth Amendment was passed ostensibly to protect the most deprived and vulnerable members of our society (the newly freed slaves), but the Supreme Court soon found ways to use it to protect the rich business interests against the working class. The relevant section of the amendment is section I, which reads ". . . nor shall any state deprive any person of life, liberty, or property, without due process of law; nor deny any person within its jurisdiction the equal protection of the laws."

The Supreme Court viewed the Fourteenth Amendment as requiring state conformity with the Bill of Rights in economic matters. As Abadinsky (2003, 65) put it, "Slowly, and over a long period of time, the Court began to apply these rights to the states. Ironically, they served to protect conservative business interests against legislative enactments designed to improve the conditions of workers." The absurd suggestion that the U.S. Congress was thinking primarily about protecting corporations when it framed the Fourteenth Amendment was first made by a lawyer working for the railroad industry in a case that is otherwise uninteresting: "Chief Justice Waite in *Santa Clara Co. v. Southern Pacific R. R. Co.* simply announced this doctrine, and corporations have been blessed and protected ever since" (Deloria and Wilkins 1999, 52).

After the precedent was set, the courts no longer needed to rely on criminal conspiracy laws to suppress labor unions and other working-class organizations. Criminal conspiracies meant trials, and trials often meant juries composed of men sympathetic to the worker's struggle. Business interests could now seek judicial injunctions against strikes with relative ease, and union members disobeying such an injunction would soon find themselves in jail for contempt of court. This method of dealing with the "union rabble" circumvented the usual legal method of settling disputes and saved business much time and money. The courts were able to use the Fourteenth Amendment in this way by defining *person* very broadly as any body of people, such as a corporation, and *property* to include business profits. By interpreting the Fourteenth Amendment this way, the courts opened the floodgates to a tide of judicial attacks on state laws that attempted to govern wages, hours, and safety provisions for workers on the grounds that such laws violated employer's "property rights."

The activity of labor unions and of Coxey's "army" (an army of unemployed workers who marched on Washington demanding economic justice in the 1890s) conjured up the ghosts of Shays' Rebellion in the minds of the moneyed classes. Here again were the "great unwashed" demanding a fair share of the American economic pie. Ideologically, the "unwashed" could not have chosen a worse time to press their claims. The "gay '90s" were saturated with the ideas of social Darwinism and Adam Smith's "invisible hand." These two philosophies coalesced as laissez-faire economics, which was strongly supported by the Court under Chief Justice Melville Fuller who held the position from 1888 to 1910. For about a forty-year period after 1889, the Court invalidated fifty acts of Congress and about four hundred state laws designed to help workers (Abadinsky 2003). The Court struck down any and all legislation designed to introduce democracy into the workplace and into the social and economic spheres of American life.

The ability of the Court to thwart the popular will, as well as its skill in interpreting legislation for means opposite to those presumably intended, is also evident in its rulings under the **Sherman Antitrust Act**. Passed by Congress in 1890 in response to outrageous exploitation of workers and "Robber Baron" violence, the act was designed to place controls on business. Few of the legislators who voted for the act wanted or expected it to have any effect, but it was popular with the electorate who voted them in or out of office. The Congress could rest easy that the courts would undo the damage their act had wrought to the power of privilege (Brinkley et al. 1991). The courts did not disappoint them.

Just as it had used the Fourteenth Amendment to protect the business elite rather than former slaves, the Court used the Sherman Act as a hammer to pound the working class rather than to control business monopolies. The Court ruled in *United States v. E. C. Knight* (1895) that the Sherman Act controlled only commerce, that manufacturing was not commerce, and therefore manufacturing monopolies did not violate the act. In *In re Debs* (1895), the court upheld the conviction and imprisonment of Eugene Debs, leader of the American Railway Union, for violating a court injunction ordering the union to halt the famous Pullman strike of 1894. Thus, in a remarkable display of doublespeak, *on the same day* that the Court ruled that manufacturing was not commerce (manufactured goods have to be transported and distributed, and that is commerce) in *Knight*, in *Debs* it ruled that trade unionism was! In *Adair v. United States* in 1908, the Court invalidated a federal law outlawing "yellow dog" contracts (contracts forced on employees requiring them to promise not to join a union as a condition of employment), saying that it violated "freedom of contract." The Sherman Act was again invoked against the unions in *Loewe v. Lawlor* (1908), ruling that the act forbade secondary boycotts by labor unions and upheld high damage payments against the union.

The late nineteenth and early twentieth centuries were replete with many decisions that hammered home the privileged position of business in American society. The Court appeared to be legitimizing the law of the jungle: The weak must bear the consequences of their weakness, the strong may enjoy the consequences of their strength, and the state should not be in the business of protecting even women and children from the predations of the entrepreneurial class. In *Lochner v. New York* (1905), for instance, the Court struck down minimum hours legislation for bakers who were being forced by employers to work up to sixteen hours each day. The Court ruled that such legislation denied employers liberty of contract. In *Hammer v. Dagenhart* (1918), the Court struck down federal legislation aimed at child labor reform (which would have cost business dearly) on the grounds that the law went beyond congressional power to regulate interstate commerce, and in *Adkins v. Children's Hospital* (1923), it struck down an act of Congress setting minimum wages for women and children as an unconstitutional violation of freedom of contract.

These cases are a small sample of the many antiworking class rulings of the Court during this period. In *no* case in which the interests of the rich business classes were opposed to the interests of the working classes did the Court find in favor of the latter. A series of decisions in the 1930s even succeeded in undermining much of President Roosevelt's effort to ameliorate the effects of the Great Depression on the poor. The most significant of these decisions came in *Schechter Poultry Corp. v. United States* (1935). This decision invalidated President Franklin Roosevelt's National Recovery Act, designed to put the unemployed back to work. In *Louisville Bank v. Radford* (1935), the Court invalidated the Frazier-Lemke Act, which provided for mortgage relief for farmers, and in *United States v. Butler* (1936), it threw out the Agricultural Adjustments Act, which provided much-needed price supports for farmers.

In short, the Supreme Court was able to use legislative amendments and acts ostensibly designed for other purposes to stifle progressive social change for so long that the United States lagged behind most other industrial democracies in passing legislation benefiting workers by as many as seventy-five years (Walsh 1988). However, the fact that the United States finally legalized trade unions and enacted many hours, wages, and safety bills points out that even an institution as powerful as the Supreme Court cannot buck pressures demanding social change indefinitely.

Perhaps fearful of an increase in riotous behavior during the Great Depression, Congress finally stripped the federal courts of their power to issue injunctions against labor unions engaged in labor disputes (although the courts have reasserted this power) in the 1932 Norris–La Guardia Act. In 1935, Congress went one step further with the passage of the National Labor Relations Act, also known as the Wagner Act, which legalized labor unions and required employers to engage in good-faith collective bargaining. The Wagner Act was declared constitutional in 1937 in *National Labor Relations Board v. Jones and Laughlin Steel Corporation*. The Court's turnabout in this case was perhaps motivated by President Franklin Roosevelt's anger at "judicial legislators" and his proposed plan to "pack" the Court. As wags of the time were fond of saying, the shift in the Court's attitude was "The switch in time that saved nine." Of the Court's behavior during the period of the New Deal, Robert Jackson (1941, xii, who was shortly to become a Supreme Court Justice) wrote "the basic grievance of the New Deal was that the Court has seemed unduly to favor private economic power and always to find ways of circumventing the efforts of popular government to control or regulate it."

The Court's partiality for rich business interests has not been so blatantly obvious since this period, although American courts in general still tend to favor business rights over labor rights. A number of scholars have noted that labor laws in the United States provide fewer protections against exploitation, injury, illness, job protection, and unemployment than the laws of the dozens of other industrial nations. Human Rights Watch, the largest human rights organization based in the United States, has frequently declared that U.S. labor laws are grossly at odds with international human rights laws (Acuff and Friedman 2006).

Two of the more recent cases demonstrate this point. In *Allied Structural Steel v. Spannous* (1978), the Court prohibited the state of Minnesota from requiring companies who leave the state to insure pension payments to retired employees, and in *National Labor Relations Board v. Bildisco* (1983), it held that companies could unilaterally breach collective bargaining contracts without waiting for rulings of bankruptcy judges if those companies found such contracts to be "burdensome." This was an invitation for companies all over the United States to engage in union busting, which many gratefully accepted (see Walsh 1988, for a review).

We have thus far looked at two sides of the triangle of reform activities that popularly elected governments have used to try to thwart excessive concentrations of wealth and power in one class: legalizing unions and regulating the activities of the rich. The redistribution of wealth via a progressive income tax system constitutes the third side of the triangle. Prior to instituting a system of income tax, the money to run the federal government (except during times of war) came mainly from the sale of federal lands and from customs taxes. As society became more complex and as the United States became a world power with all the responsibilities that come with such status, the old methods of acquiring operating funds were insufficient. Consequently, Congress passed an act imposing the federal income tax. The Supreme Court struck the act down as unconstitutional in *Pollock v. Farmer's Loan and Trust Company* (1895). Although the burdened taxpayer of today may applaud such a decision, we must remember that governments must function, and to do so, they must be funded. (Congress subsequently passed the Sixteenth Amendment in 1913 making federal income tax constitutional.) Thus, in three important cases heard in 1895 (*Pollock, E. C. Knight,* and *Debs*), the Court struck blows to each of the three principle reform activities employed by democratic governments everywhere.

Before reversing course to consider the role of the Supreme Court in inducing rather than preventing social change, we should note that the increasing demands of social change have played a major role in muting its formerly unabashed role of protector of business, the wealthy, and the elite. As Russell Galloway (1982, 181) puts it,

> It seems incontestable that the drafters of the Constitution intended to place the rights of private property in a preferred position and to assign the Supreme Court the duty of guarding that position. In other words, there was an original *explicit* intention that the Court function as a special protector of the wealthy. Thus, in order to transcend this role, The Court had to break away from the instructions contained in its own charter and redefine its purpose to fit changing social needs.

A more charitable way of looking at the matter is to say that the Supreme Court acted like the English judges during the early periods of the evolution of common law. As we saw in chapter 2, English judges became so rigidly wedded to the letter of the law that decisions were often made that grossly violated standards of equity, necessitating the developments of separate courts of equity. The various decisions involving economic issues make it plain that the Court dispensed law rather than justice during the period reviewed thus far. As Galloway implies in the quotation, after the 1930s, the justices became somewhat more sensitive to equity issues.

THE SUPREME COURT'S ROLE IN INDUCING SOCIAL CHANGE

Despite the best efforts of the Supreme Court to maintain the economic status quo, social change has been a hallmark of the American society since its beginning. The newly formed United States was too big, too empty, too wild, and too ambitious to be constrained overly much by the niceties of law, and the settlement of this land was far less orderly and "law-driven" than the settlement of Canada (Hagan and Leon 1977). Nevertheless, the law has played an active role in molding what was once a collection of semiautonomous, bickering, and sometimes warring states into a single unified and mighty nation. As for the role of the Supreme Court, as far back as the 1820s, the aristocratic French commentator Alexis de Tocqueville (1945, 156) claimed, "The peace, the prosperity, and the very existence of the Union are vested in the hands of seven Federal judges." This, doubtless, exaggeration contains some truth because the Supreme Court continually expanded the power of the federal government relative to that of the individual states, and thus served as a nation builder.

Bringing the Country Together Through Case Law

A number of important pre–Civil War Supreme Court cases did much to mold a common national identity. In these cases, the Supreme Court took the words of Article VI of the Constitution (the Supremacy Clause) and put them into practice. The **Supremacy Clause** reads, in part, "the authority of the United States shall be the supreme law of the land; and all judges in every state shall be bound thereby, anything in the Constitution or laws of any State to the contrary notwithstanding."

In *Fletcher v. Peck* (discussed earlier), the Court set the stage for its jurisdiction over state legislatures, an exercise in power stoutly resisted by the states. The Court further cemented its power in *Martin v. Hunter's Lessee* (1813). This case involved a Virginia statute that allowed the state to confiscate land owned by British Loyalists. The father of the petitioner, Philip Martin, had his land confiscated under this law. The Supreme Court ruled in favor of Martin, but Virginia refused to obey the ruling, arguing that the Court had no right to review state legislation. With the matter going before the Court again, the Justices ruled that under Article VI, the Court had the final word over all federal *and* state courts, a decision that was to become the keystone of federal judicial power (Goldinger 1990).

In *McCulloch v. Maryland* (1819), the Marshall Court "set down the classic statement of the doctrine of national authority" (McClosky 1960, 66). The case posed two questions: (1) Could the U.S. Congress charter a national bank (the Bank of the United States), and (2) if so, could the states tax it? Congress had chartered such a bank, and Maryland had taxed it in accordance with what it considered its sovereign right. The Court ruled that Congress could charter such a bank, and that the individual states could not tax it. In making this ruling, the Court had provided for an instrument for national economic stability while at the same time limiting the sovereignty of the states vis-à-vis the federal government.

In *Gibbons v. Ogden* (1824), the powers of the federal government were again pitted against the powers of the states. The basic issue in this case was whether Congress alone, or Congress and the states, could regulate interstate commerce. The Court ruled that while the individual states had the power to regulate commerce within their own borders, they had no power to regulate interstate commerce. Only the U.S. Congress, it was declared, has the constitutional authority to do so. This decision was the first one in which the Marshall Court appeared to be on the popular side (it had ruled against a hated monopoly), but "the lasting significance of *Gibbons v. Ogden* was that it freed internal transportation from the restraints of the states and thus prepared the way for the unfettered economic development of the nation by private capitalism" (Brinkley et al., 1991, 268). There is little doubt that the combined impact of the Court's rulings in *Fletcher v. Peck, Martin v. Hunter's Lessee, McCulloch v. Maryland,* and *Gibbons v. Ogden* did much to integrate and unite the states and to generate feelings among Americans of being citizens of the *United* States as well as citizens of their individual states.

Opposing this tide of national unity was a tide of disunity generated by the existence of slavery in the South. After the death of Chief Justice Marshall, Justice Roger Taney became Chief Justice in 1835. Taney was a believer in states' rights in an era in which issues of states' rights were almost all linked to the increasingly sensitive issue of slavery. In *Scott v. Sandford*, the Court upheld the position that slaves were property, and owners of property cannot be deprived of it without "due process of law." This meant that Congress had no authority to pass laws depriving persons of the right to own slaves, and on this basis, the Court held that the Missouri Compromise of 1820, which banned slavery in certain territories, was unconstitutional. This decision hardened positions in both sides of the slavery issue and helped to set the stage for the Civil War (*Scott v. Sandford* is discussed more fully in chapter 13).

Whatever the role the decision may have played in bringing on the Civil War, it played a major role in giving the presidency to Republican Abraham Lincoln in the 1860 election. Northern and Southern Democrats were bitterly divided over the decision, and each ran their own separate candidate in the election. Abraham Lincoln won 39.8 percent of the popular vote while the Democrats won 47.6 percent, divided between 29.5 percent for Northern Democrat Stephen Douglas and 18.1 percent for Southern Democrat J. C. Breckinridge (Brinkley et al. 1991, 401). The *Scott* decision did not "cause" the Civil War, but it did undermine federalist sentiment generated under the Marshall Court in favor of states' rights sentiment.

From the *Scott* decision of 1857 up to 1937, Court decisions had little or no effect on social change. As we have seen, during this period, it appeared to have only the preservation of the status quo on its mind. But in 1937, the Court upheld Washington State's minimum wage law in *West Coast Hotel Co. v. Parrish*, which marked the first time that the Court had ruled in favor of the working class in a case in which the interests of that class were opposed to the owner class. As Goldinger (1990, 42) put it, "Implicit in this reversal was the willingness of a majority of the Court to accept government authority to act to protect the general welfare of society—and to withdraw the Court from any role as the censor of economic legislation."

The Activism of the Warren and Burger Courts

The Court became a major catalyst of social change under the leadership of Chief Justice Earl Warren (1953–1969). Since in chapter 6 we discussed the activism of these courts in terms of criminal procedure rights, we limit our discussion here to noncriminal matters. One of the most famous of all Supreme Court cases was *Brown v. Board of Education of Topeka* (1954). This case has been called "the single most honored opinion in the Supreme Court's opus" (Balkin 2001, 11). Race relations in the United States up to this time were governed by the "separate but equal" doctrine enunciated by the Court in *Plessy v. Ferguson* (1896). The Court ruled in *Brown* that the *de jure* (by law) segregation of the races upheld as constitutional in *Plessy* violated the equal protection clause of the Fourteenth Amendment and was thus unconstitutional. In his written opinion, Justice Warren stated, "We conclude that in the field of public education the doctrine of 'separate but equal' has no place. Separate educational facilities are inherently unequal." Although the case dealt only with school segregation, it prepared American society for integration in all areas of social life (Mawdsley 2004).

The *Brown* ruling provoked massive resistance on the part of the Southern states, and by fall 1957, less than one fourth of the affected Southern school districts had even begun efforts to desegregate (Mawdsley 2004). Governor Orval Faubus of Arkansas even went so far as to call out the Arkansas National Guard in an attempt to prevent integration. This open defiance of federal authority, as well as the danger posed to black children, forced a reluctant President Eisenhower (an opponent of desegregation) to dispatch federal troops to Arkansas to facilitate the enrollment of black children in schools (Balkin 2001).

Writing of the impact of *Brown*, Rose (1967, 126) states, "If there had ever been a doubt…that a United States Supreme Court decision can change social behavior and social institutions, the implementation undertaken by the federal courts of the *Brown v. Board of Education* decision of 1954, should have dispelled it quickly." (See the impact of *Brown* on taxpayers in *Missouri v. Jenkins*, discussed in chapter 9.) Although the *Brown* decision was explicitly limited to segregation in the schools, in effect, it invalidated all forms of de jure segregation. *Brown* showed once again how powerful the Court is, notwithstanding its lack of purse and sword. Its ruling was upheld despite the massive resistance of the overwhelming majority of Southern whites; despite the resistance of Southern governors, congressmen, and senators; and despite the prosegregationist attitudes of the president of the United States. The will of the Court prevailed because it symbolizes the power of the Constitution as interpreted by it. As we shall see in chapter 13, however, there was considerable pressure brought to bear on the Court from the outside, including the federal government, in favor of *Brown*.

Cases that resulted in social changes of a sometimes profound nature coming from the Warren Court and the subsequent Court under Justice Warren Burger (1969–1986) are too many to recount here (most of the cases composing the "due process revolution" came out of Warren and Burger Courts, but these impacted only the criminal justice system and had limited impact on social change). Included among them are two important cases that hit at the heart of the most deeply held values of many Americans. In 1962, the Court banned prayer in public schools in *Engel v. Vitale*, and in 1973, it legalized abortion in *Roe v. Wade*. The *Engel* decision resulted in a firestorm of public protest, calls to impeach Justice Warren, and many suggestions (though no formal proposals) that it should be overruled by Congress with a constitutional amendment (Starr 2002, 95). Many public schools continued to broadcast prayers over their public address system for years after the ruling, but these systems have long since fallen silent, and the issue rarely generates any major steam today.

On the other hand, the Burger Court's decision in *Roe v. Wade* continues to polarize Americans into pro-life and pro-choice factions. Nevertheless, an increase in favorable attitudes toward abortion rights were in evidence up until 2009, at which time more Americans considered themselves pro-life (47 percent) than pro-choice (46 percent) (see chapter 10). Even in the 1980s it was already evident that although both decisions were opposed by the majority of Americans at the time of the decisions, the majority of Americans supported many of the principles enunciated in them (Barnum 1985). Over time, these rulings have become institutionalized (the establishment of a pattern of norms accompanied by state provisions for their enforcement), which facilitates public acceptance of them, particularly among younger members of the public, who have not lived in a time when school prayer was acceptable and abortion unacceptable. The ability to affect such changes in public attitudes over time underlines the legitimacy-conferring power of the Supreme Court (this is not to deny that a significant number of Americans oppose abortion and favor prayer in school). To confer legitimacy is to "create acceptance of policy among those who oppose or who are neutral about its substance and heighten acceptance among those already committed to its content" (Adamany 1973, 807). Adamany's statement sums up for us the essence of the role of law in effecting social change, a role that is likely to become more important as society becomes more and more complex and ethnically diverse.

SUMMARY

Social change is an inevitable and constant phenomenon in modern societies; it comes from many sources, and although it is welcomed by some, others stoutly resist it. Both those who favor and oppose certain changes often utilize the law in their struggles. Those who oppose change tend to view the law as arising from the customs and norms of their ancestors, and therefore law is the repository of much conventional wisdom; those who agitate for change view the law as the promoter and protector of universalistic principles of justice. Although the law is not as important as many other factors in generating social change, there is often a reciprocal relationship between the law and social change: sometimes the law causes change in society, and sometimes social change causes changes in the law. As society becomes more complex, there will be a greater role for law in the social change process.

Law has played an important part in the birth of the United States. Many British parliamentary acts were stoutly resisted by the American colonists, including the Proclamation Act, which prevented many leading figures in the American Revolution from realizing financial gains from lands ceded by the British to the Indians. Certain antislavery decisions in British courts may also have effected the decision of some of the Southern states to opt for independence. Even though the American Revolution was a revolution, many of its stated principles were "legal" in the sense that the colonists justified their actions by appealing to British legal principles.

The extensive changes in postrevolutionary Russia provide examples of both the power and limitations of law as a tool of social change. The changes in Russian society were truly revolutionary, and their implementation often required the use of terror tactics as well as law. The Soviet family was marked for particularly radical changes, which were duly accomplished. However, these changes proved disastrous, and family laws were changed again. The Soviets had no qualms about frequently changing the law, whenever it suited them to do so. The United States Supreme Court has been a major player both in facilitating and thwarting social change in the United States. The Court relies on the myths and symbols that surround it to generate legitimate authority, and hence power, and has been called "a priesthood that governs." The Court often governs—via judicial review of legislation—because decision making has been defaulted to them by legislators who, unlike the justices, are accountable to the people. There is much debate among legal scholars regarding judicial activism, with constitutional constructionists asserting that the judiciary should stick to the letter of the Constitution and constitutional liberals having a more favorable view of judicial activism.

The Supreme Court, especially for the first 150 years of its existence, was very active in preserving the privileges of the wealthy class. Under one constitutional guise or another, it consistently thwarted attempts of popularly elected legislators to better the lot of the working class, even using legislation (such as the Fourteenth Amendment and the Sherman Antitrust Act) against the very people it was designed to help. The Court consistently attacked the triangle of reforms—encouragement of unions, regulations on the activities of the owner class, and progressive taxation—that democratic governments everywhere have enacted in attempts to generate social justice. In response to Roosevelt's "Court packing" threat, the Court moved away somewhat from its antiprogressive stance, although a bias in favor of the privileged is often observed in the Court's decisions today.

The Supreme Court, in addition to its role in stifling social change vis-à-vis class relationships, has played an important role in generating change. In a series of decisions between 1810 and 1824—*Fletcher v. Peck, Martin v. Hunter's Lessee, McCulloch v. Maryland,* and *Gibbons v. Ogden*—the Court greatly enhanced federal power over the states and in doing so contributed to the unity of the nation. However, the issue of slavery addressed in the *Scott* case reversed this trend toward national unity and indirectly led to the Civil War.

The Court became a major catalyst for social change under Chief Justice Earl Warren in the 1950s and 1960s. *Brown v. Board of Education* prefaced a series of activist cases in the area of race relationships and criminal justice. Extending to the present time, the Supreme Court continues to either shock or delight

Americans as it legitimizes the formerly forbidden and illegitimizes the formerly permitted.

DISCUSSION QUESTIONS

1. Do you think that a major purpose of the law should be to generate social change as it is in socialist law? What positive and negative (in your opinion) social changes have taken place in the United States due to law rather than "natural" change?
2. What is the major difference between the stance of the government of the former Soviet Union and the stance of the government of the United States toward their respective constitutions?
3. Do you believe that the U.S. Supreme Court should function according to the ideals of strict constuctionism or those of judicial activists?
4. In your opinion, has the Supreme Court done more harm or more good for the average person in the United States over the last two hundred years?
5. Discuss a social issue not discussed in this chapter in which the law has been a major factor in bringing about social change in the United States.

References

Abadinsky, H. 2003. *Law and justice: An introduction to the American legal system.* Upper Saddle River, NJ: Prentice Hall.

Acuff, S., and S. Friedman. 2006. A new assault on worker's rights. *Mother Jones* June 28. http://www.motherjones.com/cgi-bib/print_article.

Adamany, D. 1973. Legitimacy, realigning elections, and the Supreme Court. *Wisconsin Law Review* (September) 3:780–846.

Ashford, N. 1990. Michael Oakshott and the conservative disposition. *Intercollegiate Review* 25:39–50.

Balkin, J. 2001. Is the "Brown" decision fading to irrelevance? *Chronicle of Higher Education* November 9, pp. 11–12.

Barnum, D. 1985. The Supreme Court and public opinion: Judicial decision making in the post New Deal period. *Journal of Politics* 47:652–66.

Barry, D., and C. Barner-Barry. 1978. *Contemporary Soviet politics.* Englewood Cliffs, NJ: Prentice Hall.

Bonsignore, J., E. Katsh, P. d'Errico, R. Pipkin, S. Arons, and J. Rifkin. 1989. *Before the law: An introduction to the legal process.* Boston: Houghton Mifflin.

Brinkley, A., R. Current, F. Freidel, and T. Williams. 1991. *American history: A survey.* New York: McGraw-Hill.

Corbin, A., and A. Walsh. 1988. The U.S. Supreme Court and value legitimacy: An experimental approach with older Americans. *Sociological Inquiry* 58:75–86.

Cox, A. 1981. The Court as a legitimate institution. In *Courts, law, and judicial processes,* edited by S. Ulmer, pp. 203–27. New York: Free Press.

de Tocqueville, A. 1945. *Democracy in America.* New York: Vintage.

Deloria, V., and D. Wilkins. 1999. *Tribes, treaties, and constitutional tribulations.* Austin: University of Texas Press.

Donnelly, S. 2006. Reflecting on the rule of law: Its reciprocal relations with rights, legitimacy, and other concepts and institutions. *Annals of the American Academy of Political and Social Sciences* 603:37–53.

Dunn, C. 1978. *American Democracy debated*. Morristown, NJ: Scott Foresman.

Dworkin, R. 1985. *A matter of principle*. Cambridge, MA: Harvard University Press.

Friedman, L. 1975. *The legal system: A social science perspective*. New York: Russell Sage.

Galloway, R. 1982. *The rich and the poor in Supreme Court history*. Greenbrae, CA: Paradigm Press.

Goldinger, C. 1990. *The Supreme Court at work*. Washington, DC: *Congressional Quarterly*.

Hagan, J., and J. Leon. 1977. Philosophy and sociology of crime control: Canadian-American comparisons. *Sociological Inquiry* 47:181–208.

Hazard, J., W. Butler, and P. Maggs. 1977. *The Soviet legal system*. Dobbs Ferry, NY: Oceana.

Hofstadter, R. 1948. *The American political tradition*. New York: Vintage.

Hosking, G. 1985. *The first socialist society: A history of the Soviet Union from within*. Cambridge, MA: Harvard University Press.

Jackson, R. 1941. *The struggle for judicial supremacy*. New York: Alfred A. Knopf.

Johnson, H. 2006. The rule of law in the realm and the province of New York: Prelude to the American Revolution. *History* 91:3–26.

Klingberg, F. 1968. *The anti-slavery movement in England*. New York: Archon Books.

Lerner, M. 1939. *Ideas are weapons*. New York: Viking Press.

Levine, J., and T. Becker. 1980. Toward and beyond a theory of Supreme Court impact. In *Law and society: An interdisciplinary introduction*, edited by L. Weinberg and J. Weinberg, pp. 270–77. Lanham, MD: University Press of America.

Lewis, F. 1999. *The context of judicial activism: The endurance of the Warren Court legacy in a conservative age*. Lanham, MD: Rowman and Littlefield.

Mawdsley, R. 2004. A legal history of Brown and a look at the future. *Education and Urban Society* 36:245–54.

McCann, M. 2006. Law and social movements: Contemporary perspectives. *Annual Review of Law and Social Science* 2:17–38.

McClosky, R. 1960. *The American Supreme Court*. Chicago: University of Chicago Press.

Parenti, M. 1977. *Democracy for the few*. New York: St. Martin's Press.

———. 1980. The Constitution as an elitist document. In *How Democratic is the Constitution?*, edited by R. Goldwin, and W. Schambra. Washington, D.C.: American Enterprise Institute.

Parrillo, V. 2003. *Strangers to these shores: Race and ethnic relations in the United States*. Boston: Allyn & Bacon.

Parsons, T. 1977. Law as an intellectual stepchild. *Sociological Inquiry* 47:11–58.

Pfeffer, L. 1965. *This honorable Court*. Boston: Beacon Press.

Reichel, P. 2005. *Comparative criminal justice systems*. 4th ed. Upper Saddle River, NJ: Prentice Hall.

Richards, L. 2003. *Shays' rebellion: The American Revolution's final battle*. Philadelphia: University of Pennsylvania Press.

Rodell, F. 1955. *Nine men: A political history of the Supreme Court from 1790 to 1955*. New York: Random House.

Rose, A. 1967. School desegregation: A sociologist's view. *Law and Society Review* 2:125–40.

Rosenberg, G. 1991. *The hollow hope: Can courts bring about social change?* Chicago: University of Chicago Press.

Stalin or Yeltsin? 1993. *Economist* March/April, pp. 13–14.

Starr, K. 2002. *First among equals: The Supreme Court in American life*. New York: Warner.

Tilly, C. 1984. Social movements and national politics. In *Statemaking and social movements*, edited by C. Bright and S. Harding, pp. 297–317. Ann Arbor: University of Michigan Press.

———. 2004. *Social movements, 1768–2004*. Boulder, CO: Paradigm Press.

Taylor, R. 1990. The American judiciary as a secular priesthood. *Free Inquiry* 10:37–43.

Walsh, A. 1988. "The people who own the country ought to govern it": The Supreme Court, hegemony, and its consequences. *Law and Inequality* 5:431–51.

Weber, M. 1968. *Economy and society*. New York: Bedminster.

Weinberg, J. 1980. *Law and Society*: Lanham, MD: University Press of America.

Wilson, B., and J. Cordero. 2006. Legal opportunity structures and social movements: The effects of institutional change on Costa Rican politics. *Comparative Political Studies* 39:325–351.

Woodin, G. 1974. *The shady side of America*. New York: Ace Books.

Zemans, F. 1983. Legal mobilization: The neglected role of the law in the political system. *American Political Science Review* 77:690–703.

Cases Cited

Adair v. United States, 208 U.S. 616 (1908).

Adkins v. Children's Hospital, 261 U.S. 525 (1923).

Allied Structural Steel v. Spannous, 438 U.S. 234 (1978).

Brown v. Board of Education of Topeka, 349 U.S. 294 (1954).

Bush v. Gore, 531, U.S. 98 (2000).

Engel v. Vitale, 370 U.S. 421 (1962).

Fletcher v. Peck, 6 Cranch 87 (1810).

Gibbons v. Ogden, 9 Wheaton, 1 (1824).

Griswold v. Connecticut, 381 U.S. 479 (1965).

Hammer v. Dagenhart, 247 U.S. 251 (1918).

In re Debs, 158 U.S. 564 (1895).

Joseph Knight v. Wedderburn, How. St. Tr. 1 (1778).

Lochner v. New York, 198 U.S. 45 (1905).

Loewe v. Lawlor, 208 U.S. 274 (1908).

Louisville Bank v. Radford, 295 U.S. 255 (1935).

Marbury v. Madison, 1 Cranch 137 (1803).

Martin v. Hunter's Lessee, 1 Wheaton 304 (1813).

McCulloch v. Maryland, 17 U.S. 316 (1819).

National Labor Relations Board v. Bildisco, 465 U.S. 537 (1983).

National Labor Relations Board v. Jones and Laughlin Steel Corporation, 301 U.S. 1 (1937).

Plessy v. Ferguson, 163 U.S. 537 (1896).

Pollock v. Farmer's Loan and Trust Company, 157 U.S. 601 (1895).

Roe v. Wade, 410 U.S. 113 (1973).

Santa Clara County v. Southern Pacific Railroad Company, 118 U.S. 394 (1886).

Schechter Poultry Corp v. United States, 295 U.S. 495 (1935).

Scott v. Sandford, 60 U.S. 393 (1857).

Somerset v. Stewart, 98 Eng. Rep. 499 (1772).

United States v. Butler, 297 U.S. 1 (1936).

United States v. E. C. Knight, 156 U.S. 1 (1895).

West Coast Hotel Co. v. Parrish, 300 U.S. 397 (1937).

CHAPTER 12

WOMEN AND THE LAW

by Mary K. Stohr

Although Alice Porter was fired from her job at Acme Linen in Livonia, North Carolina, for "excessive absenteeism" and "poor work performance," in reality she was fired because she got pregnant and had a child. Her company gave her two weeks' maternity leave, charging it to her vacation time. Unfortunately, her child had a number of minor health problems that necessitated Alice's absence from work to tend to its needs. No law protected Alice from Acme firing her unless the company specifically stated that it was because she got pregnant (she would be protected then by the Pregnancy Discrimination Act). To make matters worse, her husband left her and her children (four in all) and remains underemployed or unemployed on purpose to avoid paying child support, and she only has thirteen more months of welfare benefits. It seems that Alice and her children are headed for a life of poverty, a status in which women outnumber men more than two to one.

If Alice lived in most other democracies, she would have been guaranteed *by law* up to eleven months maternity leave at 90 percent of her salary and would have her former employment back without loss of seniority or social allowances. These, and many other rights, such as maternity allowances (a lump sum to cover costs of new child), family allowance (weekly sum paid per child regardless of need), and subsidized day care are guaranteed by Article II of the United Nations Convention on the Elimination of all Forms of Discrimination Against Women (UNCEFDW; see Table 12.1 later in this chapter).

The UNCEFDW recognizes that because of the biological differences between men and women, women will always be treated worse than men *unless the law intervenes and compensates for those differences.* Only women can bear children, which leads to economic or even physical vulnerability, and men's greater aggression and strength gives them the ability to dominate and abuse women. Ask yourself as you read this chapter if strictly equal treatment of men and women is just. Men do not have to put their careers on hold to become parents: why should women be punished for what they cannot help? Make no mistake: they are punished if they are treated in sex-neutral ways. The UNCEFDW mandates compensatory equality laws, not sex-neutral laws. As you read this chapter, decide whether you agree or not.

INTRODUCTION

This chapter explores how women and girls have been treated by the legal system from ancient times to the present. We trace the influence of patriarchy and how it has shaped legal practices throughout history. We show how it established a barrier against the struggle for suffrage and equality for women and girls in the nineteenth and twentieth centuries in the United States. The role of feminist legal theory, gendered law, and women's increasing involvement in the courts will be explored. Because there are many forces aligned to thwart justice and equality for women, it is critical to consider how gender influences the dispensation of rights and liberties, especially if we are interested in a different and more highly evolved world in the twenty-first century. We begin with feminist legal theory to become familiar with how various feminist scholars might analyze and evaluate the issues discussed in this chapter.

FEMINIST LEGAL THEORY

Feminism is a set of theories and strategies for social change that takes gender as its central focus in attempting to understand social institutions, processes, and relationships. It is both a social movement and a worldview of which the law is but a part, albeit a part that feminists believe can be used to right the inequities of gender. Feminist legal theory, or **feminist jurisprudence**, is simply the practice of examining and evaluating the law from a feminist perspective. For feminist legal theorists, the law is the codification of a culture's normative practices that are deeply masculine in nature since they reflect male visions, realities, and goals. Because all known societies have been controlled by males, insofar as the law has been applied to gender relationships and issues, it has been the written embodiment of patriarchy.

Patriarchy literally means "rule of the father" and is a term used to describe any social system that is male dominated at all levels from the family to the highest reaches of government, supported by the belief of overall male superiority. A patriarchal society is one in which "male" traits such as competitiveness, aggressiveness, autonomy, and individualism are lauded, and "female" traits such as intimacy, connection, cooperation, nurturance, while appreciated, are downplayed (Grana 2002). Patriarchy occupies the same despised place among most feminist scholars that capitalism occupies among Marxists. The owners of the means of production (the *bourgeoisie*) are the oppressors in Marxist theory; the owners of the means of *re*production (owners of women and girls) are the oppressors in feminist theory. This does not mean that women are powerless in a patriarchy, only that the most powerful roles in most sectors of society are held predominantly by men. Feminists believe that law is a mirror of patriarchal society and that it has been used to devalue and disenfranchise women. Patriarchies (essentially every society to various degrees) have used the law as a gender-control mechanism to assure male dominance over women and girls, largely by claiming female incompetence and by demonizing female sexuality.

Feminist jurisprudence is split by two major debates: the reformist/radical and the sameness/difference debates (Burchard 2006). Reformist feminists tend to be liberals who want to retain the current legal system and reconfigure it so that it recognizes women as equal to males. Radical feminists see the present system as so corrupted by patriarchy that it must be abandoned and replaced with one free of biases.

The sameness/difference debate revolves around the issue of whether women should be treated equally with males due to the sameness of the sexes or treated differently based on relevant differences between the sexes. In essence, the debate is about whether women are better off treated by the law as men are treated or better off if the law acknowledges the obvious differences between the sexes and treats women with these differences in mind (Grana 2002). As one feminist scholar put it, "To some, the law was unjust in its unequal treatment of equals, whereas for others its injustice lay in its equal treatment of unequals" (Haney 2000, 646). Sameness feminists accused their difference feminist sisters of trying to replicate prefeminist protectionist arguments (women need special protections because they are weak and helpless). Difference feminists accused their sameness sisters of being blind to obvious biological differences and blind to the plight of women who suffer the consequences of those differences (e.g., pregnant women in the workforce being held to the same attendance and performance standards as men).

This "damned if you do, damned if you don't" impasse led to a compromise position that asserts that the law must accept relevant gender differences but that it should not focus on the differences per se but rather on their consequences. As Burchard (2006, 5) argues, "Rights should be based on needs [e.g., paid maternity leave and the guarantee of reemployment afterwards], and if women have needs that men do not, that should not limit their rights." Or as Baer (1999, 55) put it, "Law can treat men and women alike where they are alike and different where they are different." In some cases, the law has done this; in others, it has not, as we shall see.

WOMEN AND LAW IN HISTORY: THE BIRTH OF MISOGYNY AND OTHER TRIUMPHS

Early Greek society was somewhat ambivalent about the status of women. Early Greek accounts of creation began with an earth goddess who is mother to all, with few males of power present (Coole 1993). After earth mated with sky and the lineage that produced Zeus was created, the subordination of the female goddesses began as male gods assumed the mantle of rationality and wisdom and woman were faulted for the world's woes. The Greek myth of Pandora's Box mirrors the biblical myth of Eve's apple. Pandora, the first woman on earth, had been given a box by Zeus, which she was not to open under any circumstance. But Pandora opened the box in which all evil had been contained, and evil spread around the earth. Myths such as Eve and Pandora (add Delilah, Jezabel, and Solome if you like) provide a subtle underpinning for misogyny. **Misogyny** is the hatred, devaluation, and ridicule of women, an ideology that justifies and maintains men's subordination of women.

Homer's tales of approximately 800 BCE featured traditional roles for women as domestic servants, baby makers, and sexual booty in times of war, although there was some recognition of their intelligence and strength in overcoming their trials (Coole 1993). Plato and Aristotle regarded women as inferior to men, with women thought of as the body and men as the soul. Women's appropriate sphere was the home; for men, it was the world. The life for women in Athens of the time was enclosed and controlled for the comfort and pleasure of wealthier men. In Sparta, by contrast, because of its emphasis on breeding, women had more public lives, and property was communally owned. But in general, the laws governing women in ancient Greece were repressive, as they possessed few rights or liberties and their worth was little valued.

High-status women were able to achieve some power and voice in politics when the Greek city-states were more authoritarian and hierarchical than when they were ostensibly republics (Hillard 1992). If true, perhaps this is because when the rights and liberties of men are circumscribed in autocracies, their political status may sink to that of women. Aristocratic women may wield a certain amount of power in autocratic societies because of their wealth and their positions as wives and mothers of powerful men.

Cicero, a prominent Roman politician who lived in the first century BCE, wrote that the proper place for the woman was at home as the subordinated wife of her husband and that she was to be excluded from the most important sacrifices and rites (Cicero 1985). This opinion was codified in the *Twelve Tables*, which decreed that women were subordinate to male guardianship and were to remain as minors in either their father's or their husband's households.

Similarly, in the medieval European feudal system, women were subordinate and homebound. They were allowed to own and dispose of property only if no male relative was in the picture (Grana 2002). Among the lower classes, women's lives were freer but harder, as they and their menfolk had to scramble for survival. Church theology reinforced the belief that women were and should be subordinate to their husbands because this was their "natural" state ordained by God (Coole 1993). Female submission to their husbands in everything is ordered in the Bible in Ephesians 5:22-24, Colossians 3:18, Titus 2:5, and I Peter 3:1. The apostle Paul declares that the function of women is to sexually gratify men (1 Corinthians 7:1-2) and that men were made for the glory of God and women were made for the glory of men (1 Corinthians 11:3-9).

Renaissance writers in the fifteenth century saw women as more virtuous and less worldly than men. Women were not to be involved in the world outside the home, not because they were evil (as had been assumed in the Middle Ages) but because the world was evil. Thus women were counseled to maintain the home and to avoid the corruption of public affairs (Coole 1993). The sixteenth century Reformation and the emergence of Protestantism reinforced domestic patriarchy. In Tudor England (1485–1603), women had almost no rights under either secular or religious law. They were expected to be silent, obedient, and chaste and not allowed to participate in public life. Women were homebound, uneducated, and restricted from involvement in the worlds of politics, art, or academia. What labors they were allowed to engage in were little noticed and even less appreciated. There were some women who were privately well educated, however, and others who inherited wealth when there were no male relatives (Pollock 2006).

English philosophers Thomas Hobbes and John Locke conceded some rights to women, such as the right to possessions acquired before marriage, but they were still considered naturally inferior to men in all matters (Coole 1993). Women could negotiate contracts with their husbands, but given the political and economic realities, it was unlikely that they would. When reading philosophers of this period, the reader is struck by how invisible women were.

While French philosopher Jean-Jacques Rousseau demanded equality for all men, he expressly denied it for women. He believed that women could not be citizens because they did not possess the ability to reason or judge (Coole 1993). Rousseau believed that the proper sphere for women was the private home, and the proper sphere for men was the public square. It is only in the public sphere that voices can be raised in unison and heard, and only when voices are heard can demands for rights and liberties be acknowledged. Dixon (1992, 219) reviews the acceptable roles and attitudes that women were allowed throughout history:

> Most societies do have a legitimate public role for women, but it is usually one without the most prestigious kind of power and tends to be an extension of the society's private construction of the feminine—such as a benevolent super-mother, bestowing largesse and concern on subjects; a pious wife or daughter performing a sacral function; the lady of impeccable virtue, producing perfectly pedigreed heirs. These acceptable images carry great rewards for the women involved. But the image is fragile and the first lady who tries to assume real power beyond the prescribed sphere is immediately subject to virulent attack that turns the acceptable icon upside down; ungovernable selfishness, impurity, and whorishness are the inverse of feminine generosity, piety, and chastity.

Mary Wollstonecraft (1792/1967), an early English feminist writing in *A Vindication of the Rights of Woman*, argued that we cannot know what the natural abilities of women to reason are until they are taught the same things as men. She noted that women's education and training had not been geared toward a role of citizenry and responsibility in the public sphere and that their physical appearance is emphasized to the detriment of their intelligence and strength. Wollstonecraft (1792/1967, 49–50) further argued

> Men complain, and with reason, of the follies and caprices of our sex, when they do not keenly satirize our headstrong passions and groveling vices. Behold, I should answer, the natural effect of ignorance! The mind will ever be unstable that has only prejudices to rest on, and the current will run with destructive fury when there are no barriers to break its force. Women are told from their infancy, and taught by the example of their mothers, that a little knowledge of human weakness, justly termed cunning, softness of temper, *outward* obedience, and a scrupulous

attention to a puerile kind of propriety, will obtain for them the protection of man; and should they be beautiful, everything else is needless, for, at least, twenty years of their lives.

She then makes the point that women should be educated for their own development and because they are the ones who will educate future generations. If girls were allowed to mature mentally as boys were, Wollstonecraft argued, we would find as much intellect and reason among them as we do among men.

THE RELATIVE VALUE OF CITIZENS: THE STRUGGLE FOR WOMEN'S SUFFRAGE

Due to women such as Wollstonecraft, women began to accrue legal rights throughout the nineteenth century in the same way as other undervalued persons were. In the United States, voting rights were first extended to lower-class white males under the Jacksonian reforms of the 1820s and 1830s. They were then extended by law to black males under the Fifteenth Amendment. Despite the Fourteenth Amendment's declaration that "All persons born or naturalized in the United States, and subject to the jurisdiction thereof, are citizens of the United States and of the State wherein they reside" and that no state should "deny to any person within its jurisdiction the equal protection of the laws," this basic right of citizenship was denied to women. For all practical purposes, women appear to have not been included in the definition of "person" for the purposes of allowing them their rights.

Notably, before the American Revolution, some colonies had allowed unmarried women with property to vote, but none of the new state constitutions, with the exception of New Jersey, allowed women to exercise this right (Sachs and Wilson 1978). In 1807, however, the New Jersey constitution was amended to rescind women's suffrage. It is a tragic irony that a country founded on the ideals of democracy explicitly denied it to women, minority men, and initially to white males without sufficient property.

The conception of common law that formed the basis for our system of jurisprudence decreed that adult women were not allowed to be fully functioning adults. In his *Commentaries on the Laws of England,* which formed the basis for common law in this country, Blackstone (1765–69) made known his belief that women were essentially chattel. Under the system of **coverture**, a married couple became one person, and that was, of course, the man. A married woman had no legal rights or obligations separate from those of her husband, and her whole existence was merged into that of her husband. Dusky (1996, 252–253) asserts that coverture "would later be compared to slavery, in that it effectively stripped married women of any legal rights except the right to be prosecuted for heinous crimes . . . . In general married women could not own land, retain their own wages, enter into contracts, or sue anybody."

Our founding fathers paid little heed to the pleas of the founding mothers for the vote or other citizenship rights. When asked in a letter by his wife Abigail in 1776 to "remember the ladies" when liberties and rights were accorded, John Adams (who was to become the second President of the United States) replied that "I cannot but laugh . . . you are so saucy . . . . Depend on it, we know better than to repeal our masculine systems" (Dusky 1996, 253). Abigail had been asking only that women not be at the mercy of tyrannical husbands, as common law allowed. Thomas Jefferson, the author of the Declaration of Independence, and third President of the United States, concurred with Adams, writing, "Even were our state a true democracy there would still be excluded from our deliberations women, who, to prevent deprivations of morals and ambiguity of issues, should not mix promiscuously in gatherings of men" (Dusky 1996, 254). When Jefferson wrote in the Declaration "We hold these Truths to be self-evident, that all Men are created equal, . . . " he really did mean *men*, and then only property-owning *white* men.

Thus, when Elizabeth Cady Stanton called for the right to vote for women at the 1848 woman's rights convention in Seneca Falls, New York, some of the other delegates were surprised and thought such a demand unreasonable (Dusky 1996). Most male politicians and most citizens of both sexes at the time still viewed women as too emotional, too ignorant, and too unpredictable to make rational decisions (Bailey 2006). Later in the century when the Fourteenth and Fifteenth Amendments were ratified, giving black men the vote, women's request that the word *sex* be added to the Fourteenth Amendment so that they too could vote was denied. Sojourner Truth, a famous black female orator of the time, lamented that granting black men the right to vote without giving the same right to black women would lead to continued domestic oppression of women (Dusky 1996).

The reluctance to give women the right to vote at the national level did not deter several Western states from allowing them to vote in state elections (Whittick 1979). Wyoming territory gave women the vote in 1869 and Utah in 1870; when both territories were admitted to the Union as states, these rights were confirmed. Colorado (1893) and Idaho (1896) also granted women the right to vote. Despite these advances at the state level in the West, the rest of the country did not follow suit until the ratification of the Nineteenth Amendment in 1920. When women did finally secure voting rights, it was only after a long-fought battle that spanned the globe, requiring the allegiance of diverse groups.

For instance, Susan B. Anthony and fourteen other women were prosecuted for voting illegally in 1872 (Dusky 1996). At her trial, Anthony argued that women could not be tried without a jury of their peers and that under a male-dominated judicial system, she had no voice because she had no vote. When the judge instructed the jury to find her guilty, they did. She was fined $100 and court costs. She never had to pay the fine or serve time in jail after her trial, however, as her lawyer, against Anthony's will, bailed her out. Furthermore, the judge refused to enforce the fine because he did not want her jailed. These actions (bailing her out and refusing to enforce her fine) were taken because there was concern that if she did spend time in jail, she could appeal the decision to the Supreme Court using a writ of *habeas corpus* (Sachs and Wilson 1978).

The first case relating to women's voting rights to make its way to the U.S. Supreme Court was *Minor v. Happersett* (1874) in which Virginia Minor claimed that Happersett had violated her rights by refusing to register her as a voter in Missouri. A unanimous Court rejected Minor's argument, stating that

> No argument as to woman's need of suffrage can be considered. We can only act upon her rights as they exist. It is not for us to look at the hardship of withholding. Our duty is at an end if we find it is within the power of a State to withhold. Being unanimously of the opinion that the Constitution of the United States does not confer the right of suffrage upon any one, and that the constitutions and laws of the several States which commit that important trust to men alone are not necessarily void, we affirm the judgment.

In 1902, Elizabeth Stanton, Susan B. Anthony, and Carrie Chapman Catt, all from the United States, organized an International Woman Suffrage Conference in Washington, D.C., to which five countries sent delegates. Before the next meeting of the conference in 1904 in Berlin, Anthony, Catt, and Anita Auspurg developed the following principles for conference attendees in their Declaration of Principles:

1. That men and women are born equally free and independent members of the human race; equally endowed with intelligence and ability, and equally entitled to the free exercise of their individual rights and liberty.

2. That the natural relation of the sexes is that of interdependence and cooperation, and that the repression of the rights and liberty of one sex inevitably works injury to the other, and hence to the whole race.

3. That in all lands, those laws, creeds, and customs which have tended to restrict women to a position of dependence; to discourage their education; to impede the development of their natural gifts, and to subordinate their individuality, have been based on false theories, and have produced an artificial and unjust relation of the sexes in modern society.

4. That self-government in the home and the State is the inalienable right of every normal adult, and the refusal of this right to women has resulted in social, legal, and economic injustice to them, and has also intensified the existing economic disturbances throughout the world.

5. That governments which impose taxes and laws upon their women citizens without giving them the right of consent or dissent, which is granted to men citizens, exercise a tyranny inconsistent with just government.

6. That the ballot is the only legal and permanent means of defending the rights to the "life, liberty and the pursuit of happiness" pronounced inalienable by the American Declaration of Independence, and accepted as inalienable by all civilized nations. In any

representative form of government, therefore, women should be vested with all political rights and privileges of electors. (Whittick 1979, 32)

At the time of the conference in 1904, New Zealand and Australia were the only sovereign nations that had given women the right to vote, so the Declaration was considered quite radical and not likely to garner support from most governments (Whittick 1979). The major achievement of this conference was the establishment of the International Woman Suffrage Alliance, with Carrie Catt serving as its first president.

Subsequent congresses of the Alliance from 1906 to 1914 saw it grow to delegates from twenty-four nations. By the 1910 meeting, supportive men's alliances in some European countries were also sending delegates. Delegates would leave the conferences each year and return to their native lands and agitate for the vote and other rights for women. Their form of agitation depended on the local politics and propensities of their respective countries but included reaching out to progressive politicians and party machines and campaigning door to door among the voters.

In Great Britain, women age thirty and older were given the right to vote in 1918 after much lobbying of members of Parliament (Whittick 1979). In the United States, several other states (i.e., New York, Michigan, Oklahoma, and South Dakota) other than the previously mentioned Western states had already granted female suffrage. Most other European countries that had not already granted female suffrage followed the British example in the 1920s and 1930s. Sadly, Susan B. Anthony died in 1906 without having been recognized as a full citizen with voting rights (Dusky 1996). In view of the long suffrage struggle that had preceded World War I and of women's invaluable contributions to the war effort, it became inevitable that suffrage would be achieved. After much struggle by feminists in the United States, women were given their right to vote in 1920 with the ratification of the Nineteenth Amendment, which reads, "The right of citizens of the United States to vote shall not be denied or abridged by the United States or by any State on account of sex." This is the first and only time that the U.S. Constitution explicitly recognizes that there is another sex—women. Carrie Chapman Catt, one of this country's most prominent fighters for women's rights, once remarked about the woman's suffrage movement:

> To get that word *male* out of the Constitution, cost the women of this country fifty-two years of pauseless campaign; 56 state referendum campaigns; 480 legislative campaigns to get state suffrage amendments submitted; 47 state constitutional convention campaigns; 277 state party convention campaigns; 30 national party convention campaigns to get suffrage planks in the party platforms; 19 campaigns with 19 successive Congresses to get the federal amendment submitted, and the final ratification campaign.
>
> Millions of dollars were raised, mostly in small sums, and spent with economic care. Hundreds of women gave the accumulated possibilities

of an entire lifetime, thousands gave years of their lives, hundreds of thousands gave constant interest and such aid as they could. It was a continuous and seemingly endless chain of activity. Young suffragists who helped forge the last links of that chain were not born when it began. Old suffragists who helped forge the first links were dead when it ended. (quoted in Dworkin 1993, 459–60)

WOMAN AS HUMAN AND PERSON

The lesser value for women and girls held for much of human history was reflected in Western (and other) traditions of legal thought in which women and girls were regarded as property (Bailey 2006). If a woman is property, then she can be bought, sold, traded, and replaced whenever convenient. She only exists in relation to her husband, father, and brothers, as a wife, daughter, and sister, but not as an autonomous person. If she maintains her "place," marries, and is obedient, then she is a "Madonna" to be placed on a pedestal and protected by men from the predations of other men. If she should not marry, or be widowed, divorced, or abandoned, then she was likely to be regarded as a "whore" and be subject to rape, persecution, and harassment (Ollenburger 1998).

Matilda Joslyn Gage (1893/1980), a militant humanist activist for women's suffrage in the nineteenth century, was one of the first individuals to campaign for the separation of church and state. She claimed that U.S. law was actually canon (church) law and that the church had purposefully worked for the complete subjugation of women. She made so many other dubious claims, such as that prehistoric humans lived in matriarchal (female-ruled) systems, that women were responsible for many ideas (e.g., the cotton gin) that men stole, and that the witch hunts of the fifteenth through eighteenth centuries resulted in about nine million deaths, that she destroyed much of her hard-won credibility. However, many of the points she made about witchcraft and the responses to it are worth noting:

1. That women were chiefly accused.

2. That men believing in woman's inherent wickedness, and understanding neither the mental nor the physical peculiarities of her being, ascribed all her idiosyncrasies to witchcraft.

3. That the clergy inculcated the idea that woman was in league with the devil, and that strong intellect, remarkable beauty, or unusual sickness were in themselves proof of this league. Catholics and Protestants yet agree in holding women as the chief accessory of the devil. (Gage 1980, 112)

Moreover, the church was motivated to conjure up witches and then condemn them because the killing of a witch released her family property to the church and to its prosecutors and judges (Gage 1893/1972).

RAPE AND OTHER MISOGYNOUS ATROCITIES

Laws against rape and the beating of women and girls have historically been more focused on the property rights of male owners than the suffering of the female victims (Ollenburger 1998; Wilson and Daly 1992). As Brownmiller (1975) documents in her classic historical book on rape, the rape of women and girls throughout history has been tied to their status as property. When that property becomes damaged (i.e., the loss of virginity), it was not the woman who was legally recognized as suffering a loss but her owner (i.e., father or husband), and thus it was he who must be compensated for the "damaged goods" now in his possession. As Brownmiller (1975, 18) puts it,

> Ancient Babylonian and Mosaic law was codified on tablets centuries after the rise of formal tribal hierarchies and the permanent settlements known as city-states. Slavery, private property and the subjugation of women were facts of life, and the earliest written law that has come down to us reflects this stratified life. Criminal rape, as a patriarchal father saw it, was a violation of the new way of doing business. It was, in a phrase, the theft of virginity, an embezzlement of his daughter's fair price on the market.

If a woman was not a virgin, then male rape concerns revolved less around "property damage" and more about her supposed behavior surrounding the crime. Men asked themselves questions such as how willingly the victim participated, if she had led her attacker on by provocative dress or actions, and whether she resisted with sufficient vigor. Under the Code of Hammurabi, a raped married woman might be drowned along with her attacker if her husband no longer wanted her, and the ancient Hebrews would stone both rapist and victim because her complicity in the act was assumed (Brownmiller 1975).

The efforts of feminists to obtain some legal protection against physical and sexual abuse in marriage are also linked to the conception of women as the subordinate property of men (Morash 2006). Resistance by the courts to such efforts reflects the belief that a man has a right to do what he will with his own property (wife and daughters). "Seventeenth-century judges only upheld the murder conviction of a man who beat his wife to death with a pestle [a large heavy club used for pounding and grinding wheat] because a pestle was a deadly weapon, not an appropriate instrument of correction" (Clark 1992, 188). Early American common law also recognized the "rule of thumb," which stated that a man had a right to beat his wife as long as the stick he used was no bigger in circumference than his thumb. The "rule of thumb" derives from English common law, but in 1868, a North Carolina judge in *State v. Rhodes* was still affirming this right of the husband to beat his wife.

A wife's subjugation to the authority of her husband approached that of everyone's subjugation to the sovereignty of the monarch in early English common law, as the existence of a crime called **petite treason** attests. If a husband killed his wife, the crime was simply a murder punishable by hanging. However, if a wife killed her husband, her very own "sovereign," the seriousness of the crime was elevated to that of treason (albeit, only a "little" treason), for which the punishment was burning at the stake (McIntyre 1995).

Wives across the globe have been punished severely for the crime of adultery but not generally men (Morash 2006; Wilson and Daly 1992). The gender-based criminalization of adultery in most countries reflects the proprietary interest that men have in their wives. The reasoning behind this asymmetry is given by eighteenth century English philosopher Samuel Johnson: "the man imposes no bastards upon his wife" (cited in Allman 1994, 134). In other words, if a wife should willingly mate with another man, the paternal source of offspring is in question (Johnson seems to overlook the fact that an adulterous man may impose "bastards" on some other man). If a wife should be raped, then it is better from this perspective that she be injured seriously so that her unwillingness to engage in the extramarital sex be made clear (Wilson and Daly 1992).

Things are not very different in some parts of the world even today. Islamic laws state that a woman accusing a man of rape must produce four Muslim male witnesses as evidence or potentially face charges of false accusation, for which she may receive eighty lashes. She may also face charges of adultery, for which she may be stoned to death if she is married. If the rape victim is unmarried and cannot produce the almost-impossible evidence, she receives one hundred lashes for adultery. Such draconian measures admittedly occur only rarely (for few risk further victimization by reporting the rape) and only in countries practicing fundamentalist *shari'a* law such as Sudan, Nigeria, Iran, Saudi Arabia, and Bangladesh (International Society for Human Rights 2006).

Srdja Trifkovic (2005, 9) further reveals the position of women in many Islamic societies and the extent to which they are controlled:

> The relegation of women to such an inferior position deprives Islamic societies of the talents and energies of half its people…it also entrusts the other half's crucial early years of upbringing to undereducated and downtrodden mothers. The idea of "love" is removed from those men's understanding of sexuality, which is too often reduced to hurting others by violence. Gross mutilation of little girls, known as clitorectomy [cutting off the clitoris] and rampant in Muslim Africa, and to a lesser extent in Arabia, is the direct result of a culture that deems female orgasm as indecent and threatening, because it implies mutuality.

WOMEN'S WORK AND OTHER LEGAL MATTERS

Laws seeking to treat people differently based on immutable characteristics such as race or national origin must pass the most stringent of constitutional tests (strict scrutiny), and the state must prove a compelling state interest. As we saw in chapter 3, unlike other immutable characteristics, sex has not been considered a suspect classification. Until the latter part of the twentieth century, laws treating men and women differently were evaluated by the rational basis test, meaning that because no suspect classification is implicated, a state may enact legislation impacting that class of persons if there is a rational basis for the legislation. Under the rational-basis-test standard of review, state actions are presumed to be valid and rarely struck down.

In 1971, the United States Supreme Court added the intermediary scrutiny standard of review and defined sex/gender as a quasi-suspect classification. A law passes constitutional muster under this standard only if the Court finds that it is *substantially related* to an important government purpose. The case before the Court was *Reed v. Reed* (1971) and involved an Idaho statute declaring that if a minor died intestate (dying without leaving a legal will), then a male parent executor is preferred over a female parent executor if both claim to be equally entitled to act as such. The Court reversed the ruling of the Idaho Supreme Court, stating that arbitrarily favoring equally qualified persons on the basis of a classification violated the equal protection clause of the Fourteenth Amendment.

In many sex-based distinction cases since then, the courts have turned to the sex/gender roles occupied by women and men by virtue of biological and cultural imperatives. Obviously, only women can bear children, and women tend to be the caregivers in any society. The courts would be remiss if they did not give full weight to these facts when applying the constitutional measuring rod to sex-based legislation. For instance, the Supreme Court apparently did when it upheld the Immigration and Naturalization Service's (INS) practice of making it easier for foreign-born children of female United States citizens to acquire U.S. citizenship than for foreign-born children of male United States citizens (*Nguyen v. INS* 2001). The Court agreed with the INS that there is (generally, of course) a stronger bond between mothers and children than between fathers and children and that children need their mothers more. The *Nguyen* ruling satisfies difference feminists by recognizing relevant sex differences, but sameness feminists are upset because *Nguyen's* "reliance on gender stereotypes of different parenting roles for men and women harms both, and threatens a return to the era when laws and policies based on women's 'proper' roles were used to justify restricting their participation in economic and political life" (National Women's Law Center 2001, 1).

The first wave of the feminist movement concentrated on achieving voting rights for women, while the second wave focused on other basic rights and liberties such as property, educational and employment opportunities, and "outing" male violence against women and children (Brenner 1996). Many of these changes did not occur until the 1970s when the feminist movement, following on the heels of the civil rights movement, experienced a resurgence. Supreme Court decisions after *Reed* (*Frontiero v. Richardson* 1973 and *Duren v. Missouri* 1979) established that women could administer estates, were entitled to equal benefits from the government, and had the right to serve on juries (Dusky 1996). Interestingly enough, the second woman appointed to the Supreme Court, Ruth Bader Ginsburg, was instrumental in litigating these landmark cases when she served as the head of the ACLU's Women's Rights Project in the 1970s and early 1980s (Dusky 1996).

There was a little-known period in early American history when some white women were accorded more rights than they previously had been or were to experience again until the twentieth century (Sachs and Wilson 1978). Because of the shortage of women and labor during the early colonial period, free white women were afforded rights to own and dispose of their own property and to operate a business. Sachs and Wilson (1978, 70) report that during this period in Philadelphia, "[w]omen engaged in roughly thirty different trades ranging from essential to luxury services" including "silversmiths, tin-workers, barbers, bakers, fish picklers, brewers, tanners, ropemakers, lumberjacks, gunsmiths, butchers, milliners, harnessmakers, potash manufacturers, upholsterers, printers, morticians...." However, after the Revolutionary War, women were pushed back into the home and their liberties in the areas of work, community, property ownership, and the ability to exercise control of their deceased husband's property were curtailed.

THE UNCEFDW AND THE EQUAL RIGHTS AMENDMENT

International standards, however, have recognized that gender roles are not arbitrary "stereotypes" and have endeavored to protect women's participation in economic and political life at the same time. Table 12.1 reproduces Article 11 of the **United Nations Convention on the Elimination of All Forms of Discrimination Against Women** (UNCEFDW) passed by United Nations General Assembly in 1979. The Convention became an international treaty in 1981 after the twentieth country had ratified it. Notice that the ideas in UNCEFDW support difference feminists rather than sameness feminists.

The UNCEFDW guarantees women the same kinds of rights (and then some) that feminists of both genders have been striving to introduce in the United States with the **Equal Rights Amendment** (ERA) since it was first introduced to Congress in 1923. It was not until 1972 that it was passed by Congress and then was sent to the states for ratification. The ERA never received the votes of the 38 states required to amend the Constitution and so went into a state of hibernation. There are concerted efforts underway to resurrect the ERA in several states. Ironically, the passage of the Twenty-Seventh Amendment in 1992 concerning pay raises for Congress*men* provided much of the impetus for the new ERA push. The Twenty-Seventh Amendment actually went to the states for ratification in 1789, which was 203 years before it was actually ratified (Held, Herndon, and Stager 1997). Thus there is no time limit for the ratification of an amendment once introduced.

Why do we need the ERA in a time when women have all the civil, political, and social rights that men enjoy? The problem is that these rights have been won with legislation and court decisions that, with the exception of the right to vote, can be ignored, inconsistently applied, or even rescinded at any time. The passage of the ERA would rest these rights on the solid bedrock of the Constitution and thus provide the courts with consistent and unequivocal principles with which to confront gender-equity issues. The standard of review in such cases will be elevated to strict scrutiny, and sex/gender would become a suspect classification. Finally, with the passage of the ERA, American women may begin to realize some of the benefits outlined in Article 11 of the UNCEFDW.

Table 12.1 *Article 11 of the United Nations' Convention on the Elimination of All Forms of Discrimination Against Women*

1. States Parties shall take all appropriate measures to eliminate discrimination against women in the field of employment in order to ensure, on a basis of equality of men and women, the same rights, in particular:

(a) The right to work as an inalienable right of all human beings;

(b) The right to the same employment opportunities, including the application of the same criteria for selection in matters of employment;

(c) The right to free choice of profession and employment, the right to promotion, job security and all benefits and conditions of service and the right to receive vocational training and retraining, including apprenticeships, advanced vocational training and recurrent training;

(d) The right to equal remuneration, including benefits, and to equal treatment in respect of work of equal value, as well as equality of treatment in the evaluation of the quality of work;

(e) The right to social security, particularly in cases of retirement, unemployment, sickness, invalidity and old age and other incapacity to work, as well as the right to paid leave;

(f) The right to protection of health and to safety in working conditions, including the safeguarding of the function of reproduction.

2. In order to prevent discrimination against women on the grounds of marriage or maternity and to ensure their effective right to work, States Parties shall take appropriate measures:

(a) To prohibit, subject to the imposition of sanctions, dismissal on the grounds of pregnancy or of maternity leave and discrimination in dismissals on the basis of marital status;

(b) To introduce maternity leave with pay or with comparable social benefits without loss of former employment, seniority or social allowances;

(c) To encourage the provision of the necessary supporting social services to enable parents to combine family obligations with work responsibilities and participation in public life, in particular through promoting the establishment and development of a network of child-care facilities;

(d) To provide special protection to women during pregnancy in types of work proved to be harmful to them.

3. Protective legislation relating to matters covered in this article shall be reviewed periodically in the light of scientific and technological knowledge and shall be revised, repealed or extended as necessary.

WOMEN'S REPRESENTATION IN THE LEGAL PROFESSION

Women's admittance into the legal profession has been fraught with struggle and hardship. Clearly, major victories have been achieved in the admittance of women to law schools and legal practice, while some obstacles to women's full participation remain. As Martin and Jurik (1996, 2) indicate,

> The obstacles faced by women justice workers are part of larger organizational and social patterns that construct and support women's subordination to men. Women in fields numerically dominated by men face many barriers: exclusion from informal work cultures, hostility expressed at the international level, organizational policies that promote gender

segregation, differential assignments, and sexual harassment. The confluence of these barriers produces lower pay and slower advancement for women in these fields.

These obstacles to admittance to the legal profession were based on a long tradition of excluding women from it, even though some women in colonial America performed quasi-legal work. For instance, Margaret Brent, a well-connected and capable woman, was the executor of the estate of the governor of the Maryland colony in 1638 (Morello 1986). Brent was from a wealthy family in England and settled in Maryland and made her fortune in real estate. As part of her duties as executor, she handled claims against the estate in court, settled an impending riot by soldiers who had a hefty claim against it, and appeared before the assembly asking for a vote and a voice. Despite her success and obvious ability, she was denied a vote and eventually left Maryland for Virginia, where she settled until her death on an estate she called "Peace" (Morello 1986, 7).

Other women in colonial America were also tangentially involved in court processes affecting themselves and others, primarily property matters and estates to which they had some claim. Morello (1986) notes that in 1783, a black slave woman named Elizabeth Freeman successfully argued in a Massachusetts court for her freedom. Another black woman, Lucy Terry Prince, was the first woman to argue before the Supreme Court in a 1795 case involving a land dispute (Morello 1986). But because women were essentially barred from clerkships with lawyers (a primary means of entering the profession before the proliferation of law schools), admittance to law schools, and state bar exams, it was difficult, if not impossible, for them to practice law until the latter half of the nineteenth century. Even then women did not practice law in any meaningful numbers until the latter half of the twentieth century (Bernat 1992; Friedman 1993).

Underpinning this exclusion from legal practice was the belief that feminine characteristics were not suited for the practice of law. The practice of law required rationality and an objective and unemotional demeanor. Women were viewed as lacking in the requisite logical capacity and as overly subjective and emotional. It would, of course, have been incongruent with women's citizenship status in the seventeenth, eighteenth, and nineteenth centuries to be able to practice law when they did not have the legal status of citizens.

Despite these obstacles, a few women were admitted to the study of law and to the bar by the latter half of the 1800s. In 1869, two white women (Arabella Babb Mansfield in Iowa and Myra Bradwell in Illinois) passed the bar. When Bradwell applied to practice law, she was twice denied by the Illinois Supreme Court, the first time because she was married and coverture applied and the second just because she was a woman (Friedman 1993). Bradwell appealed to the United States Supreme Court (*Bradwell v. Illinois* 1873), which upheld the right of Illinois to deny her admission to legal practice. It is instructive to read an excerpt from Justice Joseph Bradley's opinion: "Civil law, as well as nature herself, has always recognized a wide difference in the respective spheres and destinies of man and woman. The paramount destiny and mission of women are to fulfill the noble and benign offices of wife and mother. This is the law of the Creator."

Two other white women, Lemma Barkloo and Phoebe Cousins, were admitted to Washington University Law School in 1869 (Bernat 1992, 1996). One year later Ada Kepley, a white woman, graduated from the University of Chicago Law School, and the first black woman, Charlotte Ray, graduated and was admitted to the bar in 1872. In 1870, a white woman, Esther Morris, was appointed as a justice of the peace in a mining camp in Wyoming (Spohn 1990). Despite these gains, it was not until 1918 that women were allowed to join the American Bar Association and not until 1920 that women were admitted to the bar in all states. It was not until 1928 and 1950 that Columbia University and Harvard Law Schools, respectively, admitted women. Many other elite schools restricted admittance for almost as long (Martin and Jurik 1996).

Morello (1986) reports that Harlan Fiske Stone, once a dean of the school of Columbia Law School and later a Supreme Court Justice, had not permitted women to register as students when he was there. Morello also found that in the 1940s, "[R]oscoe Pound threw a woman visitor out of his class because he did not believe in teaching law to women" and that on "Ladies Day" at Harvard in the 1950s, female students were allowed to "[r]ecite on one specially selected day each semester and then only for the amusement of the professor and the male members of the class" (Morello 1986, xiv). Supreme Court Justice Ginsberg, the second woman appointed to that court, reported that even though she had graduated at the top of her class (she tied for first) from Columbia Law School in 1959, she had no job offers and was forced to take a clerkship for a federal judge (Meyers 2004).

It was not until the 1970s that women were admitted to law schools and to the practice of law in any large numbers (Law School Admission Council 2005; Martin and Jurik 1996). These increases may not have occurred at all but for the agitation by the second wave of feminists or without the passage of the 1972 amendment Title VII to the Civil Rights Act of 1964 and the Equal Employment Opportunity Act of 1972 (Harrington 1994; Spohn 1990). Title VII forbade discrimination in employment based on sex unless there was a bona fide occupational qualification (BFOQ). Also in 1972, Title IX of the Higher Education Act was passed, constraining the ability of law schools to discriminate based on sex through the threat of the loss of federal financial assistance (Martin and Jurik 1996). All of a sudden, the last vestiges of the formal legal barriers to admittance to law and its practice came tumbling down for women.

According to the Law School Admission Council (2005), the nonprofit organization that administers the Law School Admissions Test (LSAT), as of 2005 about half of the applicants to American law schools are women. The *Princeton Review: The Best Law Schools, 1998 Edition*, reported that in the mid 1990s, 44 percent of students entering law schools were women (Hollander and Tallia 1997). These figures represent major increases from even the 1970s when only 10 percent of applicants to law schools were women (Law School Admission Council 2005). In a preliminary analysis of the female student experience at Harvard Law School, Neufeld, Sanders, and Wilk (2004) found that women had a different experience in law school than men. For one thing, they were less confident in their legal skills and less likely to apply for law review than men. More women than men indicated that they hoped to work for a nonprofit or a legal services organization. In contrast, more men expected to work in prestigious law firms or businesses.

In the Princeton publication, it was also noted that 28 percent of faculty and administrators of law schools are women; 16 percent of tenured law school professors are women; 8 percent of the deans are women; 12.9 percent of the partners in law firms are women; and that women comprise 24 percent of those working in the legal profession. Linda Hirshman, a philosophy professor at Brandeis University (cited in Gest 2001), noted that about twenty law schools had female deans, and one fifth had female full professors in 2001.

Women's careers in the legal profession have shifted over time. Federal judgeships, a much sought after prize for many public service–minded lawyers, have traditionally gone to men. However, over the years, United States presidents have been increasingly more willing to nominate and appoint women. As of 2004, former-President Clinton held the record for female appointments to judgeships at 104 in his two terms, which is almost three times the number of women appointed by President George. H. W. Bush in his one term (thirty-six) or President George W. Bush in his first term (thirty-three), and over four times the number of women appointed by President Reagan in either of his terms (Maguire and Pastore 1998; Meyers 2004). According to Supreme Court Justice Ruth Bader Ginsburg, President Carter in the 1970s first broke the barrier to the appointment of women with forty federal judgeships at a time when only six women then held such positions (Meyers 2004).

Clearly, women at the turn of the millennium have made great inroads into the legal profession (Law School Admission Council 2005), although barriers to full participation have yet to be removed. There are still far fewer women serving as judges, partners in prestigious law firms, and law school faculty than expected, given their numbers in the profession (Hollander and Tallia 1997; Meyers 2004). This disparity can be explained in part by the fact that many women choose to adopt a "mommy track" when they have children. Therefore, women lawyers are more likely to choose to work fewer hours, adopt more flexible schedules, and/or take a leave of absence when their children are young. Men are less likely to make such a choice. Some disparity is also likely due to latent sexist perceptions about the abilities and propensities of women. In the 1970s, female law students had to sue to end discriminatory hiring practices by law firms (e.g., *Kohn v. Royall, Koegel, and Wells* 1973), and women had to sue their own law firms to be allowed to make partner (e.g., *Hishon v. King and Spalding* 1984) in the 1980s. Such issues remain unresolved (Hollander and Tallia 1997; Martin and Jurik 1996).

Today women outperform men in undergraduate grade point average (GPA) and do as well as men in medical, business, and other graduate/professional programs but not as well as men in law school. Some scholars report that women students claim differential treatment in law school, as they are not called on in class, and their questions and input are often ignored (Hollander and Tallia 1997). Some of the top-ranked law schools, such as Yale, and Harvard, do not even score in the top one hundred schools in terms of female representation on faculties, law reviews, and student bar associations (Hollander and Tallia 1997).

In general, women have gained equal footing in terms of sheer numbers of women involved in law careers and in the evaluations of their job satisfaction vis-à-vis their male colleagues. In her study of the perceptions of 424 female and male attorneys, Hall (1995, 121) found that they "[s]hare similar work values, career orientations, and perceptions of work. Both genders were relatively satisfied with their work because they valued the most positive aspects of their jobs." She did find perceptions of fewer promotional opportunities among women attorneys and that this affected their job satisfaction. Hall (1995) explained that women did not rate their own chances of promotion lower but rather that the chances of other women were lower.

Pollitz Worden (1997) surveyed 553 private criminal defense attorneys in Georgia and found that men and women were in basic agreement on values: "[a]lthough male respondents express more extreme advocacy of due process and defendants' rights, women and men differ little in their attitudes toward punishment issues and cynicism regarding defendants." Thus, much like research on job satisfaction, job enrichment, job commitment, stress, and work values in policing and corrections (Stohr, Lovrich, and Mays 1997; Stohr, Lovrich, and Wood 1996), women and men in the legal profession tend to be more similar than dissimilar.

THE BIAS STUDIES

Despite some similarities in experiences on the job, there are latent discriminatory attitudes that permeate America's courtrooms. In a review of over thirty state gender-bias studies, Hemmens, Strom, and Schlegel (1998, 22) found the following:

> In theory, all persons involved in court proceedings are supposed to be treated equitably. A number of states have conducted studies which indicate that in actuality men and women receive differential treatment in court. As is the case in many aspects of American society, women are most often victims of gender bias. Female litigants face an uphill battle in pursuing their cases in both civil and criminal courts.

Such bias is manifested in the beliefs, perceptions, and practices of the courtroom actors and clients. In cases of domestic violence, the California Task Force found that a majority of the male courtroom personnel (53 percent) thought that claims of abuse by female victims were "exaggerated" (Hemmens et al. 1998). Massachusetts attorneys reported that judges sometimes wondered aloud what victims did to deserve beating. Wisconsin and Minnesota attorneys reported that a victim's willingness to press charges determined whether a prosecution would go forward in many cases, despite the fact that the state is the aggrieved party and may prosecute regardless of victim involvement. In task force studies done in Nevada, New Mexico, Nebraska, Washington, Michigan, and Missouri, approximately 30 percent to 50 percent of court actors reported that women were prevented in some way from effectively pursuing court orders to protect themselves from their abusers.

Hemmens and colleagues (1998) indicate that in sexual assault cases, several gender-bias studies revealed perceptions among a number of court actors that victims of these crimes have less credibility with judges and jurors than victims of other crimes. If the victim in a sexual assault knew the offender, the offense is regarded as "less serious" and treated that way. Courtroom actors report that the sexual history of the victim is often allowed in such cases despite its irrelevance to the issue of consent.

Gender-bias studies in several states reflect perceptions of disparity in treatment in divorce, marital property, and child support that disadvantage women and children (Hemmens et al. 1998). In some states, between 30 percent to 60 percent of courtroom actors believe that men are awarded a disproportionate share of the marital property by predominately male judges in divorce cases.

Reported bias is also found in the treatment of female attorneys and judges (Hemmens et al. 1998). Female attorneys report that male judges or attorneys accord them less credibility than their male counterparts, make comments about their appearance, or subject them to sexist remarks or jokes. Female attorneys indicate that they are regarded as "bitches" if they respond as aggressively as male attorneys and are less likely to be hired or selected than similarly qualified men. The authors (Hemmens et al. 1998, 40) conclude by recognizing the extent of the gender bias and by making a recommendation that education be used to reduce it:

> The implication of gender bias is that women are still not being viewed as equal to their male counterparts. Although current laws and affirmative action plans have furthered women's equality, they cannot by themselves change the attitudes of individuals. It is the individual attitudes that require change if gender bias is to be eradicated....
>
> The task force reports on gender bias provide strong evidence that gender bias exists in all aspects of the court system, and in virtually all courts. The reports also indicate that there is a wide variation in the perception of the existence of bias, depending on the gender of the observer. Remedying gender bias requires convincing those most often guilty of it that they are acting in a biased fashion. If this can be accomplished, a major step will have been taken.

LAW, EQUALITY, AND JUSTICE

As we have discussed, there has been a concerted effort by feminists over the centuries to force the law to recognize women as people and as equal citizens entitled to all the rights and privileges that such status entails. In modern secular democracies, legal status as citizens has for the most part been achieved, as has access to all avenues of higher education in the law. What feminist scholars are now debating is the extent to which further justice can be achieved through the use of the courts and whether equality with men necessarily involves justice for women. Perhaps the best option at present would be for the United States Congress to ratify and implement the provisions of the UNCEFDW, a much easier process than a constitutional amendment.

As we have seen, the law is andocentric (male centered), and so efforts to decide issues affecting females as victims of males are likely to be stymied by the male view of what women are or should be. For instance, because women continue to be culturally defined by the old "Madonna/whore" dichotomy, rape trials often see court actors sexualizing women's bodies and failing to focus on the assault (Smart 1989). Smart also argues that the law has been used to control women's bodies (such as requiring parental consent to obtain an abortion).

A corollary to this view is that proposed by Carol Gilligan (1982) that women and men are basically different and that the law as it is currently written and practiced reflects masculine values of competitiveness, aggressiveness, and male logic.

> As we have listened for centuries to the voices of men and the theories of development that their experience informs, so we have come more recently to notice not only the silence of women but the difficulty in hearing what they say when they speak. Yet in the different voice of women lies the truth of an ethic of care, the tie between relationship and responsibility, and the origins of aggression in the failure of connection. (Gilligan 1982, 171)

Gilligan would propose that as more women enter the profession of the law, it, as well as the courts, will begin to reflect more feminine values such as cooperation, support, and care. This shift will not necessarily mean the demise in the rule of law, but it may mean there will be more *justice* in its practice.

Mackinnon (1993) also recognizes the differing frameworks that men and women experience and are shaped by but argues that a new jurisprudence and a new relationship between life and law is needed. Law should be fashioned so there is a basic equality in treatment and protection; however, to effectuate justice, law and legal procedures must also recognize the female experience, the female reality, and the female voice. Therefore, laws that truly work to protect women's and girls' abilities, access, rights, and liberties, as they do men's, will not be wholly neutral, just as laws are not and have not been neutral in conception or practice as she argues and our review of history has indicated. As we have found throughout the history of humankind, law and juridical practice have been conceived and practiced in such a way that they have disadvantaged girls and women. In the future, let it not be so.

BUILDING UNDERSTANDING

Imagine a world where one gender holds the vast majority of powerful political and corporate positions and controls most of the wealth, a world where law either forbids the involvement of the "powerless gender" in politics or business, and/or more informal controls imposed by the culture, family, and work requirements bar access to powerful positions and attainment of wealth. Imagine a world where positions in the criminal justice systems and lawmaking are largely dominated by this powerful gender as well.

Imagine the "weaker gender" being cloistered in strict Islamic countries, not allowed to own or dispose of property; to speak freely without harassment, threat of violence, or actual assault by religious adherents; totally dominated by the other gender; not believed when testifying independently in court; or not allowed to walk about, eat in restaurants, go to the theater, or shopping without escort and being shrouded with clothing. Imagine places such as India and China where the less-valued gender survives early childhood at a much lesser rate than the valued male gender because of abandonment or infanticide.

Imagine that in the United States there is a state where members of this "insignificant gender" are sometimes married to men who already have several wives and are kept in poverty and not educated so that they can not escape the abuse of themselves and their children in these marriages. Although the behavior of these men is widely known and violates the law of Utah and the Mormon Church to which they align themselves, only recently have the authorities taken meaningful steps to prosecute them.

Imagine a world where religious groups such as the Catholics and Church of Jesus Christ of Latter-day Saints exclude this "less worthy gender" from real positions of leadership in the church (elders, priests, bishops), or where Southern Baptists admonish the "less capable gender" to submit to the leadership and guidance of the wiser and more-capable-of-leadership gender. Or try to conceive of societies where one gender commits the vast majority of physical and sexual assaults and murders, and members of "a victimized gender" are victims as children and as adults, a world in which the "less violent" gender is told to stay inside, not to travel alone, and to worry from childhood on about how to avoid rape and abuse from family members, friends, and strangers. Imagine a world where "a blamed gender" is routinely told that they asked for their own abuse or are condemned because they do not leave their abusers in their traditional family when they and their children have few resources to do so and current cultural values do not support it.

Imagine a world where children and adults of the "object gender" have their bodies prostituted or trivialized in strip and topless clubs, brothels, and in print, video, and other media. This occurs even though such pornographic depictions have been tied to the sexual abuse and denigration of the suffering of the "object gender." In some Asian countries, children and adults of this gender are sold into prostitution for unscrupulous foreign members of the more abusive gender.

Can you imagine such a sexist world? Would it be possible for you to conceive of this "powerless," "weaker," "less valued," "insignificant," "less worthy and capable," "victimized," "blamed," and "object" gender as being male? If not, then why not? Why is there not a general sense of outrage that these appellations do indeed apply to women and girls right now in *our* world? The fact that many are not even concerned about such injustice for females is itself the strongest evidence of the prevalence and acceptability of injustice and privilege in *our* world.

SUMMARY

Feminist jurisprudence evaluates the law from a critical feminist perspective, noting that it is a system of control devised by men for men. All societies throughout history have been patriarchies in which women have been disadvantaged.

Feminist scholars disagree, however, on how the situation can be put right. They split primarily along reformist/radical and sameness/difference lines.

As we have reviewed the span of human history with a focus on gender issues in this chapter, it has become clear that full social and legal justice for women are hard-won prizes that have yet to be fully realized in many countries, including the United States. The ability to fully participate as citizens and to have the freedom to self-determine how one will live and negotiate in this world are not liberties that girls or women have been able to assume as their right. Such freedoms were not self-evident for women, nor did our founders intend that they be. As Elizabeth Cady Stanton stated, to the extent that such rights have finally been accorded, it has been at great cost in time, money, and lives of courageous feminist women and men.

But at the same time that Western women have achieved some legal standing, they continue to struggle against the more informal strictures that permeate homes, workplaces, courtrooms, and churches. These informal strictures limit women and girls' opportunities and shape their perceptions of themselves as less capable, able, and wise than men and boys. The repercussions of such perceptions about women and girls are stark and clear. History tells us that the abuse of women and girls arises out of a perception of their inferiority as human beings. Therefore, we might reasonably assume that those persons and entities engaged in perpetuating such perceptions are also indirectly or directly fostering the denigration of females and limiting their potential as human beings. Necessarily, these limitations on half the human population are crippling the ability of our culture to advance and flourish as it might.

A parallel issue for justicians is whether justice can mean the same thing in an environment with patriarchal overtones. Should justice be differential, as Gilligan (1982) argues in light of the special needs, backgrounds, and propensities of women? Or does justice require an adherence to equal treatment of men and women under the law as Mackinnon (1993) would have it? If we have learned anything, we should know that as a country, we will be engaged in resolving such social and legal justice issues well into the twenty-first century.

DISCUSSION QUESTIONS

1. Why do you think that women and girls are generally valued less than men and boys?
2. What central figures were involved in gaining the vote for women in this country and how long did it take?
3. Why do you think the Western states were quicker in granting suffrage to women than the Eastern states were?
4. Who was Mary Wollstonecraft and what did she argue?
5. How is the practice of rape tied to the conception of women and girls as property?
6. What do the findings of the studies by Hall and Pollitz Worden tell us about how women and men lawyers perceive their jobs?

7. What were the general conclusions of the gender-bias studies on courts by Hemmens, Strom, and Schlegel?

References

Allman, W. 1994. *The stoneage present*. New York: Simon and Schuster.

Baer, J. 1999. *Our lives before the law: Constructing a feminist jurisprudence*. Princeton, NJ: Princeton University Press.

Bailey, F. 2006. Images of women. In *Women, law, and social control*, edited by A. Merlo and J. Pollock, pp. 32–46. Boston: Allyn & Bacon.

Bernat, F. 1992. Women in the legal profession. In *The changing roles of women in the criminal justice system: Offenders, victims, and professionals*. 2nd ed., edited by I. Hoyer, pp. 307–22. Prospect Heights, IL: Waveland Press.

———. 1996. Book review of *America's first woman lawyer: The biography of Myra Bradwell* by J. Friedman. In *Women and Criminal Justice* 7:94–97.

Blackstone, W. 1765–1769. *Commentaries on the law of England*. 4 vols. London: Routledge.

Brenner, J. 1996. The best of times, the worst of times: Feminism in the United States. In *Mapping the women's movement*, edited by M. Threlfall, pp. 17–72. London: Verso.

Brownmiller, S. 1975. *Against our will: Men, women and rape*. New York: Simon & Schuster.

Burchard, M. 2006. Feminist jurisprudence. *The Internet encyclopedia of philosophy*. http://iep.utm.edu/j/jurisfem.htm.

Cicero, M. 1985. *On the Commonwealth*. New York: Macmillan.

Clark, A. 1992. Humanity or justice? Wifebeating and the law in the eighteenth and nineteenth centuries. In *Regulating womanhood: Historical essays on marriage, motherhood and sexuality*, edited by C. Smart, pp. 187–220. London: Routledge.

Coole, D. 1993. *Women in political theory: From ancient misogyny to contemporary feminism*. 2nd ed. Boulder, CO: Lynne Rienner.

Dixon, S. 1992. Conclusion: The enduring theme. Domineering dowagers and scheming concubines. In *Stereotypes of women in power: Historical perspectives and revisionist views*, edited by B. Garlick, S. Dixon, and P. Allen, pp. 209–26. New York: Greenwood Press.

Dusky, L. 1996. *Still unequal: The shameful truth about women and justice in America*. New York: Crown.

Dworkin, A. 1993. Against the Male Flood: Censorship, Pornography, and Equality. In *Feminist Jurisprudence*, edited by P. Smith. New York: Oxford University Press.

Friedman, J. 1993. *America's first woman lawyer: The biography of Myra Bradwell*. Buffalo, NY: Prometheus Books.

Gage, M. 1980. *Woman, church and state: The original expose of male collaboration against the female sex*. Watertown, MA: Persephone Press.

Gest, T. 2001. Law schools' new female face. *U.S. News and World Report*. http://www.usnews.com (accessed on February 10, 2006).

Gilligan, C. 1982. *In a different voice: Psychological theory and women's development*. Cambridge, MA: Harvard University Press.

Grana, S. 2002. *Women and (in)justice: The criminal and civil effects of the common law on women's lives*. Boston: Allyn & Bacon.

Hall, D. 1995. Job satisfaction among male and female defense attorneys. *Justice System Journal* 18:121–37.

Haney, L. 2000. Feminist state theory: Applications to jurisprudence, criminology, and the welfare state. *Annual Review of Sociology* 26:641–66.

Harrington, M. 1994. *Women lawyers: Rewriting the rules*. New York: Alfred A. Knopf.

Held, A., S. Herndon, and D. Stager. 1997. Why the Equal Rights Amendment remains legally viable and properly before the states. *William and Mary Journal of Women and the Law* 3:113–36.

Hemmens, C., K. Strom, and E. Schlegel. 1998. Gender bias in the courts: A review of the literature. *Sociological Imagination* 35:22–42.

Hillard, T. 1992. On the stage; behind the curtain: Images of politically active women in the late Roman republic. In *Stereotypes of women in power: Historical perspectives and revisionist views,* edited by B. Garlick, S. Dixon, and P. Allen, pp. 37–64. Westport, CT: Greenwood Press.

Hollander, D., and R. Tallia. 1997. *The Princeton Review: The best law schools.* New York: Random House.

International Society for Human Rights. 2006. *Shariah law, adultery and rape.* http://www.steinigung.org/artikel/shaia_adultery_rape.htm.

Law School Admission Council. 2005. *Think about law school.* http://www.lsac.org. (accessed on February 10, 2006).

Mackinnon, C. 1993. Toward feminist jurisprudence. In *Feminist jurisprudence,* edited by P. Smith, pp. 449–66. Oxford: Oxford University Press.

Maguire, K., and A. Pastore, eds. 1998. *Sourcebook of criminal justice statistics, 1997.* Washington, DC: U.S. Department of Justice.

Martin, S., and N. Jurik. 1996. *Doing justice, doing gender.* Thousand Oaks, CA: Sage.

McIntyre, L. 1995. Law and the family in historical perspective: Issues and antecedents. *Marriage and Family Review* 21:5–30.

Meyers, L. 2004. Justice Ruth Bader Ginsberg weighs in on women's progress in the legal profession—and what kept them out for so long. *Cornell News.* http://www.news.cornell.edu (accessed on February 10, 2006).

Morash, M. 2006. *Understanding gender, crime, and justice.* Thousand Oaks, CA: Sage.

Morello, K. 1986. *The invisible bar: The woman lawyer in America 1638 to the present.* New York: Random House.

National Women's Law Center. 2001. *The Supreme Court and women's rights: Fundamental protections hang in the balance.* Washington, DC: Author.

Neufeld, A., C. Sanders, and K. Wilk. 2004. A study of women's experiences at Harvard Law School. Preliminary scholarly paper submission for "Emerging Voices" workshop in "Taking Stock: Women of All Colors in Law School" conference. http://www.aals.org (accessed on February 10, 2006).

Ollenburger, J. 1998. *Sociology of women: The intersection of patriarchy, capitalism, and colonization.* Upper Saddle River, NJ: Prentice Hall.

Pollitz Worden, A. 1997. Gender and professional values in the criminal bar. *Women and Criminal Justice* 8(3):1–28.

Pollock, J. 2006. Gender, justice, and social control. In *Women, law, and social control,* edited by A. Merlo and J. Pollock, pp. 3–31. Boston: Allyn & Bacon.

Sachs, A., and J. Wilson. 1978. *Sexism and the law: A study of male beliefs and legal bias in Britain and the United States.* New York: Free Press.

Smart, C. 1989. *Women, crime and criminology: A feminist critique.* London: Routledge and Kegan Paul.

Stohr, M., N. Lovrich, and G. Mays. 1997. Service v. security focus in training assessments: Testing gender differences among contemporary women's jail correctional officers. *Women and Criminal Justice* 9:65–85.

Stohr, M., N. Lovrich, and M. Wood. 1996. Service v. security concerns in contemporary jails: Testing behavior differences in training topic assessments. *Journal of Criminal Justice* 24:437–48.

Spohn, C. 1990. Decision making in sexual assault cases: Do black and female judges make a difference? *Women and Criminal Justice* 2:83–101.

Trifkovic, S. 2005. Islam and women: *The Christian Science Monitor's* distortion and the reality. *Chronicles Magazine* January. http://www.chroniclesmagazine/News/Trikovic05/NewsST010305.html.

Whittick, A. 1979. *Woman into citizen.* Santa Barbara, CA: ABC-Clio.

Wilson, M., and M. Daly. 1992. The man who mistook his wife for chattel. In *The adapted mind: Evolutionary psychology and the generation of culture,* edited by J. Barkow, L. Cosmides, and J. Tooby, pp. 289–326. New York: Oxford University Press.

Wollstonecraft, M. 1792/1967. *A vindication of the rights of woman.* New York: Norton.

Cases Cited

Bradwell v. Illinois, 83 U.S. 130 (1873).

Duren v. Missouri, 439 U.S. 357, 364 (1979).

Frontiero v. Richardson, 411 U.S. 677 (1973).

Hishon v. King and Spalding, 467 U.S. 69 (1984).

Kohn v. Royall, Koegel, and Wells, 496 F2d 1094 (1973).

Minor v. Happersett, 88 U.S. 162 (1874).

Nguyen v. INS, 533 U.S. 53 (2001).

Reed v. Reed (1971), 404 U.S. 71 (1971).

State v. Rhodes, 61 N.C. 453 (1868).

CHAPTER 13

RACIAL MINORITIES
AND THE LAW

Kevin O'Malley was born in 1964 in Toledo, Ohio, just three months after his parents emigrated from Ireland. Jake Paterson was born in the same year, three hundred years after his ancestors were dragged to these shores in chains. With identical Law School Admission Test scores, both young men applied to the prestigious University of Michigan law school in 1986. Kevin was denied because his score was at the fifty-fifth percentile for white applicants (the cutoff is the sixtieth percentile), but Jake was admitted because his score placed him at the ninetieth percentile for black applicants.

Affirmative action is a way of trying to put things right for the Jakes of America, but is it right to do it at the expense of the Kevins? Jake's ancestors may have been wronged but not by Kevin's ancestors. Kevin's father was a line worker in a glass factory, Jake's an assistant high school principal, so need did not enter the law school's decision. Do different standards for different races drive wedges between them? Haven't we defined race-based treatment in the past as racism? Doesn't the paternalism inherent in preferential treatment imply inferiority, and doesn't it fly in the face of the American values of meritocracy and self-reliance? The Constitution is about individual rights, not group rights, so how is affirmative action justified?

One of the justifications is that schools and neighborhoods are resegregating, taking us back to a divided nation of mutually hostile groups. Do we want that, and, if not, how else can we achieve racial harmony and social equality? The worst abuses of affirmative action, such as racial quotas and different standards, have gone. Supreme Court decisions in 2003 outlawed awarding admission "points" based on race but allowed race to be taken into account if (1) there is an important state interest (such as a diverse workforce) involved, and (2) there is no other way to achieve the goal. As you read this chapter, think about whether affirmative action is the final step in acknowledging the wrong we have done to minorities in the past or if it perpetuates racist ideas of inferiority.

INTRODUCTION

The nation that was to become the United States has been bedeviled by race almost from the moment the first white settlers landed in the New World. The presence of Native American Indians, the odious practice of slavery, and the immigration of peoples from the Asian continent virtually assured that racial relations would be contentious and would require the continual actions of the law to settle the multitude of issues that arise in a multiracial/multiethnic society. These issues arose (and still arise) as peoples of different racial/ethnic groups whose collective identities differ from that of the dominant group have understandably demanded recognition of their status as equal citizens before the law and effective representation in the decision-making institutions of our society.

The United Nations Declaration on Minorities insists that the rights of minorities can only exist within the framework of democracy (Wheatley 2003). By its very nature, democracy is responsive to "the will of the people"; that is, the majority of the people. "The greatest good for the greatest number" is a noble principle in a racially homogeneous society, but in a diverse society such as the United States, the relationship between the majority will and individual rights for *all* people is problematic. This is where an independent judiciary, free of the politician's need to be responsive to those who elect him or her, should step in and apply rules of law and justice that may be at odds with the popular "will." As Immanuel Kant put it, "for law to be legitimate it must enjoy the united and consenting will of all [not just the majority]" (Wheatley 2003, 510).

To expect the courts to transcend the social and political contexts in which they are embedded is to harbor an overly romanticized vision. They can only go so far if they are not supported by the legislative and executive branches of government. In cases concerning minority rights, the Supreme Court has almost inevitably sided with what the majority of the people in the United States wanted—to keep minority group members "in their place" and to affirm the superiority of the white race. Even when state and federal legislation had been passed granting minorities certain rights, the Supreme Court justices often saw it their duty to rule that legislation unconstitutional.

AFRICAN AMERICANS

Slavery and the Law

Slavery is as old as human history, and few practices instituted by human beings are more repulsive. The first African slaves landed in America in 1619, and by 1860, they numbered 4,441,830, according to the Census of that year (Clarke 1998). The terms "slavery" or "slave" do not appear in the Constitution of the United States. In fact, it is sometimes claimed that the Declaration of Independence and the Constitution contain language that can be interpreted as having outlawed slavery (Wiecek 2000). Such claims invoke the phases reminiscent of natural law in those documents such as "inalienable rights" to buttress their claims. Others claim that the English case of *Somerset v. Stewart* (see chapter 10) should have been followed and all slaves freed because "the precedent had become part of American common law" (Wiecek 2000, 2452). Had the *Somerset* precedent been followed, slaves would have been freed and the Civil War avoided.

The Constitution does contain language clearly supporting slavery. Article I, Section 9, affirms the rights of the Southern states to allow "the migration or importation of such persons as any of the States now existing shall think proper to admit." Article I, section 2, refers to "free Persons" and "three-fifths of all other Persons," a reference based on the belief that slave labor was three fifths as productive as free labor. Slaves were only included in the count for the purpose of improving the representation of the Southern states in the House of Representatives. Finally, Article IV, section 2, states "No person held to service in one State, under the Laws thereof, escaping into another shall, in Consequence of any law or Regulation therein, be discharged from such Service of Labor, but shall be delivered up on claim of the Party whom such service or Labour be due." The need to placate the Southern states and property rights claims clearly trumped both natural law and *Somerset*, and the die was set for two-hundred-plus years of court battles aimed at securing the status of "we the people" for African Americans.

The *Amistad* Case

An important moral step in this direction was the *Amistad* case, which may be familiar to students from the 1997 movie of the same name. In 1839, African slaves being transported to Cuba aboard the Spanish ship *Amistad* revolted and killed all but two of their captors, whom they needed to navigate the ship back to Africa. The navigators took the ship to New York instead, where the remaining Africans were captured and held while the courts decided what should become of them. The case of the African captives, led by Sengbe Pieh, who has gone down in American history as Joseph Cinque, attracted attention from abolitionists anxious to gain moral support for the abolition of slavery and from Southerner slaveholders fearful of the impact of a court decision on the institution of slavery. Joseph Cinque and his fellow captives were represented by former-President of the United States John Quincy Adams, who argued for them before the Supreme Court. A federal district court judge had previously ruled in favor of Cinque, but proslavery President Van Buren ordered the prosecutor to appeal to the Supreme Court.

Adams argued that the Africans had been kidnapped in Africa and held against their will and thus had every right to act in any way necessary to secure their freedom. The contesting claim came from the Spanish government, which wanted them tried for murder and piracy, a claim with which Van Buren sympathized. Adams argued for the Africans' freedom on the basis of the natural law principles found in the Declaration of Independence, while at the same time claiming that his moral argument had no bearing on the slavery interests of the Southern states. The Court agreed with him, ordering the "kidnapped Africans" released and returned to Africa.

According to Howard Jones (2002, 25), although the Africans had been freed on a strictly legal basis (their capture was in violation of an Anglo-Spanish treaty against the slave trade), "it left the public impression that the American judicial system had dealt a severe blow to slavery by exalting the sanctity of freedom."

He further stated that the decision "constituted a landmark ruling against slavery" because "[b]lack people had brought suit on behalf of their rights as human beings and, whether on the basis of law or morality, went free." The case (*United States, Appellants v. The Libellants and Claimants of the Schooner Amistad*, 1841) exacerbated the bitter feelings between slave and nonslave states and helped to cement their respective attitudes about slavery.

The *Dred Scott* Case

Chief Justice Roger Taney was openly proslavery and saw his chance to rectify the "damage" to the institution of slavery caused by the *Amistad* case in *Scott v. Sandford* (1857). Dred Scott was born into slavery in St. Louis, Missouri. Under the **Missouri Compromise** of 1820, Missouri was the only slave state formed from the territory gained by the Louisiana Purchase. Scott was sold by his first owners to John Emerson, an army physician who took him to Illinois, a free state, and then to the free Wisconsin territory.

Scott and his wife Harriet returned to St. Louis with Emerson in 1840, ending a seven-year sojourn in free territory. In 1846, Scott petitioned for his freedom based on his stay in free territory. Such petitions were not unusual in Missouri and mostly successful for slaves who had sojourned in free states. Court rulings in such cases were typically based on *Somerset*, which, Wang (2002, 31) reminds us, ruled "that the status of 'slave' was so contrary to the common law and natural law that it could not be supported by specific positive legislation." The impact of *Somerset* was somewhat undermined by another English case (*The Slave, Grace*, 1827) in which the High Court ruled "that once a slave returned to a slave jurisdiction then the law of England would no longer be in force and his status would again be determined by the laws of the slaver jurisdiction" (Wang 2002, 32). The Missouri courts took little notice of this case at this time, but the case was cited in concurring opinions in the subsequent *Scott v. Sandford* case argued before the United States Supreme Court.

A Missouri district court awarded Scott his freedom in 1850, but Irene Emerson (John's widow) appealed to the Missouri Supreme Court. Irene's brother, John Sanford (his name was misspelled in *Scott v. Sandford*) now acted on her behalf. Unfortunately for Scott, a number of significant political changes had taken place in the meantime. Northern and Southern states were again embroiled with the issue of whether slavery should be allowed in the new territories acquired by the United States in the Mexican-American War, and proslavery Thomas Benton had become U.S. Senator for Missouri. This combination of events led the Missouri Supreme Court in 1852 to reverse the lower court decision, and it did so explicitly on political rather than legal grounds.

Lawyers for Scott then decided to take the case to the United States Supreme Court on the basis that the case was a dispute between citizens of different states (Sanford lived in New York and Scott in Missouri). At issue in the case was far more than securing Scott's freedom; it was really about securing a Supreme Court ruling on the status of slavery. Justice Taney's decision contained his opinion that under Article III of the Constitution, no black person, even if free, could be a citizen of the United States and thus could not bring suit in the federal courts. The Court could have simply denied certiorari to Scott and let the Missouri decision stand, but it plainly wanted to use the case to make a pronouncement on slavery because the issue was tearing at the heart of the nation (McClosky 1994).

The Court ruled that blacks were "altogether unfit to associate with the white race either in social or political relations; and so far inferior, that they have no rights which the white man was bound to respect" (quoted in Abadinsky, 2003, 62). Scott's claim to have been free because of his sojourn in free territory was denied because the Court said that Congress had limited jurisdiction in the territories (lands that were not yet granted statehood) and therefore could not forbid slavery in them. The claim also ran afoul on Fifth Amendment grounds that barred the law from depriving anyone of their property (as a slave, Scott was "property") without due process of law. Thus, although the issue was not before it, the Court also ruled the Missouri Compromise unconstitutional.

The constitutionality of the Missouri Compromise was a moot point in 1857 since Congress had already repealed it with the passage of the **Kansas-Nebraska Act** of 1854, which opened up areas of the West to slavery. This act was widely interpreted at the time as a precursor to legalizing slavery throughout the United States, and it precipitated its own "mini" civil war between proslavery and antislavery factions in "bleeding Kansas" (Brinkley et al. 1991, 392). What the Supreme Court had done in *Scott* was to put its stamp of approval on slavery. Some also saw the ruling as settling the issue of slavery and thus ending the movement toward sectionalism between the North and the South. Of course, it had the opposite effect, and it took the Civil War to finally put an end to slavery. Parenthetically, Scott did achieve his freedom in 1857 when the sons of his first owner purchased it for him. Sadly, he died sixteen months later (Wang 2002).

Emancipation and the Reconstruction Period

The American Civil War (which began April 12–13, 1861) was fought to preserve the Union, not to free the slaves. Of course, slavery was a major factor leading up to the war, making it almost inevitable. Northern and Southern economies and cultures had diverged in a number of fundamental ways because of slavery. The industrial North opposed slavery primarily because of the fear that its spread would imperil the economic position of free white workers, and the agricultural South supported it because it was the very foundation of its economy.

As the war progressed, the North began to see its objective as freeing the slaves as well as preserving the Union. This objective had a military as well as a moral purpose because the South relied heavily on slaves to man the factories, farms, mines, and shipyards, and a proclamation of emancipation would sow discontent and mutiny among them. The first part of Abraham Lincoln's **Emancipation Proclamation** was issued in September 1862 and freed the slaves in all states in rebellion but not in slave states loyal to the Union since it may have driven them into the arms of the Confederacy. The final Proclamation was issued in January 1863.

To forestall any postwar effort to have the Emancipation Proclamation ruled unconstitutional as a simple military order (remember, only Congress, not the executive branch, can make law), President Lincoln pressed Congress to pass the Thirteenth Amendment, banning slavery within the United States and territories, which it did in 1865. This amendment legally ended slavery in America after two hundred years. By this time, however, almost all slaves had been freed by other means, such as state legislation or federal compensation to slave owners.

Blacks fared better in the immediate aftermath of the Civil War, in the period known as **Reconstruction** (reestablishment and reorganization of the seceded Southern states). However, they were not prepared to succeed in white society even if they had been welcomed into it. Legally released from bondage, some did not leave their former masters, and others left with nothing but the clothes on their backs and a few meager possessions. The federal government made attempts to help the emancipated slaves by keeping troops in the South to protect them and by establishing the **Freedman's Bureau**. This Bureau provided former slaves with food, clothing, schools, and even land that had been abandoned or confiscated. With federal troops to protect them, for a short time "Southern blacks voted in extraordinary numbers, electing hundreds of black officeholders. Black jury service was common; streetcars were generally desegregated; and blacks finally gained access to public education" (Klarman 2004, 10).

Nevertheless, many Southern jurisdictions were seeking to recreate slavery in new legal forms that came to be known as the **Black Codes**. The codes were enacted under the assumption that blacks would not work unless compelled to do so. These codes controlled, restricted, and inhibited the movements and behavior of ex-slaves almost as totally as slavery itself had. Codes authorized local authorities to arrest unemployed blacks and to fine them for vagrancy. These vagrancy laws supplied white enterprises with a plentiful supply of black laborers because blacks arrested on any pretext had the "choice" of paying a fine or working for an employer who paid his or her fine. The employer could then work the unfortunate "vagrant without compensation until he had repaid the debt to the employer's satisfaction" (Clarke 1998, 69). Justices of the peace and law enforcement officers literally made their living arresting and sentencing "vagrants," and those who paid their fines made handsome profits from their labor.

The U.S. Congress struck back at the Black Codes by passing the *Fourteenth Amendment* in 1868, which declared that all persons born or naturalized in the United States were citizens of both the United States and of the state where they live. Congress still left the question of suffrage for blacks to the individual states, but both Northern and Southern states were very reluctant to grant it. In response to this reluctance, Congress passed the Fifteenth Amendment in 1870, granting suffrage to African American males. Section 1 of this amendment reads, "The right of citizens of the United States to vote shall not be denied or abridged by the United States or by any State on account of race, color, or previous condition of servitude."

The Emergence of Jim Crow Laws

Jim Crow laws were essentially any state or federal laws that enforced the segregation of the races. According to C. Van Woodward (1974), the origin of the term "Jim Crow" lies in an 1832 song and dance routine of the same name. The philosophical underpinning of these laws was **racism**. Racism is a form of bigotry more insidious than other forms, such as xenophobia and ethnocentrism. The latter forms involve fear and dislike of out-groups and attitudes of in-group superiority, but those attitudes may be eased by contact and assimilation. Racism, however, is not alleviated by contact and assimilation because its victims are not despised and persecuted because they have had little contact with their persecutors but usually because they have had too much. Jim Crow racism was thus a combination of overt bigotry, a belief in the innate inferiority of blacks, and support for legal and normative segregation of the races (Bobo and Kluegel 1997).

In response to increasing Jim Crowism, Congress passed the Civil Rights Act of 1875 stipulating that all persons were entitled to full access and enjoyment of all accommodations and facilities in public places. Despite this act, blacks were routinely denied access to such facilities, which led to five cases from five states coming before the Supreme Court, which were collectively referred to as *The Civil Rights Cases* (1883). In those cases, the Court ruled that the Fourteenth Amendment protected blacks only from state discrimination, not from discrimination by businesses and individuals. It also ruled that the Civil Rights Act was unconstitutional because it sought to control the legislative power of the individual states, thereby violating the Tenth Amendment, which reserves all powers not granted to the federal government to the states.

Following this decision, Southern states began enacting sweeping segregation legislation stipulating complete separation of the races in all spheres of life. Some states under Democratic control even enacted statutes such as the poll tax and literacy tests in efforts to disenfranchise (taking away the right to vote) blacks. By the 1890s, virtually all forms of integration had disappeared in the South (Klarman 2004, 11).

Segregation, Disenfranchisement, and the *Plessy* and *Williams* Cases

Most states were not overly troubled with granting *civil* rights (the right to sue, engage in contracts, own property, and so on) to blacks, but balked at granting them *political* rights (the right to vote, hold political office, or serve on juries) and, most of all, *social* rights (the right to mingle with whites in any capacity). Although social rights were less important than civil and political rights in a practical sense, the lack of them was more objectionable to blacks because it marked them as inferior and unfit to come into close proximity to whites. In common with many other states, Louisiana passed a statute decreeing that all railroad companies must provide separate but equal accommodations for black and white passengers as part of efforts to legally keep the races separate.

In 1892, a committee of mixed-race (black, white, and American Indian) Creoles calling themselves the *Comite des Citoyens* (citizen's committee) decided to test this statute by arranging for Homer Plessy to sit in a whites-only railroad car and to inform the conductor that according to Louisiana law, he was "colored." In fact, Plessey was seven eighths white and was physically indistinguishable from a white person (Davis 2002). This fact did not matter because one was either "pure" white or nonwhite, a simple racial dichotomy to which the *Comite des Citoyens* objected. Plessy was arrested, refused to identify his race, was found guilty, and appealed his case to the Supreme Court.

The issue before the Court in *Plessy v. Ferguson* (1896) was the reasonableness of the Louisiana statute; that is, in passing this bill, did the legislature act with reference to the traditions and customs of the people of Louisiana? Plessy's lawyers argued that the Fourteenth Amendment outlawed race as a legal distinction and that race was only a social construction, and because of this, no law could exist to classify anyone into a distinct racial category. The Court disagreed, ruling that "separate but equal" laws were not repugnant to the Fourteenth Amendment because they did not impact the legal equality of the races. It also dismissed Plessy's claim that race did not exist as "absurd"; Justice Brown, delivering the opinion, stated, "We consider the underlying fallacy of the plaintiff's argument to consist in the assumption that the enforced separation of the two races stamps the colored race with a badge of inferiority. If this be so, it is not by reason of anything found in the act, but solely because the colored race chooses to put that construction upon it" (quoted in Klarman 2004, 21). The Supreme Court thus placed its stamp of approval on states' efforts to deny social rights to blacks.

Two years after *Plessy*, the Court heard an important case regarding states' efforts to disenfranchise blacks. The Fifteenth Amendment prohibited the states from denying males the right to vote based on race. The issue for Southern states became how to deny blacks the vote without seeming to do it on the basis of race. Two methods were the poll tax and the literacy test. These methods reduced the black vote by 62 percent by the 1890s. They also reduced the white vote by 26 percent, but this was alleviated somewhat with the passage of "grandfather clauses," allowing anyone whose ancestors had voted to vote also (Brinkley et al. 1991). The constitutionality of these obvious shenanigans was tested in *Williams v. State of Mississippi* in 1898.

In 1896, African American Henry Williams was indicted for the crime of murder by a grand jury composed entirely of white men. Williams claimed that the way in which the jury was summoned, selected, and charged violated the Fourteenth Amendment in that it systematically excluded blacks and resulted in a biased, all-white jury. Williams was challenging the literacy tests used to exclude blacks from serving on juries as well as from voting. The Court interpreted the tests as excluding blacks on the basis of literacy, not race, because the tests also excluded illiterate whites not covered by grandfather clauses. Thus the tests did not violate the Fourteenth or Fifteenth Amendments. Determining voter eligibility standards was ruled to be within the prerogative of the individual states under the Tenth Amendment. The Court was evidently willing to let the Southern states do as they pleased with respect to voting standards as long as they did not violate the exact letter of the Fourteenth or Fifteenth Amendments. And so *Plessy* and *Williams* were sown into the patchwork of the Southern states' Jim Crow laws that stripped blacks of the rights they had gained during Reconstruction. Disenfranchisement was so effective that by "the turn of the century the last black Congressman left office, and virtually all black people in the south were disenfranchised" (Pinkney 1969, 30).

Lynching and Black Protest

Two black leaders emerged in this era of robust Jim Crowism with radically different ideas about how blacks should respond: Booker T. Washington and W. E. B. DuBois. Washington implied that black "deficiencies" rather than white discrimination were responsible for their condition and that they should appease whites by keeping their distance and engaging in hard (manual) work. This point of view was applauded by whites as a vindication of their own views, but blacks understandably did not accept it. The chief opponent of Washington's philosophy was DuBois, who counseled that blacks should aspire to higher education and not be content with manual work and that they should agitate for the restoration of their rights.

With the help of progressive whites, DuBois founded the **National Association for the Advancement of Colored People** (NAACP) in 1910. The most pressing issue for the NAACP at this time was the sadistic practice of lynching. According to the Constitutional Rights Foundation (2005), between 1892 and 1968, in the United States, 4,743 persons (over 70 percent black) were lynched. Black soldiers who had fought "to make the world safe for democracy" in World War I noted the irony in that slogan upon their return to the United States. This resulted in a rise in black militancy and in NAACP membership, but it also precipitated a violent white backlash. In the aftermath of the war, there was a revival of the Ku Klux Klan (KKK), numerous white race riots, and an increase in lynching, from thirty-six cases in 1917 to seventy-six in 1919 (Klarman 2004). Although many states had antilynching laws, the federal government did not. In 1918, Missouri Congressman Leonidas Dyer introduced the Dyer Anti-Lynching Bill in Congress, but it was halted by a filibuster in the Senate. Another antilynching law known as the Gavagan Bill was again killed by filibusters in the Senate (Constitutional Rights Foundation 2005). Incredibly, the federal government did not pass an antilynching law until the passage of the 1968 Civil Rights Act.

The most significant test of the 1968 Act came in 1981 when the FBI were called in to investigate the lynching of Michael Donald. He was chosen as a victim at random because of the anger of two young white men at a jury's failure to convict a black man for the murder of a white police officer. The FBI arrested James Knowles who confessed to the murder and who testified against his coconspirator, Henry Hays, the son of the second highest ranking KKK member in Alabama. Knowles was sentenced to life imprisonment; Hays was sentenced to death and executed in 1997. Hays was the first white man since 1913 to be executed for murdering a black man. The Southern Poverty Law Center filed a civil suit on behalf of Michael's mother, and an all-white jury found the KKK culpable for the death of Michael Donald and ordered punitive damages of $7 million. To comply with this order, the KKK had to hand over all its assets and skulk off into virtual oblivion (Spartacus 2005).

"We Shall Overcome"

World War II signaled the beginning of the end of Jim Crow. Many blacks migrated from the South to fill the vacancies left by military draftees in the factories flush with orders for war-related materials. Being confronted with less white animosity than they endured in the South, blacks became less subservient and more demanding of their basic rights. These demands, coupled with a growing belief among whites that the demands were justified, led to a series of executive, legislative, and judicial actions that began digging Jim Crow's grave, although he was still far from dead. The executive orders began with Franklin D. Roosevelt's *Fair Employment Practices Committee* and Harry Truman's *Commission on Higher Education* and his ordering of full integration in the armed forces (D'Sousa 1995). Significantly, these orders were in response to growing black militancy (such as a threatened march on Washington in 1941 in support of integration in the workplace) rather than on any real executive concern with black issues (Brinkley et al. 1991).

The first significant post–World War II Supreme Court ruling on black rights came in *Smith v. Allwright* (1944). Some states in the South held all-white primaries, legally justifying it by declaring the Democratic Party to be a "volunteer organization." The Texas Supreme Court had declared the Democratic Party of Texas to be such an organization, enabling county election official Allwright to deny Lonnie Smith the right to vote in the 1940 Texas Democratic primary. Allwright claimed that under the ruling made in *Civil Rights Cases* of 1883, the Court had no power to influence private (nonstate) discrimination. The Court disagreed, ruling that the practice violated the Fifteenth Amendment because primaries are conduced under state statutory authority.

According to Klarman (2004, 454–58), "*Smith v. Allwright* launched a revolution in politics in the urban South" because the "NAACP constantly threatened registrars and party officials with criminal liability if they defied *Smith*." As in any endeavor, success breeds success, so in many ways the *Smith* decision paved the way for the most important civil rights case of the twentieth century, *Brown v. Board of Education* (1954), which ended racial segregation in American schools.

The *Brown* decision provoked a violent backlash in the South and ushered into power politicians who ran on platforms accusing their opponents of being "soft on race" just as many current politicians accuse their opponents of being soft on crime. Several cases related to the ruling (including *Brown II* in 1955) occurred in the face of numerous efforts on behalf of various schoolboards to circumvent the ruling. Only twenty-three black children, a mere 0.001 percent of black schoolchildren, were in schools with white children in the South prior to *Brown*; in the two years afterward, there were 0.13 percent; and ten years later, (1963–1964) the proportion was only 1.2 percent (Rosenberg 1991).

Why was there such massive resistance to *Brown* relative to the minimal resistance generated by *Smith*? As indicated earlier, granting social rights to black citizens was on the top of the hierarchy of white fears. Exercising civil and political rights mixes the races only briefly for a definite purpose, but exercising social rights might do so at an unacceptably intimate level. Even during Reconstruction, all Southern schools were segregated, even as black males voted in large numbers. In the late 1940s, a plurality of Southerners supported the rights of blacks to vote and to attend professional and graduate schools with whites, while at the same time they "ferociously resisted grade school desegregation" (Klarman 2004, 456).

Congressional Activity

The picture changed dramatically after Congress passed the **Civil Rights Act of 1964**. This act gave federal officials the power to bring desegregation suits on behalf of individuals and the power to withhold federal funds to school districts practicing racial discrimination. Unlike the miniscule changes following *Brown*, 91.3 percent of Southern black schoolchildren were in desegregated schools by 1972–1973 (Rosenberg 1991, 50). Thus the legislative branch, with its power of the purse, had a much deeper impact than the judicial branch. Judicial rulings can always be ignored, wrongly interpreted, or willfully "misinterpreted," thus necessitating further legal battles and long delays, whereas the legislative branch has the ability to withhold funds almost immediately upon being made aware of a violation of its rulings.

A similar situation existed relative to voting rights after *Smith v. Allwright*. Prior to this ruling, only 5 percent of Southern blacks of voting age were registered to vote, and after the ruling, 12 percent were registered in 1947. However, the United States Congress passed the **Voting Rights Act of 1965** and things changed dramatically. This act provided for federal supervision of county voter registration sites and prohibited the use of literacy tests. (The poll tax had been declared unconstitutional by the Twenty-Fourth Amendment in 1964.) Following the passage of this act, the percentage of voting-age blacks in the South registered to vote rose to 66.9 by 1970 (Rosenberg 1991, 61).

The Supreme Court upheld the constitutionality of the 1964 Civil Rights Act in *Heart of Atlanta Motel v. United States* (1964) and the Voting Rights Act in *South Carolina v. Katzenbach* (1966). In its rulings, the Court used language 180 degrees from the language used to render similar legislative efforts unconstitutional in previous cases (United State Department of Justice, 2005b), indicating that the Court responds to the political and social pressures of the moment more than it cares to acknowledge.

The Cold War and International Pressure

Smith and *Brown* gave legitimacy, support, and impetus to black protest movements and precipitated an unprecedented level of activism. Demonstrations, marches, and sit-ins all over the South and the often vicious police response to them were viewed all over the United States through the medium of television. Watching this go on day after day generated a lot of white sympathy for the black cause, just as the novel *Uncle Tom's Cabin* had done for abolitionist sentiment over a century before. The big difference in the *Brown* case was that the audience was international as well as national, and international opinion was no longer irrelevant to American politicians.

The United States emerged from World War II as a superpower with an ideology based on the ideals of democracy and free enterprise. The Soviet Union also emerged from the war as a superpower but with communist ideals of one-party rule and state control of the economy. It was inevitable that the two countries would become enemies, but fortunately for the world at large, and for blacks in particular, the so-called **Cold War** (which lasted from the end of World War II until 1989) was fought only with propaganda. The United States and the Soviet Union were competing for "the hearts and minds of men" on the world stage, and the "Negro problem" proved to be a profound embarrassment for the United States as well as a powerful propaganda weapon for the Soviet Union (Dudziak 2000).

The U.S. government's efforts to polish its image had a large impact on civil rights policies. The State Department strongly urged civil rights reforms, and President Truman's controversial order desegregating the military was defended because segregation was "damaging to our country's reputation with millions of people around the world" (quoted in Klarman 2004, 183). Even though President Eisenhower's segregationist sentiments were well known, his government attorneys filed an amicus brief in *Brown v. Board of Education* specifically arguing that school segregation should be invalidated, not on moral grounds but because "[r]acial discrimination furnishes grist for the Communist propaganda mill" (quoted in Klarman 2004, 299). The government filed briefs in almost all racial civil rights cases coming before the Supreme Court during the period, urging it to view the issue through a Cold War lens (Dudziak 2000).

How Far Have We Come?

Racial civil, political, and social equality is now a fact enshrined in the law of the land and accepted by all but the most reactionary racists. As Bobo and Kluegel (1997, 93) put it, "Most whites now endorse integration in principle and reject discrimination, preferring instead equal treatment regardless of race. Most whites also deny that blacks are innately inferior to whites." Further indicative of present-day white acceptance is the fact that between 1967 and 1993, blacks won mayoral races in eighty-seven cities across the United States, mostly because of white support, because in two thirds of these cities blacks were a minority of the population (Thernstrom and Thernstrom 1997). Depending on one's politics or the reach of one's vision about what government and its laws can accomplish, the civil rights revolution may be seen as lying anywhere on a continuum between "a rousing success" and "still a long way to go."

If W. E. B. DuBois could gaze on what has been accomplished in the almost hundred years after the founding of the NAACP, he would be astounded at the progress we have made. He would learn of two successive African American secretaries of state, two Supreme Court justices, and countless other blacks in high-ranking positions in the government, military, business, education, and all other spheres of life. If he would be astounded by the African Americans in these positions, he would be thunderstruck, bowled over, and wordless to hear that a black man named Barack Hussein Obama, "whose name shouts its Third World otherness" (J. Harris and Davidson 2009, 2), was elected to the office of president of the United States. Although Obama garnered over 95 percent of the black vote, he could not have won without substantial white support. In fact, he received more of the white vote than Democratic candidate John Kerry received in the previous presidential election and even received the majority of the white vote in traditionally Democratic states such as Vermont (68 percent) and Oregon (60 percent) (Caswell 2009). Numerous pundits have even claimed that Obama won the race precisely *because* he is black (Ansolabehere and Stewart 2009). Obama's razor-thin résumé and his association with anti-American radicals such as Jeremiah Wright, Bill Ayers, Bernadine Dohrn, and Michael Pfleger would have been more than enough to sabotage the campaign of any white candidate.

DuBois would also be amazed to discover that not only are his people not denied access to prestigious occupations anymore, but, because of affirmative action programs, they are actually accorded preferential treatment and consequently have moved into those occupations at a more rapid rate than whites (Wilson, Sakura-Lemessy, and West 1999). He would see that we have a national holiday celebrating the life of Martin Luther King, Jr., and that Dr. King is the only individual of any race so honored, since even George Washington has been absorbed into a generic Presidents' Day.

He would be disappointed to find that there is a greater percentage of African Americans in poverty than any other racial group, but his hard-headed philosophy of self-help would preclude him from blaming this on white society (Gabbidon 2001). He would weep with joy to hear African American economist Glen Loury (1995, 200) say that "we are the most privileged, empowered people of African descent anywhere on the globe," and another African American economist, Walter Williams (2002, 2), saying that "[b]lacks spend enough money each year to make us, if we were a nation, the 14th richest." Finally, he would be most gratified to hear historians tell him that although the law has done its part in assuring equal rights, the black activism that he himself set in motion coupled with international pressure must take most of the credit.

AMERICAN INDIANS

The Early Years

Every minority group in America (and elsewhere) has a story of discrimination to tell, and the history of white malfeasance against American Indians is at least as horrific as that practiced against African Americans. By most accounts, it was worse because the United States, *as a matter of official policy*, practiced both physical and cultural genocide against the American Indians (Parrillo 2003). "If we need an index of discrimination against Native Americans," write Aguirre and Turner (1998, 105), "a tenfold drop [from their numbers prior to white expansion into their territories] in the size of the population is as good as any." The size of the Indian population before colonization in what is now the United States has been estimated to be between six and ten million, divided into approximately three hundred culturally and linguistically distinct tribes (Parrillo 2003). Much of that culture and most of those languages have been lost.

Early colonial relationships between whites and Indians ranged from peaceful coexistence to distrust and hostile confrontations. Hostilities increased as white settlers encroached more and more on Indian territories. Westward expansion saw the waxing and waning of white stereotypes of Indians. Early settlers greatly admired the Indians as "noble savages," with a "nobility of character" (D'Sousa 1995, 85). As white settlers moved west and encountered Indian opposition, the image of the "screaming, savage red man" emerged. Indians were enslaved in all thirteen colonies, with a 1708 Carolina settlement census showing 2,900 African slaves and 1,400 Indian slaves (French 2003). Indians proved more difficult than Africans to maintain in slavery, and the practice of Indian slavery soon disappeared.

The practice of physical genocide against the Indians began early. Massachusetts colony, for instance, paid cash bounties for Indian scalps, and many whites found the practice lucrative (Parrillo 2003). The Indians were still a powerful force to be reckoned with, however, and both the French and the British courted them during the French and Indian Wars (1754–1761). With the defeat of the French and with the threat of war with a growing confederation of powerful Indian tribes under the Ottawa chief, Pontiac, the British government issued the Proclamation Act of 1763. As we saw in chapter 10, the Proclamation Act forbade any further white settlement beyond the Appalachians; it also proclaimed that any land purchases from Indians without a representative of the royal government being present at the proceedings would be illegal. This essentially established the British government as the protector of Indian rights and the Indian tribes as its wards. As we have also seen, a number of historians see this act as a contributing cause of the American Revolution, although it was to become a template of the United States' own stance toward the Indians (Parrillo 2003).

In 1787, the Continental Congress passed the **Northwest Ordinance**, which provided for a survey of what was then the Northwest Territories (lands bounded by the Great Lakes, the Mississippi and Ohio rivers, Canada, and Pennsylvania) with regard to future white settlement. The Northwest Ordinance gave Congress rather than the states the sole right to trade with the Indians. Although the Ordinance promised to act in good faith toward the Indians, all of the territories were areas made off limits by the 1763 Proclamation Act.

In laying out the powers of the Congress, Article 1, Section 8 of the Constitution specifically recognizes the quasi-independent status of the Indians: the Congress shall have power "To regulate commerce with foreign nations, and among the several States, and with the Indian tribes." The **Treaty of Fort Pit** (the first of about 350 treaties made with the Indians) also implicitly recognized the sovereignty of the Indian nations and assured them that the United States had no designs on Indian lands (Wildethal 2003). This status began to change as land-hungry whites moved West and legal challenges began to arrive at the portals of the United States Supreme Court.

The Marshall Trilogy: Defining Indian Status

New definitions of Native American sovereignty emerged in three Supreme Court cases that have come to be known as the **Marshall Trilogy** (named after

Chief Justice John Marshall). Although the first of these cases (*Johnson v. McIntosh* 1823) was a land ownership dispute between whites, the Court used it to define the relationship of the federal government to the Indian nations. Joshua Johnson had purchased Indian land in 1773 under the legitimate authority of the British government, and William McIntosh purchased land from the United States in 1818, part of which overlapped Johnson's purchase. By all rules of law, Johnson should have prevailed, but the Court used the case to justify whittling away at Indian rights, violating "Euro-American individual property rights to place itself in a superior political position relative to tribal nations who were not even parties to the dispute" (Wilkins 1997, 31–32).

This "superiority" was enunciated by Marshall in an argument that has come to be known as the **Discovery Doctrine**. This doctrine asserted that the European power that "discovered" an area of the Western hemisphere is deemed to have sovereignty over it to the exclusion of other European powers and of indigenous peoples. Marshall stated that discovery gave the discovering nation and its successor, the United States, "an exclusive right to extinguish the Indian titles of occupancy, either by purchase or conquest" (quoted in Wilkins 1997, 368). The Court also asserted that Indians are merely "occupants" of the land, only "in possession" of land at the pleasure of the United States.

The next case in the trilogy, *Cherokee Nation v. Georgia* (1831), further clarified the legal status of the Indian nations. The Cherokees were one of the so-called five "civilized tribes" (the others were Choctaw, Chickasaw, Creek, and Seminole) whose lifestyle had become virtually indistinguishable from that of whites, even to the point of having a written constitution and owning black slaves. Unfortunately, their land was within the state of Georgia, which had been annexing it and asserting its authority over the Cherokee. Georgia's claims were buoyed by the 1830 **Indian Removal Act** that called for the removal of all Indians in the southeastern states to "Indian territory," an area that is now Oklahoma. The Cherokee Nation petitioned the Supreme Court for relief, citing its sovereign status as a foreign nation and its treaties with the federal government to that effect. The Court ruled that the Cherokee Nation was not a foreign nation with sovereign rights and thus did not have control of their lands, nor did it have standing to approach the Court as a Court of original jurisdiction because only sovereign political entities may do so. It further ruled that the Cherokee nation was a "domestic dependent nation" whose relationship to the government was that of ward to guardian.

The Cherokees won a legal victory in *Worcester v. Georgia* (1832), the third case in the trilogy (Samuel Worcester was a white missionary and a willing defendant in a test case against Indian removal and for Indian sovereignty). The Court defined the Cherokee in this case as a "distinct community" within the parameters of the original definition as a domestic dependent nation in which the laws of Georgia do not apply. This ruling established the doctrine that the federal government and not the individual states had authority in Indian affairs, but Georgia's encroachment on Cherokee lands continued without federal interference. Upon hearing of the Court's ruling, President Andrew Jackson is reported to have said, "John Marshall has rendered his decision, now let him enforce it" (quoted in Parrillo 2003, 250).

The Period of Removal and Physical Genocide

Under the Indian Removal Act, Indians all over the Southeast were rounded up and marched at gunpoint to Indian Territory (Oklahoma). In 1838–1839, the Cherokees were marched over one thousand miles in the dead of winter, losing 25 percent of their number to death along the way (French 2003). This event became known as the Trail of Tears and was the first of a long series of such trails or "long walks" suffered by Indian tribes across the country as the United States pursued its policy of Manifest Destiny.

Manifest Destiny was the ideological justification for the Mexican-American War (1846–1848), the annexation of Texas, the Gadsden Purchase (portions of what is today Arizona and New Mexico), and the resolution of the dispute with the British over Pacific Northwest territories. These territorial acquisitions brought many more Indian tribes, such as the Apache, Navaho, and Nez Perce, within the orbit of white American power.

In the year before the Cherokee Trail of Tears, the Dakota Sioux were expelled from thirty-five million acres of rich agricultural land east of the Mississippi River in exchange for promises of later payment. The money hallmarked for payment was instead used to assist white settlement on the land while many Sioux died from starvation and disease in their new lands (French 2003). The Dakota Sioux were moved farther west in 1851, again without the promised payment, which precipitated an Indian uprising. After being defeated, the Sioux were moved to Nebraska, where they replaced the Spotted Tail Sioux, who in turn replaced the Ponca Tribe, who were removed to Oklahoma.

This chain of events led to a significant federal court case resulting from a chief of the Ponca Tribe named Standing Bear illegally leaving the Oklahoma reservation. The two major issues in *Standing Bear v. Crook* (1879) were whether Indians had the right to leave the reservation and whether Indians were persons. General George Crook had asserted that Indians were not persons, and thus Standing Bear had no rights to petition the court for a writ of habeas corpus questioning the conditions of his arrest. The court ruled in favor of Standing Bear on both counts, stating that "an Indian is a person within the meaning of the law of the United States." According to Laurence French (2003, 13), this ruling "elevated Indians from the status of feral animals with bounties on their heads to 'persons,' albeit not equal to the white man," and signaled "the beginning of the end of physical genocide and forced the federal government to now focus on the destruction of Indian cultures instead of Indians per se."

The Assimilation Period and Cultural Genocide

The period of physical genocide on the Great Plains was marked by the wholesale destruction of the buffalo herds. This was mostly the doing of private enterprise, but it was encouraged by the government because given the almost total dependency of the plains Indians on the buffalo, the elimination of the herds would lead to the destruction of the Indians. It was the loss of the buffalo more than the losses suffered in the various wars that led to the plains Indians reluctantly moving onto the reservations where their cultures could be systematically eroded.

In 1871, Congress passed an act ending treaty making with the Indians, stating that henceforth all Indian matters would be handled by legislation (previous treaties would remain in effect unless Congress abolished them). Indian matters would thereafter be decided unilaterally by whites. The Supreme Court endorsed the right of Congress to abrogate Indian treaties in the *Cherokee Tobacco* case (1871), which upheld the federal government's right to tax Cherokee tobacco sales, in violation of an 1866 treaty. The termination of treaty making clearly stamped Indians as wards of the government and ushered in an era known as the **assimilation period**, which lasted until 1934.

Assimilation is a process of "outsiders" becoming integrated into the larger culture by adopting its values, attitudes, and practices. For the Indians, it meant giving up their cultures and becoming "civilized" and "Christianized." The agency in charge of these assimilative efforts was the **Bureau of Indian Affairs** (BIA), which was first established by the War Department in 1824. During the assimilation period, the BIA became responsible for all aspects of Indian life, such as providing food and other resources, running schools, dispensing justice, and, most importantly in the opinion of society, the eliminating of "heathen" and "godless" (i.e., nonwhite) practices.

Initially Indians dispensed their own justice for crimes committed by Indians against other Indians on the reservation. In *Ex Parte Crow Dog* (1883), the Supreme Court upheld this principle in reversing a federal district court conviction of Crow Dog who had been charged with the slaying of another Indian in Indian country. The BIA was among those who objected to this ruling, and in response, the Congress passed the **Major Crimes Act** of 1885. This act extended federal criminal jurisdiction over Indians, or any other person, in Indian country. The original seven offenses in this act became the Index crimes published yearly in the FBI's Uniform Crime Reports (French 2003). The Supreme Court upheld the constitutionality of the Major Crimes Act in *United States v. Kagama* (1886), further weakening Indian autonomy and strengthening the BIA.

The single biggest push toward the destruction of Indian cultures was probably the enactment of the **General Allotment Act** (also called the **Dawes Act**) of 1887. This act provided for the division of reservation lands into tracts that were to be allotted to individual members of the tribe in parcels of 160 acres each for a period of twenty-five years. Any land left over after the allotment would go to the United States and be sold, with the money "held in trust" by the United States government. Individuals who were able to make a success of their allotments over the twenty-five-year period would be awarded title to the land and American citizenship. Few Indians became the self-reliant farmers the act had hoped to create. Few had the background required for farming, and there was also cultural opposition to tearing up sacred ground. Additionally, whites succeeded in getting many Indians to sign over the land to them (Parrillo 2003).

Many tribes, especially the five "civilized tribes," actively resisted this transparent attempt to destroy the communal underpinnings of their cultures and were able to avoid it for a while. In response to this "intransigence," in 1898, Congress passed an act that imposed allotment of Indian lands in Oklahoma, which had been specifically designated as "Indian Territory," and severely curtailed the governing powers of the five tribes. As the Commissioner of Indian Affairs Thomas Morgan made plain in 1890, the Dawes Act had "become the settled policy of the government to break up reservations, destroy tribal relations, settle Indians upon their own homesteads, incorporate them into the national life, and deal with them not as nations or tribes or bands, but as individual citizens" (Nebraska Studies 2005). From the time of the Dawes Act to 1934, the Indians lost approximately two thirds of their lands to whites (McLemore 1983).

Indians who attempted to assimilate, however, found it difficult. Some states had Jim Crow laws for Indians as well as blacks, with separate facilities and sections in theaters and other establishments labeled "Whites," "Colored," and "Indian" (U.S. Department of Justice, 2005a), and they were denied citizenship. When John Elk, for instance, left his tribe and settled in Omaha, Nebraska, and tried to register to vote, he was rejected. In a landmark case, the Supreme Court rejected Elk's claim of his Fifteenth Amendment voting rights in *Elk v. Wilkins* (1884), stating that Indians were still in a state of "pupilage" and that the question of Indian citizenship would have to be decided by the Congress and "not for each Indian for himself" (Wildenthal 2003, 28).

The legal status of Indians hit its lowest point in *Lone Wolf v. Hitchcock* (1903). This case involved the government opening up land defined as "surplus" by the Dawes Act to white settlement. The land in question was occupied by the Comanche and Kiowa tribes in Oklahoma who naturally objected. Whites were settling the land even as the case wound its way to the Supreme Court. A unanimous Court rejected the Indian claim in upholding Congress's "plenary" (absolute, complete) power to abrogate treaties in "times of emergency," although Congress had claimed no such emergency, and the Court was unable to articulate one. In effect, the *Lone Wolf* ruling legitimized theft and was a clear violation of the taking clause of the Fifth Amendment, which provides for "just compensation" for property taken for public use.

The Beginning of the End of Cultural Genocide (With a Few Backward Steps)

The Congress finally conferred American citizenship on all Indians in the **Indian Citizenship Act** of 1924. Ten years later, in a radical turnaround in government policy, the Franklin Roosevelt administration enacted the **Indian Reorganization Act** of 1934. This act ended the practice of cultural genocide; encouraged Indians to revive their languages, religions, and customs; ended the allotment system; permitted reconsolidation of the individual plots into communal tribal lands; and gave preferences to Indians in gaining employment with the BIA. Nevertheless, tribal governments were pressured to adopt white-style political institutions, which generated internal tribal divisions, and the Interior Department still had the power to approve or reject tribal laws (Wildenthal 2003).

In 1953, Congress decided that it was time to terminate federal supervision of Indian tribes as soon as practical and passed a series of acts that are collectively known as the policy of **termination**. This policy was apparently meant to be a pro-Indian act designed to fully assimilate them into mainstream American life by encouraging individuals to leave reservations and move to urban areas. However, it had devastating consequences for terminated tribes. Federal funds for the running of reservations were promptly cut off, hospitals and other facilities shut down, tribes disintegrated, and the reservations themselves became counties of the states in which they were located and subject to state control and taxes. Although this supposedly accorded every individual Indian the same legal rights that whites enjoyed, it eliminated tribal sovereignty and law. The termination policy had the opposite effect of that which was intended in that it deprived the Indians of the resources they needed to become independent while at the same time eroding tribal sovereignty.

Because of its unpopularity among the Indians and of its negative consequences, efforts to implement termination all but ended by the 1960s, and the policy was officially renounced at President Nixon's insistence by the **Indian Self-Determination Act** (SDA) of 1975. Part of the government's turnaround may be laid at the door of increasing Indian militancy after the founding of the **American Indian Movement** (AIM) in 1968. The period between 1968 and the passage of the Self-Determination Act saw the occupation of Alcatraz Island by about six hundred Indians for a period of eighteen months, the ten-week armed standoff with the FBI at Wounded Knee on a Sioux reservation, the occupation of the BIA headquarters in Washington, D.C., and the "Trail of Broken Treaties" march on Washington. As was the case with black activism, these actions brought wide national and international exposure and sympathy to the Indian cause.

How Far Have We Come?

As is the case with African Americans, opinions relating to how far Indians have come in their quest for equality depend on one's politics and what one takes as the starting point. Certainly, Indians are less sovereign today than they were before Europeans "discovered" the Americas, but they are far more so than was the case one hundred years ago. According to Indian activist John Tahsuda (2003, 562), since the passage of the SDA we have seen refinement of self-determination policies to the point that it has become self-governance with "nearly complete control over federal programs." Similarly, since then federal and Supreme Court rulings have almost always been in favor of Indians. For instance, in *United States v. Sioux Nations of Indians* (1980), the Court ruled that the Sioux were entitled to compensation of over $100 million for the seizure of the Black Hills in 1877, and numerous other such rulings have favored Indians rights when they were opposed by individual, corporate, or state or federal government interests.

The major exceptions to generally favorable rulings have been the denial of criminal (*Oliphant v. Suquamish* 1978) and civil (*Nevada v. Hicks* 2001) jurisdiction over non-Indians in Indian country. The rationale for denying sovereignty in these areas is that the Indian Civil Rights Act of 1968 applied most of the Bill of Rights to Indians with exceptions that respected Indian tribal sovereignty but in doing so denied some rights to individuals. The act allows the establishment of tribal religions, does not require tribal criminal justice systems to provide attorneys for indigent offenders, and does not require them to provide the right to a jury trial in civil cases (Indian Civil Rights Act, 1968). By submitting to the overall sovereignty of the United States, the tribes must deal with non-Indian citizens in a manner acceptable to American law.

ASIAN AMERICANS

Asians (we focus only on the Chinese and Japanese here because they are the largest groups and arrived first) have suffered a great deal of prejudice and discrimination in the United States also. Chinese immigrants came to the United States voluntarily, and immediately upon arrival, they became the targets of legal and extralegal harassment. They were subjected to special taxes, barred from holding land or citizenship, and beaten, lynched, and driven out of towns all across the West. The conditions of their employment (sometimes referred to as the "coolie trade") often amounted to "a new system of slavery" (Kitano and Daniels 1995, 22). The Chinese also were subjected to stereotypes not much different from those applied to blacks: "They were accused of living in filth, harboring disease, being heathens, and, worst of all, being less than human. Their sexual habits were compared to those of animals; questions of character and honesty were constantly raised" (Kitano and Daniels 1995, 183–184).

The Chinese first started arriving in the United States as sojourners (immigrants who intended to eventually return home) after gold was discovered in California in 1848. Although previous legislative efforts to limit immigration from "undesirable" European countries by individual states had been ruled unconstitutional, the Congress passed the **Chinese Exclusion Act** of 1882 without legal challenge. Many Chinese still managed to enter the United States through loopholes (notably by falsely claiming U.S. relatives). The Exclusion Act was repealed by Congress in 1943, and at the same time, the Chinese were granted naturalization rights and immigration quotas (Kitano and Daniels 1995).

Although some states sometimes granted immigrant Chinese and Japanese naturalized citizenship, a California circuit court ruled *In Re Ah Yup* (1878) that only individuals of European or African origins were eligible to become citizens. The state of California even attempted to bar American-born Wong Kim Ark from reentering the United States under the Chinese Exclusion Act after he had made a short trip to China. This resulted in a landmark Supreme Court ruling that the government could not deny citizenship to anyone born in the United States (*United States v. Wong Kim Ark,* 1898). This did not mean that foreign-born Asians could become naturalized citizens; the Supreme Court explicitly stated that they could not in *Ozawa v. United States* (1922).

Asian Americans were allowed a greater level of assimilation than African Americans and had even been allowed into integrated schools by the early 1900s. The worst act of discrimination against any Asian group occurred in 1942, one month after the Japanese attack on Pearl Harbor. In response to this attack,

President Roosevelt issued Executive Order 9066 authorizing the evacuation and relocation of people of Japanese ancestry. This order was justified as a "military necessity," but very few of the many more numerous "enemy aliens" of German or Italian origin were likewise rounded up. More than 110,000 Japanese (most of them second- or third-generation Americans) were sent to camps or "relocation centers" across the Western states and forced to live under harsh physical and psychological conditions (Parrillo 2003).

Was it constitutional to imprison native-born Americans without trial because of their ancestry, even if the United States was at war with the country of their ancestry? The American Civil Liberties Union (ACLU) had been looking for a test case to answer this question and found one in Fred Korematsu. Korematsu was a second-generation American who was arrested for remaining illegally in an area deemed vulnerable to espionage and placed on five years probation. In *Korematsu v. United States* (1944), the Supreme Court ruled 6–3 that although internment was constitutionally suspect, it was justified during circumstances of wartime "emergency and peril" and that the government's need to protect against espionage outweighed Korematsu's rights. In another internment ruling (*Ex Parte Endo* 1944) handed down on the same day, however, the Court unanimously ruled that the government could not continue to detain a citizen (Mitsuye Endo) whom the government conceded was loyal to the United States.

The Endo case began the release of all detainees and the beginning of the struggle for redress. A 1948 act brought internment victims about 10 percent of what they had lost through their "relocation." Korematsu's original indictment was voided and his conviction reversed by a federal district court in 1983 (Daniels 2002). In 1988, each surviving detainee was awarded a tax-free payment of $20,000 and a formal government apology for violating their rights because of racial prejudice (Parrillo 2003).

Asian Americans Today

Compared to other racial groups, there are relatively few Chinese (2,433,000) or Japanese (797,000) in the United States today (Parrillo 2003), giving them less political "muscle" than most other minorities. Despite this lack, they have gone from being loathed as the "yellow peril" to being lauded as the "model minority." Compared with whites, Asian Americans today have a higher median family income, are more likely to be married and to have a college degree, and are less likely to be divorced (Reeves and Bennett 2003). Overall, Asians have assimilated into American culture well with relatively minimal legal conflict.

RACE, LAW, AND CONFLICT

This brief overview of the law as applied to minority issues in the United States may tend to give the reader a jaundiced view of the law. Indeed, there is much grist for the conflict view of law in this chapter, for we do not see much wheat of justice among the voluminous chaff of law. We have seen the Supreme Court put its imprimatur on slavery, segregation, the unilateral abrogation of treaties, forced assimilation, the denial of Indian sovereignty and the appropriation of their lands, and Japanese American internment. It is not too much of an exaggeration to claim that as far as minority relations go, the Court has functioned as a tool to legitimize the policies of the other two branches of government rather than as a separate branch designed to temper their excesses.

But let us not judge the errors of the past through the clearer lenses of our more enlightened times. The justices involved in the cases discussed in this chapter were men of their times who held all the prejudices that dominated those times. African Americans, Indians, Asians, women, and the white working classes were able to use the law in the latter half of the twentieth century to resist their domination, but in each case, it was activism (conflict) that provided the impetus. This conflict ranged from Rosa Parks' simple refusal to give up her seat on a Detroit bus to the worldwide propaganda conflict between the capitalist West and the communist East.

Our last task in this chapter is to examine the criminal justice system in terms of race as it exists today. The American criminal justice system has historically been shot through with racism, but is that still true? Some people insist on seeing racism wherever they look, while others consistently turn a blind eye to any suggestion that it exists.

IS TODAY'S CRIMINAL JUSTICE SYSTEM RACIST?

Claims of racism are tested most often by comparing white arrest rates with minority rates and by calculating average sentences for minorities and whites convicted of identical crimes. African Americans are arrested in numbers far exceeding what we would expect given their percentage of the general population. Comprising about 12.8 percent of the population, they consistently constitute about one third of all arrests for the FBI's index crimes contained in their annual Uniform Crime Reports (UCR). Among individuals arrested nationwide in 2005 for murder, rape, robbery, aggravated assault, burglary, larceny-theft, motor vehicle theft, and arson, African Americans constituted 47.2, 31.9, 53.3, 32.7, 27.0, 27.9, 34.1, and 20.4 percent, respectively (Federal Bureau of Investigaion 2006). Add to this the United States Department of Justice estimate that 30 percent of all African American males will be incarcerated at some time in their lives, as opposed to 4 percent of white males (Bonczar and Beck 1997), then perhaps the case can be made that the American criminal justice system is racist.

On the other hand, Asian Americans are arrested in numbers significantly less than expected from their proportion of the population. In 2005, Asian/Pacific Islanders were arrested for 1.1 percent of the homicides, 1.3 percent of the rapes, 0.6 percent of the robberies, 1.3 percent of the aggravated assaults, 1.0 percent of the burglaries, 1.3 percent of the larceny-thefts, 1.0 percent of the motor vehicle thefts, and 1.1 percent of the arsons (Federal Bureau of Investigaion 2006). This group constituted only 0.74 percent of the state and federal prison systems in 2002

(Sourcebook 2003). The Census Bureau (Reeves and Bennett 2003) reports that Asian/Pacific Islanders constitute 4.4 percent of the population, thus this group is underrepresented in the official crime figures by about the same proportion that blacks are overrepresented. Few criminologists would attribute this underrepresentation to pro-Asian bias in the criminal justice system.

Arrest data imply racial discrimination if they do not reflect the actual rate of minority offending; they do not imply it if they do reflect it. Studies comparing UCR arrest rates with victimization rates reported by the National Crime Victimization Survey (NCVS)—a semiannual survey of more than 100,000 people who are asked if they had been victims of a crime in the past six months and if so, the race and sex of the perpetrator—find that the two sources agree well with one another. For example, about 60 percent of robbery victims describe their assailants as African American, and about 60 percent of the suspects arrested for robbery are African American (Harris and Shaw 2001; O'Brien 2001).

A particularly useful study addressing this issue looked at over 335,000 violent crimes taken from the National Incident Based-Reporting System (NIBRS), which is slated to eventually replace the Uniform Crime Reports (UCR). NIBRS data identifies the race of both offenders and victims. Results from this study showed that white offenders had higher probabilities of arrest for robbery and assault (both aggravated and simple) than blacks, but there was no difference in the probability of arrest between the races for rape. The authors concluded that "disproportionately high arrest rates for black citizens is most likely attributable to differential involvement in reported crime than to racially biased law enforcement practices" (D'Alessio and Stolzenberg 2003, 1381). Differential black/white arrest rates thus appear to be due to black/white differences in participation in crime, just as arrest rates for males versus females, for young males versus older males, and for whites versus Asians reflect differences in crime participation rather than sexism, ageism, and antiwhite racism, respectively.

What about criminal sentences for African Americans? Do the more severe sentences typically received by black offenders reflect deserved punishment, or do they reflect additional punishment tacked on by a racist judiciary? Addressing this issue, criminologist Larry Siegel (2006, 578) writes, "Although critics of American race relations may think otherwise, research on sentencing has failed to show a definitive pattern of racial discrimination." Some studies do find that blacks receive harsher sentences, some that whites receive harsher sentences, and some find no race effect at all. There is widespread agreement on one point, however: the more stringent researchers are in controlling for the effects of legally relevant variables (crime seriousness and criminal record—factors that are supposed to influence the sentencing decision) the less likely they are to find racial discrimination (Siegel 2006).

On the other hand, a review of the sentencing literature by Tushar Kansal (2005, 17) concluded that "racial bias continues to pervade the U.S. criminal justice sentencing system [although] the effects of this bias are somewhat hidden, and become more apparent for certain types of defendants, such as young minority males, or for certain types of offenses, such as drug and property crimes, or may even have less to do with the race of the defendant than with the race of the victim." The issue is obviously a complex one that often evokes emotional responses and a selective view of the evidence.

Sentencing research combines a mix of variables and reports average effects. Among those average effects are a multitude of interacting variables that hide the specifics of what may be occurring. One judge may be racist and hand down harsh sentences for blacks, while another may feel duty-bound to compensate for past racial injustices by handing down lenient sentences for blacks. The net effect for all sentences handed down by these two judges will be race neutral, with each judge canceling out the effect of the other. Uhlman (1979) found that African American judges actually tend to impose harsher sentences on black defendants than white judges, and Steffensmeier and Britt (2001) found that black judges were harsher on both black and white defendants. These sentences will go into the sentencing pot with sentences given by white judges, and if we find that blacks received a higher average sentence, can we charge racism under these circumstances?

SUMMARY

The United States has had a troubled racial history that the law has struggled to come to terms with. The issue of slavery and its aftermath has kept all three branches of government busy crafting executive orders, legislative acts, and judicial rulings. The Amistad case provided some support for the abolition of slavery in the United States, but the *Dred Scott* case put the Supreme Court's stamp of approval on slavery, was interpreted by some as its approval of the expansion of this system, and hardened the respective stances of the Northern and Southern states.

The Civil War and the Emancipation Proclamation put an end to slavery, and Congress made its abolition law with the passage of the Thirteenth Amendment. The lot of the newly freed slaves appeared to have improved greatly during the Reconstruction period, a time in which the federal government, through the Freedman's Bureau, protected the lives and rights of African Americans. However, the Southern states tried to re-create slavery under the notorious Black Codes, denying blacks many rights. The Congress struck back by passing the Fourteenth Amendment, declaring blacks to be citizens of the United States, and the Fifteenth Amendment, granting blacks suffrage rights. The Southern response was to pass a variety of Jim Crow laws denying blacks civil, political, and social rights, to which the Congress replied by passing the Civil Rights Act of 1875. However, the Supreme Court ruled in the Civil Rights cases that federal authority did not extend to private acts of discrimination.

The *Plessy v. Ferguson* and *Williams v. Mississippi* cases challenged racial segregation and black disenfranchisement, respectively. The Supreme Court ruled in *Plessy* that "separate but equal" laws did not violate the Fourteenth Amendment, and in *Williams*, it ruled that voting eligibility standards are the prerogative of the individual states under the Tenth Amendment. These two rulings effectively stripped blacks of the rights that they had gained in the Reconstruction period.

The early part of the twentieth century saw the founding of the NAACP to combat the prejudice and discrimination aimed at blacks, especially the cruel practice of lynching. Many efforts were made to get the federal government to pass antilynching laws, but no such law was passed until 1968.

After World War II, things began to improve considerably. *Brown v. Board of Education* saw the beginning of the end of segregation, and Congress passed the sweeping Civil Rights Act of 1964 and the Voting Rights Act. However, much of this impetus came from the activism of blacks themselves whose struggles were beamed around the world via television. Much of the success of this activism came from efforts on the part of the government to polish its image with the international community as it struggled with the Soviet Union during the Cold War over the hearts and minds of Third World nations. Whatever the impetus, there is no doubt that the situation of blacks in the United States has improved greatly over what it was one hundred years ago.

American Indians have also suffered greatly, having endured efforts to destroy them both physically and culturally. Such efforts began early in our history as white settlers increasingly encroached on Indian territory. The government of the United States took over the role of the British as the "guardians" of the Indians, a position enunciated in the so-called Marshall Trilogy of cases in the 1830s. In these cases, the Court ruled that Indian tribes were not sovereign nations and only in possession of the lands that they occupied at the pleasure of the United States and that they were "domestic dependent nations" under the sovereignty of the United States.

The Indian Removal Act of 1830 resulted in many Indian tribes being forcibly removed to Indian Territory (Oklahoma). Many Indians died on these long treks from their homelands, and many more died because of the terrible conditions on the reservations. A Supreme Court ruling that Indians were "persons" moved the government to attempt to assimilate them into American society by inculcating white American values to "civilize" and Christianize" them. These efforts had the effect of destroying much of Native American culture. Little by little the federal government exerted more and more control over the Indian nations while still denying them citizenship rights.

This began to change with the Indian Reorganization Act of 1934, which encouraged Indians to resurrect their languages and their culture, but the termination policies of the 1950s almost destroyed tribal sovereignty again. Termination policies ended with the Indian Self-Determination Act of 1975 in response to the obvious failure of the policies and to increasing Indian militancy, led by the American Indian Movement. Since that time, the government (including the courts) has done much to improve the condition of the Indians, and they have now regained almost complete sovereignty.

Asian Americans arrived relatively late in America and have been few in number and thus have not generated a history of discrimination at the same level of African Americans and Indians. Nevertheless, they have suffered their share of bad treatment, beginning with efforts to exclude Chinese from the country as "undesirables." Both Chinese- and Japanese-born immigrants were denied citizenship for many years, a denial that the Supreme Court ruled constitutional. Japanese Americans were interned in relocation camps after the Japanese attack on Pearl Harbor, although German- and Italian-Americans were not likewise interned. Despite early setbacks, Asian Americans have done remarkably well in the United States; they earn more money than whites on average, divorce less often, are more highly educated, and commit fewer crimes than whites.

The issue of whether the American criminal justice system is still racist today was addressed in the form of comparing minority arrest rates with white rates. African Americans are arrested significantly more frequently than whites, but Asian Americans are arrested significantly less frequently. Overall, the answer appears to be that although there are obviously racist individuals in the criminal justice system, the system itself is not racist.

DISCUSSION QUESTIONS

1. Should the Founding Fathers have followed the precedent regarding slavery in *Somerset v. Stewart*? Why or why not?

2. We saw that the Supreme Court in *Scott v. Sandford* was very concerned about the danger that an antislavery ruling might tear the country apart. However, as it turned out, the proslavery ruling did so. Do you think that doing the just thing, regardless of what one thinks the consequences may be, is always preferable to doing the expedient thing?

3. Discuss whether the Southern states' circumventions of the Thirteenth, Fourteenth, and Fifteenth Amendments point to the inability of the law to effect social change in the face of concerted opposition?

4. Could the United States have expanded "from coast to coast" in ways that would not have meant the mistreatment of the Indians?

5. How important has militant activism on the part of oppressed groups been in gaining them rights relative to legal action? If militant activism is that important, how come the various Indian wars, slave uprisings, and violent worker strikes of the nineteenth century did not produce positive results?

6. Is the criminal justice system racist today? Give arguments both pro and con.

References

Abadinsky, H. 2003. *Law and justice: An introduction to the American legal system.* 5th ed. Upper Saddle River, NJ: Prentice Hall.

Aguirre, A., and J. Turner. 1998. *American ethnicity: The dynamics and consequences of discrimination.* Boston: McGraw-Hill.

Ansolabehere, S., and C. Stewart. 2009. Amazing race: How post-racial was Obama's victory? *Boston Review* January/February. Online at: http://www.bostonreview.net/BR34.1/ansolabehere_stewart.php.

Bobo, L., and J. Kluegel. 1997. Status, ideology, and dimensions of whites' racial beliefs and attitudes: Progress and stagnation. In *Racial attitudes in the 1990s: Continuity and change,* edited by S. Tuch and J. Martin, pp. 93–120. Westport, CT: Praeger.

Bonczar, T., and A. Beck. 1997. *Lifetime likelihood of going to state or federal prison.* Washington, DC: U.S. Department of Justice.

Brinkley, A., R. Current, F. Freidel, and T. Williams. 1991. *American history: A survey.* New York: McGraw-Hill.

Caswell, B. 2009. The presidency, the vote, and the formation of new coalitions. *Polity* 41:388–407.

Clarke, J. 1998. *The lineaments of wrath: Race, violent crime, and American culture.* New Brunswick, NJ: Transaction.

Constitutional Rights Foundation. 2005. "At the hands of persons unknown": Lynching in America. http://www.crf-usa.org/brown50th/lynching_america.htm.

D'Alessio, S., and L. Stolzenberg. 2003. Race and the probability of arrest. *Social Forces* 81:1381–97.

Daniels, R. 2002. Koramatsu v United States revisited: 1944 and 1983. In *Race on trial: Law and justice in American history*, edited by A. Gordon-Reed, pp. 112–29. New York: Oxford University Press.

Davis, T. 2002. Race, identity, and the law: *Plessy v Ferguson.* In *Race on trial: Law and justice in American history*, edited by A. Gordon-Reed, pp. 61–76. New York: Oxford University Press.

Deloria, V., and D. Wilkins. 1999. *Tribes, treaties, and constitutional tribulations.* Austin: University of Texas Press.

D'Sousa, D. 1995. *The end of racism: Principles for a multiracial society.* New York: Free Press.

Dudziak, M. 2000. *Cold war civil rights: Race and the image of American democracy.* Princeton, NJ: Princeton University Press.

Federal Bureau of Investigation. 2006. *Uniform crime reports, 2005.* Washington, DC: U.S. Government Printing Office.

French, L. 2003. *Native American Justice.* Chicago: Burnham.

Gabbidon, S. 2001. W. E. B. DuBois: Pioneering American criminologist. *Journal of Black Studies*, 31:581–99.

Harris, A., and J. Shaw. 2001. Looking for patterns: Race, class, and crime. In *Criminology: A contemporary handbook*, edited by J. Sheley, pp. 129–163. Belmont, CA: Wadsworth.

Harris, J., and C. Davidson. 2009. Obama: The new contours of power. *Race and Class* 50:1–19.

Indian Civil Rights Act (1968). (25 U.S.C. §§ 1301–03). Washington, DC, U.S. Government Printing Office.

Jones, H. 2002. The impact of the Amistad case on race and law in America. In *Race on trial: Law and justice in American history*, edited by A. Gordon-Reed, pp. 14–25. New York: Oxford University Press.

Kansal, T. 2005. Racial disparity in sentencing. *The Sentencing Project.* http://www.sentencingproject.org.

Kitano, H., and R. Daniels. 1995. *Asian Americans: Emerging minorities.* Englewood Cliffs, NJ: Prentice Hall.

Klarman, M. 2004. *From Jim Crow to civil rights: The Supreme Court and the struggle for racial equality.* New York: Oxford University Press.

Loury, G. 1995. *One by one from the inside out: Essays and reviews on race and responsibility in America.* New York: Free Press.

McClosky, R. 1994. *The American Supreme Court.* Chicago: University of Chicago Press.

McLemore, S. 1983. *Racial and ethnic relations in America.* Boston: Allyn & Bacon.

Nebraska Studies. 2005. http://nebraskastudies.org/0700/stories/0701_0143.html.

O'Brien, R. 2001. Crime facts: Victim and offender data. In *Criminology: A contemporary handbook*, edited by J. Sheley, pp. 59–83. Belmont, CA: Wadsworth.

Parrillo, V. 2003. *Strangers to these shores: Race and ethnic relations in the United States.* Boston: Allyn & Bacon.

Pinkney, A. 1969. *Black Americans.* Englewood Cliffs, NJ: Prentice Hall.

Reeves, T., and C. Bennett. 2003. *The Asian and Pacific Islander population in the United States: March 2002.* Washington, DC: United States Census Bureau.

Rosenberg, G. 1991. *The hollow hope: Can courts bring about social change?* Chicago: University of Chicago Press.

Siegel, L. 2006. *Criminology.* Belmont, CA: Thomson/Wadsworth.

Sourcebook. 2003. *Sourcebook of criminal justice statistics.* Washington, DC: U.S. Government Printing Office.

Spartacus. 2005. Lynching. http://www.spartacus.schoolnet.co.uk/USAlynching.htm.

Steffensmeier, D., and C. Britt. 2001. Judges' race and judicial decision making: Do black judges sentence differently? *Social Science Quarterly* 82:749–64.

Tahsuda, J. 2003. Economic self-determination: Federal policies promoting development of reservation economies. *New England Law Review* 37:559–63.

Thernstrom, S., and A. Thernstrom. 1997. *America in black and white: One nation indivisible.* New York: Simon & Schuster.

Uhlman, T. 1979. *Racial justice: Black judges and defendants in an urban trial court.* Lexington, MA: Heath.

United States Department of Justice. 2005a. Civil rights and Native Americans. http://www.policyalmanac.org/culture/archive/native_americans.shtml.

United States Department of Justice. 2005b. *Introduction to federal voting rights laws.* http://www.usdoj.gov/crt/voting/intro/intro_b.htm.

Wang, X. 2002. The Dred Scott case. In *Race on trial: Law and justice in American history*, edited by A. Gordon-Reed, pp. 26–47. New York: Oxford University Press.

Wheatley, S. 2003. Deliberative democracy and minorities. *European Journal of International Law* 14:507–27.

Wiecek, W. 2000. Somerset's case. In *Encyclopedia of the American Constitution*, edited by L. Ley and K. Karst. Vol. 5, pp. 2451–52. New York: Macmillan.

Wildenthal, B. 2003. *Native American sovereignty on trial.* Santa Barbara, CA: ABC-Clio.

Wilkins, D. 1997. *American Indian sovereignty and the U.S. Supreme Court.* Austin: University of Texas Press.

Williams, W. 2002. *The devil made me do it.* http://www.mugu.com/cgi.bin/Upstream.

Wilson, G., I. Sakura-Lemessy, and J. West. 1999. Reaching the top: Racial differences in mobility paths in upper-tier occupations. *Work and Occupations* 26:165–86.

Woodward, C. Van. 1974. *The strange career of Jim Crow.* New York: Oxford University Press.

Cases Cited

Brown v. Board of Education, 347 U.S. 483 (1954).

Brown v. Board of Education (Brown II), 349 U.S. 294 (1955).

Cherokee Nation v. Georgia, 30 U.S. 1 (1831).

Cherokee Tobacco, 78 U.S. 616 (1871).

Civil Rights Cases, 109 U.S. 3 (1883).

Elk v. Wilkins, 112 U.S. 94 (1884).

Ex Parte Crow Dog, 109 U.S. 556 (1883).

Ex Parte Endo, 323 U.S. 243 (1944).

Heart of Atlanta Motel v. United States, 379 U.S. 241 (1964).

In Re Ah Yup, 1 F. Cas. 223 (1878).

Johnson v. McIntosh, 21 U.S. (8 Wheat.)

Korematsu v. United States, 323 U.S. 214 (1944).

Lone Wolf v. Hitchcock, 187 U.S. 553 (1903).

Nevada v. Hicks (99–1994), 533 U.S. 353 (2001).

Oliphant v. Suquamish Indian Tribe, 435 U.S. 191 (1978).

Ozawa v. United States, 260 U.S. 178 (1922).

Plessy v. Ferguson, 163 U.S. 538 (1896).

Scott v. Sandford, 60 U.S. 393 (1857).

Smith v. Allwright, 321 U.S. 649 (1944).

South Carolina v. Katzenbach, 383 U.S. 301 (1966).

Standing Bear v. Crook, 25 F. Cas. 695 (1879).

The Slave, Grace, 2 Hagg. Admir. (G.B.) 94 (1827).

United States, Appellants v. The Libellants and Claimants of the Schooner Amistad,
    40 U.S. 518 (1841).

United States v. Kagama, 118 U.S. 375 (1886).

United States v. Sioux Nations of Indians, 448 U.S. 371 (1980).

United States v. Wong Kim Ark, 169 U.S. 649 (1898).

Williams v. State of Mississippi, 170 U.S. 213 (1898).

Worcester v. Georgia, 31 U.S. 515 (1832).

CHAPTER 14

COMPARATIVE LAW: LAW IN OTHER CULTURES

Over a ten-day period in September 1993, Michael Peter Fay, an eighteen-year-old American living in Singapore, went on a rampage of vandalism in which he vandalized at least eighteen cars, among various other acts. Fay pled guilty to two (out of fifty-three) counts and was sentenced to a fine, jail time, and six lashes of a rattan cane. Many Americans applauded Singapore, and opined that this tiny country could teach us a thing or two about dealing with obnoxious teenagers. Others were appalled at what they considered barbaric treatment of a juvenile and thanked God that we do not whip our miscreants in this country anymore. Whatever people's opinions may have been on the matter, if they had one, they were engaging in thinking about comparative law.

Although whipping is a common penalty in Singapore, because an American was involved it became a hot political issue in the United States in 1994. Twenty-four U.S. senators signed a letter condemning the sentence and appealing for clemency. Singaporeans resented such interference, many pointing out that Singapore was a safe and orderly society, while the United States was mired in crime. Many other commentators in both the United States and Singapore pointed to differences in the legal penalties as causes for the differences in crime between the two countries. Although both countries are common law countries, Singapore very much values the crime control model over the American due process model, and its defenders point out America pays the price for its liberal attitudes in crime and general mayhem. This is what comparative law is all about: How do two or more legal systems differ and how are they similar, and what are the consequences of those differences?

Would the United States be a safer and more civic-minded country if it adopted a Singaporean attitude toward crime? Perhaps, but are we willing to go that far? If so, how about going further and cutting off the hands of thieves and executing adulterers, as is done in some Islamic countries that are even safer than Singapore? These are some of the things to think about when we read about other systems and ask, "Why don't we do that?"

INTRODUCTION

All societies from the smallest tribe to the most populous and complex modern societies develop rules for assuring peace, order, predictability, and cultural survival. These rules and their application may differ enormously from society to society and reflect a particular culture's history and its present social, political, and economic practices, philosophies, and ideals. This chapter briefly introduces you to law as it is understood in societies other than the United States. There are many advantages to studying a familiar subject from a different point of view. Someone once said that if you only know your own culture, you do not know your own culture, and we completely agree. After all, we cannot know what "up," "tall," and "no," mean without knowing what "down," "short," and "yes" mean. We are not implying that other legal systems are directly the opposite of our system in the United States. What we are saying is that knowledge of legal systems other than our own provides us with a new understanding and appreciation of our own and will better equip us to identify both its strengths and its weaknesses.

LAW IN PRELITERATE BANDS AND TRIBES

There are still a few hundred thousand people in the world today who live in the kinds of simple hunter-gatherer, horticultural, and herding societies all our ancestors lived in ten thousand to fifty thousand years ago. These societies have no written language and are thus collectively referred to as *preliterate* societies. We have defined a crime as a violation of a criminal statute, and criminal statutes, by definition, must be written down. Since these societies have no written language and hence no statutes, can people living in preliterate societies commit crimes? Technically speaking they cannot, but they certainly can and do commit acts that are the equivalent of crimes as defined by statutes in literate societies. People in these societies obviously cannot commit acts such as tax evasion, securities fraud, embezzlement, and carjacking, but they can commit homicide and theft. Some of these preliterate cultures have homicide rates that are truly astounding when compared with the average rate of about 7.5 per 100,000 in the United States over the past two decades. For example, the Agta, a hunting and gathering society inhabiting an island in the Philippines, have an estimated rate of 326, the Yanomamo of South America have an estimated rate of 165.9, and the Kung of South Africa have an estimated rate of 29.3 (Ellis and Walsh 2000). When evaluating these rates, however, we must remember that all these societies live in very unhealthy environments lacking in even the most rudimentary medical facilities where even minor injuries can be life threatening.

Even though preliterate societies lack written codes of conduct, social control is of central concern to all organized groups, and people living in these cultures are ruled by customs as rigid and inviolable as any law. Bands are small (typically between fifty to one hundred members) groups of hunters and gathers, and tribes are larger groups (anywhere from a few hundred to many thousands) who augment hunting and gathering with agriculture.

Just as there are no written laws in preliterate societies, there are no formal agents of social control such as police or judges. There is no need for such people because usually everyone knows everyone else to some extent, and thus everyone is exposed to the informal pressures toward conformity that can be brought to bear by other members. There is also the marked absence of resource inequalities in such simple societies and thus less envy and motivation to take what is not yours. However, whenever there are proscribed and prescribed acts, and sanctions that flow from them that are sustained by authority, there is law.

The Eskimo or Inuit people inhabiting northern Canada, Alaska, and Siberia provide a good example of social control among bands. The most common crimes among the Inuit are murder and adultery (because there is very little worth stealing among the Inuit that is not readily available to all, property crime is extremely rare). Lacking formal means of redress for offended parties, the Inuit rely on self-redress. Self-redress would involve the aggrieved party (or surviving relatives if the crime was murder) killing the offender, but this would set in motion a chain reaction of interfamily murders, as it does in some preliterate societies in which homicide rates are extremely high. Such blood feuds seriously undermine the viability of band societies unless revenge murders can be carried out in such a way that the killer's identity is not blatantly obvious.

An alternate tactic that avoids bloodshed and vendettas is a unique kind of mechanism of self-redress among the Inuit called the **song duel**. The song duel involves the participants hurling sung insults at one other. These duels are so important that it is not uncommon for both parties to hire talented composers to write their songs for them just as an American might hire an attorney. The duelists "sing their insults while weaving and dancing in front of each other, and to emphasize their jibes they butt heads" (Kidder 1983, 15). The duel is witnessed by an applauding and hissing crowd, which declares one of the parties the winner on the basis of how thoroughly he has humiliated his opponent. This decision of the peers of both parties is supposed to conclude the matter just as finally as a jury or judicial decision does in developed societies. However, neither party is found "guilty" or "not guilty," nor are they forced to pay compensation. The ridicule is seen as a way to restore social relationships fractured by the wrongdoing.

The use of nondeadly duels to settle serious grievances is common among band societies, but the absence of specialized and formal agents of social control does not preclude a group response to an offender on occasion. Ostracism and banishment are terrible punishments in band societies, for they signal social and possibly physical death in the harsh and hostile environments often inhabited by bands. For intractable offenders (that small percentage of psychopathic offenders who exist in any society regardless of how close knit it may be), the Inuit may rely on some member of the band quietly pushing the offender off the ice to drown when no one else is looking (Lykken 1995).

Tribes, being larger and more complexly organized than bands, have more complex methods of social control. Because the tribe is much larger than the band, leadership and social control becomes more precisely defined. The Huron of southern Ontario will serve as our example of tribal social control. Among the Huron, each clan (a clan is a small subunit of a tribe based on kinship) was represented at a tribal council headed by a civil chief whose primary duty was to mediate disputes. Murder, theft, witchcraft, and treason were the major crime categories recognized by the Huron. Prior to the arrival of the white man's law, the Huron provided for self-redress for murder of a relative, but like the Inuit, they also feared the chain reaction nature of blood feuds. Murders (and assaults) were usually settled by fines payable not by the offender himself but by his clan. Because the murderer had burdened them with a fine, his clan kin would respond negatively toward him by ridiculing and insulting him. Such is the power of shame and dishonor in preliterate societies that this form of punishment sometimes resulted in the offender taking his own life. Fines were not levied on thieves; the recovery of stolen property and the shaming of the thief was considered punishment enough.

Whereas murder, assault, and theft were private wrongs against the individual, witchcraft and treason were crimes against the tribe. These crime categories were often used as "catch-all" categories that were useful as tools to eliminate a few persistently extreme deviants and undesirables. The punishment for these crimes was death. Executions could only be ordered by a council of chiefs, and in the case of execution for witchcraft, only with the consent of the offender's clan kin. Given this proviso, we can assume that anyone executed for "witchcraft" had exhibited truly reprehensible behavior over a long period of time and that no one mourned his or her passing (Wright and Fox 1978).

This brief discussion of band and tribal law illustrates and again emphasizes how customs deemed vital to group solidarity and survival are maintained. These customs or laws are binding obligations on all members of the social group, and if any member fails to live up to the group's behavioral expectations, he or she is subjected to pressures from the group utilizing various mechanisms to right the wrong. These mechanisms can be something as incomprehensible to us as the song duel among the Inuit or as understandable as the fine among the Huron. It is important to understand, however, that both mechanisms produce the same result—the shaming of the offender, the reinforcement of the moral rightness of the custom in the minds of group members, and the return of social tranquility.

LAW IN THE MODERN WORLD: THE FOUR TRADITIONS

There are four main traditions of law in the world today: *civil law, common law, Islamic law,* and *socialist law* (Reichel 2005). Of course, there are numerous systems of law in the world, each unique in many respects, but just about all of them are related to some degree to one of these four. Some legal systems, due to the legacy of conquest and/or colonization, and sometimes voluntary borrowing, are hybrids of one or more of these traditions, with indigenous elements also thrown into the mix. Even among members of the same legal tradition there are many specific differences, such as between England and the United States within the

Figure 14.1 Percentages of World's Nations Employing the Four Legal Traditions.

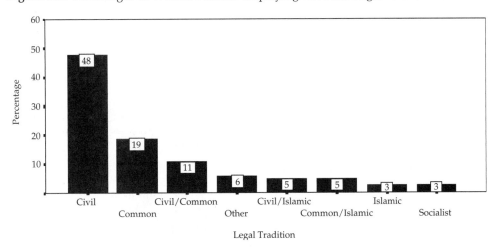

Source: Adapted from percentages provided by Reichel (2005).

common law tradition or between France and Germany within the civil law tradition. Space limitations force us to explain non–common law systems primarily by noting how they differ from American common law. The same limitations also require us to limit our discussion of these different systems to one representative nation.

Figure 14.1 gives you an idea of the representation of the various legal traditions in the world today.

Common Law

As we have seen, the common law tradition originated in England, and its influence spread around the world, mainly through British colonization. India is the world's most populous common law country, although Indian law is liberally sprinkled with indigenous Hindu law. In addition to the widespread British influence, various aspects of common law tradition have spread to formerly American-occupied countries such as the Philippines, Japan, and Italy where common law procedural principles were superimposed on a basically civil law structure. No system of law is imported whole, and Britain's daughter countries— the United States, Canada, Australia, and New Zealand—and England itself have often found it necessary to depart from some specific common law practices to varying degrees without violating its general principles. Nevertheless, it remains the major source of modern criminal law in all English-speaking countries except Scotland and South Africa, both of which employ hybrids of common and civil law (Fairchild and Dammer 2001), although it has had limited influence outside English-speaking countries. No country not colonized or defeated in war by Britain or the United States has imported the common law, whereas many have imported civil law. Friedman (1977, 47) explains that this is probably because "[t]he civil law is neat; it is compactly packaged for export. The common law is cumbersome, unsystematic; to import it, is like carrying groceries home in one's hands without a shopping bag or net."

Historical Aspects of Common Law

The origin of the English common law is traditionally traced to the Norman conquest of England in 1066. Prior to the Norman invasion, English law was a mixture of ancient custom, Church law, and remnants of Roman and Germanic law. The principles and applications of these laws varied greatly from area to area within England. Powerful feudal lords, who often settled their disputes by combat, determined the law of the land. Because the lords relied on combat, and because their subjects had few rights, law as we know it was not considered necessary. After the Norman invasion, William the Conqueror and his royal successors set out to provide the English with a law common to all (hence the term "common law"), both as a means of unifying England and increasing royal power at the expense of the feudal lords.

Norman kings did not seek to impose alien laws on the Anglo-Saxon English. The common law was fashioned from local customs and practices, shaped and formalized by judicial decisions based on the facts they had before them. As we have seen, these decisions ultimately became the basis for future judicial decisions for judges confronted with similar cases in what became known as the doctrine of precedent. Eventually these decisions, as well as the arguments made by lawyers involved in the cases, were written down and circulated for review by other judges and lawyers. Thus much of the English common law is "judge-made," or case law, which has evolved over the centuries in response to the problems of the common person. In a very real sense, common law represents the crystallization of custom as it existed at the time of its inception.

Basic Features of Common Law

Although we have already discussed common law at length, certain basic features require repeating in order that we may have a basis for comparing other legal traditions to it. Common law is distinguished from other systems of law in five important ways: (1) its unwritten nature, (2) its respect for precedent, (3) its adversarial procedures, (4) its use of grand and petit juries, and (5) its extensive use of judicial review. These distinguishing features should be viewed as differences in degree rather than in terms of absolute differences existing in one tradition and not in others. We briefly elaborate on these features.

1. *Common Law Is Unwritten.* When we say that common law is unwritten, we do not mean that it is literally not written down or that it lacks precision of meaning. Common law has a long history of producing revered documents stressing the rule of law since the time of the Magna Carta in 1215. The term "unwritten" is used to distinguish its origin in the customs of the people as formalized by judges from the written or statutory laws of the civil tradition, which were imposed on citizens from above. Common law, however, has long surrendered its lawmaking role to legislative statutes and codified criminal law while

maintaining its role in procedural law. It is in the United States that judges retain a modicum of the old common law lawmaking role rather than in England where the laws of Parliament (the British legislative body analogous to the United States Congress) are not subject to judicial review.

2. *Common Law Respects Precedent.* Common law's respect for precedent flows from its origin as case law, which reflects the accumulated wisdom of generations of judicial decisions. Precedent operates in vertical and horizontal dimensions. The vertical dimension means that lower courts in their deliberations should always consider decisions made by higher courts, and the horizontal dimension means that courts at the same level maintain consistency in their interpretations of the law. The doctrine of precedent allows for predictability, consistency, and rationality in common law.

3. *Common Law Is Adversarial.* The adversarial nature of common law stems from the "trial by combat" method of settling disputes in medieval times. In an adversarial system, both the prosecution and defense are expected to vigorously pursue their self-interest (a "victory" for the state or for their client). Judges in common law countries, particularly in the United States, function as disinterested referees, making sure that the opposing sides follow the legal rules. Judges do not control the flow of information to the court, do not generally question suspects or witnesses, and do not pass judgments of guilty or not guilty (a bench trial is an exception). Judges in other legal traditions play a much more active role.

4. *Common Law Uses Grand and Petit Juries.* Indictment by grand jury and trial by petit jury are cherished procedures in common law countries. They were traditionally viewed as bodies of citizens interposing themselves between the power of the state and the accused. The expense of grand juries, as well as the various criticisms laid against them, led to their abolition in England and Canada and to decreased use of them in the United States. Likewise, many practical considerations have led to less use of trial juries than was previously the case. The extensive use of plea bargaining, the legality of nonunanimous jury decisions, and the use of six-person juries in some states under certain circumstances make the jury less central in common law than it once was.

5. *Common Law Uses Judicial Review.* Judicial review refers to the judiciary's examination of the legality of the actions and decisions of executive and administrative officers of the government as well as appellate review of lower court decisions. The scope of judicial review is limited to various degrees in different common law countries. For instance, the United States Supreme Court can rule any state or federal law unconstitutional, but no judicial power in Britain has the power to overrule a Parliamentary act. The Supreme Court of Canada is beginning to evolve along the lines of its American counterpart, although Canada's fear of judicial lawmaking applies the brakes to excessive judicial interference in legislative business (Thompson 1985). Judicial review of criminal cases from the lower courts follows roughly similar lines in all common law countries.

Civil Law

As we see from Figure 14.1, civil law tradition is the most pervasive legal tradition in the world, being used by almost half of the world's nations. Civil law tradition is sometimes called continental law, or code law, to avoid confusion with the civil branch of law in common law countries. Variations of it are found in all countries of Western Europe except England and Wales, in all Central and South American countries, in many former non-British African colonies, and in a number of Asian countries (Fairchild and Dammer 2001). Former Warsaw Pact nations such as Poland and Hungary, as well as Russia, are also reverting to civil law systems (Danilenko and Burnham 1999). As within common law, civil law tradition encompasses a variety of systems that differ on many specifics due to its unique developmental history in each country. Some Scandinavian countries often classified as belonging to civil law tradition have systems that are a lot like civil law tradition in some respects and a lot like common law in other respects. Thus, this four-way classification of legal traditions is somewhat arbitrary in a number of cases (Reichel 2005).

Historical Origins of Civil Law

Civil law has a longer history of development than common law. Although its development is not so centered on one country as the development of common law is centered on England, it probably owes its greatest debt to ancient Rome and nineteenth-century France and Germany. The first historical example of a written code of laws can be traced back to the edicts of King Hammurabi's Code. More relevant to the development of modern civil law is early Roman law, beginning with the Twelve Tables, a compilation of rules regulating family, economic, and religious conduct, written around 450 BCE. A further advance in Roman law did not occur for almost another one thousand years when the Emperor Justinian published the *corpus juris civilis*, or Code of Justinian, in 533 CE. Modern civil law owes most to the *Code Civil des Français* (Napoleonic Code) published in 1804, for it became the blueprint for all subsequent civil law codes. This code contains four hundred codes of law and fourteen thousand pieces of legislation on all topics from criminal codes to the conduct of marriage.

Basic Features of Civil Law

The basic features of civil law are almost mirror opposites of the features of common law, although the two systems are not so far apart in practice as this statement might imply. The important historical difference between code law and common law is that the former has historically been developed after a major social upheaval that eliminated previous political regimes. The impetus for such sweeping change is usually a deep distrust and hatred of the previous status quo. For instance, French civil law developed after the French Revolution disposed of the hated *ancien régime*, and socialist law arose after the Russian Revolution overthrew the czar and old ways he stood for. The American Revolution produced no such drastic changes in the common law. The American revolutionaries had many complaints against their mother country, but they did not have a disdain for her traditions and institutions. Any differences between American and British common law have evolved slowly in response to the differing needs of the two nations.

Our discussion of civil law centers on the French system, which comes closest to the civil law prototype. A very basic philosophical difference between the American and French legal systems, particularly criminal law, is that American law, like American political ideology, emphasizes individualism, whereas French political ideology and social traditions emphasizes communitarian, and even paternalistic, values. The American criminal justice system emphasizes the rights of the accused; the French system may be characterized as a crime control system emphasizing the rights of the victimized community (Reichel 2005).

1. *Civil Law Is Written Rather Than Unwritten.* As opposed to common law's slow accumulation of case law derived from decisions based on local customs, the Napoleonic Code and its successors are all codes of conduct (statutes) written from above and imposed on citizens and subjects below. These codes are binding because they have been written down at the behest of some powerful authority, not because they are customary. In other words, writing the codes or principles of conduct down *creates* them in a civil law system, but writing them down in a common law system *reveals* the codes or principles that already exist in custom (Reichel 2005).

The comparison of principles may be overdrawn. Most law in common law countries today is code (statutory) law based on legislative fiat rather than case law. Codes in common law countries differ in one important aspect from their counterparts in civil law countries, however. In common law countries, they are viewed as *supplementing* previous law rather than abolishing it, which emphasizes the evolutionary nature of common law. In civil law countries, new codes *replace* previous law, which emphasizes the revolutionary nature of civil law. It should also be noted that the legal prescriptions and proscriptions outlined in the various civil law codes were mostly consistent with the norms and customs that prevailed at the time of their publication, so in this sense of codifying custom, civil law is not too different from common law or from any of the other legal traditions.

2. *Precedent Is Not Officially Recognized.* The doctrine of precedent emphasizes common law's ethos of tradition and slow evolutionary change and provides for flexibility by allowing judges to "make law" by their *un*precedented rulings and responses to legal issues in cases containing unique circumstances. This flexibility is not possible in civil law systems because, theoretically, the codes laid down in civil law are complete the day they are enacted and are not subject to judicial review. As such, there is no need to refer to past cases for guidance; the code itself is all the guidance needed. In practice, however, no code is so complete as to provide unambiguous guidance in all matters coming before the courts, and civil law judges often refer to and rely on case law and thus to precedent (Abadinsky 2003). The two main differences between common and civil law stances toward precedence is that in civil law, precedence is not binding and is the tool of last resort.

3. *It Is Inquisitorial Rather Than Adversarial.* This is the primary distinguishing feature of civil law vis-à-vis common law. The term *inquisitorial* conjures up images of the Spanish Inquisition, torture, and the notion that the accused is assumed guilty unless he or she can prove innocence, all of which is untrue. The

inquisitorial system is a system of extensive investigation, interviews, and interrogations carried out in civil law countries to ensure that an innocent person is not subjected to trial (Fairchild and Dammer 2001). The term *inquisition* should be thought of as denoting "inquiry," as the term *adversarial* denotes "contest." The inquisitorial focus is on truth, and not so much on procedure, so many of the procedural protections afforded suspects in common law countries either do not exist or exist in modified form.

This does not mean that the system runs roughshod over individuals. The French practice of providing attorneys for indigent defendants precedes the practice in the United States by more than half a century. It may even be more protective in some senses. For instance, to protect the accused from adverse publicity, criminal investigations are conducted in secret. No names or other information pertaining to the case are released to the press unless or until the investigation leaves authorities with little doubt that they have a strong case against the accused. These, and other such protections, have led more than one comparative legal scholar to voice the opinion that civil law is more protective of the innocent and that common law is more protective of the guilty (Fairchild and Dammer 2001; Maechling 1993). This suggests that civil law procedure is more likely to arrive at the truth and serve the purpose of justice than is common law procedure.

This "truth seeking" is accomplished by an active judicial supervision of evidence gathering and active judicial participation in the investigation of the suspect and the crime and by a cooperative rather than adversarial spirit among all participants. In an adversarial system in which the outcome may rest on the relative skills of attorneys, defendants able to bear the costs of good attorneys and related investigatory costs (expert witnesses and the like) have a significant advantage over less wealthy defendants. Such inequalities are much less relevant in a judge-controlled inquisitorial system in which judges call expert witnesses on behalf of both sides. *All* relevant evidence as to the guilt or innocence of the accused is considered, including his or her character and hearsay evidence, and nothing is automatically excluded because of so-called technicalities. The only exception to this is when evidence or confessions are obtained via physical or legal threats (Reichel 2005).

The intensive pretrial investigation minimizes the likelihood that an innocent person will be brought to trial, but it also implies a strong presumption of guilt if the investigation does lead to a trial. A trial in France is more a public review of case facts and a consideration of mitigating and aggravating circumstances for the purposes of sentencing than a forum for determining guilt or innocence. Thus, although a French *investigation* takes place under the presumption of innocence, in a sense, a French *trial* takes place with an unspoken presumption of "probably guilty." Civil law practitioners often argue that the presumption of innocence is necessary under common law because the investigation stage is not as thorough as it is under civil law (Reichel 2005). This claim is made in light of the fact that a French investigation involves the police, an examining magistrate, the prosecutor, and the defense attorney, not just the police and sometimes the prosecutor as in the United States.

Civil law advocates tend to view the various legal rights afforded to common law defendants as both unnecessary and constraining in the search for truth. American advocates of civil law argue that such rights have limited applicability to the modern United States because they were grounded in efforts to prevent abuses prevalent in medieval times. For instance, it is often argued that the Fifth Amendment prohibition against self-incrimination speaks of being *compelled* to do so via use of torture to extract confessions, but according to Maechling (1993) is used today as a ploy allowing the accused to evade responding to valid questions put to him or her by the police and prosecution.

Needless to say, a "truth-seeking" system could not operate without the input of the "star" of the show—the accused. Nevertheless, French defendants may refuse to answer questions or cooperate with the investigation because they are only expected (not required) to cooperate. French defendants are advised of their right to remain silent during pretrial proceedings, but because of the presumption that all parties involved in a case will cooperate in the investigation, it does not have the same force of meaning that it does in common law (Fairchild and Dammer 2001). Remaining silent during civil law trial proceedings, however, may be legally considered as evidence of guilt, unlike in common law countries where jurors must not draw negative conclusions from a defendant's silence.

4. *It Has Traditionally Made Little Use of Juries.* There is some use of juries in civil law countries in very serious criminal cases, but they do not have exactly the same role that they have in common law countries. Juries consist of three professional judges and nine laypersons (Fairchild and Dammer 2001). Civil law jurors can question witnesses and the accused and receive defense and prosecution summations. Given direct judicial involvement, lay jurors are more reliant on a judge's direction than are common law juries (Terrill 1999). Civil law advocates see no problem with this because judges in civil law countries are highly trained civil servants who owe their positions to education and experience, not political patronage. Judges are active participants in trials and see their job as seeking the truth by directly questioning suspects, witnesses, and other trial participants. In essence, civil law judges play to various degrees all the roles played in common law systems by judges, investigators, prosecutors, defense attorneys, and jury members.

In a jury trial, all jurors, judges, and laypersons alike are allowed to question witnesses and the accused. Jury deliberations are doubtless dominated by the professional judges on whom the laypersons must rely for explanations of law, but guilt or innocence is determined by a secret ballot in which each of the twelve votes is of equal importance. A verdict requires agreement of at least eight of the twelve jurors rather than unanimity. If the verdict is guilty, voting begins immediately on the penalty the defendant should receive. In common law countries, there is almost always at least thirty days between verdict and sentence to allow authorities (probation officers) to conduct a presentence investigation (PSI). A PSI is needed because sentences are imposed in light of information not usually admitted during trial in a common law country as well as on the basis of legally relevant factors (crime seriousness and prior record). The French trial, by way of contrast, involves judging the character of the defendant as well as the facts of the crime and his or her criminal record, so sentencing deliberations can proceed immediately following the verdict (Reichel 2005).

5. *Judicial Review Is Used Sparingly.* There can be no judicial review of legislative statutes in most instances. Although it occasionally happens, it is not nearly so widespread as it is in the United States. The French equivalent to the American Supreme Court in terms of dealing with constitutional issues is the **Conseil Constitutionnel** (the Constitutional Council). This entity is unique among national supreme courts in that it lies outside the judicial system (it is a *council,* not a court hearing cases forwarded to it from lower courts). The Council's main function is to rule on the constitutionality of *proposed* legislation, not legislation already in effect, when requested to do so by leaders of the various political parties (Fairchild and Dammer 2001). Some civil law countries tend to view the practice of judicial review of legislation as inherently antidemocratic and a violation of the separation of powers principle. There are certain civil law countries such as Germany, Italy, and Austria in which judicial power to void legislation is almost as great as in the United States, although the limited job tenure of the judges serving on those courts, as well as a civil law "hands off" tradition, tends to blunt the kind of extreme judicial activism exercised by the United States Supreme Court.

The reason that the American model of judicial review is rejected in France is that the French believe that important decisions affecting large numbers of people should be made by legislators elected by and accountable to the voters, not by appointees with lifetime tenure who are shielded from the wrath of the people. In civil law countries, courts are generally obliged to follow the statutes as written, and judges do not have the power to evaluate them; but in the United States, the content of a statute is not fully legally established until it has been construed by the courts.

Judicial decisions involving criminal matters and private and commercial disputes are appealable to higher courts or to the French equivalent of the United States Supreme Court known as the **Cour de Cassation** (*cassation* means "to break" or "to smash"). The *Cour de Cassation* sits in six chambers, each with fifteen judges (Fairchild and Dammer 2001). As the term implies, its function is to "smash" erroneous decisions made by lower courts. However, the decisions of the court, while authoritative, are not binding on the lower courts the way appellate decisions are in common law countries. Also unlike common law appellate courts whose function is to rule only on points of law, civil law appellate courts in France and in some other countries can rule on matters of both law and fact. In some instances, an appeals court may hold a new trial if new evidence is brought before it, and it can increase or decrease a criminal sentence upon appeal (Abadinsky 2003). Neither of these options is available to appeals courts in common law countries.

French law recognizes three offense categories: *crimes, delicts,* and *contraventions.* This classification determines in which court in France's three-tiered system of criminal courts the case will be heard. **Crimes** (major offenses for which the penalty can be from five years to life imprisonment) are tried in *assize* **court**, the only court that uses juries; *delicts* (less serious offenses for which the penalty can be up to five years) are tried in correctional court; and *contraventions* (minor offenses with a maximum penalty of two months in jail) are tried in **police court** (Fairchild and Dammer 2001).

Although we have been positive about French civil law, primarily because it is more of a truth-seeking system than the common law, as in any system, there is potential for abuse. The investigation into a crime is so thorough that it often takes a long time, during which the accused is typically held in custody without bail. Bail is infrequently granted in France because it operates under a crime control model and because the accused is expected to be available to help with the inquiry. Also, by the time a case gets to trial, everyone involved basically knows what is going to happen because the trial is more a forum for a review of the *known* facts (of which all parties are aware) than a forum for fact *finding*. The system is one of professional bureaucracy that lacks the same measure of lay participation favored by common law countries. The expectation of cooperation on the part of the defendant, and the negative conclusions that judge and jurors can draw if he or she does not cooperate, is something that an American due process purist finds alarming.

Socialist Law

Socialist law originated in 1917 with the Russian Revolution and the establishment of the Union of Soviet Socialist Republics (USSR). The collapse of the USSR saw the end of socialist law in Russia and its former Eastern European satellites, but variants continue to exist in China, North Korea, Vietnam, and Cuba. Socialist law is based on Marxist/Leninist ideology, and it is the only system of law that considers itself a temporary anachronism devoted to its own demise. Marxist ideology envisioned the eventual "withering away" of the state and an ensuing "dictatorship of the proletariat" in which law would not be needed. Socialist law emphasizes communal values over individual rights and is a low-tolerance crime-control model rather than a due process model. This concept of law is best exemplified by Marxist statistician Karl Pearson in an essay entitled *The Moral Basis of Socialism*, published in 1887 (as cited in Walsh 2009, 244–45): "The legislation or measures of police, to be taken against the immoral and antisocial minority, will form the political realization of Socialism. Socialists have to inculcate that spirit which would give offenders against the State short shrift and the nearest lamppost. Every citizen must learn to say with Louis XIV, *L 'etat c'est moi!*" ["I am the state!"].

The origin of such illiberal attitudes is that "archaic" concepts of individual rights and procedural limitations on state power had purchase only as long as the state and the individual were distinct entities and at odds with one another. In a socialist society the state and the laws that support it would "wither away," and whatever would be construed as the "state" thereafter would become one with and inseparable from the individual (*L 'etat c'est moi!*). Thus individuals would not be in need of bourgeois procedural protections. Indeed, procedural rights are conspicuously absent in contemporary socialist legal systems under the principle of the oneness of the state and the individual.

Since the demise of the USSR, Russia has moved away from Marxist principles, and its law has moved closer to traditional civil law. This leaves China as the largest and most important country with a socialist legal system.

Chinese Socialist Law

Ancient Chinese philosopher Confucius (551–479 BCE) expressed the attitude toward law that has pervaded Chinese thinking for centuries when he wrote, "The superior man is concerned with virtue; the inferior man is concerned with law" (quoted in Fairchild and Dammer 2001, 78). Because of the Confucian influence emphasizing informal discussion, mediation, and compromise to resolve disputes, some scholars maintain that Imperial China (221 BCE to 1911 CE) never developed a sound rational-formal legal system in the Weberian sense (Situ and Liu 1996). Others point to the **Ch'ing Code** of 1646, which contained 436 statutes and specified four thousand offenses for which punishment was prescribed, as ample evidence that Chinese law has always been at least substantively rational, that is, "guided by general rules or principles other than that of the law itself" (Marsh 2000, 283).

1. *Chinese Law Is Written and Precedent Is Not Recognized.* During the rule of Mao Zedong (1949 to 1976), the Chinese legal system borrowed heavily from the Soviet legal codes. The present system of Chinese law was established in 1954, but it was 1979 before China's first code of criminal law and procedure (the *Ch'ing Code* contained no formal procedural rules) was adopted (Davidson and Wang 1996). Under this new code of criminal procedure, the Chinese judiciary began to exercise a small measure of independent power (Situ and Liu 1996). In common with civil law, judges can only apply the law, they cannot make it. This being the case, and with even less independence than French judges, precedent in the sense of applying judge-made law has no place in the Chinese system. However, unlike the strictly worded formalism of the penal codes of common and civil law traditions, Chinese law has always had a high degree of flexibility in both substance and procedure. For instance, the **principle of analogy** allowed for punishment for acts not specified in criminal codes if the behavior was "analogous" to acts that were. This principle was rejected (at least on paper) in the 1997 revisions of Chinese law (Fairchild and Dammer 2001).

2. *The Chinese System Is Inquisitorial and Adversarial.* The Chinese system has both inquisitorial and adversarial aspects, but its emphasis is squarely on the inquisitorial process. Until 1996, the system did not operate under the presumption of innocence at either the investigatory or the trial phase, and the burden of proof rested squarely on the accused. Under the new codes, there is an assumption of innocence, and defense attorneys can now challenge the prosecutor's case (Lu and Miethe 2002). But China still stresses confession, contrition, and eventual reintegration of the defendant back into the community, which shows that Confucian ideals have not been completely lost. Chinese courts have historically placed such an emphasis on confession that they do not even allow defendants to know what evidence is to be presented against them. Any such disclosure would taint the voluntary nature of a confession because if defendants were to confess guilt after being made aware of the evidence

against them (as in an American plea bargain negotiation), they would merely be acknowledging the obvious and remorse would be hard to gauge (Reichel 2005). Amnesty International (2005) claims that torture is still sometimes used in China as a means of obtaining confessions, which, if true, hardly points to their "voluntariness."

Chinese defendants have the right to defend themselves in court, to hire a lawyer, or to entrust their defense to a relative or lay advocate. The court may appoint an advocate at its discretion, but with only about 110,000 lawyers in all of China in 2000, they are hard to come by (Reichel 2005). Dividing the number of lawyers by China's population of 1.3 billion people, it works out to about one lawyer per 12,000 citizens compared with one per 345 citizens in the United States.

Chinese advocates do not advocate for their clients in the Western sense of vigorously seeking to establish their innocence or arguing technical points of law. The function of the advocate is to see that procedural law is observed (the relative leeway allowed in its interpretation notwithstanding) during processing of the defendant and to argue for leniency before sentencing. This may be because, as Lu and Miethe (2002, 271) point out, "the stronger the defense the more severe the punishment is likely to result."

Not only this, according to a 2004 Congressional Executive Commission on China report; anything other than minimal advocacy could be risky for defense attorneys. This report claimed that Chinese prosecutors harass defense attorneys by threatening them with criminal prosecution for "evidence fabrication." Evidence fabrication is an article of the Chinese criminal code and is defined as evidence that a defense attorney relies on that is later shown to be false. It is not necessary to show that defense attorneys knew the evidence to be false to obtain a conviction. The evidence fabrication code specifically targets defense lawyers, and Chinese attorneys have understandably come to view defense work as a "high risk activity" (Congressional Executive Commission on China 2004, 2). In Lu and Miethe's (2002) study of 237 Chinese theft cases, no defense attorney maintained his or her client's innocence, but all made pleas for leniency.

3. *Chinese Law Uses a Quasi-Jury System:* Because of China's Confucian heritage, there has been a long tradition of informal social control via the sanctioning mechanisms available to **people's mediation committees** that are organized in work and neighborhood groups (Fairchild and Dammer 2001). Every adult in China belongs to one or more of these groups, and thus strong pressures toward conformity are everywhere. When citizens go beyond violating norms to committing crimes, laypersons are also involved in the formal justice system. A criminal trial in China may be held in front of what is known as a **collegial bench** composed of one to three professional judges and two to four lay people's assessors (Reichel 2005). Although assessors have a vote as to the verdict in a case, they are highly unlikely to disagree with the professional judges (Fairchild and Dammer 2001).

In May 2005, the Chinese initiated a new jury system that has been praised as a step forward by many civil rights advocates. There are many differences between what Americans' idea of jurors and jury service is and what this new system is, however. According to Chinese news sources ("Jurors to help..." 2005), many Chinese have applied to serve as lay jurors for a five-year term, notwithstanding the fact that they will only be compensated monetarily if they are not regularly employed. Candidates must be over twenty-three years old, have two years or more of college, and be of good health and of sound morality. The stated intention is to make these jurors more independent of professional judges and to "help build a more 'democratic, open, and just authoritative judiciary'" ("Jurors to help..." 2005, 1).

As in civil tradition, the Chinese trial is held mainly to review the facts and to consider sentencing options. The judges, the prosecutor, and the victim or victim's representatives may all interrogate the defendant, who does not have the right to remain silent. Following the interrogation phase is the debate phase in which the defendant literally may debate the judges, the prosecutor, or the victim. Upon the termination of the debate, the defendant is allowed to make a final statement before the judges retire to deliberate. As in civil law, the trial panel decides both the verdict and the punishment by majority vote. Unlike the civil system, difficult cases may be submitted to an adjudication committee whose decision is binding on the trial panel.

China is the world's leader in the proportion of its criminals it executes each year. The death penalty may be applied for nearly seventy different offenses, including murder, rape, economic crimes committed by high-level officials, counterrevolutionary offenses, and hooliganism. According to Amnesty International (2005), there were at least thirty-four hundred executions in China in 2004, but sources inside China put the true figure at around ten thousand. Adjusting for population size differences, the official figure (thirty-four hundred) is still over thirteen times more executions than occurred in the United States in the same year.

There are two types of death sentence: immediate and delayed. A delayed sentence is a two-year suspension of sentence during which defendants must show that they are reformed. If a person is considered rehabilitated, the sentence is usually changed to a long period of incarceration; if not, he or she is executed. An immediate sentence is carried out within seven days of imposition of the penalty. Such a sentence is imposed when in the court's opinion the defendant is beyond rehabilitation. Execution is by a single shot at the base of the skull (Felkenes 1989). Penal sanctions in China are characterized by the use of "reeducation" and forced labor camps with the stated function of resocializing inmates to rid them of "politically incorrect" thoughts and behaviors.

4. *Judicial Review Is Severely Limited.* Although politically China is not a federal system, Chinese courts are hierarchically structured at national, provincial (state), county, and local levels as they are in the United States. At the top of the hierarchy is the **Supreme People's Court** (SPC). The functions of the SPC are to handle cases affecting the entire country, supervise lower level courts, interpret statutes, and provide explanations and advisory opinions to judicial and political bodies. The SPC is unlike the U.S. Supreme Court in three important ways: (1) it is answerable for its actions to a Standing Committee of the Chinese Communist

Party (SCCCP), (2) it offers advisory opinions, and (3) it does not hear cases forwarded to it from lower courts (Davidson and Wang 1996). Its American counterpart is answerable to no one, refuses to render advisory opinions, and is kept busy by appeals forwarded from the lower courts, which constitute the vast majority of its business.

The next highest rung in the ladder is the **Higher People's Court** (HPC), which operates at the provincial level and is analogous to an American state supreme court. The HPC hears cases affecting the entire province in which it is located and hears appeals from lower courts, particularly death sentence appeals. One strange function of the HPC is to hear cases where foreigners have committed crimes or in which Chinese citizens have committed crimes against foreigners (Felkenes 1989). If you saw the movie *Red Corner*, starring Richard Gere as American entrepreneur Jack Moore accused of killing a Chinese woman, you have a good idea of the functioning of the HPC.

The **Intermediate People's Court** has exactly the same duties as the HPC at the prefecture (multicounty) level. The one major difference is that it is a court of original jurisdiction for cases involving serious crimes in the prefecture such as murder, rape, robbery, and aggravated assault.

The **Basic People's Court** (BPC) operates at the county level and is analogous to the American district (felony) court. The BPC is the workhorse of the Chinese system and handles a variety of criminal and civil cases that would be shared by district and municipal courts in the United States. The BPC also directs the work of people's mediation committees, which are informal dispute resolution committees.

There is higher judicial review of the outcome of a trial, with both the defendant and the prosecutor having the right to one appeal. The appeals court, consisting of three to five judges, reviews both the law and the facts of the case. The court may return the case to the original court for retrial, modify the original judgment, decrease or reaffirm the sentence on appeal from the defendant, or increase or reaffirm it on appeal from the prosecutor (Davidson and Wang 1996). The prosecutor's right to appeal a "not guilty" verdict reveals the lack of the right to be free of double jeopardy in China.

Given that the purpose of socialist law is to further the interests of the revolution by legalizing its dictates, it goes without saying that Chinese judges have no part in reviewing the constitutionality of legislation passed by the Chinese Communist Party. Even the judges on the Supreme People's Court are appointed by and answerable to the SCCCP. International pressures given impetus by membership in the World Trade Organization (WTO) have moved China to make promises to reform its judiciary by making it more independent and granting it the power to review administrative law (Mei-Ying Hung 2004). Note that this is only review of administrative law, the predictability and fairness of which is needed for participation in the WTO. Nevertheless, WTO membership has placed China's entire legal system under international scrutiny and may be the beginning of fundamental political reforms, without which any real legal reforms are highly unlikely (Mei-Ying Hung 2004).

Islamic Law

Islamic law exists mainly in Middle Eastern Arabic countries, most of Northern Africa, and in the Pakistani and Bangledeshi regions of the Indian subcontinent. Just as socialist law countries vary in their adherence to Marxism, Islamic countries vary in the level of their adherence to strict *Qur'anic* interpretations. Fundamentalist Iran insists on strict adherence to the *Qur'an* in theory, but in practice, it is more pragmatic, and Turkey has gone further than any other Islamic country in almost totally secularizing its laws.

1. *Islamic Law Is Written.* **Islamic law** has its origins in the collected revelations and thoughts of the Prophet Muhammad contained in Islam's Holy Book, the Qur'an (Koran). The Qur'an and its companion book containing the statements and deeds of the Prophet, the **Sunna**, contain numerous moral precepts relating in a general way to all aspects of life, but it is not per se a legal code. The generality of the Qur'an's moral precepts necessitates their augmentation by the commentary of legal scholars and case law. The Qur'an functions as a constitution, laying out general principles that must be interpreted and applied to a variety of specific cases. What emerges from the Qur'an, case law, and scholarly commentaries is called *shari'a*, "the path to follow." Saudi Arabia serves as our model nation illustrating Islamic law because the Qur'an has served as Saudi Arabia's constitution since the birth of that nation in 1926. Saudi Arabia adopted a secular abridged constitution called **Nizam** (Basic Law) compiled from administrative records and royal decrees in 1992. This document fulfills some functions of a constitution, but it is secondary to the Qur'an, contains no guarantees of rights, and is applicable mainly to administrative matters (United Nations Developmental Programme 2005).

There are three key factors that distinguish Islamic law from the other three traditions. First, it claims to be based on direct revelation from God and as such is unchangeable and binding on all people. Second, it attempts to regulate the behavior and thought processes of the individual on practically all matters. Islamic law is thus a theocratic (religious) system as opposed to the secular nature of the other legal traditions. It is total in its scope, and it requires total and unqualified submission to the will of Allah as it is laid out in the Qur'an. Third, it neither requires nor finds it desirable to achieve uniformity of law. The lack of recourse to generalized principles of law has led some Western commentators to consider it a system of ad hoc justice akin to informal dispute resolution rather than a rational and predictable system of law as we know it in the West (Abadinsky 2003).

2. *Islamic Law Is a Hybrid Inquisitorial/Adversarial System; Precedent Is Absent; and No Use Is Made of Juries.* Like the Chinese system, Saudi Arabian law is a hybrid of the inquisitorial and adversarial systems, with strong emphasis on the former. Although the system contains few procedural rules, suspects have the right to confront their accusers and are assumed innocent until proven guilty. Criminal court proceedings in Saudi Arabia are very informal by Western standards. The judge or **qadi** (or *khadi*) hears cases and makes decisions based on his own distillation of the facts and the testimony before him and on the principles

of Islamic justice as he sees them. He is not bound by precedent, not even his own, or by the decisions of higher courts. Anderson (1959, 13) tells an anecdotal story of a conversation between Muhammad, the prophet of Islam, and a qadi at Yemen relating how the qadi would make a legal decision with the tools provided by Islamic law:

> "On what," Muhammad is said to have asked, "will you base your judgments?"
>
> "On the Book of God," the Qadi replied.
>
> "But suppose there is nothing therein to help you?"
>
> "Then," said the Qadi, "I will judge by Sunna of the Prophet."
>
> "But suppose there is nothing there, either, to help you?"
>
> "Then I will follow my own opinion," the Qadi is supposed to have replied; and Muhammad is said to have thanked the Almighty that He had Vouchsafed him such a worthy emissary.

Wiechman, Kendall, and Azarian (2005, 2) applaud this, stating that "[c]ommon law is filled with precedents, rules, and limitations which inhibit creative justice. Judges under Islamic law are free to create new options and ideas to solve new problems associated with crime." This "creative," arbitrary judging is exactly what Western systems have tried to curtail since Beccaria's appeal in the eighteenth century for predictability and equity in sentencing.

Crime and Punishment

Before we proceed further with the court process, it is necessary in this tradition first to discuss crimes and their punishment, which is the fourth aspect of Islamic law that differentiates it from other systems. Unlike other legal systems that categorize the seriousness of crimes and the punishment they engender, by the severity of the damage they cause to the victim and/or to society, Islamic law characterizes offenses by the types of punishment they engender. If a punishment is prescribed by the Qur'an, it tends to be more severe than if it is not, regardless of the seriousness of the crime as Westerners might view it.

Islamic law has three classifications of crime: *Hadd, Quesas,* and *Ta'azir.* **Hadd** (plural, *Huddud*) crimes and the penalties attached to them are considered God prescribed, and no judge or legislative body can alter the penalty for them (Souryal, Potts, and Alobied 1994). *Hadd* crimes and their penalties (in parentheses) are adultery (death); fornication (whipping—eighty lashes); false accusation of any of the foregoing crimes (whipping—one hundred lashes); alcohol consumption (whipping—varies; death is possible after a third offense); apostasy—conversion from Islam to some other faith (death); theft (amputation of hand); and robbery (amputation of alternate-side hand and foot).

Hadd crimes are heard by a panel of three judges. There are variations in these sentences according to circumstance and social status. For instance, adultery carries the death penalty only for married persons; single persons receive one hundred lashes. Typically, only males are executed for apostasy, but they may be given three days to repent (under torture if necessary); females are imprisoned and may be lashed each day until they repent. A free person receives eighty lashes for drinking alcohol and slaves get forty (Fairchild and Dammer 2001). While these punishments strike Westerners as cruel and excessive, they are applied only after intense investigations carried out under strict evidentiary rules that some claim exceed any in the West (Souryal et al. 1994). Human rights groups strongly disagree with this assessment, citing vague laws, arbitrary arrests, flogging and long detention without trial, and torture to obtain confessions (International Commission of Jurists 2002).

Unlike other legal systems for which the rules of evidence remain the same for every crime, Islamic law maintains higher standards for Hadd crimes. This curiosity means that theft demands stricter rules of evidence than murder because theft is a Hadd crime and murder is not (it is a Quesas crime). A conviction for a Hadd crime requires either a confession or the eyewitness testimony of at least two adult males (sometimes two women may substitute for one male) who must be Muslims of impeccable character (Reichel 2005). Such requirements would certainly tend to minimize convictions for many crimes that take place in private, as most acts of adultery, sodomy, and fornication presumably do. These evidentiary requirements may have been purposely designed to make conviction virtually impossible for most Hadd crimes because of the harshness of the punishment. Indeed, it is considered commendable when witnesses *do not* come forward so that the accused can settle the matter privately with God (Reichel 2005).

Quesas means "equal harm" or "retaliation" and are crimes committed against individuals rather than against God. Penalties for these crimes are based on the "eye for an eye" principle. These crimes are serious ones such as murder and assault and battery, but they are crimes for which the Qu'ran does not specify a penalty. Penalties of these crimes can thus be negotiated or even forgiven upon payment of some form of restitution to the offended party or his or her survivors. If penalties are imposed, they may range from beheading (for murder), to whipping, to a prison sentence.

Ta'azir (rehabilitation) crimes include consumption of pork, bribery, provocative dress, "wifely disobedience," and traffic offenses for which the imposition of punishment is discretionary. Penalties may range from a dressing down by the judge, a short prison sentence, or some form of light corporal punishment. An important exception to these relatively light punishments is the punishment for sodomy. Although not a *Hadd* crime, sodomy is considered basically the same thing as adultery and is punished as such.

Saudi Arabian law does not normally allow legal representation in a trial, preferring that the accused speak for himself or herself. This is not as bad as it sounds because prosecutors do not subject the accused to skillful cross-examination, nor is there any jury to be swayed by emotional testimony. The qadi is the sole finder of guilt or innocence, and he may not even have to concern himself with either fact or law due to the practice of oath taking in Islamic courts. If the crime in question is a *Hadd*, the offended individual is responsible for bringing a complaint against the offender. Since few cases of adultery or burglary are likely to take place in front of two (burglary) or four (adultery) witnesses, oath taking has a central role in most trials. A series of initial statements (not made under oath) may be made by both parties in the dispute regarding various aspects of evidence and character for the qadi to evaluate. The climax of the trial comes when one of the parties challenges the other to swear an oath that he is telling the truth. Which party challenges and which swears is decided by the qadi. Whoever swears the oath wins the case, for there is no opportunity to rebut or challenge the oath. If a person declines to swear the oath, and this occurs with some regularity, he automatically surrenders the case. There is no punishment for perjury because those who falsely swear will be punished in the next life (Wiechman, Azarian, and Kendall 1995).

3. *Judicial Review Is Limited to Certain Crimes Only.* After judgment is rendered by the **Musta'galah** (ordinary courts) or **Kubra** (high courts) for *Ta'azir* crimes (in the first instance) or *Hadd or Quesas* crimes (in the second instance), the appeals process may come into play. A major function of appeals courts in other legal traditions is to try to ensure uniformity of the law, but because legal uniformity is not a concern in the Islamic tradition, in Saudi Arabia, these courts exist only to hear appeals against sentences imposed by lower courts. Such appeals, heard by panels of three to five judges, are particularly likely to occur for sentences of death, stoning, or amputation (Reichel 2005).

The formal head of the Saudi judicial system is the King of Saudi Arabia, but on a day-to-day level, the Ministry of Justice actually presides over it. The Ministry is not a court per se; it is rather an administrative body, a source of pardons, and a final body of appeal that determines if verdicts have been rendered in conformity with shari'a. Since shari'a is based on the word of God as written in the Qu'ran, the final word as to correct interpretation (a form of constitutional review in Saudi Arabia's case) rests in the hands of religious rather than secular authorities. Because the Qu'ran does not envision conflict between the interests of the rulers and the ruled and because the law is of divine origin and valid for all time, there can be no provision for judicial review of governmental actions (Fairchild and Dammer 2001).

THE FOUR TRADITIONS AND THE RULE OF LAW

A useful way of making comparisons among the four legal traditions is the degree to which the rule of law is present. Recall from chapter 2 that the rule of law has three important principles: (1) the *recognition* that there are fundamental principles and values stressing human dignity and value, (2) values and principles are articulated and *formalized* in writing and contained in revered documents, and (3) substantive laws and administrative procedures are implemented to hold the state and its agents to those fundamental values and principles.

Let us see how the representative nations of the three non–common law traditions stack up in terms of their adherence to the rule of law with reference to the indices of civil liberties quantified by Freedom House (Puddington 2007) and the Economist Intelligence Unit (2007). Both indices use up to sixty different indicators to examine many aspects of freedom and democracy across the world, but we are concerned only with each country's civil liberties score. Freedom House ranks countries on a scale of one through seven, with one indicating the highest level of civil liberty. The Economist Intelligence Unit ranks countries zero through ten, with ten indicating the highest civil liberty score. For comparison purposes, the United States (along with all other English-speaking countries) is rated 1 (the highest score) by Freedom House, and a more precise 8.53 by the Economist Intelligence Unit on civil liberty.

The fundamental principles and values of France are articulated in the 1789 document **Declaration of the Rights of Man and of the Citizen** and in the 1958 Constitution of the Fifth Republic. France thus unquestionably exhibits the first two elements of the rule of law. When addressing the third element, we have to be careful of legal ethnocentrism. The French do lack due process protections as Americans view them. These protections, however, are viewed by the French as protecting the guilty at the expense of the innocent, and the French have their own procedures for holding agents of the state responsible for implementing their revered values and principles. France does not lack due process procedures; they simply have different ones aimed more solidly (as they see it) at punishing the guilty and freeing the innocent and thus more in conformity with the principles of justice. France was rated as highly as the United States (1) on the provision of civil liberties by Freedom House and somewhat higher than the United States by the Economist Intelligence Unit (9.12 versus 8.53 for the United States).

One of the authors (Walsh) of this book was teaching in France and studying the French criminal justice system after the O. J. Simpson trial verdict (discussed in chapter 7). The verdict was a major source of conversation between him and representatives of the French criminal justice system, all of whom expressed total inability to understand the logic of both the process or the verdict. These people made it very clear why many legal people in civil law countries "find the common law to be crude, unorganized, and culturally inferior" (Reichel 2005, 156).

Islamic law recognizes fundamental values and principles, and those values and principles have been committed to writing in the Qur'an. Thus Islamic law conforms to the first two requirements of the rule of law. However, the provision of procedures for implementing those values and principles has not been a major concern in Islamic law. Some Islamic countries that have secularized their laws provide moderate (e.g., Turkey) due process rights, but states that maintain strict shari'a have no procedures to review the acts of their government and its agents and to hold them accountable. This lack is the result of the Muslims' Qur'anic duty to give allegiance to the existing civil authority regardless of how just or unjust it may be. It is assumed that Allah will punish unjust actions in due course. Islamic law thus does not operate under the rule of law because its written principles and values are not backed by formal procedures for holding the government accountable to them. Saudi Arabia was rated a six (the second-lowest score; recall that seven is the worst score) on civil liberties by Freedom House and a very low 1.76 (out of ten) by the Economist Intelligence Unit.

Socialist law is different from the other three traditions in that it fails to meet any of the criteria for operating under the rule of law. The rule of law is absent by design in socialist law because it subordinates itself to social policy and does not even recognize any fundamental values and principles that could be written down to serve as the basis for holding authorities accountable. As we have seen, there are certain procedural rules under socialist law, but these are followed or not followed according to the needs of the state at the moment. China has legislated various reforms since it joined the WTO, but how or if they will be implemented remains to be seen. China was rated a six on civil liberties by Freedom House and even lower than Saudi Arabia (1.18) by the Economist Intelligence Unit.

It is interesting to note that each of our representative nations opposes American-style judicial review of governmental actions but for vastly different reasons. The French oppose it because it thwarts the will of the people as expressed by the legislature; the Chinese oppose it because it interferes with the wishes of the Communist Party; and the Saudis oppose it because the law is the word of God and thus cannot be amended by any mere mortal. Strictly speaking, however, the French hold their government to the rule of law by the scrutiny of the *Conseil Constitutionnel*, prior to the implementation of proposed legislation rather than afterward, as in the United States. Judicial review of substantive and procedural criminal law is, however, an integral part of all modern common and civil law systems regardless of whether or not judicial review of legislation is permitted in a given country.

To conclude, France is a modern democratic nation that functions under the rule of law. On the other hand, both China and Saudi Arabia are traditional autocratic systems. They are both ruled by law, for there is no other way a nation can survive. However, being ruled *by* law is not the same as functioning under the rule *of* law. Rule *by* laws unencumbered by anything as inconvenient as respect for universal human rights brings with it only a stifling constraint of liberty; the rule *of* law implies a liberating constraint.

THE CONVERGENCE OF SYSTEMS

As the world becomes more complex and interdependent, its cultures will inevitably converge more and more, which probably means that the various legal systems will become more and more similar in all places. One of the most positive trends in criminal law around much of the world is an increased concern for individual rights and the rule of law. The interpenetration of cultures means widespread exposure to the methods other countries use to settle disputes and to define and punish criminals. Such exposure will inevitably lead to cross-fertilization and perhaps a better balance between individual and community rights than has heretofore existed. This trend was already in evidence nearly forty years ago when Merryman (1969, 134) wrote,

> In a sense, it can be said that the evolution of criminal procedure in
> the last two centuries in the civil law world has been away from the

extremes and abuses of the inquisitorial system, and that the evolution in the common law world during the same period has been away from the abuses and excesses of the accusatorial [adversarial] system. The two systems, in other words, are converging from different directions toward roughly equivalent mixed systems of criminal procedure.

Does this convergence also apply to the socialist and Islamic traditions? The short answer is "probably yes." It is more and more difficult for individual nations to participate in the community of nations without conducting themselves according to rational-formal law. The need for uniformity in commercial law is already in evidence. China's acceptance on paper of the international community's "suggestions" on civil rights reforms upon China's entry in the WTO is a case in point. Countries in the Islamic tradition that have strongly pursued modernization have discouraged the use of Islamic law, and despite the zealous embrace of Islamic fundamentalism by Iran, that country has not totally abandoned the civil law aspects of its system. Because Islam forbids certain business practices (i.e., payment of interest), even Saudi Arabia has had to make concessions to the exigencies of international trade and banking (Fairchild and Dammer 2001).

There are, or course, also substantial cultural barriers to convergence in areas other than commercial law. Only greater secularization of Islamic nations will temper the harsh criminal code of Shari'a as well as extend human rights to women, religious minorities, and gays in those countries. Unfortunately, at the time of writing, such rights appear to be decreasing rather than increasing, as shari'a law is experiencing a robust resurgence in many Islamic countries around the world (Coleman 2006; Puddington 2007).

The establishment of supranational courts such as the **International Court of Justice**, also known as the World Court, situated in The Hague, Holland, and the European Court of Human Rights, situated in Strasbourg, France, provides further evidence for the convergence of systems. The World Court, the judicial body of the United Nations, rules on international law, although nations often see fit not to abide by its rulings if those rulings are not in their national interest. Given the lack of an executive mechanism to enforce its rulings, we might ask if the World Court is truly a court in the traditional sense.

The European Court of Human Rights, which is the court of final appeals among the nations of the European Union, does find its ruling respected by member nations of the European Union. All member nations with the exception of Britain are civil law nations, which will probably mean that the Court of Human Rights will tend to move English common law closer to the continental civil system (Kenney 1998). This may mean that other Commonwealth countries such as Australia and Canada may also move more toward civil law, possibly leaving the United States as the sole common law nation left in the world. Nevertheless, because of a great deal of cross-fertilization among the various traditions, there is much that is "civil" about the American system and much that is "common" among civil law countries. There will probably always be some differences in legal systems from society to society, however. The trajectory of modernism and international legal conformity will clash with the reluctance to dispense with deep-seated cultural beliefs in many nations, especially in nations with legal traditions based on religious prescriptions, leaving the study of comparative law an interesting one for many years to come.

SUMMARY

Even the simplest of societies need rules to live by, whether or not those rules are written down and formalized as law. Band and tribal cultures rely mostly on informal methods of enforcing rules, such as shame and ridicule, which are very effective in small-scale social groups in which everybody knows everybody else.

There are four main traditions of law in the world today, and we examined them in terms of how the three non–common law traditions differed from common law, focusing on France (civil law), China (socialist law), and Saudi Arabia (Islamic law). Civil law is the most common (48 percent of nations) legal tradition in the world, followed by common law (19 percent), with Islamic and socialist next, each with 3 percent. The remaining nations have mixtures of the four traditions.

Civil and socialist law both arose out of the revolutionary tradition of the French and Russian Revolutions, respectively, and represent the complete abandonment of the status quo as it existed prior to those events. This is contrasted with common law, which has evolved piecemeal over the centuries without any major traumatic breaks. We noted that French civil law tradition differs from common law in several ways. The French legal system has been characterized as a "truth-seeking" system in which all sorts of evidence is admissible and in which the innocent are more likely to be set free and the guilty found guilty than is the case in a common law system.

Socialist law is a system of law that is subordinate to the social policy goals of the ruling communist party and under which suspects are granted very few due process rights. Since the breakup of the Soviet Union and the Russian rejection of communism, the major socialist law country remaining today is China. The Chinese system places emphasis on confession and reintegration into the community. Defendants are not told of the evidence against them; they usually defend themselves in court by the debate process; and the prosecutor can appeal a "not guilty" verdict. A large number of crimes in China carry the death penalty, and the number of criminals executed annually in China exceeds the number from any other country from which data are available.

Islamic law is based on the *Qur'an*, the Islamic holy book, and the *Sunna*, which together comprise the *Shari'a*, "the path to follow." Islamic law is a theocratic system, and Saudi Arabia has adopted the Qur'an as its constitution and insists on strict adherence to its principles. Rather than categorizing crimes according to the degree of damage done to the individual or society, Islamic law categorizes them by the punishment for them prescribed in the Qur'an. There are three broad classes of crimes—*Hadd*, *Quesas*, and *Ta'azir*. *Hadd* crimes carry the most severe penalties, which cannot be changed by man since they are pre-scribed by God. Because there is no penalty prescribed for murder (a *Quesas* crime) in the Qur'an, it is possible to receive a more lenient sentence for murder than for crimes such as adultery, sodomy, or apostasy, all of which carry the death penalty. Because of the severity of the penalty for such crimes, standards of evidence are said to be extremely high, and it is often preferred that a person accused of such a crime settle the matter privately with God. Oath swearing is the major means of deciding a case in a Saudi court, which has few formal legal rules.

In terms of how our representative nations followed the rule of law, we found that France offers extensive protections to the accused, although they are somewhat different from the protections offered in the United States. Saudi Arabia conforms to the first two principles of the rule of law but falls down on the third (laws and procedures to hold the state and its agents accountable). China fares poorly on all three elements of the rule of law, although there are indica-tions that the concept of due process may be taking hold there.

As the various nations of the world become more economically integrated, we can expect to see a degree of convergence of legal systems. This has been going on for some time because of legal cross-pollination. There is fairly univer-sal agreement that economic advancement requires a rational-formal legal sys-tem, and many nations formerly not employing such a system are doing so, if only in the area of commercial law thus far. It was also noted that the various supranational courts that have sprung up over the last century will also tend to move disparate systems closer to each other over time.

DISCUSSION QUESTIONS

1. Why would, or would not, the practice of shaming as it occurs in preliterate cultures work in the United States to deter crime?
2. Would civil law as exemplified in the French system work in the United States? Are there any aspects of the French system you would like to see incorporated into American law?
3. What is the major advantage of civil law over common law, and what is the major disadvantage? Look at the question from both a due process and crime control perspective.
4. Do you think it would be an improvement over our current legal system if we adopted a theocratic system based on the Bible and even made the Bible our constitution?
5. If you are guilty of a capital offense, would you rather be tried in Saudi Arabia or China?
6. Because adherence to international laws and courts necessarily means surrendering some aspects of national sovereignty, should the United States pay any attention at all to World Court decisions that run counter to its interests?

References

Abadinsky, H. 2003. *Law and justice: An introduction to the American legal system.* Upper Saddle River, NJ: Prentice Hall.

Amnesty International. 2005. *Death penalty: 3,977 executed in 2004.* London: Author.

Anderson, J. 1959. *Islamic law in the modern world.* Westport, CT: Greenwood Press.

Coleman, I. 2006. Women, Islam, and the new Iraq. *Foreign Affairs,* February. http://www.foreignaffairs.org/20060101faessay85104/isobel-coleman-islam.

Congressional Executive Commission on China. 2004. *Defense lawyers turned defendants: Zhang Jianzhong and the criminal prosecution of defense lawyers in China.* http://www.cecc.gov/pages/news/zhang_052703.php.

Danilenko, G., and W. Burnham. 1999. *Law and the legal system of the Russian Federation.* New York: Juris.

Davidson, R., and Z. Wang. 1996. The court system in the People's Republic of China with a case study of a criminal trial. In *Comparative and international criminal justice systems,* edited by O. Ebbe, pp. 139–53. Boston: Butterworth-Heiemann.

Economist Intelligence Unit. 2007. *The Economist Intelligence Unit's index of democracy.* http://www.economist.com/media/pdf/DEMOCRACY_INDEX_2007_v3.pdf

Ellis, L., and A. Walsh. 2000. *Criminology: A global perspective.* Boston: Allyn & Bacon.

Fairchild, E., and H. Dammer. 2001. *Comparative criminal justice systems.* Belmont, CA: Wadsworth.

Felkenes, G. 1989. Courts, sentencing, and the death penalty in the PCR. In *Social control in the People's Republic of China,* edited by R. Troyer, J. Clark, and D. Rojek, pp. 141–58. New York: Praeger.

Friedman, L. 1977. *Law and society: An introduction.* Englewood Cliffs, NJ: Prentice Hall.

International Commission of Jurists. 2002. *Saudi Arabia.* www.icj/news.multi.php.mot=.

Jurors to help to decide court verdicts. 2005. *China Daily,* April, 24, p. 1. http://en.cn./National/Law/200504/25/t20050425_3689256.shtml.

Kenney, S. 1998. The European Court of Justice: Integrating Europe through law. *Judicature* 81:250–55.

Kidder, R. 1983. *Connecting law to society.* Englewood Cliffs, NJ: Prentice Hall.

Lu, H., and T. Miethe. 2002. Legal representation and legal processing in China. *British Journal of Criminology* 42:267–80.

Lykken, D. 1995. *The antisocial personalities.* Hillsdale, NJ: Lawrence Erlbaum.

Maeching, C. 1993. The adversarial system should be replaced. In *Criminal justice, Opposing viewpoints,* edited by M. Biskup, 35–42. San Diego, CA: Greenhaven.

Marsh, R. 2000. Weber's misunderstanding of traditional Chinese law. *American Journal of Sociology* 106:281–302.

Mei-Ying Hung, V. 2004. China's WTO commitment on independent judicial review: Impact on legal and political reforms. *American Journal of Comparative Law* 52:77–132.

Merryman, J. 1969. *The civil law tradition: An introduction to the legal systems of Western Europe and Latin America.* Stanford, CA: Stanford University Press.

Puddington, A. 2007. *Freedom in the world 2007.* Freedom House. http://www.freedomhouse.org/uploads/press_release/fiw07_overview_final.pdf

Reichel, P. 2005. *Comparative criminal justice systems: A topical approach.* 4th ed. Upper Saddle River, NJ: Prentice Hall.

Situ, Y., and W. Liu. 1996. An overview of the Chinese criminal justice system. In *Comparative and international criminal justice systems,* edited by O. Ebbe, 125–37. Boston: Butterworth-Heiemann.

Souryal, S., D. Potts, and A. Alobied. 1994. The penalty of hand amputation for theft in Islamic justice. *Journal of Criminal Justice* 22:249–65.

Terrill, R. 1999. *World criminal justice systems*. Cincinnati, OH: Anderson.

Thompson, W. 1985. *Canada 1985*. Washington, DC: Stryker-Post.

United Nations Developmental Programme. 2005. *Programme for governance in the Arab region*. http://www.pogar.org/countries/constitution.asp?cid=16.

Walsh, A. 2009. *Biology and criminology: The biosocial synthesis*. New York: Routledge.

Wiechman, D., M. Azarian, and J. Kendall. 1995. Islamic courts and corrections. *International Journal of Comparative and Applied Criminal Justice* 19:33–46.

Wiechman, D., J. Kendall, and M. Azarian. 2005. *Islamic law: Myths and realities*. http://muslim-canada.org/Islam_myths-htm.

Wright, B., and V. Fox. 1978. *Criminal justice and the social sciences*. Philadelphia: W. B. Saunders.

APPENDIX A

CONSTITUTION OF THE UNITED STATES OF AMERICA

We the People of the United States, in Order to form a more perfect Union, establish Justice, insure domestic Tranquility, provide for the common defense, promote the general Welfare, and secure the Blessings of Liberty to ourselves and our Posterity, do ordain and establish this Constitution for the United States of America.

Article. I.

Section. 1.

All legislative Powers herein granted shall be vested in a Congress of the United States, which shall consist of a Senate and House of Representatives.

Section. 2.

The House of Representatives shall be composed of Members chosen every second Year by the People of the several States, and the Electors in each State shall have the Qualifications requisite for Electors of the most numerous Branch of the State Legislature.

No Person shall be a Representative who shall not have attained to the Age of twenty five Years, and been seven Years a Citizen of the United States, and who shall not, when elected, be an Inhabitant of that State in which he shall be chosen.

Representatives and direct Taxes shall be apportioned among the several States which may be included within this Union, according to their respective Numbers, which shall be determined by adding to the whole Number of free Persons, including those bound to Service for a Term of Years, and excluding Indians not taxed, three fifths of all other Persons. The actual Enumeration shall be made within three Years after the first Meeting of the Congress of the United States, and within every subsequent Term of ten Years, in such Manner as they shall by Law direct. The Number of Representatives shall not exceed one for every thirty Thousand, but each State shall have at Least one Representative; and until such enumeration shall be made, the State of New Hampshire shall be entitled to chuse three, Massachusetts eight, Rhode-Island and Providence Plantations one, Connecticut five, New-York six, New Jersey four, Pennsylvania eight, Delaware one, Maryland six, Virginia ten, North Carolina five, South Carolina five, and Georgia three.

When vacancies happen in the Representation from any State, the Executive Authority thereof shall issue Writs of Election to fill such Vacancies.

The House of Representatives shall chuse [sic] their Speaker and other Officers; and shall have the sole Power of Impeachment.

Section. 3.

The Senate of the United States shall be composed of two Senators from each State, chosen by the Legislature thereof for six Years; and each Senator shall have one Vote.

Immediately after they shall be assembled in Consequence of the first Election, they shall be divided as equally as may be into three Classes. The Seats of the Senators of the first Class shall be vacated at the Expiration of the second Year, of the second Class at the Expiration of the fourth Year, and of the third Class at the Expiration of the sixth Year, so that one third may be chosen every second Year; and if Vacancies happen by Resignation, or otherwise, during the Recess of the Legislature of any State, the Executive thereof may make temporary Appointments until the next Meeting of the Legislature, which shall then fill such Vacancies.

No Person shall be a Senator who shall not have attained to the Age of thirty Years, and been nine Years a Citizen of the United States, and who shall not, when elected, be an Inhabitant of that State for which he shall be chosen.

The Vice President of the United States shall be President of the Senate, but shall have no Vote, unless they be equally divided.

The Senate shall chuse their other Officers, and also a President pro tempore, in the Absence of the Vice President, or when he shall exercise the Office of President of the United States.

The Senate shall have the sole Power to try all Impeachments. When sitting for that Purpose, they shall be on Oath or Affirmation. When the President of the United States is tried, the Chief Justice shall preside: And no Person shall be convicted without the Concurrence of two thirds of the Members present.

Judgment in Cases of Impeachment shall not extend further than to removal from Office, and disqualification to hold and enjoy any Office of honor, Trust or Profit under the United States: but the Party convicted shall nevertheless be liable and subject to Indictment, Trial, Judgment and Punishment, according to Law.

Section. 4.

The Times, Places and Manner of holding Elections for Senators and Representatives, shall be prescribed in each State by the Legislature thereof; but the Congress may at any time by Law make or alter such Regulations, except as to the Places of chusing Senators.

The Congress shall assemble at least once in every Year, and such Meeting shall be on the first Monday in December, unless they shall by Law appoint a different Day.

Section. 5.

Each House shall be the Judge of the Elections, Returns and Qualifications of its own Members, and a Majority of each shall constitute a Quorum to do Business; but a smaller Number may adjourn from day to day, and may be authorized to compel the Attendance of absent Members, in such Manner, and under such Penalties as each House may provide.

Each House may determine the Rules of its Proceedings, punish its Members for disorderly Behaviour, and, with the Concurrence of two thirds, expel a Member.

Each House shall keep a Journal of its Proceedings, and from time to time publish the same, excepting such Parts as may in their Judgment require Secrecy; and the Yeas and

Nays of the Members of either House on any question shall, at the Desire of one fifth of those Present, be entered on the Journal.

Neither House, during the Session of Congress, shall, without the Consent of the other, adjourn for more than three days, nor to any other Place than that in which the two Houses shall be sitting.

Section. 6.

The Senators and Representatives shall receive a Compensation for their Services, to be ascertained by Law, and paid out of the Treasury of the United States. They shall in all Cases, except Treason, Felony and Breach of the Peace, be privileged from Arrest during their Attendance at the Session of their respective Houses, and in going to and returning from the same; and for any Speech or Debate in either House, they shall not be questioned in any other Place.

No Senator or Representative shall, during the Time for which he was elected, be appointed to any civil Office under the Authority of the United States, which shall have been created, or the Emoluments whereof shall have been encreased during such time; and no Person holding any Office under the United States, shall be a Member of either House during his Continuance in Office.

Section. 7.

All Bills for raising Revenue shall originate in the House of Representatives; but the Senate may propose or concur with Amendments as on other Bills.

Every Bill which shall have passed the House of Representatives and the Senate, shall, before it become a Law, be presented to the President of the United States: If he approve he shall sign it, but if not he shall return it, with his Objections to that House in which it shall have originated, who shall enter the Objections at large on their Journal, and proceed to reconsider it. If after such Reconsideration two thirds of that House shall agree to pass the Bill, it shall be sent, together with the Objections, to the other House, by which it shall likewise be reconsidered, and if approved by two thirds of that House, it shall become a Law. But in all such Cases the Votes of both Houses shall be determined by yeas and Nays, and the Names of the Persons voting for and against the Bill shall be entered on the Journal of each House respectively. If any Bill shall not be returned by the President within ten Days (Sundays excepted) after it shall have been presented to him, the Same shall be a Law, in like Manner as if he had signed it, unless the Congress by their Adjournment prevent its Return, in which Case it shall not be a Law.

Every Order, Resolution, or Vote to which the Concurrence of the Senate and House of Representatives may be necessary (except on a question of Adjournment) shall be presented to the President of the United States; and before the Same shall take Effect, shall be approved by him, or being disapproved by him, shall be repassed by two thirds of the Senate and House of Representatives, according to the Rules and Limitations prescribed in the Case of a Bill.

Section. 8.

The Congress shall have Power To lay and collect Taxes, Duties, Imposts and Excises, to pay the Debts and provide for the common Defence and general Welfare of the United States; but all Duties, Imposts and Excises shall be uniform throughout the United States;

To borrow Money on the credit of the United States;

To regulate Commerce with foreign Nations, and among the several States, and with the Indian Tribes;

To establish an uniform Rule of Naturalization, and uniform Laws on the subject of Bankruptcies throughout the United States;

To coin Money, regulate the Value thereof, and of foreign Coin, and fix the Standard of Weights and Measures;

To provide for the Punishment of counterfeiting the Securities and current Coin of the United States;

To establish Post Offices and post Roads;

To promote the Progress of Science and useful Arts, by securing for limited Times to Authors and Inventors the exclusive Right to their respective Writings and Discoveries;

To constitute Tribunals inferior to the supreme Court;

To define and punish Piracies and Felonies committed on the high Seas, and Offences against the Law of Nations;

To declare War, grant Letters of Marque and Reprisal, and make Rules concerning Captures on Land and Water;

To raise and support Armies, but no Appropriation of Money to that Use shall be for a longer Term than two Years;

To provide and maintain a Navy;

To make Rules for the Government and Regulation of the land and naval Forces;

To provide for calling forth the Militia to execute the Laws of the Union, suppress Insurrections and repel Invasions;

To provide for organizing, arming, and disciplining, the Militia, and for governing such Part of them as may be employed in the Service of the United States, reserving to the States respectively, the Appointment of the Officers, and the Authority of training the Militia according to the discipline prescribed by Congress;

To exercise exclusive Legislation in all Cases whatsoever, over such District (not exceeding ten Miles square) as may, by Cession of particular States, and the Acceptance of Congress, become the Seat of the Government of the United States, and to exercise like Authority over all Places purchased by the Consent of the Legislature of the State in which the Same shall be, for the Erection of Forts, Magazines, Arsenals, dock-Yards, and other needful Buildings;—And

To make all Laws which shall be necessary and proper for carrying into Execution the foregoing Powers, and all other Powers vested by this Constitution in the Government of the United States, or in any Department or Officer thereof.

Section. 9.

The Migration or Importation of such Persons as any of the States now existing shall think proper to admit, shall not be prohibited by the Congress prior to the Year one thousand eight hundred and eight, but a Tax or duty may be imposed on such Importation, not exceeding ten dollars for each Person.

The Privilege of the Writ of Habeas Corpus shall not be suspended, unless when in Cases of Rebellion or Invasion the public Safety may require it.

No Bill of Attainder or ex post facto Law shall be passed.

No Capitation, or other direct, Tax shall be laid, unless in Proportion to the Census or enumeration herein before directed to be taken.

No Tax or Duty shall be laid on Articles exported from any State.

No Preference shall be given by any Regulation of Commerce or Revenue to the Ports of one State over those of another; nor shall Vessels bound to, or from, one State, be obliged to enter, clear, or pay Duties in another.

No Money shall be drawn from the Treasury, but in Consequence of Appropriations made by Law; and a regular Statement and Account of the Receipts and Expenditures of all public Money shall be published from time to time.

No Title of Nobility shall be granted by the United States: And no Person holding any Office of Profit or Trust under them, shall, without the Consent of the Congress, accept of any present, Emolument, Office, or Title, of any kind whatever, from any King, Prince, or foreign State.

Section. 10.

No State shall enter into any Treaty, Alliance, or Confederation; grant Letters of Marque and Reprisal; coin Money; emit Bills of Credit; make any Thing but gold and silver Coin a Tender in Payment of Debts; pass any Bill of Attainder, ex post facto Law, or Law impairing the Obligation of Contracts, or grant any Title of Nobility.

No State shall, without the Consent of the Congress, lay any Imposts or Duties on Imports or Exports, except what may be absolutely necessary for executing it's inspection Laws: and the net Produce of all Duties and Imposts, laid by any State on Imports or Exports, shall be for the Use of the Treasury of the United States; and all such Laws shall be subject to the Revision and Controul of the Congress.

No State shall, without the Consent of Congress, lay any Duty of Tonnage, keep Troops, or Ships of War in time of Peace, enter into any Agreement or Compact with another State, or with a foreign Power, or engage in War, unless actually invaded, or in such imminent Danger as will not admit of delay.

Article. II.

Section. 1.

The executive Power shall be vested in a President of the United States of America. He shall hold his Office during the Term of four Years, and, together with the Vice President, chosen for the same Term, be elected, as follows:

Each State shall appoint, in such Manner as the Legislature thereof may direct, a Number of Electors, equal to the whole Number of Senators and Representatives to which the State may be entitled in the Congress: but no Senator or Representative, or Person holding an Office of Trust or Profit under the United States, shall be appointed an Elector.

The Electors shall meet in their respective States, and vote by Ballot for two Persons, of whom one at least shall not be an Inhabitant of the same State with themselves. And they shall make a List of all the Persons voted for, and of the Number of Votes for each; which List they shall sign and certify, and transmit sealed to the Seat of the Government of the United States, directed to the President of the Senate. The President of the Senate shall, in the Presence of the Senate and House of Representatives, open all the Certificates, and the Votes shall then be counted. The Person having the greatest Number of Votes shall be the President, if such Number be a Majority of the whole Number of Electors appointed; and if there be more than one who have such Majority, and have an equal Number of Votes, then the House of Representatives shall immediately chuse by Ballot one of them for President; and if no Person have a Majority, then from the five highest on the List the said House shall in like Manner chuse the President. But in chusing the President, the Votes shall be taken by States, the Representation from each State having one Vote; A quorum for this purpose shall consist of a Member or Members from two thirds of the States, and a Majority of all the States shall be necessary to a Choice. In every Case, after the Choice of the President, the Person having the greatest Number of Votes of the Electors shall be the Vice President. But if there should remain two or more who have equal Votes, the Senate shall chuse from them by Ballot the Vice President.

The Congress may determine the Time of chusing the Electors, and the Day on which they shall give their Votes; which Day shall be the same throughout the United States.

No Person except a natural born Citizen, or a Citizen of the United States, at the time of the Adoption of this Constitution, shall be eligible to the Office of President; neither shall any Person be eligible to that Office who shall not have attained to the Age of thirty five Years, and been fourteen Years a Resident within the United States.

In Case of the Removal of the President from Office, or of his Death, Resignation, or Inability to discharge the Powers and Duties of the said Office, the Same shall devolve on the Vice President, and the Congress may by Law provide for the Case of Removal, Death, Resignation or Inability, both of the President and Vice President, declaring what Officer shall then act as President, and such Officer shall act accordingly, until the Disability be removed, or a President shall be elected.

The President shall, at stated Times, receive for his Services, a Compensation, which shall neither be increased nor diminished during the Period for which he shall have been elected, and he shall not receive within that Period any other Emolument from the United States, or any of them.

Before he enter on the Execution of his Office, he shall take the following Oath or Affirmation:—"I do solemnly swear (or affirm) that I will faithfully execute the Office of President of the United States, and will to the best of my Ability, preserve, protect and defend the Constitution of the United States."

Section. 2.

The President shall be Commander in Chief of the Army and Navy of the United States, and of the Militia of the several States, when called into the actual Service of the United States; he may require the Opinion, in writing, of the principal Officer in each of the executive Departments, upon any Subject relating to the Duties of their respective Offices, and he shall have Power to grant Reprieves and Pardons for Offences against the United States, except in Cases of Impeachment.

He shall have Power, by and with the Advice and Consent of the Senate, to make Treaties, provided two thirds of the Senators present concur; and he shall nominate, and by and with the Advice and Consent of the Senate, shall appoint Ambassadors, other public Ministers and Consuls, Judges of the supreme Court, and all other Officers of the United States, whose Appointments are not herein otherwise provided for, and which shall be established by Law: but the Congress may by Law vest the Appointment of such inferior Officers, as they think proper, in the President alone, in the Courts of Law, or in the Heads of Departments.

The President shall have Power to fill up all Vacancies that may happen during the Recess of the Senate, by granting Commissions which shall expire at the End of their next Session.

Section. 3.

He shall from time to time give to the Congress Information of the State of the Union, and recommend to their Consideration such Measures as he shall judge necessary and expedient; he may, on extraordinary Occasions, convene both Houses, or either of them, and in Case of Disagreement between them, with Respect to the Time of Adjournment, he may adjourn them to such Time as he shall think proper; he shall receive Ambassadors and other public Ministers; he shall take Care that the Laws be faithfully executed, and shall Commission all the Officers of the United States.

Section. 4.

The President, Vice President and all civil Officers of the United States, shall be removed from Office on Impeachment for, and Conviction of, Treason, Bribery, or other high Crimes and Misdemeanors.

Article. III.

Section. 1.

The judicial Power of the United States shall be vested in one supreme Court, and in such inferior Courts as the Congress may from time to time ordain and establish. The Judges, both of the supreme and inferior Courts, shall hold their Offices during good Behaviour, and shall, at stated Times, receive for their Services a Compensation, which shall not be diminished during their Continuance in Office.

Section. 2.

The judicial Power shall extend to all Cases, in Law and Equity, arising under this Constitution, the Laws of the United States, and Treaties made, or which shall be made, under their Authority;—to all Cases affecting Ambassadors, other public Ministers and Consuls;—to all Cases of admiralty and maritime Jurisdiction;—to Controversies to which the United States shall be a Party;—to Controversies between two or more States;—between a State and Citizens of another State;—between Citizens of different States;—between Citizens of the same State claiming Lands under Grants of different States, and between a State, or the Citizens thereof, and foreign States, Citizens or Subjects.

In all Cases affecting Ambassadors, other public Ministers and Consuls, and those in which a State shall be Party, the supreme Court shall have original Jurisdiction. In all the other Cases before mentioned, the supreme Court shall have appellate Jurisdiction, both as to Law and Fact, with such Exceptions, and under such Regulations as the Congress shall make.

The Trial of all Crimes, except in Cases of Impeachment, shall be by Jury; and such Trial shall be held in the State where the said Crimes shall have been committed; but when not committed within any State, the Trial shall be at such Place or Places as the Congress may by Law have directed.

Section. 3.

Treason against the United States, shall consist only in levying War against them, or in adhering to their Enemies, giving them Aid and Comfort. No Person shall be convicted of Treason unless on the Testimony of two Witnesses to the same overt Act, or on Confession in open Court.

The Congress shall have Power to declare the Punishment of Treason, but no Attainder of Treason shall work Corruption of Blood, or Forfeiture except during the Life of the Person attainted.

Article. IV.

Section. 1.

Full Faith and Credit shall be given in each State to the public Acts, Records, and judicial Proceedings of every other State. And the Congress may by general Laws prescribe the

Manner in which such Acts, Records and Proceedings shall be proved, and the Effect thereof.

Section. 2.

The Citizens of each State shall be entitled to all Privileges and Immunities of Citizens in the several States.

A Person charged in any State with Treason, Felony, or other Crime, who shall flee from Justice, and be found in another State, shall on Demand of the executive Authority of the State from which he fled, be delivered up, to be removed to the State having Jurisdiction of the Crime.

No Person held to Service or Labour in one State, under the Laws thereof, escaping into another, shall, in Consequence of any Law or Regulation therein, be discharged from such Service or Labour, but shall be delivered up on Claim of the Party to whom such Service or Labour may be due.

Section. 3.

New States may be admitted by the Congress into this Union; but no new State shall be formed or erected within the Jurisdiction of any other State; nor any State be formed by the Junction of two or more States, or Parts of States, without the Consent of the Legislatures of the States concerned as well as of the Congress.

The Congress shall have Power to dispose of and make all needful Rules and Regulations respecting the Territory or other Property belonging to the United States; and nothing in this Constitution shall be so construed as to Prejudice any Claims of the United States, or of any particular State.

Section. 4.

The United States shall guarantee to every State in this Union a Republican Form of Government, and shall protect each of them against Invasion; and on Application of the Legislature, or of the Executive (when the Legislature cannot be convened), against domestic Violence.

Article. V.

The Congress, whenever two thirds of both Houses shall deem it necessary, shall propose Amendments to this Constitution, or, on the Application of the Legislatures of two thirds of the several States, shall call a Convention for proposing Amendments, which, in either Case, shall be valid to all Intents and Purposes, as Part of this Constitution, when ratified by the Legislatures of three fourths of the several States, or by Conventions in three fourths thereof, as the one or the other Mode of Ratification may be proposed by the Congress; Provided that no Amendment which may be made prior to the Year One thousand eight hundred and eight shall in any Manner affect the first and fourth Clauses in the Ninth Section of the first Article; and that no State, without its Consent, shall be deprived of its equal Suffrage in the Senate.

Article. VI.

All Debts contracted and Engagements entered into, before the Adoption of this Constitution, shall be as valid against the United States under this Constitution, as under the Confederation.

This Constitution, and the Laws of the United States which shall be made in Pursuance thereof; and all Treaties made, or which shall be made, under the Authority of the United States, shall be the supreme Law of the Land; and the Judges in every State shall be bound thereby, any Thing in the Constitution or Laws of any State to the Contrary notwithstanding.

The Senators and Representatives before mentioned, and the Members of the several State Legislatures, and all executive and judicial Officers, both of the United States and of the several States, shall be bound by Oath or Affirmation, to support this Constitution; but no religious Test shall ever be required as a Qualification to any Office or public Trust under the United States.

Article. VII.

The Ratification of the Conventions of nine States, shall be sufficient for the Establishment of this Constitution between the States so ratifying the Same.

THE AMENDMENTS

The Preamble to the Bill of Rights

Congress of the United States begun and held at the City of New York, on Wednesday the fourth of March, one thousand seven hundred and eighty nine.

THE Conventions of a number of the States, having at the time of their adopting the Constitution, expressed a desire, in order to prevent misconstruction or abuse of its powers, that further declaratory and restrictive clauses should be added: And as extending the ground of public confidence in the Government, will best ensure the beneficent ends of its institution.

RESOLVED by the Senate and House of Representatives of the United States of America, in Congress assembled, two thirds of both Houses concurring, that the following Articles be proposed to the Legislatures of the several States, as amendments to the Constitution of the United States, all, or any of which Articles, when ratified by three fourths of the said Legislatures, to be valid to all intents and purposes, as part of the said Constitution; viz.

ARTICLES in addition to, and Amendment of the Constitution of the United States of America, proposed by Congress, and ratified by the Legislatures of the several States, pursuant to the fifth Article of the original Constitution.

AMENDMENT I

Congress shall make no law respecting an establishment of religion, or prohibiting the free exercise thereof; or abridging the freedom of speech, or of the press; or the right of the people peaceably to assemble, and to petition the Government for a redress of grievances.

AMENDMENT II

A well regulated Militia, being necessary to the security of a free State, the right of the people to keep and bear Arms, shall not be infringed.

AMENDMENT III

No Soldier shall, in time of peace be quartered in any house, without the consent of the Owner, nor in time of war, but in a manner to be prescribed by law.

AMENDMENT IV

The right of the people to be secure in their persons, houses, papers, and effects, against unreasonable searches and seizures, shall not be violated, and no Warrants shall issue, but upon probable cause, supported by Oath or affirmation, and particularly describing the place to be searched, and the persons or things to be seized.

AMENDMENT V

No person shall be held to answer for a capital, or otherwise infamous crime, unless on a presentment or indictment of a Grand Jury, except in cases arising in the land or naval forces, or in the Militia, when in actual service in time of War or public danger; nor shall any person be subject for the same offence to be twice put in jeopardy of life or limb; nor shall be compelled in any criminal case to be a witness against himself, nor be deprived of life, liberty, or property, without due process of law; nor shall private property be taken for public use, without just compensation.

AMENDMENT VI

In all criminal prosecutions, the accused shall enjoy the right to a speedy and public trial, by an impartial jury of the State and district wherein the crime shall have been committed, which district shall have been previously ascertained by law, and to be informed of the nature and cause of the accusation; to be confronted with the witnesses against him; to have compulsory process for obtaining witnesses in his favor, and to have the Assistance of Counsel for his defence.

AMENDMENT VII

In Suits at common law, where the value in controversy shall exceed twenty dollars, the right of trial by jury shall be preserved, and no fact tried by a jury, shall be otherwise re-examined in any Court of the United States, than according to the rules of the common law.

AMENDMENT VIII

Excessive bail shall not be required, nor excessive fines imposed, nor cruel and unusual punishments inflicted.

AMENDMENT IX

The enumeration in the Constitution, of certain rights, shall not be construed to deny or disparage others retained by the people.

AMENDMENT X

The powers not delegated to the United States by the Constitution, nor prohibited by it to the States, are reserved to the States respectively, or to the people.

AMENDMENT XI (1795)

The Judicial power of the United States shall not be construed to extend to any suit in law or equity, commenced or prosecuted against one of the United States by Citizens of another State, or by Citizens or Subjects of any Foreign State.

AMENDMENT XII (1804)

The Electors shall meet in their respective states and vote by ballot for President and Vice-President, one of whom, at least, shall not be an inhabitant of the same state with themselves; they shall name in their ballots the person voted for as President, and in distinct ballots the person voted for as Vice-President, and they shall make distinct lists of all persons voted for as President, and of all persons voted for as Vice-President, and of the number of votes for each, which lists they shall sign and certify, and transmit sealed to the seat of the government of the United States, directed to the President of the Senate;—the President of the Senate shall, in the presence of the Senate and House of Representatives, open all the certificates and the votes shall then be counted;—The person having the greatest number of votes for President, shall be the President, if such number be a majority of the whole number of Electors appointed; and if no person have such majority, then from the persons having the highest numbers not exceeding three on the list of those voted for as President, the House of Representatives shall choose immediately, by ballot, the President. But in choosing the President, the votes shall be taken by states, the representation from each state having one vote; a quorum for this purpose shall consist of a member or members from two-thirds of the states, and a majority of all the states shall be necessary to a choice. And if the House of Representatives shall not choose a President whenever the right of choice shall devolve upon them, before the fourth day of March next following, then the Vice-President shall act as President, as in case of the death or other constitutional disability of the President. The person having the greatest number of votes as Vice-President, shall be the Vice-President, if such number be a majority of the whole number of Electors appointed, and if no person have a majority, then from the two highest numbers on the list, the Senate shall choose the Vice-President; a quorum for the purpose shall consist of two-thirds of the whole number of Senators, and a majority of the whole number shall be necessary to a choice. But no person constitutionally ineligible to the office of President shall be eligible to that of Vice-President of the United States.

AMENDMENT XIII (1865)

Section 1.

Neither slavery nor involuntary servitude, except as a punishment for crime whereof the party shall have been duly convicted, shall exist within the United States, or any place subject to their jurisdiction.

Section 2.

Congress shall have power to enforce this article by appropriate legislation.

AMENDMENT XIV (1868)

Section 1.

All persons born or naturalized in the United States, and subject to the jurisdiction thereof, are citizens of the United States and of the State wherein they reside. No State shall make or enforce any law which shall abridge the privileges or immunities of citizens of the United States; nor shall any State deprive any person of life, liberty, or property, without due process of law; nor deny to any person within its jurisdiction the equal protection of the laws.

Section 2.

Representatives shall be apportioned among the several States according to their respective numbers, counting the whole number of persons in each State, excluding Indians not taxed. But when the right to vote at any election for the choice of electors for President and Vice-President of the United States, Representatives in Congress, the Executive and Judicial officers of a State, or the members of the Legislature thereof, is denied to any of the male inhabitants of such State, being twenty-one years of age, and citizens of the United States, or in any way abridged, except for participation in rebellion, or other crime, the basis of representation therein shall be reduced in the proportion which the number of such male citizens shall bear to the whole number of male citizens twenty-one years of age in such State.

Section 3.

No person shall be a Senator or Representative in Congress, or elector of President and Vice-President, or hold any office, civil or military, under the United States, or under any State, who, having previously taken an oath, as a member of Congress, or as an officer of the United States, or as a member of any State legislature, or as an executive or judicial officer of any State, to support the Constitution of the United States, shall have engaged in insurrection or rebellion against the same, or given aid or comfort to the enemies thereof. But Congress may by a vote of two-thirds of each House, remove such disability.

Section 4.

The validity of the public debt of the United States, authorized by law, including debts incurred for payment of pensions and bounties for services in suppressing insurrection or rebellion, shall not be questioned. But neither the United States nor any State shall assume or pay any debt or obligation incurred in aid of insurrection or rebellion against the United States, or any claim for the loss or emancipation of any slave; but all such debts, obligations and claims shall be held illegal and void.

Section 5.

The Congress shall have the power to enforce, by appropriate legislation, the provisions of this article.

AMENDMENT XV (1870)

Section 1.

The right of citizens of the United States to vote shall not be denied or abridged by the United States or by any State on account of race, color, or previous condition of servitude.

Section 2.

The Congress shall have the power to enforce this article by appropriate legislation.

AMENDMENT XVI (1913)

The Congress shall have power to lay and collect taxes on incomes, from whatever source derived, without apportionment among the several States, and without regard to any census or enumeration.

AMENDMENT XVII (1913)

The Senate of the United States shall be composed of two Senators from each State, elected by the people thereof, for six years; and each Senator shall have one vote. The electors in each State shall have the qualifications requisite for electors of the most numerous branch of the State legislatures.

When vacancies happen in the representation of any State in the Senate, the executive authority of such State shall issue writs of election to fill such vacancies: *Provided*, That the legislature of any State may empower the executive thereof to make temporary appointments until the people fill the vacancies by election as the legislature may direct.

This amendment shall not be so construed as to affect the election or term of any Senator chosen before it becomes valid as part of the Constitution.

AMENDMENT XVIII (1917)

Section 1.

After one year from the ratification of this article the manufacture, sale, or transportation of intoxicating liquors within, the importation thereof into, or the exportation thereof from the United States and all territory subject to the jurisdiction thereof for beverage purposes is hereby prohibited.

Section 2.

The Congress and the several States shall have concurrent power to enforce this article by appropriate legislation.

Section 3.

This article shall be inoperative unless it shall have been ratified as an amendment to the Constitution by the legislatures of the several States, as provided in the Constitution, within seven years from the date of the submission hereof to the States by the Congress.

AMENDMENT XIX (1920)

Section 1.

The right of citizens of the United States to vote shall not be denied or abridged by the United States or by any State on account of sex.

Section 2.

Congress shall have power to enforce this article by appropriate legislation.

AMENDMENT XX (1933)

Section 1.

The terms of the President and the Vice President shall end at noon on the 20th day of January, and the terms of Senators and Representatives at noon on the 3d day of January, of the years in which such terms would have ended if this article had not been ratified; and the terms of their successors shall then begin.

Section 2.

The Congress shall assemble at least once in every year, and such meeting shall begin at noon on the 3d day of January, unless they shall by law appoint a different day.

Section 3.

If, at the time fixed for the beginning of the term of the President, the President elect shall have died, the Vice President elect shall become President. If a President shall not have been chosen before the time fixed for the beginning of his term, or if the President elect shall have failed to qualify, then the Vice President elect shall act as President until a President shall have qualified; and the Congress may by law provide for the case wherein neither a President elect nor a Vice President shall have qualified, declaring who shall then act as President, or the manner in which one who is to act shall be selected, and such person shall act accordingly until a President or Vice President shall have qualified.

Section 4.

The Congress may by law provide for the case of the death of any of the persons from whom the House of Representatives may choose a President whenever the right of choice shall have devolved upon them, and for the case of the death of any of the persons from whom the Senate may choose a Vice President whenever the right of choice shall have devolved upon them.

Section 5.

Sections 1 and 2 shall take effect on the 15th day of October following the ratification of this article.

Section 6.

This article shall be inoperative unless it shall have been ratified as an amendment to the Constitution by the legislatures of three-fourths of the several States within seven years from the date of its submission.

AMENDMENT XXI (1933)

Section 1.

The eighteenth article of amendment to the Constitution of the United States is hereby repealed.

Section 2.

The transportation or importation into any State, Territory, or Possession of the United States for delivery or use therein of intoxicating liquors, in violation of the laws thereof, is hereby prohibited.

Section 3.

This article shall be inoperative unless it shall have been ratified as an amendment to the Constitution by conventions in the several States, as provided in the Constitution, within seven years from the date of the submission hereof to the States by the Congress.

AMENDMENT XXII (1951)

Section 1.

No person shall be elected to the office of the President more than twice, and no person who has held the office of President, or acted as President, for more than two years of a term to which some other person was elected President shall be elected to the office of President more than once. But this Article shall not apply to any person holding the office of President when this Article was proposed by Congress, and shall not prevent any person who may be holding the office of President, or acting as President, during the term within which this Article becomes operative from holding the office of President or acting as President during the remainder of such term.

Section 2.

This article shall be inoperative unless it shall have been ratified as an amendment to the Constitution by the legislatures of three-fourths of the several States within seven years from the date of its submission to the States by the Congress.

AMENDMENT XXIII (1961)

Section 1.

The District constituting the seat of Government of the United States shall appoint in such manner as Congress may direct:

A number of electors of President and Vice President equal to the whole number of Senators and Representatives in Congress to which the District would be entitled if it were a State, but in no event more than the least populous State; they shall be in addition to those appointed by the States, but they shall be considered, for the purposes of the election of President and Vice President, to be electors appointed by a State; and they shall meet in the District and perform such duties as provided by the twelfth article of amendment.

Section 2.

The Congress shall have power to enforce this article by appropriate legislation.

AMENDMENT XXIV (1964)

Section 1.

The right of citizens of the United States to vote in any primary or other election for President or Vice President, for electors for President or Vice President, or for Senator or Representative in Congress, shall not be denied or abridged by the United States or any State by reason of failure to pay poll tax or other tax.

Section 2.

The Congress shall have power to enforce this article by appropriate legislation.

AMENDMENT XXV (1967)

Section 1.

In case of the removal of the President from office or of his death or resignation, the Vice President shall become President.

Section 2.

Whenever there is a vacancy in the office of the Vice President, the President shall nominate a Vice President who shall take office upon confirmation by a majority vote of both Houses of Congress.

Section 3.

Whenever the President transmits to the President pro tempore of the Senate and the Speaker of the House of Representatives his written declaration that he is unable to discharge the powers and duties of his office, and until he transmits to them a written declaration to the contrary, such powers and duties shall be discharged by the Vice President as Acting President.

Section 4.

Whenever the Vice President and a majority of either the principal officers of the executive departments or of such other body as Congress may by law provide, transmit to the President pro tempore of the Senate and the Speaker of the House of Representatives their written declaration that the President is unable to discharge the powers and duties of his office, the Vice President shall immediately assume the powers and duties of the office as Acting President.

Thereafter, when the President transmits to the President pro tempore of the Senate and the Speaker of the House of Representatives his written declaration that no inability exists, he shall resume the powers and duties of his office unless the Vice President and a majority of either the principal officers of the executive department or of such other body as Congress may by law provide, transmit within four days to the President pro tempore of the Senate and the Speaker of the House of Representatives their written declaration that the President is unable to discharge the powers and duties of his office. Thereupon Congress shall decide the issue, assembling within forty-eight hours for that purpose if not in session. If the Congress, within twenty-one days after receipt of the latter written declaration, or, if Congress is not in session, within twenty-one days after Congress is required to assemble, determines by two-thirds vote of both Houses that the President is unable to discharge the powers and duties of his office, the Vice President shall continue to discharge the same as Acting President; otherwise, the President shall resume the powers and duties of his office.

AMENDMENT XXVI (1971)

Section 1.

The right of citizens of the United States, who are eighteen years of age or older, to vote shall not be denied or abridged by the United States or by any State on account of age.

Section 2.

The Congress shall have power to enforce this article by appropriate legislation.

AMENDMENT XXVII (1992)

No law, varying the compensation for the services of the Senators and Representatives, shall take effect, until an election of representatives shall have intervened.

APPENDIX B

STUDENT-FRIENDLY LEGAL WEB SITES

Findlaw.com: http://www.findlaw.com
One of the best sites, but tends toward "legalese."

Law Guru: http://www.lawguru.com
Perhaps the best site because of its links to other search engines.

Duhaime's Law Dictionary: http://www.duhaime.org.diction.htm
Good definitions (and more) of all legal terms.

Everybody's Law Dictionary: http://www.nolo.com/dictionary/worldindex.cfm
Legal definitions in plain English.

Alabama Law Review: http://www.law.ua.edu/lawreview
Provides full-text articles free of charge.

American University International Law Review: http://www.wcl.american.edu/pub/ilr/home.htm
This journal provides international legal perspectives.

American University Law Review: http://www.wcl.american.edu/pub/journals/lawrev/aulrhome.htm
Some full-text articles available free of charge. This is America's oldest and largest legal journal.

Cardozo Law Review: http://www.cardozo.yu.edu/cardlrev/index.html
Provides full-text articles free of charge.

Indiana Law Journal: http://www.law.indiana.edu/ilj/ilj.html
Some full-text articles available free of charge.

U.S. Supreme Court: http://www.supremecourtus.gov
Provides up to date access to Court decisions and many other things relevant to the Court: well worth a visit.

Law and Society Association: http://www.lawandsociety.org/
Web site includes many interesting posted items as well as access to the journal link to their JSTOR journal.

GLOSSARY

Abortion: The intentional termination of a pregnancy by the removal or expulsion of an embryo/fetus from the uterus resulting in its death.

Acceptance: The agreement to terms of a contract offer or promise.

Acquittal: An acquittal or "not guilty" decision means that the state was unable to meet the high burden of proof necessary for a conviction.

Actus reus: Meaning "a guilty act," it refers to the three forms of the criminal act: (1) voluntary bodily movements, (2) an omission in the face of a duty to act, and (3) possession.

Adequate provocation: Defined as a killing, which occurs after such provocation, as the law deems sufficient—that which could cause even a reasonable person to react violently.

Administrative law: A body of law (also known as regulatory law) created by administrative agencies by the powers granted to them by Congress.

Administrative Procedure Act: This 1946 act established the procedural standards federal agencies must follow when adjudicating violations of administrative law.

Administrative regulations: Forms of legislation, which, under certain circumstances, may have the force of law.

Adverse possession: Legal doctrine that allows someone to take the real property of another if they have used it openly and continuously for a period of time.

Affirmative defense: Defenses in which the defendant has the burden of production and the burden of persuasion.

Alford plea: A plea in which the defendant enters a guilty plea but at the same time officially denies having committed the crime to which he or she is pleading.

Alibi: When the defendant asserts he or she is not the person who committed the act charged or a claim that the state has failed to meet its burden of proof on a particular element of the offense charged.

All property: A family law model for dividing property after a divorce; states using this model divide equally all property held jointly regardless of when it was acquired.

American Indian Movement (AIM): Radical activist Indian organization founded in 1968.

Amicus curiae briefs: Briefs presented to the Court arguing in favor of one side or the other by interested parties not directly involved with the case.

Annulment: A legal determination that a valid marriage never existed between the parties.

Anomie: A condition of relative normlessness or social deregulation in society.

Anticipatory offense: An offense where criminal liability exists, even in the absence of the anticipated harm, such as attempt, solicitation, and conspiracy.

Arrest: An arrest occurs when a reasonable person would conclude that the police in some way had restrained his or her liberty so that the person was not free to leave.

Arson: Setting fire to a structure with the intent to burn the structure, in whole or in part.

Articles of Confederation: The 1781 document that was the first attempt at creating a unified United States.

Assault and battery: Under the common law, assault was either (1) an attempt or (2) a threat to inflict immediate harm by a person with the present means of carrying out the attempt or threat.

Assimilation period: Period in which the U.S. government attempted to integrate the Indians into white society by "civilizing" and "Christianizing" them.

Assize court: French court in which the most serious crimes are tried.

Attenuation exception: An exception to the exclusionary rule (or its "fruit of the poisonous tree" offshoot) that states that illegal evidence is admissible if it is attenuated (weakened) by it being sufficiently remote from the initial illegality.

Bailment: The temporary transfer of possession of personal property to another for a particular purpose.

Basic People's Court: Chinese court analogous to American district (felony) court.

Beliefs: Ideas we have about how the world operates and what is true and false.

Bill of Rights: The first 10 Amendments to the U.S. Constitution.

Bills of attainder: Legislation imposing punishment without trial.

Binding out: The practice of assigning children to foster parents as indentured servants.

Black Codes: Various legal codes enacted by the Southern states to control, restrict, and inhibit the movements and behavior of ex-slaves.

Booking: An administrative procedure that involves making an entry in the police blotter at the station indicating the just-arrested suspect's name, arrest time, offense, and the taking of the suspect's fingerprints and photograph.

Breach of contract: The failure to comply with the terms of a valid contract.

Bridewells: Early English institutions for housing and training youthful offenders.

Burden of production: Refers to the duty to produce evidence. Thus, in every criminal case, the prosecution must introduce evidence showing the defendant, in all likelihood, committed the crime with which he or she has been charged.

Burden of Proof: The obligation to prove allegations presented in a court of law. In a criminal case, it is the prosecution.

Bureau of Indian Affairs (BIA): Agency responsible for all aspects of Indian life, especially during the assimilation period.

Burglary: Must be an unlawful entry accompanied by the present intent to commit another crime once inside. It may occur at all hours of the day and is not limited to dwellings but also may occur in virtually any structure.

Castle Doctrine: An exception to the general rules of self-defense, it states that persons attacked in their home need not retreat from a potentially deadly invasion and/or attack.

Causation: The legal principle that the criminal act is the act that is the cause of the harm. There are two types of causation: factual and legal.

Cesare Beccaria: Italian nobleman and lawyer famous for his book *On crime and Punishment* advocating for reform of the criminal justice system.

Challenge for cause: A challenge in which a valid reason for wanting to dismiss a potential jury member is shown to the court's satisfaction. Usually involves demonstrating that a potential juror cannot be unbiased or impartial.

Charismatic authority: A type of authority underlain by mythical, quasi-supernatural qualities.

Chevron deference: The principle enunciated by the Supreme Court that courts must defer to agency interpretations of their own laws.

Child Savers: Liberals whose goal was to reform the juvenile justice system.

Chinese Exclusion Act: An 1882 act barring Chinese from immigrating to the United States.

Ch'ing Code: Early (1646) Chinese law code containing many statutes and offenses.

CHINS: Acronym for "child in need of supervision;" a status offender.

Civil law: The area of law common law regulating the conduct of private parties and their relationships.

Civil law or code law: World's most popular legal tradition; written law.

Civil Rights Act of 1875: Congressional Act stipulating that all persons were entitled to full access and enjoyment of all and facilities in hotels, inns, theaters, and public conveyances. Was declared unconstitutional in the *Civil Rights Cases* of 1883.

Civil Rights Act of 1964: Sweeping Congressional act that ensured civil, political, and social rights for blacks.

Clear and convincing evidence: A standard of proof in civil law that falls between the usual *preponderance of evidence* and criminal law's *beyond a reasonable doubt.*

Code Civil des Français: Also known as the Napoleonic Code. It became the blueprint for all subsequence civil law codes.

Codes: Legislative enactments, or bills, often referred to as *statutes.*

Cold War: Period from the end of World War II to 1989. A propaganda war "fought" largely between the United States and the Soviet Union.

Collegial bench: Comprises one to three professional judges and two to four lay *people's* assessors who sit in judgment of Chinese individuals accused of serious crimes.

Common law: A common law system was developed in England by the thirteenth century. Common law was judge-made law. That is, it was law created by judges as they heard cases and settled disputes.

Common law marriage: A legally binding marriage despite the absence of legal documents; allowed in only a handful of states today.

Comparative negligence: A legal doctrine that attempts to apportion the responsibility for negligent conduct among the parties involved.

Compensatory style: A form of social control in which some person or group has accused another person or group of breaching an obligation and brings the matter before the courts seeking compensation.

Complaint: An accusation on a formal document that may be filled out by an officer or a private citizen accusing a specified person or persons of committing a specified act or acts. If an arrest is made first, a complaint will be sworn out afterwards, usually by the arresting officer. The complaint serves as the charging document for the preliminary hearing.

Complicity: Sets forth the situations where more than one person may be held liable for criminal activity. Complicity still requires all the elements of criminal liability (intent, act, harm, and causation), but allows liability to attach to someone else's conduct.

Conciliatory style: A form of social control using the law to remedy a breach in a formerly harmonious relationship. Blame is not usually assigned in such matters.

Concurrence: The union of the criminal act (*actus reus*) and criminal intent (*mens rea*).

Conflict perspective: Perspective emphasizing that conflict mostly characterizes society, in which resources are limited and people seek to maximize their interests.

Conseil Constitutionnel: France's constitutional court determining constitutionality of *proposed* legislation only.

Consensus perspective: A perspective emphasizing that consensus mostly characterizes society, where being part of a shared culture contributes to social stability.

Consent: A defense to some crimes in which a person granting consent is harmed. A claim of consent must demonstrate that it was voluntary, knowing, and intelligent.

Conspiracy: An agreement between two or more people for the purpose of committing a crime.

Constitution: A document that legalizes the existing political order and legitimizes its ideology, provides a framework for the administration of government, regulates social and institutional behavior, and enumerates national goals and aspirations.

Constrained view: A view of the Supreme Court that maintains that it can rarely produce significant social change because its practical powers are limited.

Contract: A legally enforceable promise.

Contract law: A form of civil law governing the conduct of business, which deals with the enforceability of private agreements between individuals and between organizations.

Contrast effect: The contrast between the circumstances of punishment suffered and an offender's usual life; the greater the contrast, the greater the deterrent effect.

Contraventions: In the French criminal justice system, *contraventions* are similar to minor misdemeanors in the American system. They carry a maximum penalty of two months in jail.

Contributory negligence: A legal rule now mostly out of favor that states that if an injured party was in any way partially responsible for his or her injuries, he or she was barred from collecting from the tortfeasor.

Convention on the Elimination of All Forms of Discrimination Against Women: United Nations charter designed to accomplish what its title implies. The United States is one of the few countries that have not ratified the Convention.

Conviction: Result of a criminal trial in which the person accused has been found or has pleaded guilty.

Corpus delecti: Refers to the five elements of criminal liability, each of which must be established beyond a reasonable doubt.

Corpus Juris Civilis: Roman legal code also known as the Code of Justinian.

Correctional court: French courts trying crimes carrying up to five years in prison.

Cour de Cassation: France's highest appeals court hearing criminal cases.

Courts of Chancery: Early English courts in which judges were directed to view each case as unique, to be flexible and empathetic, and to think in terms of *standards* of fairness rather than *rules* of law.

Coverture: A legal term that describes the legal subsuming of the female person into the male in marriage.

Crime control model: Criminal justice model emphasizing community protection from criminals and that civil liberties can only have meaning in a safe, well-ordered society.

Criminal law: The body of law that regulates conduct and provides penalties (including fines and imprisonment) to be imposed on those who violate the laws; sometimes referred to as the criminal code or penal code.

Culture: The totality of learned socially transmitted behaviors, ideas, values, customs, artifacts, and technology of groups of people living in a common society.

Curtilage: The land and buildings immediately surrounding and intimately associated with a dwelling.

Custody: Defined as when the suspect has been subjected to a formal arrest or equivalent restraints on his freedom of movement.

De facto: "According to practice." Some practice that exists in fact but not by law.

De jure: "According to law." Something conforming with legal requirements or statutes.

De minimis intrusion: To balance the limited intrusion on individual rights against the heightened public interest in the subject, with the governmental interest outweighing the principle of *de minimis* (literally, *the least*).

Declaration of the Rights of Man and of the Citizen: Revolutionary document integrated into the French constitution.

Defense of Marriage Act: A 1996 federal act defining marriage as a contract that only people of opposite sexes can enter into.

Delinquent: A minor who commits acts that are crimes when committed by adults.

Delicts: In the French criminal justice system, delicts are similar to the less serious felonies in the American system. They carry a maximum penalty of up to fives years in prison and are tried in correctional court.

Direct-formal social control: Social control via the direct formalities of law (i.e., punishment legally applied to the transgressor).

Direct-informal social control: Social control via the informal application of stigma applied to the transgressor.

Discovery doctrine: Justice Marshall's doctrine asserting white sovereignty over the Indians by virtue of being heir to the European power that "discovered" America.

Disenfranchisement: Taking away the right to vote.

Disorderly conduct: A catch-all phrase and has been held to include acts as diverse as public drunkenness, vagrancy, playing loud music, and fighting.

Distributive justice: The form of justice concerned with how a political entity such as a nation distributes its resources.

Double jeopardy: The legal principle that states a jurisdiction may not (1) prosecute someone again for the same crime after the person has been acquitted, (2) prosecute someone again for the same crime after the person has been convicted, and (3) punish someone twice for the same offense.

Dual property: A family law model for dividing property after a divorce; states using this model divide equally all property held jointly that was acquired during the marriage.

Dual sovereignty doctrine: Under the dual sovereignty doctrine, a person can be prosecuted in both federal and state court for the same offense or in the courts of different states for the same offense if certain circumstances surrounding the offense occurred in more than one state.

Due process: A set of instructions informing agents of the state how they must proceed in their investigation, arrest, questioning, prosecution, and punishment of individuals who are suspected of committing crimes; a principle binding the state to follow certain procedures designed to protect individual rights before it may deprive individuals of life, liberty, or property.

Due process model: Concerned primarily with the protection of individual privacy. It emphasizes the importance of the formal legal process as a means of ensuring mistakes are kept to a minimum, and it operates on the presumption of innocence.

Duress: Duress may be raised as a defense in a limited number of situations, which vary by jurisdiction, but generally include situations involving the threat of serious, imminent harm to oneself where the act is less serious than the threatened harm.

Durham rule: This rule is met when the act was caused by the defendant's mental illness.

Dynamic view: A view of the Supreme Court maintaining that it can be more effective than other government branches in bringing about social change because it is free of election concerns and can act in the face of public opposition.

Easement: A limited right to use another's real property for a specific purpose and time period.

Effects: Include papers, cars, and other like items. Items sought may include contraband; fruits of the crime; instrumentalities of the crime such as weapons, burglar's tools, or the getaway car; or evidence of the crime.

Emancipation Proclamation: Executive proclamation issued in 1862 and in 1863 by Abraham Lincoln, freeing all slaves in the United States.

Eminent domain: The right and power of government to take private property with just compensation for public purposes.

Entrapment: A defense to criminal liability in which the defendant asserts he or she committed the crime only because the government encouraged them to do so. According to the Supreme Court, it occurs when (1) the crime is the result of "the creative activity" of law enforcement, and (2) the prosecutor cannot prove beyond a reasonable doubt that the defendant was "independently predisposed" to commit the crime.

Environmental justice: The fair treatment and meaningful involvement of all people, regardless of race, color, national origin, or income, with respect to the development, implementation, and enforcement of environmental laws, regulations, and policies.

Equal protection clause: Interpreted to preclude states from making unequal, arbitrary distinctions between people. It does not ban reasonable classifications, but it does prohibit classifications that are either without reason or based on race or gender.

Equal Rights Amendment: A proposed amendment to the United States Constitution that would guarantee women certain rights.

Equity: A concept akin to *fairness* or *justice* that served as the basis of the Courts of Chancery in England.

European Court of Human Rights: Multinational court concerned with human rights issues in the European Union.

Evolutionary perspective: Perspective of natural law that considers it natural because it flows from the evolved nature of the species.

Ex parte: A court hearing in the presence of only one of the parties to a case.

Ex post facto law: Criminalizing an act already completed but not previously forbidden by the penal law.

Exclusionary rule: A judicially created remedy for violations of the Fourth Amendment, it provides that any evidence obtained by the government in violation of the Fourth Amendment guarantee against unreasonable searches and seizures is not admissible in a criminal trial to prove guilt.

Excuse defense: One in which defendants admit that what they did was wrong but argue that under the circumstances, they are not responsible for the improper conduct.

Exigent circumstance: A critical or urgent situation that justifies the failure to obtain a warrant.

Expressive conduct: Conduct such as written statements and some physical acts intended to make a point ("symbolic speech") protected by the First Amendment.

Extortion: A taking of property accomplished by the threat of future harm to person, property, or reputation.

Factual cause: Refers to the idea that "but for" the actor's conduct, the harm would not have occurred. It is an initial act that sets a series of other acts in motion that leads to some harm. Factual causation is a necessary but not sufficient element for the imposition of criminal liability. A legal cause also must exist.

False consciousness: In Marxist philosophy, the acceptance of a belief system among the working classes that is contrary to their class interests.

Family law: The set of laws involving marriage, child custody, and other issues arising in personal relationships.

Fee simple absolute estate: One in which the property interest does not revert to the original owner.

Fee simple estate: An interest in real property that ends when the person dies—at which time the interest reverts to the original owner of the property.

Felony murder rule: A rule in which an individual may be held liable for an unintended killing that occurs during the commission of a dangerous felony, such as robbery or rape. There is no requirement of intent to either kill or inflict serious injury. It is enough if the person was engaged in what is considered a dangerous felony, or a felony in which serious injury is a reasonably foreseeable outcome. In most states, felony murder is treated as second degree murder.

Feminism: A set of theories and strategies for social change that takes gender as their central focus in attempting to understand social institutions, processes, and relationships.

Feminist jurisprudence: The practice of examining and evaluating the law from a feminist perspective.

Forgery: False legal writing or altering of an existing legal document.

Formal irrationality: Legal decisions based on formal rules but not based on reason or logic.

Formal rationality: Legal decisions based on formal rules and on reason and logic.

Forms: Refers to Plato's belief that the objects and ideas in the world are only imperfect representations of the archetypal objects and ideas in the real world.

Fourteenth Amendment: Guarantees "due process" and has been interpreted by the U.S. Supreme Court to incorporate much of the Bill of Rights.

Fourth Amendment search: The examination of an individual's house, person, or effects to discover items related to criminal activity and only applies to areas where persons have a reasonable expectation of privacy, such as in a person's home.

Fourth Amendment seizure: States that citizens have a right to be free from "unreasonable" searches and seizure and that warrants shall be issued only upon a showing of "probable cause."

Freedman's Bureau: During the Reconstruction, Bureau set up by the federal government to provide former slaves with food, clothing, schools, and other requirements.

Freehold estate: One wherein a person owns a piece of property as distinguished from only a right to use property (as in a rental agreement).

Fruit of the poisonous tree: An appendage to the exclusionary rule that dictates that any evidence indirectly gained by an illegal police action must be excluded.

Fundamental rights: Rights that the Supreme Court has determined are "essential to the concept of ordered liberty."

Gender bias: Refers to differential treatment based on one's gender.

General Allotment Act (or Dawes Act): Act dividing up reservation lands into allotments given to individual Indians as part of the assimilation process.

General deterrence: The supposed preventive effect of punishment on those who have witnessed it but not experienced it.

General warrant: A warrant employed by the British prior to the American Revolution; that did not spell out what specifically was being looked for and why.

Good faith: An assumption that all of the parties are making promises that they mean to keep and that these promises are made based on a common understanding of what will be required to meet the obligations incurred according to standards of fair dealing in trade.

Good faith exception: The exclusion of evidence obtained by police who have not knowingly violated the Fourth Amendment and who relied in "good faith" on other actors in the criminal justice system does not serve the purpose of deterring police misconduct, the primary goal of the exclusionary rule.

Grand jury: A group of citizens who listen to the case presented by a prosecutor and determine whether there is sufficient evidence to grant an indictment.

Habeas corpus: A document challenging the legality of a person's detention.

Hadd Crimes (plural, Huddud): Islam's most serious crimes with mandated punishments as defined by God.

Hammurabi's Code: The first known legal codes.

Harm: The result of the act, the injury to another.

Harm principle: A principle first enunciated by John Stuart Mill stating that people should enjoy any and all liberties, even those harmful to themselves, as long as their behavior does not cause harm to others.

Harrison Narcotics Act: A 1914 act regulating drug use in the United States that was the benchmark act for changing America's attitudes toward drugs.

Henry II: English king (1154–1189) often referred to as the "father of the common law."

Henry de Bracton: English judge who compiled judicial rulings to show how precedent may guide future rulings; he is often referred to as the father of case law.

Higher People's Court: Chinese court analogous to an American state supreme court.

Homicide: A broad, all-inclusive term for any killing of another human being.

Hung jury: A situation that occurs when the trial jury is unable to reach a unanimous verdict in a case that requires unanimity.

Immunity: In law, the concept that some people (judges for actions that fall within the purview of judicial duties) or entities (sovereign states) are immune from legal prosecution for their actions.

Imperfect: Refers to an affirmative defense resulting in a reduction of the charge; or they may simply serve to mitigate the punishment.

In re: Literally, "in the matter of"; used in nonadversarial court proceedings.

Incapacitation: A philosophy of punishment justified by the inability of incarcerated criminals to victimize people outside the prison walls.

Inchoate crimes: Crimes that occur in preparation for an offense. Inchoate means "to begin" or "to partially put into operation."

Indian Citizenship Act: Act granting U.S. citizenship to Indians in 1924.

Indian Civil Rights Act: A 1968 act that applied the most of the Bill of Rights to Indians with exceptions that respected Indian tribal sovereignty.

Indian Removal Act: Congressional act mandating the removal of all Indians in the southeastern states to "Indian territory" (now the state of Oklahoma).

Indian Reorganization Act: A 1934 act that ended the practice of cultural genocide and encouraged Indians to revive their languages, religions, and customs.

Indian Self-Determination Act: A 1975 act ending the termination policy of the 1950s.

Indictment: A document formally charging the defendant with a crime handed down by a grand jury after hearing the evidence presented by the prosecutor.

Indirect-formal social control: Social control via the threat of legal sanctions perceived by individuals who have not transgressed the law.

Indirect-informal social control: Social control by reinforcing norms.

Inevitable discovery exception: An exception to the exclusionary rule that permits the introduction of illegally obtained evidence if the police can demonstrate that they would have discovered the evidence by legal means anyway.

Information: A substitute for an indictment in which charges against a defendant are filed directly with the court by the prosecutor, thus bypassing the grand jury.

Initial appearance: The first court appearance by a suspect/defendant, which takes place in a municipal or justice of the peace court. It is here that suspects are informed of their constitutional rights, the nature of the charges against them, and a bail decision is made.

Inquisitorial system: Investigatory criminal justice system characterized by cooperation between all parties in an effort to reach the truth.

Insanity: A defense to criminal liability in most jurisdictions. A person who is found by the jury to be insane is not liable for his or her actions because they lack mens rea. It is a legal term to describe mental illness. There are several different tests for insanity, depending on the jurisdiction.

Intellectual property: Ideas or concepts developed by an individual or group.

Intent: What a person meant to happen when they engaged in particular conduct.

Intentional tort: An injury purposely caused by a tort defendant.

Intermediate People's Court: Chinese court that carries out the same functions as the higher people's court at the prefecture (multicounty) level. The major difference is that it is a court of original jurisdiction for cases involving serious crimes such as murder and rape.

Intermediate scrutiny: A level of review developed by the Supreme Court to rview government actions that may affect an individual's constitutional rights. The test is whether a law is "substantially related to an important government purpose."

International Court of Justice: Also known as the World Court, it is the judicial body of the United Nations. Deals with legal disputes among United Nations member states.

Inventory search: A warrantless search, as a matter of policy, police impound and/or inventory vehicles after the driver is arrested and is intended to protect the property of the arrestee as well as the department from lawsuits alleging theft of personal property within the vehicle.

Investigative detention: See "Stop and frisk."

Involuntary commitment: The use of legal means to commit someone to a mental institution against his or her will.

Irresistible impulse: Defined as when a defendant could not control his or her conduct.

Islamic Law: A theocratic system of law based on the *Qur'an,* the *Sunna,* and *Shari'a.*

Jim Crow laws: Any state or federal laws that enforced the segregation of the races in various areas of American life.

Judicial activism: Accusation made against judges when it is believed they have decided a case based on principles other than constitutional ones.

Judicial review: The power of the courts to examine a law to determine whether it is constitutional.

Judicial waiver: Transfer of a juvenile to criminal court decided by juvenile court judge at his or her own discretion after a full inquiry into the matter.

Jury consultants: Experts hired by attorneys to help them determine what type of person is more likely to favor their side.

Jus cogens: International standards of justice; closely tied to the idea of universal natural law, it means "compelling" or "higher law."

Justice: According to Aristotle, "justice consists of treating equals equally and unequals unequally according to relevant differences."

Justification defense: One in which the defendant admits he or she is responsible for the act which occurred but claims that under the circumstances the act was not criminal.

Kansas-Nebraska Act: Repealed the Missouri Compromise and opened up areas of the West to slavery.

Knock and announce requirement: Police officers executing an arrest (or search) warrant at a private dwelling are required to "knock and announce" their presence and purpose and provide occupants of a dwelling a reasonable amount of time to answer the door.

Kubra: The high courts in Islamic law that hear serious (Hadd) offenses.

Larceny: The unlawful taking and carrying away of another's personal property, with the intent to permanently deprive the rightful owner of its possession. Includes taking by stealth, by force, by fraud, and by false pretenses.

Law: A written body of general rules of conduct applicable to all members of a defined community, society, or culture, which emanate from a governing authority and which are enforced by its agents by the imposition of penalties for their violation.

Legal cause: Also referred to as proximate cause. The proximity in time between the accused's actions and the ultimate degree of harm caused to the victim. The question often asked in such cases is "for which act does it seem fair and just to hold the actor accountable?" Consequences of an act that are not reasonably foreseeable to the actor are "intervening causes" and may serve to relieve the actor of criminal liability.

Legal realism: The study of legal decision making. It explores how law is applied and the implications of that application: not law "as written," but law "as practiced."

Legitimacy: The ability to command compliance with rules despite the lack of objective means to compel it.

Lettres de cachet: Notorious sealed letters issued under the Code Louis in France ordering the arrest and incarceration of anyone displeasing powerful individuals.

Lineup: "Critical stage" in the criminal proceedings where the suspect(s), along with other individuals of the same appearance, are lined up for witnesses or the victim of the offense to identify as the culprit.

Lunge area: Referring to the immediate vicinity of the suspect.

Magna Carta: The "Great Charter" of 1215 limiting the power of the English sovereign and asserting certain rights on the part of the barons.

Major Crimes Act: An 1885 act that extended federal criminal jurisdiction over Indians and other persons in Indian country.

Mala in se crimes: Crimes that are universally condemned because they are inherently evil.

Mala prohibita crimes: Crimes that are defined as bad simply because they are forbidden.

Manslaughter: voluntary: An intentional killing that occurs either (1) under a mistaken belief that self-defense required the use of deadly force or (2) in response to adequate provocation while in the sudden heat of passion; **involuntary:** a criminal homicide where an unintentional killing results from a reckless act.

Marshall Trilogy: Three Supreme Court cases that defined the legal status of Native American sovereignty.

McNaughten rule: The first, and still most common, test for insanity. Under it, a defendant is not criminally liable if he or she did not know either what he or she was doing or know that it was wrong.

Mechanical solidarity: According to Durkheim, the form of social solidarity found in premodern societies.

Mens rea: "Guilty mind." Liability generally does not attach based on action alone; there also must exist some sort of guilty mind.

Miller Test: A test specifying what material must be to be considered obscene. (1) The material must appeal to prurient interests as determined by the "average person" applying "contemporary community standards." (2) It must describe-illustrate sexual activity in a "patently offensive" way. And (3) it has to lack any serious literary, artistic, scientific, or political value.

Miranda warnings: Warning given by police to arrested suspects, informing them of both the privilege against self-incrimination and the right to counsel. Evidence obtained by the police during a custodial interrogation of a suspect could not be used at trial unless the suspect first was informed of these rights.

Misogyny: The hatred, devaluation, and ridicule of women.

Missouri Compromise: An act admitting Missouri into the union as a slave state but restricting the spread of slavery in certain other areas of the Louisiana Purchase territories.

Mistrial: A situation in which a trial is terminated because of a legal error that occurs during a trial that unfairly prejudices the defendant. A new trial may be held at a later date.

Model Penal Code: In relation to modern criminal law, it sets forth four levels of intent: purposeful, knowing, reckless, and negligent.

Motive: The cause or reason why an act is committed.

Movables: Personal property; property not permanently connected to the land.

Murder (first and second degree): A killing that occurs (1) purposefully, or (2) knowingly, or (3) recklessly under circumstances exhibiting extreme indifference to human life. First-degree murder encompasses those killings that are deliberate and premeditated. Second-degree murder includes any killings that are intentional but not premeditated or planned.

Musta'galah: Type of court in Islamic law that hears minor (ta'azir) offenses.

Musta'galah court: Lower court in Saudi Arabia for ta'azir crimes.

National Association for the Advancement of Colored People (NAACP): Founded in 1910 by W. E. B. DuBois, to advance the causes of African Americans.

Natural law: A theory or philosophy of law often contrasted with positive law maintaining that there is a law that is either God given or one that flows from the evolved nature of *Homo sapiens*.

Naturalistic fallacy: The fallacy of confusing what *is* with what *ought* to be.

Negligence: A failure to act with the appropriate level of care.

Negligent homicide: An unintentional killing in which the defendant should have known that he or she was creating a substantial risk of death by his or her conduct, which itself deviated from the ordinary level of care owed to others.

Nizam: Abridged secular Saudi Arabian constitution applicable mainly to administrative matters. It is secondary to the Qur'an and contains no bill of rights.

No-fault divorce: Divorce granted without assigning fault for the breakup of the marriage.

Nolo contendere: A plea in which the defendant accepts whatever punishment the court would impose on a guilty defendant but refuses to admit liability. Also referred to as a "no contest" plea. It is frequently used by defendants who fear being exposed to civil liability for their criminal misdeeds and a guilty plea would so expose them.

Norm: The action component of a value or a belief that prescribes and proscribes behavior as acceptable or unacceptable.

Northwest Ordinance: Provided for a survey of the Northwest Territories and gave the U.S. Congress rather than the states the sole right to trade with Indians.

Nuisance: Using one's property in such a way that it has an unreasonable, adverse affect on other property owners.

Obiter dicta: Statements in a court's decision made in support of the ratio decidendi but that do not establish precedent.

Obscenity: A legal term for any subcategory of pornography that is not constitutionally protected, such as child pornography.

Offer: When a party agrees to do something; required for a valid contract.

On the street encounter: Police may ask questions of anyone in public, and doing so does not constitute an arrest or even a seizure. In such "on-the-street encounters," citizens remain free to leave and even ignore the police officer's question.

Open fields exception: Refers to everything that is *not* defined as being within the curtilage.

Ordered liberty: See *Fundamental rights*.

Ordinary care: The level of care required to avoid committing a negligent act and being civilly liable in tort law.

Organic solidarity: According to Durkheim, the form of social solidarity found in modern societies.

Original position: John Rawls' version of Hobbes' and Locke's precontractual state of nature.

Overbreadth doctrine: A criminal law violates the overbreadth doctrine when it fails to narrowly define the specific behavior to be restricted.

Parens patriae: The obligation of the state to care for people in need of care and protection, such as children and the mentally ill.

Particularity requirement: Means that the warrant must make clear on its face who or what is to be searched or seized, so as to limit the discretion of the police officer.

Paterna pietas: *Literally*, father love.

Patria potestas: Literally, *fatherly power:* the power of the father over his family.

Patriarchy: A system whereby males are promoted and supported over females.

Penal code: Commonly referred to as criminal law.

Penal style: Style of social control attained by punishing violators of the criminal law.

People's mediation committees: Committee of individuals organized in work and neighborhood groups to ensure rule conformity.

Peremptory challenge: One for which no reason need be given. While challenges for cause are unlimited, peremptory challenges are usually limited to a certain number. The Supreme Court has held that peremptory challenges may not be used to exclude potential jurors on the basis of race (*Batson v. Kentucky*, 1986) or gender (*J. E. B. v. Alabama*, 1994).

Petite treason: A charge made under early common law against women who murdered their husbands. It was considered worse than an ordinary murder because she had committed it against her "sovereign master."

PINS: Acronym for "person in need of supervision;" a status offender.

Plain view exception: Exception to the exclusionary rule. "Objects falling in the plain view of an officer who has a right to be in a position to have that view are subject to seizure."

Plaintiff: Person alleging that the defendant has harmed him or her in some way and who seeks damages for the injury.

Plato's Forms: The true and ultimate immaterial reality underlying all things. All observable things are imperfect copies of the true essence of these forms.

Plea bargaining: Process in which the defendant in a criminal case pleads guilty in exchange for a more lenient sentence than he or she would otherwise face.

Police court: Lowest-level French trial court for crimes with maximum penalty of two months in jail.

Pornography: The depiction of sexual behavior in pictures, writing, film, or other material intended to cause sexual arousal.

Positive Law: Human-made law arising from social norms; contrasted with natural law.

Precedent: The decision of a court that governs the court issuing the decision and any lower courts in subsequent cases.

Prefrontal cortex: The brain's "CEO," serving functions such as modulating emotional states that come from the brain's emotional centers and making reasoned judgments and plans.

Preliminary hearing: The second step in the trial process, after the initial appearance. Here, the magistrate determines if there is probable cause to believe that an offense was committed and that it was the defendant who committed it. If probable cause is established, the defendant is "bound over" for trial. The preliminary examination is a formal adversarial proceeding, conducted in open court. The Supreme Court has defined it as a "critical stage" of the prosecution, which means the defendant has a right to have his or her lawyer present.

Preponderance of the evidence: The standard of proof in civil cases.

Principle of Analogy: Chinese legal principle allowing for punishment of acts not specified by criminal codes but that are "analogous" to them.

Probable cause: A legal concept referring to the amount of proof a police officer must have to search or arrest someone.

Procedural law: The rules the state must follow when investigating suspects or prosecuting someone who has committed a crime. It comprises the rules that govern the manner in which the state may go about depriving an individual of his or her liberty.

Proclamation Act: A 1763 act passed by the British Parliament forbidding white settlement in America west of the Appalachians.

Progressives: A nineteenth-century group of liberal reformers who argued for the professionalization of public service.

Prohibition: A name given to the combination of the Eighteenth Amendment and the Volstead Act of 1919 outlawing the manufacture and sale of alcohol in the United States.

Promises: The basis of contracts and are legally binding.

Property: The right of ownership or possession of an item, which may be real, personal, or intangible.

Property law: A form of civil law that focuses on the ownership and acquisition of property through conveyances and inheritances.

Prosecutorial discretion: Type of waiver (also known as a *direct file*) allowing prosecutors to file certain juvenile cases in either juvenile or adult court.

Prostitution: The provision of sexual services in exchange for money or other tangible reward. A *prostitute* is a person who engages in prostitution as a source of income.

Proximate cause: The legal principle that the criminal act is the one that is the most significant and it seems fair and just to hold the actor accountable for his or her actions.

Public morals offenses: Those in which the moral health of society is injured. These include consensual sexual acts such as adultery, prostitution, and obscenity.

Public order offenses: Those in which the injury is to the peace and order of society. These include disorderly conduct, unlawful assembly, and vagrancy punishment for the guilty.

Punishment: A formal method of social control imposing painful sanctions on those who have broken the law.

Punitive damages: Monetary awards beyond compensation that are designed to punish the defendant and to deter others.

Qadi (or Khadi): Islamic judge.

Quesas crimes: In Islamic law, serious non-Hadd crimes for which punishment is not prescribed in the Qur'an, Islam's holy book.

Racism: A belief in the innate inferiority of persons of another race and discriminatory behavior consistent with that belief.

Ranulf de Glanvill: Henry II's chief justice, who wrote a book detailing the transition from substantive irrationality decision making to legal decision making in common law.

Rape: Carnal knowledge of a female forcibly and against her will.

Ratio decidendi: The legal principle on which a case is decided.

Rational basis review: A less restrictive basis of judicial review used when neither a fundamental right nor a suspect classification is implicated in enacted legislation. Legislation must have a rational basis.

Rational-legal authority: A form of authority derived from rules rationally and legally enacted.

Real property: Land and items permanently attached to the land.

Reasonable expectation of privacy: Fourth Amendment provision applies to areas where persons have a reasonable expectation of privacy. There are subjective and objective components: (1) a subject must have a subjective expectation of privacy, and (2) society must view that expectation as reasonable.

Reconstruction: A period of reestablishment and reorganization of the seceded Southern states after their defeat in the Civil War.

Rehabilitation: A philosophy of punishment that seeks to restore criminals to constructive activity through treatment programs designed to change thinking patterns.

Reintegration: A philosophy of punishment based on concrete programming, such as job training and education, designed to prepare criminals to reenter the free community as well equipped as possible to avoid commiting crime in the future.

Res judicata: Civil law analogue of the prohibition against double jeopardy. Once a case has been through all possible appeals, it is decided forever.

Restitutive justice: According to Durkheim, the form of justice found in modern societies.

Restorative justice: An approach to criminal justice aiming to repair the harm done by an agreeable restorative solution.

Retreat doctrine: A doctrine stating that a person must retreat rather than use deadly force in a situation if doing so is possible without endangering the person's life.

Retribution: The justification for punishment exemplified by the "eye for an eye" concept; punishment must match the degree of harm inflicted on the victim.

Retributive justice: Form of justice concerned with how a society's system of law goes about determining guilt or innocence, and then how it goes about determining the proper (just) sentence.

Risk society: A society organized in response to internally manufactured risks.

Rule of Four: A Supreme Court rule that requires that only four of the nine justices need to vote to accept a petition for a writ of certiorari for it to be issued—even though it takes five of nine justices for a majority to decide the case.

Rule of law: The principle that law, not men, govern and that no one is above the law.

Sarbanes-Oxley Act: Act passed by Congress in 2002 designed to crack down on white-collar crime.

Search incident to arrest exception: Deals with the scope of the search, includes anywhere on the person and the "lunge area," or immediate vicinity of the suspect.

Selective incorporation: A piecemeal evolutionary approach to incorporation.

Self-defense: A defense to criminal liability that states that a person may use force to repel an imminent, unprovoked attack in which they reasonably believed they were about to be seriously injured. The defendant may only use as much force as is necessary to repel the attack.

Shari'a: In Islam, "the path to follow"; rules of conduct revealed by Allah.

Sherman Antitrust Act: Passed by Congress in 1890 and designed to place controls on business.

Silver platter doctrine: Refers to evidence seized illegally without fear of its exclusion in state criminal proceedings.

Sir Edmund Coke: Chief Justice of England during the seventeenth-century reign of James II. Often called the "father of due process."

Social change: Any relatively enduring alteration in social relationships, behavior patterns, values, norms, and attitudes occurring over time.

Social contract: Hypothetical contract between individuals creating a state that could protect them from predation and exploitation.

Social control: Any action that influences conduct toward conformity, whether or not the persons being influenced are aware of the process.

Social movement: A sustained series of interactions between power holders and persons claiming to speak on behalf of a constituency lacking formal representation making publicly visible demands for changes in the distribution or exercise of power and backing those demands with public demonstrations of support.

Socialist law: System of law based on Marxist principles and developed in the former Soviet Union. Socialist law subordinates the rule of law to the requirements of the state.

Sodomy: Anal sex between two people of either sex. An expanded definition includes fellatio (mouth–penis contact) and sometimes cunnilingus (mouth–vagina contact).

Solicitation: involves the intent to induce another to commit a crime.

Song duel: Method of restoring peace among the Eskimo (Inuit) peoples by the perpetrator of a crime and the victim hurling singsong insults at one another.

Sovereign immunity: The doctrine that prohibits citizens from suing their government.

Soviet legalism: "Strict and unflinching observance and fulfillment of Soviet laws by all organs of the socialist state and public organizations, institutions and all citizens, in all circumstances, and at all times."

Specific deterrence: The supposed preventative effect of imposed punishment on the future behavior of the person punished.

Specific performance: In civil law, when a court orders someone to do (or not do) something.

Standard of Proof: The amount of evidence that the prosecution in a criminal case or a plaintiff (usually) must present in a trial to prevail; in a criminal case, it is *beyond a reasonable doubt*; in a civil or juvenile case, the *preponderance of evidence*.

Standing exception: Exception to the exclusionary rule under which a person must have the legal right to claim violation of his or her rights by virtue of being personally harmed by police illegality.

Standing mute: When a defendant refuses to enter a plea of any kind. In these instances, the court enters a "not guilty" plea on behalf of defendant, thus preserving the constitutional right to trial.

Stare decisis: The legal basis for adhering to precedent: "Let the decision stand."

Status offenses: Noncriminal offenses such as truancy and ungovernable that apply only to individuals whose status is that of a juvenile.

Statute: Legislative enactments or bills.

Statutory exclusion: An automatic waiver (also called a *legislative waiver*) applied when state legislatures have statutorily excluded serious offenses from the juvenile courts based on age.

Stop and frisk: Involves a police officer stopping people in public and questioning them as to their identity and activity, followed in some circumstances by a limited "pat-down" search of their outer clothing.

Strict constructionism: A philosophy maintaining that judges must seek to discover and adhere to the "original intent" of the Framers of the Constitution when making decisions.

Strict liability: Imposes accountability without proof of criminal intent in situations where society deems it fair to do so, such as violations of drug and alcohol sales laws.

Strict liability: Liability without consideration of the intent of the defendant.

Strict scrutiny review: A rigorous standard of review exercised by the courts for cases involving legislation curtailing fundamental rights or a suspect classification.

Substantial capacity test: Defined as when the defendant lacks substantial capacity to appreciate the wrongfulness of his or her conduct or to know how to control it.

Substantive due process: A constitutional principle that holds that in addition to procedural rights, the law must protect substantive rights, such as the right to possess or to say or do certain things.

Substantive irrationality: Legal decisions on a case-by-case basis without a set of legal principles.

Substantive law: Defined by statute, it prescribes (what we should do) and proscribes (what we should not do) various types of conduct.

Substantive rationality: Legal decisions on a case-by-case basis with a set of rules.

Suffrage: The right to vote.

Sunna: Companion book to the Qur'an containing numerous moral precepts relating to all aspects of Islamic life.

Supremacy Clause: A clause in the United States Constitution stating that the authority of the United States (not the individual states) shall be the supreme law of the land.

Supreme People's Court: China's highest-level court. Deals with important national matters and appeals from lower courts.

Suspect classification: An unconstitutional distinction made between individuals on the basis of race, religion, or national origin in a law or policy.

Suspect classification: Means that the state cannot enact or enforce laws aimed at restricting the rights of so-called *suspect classifications*, which are groups of people who historically have been ill-treated. *See also* Equal protection clause.

Symbols: A concrete physical manifestation that "stands for" an abstraction.

Ta'azir: In Islamic law, *ta'azir* offenses are "rehabilitation" offenses such as eating pork or dressing provocatively.

Ta'azir crimes: In Islamic law, minor crimes for which punishment is discretionary and lenient by Islamic standards.

Technology: The totality of the knowledge and techniques a people employ to create the material object of their sustenance and comfort.

Tenancy in common: Exists when multiple parties share equally in the ownership or possession of real property.

Termination: Policy aimed at terminating federal supervision of Indian tribes in the 1950s.

Terry stop: A short pat-down; see stop and frisk section and definition.

Therapeutic style: Style of social control aimed at those considered in need of treatment rather than punishment; a remedial style.

Tort law: The body of civil law associated with harm caused to plaintiffs by the action or inaction of defendants.

Tort reform: Efforts by insurance companies and other businesses to limit frivolous lawsuits and excessive punitive damages.

Total incorporation: Under the total incorporation approach, the due process clause of the Fourteenth Amendment made the entire Bill of Rights applicable to the states.

Total incorporation plus: Under total incorporation plus, the due process clause of the Fourteenth Amendment includes all of the Bill of Rights and includes other rights not specified in it.

Traditional authority: A type of authority that rests on long-standing usage and custom.

Transcendental perspective on natural law: A perspective on natural law that law originates in some transcendental realm (such as God) and must be followed by all.

Transcendentalism: A philosophy emphasizing the primacy of the spiritual over the material (the spirit transcends the material).

Transferred intent: Applies to situations where a person intended to harm A but in error harmed B.

Treason: The act of opposition to one's government, either by waging war against or helping the enemies of such government.

Treaty of Fort Pit: First treaty made with the Indians. It implicitly recognized the sovereignty of the Indian nations and assured them that the United States had no designs on Indian lands.

Trespass: Going into someone's house or simply onto their property unlawfully.

Trial de novo: Literally, a new trial. It is a trial held as if no prior trial has been held. Often used as an appeal from small claims courts.

Uniform Commercial Code: A code of law concerning contracts designed to standardize trade and contract practices among merchants and businesses.

Uniform Crime Reports (UCR): The Federal Bureau of Investigation's annual report of crimes committed in the United States. It comprises Part I and Part II offenses. The UCR defines eight crimes (murder, rape, robbery, aggravated assault, burglary, larceny/theft, motor vehicle theft, and arson) as Part I offenses. Part II offenses are a mixture of mala prohibita offenses and less serious mala in se offenses.

Unlawful assembly: Disorderly conduct in a group setting, this includes groups assembled in public without the necessary permits, as well as riots.

USA Patriot Act: Act passed in response to 9/11 terrorist attacks against the United States and expanded the authority of law enforcement to fight terroism.

Uttering: The passing of a false legal document to another, with knowledge of its falsity and the intent to defraud.

Values: Normative standards shared by the culture about what is good and bad, correct and incrorrect, moral and immoral, normal and deviant.

Veil of ignorance: A concept in Rawls' theory of justice that asks what kind of society people would endeavor to make if they were completely ignorant of their future place in it (forced to choose behind the veil of ignorance).

Venire: Latin for "to cause" or "to make come" (to the courthouse). Prospective jurors are examined by the judge and/or the attorneys for the prosecution and defense to determine whether they have any bias, prejudice, or interest that would prevent the potential juror from being impartial.

Vicarious liability: Refers to the imputation of accountability from one person to another, usually the individual's superior.

Vice crime: Any consensual act that offends the moral standards of the community that has defined the act as worthy of condemnation and legal control.

Void for vagueness doctrine: A statute is void for vagueness if it fails to clearly define both the act prohibited and the appropriate punishment in advance.

Voire dire: Latin for "to speak the truth." It refers to the process of questioning potential jurors to determine whether they are fit to serve on a jury.

Voting Rights Act of 1965: Act providing federal supervision of voter registration sites and prohibiting the use of literacy tests.

Waived: A term used to describe a juvenile being transferred (waived) from juvenile to adult court because of the seriousness of the crime.

White-Collar Crime Penalty Enhancement Act: Act passed in conjunction with the Sarbanes-Oxley Act. It enhanced penalties for white-collar crimes and relaxed evidentiary rules for prosecuting them.

William Blackstone: English judge and philosopher whose *Commentaries on the Laws of England* organized common law into the structure it has today.

Writ of mandamus: A court order compelling a public official to do his or her duty.

TABLE OF CASES

Adair v. United States, 299
Adams v. New York, 153
Adkins v. Children's Hospital, 299
Alabama v. White, 140
Allied Structural Steel v. Spannous, 300
American Booksellers Association, Inc. v.
    Hudnut, 264
Amistad case. See United States, Appellants v. The
    Libellants and Claimants of the Schooner Amistad
Apodaca v. Oregon, 102
Argersinger v. Hamlin, 147
Arizona v. Evans, 157
Arizona v. Hicks, 144
Arizona v. Roberson, 150
Ashcroft v. Free Speech Coalition, 264
Atkins v. Georgia, 214
Atkins v. Virginia, 236

Barker v. Wingo, 70–71
Barron v. Baltimore, 77
Batson v. Kentucky, 101
Berkemer v. McCarty, 149
Bordenkircher v. Hayes, 234
Bowers v. Hardwick, 248, 258–59
Boyd v. United States, 153
Bradwell v. Illinois, 326
Breed v. Jones, 211–12
Brewer v. Williams, 50–51, 53
Brinegar v. United States, 138
Brown v. Board of Education of Topeka, 247–48,
    250, 304, 306, 346, 348, 361
Brown v. Board of Education of Topeka
    (Brown II), 346
Brown v. Mississippi, 51, 53
Burch v. Louisiana, 102
Bush v. Gore, 35, 295

California v. Beheler, 148
California v. Ciraolo, 145
California v. Greenwood, 145
Carroll v. United States, 143
Chaplinsky v. New Hampshire, 65
Cherokee Nation v. Georgia, 351
Cherokee Tobacco, 353
Chevron U.S.A., Inc. v. Natural Resources Defense
    Council, Inc., 186
Chimel v. California, 142–43
Chisholm v. Georgia, 83

City of Oakland v. The Oakland Raiders, 172–73
Civil Rights Cases, 346
Coker v. Georgia, 127, 236
Coleman v. Thompson, 239
Communist Party v. Subversive Activities
    Control Board, 243
Crawford v. Washington, 151

Delaware v. Prouse, 141
Dennis v. United States, 243
District of Columbia v. Heller, 66
Doe v. Bolton, 268
Dred Scott case. See Scott v. Sandford
Dudgeon v. The United Kingdom, 259
Duren v. Missouri, 323

Eddings v. Oklahoma, 212–13
Edwards v. Arizona, 150
Elk v. Wilkins, 354
Engel v. Vitale, 305
Entick v. Carrington, 73
Escobedo v. Illinois, 148
Everson v. Board of Education, 65
Ex Parte Crouse, 204
Ex Parte Crow Dog, 353
Ex parte Endo, 357

Fletcher v. Peck, 297, 302–3, 306
Florida v. Wells, 144
Frontiero v. Richardson, 323
Furman v. Georgia, 236

Georgia v. Randolph, 143
Gibbons v. Ogden, 303, 306
Gideon v. Wainwright, 147
Gitlow v. New York, 243
Gonzales v. Carhart, 269
Gregg v. Georgia, 115, 236
Griffin v. California, 70
Griswold v. Connecticut, 73, 78–79, 114, 291

Haley v. Ohio, 208
Hammer v. Dagenhart, 299
Harris v. McRae, 268
Harris v. New York, 150
Harris v. United States, 144
Heart of Atlanta Motel v. United States, 347
Hester v. United States, 144

Hishon v. King and Spalding, 328
Hodgson v. Minnesota, 268
Horton v. California, 144
Hurtado v. California, 68, 99

Illinois v. Gates, 138
Illinois v. Perkins, 150
In Re Ah Yup, 356
In Re Debs, 299, 301
In Re Gault, 209–10, 215
In Re Winship, 210–11, 215

Jacobellis v. Ohio, 262
J.E.B. v. Alabama, 101, 115
Johnson v. Louisiana, 192
Johnson v. McIntosh, 351
Johnson v. Zerbst, 147
Joseph Knight v. Wedderburn, 287

Kansas v. Hendricks, 246
Katz v. United States, 141–42
Kelo v. City of New London, 70
Kent v. United States, 208–9, 215, 219
Kirby v. Illinois, 71, 151
Kohn v. Royall, Koegel, and Wells, 328
Korematsu v. United States, 357

Lawrence v. Texas, 73, 112, 114, 258–59, 276
Lemon v. Kurtzman, 65
Lochner v. New York, 299
Loewe v. Lawlor, 299
Lone Wolf v. Hitchcock, 354
Louisville Bank v. Radford, 300
Loving v. Virginia, 178–79
Lubitz v. Wells, 170

Malloy v. Hogan, 70
Mapp v. Ohio, 57, 80, 153–55
Marbury v. Madison, 81–82, 293
Martin v. Hunter's Lessee, 302–3, 306
Maryland v. Wilson, 141
McClesky v. Kemp, 240
McCulloch v. Maryland, 302–3, 306
McKeiver v. Pennsylvania, 211
McNeil v. Wisconsin, 150
Michigan Department of State Police v. Sitz, 141, 149
Michigan v. Chesternutt, 139
Miller v. California, 65, 263, 277
Minnesota v. Dickerson, 140
Minor v. Happersett, 317–18
Miranda v. Arizona, 148–50, 159
Missouri v. Jenkins, 246
Missouri v. Jenkins II, 248

Montana v. Egelhoff, 123
Moran v. Burbine, 150
Mortensen v. United States, 260
Muller v. Oregon, 35

Nardone v. United States, 154
National Cable & Telecommunications v. X Internet Services, 186
National Labor Relations Board v. Bildisco, 300
National Labor Relations Board v. Bildisco & Bildisco, 176–77
National Labor Relations Board v. Jones and Laughlin Steel Corporation, 300
Nevada v. Hicks, 355
New York v. Belton, 143
New York v. Quarles, 149
Nguyen v. INS, 323
Nix v. Williams, 51, 157–58

Ohio v. Robinette, 141
Oliphant v. Suquamish Indian Tribe, 355
Oregon v. Elstad, 150
Ozawa v. United States, 356

Palko v. Connecticut, 75, 79
Papachristou et al. v. City of Jacksonville, 115, 131
Payton v. New York, 139
Pennsylvania v. Mimms, 141
Penry v. Lynaugh, 236
People v. Defoe, 155
Pierson v. Post, 172
Planned Parenthood of Southeastern Pennsylvania v. Casey, 268
Planned Parenthood v. Danforth, 268
Plessy v. Ferguson, 304, 343–44, 360
Pointer v. Texas, 151
Pollock v. Farmer's Loan and Trust Company, 301
Powell v. Alabama, 147
Powell v. Texas, 116

Rakas v. Illinois, 155–56
Reed v. Reed, 323
Regina v. Hicklin, 263
Rex v. Beare, 267
Rex v. Hadfield, 123
Rex v. M'Naghten, 123
Reynolds v. United States, 178
Rhode Island v. Innis, 149
Riggs v. Palmer, 43
Ring v. Arizona, 103
Robinson v. California, 116
Roe v. Butterworth, 260
Roe v. Wade, 73, 78, 114, 268, 270, 291, 305

Roper v. Simmons, 213, 236
Roth v. United States, 263
Rummel v. Estelle, 115
Rylands v. Fletcher, 189

Santa Clara Co. v. Southern Pacific R. R. Co., 298
Scales v. United States, 243
Schall v. Martin, 212
Schechter Poultry Corp. v. United States, 300
Schenck v. United States, 243
Scott v. Sandford, 294, 303, 306, 340–41, 360
Segura v. United States, 156
Sherman v. U.S., 124
Skinner v. State of Oklahoma, 178–79
Slaughterhouse cases, 77
Slave, Grace, The, 340
Smith v. Allwright, 346–47
Somerset v. Stewart, 287
South Carolina v. Katzenbach, 347
South Dakota v. Opperman, 144
Stack v. Boyle, 72
Standing Bear v. Crook, 352
Stanford v. Kentucky, 213, 236
State v. Rhodes, 321
Stenberg v. Carhart, 268–69
Strickland v. Washington, 71
Sullivan v. O'Connor, 176

Tennessee v. Garner, 122, 139
Terry v. Ohio, 140
Texas v. Brown, 144
Texas v. Johnson, 65, 78, 112
Thompson v. Oklahoma, 213

Turner v. Safley, 178
Twining v. New Jersey, 79

*United States, Appellants v. The Libellants and
    Claimants of the Schooner Amistad*, 339–40, 360
United States v. Butler, 300
United States v. E. C. Knight, 299, 301
United States v. Kagama, 353
United States v. Karo, 144
United States v. Knights, 145
United States v. Leon, 157
United States v. Salerno, 72
United States v. Sioux Nations of Indians, 355
United States v. Wade, 150
United States v. Weitzenhoff, 189
United States v. Wong Kim Ark, 356

*Virginia State Board of Pharmacy v. Virginia
    Citizens Consumers Council, Inc.*, 65

Washington v. Texas, 152
Webster v. Reproductive Health Services, 268
Weeks v. United States, 153, 155
West Coast Hotel Co. v. Parrish, 303
Williams v. Florida, 102
Williams v. State of Mississippi, 344, 360
Wilson v. Arkansas, 139
Wolf v. Colorado, 57, 79, 154
Wong Sun v. United States, 156
Woodson v. North Carolina, 236
Worcester v. Georgia, 351

Zablocki v. Redhail, 178

INDEX

abandoned property, 145
abortion rights, 5, 73, 266–70, 277, 305
absolutism, 41
accessories, 120
ACLU. See American Civil Liberties Union
acquittal, 69
actual cause, 170
actus reus (criminal act), 116, 122
Adams, Abigail, 316–17
Adams, John, 23, 81, 244, 296, 316–17
Adams, John Quincy, 339
adequate provocation, 126
administrative law, 181–87, 183–84*t*
   corporate crime and, 190–91
Administrative Procedure Act (APA), 182
adultery, 226–27, 256–57, 275–76, 322, 385–87
adversarial system, 372–73, 376, 380, 384, 390
adverse possession, 173–74
affirmative action, 287, 330, 337, 349
affirmative defenses, 121
African Americans, 338–49
   protests by, 345–47
   suffrage for, 342–44
age defense, 122–23
aggravated assault, 127
Agta people, 368
AIM. *See* American Indian Movement
alcohol, 270–73
Alford plea, 100
alibi, 121
Alito, Samuel, 94–95
Allott, Phillip, 2
all-property model, 180
altruistic punishment, 40
amending Constitution, process of, 82–83
amendments to Constitution, 64–74
   First Amendment, 64–66, 154
   Second Amendment, 66–67, 80
   Third Amendment, 67, 79
   Fourth Amendment, 67–68, 79–81, 137, 141,
      152–55, 166
   Fifth Amendment, 68–70, 136–37, 148, 166,
      341
   Sixth Amendment, 70–71, 137, 147–48, 158,
      166
   Seventh Amendment, 72, 80
   Eighth Amendment, 72, 115, 137, 215
   Ninth Amendment, 72–73
   Tenth Amendment, 73, 181, 343
   Eleventh Amendment, 83
   Thirteenth Amendment, 74, 342, 360

Fourteenth Amendment, 74–75, 77–80, 114,
   136–37, 154, 178, 208, 297–301, 342–44
Fifteenth Amendment, 73, 317, 342, 344, 354,
   360
Eighteenth Amendment, 283
Nineteenth Amendment, 317, 319
Twenty-First Amendment, 273
Twenty-Seventh Amendment, 324
Twenty-Fourth Amendment, 347
American Bar Association, 327
American Civil Liberties Union (ACLU), 235,
   261, 323, 357
American Indian Movement (AIM), 355
American Indians, 338, 349–56
   early years of, 349–50
   genocide of, 349–50, 352–55
   removal of, 352–55
   slavery of, 350
American Medical Association, 267
American Psychiatric Association (APA), 245,
   257–58
American Revolution, 14, 24, 286–88, 306, 374
Amistad Case, 339–40
Amnesty International, 237, 381–82
analogy, principle of, 380
annulment, 180
Anthony, Susan B., 317–19
APA. *See* Administrative Procedure Act;
   American Psychiatric Association
appeals, 103–4
   courts of, 92–93, 95, 97
appellate jurisdiction, 90
Aristotle, 12–13, 21–22
   justice and, 24, 28–31, 33, 51–52
   on women, 314
arrest, 139–41, 239
arson, 113, 128–29, 358
Article III courts, 90
Articles of Confederation, 62–63
Asian Americans, 356–57, 361–62
assault, 127–28. *See also* rape
   aggravated, 127
   child sexual, 127
   sexual, 126–27, 329, 332
   simple, 127
assembly
   freedom of, 64–65, 114
   unlawful, 131
assent requirement, 176
assize court, 378
Assize of Clarendon, 71

attempt, 119–20
attenuation exception, 156
Augspurg, Anita, 318
authority
    rational-legal, 293–94
    traditional v. charismatic, 292
Ayers, Bill, 349

bailment, 174
bail setting, 72, 80, 96
Basic People's Court (BPC), 383
battery, 128
Beccaria, Cesare Bonesana, Marchese di, 53, 385
    Dei Delitti e della Pene (*On Crimes and
        Punishment*), 47–48
beliefs, 4, 6*f*
Bentham, Jeremy, 12
Benton, Thomas, 340
Bernstein, Daniel, 60
Berrigan, Philip, 101
BIA. *See* Bureau of Indian Affairs
bigamy, 177
bilateral contracts, 176
billeting, of soldiers, 67
Bill of Rights, 48, 63, 77–80, 83–84, 137
bills of attainder, 63, 115
binding out, 202
Black, Donald, 226, 231, 244, 249
Black, Hugo, 78
Black Codes, 298, 342, 360
Blackmun, Harry, 211
Blackstone, William, 136–37
    Commentaries on the Laws of England, 60, 316
Blake, Robert, 101
booking, 98
BPC. *See* Basic People's Court
Bracton, Henry de, *On the Laws and Customs of
        England*, 58–59
Bradley, Joseph, 326
brain maturation, 200–201, 214, 219
Brandeis, Louis, 94
breach of contract, 176
Brennan, William, 80, 210
Brent, Margaret, 326
Breyer, Stephen, 268
British High Court, 73
British law, 285–88, 371
    slavery in, 285, 287, 306
Brown, Henry Billings, 344
Brownmiller, Susan, 321
Brown-Simpson, Nicole, 165
burden of production, 121
burden of proof, 76, 136, 166
Bureau of Indian Affairs (BIA), 353–55
Burger, Warren, 51, 215, 285, 304–5
burglary, 129–30
Burke, Edmund, 288
Bush, George H. W., 188, 328

Bush, George W., 35, 189, 191, 295, 328
business interests, 297–301

Cardozo, Benjamin, 155
Carter, David O., 179
Carter, Jimmy, 328
castle doctrine, 121
Catt, Carrie Chapman, 318–19
causation, 118
caveat emptor, 43, 181
certiorari, writ of, 94, 341
challenges for cause, 191
charismatic authority, 292
Charles I (king of England), 13
Chevron deference rule, 186, 193
child custody, 180
Child Savers, 204–5
child sexual assault, 127
China, death penalty in, 382, 391
Chinese Americans, 356–57, 361–62
Chinese Exclusion Act of 1882, 356
Chinese socialist law, 379–83, 389
Ch'ing Code of 1646, 380
Churchill, Winston, 281
Cinque, Joseph, 339
circuit courts. *See* courts of appeals
civil law, 43, 89, 163–95
    v. criminal law, 164–67, 166*t*
    in France, 371, 374–79, 391
    tradition of, 370, 373–79, 388
civil liberties, 50, 71, 223, 242, 387–89
Civil Rights Act of 1875, 343, 360
Civil Rights Act of 1964, 347, 361
Civil Rights Act of 1968, 345
Civil War, 45, 74, 260, 338, 341–42
Clark, Tom, 153
class conflict, 12, 22–23, 30
Clinton, Bill, 188, 328
clitorectomy, 322
Code Civil des Français, 374
Code Louis of 1670, 46–47, 53, 71, 136
Code Napoléon of 1804, 46
Code of Hammurabi. *See* Hammurabi, Code of
Code of Justinian, 374
Coke, Edmund, 48
Cold War, 243, 347–48, 361
collective conscience/collective consciousness, 19
collegial bench, 381
Columbus, Christopher, 4
Comite des Citoyens, 343–44
Commentaries on the Laws of England
        (Blackstone), 60, 316
commercialized vice crime, 259–62
commitment, involuntary, 166
common law, 37, 42–43, 50–52, 58–59, 172
    Magna Carta and, 58, 372
    marriage in, 179
    tradition of, 370–73, 388

Communism, 241–43, 289–90
comparative law, 367–94
compensatory social control, 231
compulsory process, 152
conciliatory social control, 231
concurrence, 117–18
conflict perspective, 22–23, 25
conflict theorists, 21
confrontation of witnesses, 151
Confucius, 380
Conseil Constitutionnel, 389
consensus perspective, 21–22, 25
consensus theorists, 20–21
consent, 121–22, 142–43, 171
conspiracy, 120
Constitution, U. S., 62–63. *See also* amendments
    to Constitution
  amending, process of, 82–83
  freedom of contract clause of, 43
  rights in, 63, 64*t*
  Supremacy Clause of, 302
  Supreme Court and, 35, 81–82, 290
constitutionalism, 73
constitutionality, and Supreme Court, 61, 80,
    137, 338
Constitutional Rights Foundation, 345
constitutions, 60–61
constructionism, strict, 294–95
contract law, 164, 168*f*, 174–77, 297
contrast effect, 228
contraventions, 379
corporate crime, 190–92
correctional court, 379
corroborating evidence, 152
counsel, right to, 71, 146–51, 149*f*
Cour de Cassation, 378
Court of Chancery, 42–43
courts of appeals
  federal, 92–93
  state, 95, 97
coverture, 316, 326
Crawford, William, 287
crime(s), 199*f*, 378. *See also specific crimes*
  commercialized vice crime, 259–62
  corporate, 190–92
  definition of, 112–14
  environmental, 189–90
  Hadd crimes, 385–86, 392
  against humanity, 27
  inchoate, 119–20
  natural, 44–45
  parties to, 120
  against persons, 125–28
  against property, 128–31
  against public order and morality, 13, 131
  Quesas crimes, 386, 392
  Ta'azir crimes, 386, 392
  United States as soft on, 233–34, 233*f*

  vice crime, 254–56
  victimless, 118, 254–56, 266–67, 276
Crime Control Model, 49, 136
criminal intent, 116–17, 122
criminal justice system
  Packer and, 48–51, 53
  racism and, 358–60
  social control and, 232–33
criminal law, 61, 89, 111–33
  v. civil law, 164–67, 166*t*
  limitations on, 114–15
  sources of, 114
criminal liability, 115–18
  defenses to, 121–24
criminal offenses, elements of, 116–18
criminal procedure law, 135–61
criminal process, 98–100
Crook, George, 352
cruel and unusual punishment, 48, 72, 115, 213–15
culpability, 201
culture, 3–9
cumulative evidence, 152
curfews, 75
curtilage, 144–45
custody, 148–49

Dawes Act of 1887, 353–54
day-fine system, 31
DEA. *See* Drug Enforcement Administration
deadly force, 139
death penalty, 72, 103, 115, 127, 236*f*
  in China, 382, 391
  debate on, 235–40
  in Islamic law, 385–86, 392
  for juveniles, 212
  in preliterate societies, 369–70
Debs, Eugene, 299
decision-making typology, 18–19, 18*t*
Declaration of Independence, 38, 50, 288,
    317–18, 338–39
Declaration of the Rights of Man and of the
    Citizen, 388
defense(s)
  affirmative, 121
  age, 122–23
  to criminal liability, 121–24
  duress, 122
  excuse defenses, 122
  insanity, 122–24
  intoxication, 122–23
  involuntary intoxication, 122–23
  justification defenses, 121
  procedural, 124–25
  self-defense, 121
  voluntary intoxication, 122–23
defense attorneys, 107
Defense of Marriage Act (DOMA),
    178–79, 193

Dei Delitti e della Pene (*On Crimes and Punishment*) (Beccaria), 47–48
delicts, 378–79
delinquents, 198
democratization, 285
desegregation, of schools, 88, 246–48, 250, 346–47
detention, 139
developmental factors, 200
Devlin, Patrick, 266
discouraged behavior, 6f
Discovery Doctrine, 351
Disraeli, Benjamin, 283
distributive justice, 28–30
district courts, 91–92, 91f
diversity of citizenship, 92
divine right of kings, 38
Division of Labor in Society (Durkheim), 19
divorce law, 179–81
DNA evidence, 166, 240
doctrine of transferred intent, 117
Dohrn, Bernardine, 349
DOMA. *See* Defense of Marriage Act
Dometius Ulpanius, 28
Donald, Michael, 345
Donnelly, Samuel, 45
double jeopardy, 68–69, 169, 211–12
Douglas, William O., 73, 79, 87, 291
Dred Scott Case, 340, 360
Drug Enforcement Administration (DEA), 274
drugs, illicit, 273–75
dual-property model, 180
dual sovereignty doctrine, 69
DuBois, W. E . B., 345, 348
due process, 46–53, 136, 208–12
    model of, 49–51, 136
    substantive, 78, 114
duress defense, 122
Durham rule, 123
Durkheim, Émile, 16, 19–20, 23, 40, 266
    Division of Labor in Society, 19
Dyer, Leonidas, 345
Dyer Anti-Lynching Bill, 345
Dylan, Bob, 228

easement, 173
ECHR. *See* European Court of Human Rights
Economist Intelligence Unit, 387–89
Economy and Society (Weber), 17
Edward I (king of England), 101
Eisenhower, Dwight D., 304, 348
Ellis, L., 113, 191
Emancipation Proclamation, 295, 341, 360
Emerson, John, 340
eminent domain, 70
en banc hearings, 93
encouraged behavior, 6f
Endo, Mitsuye, 358

Engels, Friedrich, 25
    The German Ideology, 22
entrapment, 124–25
enumerated powers, 73
environmental crime, 189–90
environmental justice, 186–90
Environmental Protection Agency (EPA), 186–89
EPA. *See* Environmental Protection Agency
Equal Employment Opportunity Act of 1972, 327
equality, 330–31, 348–49
equal protection, 35, 74
Equal Rights Amendment (ERA), 324–25
equity, 42–44
ERA. *See* Equal Rights Amendment
Eratosthenes, 4
Espionage Act of 1917, 242
ethnocentrism, 37, 343, 388
European Court of Human Rights (ECHR), 197, 259, 390
evidence
    cumulative v. corroborating, 152
    DNA evidence, 166, 240
    ex parte, 151
    preponderance of, 165, 205
evolutionary perspective, of natural law, 39–41
exclusionary rule, 152–58, 158f
    inevitable discovery exception to, 51, 157–58
excuse defenses, 122
ex parte evidence, 151
ex post facto laws, 27, 63, 115, 289
extortion, 128

factual cause, 118
failure to act, 116
false consciousness, 23
family law, 164, 177–81, 289–90
FAS. *See* fetal alcohol syndrome
Faubus, Orval, 304
Fay, Michael Peter, 367
federal courts, 90–95, 91f, 93f
    of appeals, 92–93
Federal Energy Regulatory Commission (FERC), 182
Federalism, 63, 73, 105
Federalist Papers, 90
fee simple absolute estate, 173
fee simple estate, 163
felony murder rule, 126
felony sentencing worksheet (FSW), 31–33, 32f
feminist jurisprudence, 312–13
feminist legal theory, 313
FERC. *See* Federal Energy Regulatory Commission
fetal alcohol syndrome (FAS), 271
Fikentscher, W., 41
Finkel, N., 36–37
firearms possession, 66
flag-burning statutes, 112

folkways, 5, *6f*
Ford Motor Company, 163
forgery, 128
formal irrationality, 17–18
formal rationality, 17–18, 38
forms/ideas, Plato's theory of, 11
Fortas, Abe, 209–10
France, Anatole, 30
France, civil law in, 371, 374–79, 391
Frankfurter, Felix, 79
Franklin, Benjamin, 228, 270–72, 287
Freedman's Bureau, 342, 360
freedom
    of assembly, 64–65, 114
    of contract clause, of Constitution, 43
    of press, 64–66
    religious, 64–65
    of speech, 64–65, 114
Freedom House, 387–89
freehold estate, 173
Freeman, Elizabeth, 326
French Revolution, 14, 24, 47, 288, 374
Freud, Sigmund, 273
"fruit of the poisonous tree," 154
FSW. *See* felony sentencing worksheet
Fuller, Melville, 298
Full Faith and Credit Clause, 179
fundamental rights, 75, 79

Gadsden Purchase, 352
Gage, Matilda Joslyn, 320
Garofalo, Raffaele, 44–45, 52
Gavagan Bill, 345
gender-bias studies, 329–30
gender discrimination, 329–32
gender segregation, 325–26
General Allotment Act of 1887, 353
general jurisdiction, 89
genocide, of American Indians, 349–50, 352–55
geographical jurisdiction, 89
George III (king of England), 123, 247, 288
The German Ideology (Marx and Engels), 22
Gilligan, Carol, 331, 333
Ginsburg, Ruth Bader, 94–95, 323, 327–28
globalization, 8
global warming, 8
Glorious (English) Revolution, 14, 24, 45, 47, 288
"Golden Mean," 51
Golden Rule, 5, 22, 38, 296
good faith, 176
good faith exception, 156–57
grand juries, 68–69, 71, 80, 99
Great Depression, 78, 88, 273, 300
gun control legislation, 66
Gyges allegory, 228–29

habeas corpus, 63
    Magna Carta and, 104

Hadd crimes, 385–86, 392
Hamilton, Alexander, 90, 296
Hammurabi, Code of, 9–10, 23, 374
    abortion and, 267
    prostitution and, 259
    rape and, 321
    retributive justice and, 58
    substantive rationality and, 18
Hanson, John, 63
Harding, Warren, 272
harm principle, 118, 255
Harre, R., 36–37
Harrisburg Seven, 101
Harrison Narcotics Act of 1914, 112, 273–74
Hawthorne, Nathaniel, *The Scarlet Letter*, 226–28, *227f*
Hays, Henry, 345
Hemmens, Craig, 329
Henry II (king of England), 58, 100
Hicklin test, 263
hierarchical jurisdiction, 89
Higher People's Court (HPC), 383
Hinckley, John, 124
Hitler, Adolf, 27
Hobbes, Thomas, 3, 19, 24, 136, 315
    Leviathan, 12–15
Holmes, Oliver Wendell, 34, 65
homicide, 125–26, 234, 274, 368–69
homosexuality, 256–59
Hoover, Herbert, 272
HPC. *See* Higher People's Court
Hughes, Charles Evans, 290
human nature, 12–14, 38, 41, 44, 217
human rights, 45, 259, 389–90
Human Rights Watch, 300
hung jury, 69, 102
Huron people, 369–70
Hussein, Saddam, 1

ideal types, 21
illicit drugs, 273–75
Immigration and Naturalization Service (INS), 323
immunity, 171
incapacitation, 230
incarceration rates, *233f*
inchoate crime(s), 119–20
incorporation
    selective, 79–80
    theories of, *80f*
independent source exception, 156
Indian Citizenship Act of 1924, 354
Indian Removal Act, 351–52, 361
Indian Reorganization Act of 1934, 354, 361
Indian Self-Determination Act (SDA) of 1975, 355, 361
indictments, 68–69

inevitable discovery exception, to exclusionary
      rule, 51, 157–58
infanticide, 332
information, 69
inquisitorial system, 375–77, 380, 384
INS. *See* Immigration and Naturalization
      Service
insanity defense, 122–24
Intermediate People's Court, of China, 383
intermediate scrutiny standard, 75–76
International Court of Justice, 390
International Woman Suffrage Conference,
      318–19
interrogation, 149
intoxication defense, 122–23
Inuit people, 369
involuntary commitment, 166
involuntary intoxication defense, 122–23
Iraq, 1–2
irrationality, 17
irresistible impulse, 124
Islamic law, 37–38, 253, 322, 331
      death penalty in, 385–86, 392
      tradition of, 384–88

Jackson, Andrew, 105, 351
Japanese Americans, 356–57, 361–62
Jay, John, 90, 95, 296
Jefferson, Thomas, 15, 81, 241, 317
Jim Crow laws, 342–46
John (king of England), 58
Johnson, Joshua, 351
Jones, Howard, 339–40
judges, 104–5, 106*t*
judicial activism, 295, 304–5
judicial review, 75–76, 76*f*, 80–84, 373, 378
judicial social control, 246–48
judicial waiver, 207
Judiciary Act of 1789, 82, 90, 95, 105
jurisdiction, 88–90
      types of, 89–90
jury(ies)
      grand juries, 68–69, 71, 80, 99
      selection of, 101–2, 344
      trial by, 72, 100–101, 373, 377
jus cogens, 38, 237
justice
      Aristotle and, 24, 28–31, 33, 51–52
      definitions of, 28–33
      distributive, 28–30
      environmental, 186–90
      law and, 27–55, 330–31
      repressive, 20
      restitutive, 20
      restorative, 215–18
      retributive, 20, 30–33, 32*f*, 58, 229–30
justices, of Supreme Court, U. S., 87, 94–95
justification defenses, 121

juvenile law, 164, 197–222, 199*f*, 206*t*, 226
      death penalty and, 212
      Supreme Court and, 214*f*

Kansas-Nebraska Act of 1854, 341
Kant, Immanuel, 36, 338
Kelly, Donald, 16
Kennedy, Anthony, 94, 213–14, 246–48, 250, 259
Kent, Chancellor, 34–35, 42
Kerry, John, 349
King, Martin Luther, Jr., 349
Kissinger, Henry, 101
KKK. *See* Ku Klux Klan
"knock and announce" rule, 135
knowing intent, 117, 125
Knowles, James, 345
Korematsu, Fred, 357
Kubra courts, 387
Ku Klux Klan (KKK), 345
Kung people, 368
Kyoto Protocol, 189

labor unions, 295, 298–301, 306
laissez-faire, 181
language, 8–9
larceny, 130–31
law, 6*f*. *See also* civil law; criminal law;
      Islamic law; juvenile law
      administrative, 181–87, 183–84*t*, 190–91
      British, 285–88, 306, 371
      Chinese socialist, 379–83, 389
      common, 37, 42–43, 50–52, 58–59, 172, 179,
            370–73, 388
      comparative, 367–94
      contract, 164, 168*f*, 174–77, 297
      definitions of, 3
      divorce, 179–81
      on family, 164, 177–81, 289–90
      France, civil law in, 371, 374–79, 391
      justice and, 27–55, 330–31
      on marriage, 177–79
      natural, 6, 12, 27, 36–42
      positive, 6, 12, 38
      procedural, 111
      on property, 164, 172–74, 192
      race and, 357–58
      real property law, 168*f*, 172–74
      regulatory, 187–90
      rule of, 45–47, 53, 387–89
      on search and seizure, 138, 146*f*
      slavery and, 338–41, 360
      social change and, 284–86, 286*f*
      as social control mechanism, 226–32
      sociological perspectives of, 16–20
      sources of, 60–62, 61*f*
      substantive, 111–12
      tort law, 164, 167–72, 168*f*, 192
      women and, in history, 313–16

law enforcement, special needs of, 145–46
Law for the Protection of German Blood
    and Honor, 27
Laws (Plato), 45
Law School Admission Council, 327
legal capacity requirement, 175
legal cause, 118
legality requirement, 176
legal positivists, 6, 10–13, 27, 41
legal profession, women in, 325–29
legal realism, 34–36, 52
legal traditions, four, 370–87, 371f
    convergence of, 389–91
    rule of law and, 387–89
lettres de cachet, 46–49, 71
Leviathan (Hobbes), 12–15
liability, 169
    criminal, 115–18
    criminal, defenses to, 121–24
    without fault, 119
    strict, 119
    vicarious, 119
Lincoln, Abraham, 2, 303
literacy tests, 343–44
Little, Joan, 101
Locke, John, 12–15, 19, 24, 136, 315
    The Second Treatise on Government, 14
Louisiana Purchase, 340
Loury, Glen, 349
lynching, 345, 361

Madison, James, 15, 90, 296
Magna Carta, 45, 48, 71
    common law and, 58, 372
    habeas corpus and, 104
    jury selection and, 102
Major Crimes Act of 1885, 353
mala in se, 44, 52, 112–13, 113f, 276
mala prohibita, 44, 52, 113, 113f, 256
malice aforethought, 125
Manifest Destiny, 352
manslaughter, 125–26
Mao Zedong, 380
Mapp, Dollree, 57, 154
Mapplethorpe, Robert, 263
marriage law, 177–79
    in common law, 179
Marshall, John, 81–82, 95, 303, 350–51
Marshall, Thurgood, 94
Marshall Trilogy cases, 350–51, 361
Marx, Karl, 7, 16, 25, 289
    The German Ideology, 22
Marxism, 22, 29, 312, 379–80, 389
maternity leave, 311
McIntosh, William, 351
mechanical solidarity, 19
mens rea (criminal intent), 116–19, 122
mental illness, 244–46

Miles, T., 34
Mill, John Stuart, *On Liberty*, 255–56, 276
Miller Test, 263, 277
Minor, Virginia, 317–18
Miranda warnings, 69, 148–50, 159
misogyny, 313–16, 321–22
Missouri Compromise of 1820, 82, 303,
    340–41
mistrial, 69
M'Naghten rule, 123
Model Penal Code, 116–17, 125
modernization, 8
The Moral Basis of Socialism (Pearson), 379
moral relativism, 37
moral universality, 41
mores, 5, 6f
Morgan, Thomas, 354
motive, 117
movables, 174
murder, 125–26
Musta'galah courts, 387

NAACP. *See* National Association for the
    Advancement of Colored People
Napoleonic Code, 374
National Association for the Advancement of
    Colored People (NAACP), 235, 345–46,
    348, 361
National Center for State Courts, 96
National Crime Victimization Survey
    (NCVS), 359
National Crime Victimization Surveys
    (NCVS), 265
National Incident Based-Reporting System
    (NIBRS), 359
Native Americans. *See* American Indians
naturalistic fallacy, 39
natural law, 6, 12, 27, 36–42
    evolutionary perspective of, 39–41
    transcendental perspective of, 37–39
Natural Resources Defense Council
    (NRDC), 186
Nazi regime, 27, 239, 243
NCVS. *See* National Crime Victimization Survey;
    National Crime Victimization Surveys
negligence, 169–70
negligent homicide, 125–26
negligent intent, 117
New Deal legislation, 78, 182
NIBRS. *See* National Incident Based-Reporting
    System
Nixon, Richard, 188
Nizam (basic law), 384
no-fault divorce, 179–80
nolo contendere, 99–100
Norman conquest, 372
normative standards, 5–6
norms, 5–6, 6f

Northwest Ordinance, 350
NRDC. *See* Natural Resources Defense Council

oath-taking, 386–87, 392
Obama, Barack, 179, 189, 348
obiter dicta, 60
obscenity, 262–65, 276–77
Occupational Safety and Health Administration
   (OSHA), 185
O'Connor, Sandra Day, 95
Office of Juvenile Justice and Delinquency
   Prevention (OJJDP), 215–16
OJJDP. *See* Office of Juvenile Justice and
   Delinquency Prevention
On Liberty (Mill), 255–56, 276
On the Laws and Customs of England (Bracton),
   58–59
open fields, 144–45
ordinary care, 169
organic solidarity, 19
original jurisdiction, 90
OSHA. *See* Occupational Safety and Health
   Administration
overbreadth doctrine, 114–15

Packer, Herbert, 48–51, 53
Palmer, Elmer, 43–44
parens patriae doctrine, 123, 202, 205, 208–12, 219
Parenti, Michael, 242, 296
Parks, Rosa, 358
Parsons, Talcott, 290
Partial-Birth Abortion Ban Act of 2003, 269
particularity, 138
parties to crime, 120
patria potestas, 201
patriarchy, 312, 332
Patriot Act, 223, 243–44
Pearson, Karl, *The Moral Basis of Socialism*, 379
penal social control, 231–32
people's mediation committees, 381
peremptory challenges, 101
personal jurisdiction, 89
personal property, 172, 174
petite treason, 321
PFC. *See* prefrontal cortex
Pfleger, Michael, 349
plaintiffs, 165
plain view, 144
Planned Parenthood League of Connecticut, 73
Plato, 10–13, 22, 24, 37, 228
   Laws, 45
   The Republic and Other Works, 22
   on women, 314
plea bargaining, 234–35
Plessy, Homer, 343–44
Plutarch, 23
plutocracy, 295
police court, 379

political dissent, social control of, 240–44, 249
poll taxes, 343–44
Pontiac (Ottawa chief), 350
pornography, 262–66
Porter, Alice, 311
positive law, 6, 12, 38
positivists, legal, 6, 10–12, 27, 41
possession, as criminal act, 116
Powers, Pamela, 50–51
precedent, 59–60, 94, 373, 375
prefrontal cortex (PFC), 200
Pregnancy Discrimination Act, 311
preliminary hearing, 98
preliterate societies, 368–70
preponderance of evidence, 165, 205
presentence investigation report (PSI), 103, 377
press, freedom of, 64–66
pretrial proceedings, 98–100, 148–51
Prince, Lucy Terry, 326
principle of analogy, 380
privacy
   reasonable expectation of, 142
   rights of, 73, 78–80, 178, 291
probable cause, 68, 98, 108, 139
procedural law, 111
Proclamation Act of 1763, 287, 306, 350
Prohibition, 45, 272, 276–77, 281
property law, 164, 172–74, 192
prosecutorial discretion, 207
prosecutors, 105–7
prostitution, 259–62
protests, by African Americans, 345–47
proximate cause, 118, 170
PSI. *See* presentence investigation report
public order offenses, 254
public policy, 88
punishment philosophies, 227–30, 231*t*
punitive damages, 165–66
purposeful intent, 117, 125

qadi, 384–85
Quesas crimes, 386, 392
Qur'an (Koran), 38, 384–88, 391–92

race, and law, 357–58
racial segregation, 296, 304, 342–43, 358, 360–61
   in military, 348
racism, 232, 270, 283, 337
   criminal justice system and, 358–60
   Jim Crow laws and, 343
Ranulf de Glanvill, *Treatise on the Laws and
   Customs of the Realm of England*, 58
rape, 126–27, 265, 265*f*, 321–22
   Code of Hammurabi and, 321
   statutory, 119, 126, 253
ratio decidendi, 59
rationality, 17
rational-legal authority, 293–94

Rawls, John, 15–16
Reagan, Ronald, 124, 328
real property law, 168*f*, 172–74
reasonableness clause, 138
reckless intent, 117, 125
Reconstruction, 73, 298, 341–42, 344, 346
Red Corner (film), 383
redress of grievances, 64–65, 88
Reformation, 314
regulatory law, 187–90
rehabilitation, 230, 233
Rehnquist, William H., 95
Reichel, Philip, 43, 45–46
reintegration, 230
relativism, moral, 37
reliance, 175
religious freedom, 64–65
removal, of American Indians, 352–55
repressive justice, 20
reproductive success, 39
The Republic and Other Works (Plato), 22
res judicata, 169
restitutive justice, 20
restorative justice, 215–18
retreat doctrine, 121
retributive justice, 20, 30–33, 32*f*, 58, 229–30
rights. *See also* Bill of Rights
    abortion rights, 5, 73, 266–70, 277, 305
    in Constitution, 63, 64*t*
    fundamental, 75, 79
    human, 45, 259, 389–90
    privacy, 73, 78–80, 178, 291
    right to counsel, 71, 146–51, 149*f*
    social, 343–44
    sources of, 62
    Supreme Court and, 65
    voting, 316–20, 342–44
risk society, 8
robbery, 128
Roberts, John, 94–95
Rodriguez Lopez, J., 36–37
Roman Catholic Church, 4, 202, 267, 332
Roosevelt, Franklin D., 78, 87, 182, 346, 354, 357
Rosenberg, Gerald, 291
Rousseau, Jean-Jacques, 315
rule of four, 94
rule of law, 45–47, 53
    four legal traditions and, 387–89
Russian Revolution, 288, 374, 379, 391

Sabah, Jawad, 1–2
Sarbanes-Oxley Act, 191, 193
Scalia, Antonin, 66–67, 94, 214, 236, 269
The Scarlet Letter (Hawthorne), 226–28, 227*f*
SCCCP. *See* Standing Committee of the
    Chinese Communist Party
school desegregation, 88, 246–48, 250, 346–47
Schwartz, Bernard, 48

Scott, Dred, 340–41
Scott, Harriet, 340
SDA. *See* Indian Self-Determination Act of 1975
search and seizure law, 138, 146*f*
searches, 141–45
SEC. *See* Securities and Exchange
    Commission
The Second Treatise on Government (Locke), 14
Securities and Exchange Commission (SEC),
    185, 191
Sedition Act of 1798, 241
segregation
    gender, 325–26
    racial, 296, 304, 342–43, 348, 358, 360–61
    school desegregation, 88, 246–48, 250, 346–47
seizure, 139, 146*f*
selective incorporation, 79–80
self-defense, 121
self-incrimination, 69–70, 148
sentencing, 103
    guidelines for, 31–33, 32*f*, 52
"separate but equal" doctrine, 304, 343–44, 360
serotonin levels, 200
sex offenders, 215, 256
sexual assault, 126–27, 329, 332. *See also* rape
sexual orientation, 258
shadow government, 181
shari'a, 322, 384, 387–88, 390–91
Shays' Rebellion, 297–98
Sherman Antitrust Act, 299, 306
Siegel, Larry, 359
simple assault, 127
Simpson, O. J., 101, 165–66, 169, 388
slavery, 74, 294–95, 303
    of American Indians, 350
    British law and, 285, 287, 306
    Emancipation Proclamation, 295, 341, 360
    law and, 338–41, 360
"slayer statutes," 44
social change, 281–309
    law and, 284–86, 286*f*
    Supreme Court and, 290–95, 302–5
social contract theory, 13, 15, 19, 24, 136
social control, 223–52
    criminal justice system and, 232–33
    defined, 224
    judicial, 246–48
    law as mechanism of, 226–32
    of political dissent, 240–44, 249
    therapeutic, 231, 244–46
    typology of, 224–25, 227*f*, 249
social engineering, 288–90
socialism, 242
socialist law, 379–83, 389
social rights, 343–44
social solidarity, 19–20
Society for the Evolutionary Analysis
    of Law, 41

sociological perspectives, of the law, 16–20
sodomy statutes, 73, 112, 256–59, 276, 386
solicitation, 120
solidarity, social, 19–20
Solon, 261
song duels, 369
Sotomayor, Sonia, 35–36, 94–95
Southern Poverty Law Center, 345
Soviet social engineering, 288–90
Spanish Inquisition, 68, 71
SPC. *See* Supreme People's Court
speech, freedom of, 64–65, 114
speedy trial, 70–71, 92
Speedy Trial Act of 1974, 71
Standard of Review, 75–76, 76*f*
Standing Bear (Ponca chief), 352
Standing Committee of the Chinese
    Communist Party (SCCCP), 382–83
standing exception, 155–56
Stanton, Elizabeth Cady, 317–18, 333
Star Chamber, 68, 71
stare decisis, 57, 59–60, 83
state courts, 95–98, 96*f*
    of appeals, 95, 97
status offenses, 198
status quo, and Supreme Court, 94, 295–301
Statute of Winchester (1275), 48, 72
statutory exclusion, 207
statutory rape, 119, 126, 253
Stevens, John Paul, 67
Stewart, Potter, 215, 262
Stohr, Mary K., 311–36
Stone, Harlan Fiske, 327
"stop and frisk," 140
strict constructionism, 294–95
strict liability, 119
strict scrutiny review, 75
subject matter jurisdiction, 89
substantial capacity test, 124
substantive due process, 78, 114
substantive irrationality, 17–18, 38
substantive law, 111–12
substantive rationality, 17–18
suffrage
    for African Americans, 342–44
    for women, 316–20
Sunstein, C., 34
Supremacy Clause, of Constitution, 302
Supreme Court, U. S., 94–95
    constitutionality and, 61, 80, 137, 338
    Constitution and, 35, 81–82, 290
    dynamic and constrained views of, 291–92
    justices of, 87, 94–95. *See also specific justices*
    juvenile law and, 214*f*
    legitimacy of, 292–94
    rights and, 65
    social change and, 290–95, 302–5

status quo and, 94, 295–301
    strict constructionism and, 294–95
Supreme People's Court (SPC), 382–83
surveillance, 223
suspect classifications, 74
symbols, 6–7

Ta'azir crimes, 386, 392
Tahsuda, John, 355
Taney, Roger, 94, 294, 303, 340
Tappan, Paul, 112
technology, 7–8
tenancy in common, 173
Ten Commandments, 5, 37
termination policy, 355
Texas State Court System, 96*f*
theft, 130–31
theory of forms, 11
therapeutic social control, 231, 244–46
Thomas, Clarence, 94
Tocqueville, Alexis de, 284
tort law, 164, 167–72, 168*f*
    reform of, 171–72, 192
torture, 47
trade unions, 30
traditional authority, 292
"Trail of Broken Treaties" march, 355
transcendental perspective, of natural law,
    37–39
treason, 114
*Treatise on the Laws and Customs of the Realm of
    England* (Ranulf), 58
Treaty of Fort Pitt, 350
trial(s)
    de novo, 96–97
    by jury, 72, 100–101, 373, 377
    overview of, 102
    speedy, 70–71, 92
Truman, Harry S., 346, 348
Truth, Sojourner, 317
Twelve Tables, 58, 314, 374
two-party requirement, 175

UCR. *See* Uniform Crime Reports
UNCEFDW. *See* United Nations Convention
    on the Elimination of All Forms of
    Discrimination Against Women
Uniform Commercial Code, 175
Uniform Crime Reports (UCR), 113, 190, 198,
    358–59
United Nations Convention on the
    Elimination of All Forms of
    Discrimination Against Women
    (UNCEFDW), 311, 324, 325*t*, 330
United States. *See also* Constitution, U. S.;
    Supreme Court, U. S.
    as soft on crime, 233–34, 233*f*

universality, moral, 41
unlawful assembly, 131
unreasonable searches and seizures, 67, 80–81

vagrancy, 131, 202–3, 342
values, 4–5, 6*f*
Van Buren, Martin, 339
Van Woodward, C., 342–43
vehicle stops, 141–43
vehicular homicide, 126
vicarious liability, 119
vice crime, 254–56
  commercialized, 259–62
victimless crimes, 118, 254–56, 266–67, 276
victim-offender reconciliation programs (VORPS), 217
A Vindication of the Rights of Woman (Wollstonecraft), 315–16
void for vagueness, 115
Volstead Act, 45, 272
voluntary intoxication defense, 122–23
VORPS. *See* victim-offender reconciliation programs
voting rights, 316–20, 342–44
Voting Rights Act of 1965, 347, 361

Waite, Morrison, 298
Walsh, Anthony, 40, 113, 191, 388
"war on drugs," 92
warrants, 138, 142
Warren, Earl, 78, 80, 285, 304–6
Washington, Booker T., 345
Washington, George, 287, 349
Weber, Max, 16–19, 18*t*, 21–23, 34, 38
  Economy and Society, 17
White, Byron, 247

White-Collar Crimes Penalty Enhancement Act, 191, 193
White-Slave Traffic Act, 260
WHO. *See* World Health Organization
Williams, Henry, 344
Williams, Robert, 50–51
Wilson, Woodrow, 242
witchcraft, 4, 68, 320, 370
witnesses, confrontation of, 151
Wollstonecraft, Mary, *A Vindication of the Rights of Woman*, 315–16
women
  Aristotle on, 314
  law and, in history, 313–16
  in legal profession, 325–29
  as persons, 320–21
  Plato on, 314
  suffrage for, 316–20
  work and, 322–24
Women's Rights Project, 323
Women's Temperance Union, 272
Wong Kim Ark, 356
work, and women, 322–24
workhouses, 203
World Court, 390
World Health Organization (WHO), 275
World Trade Organization (WTO), 383, 390
Wright, Jeremiah, 349
writ of mandamus, 247
WTO. *See* World Trade Organization

xenophobia, 283, 343

Yanomamo people, 368
Yeltsin, Boris, 288–89

Zemans, Frances, 284